OUTLINES OF MUHAMMADAN LAW

LAW IN INDIA SERIES

series advisors: Rajeev Dhavan, S.P. Sathe

As well as catering to professional lawyers, advocates and judges, the *Law in India* series is aimed at legal academics and students whose engagement with the law, in South Asia particularly, reaches beyond standard black letter law towards an understanding of how laws and legal institutions have an impact upon society as a whole.

The series includes high quality, authoritative texts by leading lawyers and academics across the globe. Each volume is vetted and approved by a team of international legal experts to ensure the highest levels of scholarship and accuracy.

Other books in the series:

Flavia Agnes, *Law and Gender Inequality: The Politics of Women's Rights in India*

J.Duncan M. Derrett, *Religion, Law and the State in India*

Asaf A.A. Fyzee, *Outlines of Muhammadan Law, 4/e* *

Robert Hayden, *Arguments and Disputes in a Nomad Caste Council*

Robert Lingat (transl. and ed., J.D.M. Derrett), *Classical Law in India**

C.J. Nirmal (ed.), *Human Rights in India: Historical, Social and Political Perspectives*

Monroe E. Price and Stefaan Verhulst (eds), *Broadcasting Reform in India: Media Law from a Global Perspective*

B. Sivaramayya, *Matrimonial Property Rights*

Stanley Yeo, *Unrestrained Killings and the Law: Provocation and Excessive Self-Defence in India, England and Australia*

* available as Oxford India Paperbacks

OUTLINES OF MUHAMMADAN LAW

Fourth Edition

ASAF A.A. FYZEE

OXFORD
UNIVERSITY PRESS

OXFORD
UNIVERSITY PRESS

YMCA Library Building, Jai Singh Road, New Delhi 110001

Oxford University Press is a department of the University of Oxford. It furthers the University's objective of excellence in research, scholarship, and education by publishing worldwide in

Oxford New York
Athens Auckland Bangkok Bogota Buenos Aires Calcutta
Cape Town Chennai Dar es Salaam Delhi Florence Hong Kong Istanbul
Karachi Kuala Lumpur Madrid Melbourne Mexico City Mumbai
Nairobi Paris Sao Paolo Singapore Taipei Tokyo Toronto Warsaw
with associated companies in Berlin Ibadan

Oxford is a registered trade mark of Oxford University Press
in the UK and in certain other countries

Published in India
By Oxford University Press, New Delhi

Second impression 1999

First published 1949
Oxford India Paperbacks 1999
Second Impression 1999

ISBN 019 564 8145

Typeset in Garamond
Printed by Rekha Printers Pvt Ltd, New Delhi
Published by Manzar Khan, Oxford University Press
YMCA Library Building, Jai Singh Road, New Delhi 110 001

PREFACE TO THE FOURTH EDITION

THIS edition has been brought up to the end of 1970. It is unfortunate that Pakistani cases from 1961 to 1970 have not been included; they are not available in India at present, at least not to my knowledge. Nor have I been able in Bombay to consult learned periodicals published in Europe and America such as *Studia Islamica* and *Orient* (Paris), *Saeculum* (Munich), *Oriens* (Istanbul) and *Der Islam* (Berlin), among others. With such handicaps, it is impossible to produce a satisfactory edition, as the development of the law is intimately connected with social and cultural changes.

Since the last edition of this book, a new edition, the fourth, of Tyabji on *Muslim Law* has appeared after 29 years; this has necessitated a large number of alterations in the references and I hope that not many mistakes still remain undetected. A companion to this volume, *Cases in the Muhammadan Law of India and Pakistan* (Clarendon Press, Oxford, 1965), gives in a handy form all the most important cases necessary for the student. And a little known branch of the law applicable to Dā'ūdī and Sulaymānī Bohoras has been treated in a summary fashion in my *Compendium to Fatimid Law* (Simla, India, 1969).

The most regrettable event for students of the *fiqh* has been the death of Joseph Schacht on 1 August 1969 at New Jersey.* He belonged to a brilliant group of contemporary scholars; but probably few of them will deny his pre-eminence in his chosen field. His *Origins* (1950) and *Introduction* (1964) will long be studied and referred to as monumental works of erudition and originality.

I am indebted to my cousin Dāniyāl Laṭīfī, Bar-at-law of the Supreme Court, New Delhi, for drawing my attention to mistakes and latest decisions, and to my nephew Qays

* *The Times* (London), 8 August 1969

Ṭayyibjī, Advocate (O.S.), for revising the text of Appendixes A and B.

The publication of this edition has been held up for unforeseeable reasons. Conditions prevailing in the country are making it almost impossible to keep abreast with the modern contributions to Islamic law in the different parts of the world. The book was written some twenty years ago; probably a new book should now be attempted, or at least a fresh mind entrusted with the task of editing it,

For we are but harvest in a field,
And the Reaper comes when the corn is ripe.

—al-Ṭirimmāḥ

A.A.A.F.

Bombay
15th November 1971

PREFACE TO THE FIRST EDITION

No apology appears to be necessary for this book. There are, indeed, a number of standard works on the subject—Ameer Ali, Wilson, Tyabji and Mulla, for instance; none of them, however, is written for the elementary student; they aim rather at instructing the practitioner or aiding the Judge. The need for a systematic and brief textbook on Muhammadan law as administered in India has been greatly felt in recent years both by students and by teachers; and the author has, after fifteen years of teaching experience, endeavoured to make a beginning in this direction.

Muhammadan law is often conceived as a conglomeration of chaotic rules based in the main on the arbitrary dictates of a revengeful Semitic deity, and on the decisions—sometimes apocryphal, often without reason—of the Prophet of Islam, coupled with the *fatwas* and deductions of fanatical *mullas* and *muftis* and *kazis* throughout the Middle Ages.* Such a

* The expression 'palm tree justice', sometimes used derisively for Islamic law, arose out of certain words used by Lord Justice Goddard in a well-known English case cited by Prof. Noel J. Coulson in his brief but instructive volume, *Conflicts and Tensions in Islamic Jurisprudence* (Chicago, 1969), pp. 40 and 57—A.A.A.F.

view can only be held by those who possess a superficial acquaintance with the rules of law and a deplorable ignorance of the social and historical factors which existed during the centuries in which the law of Islam flourished and developed. A satisfactory textbook cannot possibly neglect the historical and cultural elements, and must try to expound the law in its social and political background. The author is fully alive to the difficulties of the task and conscious of the many shortcomings in his work; nevertheless he has made a beginning, and he hopes that others, more competent, will complete the task.

The treatment is elementary and not historical; only the first principles of the law in India are discussed; and the needs of a university student have always been kept in view. By a 'university student' I do not merely mean a law student cramming away for his degree, but any serious student of the law of Islam who is willing to approach the subject from the viewpoint of the conditions prevailing in India; and possibly it may also serve as a 'refresher course' for practising lawyers (*a*).

In the writing of this book I have made every possible endeavour to be brief, lucid and precise; for I have a horror of undue prolixity. One's style ought never, in the exquisite phrase of Virginia Woolf, 'be allowed to settle into stagnancy or swell into turbidity';(*b*) and, in the manner of presentation, I have kept before me three models of almost unapproachable excellence—*Kenny on Crimes, Anson on Contracts* and *Dicey on the Constitution*. Such mastery of subject, grace of exposition and distinction of style can only be achieved by inspiration or by accident—the accident that comes from a combination of rare talents. But one can at least emulate the great masters whose renown has deservedly grown almost to legendary proportions, and who guide one's faltering steps by the light they shed. English is now a world language, used by millions, and yet the acquisition of an individuality

(*a*) To use Lord Macmillan's phrase, C. M. Schmitthoff, *English Conflict of Laws* (London, 1945), Foreword, p. vi.

(*b*) *The Common Reader*, First Series, 5th Uniform Edition, 1945, p. 68.

in style is given to but few. Nevertheless, I hope I have avoided, in some measure at least, the twin pitfalls of a jejune brevity and a diffuse garrulousness, to be found in some of our textbooks. At any rate, the reader may be assured that not a paragraph has escaped unremitting attention and careful pruning.

The Introduction in this book is based upon an earlier booklet of mine entitled *Introduction to the Study of Mahomedan Law*, published by the Oxford University Press in 1931. Although the topics dealt with are the same, it has been carefully revised and in parts rewritten, and a number of newer references added. I adhere to my earlier view that, in order to understand a system of jurisprudence like that of Islam, the student must have an opportunity to acquaint himself with the historical and cultural background of the law; and I venture to hope that in the universities, at any rate, the importance of this aspect will not be overlooked. For the general reader, the Introduction should, in my estimation, prove to be of popular interest.

Citations have been reduced to a minimum and only the most important decisions have been referred to. Where a clear and positive rule of law has been correctly stated by one of the standard works, care has been taken not to overload the footnotes and add additional cases or ancient texts. In addition to the works mentioned above, older textbooks such as Macnaghten and Sircar, modern writers such as Fitzgerald and others have been gratefully used and due acknowledgement made.

It is necessary to explain that by 'India' is meant the area comprising both the Union of India and the Dominion of Pakistan. The book was completed in March 1947, prior to the partition of India into two self-governing Dominions. The proper term at that time would have been 'British India'. But 'India' is now preferable for various reasons: first, by 'India' is meant a geographical entity well known all over the world, and 'India and Pakistan' would be a cumbersome expression;

secondly, 'British India' is no longer an accurate term; and thirdly, although the Muhammadan law as stated in this book is to be found in the judgments of British Indian courts, it is also the law, with but few minor exceptions, of the Indian States; for it is an invariable convention that the courts in the Indian States freely cite and follow the law as laid down by the High Courts in British India. Thus, on the whole, the brief word 'India' is to be preferred to all the other alternatives in an elementary work.

Although a few later cases have been added during the course of printing, case references have been brought down to the end of 1946; but, as is well known, parts of certain reports were not available, and it is possible that some cases of importance remain unnoticed. Having regard to the conditions prevailing after the war, I crave the indulgence of the critical reader in this respect.

As regards references, the Bibliography gives sufficient information concerning the leading authorities used; in other cases, full titles are given. The system of transliteration is the one commonly used by writers in English, and recommended by the Royal Asiatic Society, London; common words, however, like 'wakf', 'kazi' and 'Koran', are left in their usual garb.

The elision of the final *t* in certain Arabic and Persian words requires explanation. Let us take, for example, the words Imamate, *imāmat* and *imāma*; or Caliphate, *khilāfat* and *khilāfa*. Similarly, Shariat, *sharī'at* and *sharī'a*; also *'āriya(t)*, *ṣadaqa(t)*, *da'wa(t)*. 'Imamate', 'Caliphate', and 'Shariat' are forms commonly employed in English; *imāmat*, *khilāfat*, *sharī'at* are in general use in Persian and Urdu; *imāma*, *khilāfa*, *sharī'a* are the pausal forms in classical Arabic. They are also written 'imāma*h*', 'khilāfa*h*' and 'sharī'a*h*'. The elision of the penultimate *t*, and its change into a form of *h* at the end of a word, is a well-known rule of Arabic grammar; and I hope that this explanation is sufficiently simple and will not cause further confusion.

European scholars usually refer to Flügel's edition of the Koran—*Corani Textus Arabicus*, 2nd edition, by G. Flügel, Leipzig, 1841, and subsequent impressions. This edition is somewhat scarce in India, and I have therefore referred to *The Meaning of the Glorious Koran*, 2 Volumes, Text and Translation, Hyderabad, 1938. The text is that of the famous Egyptian Edition, A.H. 1342, known as 'The King's Koran', and the translation by M. Pickthall is extremely accurate.

My sincere gratitude is due to Mrs Freda Ramsay who very kindly read the typescript, and made many suggestions for the improvement of the language. My former pupils, Mr K. S. Cooper and Mr P. N. Bhagwati*, Advocates (O.S.) of the High Court, Bombay, have kindly read the book, chapter by chapter, while it was being written and I have benefited by their advice and criticism. Mr K. S. Cooper has, in addition, laid me under a debt of gratitude by preparing the Index of Subjects. Finally, the Oxford University Press have done everything in their power to have the book printed accurately and expeditiously, and I should like to offer to them my deep acknowledgements.

A.A.A.F.

Public Service Commission
Bombay
6 August 1948

* Now Judge, Supreme Court of India.

حرم‌جویان دری را می‌پرستند
فقیهان دفتری را می‌پرستند
برافکن پرده تا معلوم گردد
که یاران دیگری را می‌پرستند

O ye who believe! Be ye staunch in justice, witnesses for Allah, even though it be against yourselves or your parents or your kindred, whether rich or poor, for Allah is nearer akin to you than either.

Koran, iv, 135 (ed. Flügel, iv, 134)

Jurisprudence is the soul's cognizance of its rights and obligations.

Abū Ḥanīfa

It is an accepted fact that the terms of law vary with the change in the times.

Mejelle, Article 39 (C. A. Hooper, *Civil Law of Palestine and Trans-Jordan*, Vol. 1, Jerusalem, 1933)

[The Persian quatrain cited at p. xiv is by 'Urfī, see Shiblī Nu'mānī, *Shi'r al-'Ajam*, III (A'ẓamgadh, 1920), 124.]

CONTENTS

III. DOWER (*MAHR*)

IV. DISSOLUTION OF MARRIAGE

V. PARENTAGE AND LEGITIMACY

VI. GUARDIANSHIP

VII. MAINTENANCE

VIII. GIFTS

INDEXES

TABLES AND DIAGRAMS

INTRODUCTION TO THE STUDY OF MUHAMMADAN LAW

General Observations

MUHAMMADAN law as it exists today is the result of a continuous process of development during the fourteen centuries of the existence of Islam. According to the classical theory, it consists of the express injunctions of the Koran; of the legislation introduced by the 'practice' (*sunna*) of the Prophet; and of the opinions of lawyers. In certain cases the opinion of jurists may coincide on a point, and this is known as *ijmā'* or consensus; in others, it may not—this is called *qiyās* or analogical deduction. This theory requires modification in view of the latest investigations into the early history of Islamic jurisprudence. Joseph Schacht has propounded the view that *sunna* is not so much the practice introduced by the Prophet Muhammad, as the practice of the Umayyads of Damascus, supported by traditions of the Prophet—mostly apocryphal—and, in some cases, pre-Islamic custom accepted by the Prophet (*a*). Islamic law is not a systematic code, but a living and growing organism; nevertheless there is amongst its different schools a large measure of agreement, because the starting point and the basic principles are identical. The differences that exist are due to historical, political, economic and cultural reasons, and it is, therefore, obvious that this system cannot be studied without a proper regard to its historical development (*b*).

Now, first, an apology for the term 'Muhammadan' law. The word itself is unsatisfactory and, spell it how you will,

(*a*) J. Schacht, *Origins of Muhammadan Jurisprudence* (Oxford, 1950). Later referred to as 'Schacht'.

(*b*) C. Snouck Hurgronje, 'Le droit Musulman' in *Revue de l'Histoire des Religions* (Paris, 1898), 2, a very valuable article by a leading Dutch orientalist; *Law in the Middle East*, ed. M. Khadduri and H. J. Liebesny, vol. I, *Origin and Development of Islamic Law* (Washington, 1955). This work is abbreviated as *LME*, I, in the pages that follow. A very good general introduction by an 'old master' is Ibn Khaldūn, *Muqaddima*, (tr. F. Rosenthal), III, 1-32. A sound modern treatment will be found in J. N. D. Anderson and N. J. Coulson, 'Islamic Law in Contemporary Cultural Change,' *Saeculum* (Munich), XVIII (1967), 14-92.

it does not improve. This ugly term as well as its variants Moohummudun (Baillie), Mahomedan (the Judicial Committee of the Privy Council and most Indian High Courts), Mahommedan (Ameer Ali), Anglo-Muhammadan (Wilson), Mohammedan (Nicholson), Muslim (Tyabji) and occasionally Mussalman (various Indian Acts), are all open to serious objection. Strictly speaking, the religion taught by the Prophet was Islam, not Muhammadanism; and the people who believe in it are Muslims, not Muhammadans. The system developed by the Muslim doctors is *fiqh*, and I wish to make it clear that the term 'Islamic law' is used synonymously with it. 'Muhammadan law' is, however, a useful expression so far as India is concerned; for here, as in many other countries, not the whole of the *fiqh*, but only a certain part of it, is applied to the Muslims. By Muhammadan law, therefore, is meant *that portion of the Islamic Civil Law which is applied in India to Muslims as a personal law*. And, in choosing the spelling, I have tried to follow the modern practice (Mahmood J., Abdur Rahim, Schacht) and would most certainly be branded as a pedant by the middle-aged lady referred to by Fowler (*c*).

I. Pre-Islamic Arabia (*cc*)

The Beduin of the desert (*ccc*) has changed but little in the two or three thousand years within historic memory. A true son of the desert, the influences of nature have left upon his character an indelible mark. The climate of the desert is inhospitable in the extreme and water is scarce; the burning sun and the hot sands are things to which he has to grow accustomed. We in the cities can hardly realize the degree of hardship which the denizens of the desert have to suffer. In towns there are roads and streets, but in the desert the rising and the setting sun and the shadows it casts by day, and the position of the moon and the stars by night, are the sole

(*c*) Fowler, *Modern English Usage*, s.v. 'Mahomet'.

(*cc*) *Cambridge History of Islam*, I (Cambridge, 1970), Chap. i.

(*ccc*) 'Badw', *Ency. of Islam*, I (rev. ed.), 872; W. Thesiger, *Arabian Sands* (London, 1959), 82, 230 sqq.; R. Fedden, *Syria and Lebanon* (London, 1965), 146 sq.

guides. The Arab roams about in the desert sands in search of water or pasturage, and in doing so the spirit of independence and freedom is born in him. Face to face with hardship he develops characteristics which are peculiar to the desert nomads. If his land is inhospitable, he considers hospitality one of the greatest virtues. Courage and bravery are qualities greatly admired by everyone who is either free or nobly born. No abuse can be greater to the Arab than to call him a coward. Arab hospitality and Arab bravery are proverbial. An Arab takes a peculiar pride in his lineage, and when anyone of his line or tribe is hurt or killed, he considers revenge almost a religious duty. Vendetta is the Arab's master passion. The three Arabian virtues, extolled universally by the ancient poets, are hospitality, fortitude and manliness (*d*).

He loves his animals, his sheep and camels and horses, with the love of an idyllic nature; and yet, in the picturesque phrase of Sprenger, the Beduin is a parasite of the camel (*e*). In the pre-Islamic poetry that has been handed down to us, beautiful descriptions of animals abound. The horse, the camel and the gazelle, each one of them is painted with delight by the poet.

And what were the chief joys of an Arab? How did he live? What were his pastimes and his duties? The best answer to these questions is contained in the immortal lines of the *Mu'allaqa* of Ṭarafa where he says:

Canst thou make me immortal, O thou that blamest me so
For haunting the battle and loving the pleasures that fly?
If thou hast not the power to ward me from Death, let me go
To meet him and scatter the wealth in my hand, ere I die.

Save only for three things in which noble youth take delight,
I care not how soon rises o'er me the coronach loud:

(*d*) *ḍiyāfa, ḥamāsa, murū'a.* P. K. Hitti, *History of the Arabs*, 1st ed. (London, 1937), 25; Nicholson, *Lit. His. Arabs*, 82 sqq. and index; Ig. Goldziher, *Muhammedanische Studien*, Vol. I, ch. i.

(*e*) H. Lammens, *Islam* (English translation), 3.

Wine that foams when the water is poured on it, ruddy, not bright,
Dark wine that I quaff stol'n away from the cavilling crowd;
And then my fierce charge to the rescue on back of a mare
Wide-stepping as wolf I have startled where thirsty he cowers;
And third, the day-long with a lass in her tent of goat's hair
To hear the wild rain and beguile of their slowness the hours (*f*).

In other words—wine, woman and war.

The Arabs of today present a different picture: about 75 per cent of them pursue agriculture and cultivate the soil; 15 per cent live in towns; 10 per cent are nomads, invariably the Beduin. But the life of the desert nomads is undergoing a rapid change. A considerable proportion of them are taking to agriculture and are lured by the salaries offered by the various oil companies. The result is that, unless they are segregated or protected, the Beduin of classical Arabia will in time disappear from the face of the earth, and with them their peculiar virtues—manliness, bravery and hospitality (*ff*).

As a race, the Arabs are at once the most ancient, as they are in many ways the purest, surviving type of the Semites, a great conquering and migrating race of antiquity (*g*). It cannot be decided with certainty whether their tongue is the most ancient of the Semitic languages but, compared with other languages in the same group, classical Arabic is rich in grammatical forms and preserves intact many ancient philological usages. It possesses a rich and varied literature, of which the

(*f*) Nicholson, *Translations from Eastern Poetry and Prose* (Cambridge, 1922), 8.

(*ff*) Don Peretz, *The Middle East Today* (New York, 1963), 15-21. The Arab character is well depicted in two works by J. G. Glubb (Glubb Pasha), *Story of the Arab Legion* (London, 1948) and *A Soldier with the Arabs* (London, 1957).

(*g*) Robertson Smith, *Kinship*, 276; Majid Khadduri, *Law of War and Peace in Islam* (London, 1940), 23-4.

Arabs are justly proud. They consider their mother tongue the best of all the languages. Physically the Arabs are one of the strongest and noblest races of the world. Baron de Larrey, surgeon-general to Napoleon, remarked: 'Their physical structure is in all respects more perfect than that of the Europeans; their organs of sense exquisitely acute, their size above the average of men in general; their figure robust and elegant, their colour brown; their intelligence proportionate to their physical perfection and without doubt superior, other things being equal, to that of other nations.'(*h*) They used to be very defective in organizing power and incapable of combined action. The Prophet, however, put new life into them, and one of the most remarkable achievements of Islam was to unify the warring tribes and inspire them with a common ideal.

In trying to study the social condition of the ancient Arabs it is necessary to realize the position of women in pre-Islamic Arabia. Muslim authors as a rule maintain that the position of women at the time of the Prophet was no better than that of animals: they had no legal rights; in youth they were the goods and chattels of the father; after marriage the husband became their lord and master (*i*). Polygamy was universal, divorce was easy and female infanticide was common (*j*). European scholars generally, following Goldziher and Sir Charles Lyall, are of opinion that this picture is overdrawn. They maintain that Islam robbed Arabian woman of her ancient liberty; and relying on the poetry and proverbs of the days of *jāhiliyya* they show that the ideal Arab woman was an embodiment of modesty, fortitude, virtue and beauty, and that the men honoured and respected her (*k*). They further show that the

(*h*) *Ency. Brit.* 13th ed., II, 284, s.v. 'Arabs'; see also 'Semitic Languages' for linguistic information; and, for a general account of Arabia, cf. 'Arabia' in *Ency. of Islam*.

(*i*) R. Levy, *Social Structure of Islam* (Cambridge, 1957), 91.

(*j*) Abdur Rahim, *Muh. Jur.*, 9 sqq.: on infanticide (*wa'd*), the best short account is R. Smith, *Kinship*, 291, Additional Note C.

(*k*) Lyall, *Ancient Arabian Poetry*, Introduction, p. xxxi; Nicholson, *Literary History of the Arabs*, 1st ed., 87 sqq.; Smith, *Rābi'a the Mystic*, 111; *Ency. Brit.*, 13th ed., II, 284, s.v. 'Arabs'; R. Levy, op. cit., ch. ii.

word *jāhiliyya* does not mean the period of 'ignorance', but rather of 'wildness' or 'intrepidity'.(*l*)

The real explanation seems to be that about a hundred years prior to the Prophet, when the classical poets wrote, Arabia was civilized to some extent and women were treated favourably: they enjoyed some rights and a certain measure of freedom. That civilization slowly disappeared; the Arabs of the desert forgot all forms of religion and morality, and idolatry of a crude type generally prevailed. The privileges which the free Arab women of the desert used to enjoy were lost, and their legal rights cut down. Thus the time was peculiarly ripe for the acceptance of a simple and rational faith like Islam, which gave to women many important rights (*m*). In *Moonshee Buzloor Ruheem* v. *Shumsoonnissa Begum*, Sir James Colville, delivering the judgment of the Privy Council, gave expression to the following views: 'The Mahomedan Wife, as has been shown above, has rights which the Christian —or at least the English—Wife has not against her Husband.'(*n*)

II. Ancient Arabian Customs

We must now consider whether law, or custom having the force of law, existed in ancient Arabia. In pre-Islamic times law proper, as we understand it today, was unknown. Tribes and chieftains acted in accordance with tradition and convention. Abdur Rahim in his *Muhammadan Jurisprudence* (*o*) has examined a number of such customs and many of them are interesting from a comparative point of view. It will be observed how in many institutions, marriage for example,

(*l*) *Jahl* is contrary to *ḥilm* (kindness, consideration, restraint) and not to *'ilm* (knowledge). This was proved long ago by Goldziher, Nicholson, *Lit. Hist.*, 1st ed., 30.

(*m*) Ameer Ali, *Spirit of Islam*, 2nd ed., 255-6.

(*n*) (1867) 11 M. I. A. 551, 612; *Cases*, 281, 297. The position has entirely changed, however, in the last fifty years, notably after the Married Women's Property Acts.

(*o*) *Tagore Law Lectures* 1907, (London/Madras) 1911, pp. 2-16.

there is a curious similarity between some pre-Islamic Arab customs and certain kinds of marital relationship known among the ancient Hindus. Apart from this, we shall find many of these customs adopted wholly or with modifications by the law of Islam. One striking example is the principle of agnacy or *ta'ṣīb*, which is fundamental in the Sunnite law of inheritance (*p*).

At the time of the advent of Islam, Arab society was generally nomadic. No settled form of government or administration of law existed. The population consisted of two classes: there were the desert nomads who led a more or less roving life and were called Beduins, and there were the town-dwellers who to some extent led a more settled form of existence. The tribe was the principal unit, and therefore the tribal chief exercised great power and influence. Generally he was elected because of his nobility of birth or wisdom or courage (*q*). There was no regular manner in which his behests were carried out; he relied mainly on the force of his character and tribal opinion. The commonest offences were tribal; for example, one member of a tribe killing a member of another tribe. In such circumstances the chief of the tribe that had suffered would call upon the leader of the offender's tribe to surrender the criminal so that he might suffer the penalty of death. If the tribes were friendly, some sort of arrangement was arrived at; if not, there would be guerilla warfare between them. In certain cases blood-money was fixed, and the offender's tribe had to pay a price in consonance with the dead man's position. Generally speaking two kinds of custom having the force of law may be recognized: inter-tribal customs, and customs which regulated the relation of the individual to his own tribe. We are mostly concerned with the latter class.

We have not much knowledge of the procedure followed in deciding cases. Generally the plaintiff had to substantiate his

(*p*) Tyabji, 800 sqq. Tyabji's exposition of the law of inheritance is of great value.

(*q*) R. Levy, op. cit., 271 sqq.

claim. If he had no evidence, the defendant, where he denied the charge, would be given the oath; and on taking it, he would be absolved from all liability. Occasionally, diviners would be consulted, and torture was also resorted to. Oaths were held in great reverence, and were often used for settling disputes (*r*).

Among the most interesting of ancient Arabian customs were those that regulated the relations between the sexes and the filiation of children. Side by side with the regular form of marriage, various other connexions between members of the opposite sex were common. Abdur Rahim, citing the *Kashf al-Ghumma,* tells us of four types of Arabian marriages (*s*): (i) A form of marriage similar to that sanctioned by Islam; a man would ask another for the hand of his daughter or ward, and then marry her by giving her a certain dower. (ii) A man desiring noble offspring would ask his wife to send for a great chief and have intercourse with him. During the period of such intercourse the husband would stay away, but return to her after pregnancy was well advanced. (iii) A number of men, less than ten, would be invited by a woman to have intercourse with her. If she conceived, and was delivered of a child, she had the right to summon all the men and they were bound to come. She would then say, 'O so and so, this is your son.' This established paternity conclusively and the man had no right to disclaim it. (iv) Common prostitutes were well known. They used to have a definite number of visitors and their tents had a special flag as a sign of their calling. If a woman of this class conceived, the men who frequented her house were assembled, and the physiognomists decided to whom the child belonged (*t*).

Mut'a or temporary marriage was a common practice. From a study of *ḥadīth* it would seem that *mut'a* was a form of legalized prostitution tolerated by the Prophet in the earlier

(*r*) Abdur Rahim, *Muh. Jur.*, 6.

(*s*) ibid., 7; *Alberuni's India,* tr. Sachau (London, 1914), 108 sq.

(*t*) R. Levy, op. cit. 118 sqq.

days of Islam, but later on he prohibited it (*u*). It is to be noted that only one school of Muhammadan law, the Ithnā 'Asharī, allows such marriages today. Not only the Sunnite schools but all the other Shiites, notably the Ismailis and Zaydīs, consider such marriages illicit (*v*).

Few of the conjugal relations described above can be called 'marriages' in the modern acceptation of the term. It is more appropriate today to consider them as forms of legalized prostitution or of tribal sexual behaviour recognized by custom. The second form of marriage mentioned by Abdur Rahim reminds us of the ancient Hindu practice of *niyoga*. Widely different peoples have, it seems, possessed, in times past, similar institutions before coming to the modern —and not merely the Christian—idea of marriage, 'the voluntary union for life of one man and one woman, to the exclusion of all others'.(*w*)

Dower was one of the necessary conditions of marriage in the regular form. But the amount was paid more often to the guardian or the father than to the woman herself, and for this reason the marriage contract was for all practical purposes a sale (*x*). In Islam, however, *mahr* is a bridal gift and the idea of sale has disappeared almost entirely, although the classical texts do contain vestiges of the original conception of marriage as being a form of sale. The husband could avoid his liability to pay dower in various ways. A man would give his daughter or sister in marriage to another in consideration of the latter giving his daughter or sister in marriage to the

(*u*) Wensinck, *Early Muhammadan Tradition*, 145; R. Levy, op. cit., 115.

(*v*) *Majmū' al-Fiqh*, ed. Griffini, §718; Fyzee in (1931) 33 Bom. Law Rep. Jl:. 30; *Da'ā'im al-Islām*, ii, §§858-9; *Fatimid Law*, §95 sqq.

(*w*) Dictum of Lord Penzance in *Hyde* v. *Hyde* adopted and approved in *Nachimson* v. *Nachimson* [1930] P. 85 and 217. It must, however, be admitted that the impact of the modern law of divorce has greatly weakened the force of this dictum in the present century, see P. M. Bromley, *Family Law* (London, 1957), 2. Hitti mentions a case of polyandry by brothers in South Arabia, *History of the Arabs*, 1st ed., 48.

(*x*) '*Mahr*' in *Ency. of Islam*, III, 137; Tyabji §92. Robertson Smith explains the difference between *mahr* and *ṣadāq*, *Kinship*, 2nd ed., 93, 111, and see Levy, op. cit., 113.

former. This was called *shighār* (*y*). In this case no dower was paid. Unchastity on the part of the wife was also a reason for debarring her claim for dower. A false charge was, therefore, sometimes brought against her and her dower forfeited before divorce.

Woman was never a free agent in marriage. It was the father or other male guardian who gave her in marriage, and her consent was of no moment. There was no limit to the number of wives a man could have. Divorce was a matter of a few words, and there were many forms of dissolution of marriage, some of which have been adopted by Islam.

The Arabian law of property has very little practical value now, and therefore we shall pass on to inheritance and succession. An Arab could dispose of all his property by will. He could in many instances cut off his nearest relations. In the law of inheritance the cardinal rule was that no female could take; only the males inherited and, even among males, only agnates, such as son, father, grandfather, brother, cousin, etc.; cognates were entirely excluded. These constituted the first class of heirs. The second class consisted of adopted sons and relations, who stood on the same footing as natural-born sons. The third class consisted of heirs by contract. Two Arabs, for services rendered to each other or for mutual affection, would enter into a contract that in the event of the death of the one the other would succeed to his estate (*z*).

This brief summary of pre-Islamic customs will suffice to show how far-reaching and humane were the reforms brought about by the Prophet and the religion he taught (*a*).

(*y*) Abdur Rahim, 8; Levy, op. cit., 105; Robertson Smith, *Kinship*, 112.

(*z*) Abdur Rahim, 15.

(*a*) See generally in *LME*, I, 28 sqq. Modern Conditions: A valuable addition to our knowledge are seven articles by Aḥmad bin Muḥammad Ibrāhīm, Att.-Gen. of Singapore, under the general caption: "The Status of Muslim Women in Family Life in Malaysia and Brunei'—(1963) 5 *Malaya Law Review*, 313-37; (1963) 6 *Mal. L. R.*, 40-82; (1964) 6 *Mal. L. R.*, 353-86; (1965) 7 *Mal. L. R.* (54-94; (1965) 7 *Mal. L. R.* 299-313; (1966) 8 *Mal. L. R.* 46-85; (1966) 8 *Mal. L. R.* 233-69.

For Iran, see Doreen Hinchcliffe, 'The Iranian Family Protection Act', *Intern. and Comp. Law Quar.*, 1968, 17, 516-21,

III. Advent of Islam

At the time of the Prophet and just before he preached the new faith, we can distinguish several kinds of religious belief in Arabia. None of them was of an advanced type. First let us consider ancient Arabian paganism or heathenism. 'The paganism of the Arabs was in general of a remarkably crude and inartistic kind, with no ritual pomp, no elaborate mythology and, it hardly needs be said, no tinge of philosophical speculation.'(*b*) Strictly speaking, this paganism was not a fixed system at all; on the one hand, the most primitive beliefs were akin to animism and totemism; and on the other, the religion of the more advanced Arabs bore a great resemblance to that of the Sabians (*c*).

Then we come to organized religion; there were colonies of Christian sectarians in the north and also at Najrān in the south, Jewish communities were to be found in the north-west, and Zoroastrian communities in the neighbourhood of the Persian Gulf. In the majority of cases, it was merely the outward form, the traditional ritual of each faith, that was preserved; the people had forgotten the true principles of their religion and lost contact with spirituality. In their heart of hearts, they remained true sons of the desert; believing in free love, considering vengeance a sacred duty, loving a life of pleasure; wild, passionate, hospitable; and above all, freedom-loving and courageous (*d*).

We now come to an interesting and significant fact: significant because in some ways it explains and anticipates the birth of Islam. Round about Mecca there arose a group of men

(*b*) Prof. A. A. Bevan on 'Mahomet', *Camb. Med. Hist.*, II, 302, 303. This is the best short account of the Prophet from the pen of a non-Muslim critic that we have.

(*c*) The Sabians were half Christian and half heathen; and the appellation 'Sabian', Arabic *Ṣābi'ūn*, was a derived name given to the earliest followers of the Prophet, *Camb. Med. Hist.*, II, 309; C. C. Torrey, *Jewish Foundation of Islam* (New York, 1933), 3, an extremely valuable and suggestive study. The Sabians (*Ency. Brit.*, 14th ed., Vol. 23, p. 964) must not be confused with the Sabaeans, an ancient tribe in the Yemen (*Ency. Brit.*, 14th ed., Vol. 23, p. 955).

(*d*) A recent work throws a great deal of light on the Beduin: H. R. P. Dickson, *The Arab of the Desert* (London, 1949).

who were dissatisfied with the prevailing forms of worship and belief, who were monotheistic and devoted themselves to religious meditation. These people were called *ḥanīfs*, a term of which the precise meaning and origin are obscure. The *ḥanīfs* hardly formed a community of their own and our information concerning them is, unfortunately, extremely meagre; nor do we know for certain what their relations were with the earliest converts to Islam (*e*).

This then was the background when the Prophet preached his religion. It is not my purpose to give here any detailed exposition of the tenets of Islam. But this faith has a particular appeal to the modern mind. It is a socialistic and a democratic creed: socialistic, because it divides the estate of a person after his death compulsorily and distributes it among his nearest relations, male and female; democratic, because it preaches equality among human beings and the brotherhood of man. Now as, in Islam, laws are intermixed with religion, a few words must be said regarding its basic principles, failure to understand which would mean failure to appreciate the true spirit of Islam. The French proverb, 'To understand is to forgive', is never truer than in matters concerning religion.

First of all, the Prophet himself never claimed that Islam was a new religion. He asserted, on the other hand, that it was as old as the hills. *Islām* is a word which in Arabic means 'Submission to the will of God', and from the way in which the verb *aslama* (lit., he submitted) is used in Arabic, it appears that it further signifies the *deliberate adoption* of a new faith (*f*). The word *muslim* is a noun of action, meaning 'one who adopts the faith of *islām*'. Therefore the appellation 'Muslim law', with due respect to the Supreme Court of India

(*e*) '*Ḥanīfs*' in *Ency. of Islam*, II, 258; *Camb. Med. Hist.*, II, 306; and A. Jeffery, *Foreign Vocabulary of the Qur'ān* (Baroda, 1938), 112-15. As to early origins and especially the influence of Judaism, see C. C. Torrey, *Jewish Foundation of Islam*, 3-8.

(*f*) Prof. A. A. Bevan, *Camb. Med. Hist.*, II, 309, fn. 1; A. J. Wensinck, *The Muslim Creed* (Cambridge, 1932), 9; A. Jeffery, *Foreign Vocabulary of the Qur'ān* (Baroda, 1938), 62.

and Tyabji, is not accurate. It is a rational human being who alone can be designated as a *muslim*. The correct term in English would be 'Islamic law'.

In Koranic theory Islam is a religion which has existed since the beginning of the world and will exist till the day of Resurrection. From time to time this religion is corrupted. People forget the principles of the true faith, and God in His infinite mercy sends to them a Reformer, a *rasūl* or a Messenger, in order that he may point out the way and warn the people. Such were Adam, Abraham, Ishmael, Moses and Jesus the son of Mary. Such was also Muḥammad, the son of 'Abdallāh, who claimed that he was merely a man like others, liable to err in human affairs, but divinely guided and inspired in matters of religion (*g*).

The next principle of the utmost importance is *tawḥīd* or the dogma of the unity of God. If there is one thing in which Islam will not temporize or compromise, it is the dogma of the absolute unity of God. The religion of Islam is essentially monotheistic, the religion of one God in direct contradistinction to the ancient Arabian polytheism or paganism. The doctrine of *tawḥīd*, because of its immutability, is, according to Iqbal, the principle of permanence in the world of Islam (*h*). Strict monothesism, it may be added, is also the creed of Jews and Christians.

The third principle is *brotherhood* (*i*). From the practical point of view, the principle of brotherhood which Islam has preached—and not only preached but made real—is one of its greatest glories. Almost all religions have taught brotherhood in different ways, but no religion in history can boast of having made brotherhood so real and actual in everyday life. In his last sermon, the Prophet told his people that excellence consisted only in deed. Pride of colour or race was utterly

(*g*) Wensinck, *Early Muhammadan Tradition*, 168. The Koran proclaims the absolute equality of all Apostles, ii, 136 and iii, 84.

(*h*) Iqbal, *Reconstruction in Islam* (Lahore, 1930), 207; (Oxford, 1934), 147-9.

(*i*) R. Levy, op. cit., 53 sqq.; Koran, xlix, 10.

condemned. 'The Arab is not superior to the non-Arab; the non-Arab is not superior to the Arab. You are all sons of Adam, and Adam was made of Earth. Verily all Muslims are brothers . . . If a deformed Abyssinian slave holds authority over you and leads you according to the Book of Allah, hear him and obey.' Nowhere has the true spirit of Islam been so tersely summarized as in this the last speech of the founder of Islam (*j*).

As students of law, we would do well to consider the striking tribute which has been paid to Islam by a great European authority on Muslim law, Count Léon Ostrorog, in concluding his lectures on *The Angora Reform* in the University of London: 'However that may be, Islam, with its glorious history, its magnificent literature, its simple, stoical tenets, will certainly remain, for many millions, at the very least an ideal, a moral doctrine, teaching men to be clean, abstemious, brave and charitable, proclaiming as fundamental commandment the noble Quranic verse: *Verily God commands you to be just and kind!*—a religion, nothing more, but such a religion that even those who do not profess it, but have studied it with a certain care, render it the tribute of a deep sympathy and a profound respect.'(*k*)

IV. Origin of Muslim Law

(A) *Sharīʿat.*—Coming to law proper, it is necessary to remember that there are two different conceptions of law. Law may be considered to be of divine origin as is the case with the Hindu law and the Islamic law, or it may be conceived as man-made. The latter conception is the guiding principle of all modern legislation; it is, as Ostrorog has pointed out, the Greek, Roman, Celtic or Germanic notion

(*j*) Ibn Hishām, *Sīra*, ed. Wüstenfeld, 968-9. Accretions to the main text will be found in a number of *ḥadīth*-texts, and they are reflected in the translations such as those of Muir, *Life of Mohammad* (4th ed., 1923), 472-4, and Ameer Ali, *Spirit of Islam*, 113-14. See also Shiblī, *Sīrat*, II, 118-32; and Fyzee, *A Modern Approach to Islam* (Bombay, 1963), 37 sqq.

(*k*) Ostrorog, *The Angora Reform*, 99.

of law (*l*). We may be compelled to act in accordance with certain principles because God desires us to do so, or, in the alternative, because the King or the Assembly of wise men or the leaders of the community or social custom demand it of us for the good of the people in general. In the case of Hindu law, it is based, first, on the Vedas, that is *sruti*, meaning 'that which is heard'; secondly, it is based on the *smriti* or 'that which is remembered' by the sages or *rishīs*. Although the effect of custom is undoubtedly great, yet *dharma*, as defined by Hindu lawyers, implies a course of conduct which is approved by God.

Now, what is the Islamic notion of law? In the words of Mr Justice Mahmood, 'It is to be remembered that Hindu and Muhammadan law are so intimately connected with religion that they cannot readily be dissevered from it.'(*m*) There is in Islam a doctrine of 'certitude' (*'ilm al-yaqīn*) in the matter of Good and Evil (*n*). We in our weakness cannot understand what Good and Evil are unless we are guided in the matter by an inspired Prophet. Good and Evil, technically as the Muslim doctors have it, *ḥusn*, beauty and *qubḥ*, ugliness, are to be taken in the ethical acceptation of the terms (*o*). What is morally beautiful, that must be done; and what is morally ugly must not be done. That is law or *sharī'at* and nothing else can be law. But what is absolutely and indubitably beautiful, what is absolutely and indubitably ugly? These are the important legal questions; and who can answer them? Certainly not man, say the Muslim legists. We have the Koran which is the very word of God. Supplementary to it we have *ḥadīth*, which are traditions of the Prophet—the records of his actions and his sayings—from which we must derive help and inspiration in arriving at legal decisions. If there is nothing either in

(*l*) Ostrorog, *The Angora Reform*, 15 sqq.

(*m*) *Gobind Dayal* v. *Inayatullah* (1885) 7 All. 775, 781; *Cases*, 429, 434-35. A similar view concerning *dharma* will be found in S. C. Banerjee, *Hindu Law of Marriage and Stridhana* (Tagore Lectures for 1878, 5th ed. Calcutta, 1923), 1-3.

(*n*) Ostrorog, *The Angora Reform*, 16.

(*o*) For a Shiite view see *al-Bābu'l-ḥādī 'Ashar* (tr. Miller), §111.

the Koran or in the *ḥadīth* to answer the particular question which is before us, we have to follow the dictates of secular reason *in accordance with certain definite principles*.

These principles constitute the basis of sacred law or *sharī'at* as the Muslim doctors understand it. And it is these fundamental juristic notions which we must try to study and analyse before we approach the study of the Islamic civil law as a whole, or even that small part of it which in India is known as 'Muhammadan law'.

Modern jurists emphasize the importance of law for understanding the character and ethos of a people. 'Law', says a modern jurist, 'streams from the soul of a people like national poetry, it is as holy as the national religion, it grows and spreads like language; religious, ethical, and poetical elements all contribute to its vital force'(*p*); it is 'the distilled essence of the civilization of a people' (*q*); it reflects the people's soul more clearly than any other organism (*r*). This is true of Islam more than of any other faith. The *sharī'at* is the central core of Islam; no understanding of its civilization, its social history or its political system is possible without a knowledge and appreciation of its legal system (*s*).

Sharī'a[*t*] (lit., the road to the watering place, the path to be followed), as a technical term, means the Canon law of Islam, the totality of Allah's commandments. Each one of such commandments is called *ḥukm* (pl. *aḥkām*). The law of Allah and its inner meaning is not easy to grasp; and *sharī'at* embraces all human actions. For this reason it is not 'law' in the modern sense; it contains an infallible guide to ethics. It is fundamentally a DOCTRINE OF DUTIES (*t*), a code of obligations. Legal considerations and individual rights have a

(*p*) C. K. Allen, *Law in the Making* (Oxford, 1927), 54; 5th ed., 90.

(*q*) A. S. Diamond, *Evolution of Law and Order* (London, 1949), 303.

(*r*) D. Hughes Parry, *Haldane Memorial Lecture*, 1951, 3.

(*s*) Schacht, *Esquisse*, 9, and *LME*, I, 28.

(*t*) This was pointed out by Snouck Hurgronje, who, according to Goldziher, is the 'founder' of the historical criticism of *fiqh*. See *Ency. of Islam*, II, 105; *LME*, I, 31.

secondary place in it; above all, the tendency towards a religious evaluation of all the affairs of life is supreme.

According to the *sharī'at*, religious injunctions are of five kinds, *al-aḥkām al-khamsa.*(*tt*) . Those strictly enjoined are *farḍ*, and those strictly forbidden are *ḥarām*. Between them we have two middle categories, namely, things which you are advised to do (*mandūb*), and things which you are advised to refrain from (*makrūh*), and finally there are things about which religion is indifferent (*jā'iz*) (*u*). The daily prayers, five in number, are *farḍ;* wine is *ḥarām;* the additional prayers like those on the *'īd*, are *mandūb;* certain kinds of fish are *makrūh*; and there are thousands of *jā'iz* things, such as travelling by air. Thus the *sharī'at* is totalitarian; all human activity is embraced in its sovereign domain. This fivefold division must be carefully noted; for, unless this is done, it is impossible to understand the distinction between that which is only morally enjoined and that which is legally enforced. Obviously, moral obligation is quite a different thing from legal necessity, and if in law these distinctions are not kept in mind, error and confusion are the inevitable result. This has been forcibly pointed out by Mr Justice Mahmood in the leading case of *Gobind Dayal* v. *Inayatullah* (*v*).

(B) ***Fiqh: The Classical Theory.***—The law in Islam is called *fiqh*; it is the name given to the whole science of jurisprudence because it implies the exercise of intelligence in deciding a point of law in the absence of a binding *naṣṣ* (command) from the Koran or *sunna*. *Fiqh* literally means 'intelligence', and *faqīh* is a 'jurist', a person skilled in the law. There is thus a difference between *'ilm*, knowledge, and *fiqh*, which requires both intelligence and independent

(*tt*) Kemal A. Faruki, *al-aḥkām al-khamsa:* The Five Values, *Jl. Islamic Research Institute Pakistan,* V (1966), 43-8.

(*u*) *Ency. of Islam*, s.v. *'Sharī'a*, IV, 322; and *al-Bābu'l-ḥādī 'Ashar* (tr. Miller), §113; Levy, op. cit., 202-3; Aghnides, 109 sqq., Fitzgerald, *LME*, I, 98.

(*v*) (1885) 7 All. 775, 805; *Cases*, 429, 453 sq. A good description of *sharī'at* in Indian conditions will be found in M. Mujeeb, *The Indian Muslims* (London, 1967), 56 sqq.

judgment. A man may be learned, *'ālim* (pl. *'ulamā,* commonly called *ulema*), but to be a *faqīh* (pl. *fuqahā'*), he must possess the quality of independent judgment, the capacity to discern between the 'correct' and binding rule of law, and the 'weak' or unsupported opinion of a classical author. The terms *fiqh* and *fuqahā'* may also have been suggested by the Latin terms (*juris*) *prudentia* and (*juris*) *prudentes*; for a study of the *fiqh* reveals that traces of Roman, Jewish and Persian laws have been incorporated in it (*w*).

We have now to see how the Islamic lawyers have defined the term *fiqh*. Abū Ḥanīfa's definition stresses the moral aspect: *fiqh* is the soul's cognizance of its rights and obligations (*x*). The Turkish *Mejelle* (Art. 1) defines it as 'the knowledge of practical legal questions' (*y*). Most Islamic authorities, however, define it in terms of its four basic constituents (*z*), and we may therefore say that:

Fiqh or the science of Islamic Law is the knowledge of one's rights and obligations derived from the Koran, or the *sunna* of the Prophet, or the consensus of opinion among the learned (*ijmā'*), or analogical deduction (*qiyās*) (*zz*).

This is the classical view and is said to be founded on the oft-quoted tradition of Mu'ādh. The Prophet sent Mu'ādh, one of his Companions, as governor of a province and also appointed him as the distributor of justice. No trained lawyers existed then and the Prophet asked: 'According to what shalt thou judge?' He replied:

'According to the scriptures of God.'

'And if thou findest nought therein?'

'According to the Tradition of the Messenger of God.'

(*w*) Goldziher on 'Fiḳh,' *Ency of Islam,* 1st ed., II, 102, Wensinck, *Muslim Creed*, 110 sqq. has a valuable discussion on the term *fiqh* in *ḥadīth* literature.

(*x*) Taftāzānī, *Talwīḥ* I, (Cairo, A.H. 1327) 10 (margin). For this author see N. P. Aghnides, *Mohammedan Theories of Finance*, Intr., 176, No. 15.

(*y*) Mahmassani, S., *Philosophy of Jurisprudence in Islam* (Leiden, 1961), 8.

(*z*) Abdur Rahim, 48; Schacht, *Esquisse*, 53.

(*zz*) Shāfi'ī, *Risāla*, tr. M. Khadduri, 78, §27.

'And if thou findest nought therein?'

'Then I shall strive to interpret with my reason.'

And thereupon the Prophet said:

'Praise be to God who has favoured the messenger of His Messenger with what His Messenger is willing to approve.'(*a*)

Possibly of late origin, this is an important tradition emphasizing the principle that the exercise of independent judgment, within certain limits, is not only permissible but praiseworthy. The Koran has to be interpreted, the actions and sayings of the Prophet duly considered, and judgment exercised in accordance with legal theory in case the Koran and *sunna* are silent on the question. A noteworthy feature of the *ḥadīth* is that the Koran is given pre-eminence and next comes the practice of the Prophet. Although consensus is not mentioned specifically, it prepares the way for it, for *ijmāʿ* emphasizes the importance the Arabs gave to the 'prevalent usage' of the community. And finally, if all these sources fail, then the opinion of a distinguished jurist may also have the force of law.

The Koran according to this theory is the first source of law. Its importance is religious and spiritual, no less than legal, as it is, in Muslim belief, the Word of God. When a verse of the Koran is cited, the Muslim authors say: 'God says, Mighty and Glorious is He' or 'Says God, the Blessed and Exalted'. It is for this reason that the verses of the Koran (*āyāt*), although only a few of them deal specifically with legal questions, are held to be of paramount authority (*b*). In interpreting the Koranic verses, one important principle has to be observed. Some verses are deemed to be the abrogating (*nāsikh*) verses and some to be the abrogated (*mansūkh*) ones. Generally speaking the earlier verses are deemed to be repealed by the later ones. The textbooks on

(*a*) Ostrorog, op. cit., 21; Wensinck, *Early Mdn. Trad.*, 156; Khadduri, *Law of War and Peace in Islam*, 28; Abdur Rahim, 140-1. Schacht has discussed its origin, 105-6. Jazīrī, I (Intr. to 2nd ed.), 14.

(*b*) Wilson has given a useful collection of Koranic verses dealing with legal questions, Appendix D.

Islamic law give a good deal of attention to problems of interpretation and discuss exhaustively the question of how the rule of law is to be deduced when several Koranic verses deal with the same or a similar problem, or when one verse affects another, directly or indirectly (*c*).

The second source of law is the *sunna*, the practice of the Prophet. The word *sunna* was used in pre-Islamic times for an ancient and continuous usage, well established in the community (*sunnat al-umma*); later, the term was applied to the Practice of the Prophet (*sunnat al-nabī*). The word *sunna* must be distinguished from the term *ḥadīth*, for a promiscuous use of the two terms leads sometimes to confusion of thought. *Ḥadīth* is the story of a particular occurrence; *sunna*, the rule of law deduced from it is the 'practice' of the Prophet, his 'model behaviour'. The two sources, Koran and *sunna*, are often called *naṣṣ* (binding ordinance), and represent direct and indirect revelation (*d*). According to Wensinck, *ḥadīth* is the mirror of Muslim society (*e*), and although modern research tends to show that a large proportion of the traditions ascribed to the Prophet are of late origin and doubtful, their importance in establishing the usage of the community and as a formative element in law must never be minimized.

The third source of law is *ijmā'*, consensus of opinion among the learned of the community. Although the Muslim legists give it the third place in descending order, modern critics consider it to be the most important element in Islamic law, and an examination of the corpus of the *fiqh* reveals that a major portion of the law consists of the concurrent opinions of scholars on legal questions. Snouck

(*c*) Mahmassani, op. cit., 66; Abdur Rahim, 77.

(*d*) Schacht, 16 and 58 sqq.; distinction between *ḥadīth* and *sunna*, *Ma'ārif* (Azamgadh, U.P.), 1929, Vol. 24, 91. Shāfi'ī said that *sunna* explains the Koran, *Risāla* (tr. Khadduri), 72, §23. See also S. M. Yousuf, 'The Sunnah: its Transmission, Development and Revision', *Islamic Culture* [*Hyderabad*] XXXVII (1963), 271-82, and *Ḥadith* by J. Robson, *Ency. of Islam*, III (rev. ed.) 23-8.

(*e*) Wensinck, *Muslim Creed*, 1. Generally see *Ency. of Islam*, 1st ed., IV, 555.

Hurgronje considers it to be 'the foundation of foundations' and the movable element in the law (*f*). A tradition of the Prophet tersely summarizes the principle: 'My community will never agree on an error'(*g*) and several Koranic texts are adduced in its support (*h*). But we shall see later that *ijmā'*, representing as it does the majority view among scholars, was allied to the pre-Islamic *sunna*, the prevalent usage, and thus became during the centuries to follow the most fruitful source of law (*i*).

The fourth and last source of law is *qiyās*, analogical deduction. It is derived from the Jewish term *hiqqīsh*, from an Aramaic root, meaning 'to beat together'(*j*). In Arabic usage the word means 'measurement' and therefore 'analogy'. The terms *ra'y* and *qiyās* are often used by lawyers and it is well to know their exact significance. According to Schacht, 'Individual reasoning in general is called *ra'y*, 'opinion'. When it is directed towards achieving systematic consistency and guided by the parallel of an existing institution or decision it is called *qiyās*. When it reflects the personal choice of the lawyer, guided by his idea of appropriateness, it is called *istiḥsan* or *istiṣlaḥ*, 'preference' (*k*).

The exercise of opinion, the drawing of conclusions, and the use of discretion were used in the law of Islam from the earliest days, and in Sunnite law, the method of deduction forms the fourth and last source of law. There are other sources of law as well, often in the nature of judicial discretion exercised by English judges on matters of public policy, such as *istiṣlāḥ*, *istidlāl*, *istiṣḥāb*, and *istiḥsān*, but they are unnecessary for our purposes. They mainly reflect

(*f*) *Selected Works*, 289.

(*g*) Abdur Rahim, 115; Wensinck, *Muslim Creed*, 113; for criticism of this *ḥadīth*, see Schacht, 42, 91. According to Shāfi'ī, *qiyās* and *ijtihād* run parallel and have equal value, Malcolm H. Kerr, *Islamic Reform* (Cambridge, 1966), 76.

(*h*) Mahmassani, 76.

(*i*) For *ijmā'* generally, Schacht, 82 sqq., and D. B. Macdonald, *Ency. of Islam*, 1st ed., II, 448.

(*j*) *Schacht*, 99.

(*k*) ibid., 98.

the difference of opinion among jurists in matters where discretion can be exercised and lead to refinements and distinctions which have become questions of controversy among the adherents of various schools. It may, however, be pointed out that all forms of *ra'y* and *qiyās* are entirely rejected by the Ithnā 'Asharī and the Fatimid schools of Shiite law (*l*).

In addition to the four formal sources, there are others which may be termed the material sources of law, and these cannot be neglected. First, pre-Islamic custom. There is considerable authority for the proposition that beneficial customs, although ancient and pre-Islamic, are to be retained (*m*). Secondly, some elements of Roman law seem to have been engrafted on to the Islamic system (*n*). Thirdly, evidence of the retention of the customs of different peoples and countries is also to be found, as in Java and Indonesia, Africa, Egypt and in our own country; this is known as *'āda* or *'urf* (*o*). Customs are also accepted under the guise of *ijmā'*. And lastly, English law is introduced by the expression 'justice, equity and good conscience' to be found in numerous statutes (*p*).

The gradual infiltration of English law into the fabric of Muhammadan law in India has been well described by Hamilton J. (Kenya, East Africa) in a case dealing with the law of Wakf. 'A study of the question shows that while the Mohamedan law, uninfluenced from outside sources, per-

(*l*) Generally see Schacht, 98 sqq., and *Ency. of Islam*, s.v. Ḳiyās; Mahmassani, 79. For Shiite doctrine, *LME*, I, 122 sqq.; *Fat. Law*, xlvi sq.

(*m*) *LME*, I, 28 sqq., Mahmassani, op. cit., 91.

(*n*) 'The Alleged Debt of Islamic to Roman Law' by S. V. Fitzgerald, *Law Quar. Rev.* for 1951, 81, and Mahmassani, op. cit., 136.

(*o*) See *'amal*, *Ency. of Islam*, rev. ed., I, 427. On custom in general, see Levy, *Social Structure of Islam*, Ch. vi; Mahmassani, op. cit., 130; C. Snouck Hurgronje, *Selected Works*, 290, and *LME*, I, 110. Coulson, *History*, 147.

(*p*) See below, Chapter I, §1. There are also laws made by the state, Mujeeb, *Indian Muslims* (London, 1967), 37. For an exhaustive historical discussion see 'Justice, Equity and Good Conscience', by J. D. M. Derrett in J. N. D. Anderson (ed.), *Changing Law in Developing Countries* (London, 1963), 114-53.

mitted perpetuities and the erection of wakfs for family aggrandizement solely, the influence of English judges and of the Privy Council has gradually encroached on this position until decisions given quite recently have decided that such wakfs are illegal. . . The Mohamedan law in East Africa has, however, not been subjected to the same modifying influence as in India, and remains the same as when the Min Haj (*Minhāj al-Ṭālibīn*) was written in the sixth century of the Hejira.'(*q*)

While we are discussing the nature of *fiqh*, it must also be pointed out that this science has been divided into two portions. The *uṣūl*, literally the Roots (*r*) of the law, and the *furū'*, the Branches (*s*) of the law. The science of *uṣūl* deals with the first principles of interpretation and may be likened to our modern jurisprudence, while the science of *furū'* deals with particular injunctions—*aḥkām*—or the substantive law, as we would call it, which really follows from the science of *uṣūl*. The science of *uṣūl* deals with the sources of the law and its interpretation; the science of *furū'* deals with the law as it is actually applicable in courts of justice; for instance, the law of marriage, the law of *wakf* or the law of inheritance. It is, therefore, necessary to realize that in Islamic law there is a very clear distinction between the first principles and the rules deduced from their application (*t*).

We have now seen what *sharī'at* is and what, in essentials, is the definition of *fiqh*. What is the distinction, if any, between them? *Sharī'at* is the wider circle, it embraces in its orbit *all* human actions; *fiqh* is the narrower one, and deals with what are commonly understood as legal acts. *Sharī'at* reminds us always of revelation, that *'ilm* (know-

(*q*) Cited by Lord Simonds in *Fatuma binti Mohamed* v. *Mohamed bin Salim* [1952] A.C.1, 14. See Nawawī, *Minhaj Et Talibin*, Eng. trans., by L. W. C. van der Berg (London, 1914).

(*r*) Or 'foundations'.

(*s*) Or 'applications'.

(*t*) Goldziher on Fiḳh, *Ency. of Islam*, 1st ed., II, 104; this is the most valuable general article on the subject. Mahmassani, 63 sqq.; Abdur Rahim's *Muhammadan Jurisprudence* is a modern textbook on *uṣūl*.

ledge) which we could never have possessed but for the Koran or *ḥadīth*; in *fiqh*, the power of reasoning is stressed, and deductions based upon *'ilm* are continuously cited with approval. The path of *sharī'at* is laid down by God and His Prophet; the edifice of *fiqh* is erected by human endeavour. In the *fiqh*, an action is either legal or illegal, *yajūzu wa mā lā yajūzu*, permissible or not permissible. In the *sharī'at*, there are various grades of approval or disapproval. *Fiqh* is the term used for the law as a science; and *sharī'at*, for the law as the divinely ordained path of rectitude. It must, however, be candidly confessed that the line of distinction is by no means clearly drawn, and very often the Muslim doctors themselves use the terms synonymously; for the criterion of all human action, whether in the *sharī'at* or in the *fiqh*, is the same—seeking the approval of Allah by conforming to an ideally perfect code (*u*).

(C) ***Fiqh: The Modern Theory.***—The Classical Theory of the sources and constitution of Islamic law was formulated as a system first by Shāfi'ī, although traces of it can be found from the earliest times. Since its formulation it has been accepted universally by Islamic scholars, both ancient and modern (*v*). During the last century, however, Ignaz Goldziher began the scientific criticism of the *ḥadīth* literature, and he may be said to be the originator of the Modern Theory. Goldziher was followed by Bergsträsser and Schacht, who has by his careful study of the works of Shāfi'ī established the main features of the modern theory in his *Origins of Muhammadan Jurisprudence* (Oxford, 1950). A brief account of his theory is given in the following pages, based on the above work; his *Esquisse d'une Histoire du Droit Musulman* (1953) and his two articles in *Law in the Middle*

(*u*) Levy says that *fiqh*, plus *kalām* (scholastic philosophy) combine and constitute *sharī'at, Social Structure*, 150.

(*v*) *Ancient authorities:* Taftāzānī, *Talwīḥ* (Cairo, A.H. 1327), 2 vols.; Ibn Khaldūn, *Muqaddima*, tr. F. Rosenthal, III, 1-32.

Modern authorities: C. Snouck Hurgronje, 'Le Droit Musulman', 1898, see *Selected Works* (Leiden, 1960); Abdur Rahim, *Muhammadan Jurisprudence*, 1907; S. Mahmassani, *Philosophy of Jurisprudence in Islam*, tr. Farhat J. Ziadeh (Leiden, 1961).

East, Volume I, *Origin and Development of Islamic Jurisprudence* (1955), chapters ii and iii (*w*).

The spirit of the law in Islam is religious and ethical, drawing its inspiration from the Koran and the teaching of the Prophet. But the content of the law is based upon pre-Islamic customs and usages. The matter is non-Islamic, but the spirit is Islamic. Beduin law was primitive, but in Mecca and Medina, trade flourished and a more elaborate system of customary law came to be recognized. This was known as the *sunna* of the people and was applied by *ḥakams*, arbitrators, for there were no regular courts or judges. The institution of cadis came later; some were appointed by the Prophet himself, but the real cadis came into existence only during the early Umayyad times.

The Prophet of Islam did not create a new system of law; he took the existing *sunna*, the 'prevalent usage'(*x*), and modified it in two ways. First, by direct revelation, that is, the ordinances of the Koran; and second, by his teaching and traditions (*ḥadīth*, pl. *aḥādīth*). Of these teachings, despite the monumental labours of the traditionists, we have no authentic record; for, on closer examination, the well-known traditions in the authoritative collections appear to have 'grown' later, in the second or third century A.H., and we cannot say for certain whether they represent the Prophet's actual words and actions. Modern research tends to show that a major portion of the traditions attributed to the Prophet is apocryphal.

When the Islamic state was firmly established, the need for cadis arose, and the *ḥakams* were displaced by these officials. The law was, however, the special preserve of the 'specialists', the *fuqahā'*, who endeavoured to reconcile the ancient usage with Islamic teaching. There was thus a conflict between the

(*w*) Detailed references have been avoided so as to give continuity to this brief summary.

(*x*) Schacht calls it the 'living tradition'. I, however, prefer the expression 'prevalent usage' and restrict the use of the word 'tradition' to the traditions (*aḥādīth*) ascribed to the Prophet Muḥammad.

prevalent usage and some of the rules laid down by the Prophet and his early Companions. The law was studied specially in three ancient centres, namely, Iraq, Hijaz and Syria, and 'the real distinguishing features between the ancient schools of law is neither the personal allegiance to a master, nor, as we shall see later, any essential difference in doctrine, but simply their geographical distribution'.(*y*)

The first two founders of the schools of Sunnite law were Abū Ḥanīfa and Mālik; the former represents the Iraq school and the latter, the school of Hijaz. Shāfi'ī, the founder of the third school, was the pupil of Mālik, but differed from him regarding *sunna*. It was Shāfi'ī who defined *sunna* as 'the model behaviour of the Prophet', which, if it conflicted with the prevalent usage, was to be accepted without any reserve. For Shāfi'ī, the most important source of law is the teaching or the practice of the Prophet; thus he gives the utmost importance to the traditions of the Prophet, and admits the traditions of the Companions and Successors only as a secondary source. A critical study of the traditions, however, shows that traditions of the Companions and Successors are earlier than those ascribed to the Prophet.

While the first four schools of law, Hanafi, Mālikī, Shāfi'ī, and Ḥanbalī were founded in the second century, the canonical traditionists worked in the third century. The six 'correct' books of the Sunnites are the work of Bukhārī, Muslim, Abū Dāwūd, Tirmidhī, Ibn Māja and Nasā'ī. The four authoritative books of the Twelver Shī'a by Kulaynī, Ibn Bābawayhi and Ṭūsī are still later and were composed during the fourth and the first half of the fifth century (*z*). The Muslim traditionists, it is related, made great efforts to sift the true from the false traditions, but their labours were inadequate and their methods imperfect. Goldziher has shown, in his ***Muhammedanische Studien***, that the great majority of traditions even in the classical collections are

(*y*) Schacht, *Origins*, 7.

(*z*) Fyzee, *Shiite Creed* (Oxford, 1942), 6.

documents not of the time to which they claim to belong, but of the successive stages of the development of the doctrines during the first centuries of Islam. Schacht has carried the investigation further and demonstrated that traditions unknown to earlier masters have been quoted by later authorities; he has also proved that traditions from Companions and Successors are earlier than those from the Prophet. In his own words:

> This book (*Origins of Muhammadan Jurisprudence*) will be found to confirm Goldziher's results, and to go beyond them in the following respects: a great many traditions in the classical and other collections were put into circulation only after Shāfi'ī's time; the first considerable body of traditions from the Prophet originated towards the middle of the second century, in opposition to slightly earlier traditions from Companions and other authorities, and to the 'living tradition' of the ancient schools of law; traditions from Companions and other authorities underwent the same process of growth, and are to be considered in the same light, as traditions from the Prophet; the study of *isnāds* often enable us to date traditions; the *isnāds* show a tendency to grow backwards and to claim higher and higher authority until they arrive at the Prophet; the evidence of legal traditions carries us back to about the year 100 A.H. only; at that time Islamic legal thought started from late Umaiyad administrative and popular practice, which is still reflected in a number of traditions (*a*).

If this is the correct position—and until the contrary is proved, we must assume that it is true—Imām Shāfi'ī's and Imām Aḥmad ibn Ḥanbal's insistence on the correct traditions assumes a new meaning for us. The *ḥadīth* may thus be one of two things: (i) a reform advocated by the Prophet in opposition to the prevalent usage, or (ii) a practice put forward by certain jurists to support their own theoretical views or the prevalent usage of a particular community.

As this is an elementary treatment of a vast and complicated subject, we shall not go into the details of the various schools and the methods by which they accepted or rejected the traditions; but we may note broadly that the ancient schools of law accepted the prevalent usage as the *sunna*.

(*a*) Schacht, *Origins*, 4-5.

The Iraqians speak of the traditions of the Prophet, and the Medinese sometimes accept the usage of the people. They also use *ra'y* for arriving at the correct rule. It is Shāfi'ī who introduces the normative element in *ḥadīth*, and says that a clear tradition of the Prophet overrules the prevalent usage of the community, and this became ultimately the established doctrine of Islamic law.

The force of tradition was, however, cut down by the parallel development of the doctrine of Consensus. The people at large adhered to the commonsense view that a majority of the people, the *umma* of the Prophet, cannot be wrong; and this was reflected in a *ḥadīth* from the Prophet: 'My people will never agree on an error,' but Imām Shāfi'ī does not know of it. The wording is similar to some of Shāfi'ī's statements and it emerges as a full-fledged tradition in the third century (*b*). The doctrine of Consensus draws its strength from the customs and usages of the ancient Arabs, and the importance given to it by C. Snouck Hurgronje as 'the foundation of foundations' is justifiable by the subsequent development of the law. The Koran and *sunna* look to the past; Consensus and *qiyās* deal with the future of Islamic jurisprudence.

We are now in a position to comprehend the general situation: (1) that the *prevalent usage* (the 'living tradition' of Schacht) of the ancient schools, based on individual reasoning, came first; (2) that it was put under the aegis of the Companions; (3) that traditions from the Prophet, put into circulation by the traditionists of the second century, disturbed this placid current of prevalent usage; and (4) that it was Shāfi'ī who secured for these traditions the supreme authority they enjoy.

A deciding factor in the argument of Schacht is that if a tradition of the Prophet is not cited by an earlier authority, it was unknown to him and that it must have been forged later. This is a plausible view; but an absolute acceptance of

(*b*) Schacht, *Origins*, 91.

this presumption can lead to a serious difficulty. It may be argued that, in some cases at least, the traditionists by their incessant search discovered authentic material not known to earlier jurists. With this slight reservation the general theory put forward by Schacht may be accepted without hesitation.

A number of traditions ascribed to the Prophet have come down to us in the form of aphorisms or legal maxims. Many of them can be demonstrated to be of late origin and cannot be accepted without reserve. They are not uniform as to provenance or chronology; but as a rule they embody legal usage of early times, and take the form of traditions much later. Familiar examples are 'There is no valid marriage without a *walī*', and 'My community will not agree on an error'.

The essential features of the old Islamic jurisprudence, namely, the validity of prevalent usage (*sunna* of the people); a body of common doctrine with some degree of systemization; legal maxims in the form of traditions—all these were in existence in the beginning of the second century. The *science* of Islamic law grew from the later part of the Umayyad period, taking the prevalent usage as its raw material, and accepting or amending it as the need arose. Two observations of Schacht must, however, be borne in mind:

First: legal practice in the several parts of the Umaiyad empire was not uniform, and this accounts for some of the original differences in doctrine between the ancient schools of law. Secondly: although the dynasty and most of the Arab ruling class were Muslims, and although some elementary legal rules enacted in the Koran were more or less followed, the legal practice during the earlier part of the Umaiyad period cannot yet be called Muhammadan law. Muhammadan law came into existence only through the application of Muhammadan jurisprudence to the raw material supplied by the practice. It will be shown that legal norms based on the Koran, which go beyond the elementary rules, were introduced into Muhammadan law almost invariably at a secondary stage (*c*).

(*c*) ibid., 190-91.

Without going into the elaborate examination of the various schools and the conclusions to be drawn therefrom, we shall state the general theory in the words of its most prominent exponent:

Muhammadan law came into existence through the working of Muhammadan jurisprudence on the raw material which consisted of the popular and the administrative practice of late Umaiyad times and was endorsed, modified or rejected by the earliest lawyers. These lawyers and their successors were guided by a double aim: by the effort to systematize . . . an effort which we have considered in the preceding chapter . . . and by the tendency to 'Islamize', to impregnate the sphere of law with religious and ethical ideas, to subject it to Islamic norms, and to incorporate it in the body of duties incumbent on every Muslim. In doing this, Muhammadan law achieved on a much wider scale and in a vastly more detailed manner what the Prophet in the Koran had tried to do for the early Islamic community of Medina. Those two parallel and closely connected aims underlie much of the development of Muhammadan law during its formative period, as Bergsträsser has pointed out.

The tendency to Islamize took various forms: it made the ancient lawyers criticize Umaiyad popular and administrative practice, it made them pay attention to the (formerly disregarded) details and implications of Koranic rules, it made them attribute the 'living tradition' of their schools of law to the Prophet and his Companions, it made them take account of the rising tide of traditions ascribed to the Prophet, it provided them with part of the material considerations which entered into their systematic reasoning. Much as the ancient schools of law represented an Islamizing movement of opposition . . . though of course not necessarily political opposition . . . to late Umaiyad practice, the traditionists and the opposition groups within the ancient schools formed a still more thoroughly Islamizing minority which was partly successful and, when this happened, became indistinguishable from the majority. But the Islamizing process by which Muhammadan law as such emerged was not a monopoly of the traditionists or, within the ancient schools of law, of the school of Medina (*d*).

. . . that technical legal thought, as a rule, tended to become increasingly perfected from the beginnings of Muhammadan

(*d*) ibid., 283-4.

jurisprudence up to the time of Shāfi'ī, and that material considerations of a religious and ethical kind, whether they were from the beginning or introduced at a later stage, usually tended to become fused with systematic reasoning. In both respects, the work of Shāfi'ī represents the zenith of development, and the reader will, I hope, take it on trust that technical legal thought in Muhammadan jurisprudence hardly ever approached and never surpassed the standard he set (*e*).

The limitations and faults of Shāfi'ī's reasoning cannot detract from the unprecedentedly high quality of his technical legal thought which stands out beyond doubt as the highest individual achievement in Muhammadan jurisprudence (*f*).

In the Epilogue Schacht says: 'After the work of Goldziher there remained no doubt that the conventional picture concealed rather than revealed the truth; and I trust the sketch by which I have tried to replace it comes nearer to reality.' The classical theory as it emerges, after fourteen centuries of development, gives prime importance to the religious and ethical teaching of the Koran and the Prophet; it has thus a certain value for the lawyer, the historian and the student of civilization. The modern critical theory goes to the roots of the law as they are to be found in the history of its growth and its institutions. It pays little regard to ethical and spiritual norms. Thus it has a scientific value, but it cannot stand alone. A careful study of both the theories is essential for a modern, critical student of the law; and it is to be hoped that some other scholar will study the work of the Ḥanbalī school, such as the legal thought of Ibn Taymiyya or Ibn Qayyim, and the jurists of the Ithnā 'Asharī school, such as Ibn Bābawayhi and Ṭūsī, with the same learning, penetration and objectivity as that shown by Schacht in his examination of the work of Shāfi'ī. Such an investigation will go far towards the deeper understanding of the problems connected with the development of Islamic law in all their complexity (*ff*).

(*e*) ibid., 287.

(*f*) ibid., 324.

(*ff*) For a recent discussion see Anderson and Coulson, op. cit., 1-36, and N. J. Coulson, *A History of Islamic Law* (Edinburgh, 1964).

V. Development of Muslim Law

(A) *Formation of Sunnite schools: The five periods.*—It is now proposed briefly to deal with the most important periods of the development of Islamic law. Abdur Rahim, in his *Muhammadan Jurisprudence*, following the usual classification, divides the course of Muhammadan law into four different periods. On the other hand, al-Khuḍarī, in his history of *fiqh*, divides the history of Islamic law into six periods (*g*). The classification of al-Khuḍarī is to be preferred, but for the sake of simplicity and because it would be out of place to enter into historical details concerning this particular question, the classification of Abdur Rahim, which is generally accepted, is adopted here. But historical analysis compels us to add another, the fifth, commencing with the *abolition of the Caliphate* in 1924. Thus there are five periods in the history of Islamic law.

The first period is the one between A.H. 1 and 10, viz. the last ten years of the Prophet's life. This is the most important period so far as the first two sources of the law, the Koran and the *ḥadīth*, are concerned. The Prophet had conquered Medina and Mecca, and in the last few years of his life he took upon himself the task of legislation. Most of the legal verses of the Koran were revealed at that time and some of his most important judicial decisions and traditions relate to that period. With reference to the binding force of tradition, it is convenient here to say a word about the theory of inspiration, *waḥy*, in Islamic law. Inspiration may be of two different kinds; it may be manifest (*ẓāhir*) or it may be implied (*bāṭin*) (*h*). The verses of the Koran are direct inspiration—in the theory of Islam they are the very words of God. The actions and the sayings of the Prophet stand on a different level. In Islamic theory these actions and sayings

(*g*) Muḥammad al-Khuḍarī, *Ta'rīkh al-tashrī' al-islāmī*, 3rd ed., Cairo, 1930/1348, p. 4; abridged Urdu translation, *Tārīkh-e fiqh-e islāmī*, by Mawlānā 'Abdu's-Salām (Azamgadh), A.H. 1346. The best general account is by Schacht in *LME*, I, 57 sqq.

(*h*) Abdur Rahim, op. cit., 69 sqq.

were also inspired but the inspiration was indirect, that is to say, we have to look to all the surrounding circumstances of a particular action or saying of the Prophet before we can arrive at the true principle behind it, and that principle was inspired in the sense that it also was suggested or commanded by God. The traditions are therefore supposed to be indirect revelation (*i*).

The next period of great significance from the point of view of the law is the period A.H. 10 to 40, the thirty years of the Orthodox Khilāfat, the Khilāfat (Caliphate) of the first four Caliphs or successors of the Prophet. The two things which are apparent in this period are the close adherence to ancient practice under the fiction of adherence to *sunna*, and secondly, the collection and the editing of the text of the Koran, the final recension whereof took place in the reign of 'Uthmān, the third Caliph. It is that Koran—'Uthmān's edition—which exists absolutely pure and without corruption to this day, and this may be called the authorized text.

The third period of Islamic law, which takes us from A.H. 40 to the third century of the *hijra*, is a period which is still more important, because in this period the work of collecting the traditions took place, and the collections of Bukhārī and Muslim, for instance, came to be recognized as authoritative. During the earlier part of this period there appear the four schools of Sunnite law which are well known and considered equally 'orthodox'(*j*). First, the Ḥanafī (*k*) school named after Imām Abū Ḥanīfa (80/699 to 150/766), the oldest and supposedly the most liberal of the four schools, the special characteristic of which was reliance

(*i*) Modern research tends to the view that a considerable body of traditions attributed to the Prophet may be spurious; nevertheless, a good many of them reflect the actual practice of jurists of authority.

(*j*) W. H. Morley, *Administration of Justice in British India* (London, 1858), 247; *LME*, I, 70; Schacht, *Esquisse*, 59-60.

(*k*) *Ḥanafī* not *ḥanīfī*, nor *Hânâfi*, as commonly mispronounced and misspelt: see [1955] 2 Cal., 109, 124. The word is so common that it is spelt Hanafi in this book, without any accents.

on the principles of *qiyās* or Analogical Deduction. Many scholars think that he was the founder of *qiyās*; this is incorrect. He employed *qiyās* more because the science of *ḥadīth* had not developed fully by that time, and no recognized collections were available. In essentials, his system does not differ from the others. His two disciples were the Cadi Abū Yūsuf and Imām Muḥammad al-Shaybānī, both jurists of the first rank (*l*).

The Kūfa school of Imām Abū Ḥanīfa is to be distinguished from the Medina school of Mālik ibn Anas (90 or 97/713 to 179/795), the next in point of time which did not place much reliance on *qiyās* and represents more the *ijmā'* and practice of Medina than any system worked out by Imām Mālik alone. His chief book, the *Muwaṭṭa'*, is the oldest corpus of Sunnite law extant and is of interest because it forms a link between the *fiqh* literature of earlier days and the *ḥadīth* collections of later times. According to Schacht, Mālik's tendency to consistent systematic reasoning is secondary to his dependence on prevalent usage by tradition. His reasoning is inspired 'by material considerations, by practical expediency, and by the tendency to Islamize' (*m*).

The third school which we have to consider is the school of Imām Shāfi'ī (150/767 to 204/820). He was a pupil of Imām Mālik and of Imām Muḥammad, the pupil of Abū Ḥanīfa. Modern critics place Imām Shāfi'ī very high as a jurist; he is one of the greatest jurists of Islam, and the creator of the Classical Theory of Islamic Jurisprudence. Shāfi'ī is generally regarded as the founder of the science of *uṣūl*; and he perfected the doctrine of *ijmā'*. al-Shāfi'ī may be described as an eclectic who acted as an intermediary

(*l*) Juynboll in *Ency. of Islam*, I, 90. For the best modern discussion of the Imām and his disciples see Schacht, 239, 294, 301 and index; also his *Esquisse*, 57. A full but uncritical account of his life will be found in Shiblī Nu'mānī, *Sīrat al-Nu'mān* (Azamgadh, 1936, Urdu).

(*m*) Schacht in *Ency. of Islam*, III, 205, and his *Origins*, 6 sqq., and 311 sqq. and *Esquisse*, 58. The traditional account of his life will be found in *Ḥayāt-e Mālik* by Sayyid Sulaymān Nadwī, 3rd ed., Azamgadh (India), 1940. See also J. Schacht, 'Ḥanafiyya', *Ency. of Isl.*, III (rev. ed.), 142.

between independent legal investigation and the traditionism of his time. Not only did he work through the legal material available, but in his *Risāla,* he also investigated the principles and methods of jurisprudence.'(*n*)

Finally we come to Imām Aḥmad ibn Ḥanbal (164/780 to 241/855). Originally the pupil of Imām Shāfi'ī, he represents the most extreme reaction (except Dā'ūd al-Ẓahirī) from the school of what was called *ahl al-ra'y,* 'the people of opinion', and strictly adhered to the principle of following the *ḥadīth* literally. He was a man of very saintly character and more of a traditionist than a lawyer. Ṭabarī the historian refused to recognize him as a jurist (*faqīh*), considering him a mere traditionist (*muḥaddith*). Goldziher doubts whether he can be said to have founded a new school of law, but he is undoubtedly recognized as an Imām by the Sunnites (*o*).

It must not be supposed that these were the only Imāms or Founders of the law. There were others too who attained the rank of Imām or *mujtahid*, but whose schools did not survive; such were Dā'ūd ibn 'Alī al-Ẓāhirī, al-Awzā'ī (*p*), Sufyān al-Thawrī and Abū Thawr (*q*).

The vast majority of Muslims in India, Pakistan, Afghanistan and Turkey are Hanafis. The Shāfi'īs are to be found on the coast-line of Arabia and India, in South Arabia, Lower Egypt, East Africa and South-East Asia. For instance, the Koknīs of Bombay, the Moplahs (Mapillahs) of Malabar, the Moors of Ceylon and the Arabs in Java are all Shāfi'īs. North Africa, the *maghrib* of the Muslim authors (Maghreb, in Europe), and West Africa are wholly of Mālikī persuasion.

(*n*) Heffening in *Ency. of Islam*, IV, 253. See also Ḥāfiẓ Md. Na'īm Nadwī Ṣiddīqī, *Imām Shāfi'ī awr unkī khidmāt, Ma'ārif* (Azamgadh, India), Jan. and Feb. 1968, pp. 25-40 and 98-110. Shāfi'ī's *Risāla* has been translated into English by M. Khadduri (Baltimore, 1961).

(*o*) Goldziher in *Ency. of Islam*, I, 188. 'Ḥanābila', H. Laoust, in *Ency. of Islam,* III (rev. ed.), 158.

(*p*) This jurist offers some of the oldest solutions in Islamic Jurisprudence, Schacht, 288.

(*q*) Aghnides, op. cit., 133.

We have no Mālikīs in India. The so-called Wahhābīs, the followers of Ibn Sa'ūd, Sultan of Najd, are Ḥanbalīs; but, except in the centre of Arabia, as leaders in a puritanical movement, the Ḥanbalīs are nowhere else to be found (*r*).

(B) *Evolution of* Ijtihād *and* Taqlīd.—We now come to the fourth period, a period not only long and varied, but also one of general decadence. It extends from the third century of the Hijra to 1922/1924.

Strictly the fourth period extends only to 1922, the abolition of the Sultanate, or 1924, the abolition of the Caliphate by the Turkish Republic. For, after that, Sunnite Islam had no generally recognized head, and we may be said to be living since then in the fifth period, a period wherein great inroads have been made by the secular law (*qānūn*) into the domain of the sacred law (*sharī'at*) in all Muslim countries. This tendency, it is submitted, is likely to increase, until ultimately the law will largely be secularized (*rr*).

After the four recognized schools had been founded, later scholars applied themselves to the methods laid down by the founders and developed each system in a particular manner; but no individual jurist was ever afterwards recognized as having the same rank as the founder himself. On the one hand the doctrine of *taqlīd* (following or imitation) came into prominence; on the other, the limits of *ijtihād*, the power of independent interpretation of law, were greatly restricted. The earlier jurists had greater powers; the later ones could not cross the barrier and were classified as of lower and lower rank. The classification of the lawyers of this period is very elaborate; seven different grades are recognized, beginning from the Imāms as founders down to the ordinary juris-

(*r*) *Ency. of Islam,* II, 104. As regards the distribution of the schools see Schacht, *Esquisse,* 57 sqq. F. Rahman, *Islam* (London, 1966) gives the total number of Muslims as 600 m., but the usual count is as follows: 384 m. Sunnites, 40, Shiites; 1 Khārijites, *Revue de l'Academie Arabe de Damas*, 1967, XLII, 196.

(*rr*) Anderson and Coulson, op. cit., 37 sqq; M. Mujeeb, *The Indian Muslims* (London, 1967), 37.

consult or *muftī* (*s*). Practically, in every case the later lawyers were considered lower in grade; until, after a time, the exercise of independent judgement was not permitted at all. This is known as 'The Closure of the Gate of Interpretation' during the fourth/tenth century (*t*).

The fifth period commences with the abolition of the Caliph/Sultan. As there is no one to execute the behests of the *sharī'at*, a new situation arises and legal fictions have to be created. The *sharī'at* becomes a moral code and loses its juristic sanction, for how can we conceive of a law without someone to administer it and execute its decrees? Thus, with the changing of time, Islamic law all over the world must now be considered in a different light, juristically (*u*).

We must now consider the doctrines of *ijtihād* and *taqlīd*. *Ijtihād* literally means 'exerting one's self to the utmost degree to attain an object', and technically, 'exerting one's self to form an opinion in a case or as to a rule of law' (*v*). Islamic law was not a corpus of legislative activity but a science developed by juristic thought. Hence, the considered opinion of individual specialists often becomes part of the law. In his polemics and discussions, Imām Shāfi'ī, while acknowledging and defending the *sunna* of the Prophet, expresses himself solidly against the unthinking and unquestioning acceptance of the opinions of men (*w*). In the early days of Islam many individuals were known as *mujtahids* or those who exercised independent judgment; but this power was cut down by the parallel doctrine of *taqlīd*. *Taqlīd* (literally, imitation) means 'following the opinion of another person without knowledge of the authority for such

(*s*) Aghnides, op. cit., 121-3; Abdur Rahim, op. cit., 168, 182 sqq.

(*t*) *LME*, I, 73; Schacht, *Esquisse*, 63 sqq.; *Origins*, 116.

(*u*) M. K. Nawaz, 'A Re-examination of some Basic Concepts of Islamic Law and Jurisprudence', *Indian Year Book of Intern. Affairs*, (Madras, 1963), 205.

(*v*) *Ency. of Islam*, II, 448; Abdur Rahim, op. cit., 168. Shāfi'ī, *Umm*, VII, 203-4; Coulson, *History*, 182, 202 and elsewhere.

(*w*) Schacht, 6. For Shāfi'ī's classical precept to Muzanī against blindly following himself or any one else, see *Umm*, I, 1 (top).

opinion' (*x*). A Muslim had to follow the law; every man in the street could not be learned in the rules of *sharī'at*; being ignorant, he was asked to follow the opinion of those who knew better. Those who knew better, the '*ulamā*', were denied independence of judgment in any vital matter. Hence the vicious circle of *taqlīd* (*y*).

There is nothing, as Abdur Rahim has shown, in the theory of Islam to force the principle of blind imitation on the Muslims (*z*). In fact, it is only due to political and other causes that they still consider themselves bound by older views, while the letter of the law allows them liberty to develop their system of jurisprudence. Therefore, to say that legally no one can have the rank of *mujtahid* at present is wrong; the practical difficulty, however, that there is no chance of anybody being recognized as such today, remains. Unless a bold step is taken, as suggested by that thinker and poet, Iqbal, in his *Reconstruction in Islam*, the *sharī'at* will remain a fossil (*a*). He suggests that the principles of *ijmā'* should be applied and that the power of *ijtihād* should reside not in one individual, but in a body of learned Muslim scholars of advanced views, who may interpret the law so that it falls in line, as far as possible, with modern legal and social ideas. Since the Turkish Revolution of 1922, efforts in this direction by legislative activity are constantly being made in almost all the countries of the Middle East and

(*x*) Abdur Rahim, op. cit., 171.

(*y*) A few derived terms may be explained here, as they are often used in Islamic legal literature. From *ijtihād*, we have *mujtahid*, literally, 'one who strives incessantly (to attain the truth)', i.e., one who is entitled to express an independent opinion; and from *taqlīd* is derived *muqallid*, one who follows the opinion of another. These terms are used with reference to human beings, for all mankind is under *taklīf*, which means, the obligation to follow the law. Hence, every man being sane and adult is a *mukallaf*—a person on whom an obligation rests—and God is the *mukallif*, one who casts the obligation of obedience upon mankind.

(*z*) Abdur Rahim, 173. See generally, Schacht, *Esquisse*, 63 sqq., and Mahmassani, 92 sqq., and his valuable remarks on the evolution of laws, in Part iv, 105 sqq.

(*a*) (Lahore, 1930) 242-4; (Oxford, 1934) 141 sqq.

Africa (*b*). A theoretical separation of *law* and *religion* in Islam appears to be a possible solution (*bb*).

VI. The Shī'a: History and Sub-Schools

We must now proceed to consider what is generally known as the Shiite law (*c*). This requires separate treatment, particularly because very few authorities give adequate information concerning it (*d*). The term *shī'a* by itself means 'faction', and being an abbreviation of the term *shī'at 'Alī*, it means specifically that party which, after the death of the Prophet, attached itself to Ali, the son-in-law of the Prophet, considering him the successor of the Prophet both in temporal and in religious matters, and denying the rightful succession of the first three caliphs (*e*). The Shiites deny the principle of

(*b*) Shaykh Muḥammad 'Abduh, an Egyptian theologian, put forward the right of independent investigation at the close of the nineteenth century. His views are discussed by C. C. Adams in *Islam and Modernism in Egypt* (Oxford University Press, 1933), 132 sqq. A discussion of the problem will be found in Professor H. A. R. Gibb's *Modern Trends in Islam* (Chicago-Cambridge, 1947). See also J. Schacht, 'Islamic Law in Contemporary States', *Amer. Jl. of Comparative Law*, 1959, vol. 8, 133-47; J. N. D. Anderson, *Islamic Law in the Modern World* (London, 1959) and *Islamic Law in Africa* (London, 1954); J. N. D. Anderson, 'The Significance of Islamic Law in the World Today', *Amer. Jl. of Comparative Law*, 1960, 187; A. A. A. Fyzee, 'The Relevance of Muhammadan Law in the Twentieth Century', *Cambridge L.J.*, 1963, 261-69; Anderson and Coulson, 'Islamic Law in Contemporary Cultural Change', *Saeculum*, op. cit.

(*bb*) A theoretical separation between *law* and *religion* in Islam has been advocated by me in *A Modern Approach to Islam* (Bombay, 1963).

(*c*) The term *Shī'a* is a noun and cannot be used as an adjective. The terms 'Shia law', 'Shia books', 'Shia tenets' and 'Shias' are, therefore, all objectionable, although commonly used. The correct forms would be 'Shī'ī' or 'Shī'ite' law, and 'Shī'īs' or 'Shī'ites'; cf. 'Sunna' and 'Sunni' or 'Sunnite', for example. The adjective 'Shiite' is adopted throughout in this book as it is a common English word, see the *Concise Oxford Dictionary*, 5th ed., 1964.

(*d*) W. H. Morley, *Administration of Justice in British India* (London, 1858), 250. For general principles see my 'Shī'ī Legal Theories', *LME*, I, 113-31.

(*e*) There is no thorough account of the Shī'a, but the best summary of what is known is by Strothmann in *Ency. of Islam*, IV, 350, s.v. 'Shī'a'. See also D. M. Donaldson, *The Shiite Religion* (London, 1933), Asaf A. A. Fyzee, *A Shiite Creed*, Islamic Research Association Series, No. 9 (Oxford University Press, 1942), and J. N. Hollister, *The Shia of India* (London, 1953).

election by the people in the matter of the Imāmate, and hold that the Prophet appointed Ali as his vicegerent on a certain occasion. (*ee*) Out of 600 million adherents of the Islamic faith (*f*), the Shiites number about 30 million (*g*); these figures are, however, somewhat doubtful, and the exact proportion of the Shiites to the rest of the Muslims cannot be determined with exactitude. The Shiites are divided into a large number of sub-schools, the two most important of which, so far as India is concerned, are the Ismailis and the Ithnā 'Asharīs (*h*). A short pedigree of the first Imāms (given in the genealogical table on p. 42) will make things clear.

Of the Shiite sects today, the Zaydīs are represented in south Arabia, mostly in the Yemen, and exhibit a curious and interesting fusion of Shiite and Sunnite principles. It will be seen from the genealogical table that the first principal difference among the Shiites arose after the fourth Imām, Zayn al-'Ābidīn. One of his sons, Zayd (d. A.H. 122) was accepted as Imām by certain people. Thus arose the present Zaydī sect. To this Zayd is attributed the *Majmū'al-Fiqh*. It is unfortunate that it has reached us in a spurious form; else it would have been the earliest extant manual of Islamic law, Mālik's *Muwaṭṭā'* being the second in point of time (*i*). The majority, however, followed Imām Muḥammad al-Bāqir, and after him Imām Ja'far al-Ṣādiq, who is distinguished not merely as Imām of the Shiites, but also as a man well versed in law and science. After the death of Imām Ja'far, again a difference arose, the majority following Imām Mūsā Kāẓim and

(*ee*) *Fat. Law*, Intr., XL sqq.

(*f*) F. Rahman *Islam* (London, 1966), 9; Hazard, *Atlas of Islamic History* (Princeton, 1951).

(*g*) L. Massignon, *Annuaire du Monde Musulman*, 4th ed., 1954, pp. xi and 428.

(*h*) See *Kitāb Firaq al-shī'a* (Die Sekten der Schī'a) of al-Ḥasan b. Mūsā al-Naubakhtī, ed. H. Ritter, Bibliotheca Islamica, Band 4, Leipzig-Istanbul, 1931.

(*i*) It has been edited by Griffini in Milan and also printed in Cairo. See Goldziher on '*Fiqh*', *Ency. of Islam*, II, 103. Strothmann has given us two careful and thorough studies of Zaydī law. See also Schacht, *Esquisse*, 61 sq.

through him six other Imāms, thus making the twelve Imāms of the sect known as Twelvers (in Arabic, *ithnā 'asharī*).

The minority, after the death of Imām Ja'far, the sixth Imām, did not acknowledge Imām Mūsā Kāẓim but adhered to the claims of his elder brother Ismā'īl and are today known as Ismā'īlīs; they are generally, but inaccurately, known as the Seveners (*sab'iyya*). In India they consist of two main groups, (i) the Khojas, or *Eastern* Ismailis, representing the followers of the present Aga Khan (*ii*), who is believed to be the forty-ninth Imām in the line of the Prophet (*j*), and (ii) the *Western* Ismailis who are popularly called Bohoras, and may be divided into Dā'ūdīs and Sulaymānīs and various other small groups. It must, however, be pointed out that the word *bohōra* merely means a 'merchant', and does not signify any particular school of Muhammadan law (*k*). There are Hindu Bohoras, Sunni Bohoras of Rander and other Bohoras of the Ismaili religion. The Eastern Ismailis are also to be found in East Africa,

(*ii*) His Royal Highness Prince Karim Aga Khan. This is the title awarded to him by the Iranian Government.

(*j*) cf. 'Ismaīliya', *Ency. of Islam*, II, 549 and *Sup.*; Ed. A. S. Arberry, *Religion in the Middle East*, vol. 2, (Cambridge, 1969), 'The Ismā'īlīs' by A. A. A. Fyzee, pp. 318-29. W. Ivanow, *Ismailitica*, 69, 76; for History, see *Adv.-Genl.* v. *Muhammad Husen Huseni* (known as the *Aga Khan Case*), (1886) 12 Bom. H. C. R. 323; *Cases*, 504-49 and *Haji Bibi* v. *H. H. Sir Sultan Mahomed Shah, the Aga Khan* (1908) 11 Bom. L. R. 409. The first case lays down that Khojas are Ismailis and not Sunnites; the second makes it clear that they are not Ithnā 'Asharīs, and distinguishes between the Seveners and the Twelvers. W. Ivanow has written several papers and edited texts relating to the Ismailis.

(*k*) cf. Asaf A. A. Fyzee, *Ismaili Law of Wills* (Oxford University Press, 1933), 3, note 2; 'Bohoras', *Ency. of Islam* (rev. ed.), 1960, I, 1254. For the history, tenets and books of the Dā'ūdī Bohoras, and the powers of the Mullaji Saheb, their *Dā'ī'l-Muṭlaq*, see *Adv.-Genl.* v. *Yusufalli* (1921) 24 Bom. L. R. 1060. Our knowledge of the Ismaili law is very meagre; Tyabji, *Muh. Law*, 3rd ed., 26. Their chief legal text, *Da'ā'im al-Islām*, has been edited by me in the original Arabic, Dar el-Maaref, Cairo, Vol. I, 1951; Vol. II, 1961. A translation of this text is being prepared by me. Four extracts with translations have been published; (i) on *Bequests to Heirs* in (1929) Jl. Bom. Br. R. A. S., 141, and (1929) 31 Bom. Law Rep. Jl., 84; (ii) on *Mut'a* in (1931) 33 Bom. Law Rep. Jl., 30. On both these points the Ismaili law agrees with the Hanafi rule ; (iii) *Wills* in (1932) 34 Bom. Law Rep. Jl., 89 and the author's *Ismaili Law of Wills* (Oxford University Press, 133); (iv) *Marriage of Minors* in (1936) 38 Bom. Law Rep. Jl., 41; and generally, *Compendium of Fatimid Law* (Simla, 1969).

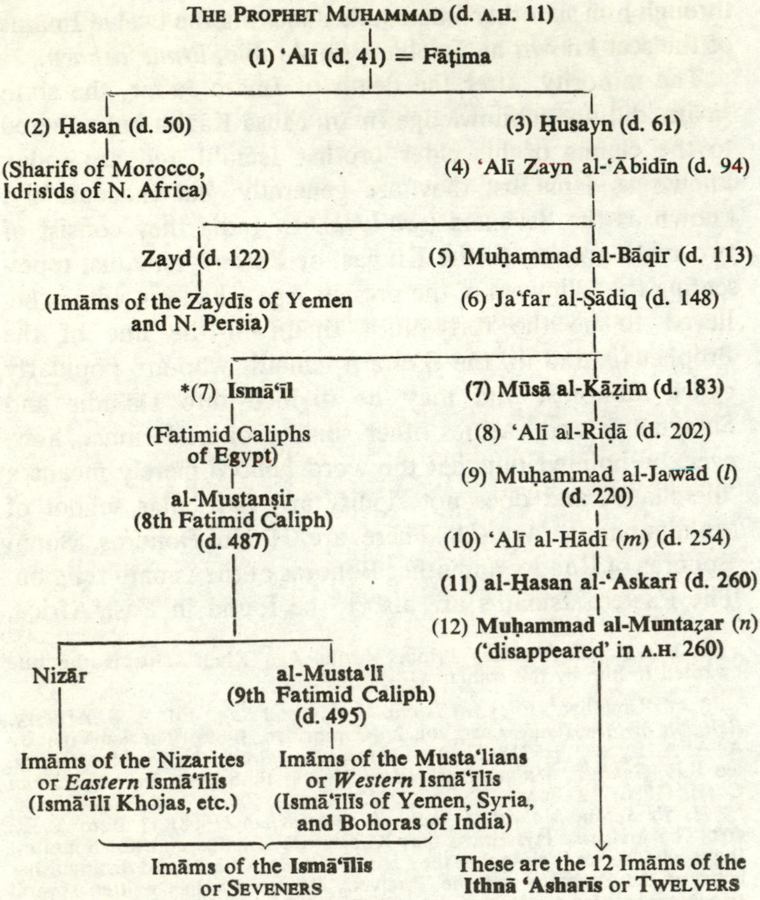

Central Asia, Persia, Syria and the Frontier Provinces. The Western Ismailis are spread over Syria, Southern Arabia, particularly the Yemen, and round the Persian Gulf.

The majority of the Shī'a belong to the Ithnā 'Asharī school. It is the religion of the majority in Iran, and of

(*l*) Or al-Taqī, D. M. Donaldson, op. cit., 188 sqq.

(*m*) Or al-Naqī, D. M. Donaldson, op. cit., 209 sqq.

(*n*) Also called *al-ḥujja* (the Proof), *al-qā'im bi-amri'l-lāh* (the Upholder of the Divine Command) and *ṣaḥib al-zamān* (the Master of Time); see Fyzee, *A Shiite Creed,* 95, and references.

a number of princely families in India. Some of the Nawabs of Lucknow, Murshidabad and the Deccan follow this school; and this branch of Muslim law is well known and recognized in India. The word 'Shī'a' is in India applied in general to the Ithnā 'Asharī school of Shiites, and hardly ever to any other. Sulaiman J. of the Allahabad High Court has laid down that 'Shia' law (*Ithnā 'Asharī*) was as much the law of India as any other branch of the law, and that therefore he would not allow any experts or *mujtahids* to go into the box and give expert evidence on it as if it were a branch of foreign law (*o*).

VII. Imāmat: Shiite Notion of Law

The fundamental difference between the Shiite and the Sunnite theology is the doctrine of Imāmat developed by the former. According to the Sunnite doctrine, the leader of the Muslims at any given moment is the *khalīfa* or caliph, literally, the 'successor' of the Prophet. He is more of a temporal ruler than a religious chief; for in religious matters he has simply to follow the path of *sharī'at*. He is a mere mortal; he must possess certain qualifications for election to his high office, and remains caliph so long as he performs his duties in accordance with the law; if he is found unfit, he may be deprived of the caliphate (*p*). The caliphate was abolished after the Turkish revolution in 1924, and the majority of Sunnite theologians have borne the loss without much mental discomfort.

The concept of *imām* (lit., leader) among the Shī'a, however, is totally different (*q*). Here temporal affairs take a

(*o*) *Aziz Bano* v. *Mahomed Ibrahim* (1925) 47 All. 823, 835; approved by the Judicial Committee in *Masjid Shahid Ganj* v. *Shiromani Gurdwara* (1940) 67 I.A. 251, 42 Bom. L.R. 1100.

(*p*) Arnold, *The Caliphate*, 71-2; *Ency. of Islam*, 1st ed., II, 881; Levy, *Sociology of Islam*, I, 295-300, 311 sqq.

(*q*) Definition and conditions of Imāmat, *al-Bābu'l-Ḥādī 'Ashar*, §174. Levy, op. cit., 301 sqq.; D. M. Donaldson, *The Shiite Religion* (London, 1933). Chapters I on 'The Question of Succession' and XXIX on 'The Doctrine of Imamate'; Fyzee, *A Shiite Creed* (Islamic Research Association Series, No. 9, Oxford University Press, 1942), Chapters 34-6 and index, and *LME*, I, 114 sqq.; Hollister, op. cit., 32.

secondary place; the Imām is the final interpreter of the law on earth. He is 'leader' not by the suffrage of the people, but by divine right, because he is a descendant of the Prophet—or rather of Ali. In some sects like the Zaydīs, he is merely a human being; in others, like the Ithnā 'Asharīs, the Twelfth Imān partakes of the divine essence. He is the *ghā'ib* and *muntaẓar*—'he who has vanished' and 'he who is awaited'—but he lives and is deathless, and will appear at a pre-ordained time and 'will fill the earth with justice just as it is (now) full of injustice'.(*r*) Among the Western Ismailis, the Imām is '*maṣtūr*', hidden, from the sight of the uninitiated, but not immortal. On account of persecution, one of the earlier Imāms went into hiding; his descendants have continued to rule over the true believers to this day, and will go on doing so for ever, but he can only be recognized by the higher Initiates, the *dā'īs*. The Eastern Ismailis identify their Imām, for all practical purposes, with God; they hold that Ali was more God than man, while the Prophet is given a secondary position to him as *ḥujjat* (*s*). The 'Alī Ilāhīs and the Druzes are even more frankly believers in the principles of incarnation and epiphany.

The Imām of the Shī'a is therefore similar in some respects to the *quṭb* or *insān al-kāmil* of the Ṣūfīs, the *bāb* of the Bābīs, and the *ghawth* of the Dervishes. Originally the Imām, being a descendant of Ali, was supposed to be the repository of the secret doctrines and teaching of Islam imparted by the Prophet to his favourite son-in-law. But later, in Islam as in many other faiths, the simplicity of the original creed apparently failed to satisfy certain spiritually-minded and philosophically-inclined men; in particular, the urge to find an intermediary between man and God—partaking of the

(*r*) Shahrastānī, *Milal wa'n-Niḥal*, ed. Cureton, 133; D. M. Donaldson, *The Shiite Religion*, 226; R. Strothmann, *Staatsrecht der Zaiditen*, 48, note. Definition and conditions of Imāmat, *al-Bābu'l-Ḥādī 'Ashar*, §211 (last lines), and Fyzee, *A Shiite Creed*, index.

(*s*) W. Ivanow, *Ismailitica*, 68. This, it seems, is not usual; *Salmān-i Fārisī* is ordinarily the *ḥujjat* of Ali; *Fat. Law*, Intr., xxxviii sqq.

essence of both, not quite God and yet somehow greater than man—was deeply felt.

It is unnecessary to go into the other doctrinal differences between Shiites and Sunnites. Those interested in the subject may refer to Wensinck's *The Muslim Creed* (Cambridge, 1932), and compare it with the creed of Ibn Bābawayhi, known as Shaykh Ṣadūq (*t*), or the later *al-Bābu'l-Ḥādī 'Ashar* by 'Allāma-i-Ḥillī (*u*). But one particular Shiite theory, the distinction between *īmān* and *islām*, may be mentioned, because it has been discussed in a court of law with reference to the validity of marriages between Shiites and Sunnites. The Shiites, relying on a text of the Koran (*v*), say that the two words are not synonymous, and in this respect differ from the Sunnites (*w*). Mankind may be divided first into two classes: Believers (*muslims*) and non-Believers (*ghayr muslims*). Muslims should again be divided into *mu'mins* (possessors of *īmān*, true believers) and *muslims*, the generality of believers. Belief in one God and the apostleship of Muhammad constitutes *islām* (*x*), and those who accept this are Muslims. But *īmān* consists of, first, *islām*, acceptance of the above dogma, plus secondly, *knowledge* of the true faith, consisting of the belief in a God-appointed necessarily-existent, and sinless (*ma'ṣūm*) Imām, and the theory of Imāmat (*y*); and thirdly, *action* in accordance with this true belief. Islam therefore is the wider circle; *īmān* the narrower one: a *mu'min* is necessarily also a *muslim*, but a

(*t*) Tr. by me, *A Shiite Creed* (Oxford University Press, 1942).

(*u*) Tr. by W. M. Miller, London, R. A. S., 1928.

(*v*) Qur'ān, xlix, 14; *al-Bābu'l-Ḥādī 'Ashar*, §19 and note; Wensinck. *Muslim Creed* (Cambridge, 1932), 34; Ameer Ali, II, 22; Aghnides, 137 The *Da'ā'im al-Islām* of Cadi Nu'mān discusses this question fully in the first book, *dhikr al-īmān* in Vol. I, pp. 3, 15-17.

(*w*) Article on '*Imān*', in *Ency. of Islam*, II, 474; Macdonald, op. cit., 312.

(*x*) *Narantakath* v. *Parakkal* (1922) 45 Mad. 986, 991, 1001 and *Cases*, 7; Ameer Ali, II. 22.

(*y*) *al-Bābu'l-Ḥādī 'Ashar*, §179; for a philosophical definition of *īmān*, see *Rasā'il Ikhwān al-Ṣafā'*, Cairo, 1928/1347, IV, 128; Wensinck, *Muslim Creed* (Cambridge, 1932), 125, Art. 1, which is identical with the definition in the *Da'ā'im*, a Fatimid text, I, 3.

muslim is not necessarily a *mu'min*. Islam is the religion of the multitude; *īmān*, the faith of the chosen few. Islam—say the Shī'a—is the religion of the Prophet in its ordinary form; *īmān* is the name of its essence, its more perfect and nobler form. (*yy*).

This doctrine assumes importance when considered in relation to the law of marriage or *nikāḥ*. The argument may be stated as follows: a Muslim man may validly marry a non-Muslim woman under certain circumstances (*z*), but a Muslim woman cannot under any circumstances marry a non-Muslim. A man, say the doctors of the law, may under given conditions marry a woman who in faith is his inferior; not so the woman—she can only marry an equal (*kuf'*). Hence, say the Shiites, a *mu'min* (Shiite) man may marry a *muslim* (Sunnite or Shiite) woman; but a *mu'min* woman cannot marry anyone but a *mu'min* man. Such a contention was raised by an Ithnā 'Asharī wife against her Ḥanafi husband in a well-known Allahabad case (*a*); but Sulaiman J., in a learned and elaborate judgment based on the authority of the leading Shiite text, *Sharā'i' al-Islām* (popularly called Sharaya-ool-Islam, and even Suraya), disallowed it, and held that such a marriage was, from the viewpoint of the Shī'a, perfectly valid in law, although the pious may consider it undesirable or *makrūh*. The reverse case does not arise, because Sunnites make no such distinction between *islām* and *īmān*, and the validity of the marriage of a Sunnite woman with a Shiite man is now, so far as the Indian courts are concerned, beyond dispute (*b*).

What, therefore, is the definition of the law according to the Shī'a? They certainly accept the authority of the Koran, the Word of God, and the *sunna* of the Prophet. No *ḥadīth*

(*yy*) *Fat. Law*, Intr., xxxix.

(*z*) He may marry a *kitābiyya*, that is a Jewish or a Christian woman. Some of the Shī'a consider the *majūs* (Zoroastrians) also as among the *ahl al-kitāb*, *Ency. of Islam*, III, 665b; *Fat. Law* §148-49.

(*a*) *Aziz Bano* v. *Md. Ibrahim* (1925) 47 All. 823, 825, 836.

(*b*) Mulla, §258. The Fatimid law permits such marriages in time of necessity, *Da'ā'im*, II §732, note; *Fat. Law* §23.

is ordinarily accepted by them unless related by an Imām descended from the Prophet. But they say that only the Imām, and in his absence the *mujtahids* (*c*), his servants and teachers of the True Faith, can tell us what the correct interpretation of the law is. The Imām is the law-giver himself, the speaking (*nāṭiq*) Koran; he may in a proper case even legislate, make new laws and abrogate old ones; but as he is hidden or evanescent, the *mujtahids,* who are present at all times and in each country, are his agents, the recognized interpreters of the law in accordance with the canonical tradition. *Ijtihād*, therefore, has an altogether different signification in Shiite law; as Macdonald says, 'The Shiites still have *mujtahids* who are not bound to the words of a Master, but can give decisions on their own responsibility. These seem to have in their hands the teaching power which strictly belongs to the Hidden Imām. They thus represent the principle of authority which is the governing conception of the Shī'a.'(*d*) Among Sunnites, however, *mujtahids* have not existed since the fourth century of the Hijra; and the doctrine of *ijtihād* is jealously guarded and strictly construed by them (*e*). No matter how learned a scholar may be among the Shiites, his opinion has no value unless he attains the rank of a *mujtahid*, and therefore derives authority from the Imām and acts on his behalf. This does not mean that in practice the *mujtahid* can interpret the law with greater freedom than his Sunnite counterpart; it is a well-known fact that *taqlīd* has entered the Shiite mind to the same extent as amongst the Sunnites, and imitation is as much the rule in the one as in the other. The doctrine of *qiyās* is not accepted by the Shī'a, nor of *ijmā'*, as understood among the Sunnites (*f*).

Thus law, in the estimation of the Shiite doctors, consists

(*c*) The Shiite *mujtahids* are in fact very similar to the Sunnite *qāḍīs* (kazis). For an account of *mujtahids,* their course of studies and other information, see C. Frank, *Ueber den Schiitischen Mudschtahid* in *Islamica*, 1962, II, 171-92.

(*d*) Macdonald, *Muslim Theology*, 116.

(*e*) ibid., 38.

(*f*) LME, I, 127.

of rules for human conduct, based on the authoritative interpretation of the Koran and the *sunna* and the decisions of the Imāms by the *mujtahids*, who are the servants of the Imām of the time, derive their authority from him and act in his name. Nu'mān, the Fatimid jurist, says unequivocally that the law is founded upon (1) the Koran, (2) the *sunna*, and (3) the dictum of the *imāms* (*qawl al-a'imma*) (*g*).

It will be observed that the use of the term 'sect' for the two divisions has been studiously avoided, because, as has been pointed out by Goldziher, there are really no 'sects' in Islam but only 'schools', *madhāhib* (sing. *madhhab*), of Muslim law (*h*). Strictly speaking, belief in the one and only God and the apostleship of the Prophet Muhammad are the only two beliefs necessary in Islam (*i*). In the theory of the law all Muslims are brothers and equals, and differences in opinion on questions of law do not constitute them, speaking legally of course, into separate sects of the kind which we find in Hindu law.

VIII. The Last Phase: Muhammadan Law

Coming down to the times of the Muhammadan supremacy in India, we find that as the Mughal emperors were Hanafis, the *Kazis* (*j*) appointed by them administered the Hanafi law. Hanafi law was, in the Mughal times, the law of the land. This continued till the establishment of the British rule, when the influence of English common law and the principles of equity became more and more apparent (*k*). The Muhammadan law was applied as a branch of personal

(*g*) *Fat. Law*, Intr., xlvi sq.

(*h*) Goldziher, *Vorlesungen*, 1st ed., 51; *Ency. of Islam*, II, 104.

(*i*) *Narantakath* v. *Parakkal* (1922) 45 Mad. 986, *Cases*, 57 and below, §2, 'Definition of a Muslim'.

(*j*) Strictly *qāḍīs*. In England *cadi*, and in India *kazi*, is commonly used. The history and powers of this functionary are discussed below in §61(7) 'Kazi'. An account of the administration of justice under Muslim rule is given by M. B. Ahmad in *Administration of Justice in Medieval India* (Aligarh, 1941).

(*k*) Sir George Rankin, *Background to Indian Law* (Cambridge, 1946), 38-9.

law to those who belonged to the Muslim persuasion in accordance with the principles of their own school or sub-school.

In the earlier days of British rule, the influence of Islamic law, pure and simple, was felt everywhere (*l*). Originally the East India Company had merely the right of collecting the revenue. The administration of justice, civil and criminal, remained as it had been under the Muslim rule. The law-officers were mostly Muslims; the criminal law was Muslim; in civil matters, the Islamic law was applied to Muslims and the Hindu law to Hindus in accordance with the opinions of *maulvis* and *pandits* attached to the courts. This policy was further developed in the British régime, and we have in the famous Regulation II of 1772 the provision that 'in all suits regarding inheritance, succession, marriage and caste and other usages or institutions, the laws of the Koran with respect to Mahomedans, and those of the Shaster with respect to the Gentoos (Hindus), shall be invariably adhered to'. (*m*) Where the personal laws of the parties differed, the law of the defendant was applicable (*n*).

The Islamic criminal law, although successively modified, remained in force somewhat longer; and not till the year 1862, when the Indian Penal Code and the Code of Criminal Procedure came into force, did it entirely disappear. (*o*) As regards evidence, too, the Islamic law was not entirely abolished till the passing of the Evidence Act in 1872.

It is unnecessary to go into the history of the various enactments or to show how continuously the law has been and is even now being secularized. The personal law of the various communities has been applied, until, with differing social conditions, the need for a change is apparent. On the

(*l*) For history see W. H. Morley, *Administration of Justice in British India* (London, 1858); Sir Charles Fawcett, *First Century of British Justice in India* (London, 1934); Sir George Rankin, *Background to Indian Law* (Cambridge, 1946).

(*m*) Wilson, *Anglo-Muhammadan Law*, 6th ed., 25 sqq.

(*n*) Sir George Rankin, *Background to Indian Law*, 9, 12-14.

(*o*) For Criminal Law, see *LME*, I, 223 sqq.

one hand, certain portions of the law were abolished, such as slavery and forfeiture of rights on apostasy; and at the same time, newer ideas have been developed. In certain cases, for example the Wakf Act of 1913, where the courts had departed from the ancient rules regarding *Wakfs* or religious endowments to lineal descendants, the legislature intervened and passed an Act by which the original rules of Islamic law were made applicable (*p*). The result is that today the Muhammadan law of Marriage, Divorce, Dower, Legitimacy, Guardianship, Gifts, *Wakfs*, Wills and Inheritance is applied to Muslims everywhere in India. The law of Pre-emption is not applicable in Madras; but it is applied elsewhere, and, in some instances, in the north of India, even to Hindus by custom.

As regards custom, the Shariat Act, 1937, has had the effect of abrogating it and restoring to Muslims their own personal law in almost all cases.

And here it must not be forgotten that the Muhammadan law to be applied in India is the law that is to be found in well-known legal texts, such as the *Hedaya* and the *Fatāwā 'Ālamgīrī* and others which have acquired a special kind of authority in India; new rules of law cannot now be deduced by lawyers of eminence. It is for this reason that their lordships of the Privy Council in an important case said that they 'have endeavoured to the best of their ability to ascertain and apply the Mahomedan law, *as known and administered in India*'.(*q*) They did not rely in that case on 'the opinion of that learned Mahomedan lawyer' (Ameer Ali J.) which was founded on 'texts of an abstract character and upon precedents very imperfectly stated'. In another leading case, overruling the opinion of so great a judge as Mahmood J., Sir Arthur Wilson said:

(*p*) This Act was originally not retrospective. Subsequently, by another Act, XXXII of 1930, it was made so, and therefore the original rules of Islamic law now apply to *Wakfs*, whatever the date of their creation.

(*q*) *Abul Fata* v. *Russomoy Dhur Chowdhury* (1894) 22 I.A 76, 86-7; *Cases*, 388, 395.

In *Abul Fata* v. *Russomoy Dhur Chowdhury*, in the judgment of this Committee delivered by Lord Hobhouse, the danger was pointed out of relying upon ancient texts of the Mahomedan law, and even precepts of the Prophet himself, of taking them literally, and deducing from them new rules of law, especially when such proposed rules do not conduce to substantial justice. That danger is equally great whether reliance be placed upon fresh texts newly brought to light, or upon logical inferences newly drawn from old and undisputed texts. Their Lordships think it would be extremely dangerous to accept as a general principle that new rules of law are to be introduced because they seem to lawyers of the present day to follow logically from ancient texts, however authoritative, when the ancient doctors of the law have not themselves drawn those conclusions. (*r*).

This attitude, natural enough in India, where the majority of Muslims, being orthodox, were averse to any change in the 'holy' *sharī'at*, is the result of the combined effects of the doctrine of *taqlīd*, as understood by the later Islamic jurists and the common law doctrine of precedent, which tells the judge to interpret and follow, rather than create and expand the law. It has had, during the two centuries of British rule, the effect of keeping the law stationary and static except for two broadening influences: legislation, and the healthy introduction of the principles of English equity (*s*). Thus the Muhammadan law, as received in India, is the *sharī'at*, modified by the principles of the English common law and equity, in the varying social and cultural conditions of India; and during the centuries, it has tended to become a discrete system, somewhat at variance with its original sources (*ss*).

From the general history of legislation in these matters, two conflicting sets of principles arise. First, as far as possible, government does not wish to interfere with the personal law of the various communities, as it would tend to create great dissatisfaction; and secondly, changing social conditions, the

(*r*) *Baker Ali Khan* v. *Anjuman Ara Begum* (1903) 30 I.A. 94 at 111-12; *Cases*, 4, 17. For interpretation of conflicting texts, see §5, below.

(*s*) On the distinctive character of Anglo-Muhammadan law, see Schacht, *Esquisse*, 86, and *LME*, I, 82.

(*ss*) See my *The Reform of Muslim Personal Law in India*, Bombay, 1971.

effect of European education, the contact in commercial and other centres with Europeans and their legal notions—in sum, modern civilization—produce a desire in the minds of some to see that reforms are carried out. This can only be done by appropriate legislation, but the task is not easy. Even in the case of such legislation as the Hindu Code and the Special Marriage Act, 1954, there are large numbers of both Hindus and Muslims whose religious susceptibilities have been touched. Reform, therefore, becomes a matter of difficulty (*t*).

It is sometimes suggested that the Muhammadan law in India should be codified (*u*). In theory this is easy; we have only to bring together a dozen men learned in the various branches of Islamic law, and draft a Code giving us the law in the shape of clear-cut propositions. This has been done in Egypt (*v*), Turkey, Iran and Palestine with success; and, it is asked, why not here too? (*w*) To the reformer this would be a great opportunity for doing away with everything suggesting a state of affairs that flourished some centuries ago and for breaking off with the past. But, in the first place, the members of each community would desire their own particular laws to be applied to them; secondly, so few of our legal texts have been critically edited in the original Arabic or translated accurately into any language, English or vernacular, that the discovery of the proper rules in certain branches of the law would involve considerable research; and for that

(*t*) See the valuable essay of Derrett, 'Future of Muhammadan Law in India', in *Religion, Law and the State in India* (New York, 1968), 513-54.

(*u*) As was done by a great jurist and draftsman, Dr. 'Abd al-Razzāq al-Sanhūrī, well-known in Cairo as Sanhury Pasha for Egypt, Syria, Iraq and Libya. M. Khaddūrī, *Isl. Jurisprudence* (Shāfi'ī's *Risāla*), viii.

(*v*) J. N. D. Anderson, 'Law, Reform in Egypt, 1850-1950', in P. M. Holt (ed.), *Political and Social Change in Modern Egypt* (Oxford, 1968), 209.

(*w*) 'The Movement towards Codification in Turkey, Cyprus and the Arab World' by Prof. J. N. D. Anderson in *The Indian Year Book of International Affairs,* 1958, Vol. VII (Madras), 125; H. J. Liebesny, 'Stability and Change in Islamic Law', *MEJ,* Vol. 21, 1967, 16-34; Anderson and Coulson, op. cit., 37 sqq.; N. J. Coulson, *Succession in the Muslim Family,* Cambridge, 1971; Tahir Mahmood, *Family Law Reform in the Muslim World,* New Delhi, 1972.

time and money would be needed. (*x*) To all these difficult questions no hard and fast answers can be given. Partial codification as in Egypt, and the Dissolution of Muslim Marriages Act, 1939, in India, is one kind of remedy. And another, a more feasible one, is permissive legislation, which will gradually bring all communities under one uniform law (*xx*).

One of the most penetrating modern discussions of Islamic law is contained in the course of three lectures delivered in the University of London by Count Léon Ostrorog on *The Angora Reform* in 1927. His admiration for the system is unbounded; and I might fitly conclude by adopting his words:

> Considered from the point of view of its logical structure, the system (Islamic law) is one of rare perfection, and to this day it commands the admiration of the student. Once the dogma of the revelation to the Prophet is admitted as postulate, it is difficult to find a flaw in the long series of deductions, so unimpeachable do they appear from the point of view of Formal Logic and of the rules of Arabic Grammar. If the contents of that logical fabric are examined, some theories command not only admiration but surprise. Those Eastern thinkers of the ninth century laid down, on the basis of their theology, the principle of the Rights of Man, in those very terms, comprehending the rights of individual liberty, and of inviolability of person and property; described the supreme power in Islam, or Califate, as based on a contract, implying conditions of capacity and performance, and subject to cancellation if the conditions under the contract were not fulfilled; elaborated a Law of War of which the humane, chivalrous prescriptions would have put to the blush

(*x*) N. J. Coulson, 'The Concept of Progress and Islamic Law', *Quest* (Bombay), 1964, 16-25; and also his 'Islamic Family Law: Progress in Pakistan', *Changing Law in Developing Countries*, op. cit., 240. For reforms in Pakistan, see D. Pearl, 'Family Law in Pakistan', *Journal of Family Law*, Louisville, 1969, 165-89, and 'Within the limits prescribed by Allah', *South Asian Review*, vol. 3, 1970, 313-22. For other countries, J. N. D. Anderson 'The Role of Personal Statutes in Social Development in Islamic Communities', *Comp. Studies in Society and History*, vol. 13, 1971, 16-31.

(*xx*) For a full discussion of urgent reforms needed in India, see Asaf A. A. Fyzee, 'The Reform of Muslim Personal Law in India', Bombay, 1971; for an Urdu version, see *Islām awr 'aṣr-e Jadīd* (New Delhi), Oct. 1971, 12-40 and the editorial, 5-11.

certain belligerents in the Great War; expounded a doctrine of toleration of non-Moslem creeds so liberal that our West had to wait a thousand years before seeing equivalent principles adopted. Such a height and scope of conceptions may well have sufficed to inspire silent submission in any minds not endowed with constructive genius to an equal degree; but events moreover occurred that seem to have exerted the influence of a crushing and decisive factor (y).

(y) Ostrorog, *The Angora Reform*, 30-1. For international law in Islam, see M. Khadduri, *War and Peace in the Law of Islam* (Baltimore, 1955), 'International Law' in *LME*, I, 349, and *The Islamic Law of Nations* (Shaybānī's *Siyar*), Baltimore, 1966.

CHAPTER I

APPLICATION AND INTERPRETATION

§1. Application of Muhammadan Law—Shariat Act, 1937
§2. Definition of a 'Muslim'
§3. Conversion to Islam and Custom
§4. Three Commercial Communities: Khojas, Bohoras, Memons
§5. Schools of Law—Principles of Interpretation

§1. Application of Muhammadan Law—Shariat Act, 1937

MUHAMMADAN law was applied to Muslims in British India as a matter of policy. This policy was the result of the adoption of a tradition inherited from the Mughal rulers of India, who applied the Hindu and Islamic laws to their subjects conformably with their own views, to safeguard and guarantee to each of these communities the practice of its own religion (*a*). An early statement of this view is to be found in a letter written by Sir William Jones, the Calcutta judge and orientalist in 1788.

'Nothing,' says Sir William Jones, 'could be more obviously just than to determine private contests according to those laws which the parties themselves had ever considered as the rules of their conduct and engagements in civil life; nor could any thing be wiser than, by a legislative act, to assure the Hindu and Muselman subjects of Great Britain that the private laws which they severally hold sacred, and a violation of which they would have thought the most grievous oppression, should not be superseded by a new system, of which they could have no knowledge, and which they must have considered as imposed on them by a spirit of rigour and intolerance.'(*b*)

The policy of the British was dictated by three main considerations. First, they did not desire any break with the past; secondly, their chief object was to have security in social conditions so as to facilitate trade; and thirdly, they had no desire

(*a*) M. B. Ahmad, *Administration of Justice in Medieval India* (Aligarh, 1941), 32-3; 90-4.
(*b*) W. H. Morley, *Administration of Justice in British India* (London, 1858), 193.

to interfere with the religious susceptibilities of their subjects. Morley says, for instance:

In considering the propriety of altering or abrogating the Hindu or Muhammadan laws, all preconceived notions of the relative excellence of the English and native systems of jurisprudence should be taken as secondary considerations; nor should it be called in question whether such systems are in themselves good or bad; for it should never be forgotten, that, in the present state of society in India, they are undoubtedly the best adapted to the wants and prejudices of the people who form the great bulk of the population of the country; that they are an integral part of the faith of that people, and that, though we may not be bound by absolute treaty, we have virtually pledged ourselves to preserve them by repeated proclamations and enactments (*c*).

The earliest trace of the acceptance of this policy is to be found in the charter of George II, granted in 1753 (*d*). In Warren Hastings's plan for the administration of justice, proposed and adopted in 1772 when the East India Company took over the management of their territories in India, it was provided that *maulvis* and *pandits* should attend the courts to expound the law and to assist in the administration of justice. And later, by Sec. 27 of the celebrated Regulation of 1780, it was laid down 'That in all suits regarding inheritance, marriage and caste, and other religious usages or institutions, the laws of the Koran with respect to Mahomedans, and those of the Shaster with respect to Gentoos, shall be invariably adhered to.'(*e*) If only one of the parties were a Hindu or a Muslim, the laws and usages of the defendant were to be applied (*f*).

The subsequent history of this policy is beyond the scope of this work and the curious may follow it up in the pages of Morley, Ilbert, Abdur Rahim (*g*), Rankin (*h*) and other

(*c*) Morley, 197. (*d*) ibid., 177. (*e*) ibid., 177-8.

(*f*) Sir George Rankin, *Background to Indian Law* (Cambridge, 1946), 9. See *Robasa* (*Robaba*) v. *Khodadad* (1946) 48 Bom. L.R. 864, 878. See also the observations of Mahmood J.. in *Gobind Dayal's Case, Cases,* 431-2; M. Mujeeb, *Indian Muslims,* 42.

(*g*) *Muhammadan Jurisprudence*, 37-47.

(*h*) Sir George Rankin, *Background to Indian Law* (Cambridge, 1946).

writers. The present position may be summarized briefly. In India the *sharī'at* laws are not applied in their entirety; only a portion is made applicable, and this may be conveniently divided as follows:

(i) Rules which are *expressly* applied, for example inheritance and succession.

(ii) Rules which are applied as a matter of *justice, equity and good conscience* (*i*), for example pre-emption, within a limited scope, all over India, except in Tamil Nadu.

Recently it has been held that certain parts of the laws of England have been preserved by the Constitution of India, Art. 372(1); and that such parts of the English law as were in force before the commencement of the constitution, and have not been altered, repealed or amended, remain the law of the land until they are expressly repealed (*j*).

(iii) Rules which are *not applicable*, for example criminal law, law of evidence, slavery, etc.

[For further particulars, see Tyabji, Chapter 2; Wilson, Chapter 1; Mulla, Chapter 1. The impact of English law on the application of Muhammadan law in India has not been studied exhaustively, but a beginning will be found in *Cases*, Introduction.]

(*i*) An expression which means rules derived from the English common law and equity, in so far as they are in consonance with Muhammadan law. Pollock, *Expansion of Common Law*, 133; Holdsworth, *Some Makers of English Law*, 3: Sir George Rankin, op. cit., 38-9: *Hamira Bibi* v. *Zubaida Bibi* (1916) 43 I.A. 294, 301-2; *Waghela* v. *Masludin* (1887) 14 I.A. 89, 96; and Tyabji §16. But apart from such noble sentiments, it must be admitted that the pungent remark of Stephen has considerable force:

'Practically these attractive words mean little more than an imperfect understanding of imperfect collections of not very recent editions of English text-books', Sir George Rankin, op. cit., 119.

In *Moonshee Buzloor Ruheem* v. *Shumsoonnissa Begum*, Sir James Colville reacted strongly in favour of 'equity and good conscience' where the wife, 'be the conduct of the Husband ever so bad', has no relief: *Cases*, 298-9 (bottom).

For an historical account, see J. D. M. Derrett, 'Justice, Equity and Good Conscience', in *Changing Law in Developing Countries*, edited by J. N. D. Anderson (London, 1963), pp. 114-53.

(*j*) *Bank of India* v. *Bowman* (1955) 57 Bom. L.R. 345, 364.

See also 'The Migration of the Common Law', by Mr Justice Vivian Bose, *Law Quar. Rev.* (1960), 59, and M. C. Setalvad, *The Common Law in India*, Hamlyn Lectures, 1960, 62 and elsewhere.

Shariat Act, XXVI of 1937

The most important and far-reaching enactment passed within recent years, dealing with the application of Muhammadan law in India, is the Shariat Act, 1937. It came into operation on 7 October 1937, and is applicable throughout India, except in the North-West Frontier Province (*k*), which has an act of its own. It is a short enactment of six sections which aims at restoring the law of Islam to all Muslim communities residing in India, and doing away with customs contrary to the *sharīʿat*. It is applicable to every Muslim, regardless of the school to which he belongs, but a peculiar feature is that, even for the limited purposes of the law, the word 'Muslim' is not defined. It is applicable to all kinds of property, but there are three main exceptions: (i) agricultural land; (ii) testamentary succession in certain communities; and (iii) charities, other than *wakfs*. We shall now consider some of its provisions in detail (*l*).

Sec. 2 runs as follows: 'Notwithstanding any custom or usage to the contrary, in all questions (save questions relating to agricultural land) regarding intestate succession, special property of females, including personal property inherited or obtained under contract or gift or any other provision of Personal Law, marriage, dissolution of marriage, including *talaq*, *ila*, *zihar*, *lian*, *khula* and *mubaraat*, maintenance, dower, guardianship, gifts, trusts and trust properties, and *wakfs* (other than charities and charitable institutions and charitable and religious endowments) the rule of decision in cases where the parties are Muslims shall be the Muslim Personal Law (*Shariat*).'

The first part of this section largely abrogates custom. Muslim communities following customs at variance with Islamic law are compelled to follow the *sharīʿat*. Later we have the exception regarding agricultural land. The words 'intestate succession' show clearly that the power of testamentary succession enjoyed by certain communities is not

(*k*) A province now forming part of Pakistan.

(*l*) The text of the Shariat Act, 1937, will be found in Appendix A.

taken away (*m*). If a female receives property and by customary law the property is to revert to the heirs of the last male owner, such custom is abolished and she holds it in all respects as an heir at Muhammadam law (*n*).

The Supreme Court has decided that the words 'the rule of decision' in Sec. 2 are mandatory; the injunction is addressed to the court, and the intention of the legislature is that the Act should apply to all suits, proceedings and even appeals which were *pending* on the date when the Act came into operation in addition to suits and proceedings filed *after* that date (*o*).

Sec. 3 of the Shariat Act lays down that if a person belonging to a community whose customs regarding 'adoption, wills and legacies' prevail, makes a certain declaration, he will thereafter be governed in all respects by Muhammadan law. This section is applicable to certain communities in the Punjab and Sind where adoption prevails; and to Khojas in Bombay, as regards wills. A Khoja can, by custom, will away the whole of his property. But by making this declaration, he loses this right and is governed in all respects by Muhammadan law. Until the passing of the Cutchi Memons Act, 1938, the Cutchi Memons could also dispose of the whole of their property by will. Since the Act of 1938, the Cutchi Memons have been governed in all respects by Muhammadan law. Thus this section aims at compelling the Muslim communities to give up rights contrary to the Muhammadan law, to merge into the general Islamic community, and to be governed exclusively by the laws of the *sharī'at*.

The Shariat Act (including the Madras amendments) does not abolish the rights and incidents of a Moplah Marumaka-

(*m*) These communities, to be found in Western India, are Khojas and Memons. In Northern India, customary law at variance with the *sharī'at* and in Southern India, among the Moplas, Marumakathayam law are abolished, to the extent provided by the Shariat Act. Mulla §6; Tyabji §2(8)(a) and generally §9 has a full discussion on custom.

(*n*) Mulla, p. 5.

(*o*) *C. Mohammed Yunus* v. *Syed Unissa* [1962] 1 S.C.R. 67.

thayam *tarwad* in Madras. It abrogates custom only to the extent mentioned in Sec. 2 and 3 of the Central Act and Sec. 2 of the local Act (*p*). In the former state of Hyderabad no custom in derogation of the Muhammadan law can be pleaded regarding the rights of inheritance (*q*).

Sec. 5 has been repealed and, since 1939, the Calcutta case, *Burhan* v. *Khodeja,* represents the law correctly and suits can now be filed in courts lower than district courts (*r*).

§2. Definition of a 'Muslim'

If the Muhammadan law is to be applied to Muslims, the next question that arises is: Who, for the purposes of the administration of justice, is to be considered a Muslim? The courts are entirely unconcerned with theological refinements; the law treats all religions with equality (*s*); there is no state religion in the republic of India. We have to discover if possible some objective tests to answer this question.

A good discussion of the subject is to be found in Aghnides, where he explains that there are at least three divergent views on the subject: (i) he who believes in Muhammad as a prophet belongs to the Muslim community; or (ii) every person who says 'there is no God but God, and Muhammad is the Prophet of God' is a Muslim; or (iii) al-Baghdādī and other theologians hold that in addition to the belief in God and the Prophet, a number of other beliefs are also necessary (*t*).

But the doctrine of the courts is simple: 'The Mahommedan law applies to all Musulmans whether they are so by birth or by conversion . . . Any person who professes the religion of Islam, in other words, accepts the unity of God

(*p*) *Abdurahiman* v. *Avooma* [1956] Mad. 903.

(*q*) Mulla §17; see §4 (A), below.

(*r*) [1936] 2 Cal. 79; Mulla §6(*3*).

(*s*) '. . . Brahmin, Buddhist, Christian, Mahommedan, Parsee and Sikh are one nation, enjoying equal political rights and *having perfect equality before the tribunals*, they coexist as separate and very distinct communities, having distinct laws affecting every relation of life.' *Skinner* v *Orde* (1871) 14 M.I.A. 309, 323; *Robaba* v. *Khodadad* (1946) 48 Bom. L.R. 864, 869; and Tyabji §8. Constitution of India, Art. 25.

(*t*) *Aghnides*, 134-7.

and the prophetic character of Mohammad is a Moslem and is subject to Musulman law' (*u*). This opinion of Ameer Ali, an eminently simple and logical view, has now been accepted by the Indian courts.

In a Madras case, decided by two judges, one a European and the other a Hindu, it was laid down that the essential doctrine of Islam is (i) that there is but one God and (ii) that Muhammad is His Prophet (*v*). This is the indispensable minimum; a belief short of this is not Islam; a belief in excess of this is, for the law courts at least, a redundancy.

It is not necessary that a Muslim should be born a Muslim; it is sufficient if he is a Muslim by profession or conversion (*w*). According to the theory of Islam, religion depends upon belief; a believer may renounce Islam just as an unbeliever may accept Islam. It is for the courts to decide whether a person is or is not a Muslim, and this depends upon the facts of each case.

In the first instance, if a man is born a Muslim, the presumption is that he is a Muslim. According to the *sharī'at* if one of the parents is a Muslim, the child is to be treated as a Muslim (*x*); but in India, it has been held that a child is presumed to belong to the religion of the father (*y*).

Secondly, a court of law is not concerned with peculiarities in belief, orthodoxy or heterodoxy, so long as the minimum of belief exists. It has been held, for instance, that despite their peculiar beliefs the Aḥmadīs are Muslims (*z*). The facts of this case are peculiar and show how a very important point relating to one branch of the law may some-

(*u*) Ameer Ali, II, 22 (italics mine). Ameer Ali points out that many Muslim divines considered Raja Ram Mohun Roy a Muslim, ibid., 88 (notes).

(*v*) *Narantakath* v. *Parakkal* (1922) 45 Mad. 986; *Cases*, 57; Abdur Rahim, 249; Tyabji §1; Mulla §19. The same is the view in Pakistan, *Atia Waris* v. *Sultan Ahmad* PLD 1959 (W.P.) Lahore 205.

(*w*) *Abraham* v. *Abraham* (1863) 9 M.I.A. 195, 239-40; *Cases*, 39, 46-7; *K. P. Chandrashekharappa* v. *Govt. of Mysore* A.I.R. (1955) Mysore 26.

(*x*) Baillie, II, 265; Ameer Ali, II, 176.

(*y*) *Skinner* v. *Orde* (1871) 14 M.IA. 309; *Cases*, 254.

(*z*) *Narantakath* v. *Parakkal* (*supra*).

times be hidden under the cover of another. The case is indexed as one on bigamy under Sec. 79 and 494 of the Indian Penal Code, and yet it is the clearest authority for the proposition that belief in monotheism and the prophetic mission of the Prophet Muhammad are the essentials of Islam.

A Moplah woman married a man who after some time became an Aḥmadī. Moplahs are strict Muslims and this change of doctrine on the part of the husband was considered an act of apostasy. Now, by the strict letter of the *sharī'at*, apostasy on the part of one of the spouses completely severs the marital tie. The wife thereupon married another husband. This question became a matter of public importance to the Muslim community; some holding that there was no bigamy, whereas the Aḥmadīs, always claiming to be Muslims, asserted that this was a clear case of bigamy on the part of the wife. On a prosecution for bigamy against the wife, the lower court upheld the contention that conversion to the Aḥmadī faith, being considered by the generality of Muslims as an act of apostasy, had in law the effect of severing the marital tie and that the second marriage was therefore perfectly valid. The prosecution thus failed. The High Court in revision, however, carefully examined the tenets of the Aḥmadiyya and found that they did believe in the two fundamental dogmas of Islam. They therefore disapproved of the views of those people who 'are too prone to charge others with unbelief and treat them as heretics' (*a*), and held that conversion to Aḥmadism is not an act of apostasy on the part of a Muslim and that therefore the woman had committed bigamy. In view, however, of the peculiar circumstances of the case the High Court did not order a new trial.

In a Lahore case, *Jiwan Khan* v. *Habib* (1933) 14 Lahore 518, it was contended that Shiites, who use abusive language against the first three caliphs, are not true Muslims and should not be allowed to pray in a Sunnite mosque. The

(*a*) ibid., 999.

High Court decided, first, that 'it is a well-recognized principle of Mahomedan law that a mosque does not belong to any particular sect', and that every Muslim has a right to worship in it (*b*), and secondly, that Shiites, despite their peculiar beliefs, do accept the fundamental dogmas of Islam, to wit, the unity of God and the mission of Muhammad as a prophet (*c*), and are clearly within the pale of Islam. The High Court therefore refused the application. The sane and broadminded view of the courts has to a large extent done away with the pernicious influence of reactionary and disruptive forces, so far as the law is concerned.

The third question that arises is: What are the tests of a true conversion? When can we say that a man has either accepted Islam or rejected it? Islam depends upon belief, but it is well known that 'the thought of man is not triable'. (*d*) No hard and fast rules can be laid down so far as external tests are concerned. Circumcision is one of the tests, but it is by no means final (*e*); particular forms of belief and observance of ceremonial law may also be taken into consideration (*f*), but as Lord Macnaghten said, 'No court can test or gauge the sincerity of religious belief.' (*g*) In order to be treated as a Muslim, a man must profess to be a Muslim (*h*), and secondly, the conversion must not be colourable. In the leading case of *Skinner* v. *Orde*, one Helen Skinner was married in Christian form to George Skinner. Later, after the death of George Skinner, Helen Skinner cohabited with John Thomas John, a Christian married to a Christian wife who was alive. In order to legalize their union, John and Helen went through the ceremony of conversion to the Muhammadan faith, and the Privy Council held that such a marriage was of doubtful validity (*i*). Hence a pretended con-

(*b*) 14 Lahore 518, 521-2.
(*c*) ibid., 523.
(*d*) Brian C.J. cited by Tyabji, p. 7.
(*e*) Tyabji loc. cit.
(*f*) Wilson §12.
(*g*) *Abdool Razack* v. *Aga Mahomed* (1893) 21 I.A. 56, 64; *Cases*, 68, 72.
(*h*) Tyabji §1(a); Wilson §11.
(*i*) *Skinner* v. *Orde* (1871) 14 M.I.A. 309, *Cases*, 254, 259.

version, for the purpose of eluding the personal law of the parties, will be considered a fraud upon the law and will not be permitted by the courts.

Nevertheless, the importance of a formal profession remains, for on a valid and proper conversion to Islam, the Muhammadan law is applicable.

In another leading case, *Abdool Razack* v. *Aga Mahomed* (*j*), Lord Macnaghten, in emphasizing the importance of the profession of Islam, lays down.

It was a mistake . . . to talk of conversion. No court can test or gauge the sincerity of religious belief. In all cases where, according to Mahomedan law, unbelief or difference of creed is a bar to marriage with a true believer, it is enough if the alien in religion embraces the Mahomedan faith. Profession with or without conversion is necessary and sufficient to remove the disability.

Therefore it may be said that a formal profession of Islam is sufficient, unless (i) the conversion is a pretended or colourable one, for the purpose of perpetrating a fraud upon the law, or (ii) the whole of the man's conduct and the evidence of surrounding facts is such as to run counter to the presumption of conversion to Islam (*k*).

In a Privy Council case from Ceylon, Lord Upjohn made the following illuminating remarks:

Ceylon is a country of many races, many creeds and has a number of Marriage Ordinances and Acts . . . In their lordships' view, in such countries there must be an inherent right in the inhabitants domiciled there to change their religion and personal law and so to contract a valid polygamous marriage if recognised by the laws of the country notwithstanding an earlier marriage. If such inherent right is to be abrogated, it must be done by statute. Admittedly there is none (*l*).

§3. Conversion to Islam and Custom

We have seen that conversion to Islam is mainly a question of fact, and that it is for the courts to decide whether the

(*j*) (1893) 21 I.A. 56, 64; *Cases* 68, 72.
(*k*) Tyabji, p. 8; Wilson §§11, 12.
(*l*) *Attorney-General of Ceylon* v. *Reid* [1965] 1 All E.R. 812, 817.

profession of Islam is colourable or not; for the Muhammadan law is applicable immediately on conversion to Islam. Now in India we have three different classes of Muslims: (i) there are the ordinary Muslims to whom the whole body of Muhammadan law applies; (ii) there are Muslims who are not subject to Islamic law in all respects, but who are governed by custom in certain matters. These are, for example, the Khojas, the Sunni Bohoras of Gujarat and Molesālam Girāsias of Broach (*m*). These communities preserve to some extent their own customary laws. A Khoja can bequeath the whole of his property; and in regard to agricultural land, the Khojas, the Sunni Bohoras and Molesālam Girāsias are still governed by custom.

The position with regard to the Cutchi Memons is a somewhat complicated one and will be considered later. They are at present entirely governed by Muhammadan law.

(iii) Moreover there are amphibious communities which cannot be said to be either wholly Hindu or wholly Muslim. Such, for instance, are the Meos of Rajasthan and the Satpanthis of Madhya Pradesh, and their religious status is likely to raise some very difficult questions of law (*n*).

(*m*) Mulla §24; §26 states the law inaccurately.

(*n*) R. H. Hutton rightly observes 'that there is thus a very real difficulty sometimes in deciding whether a particular body is Muslim or Hindu' (*Census of India*, 1931, Vol. I, Part I, Report, pp. 380-1). He gives as illustrations the Satpanthis and Pīrpanthis of Gujarat, Kachh and Khandesh, who are by caste Mātia Kunbis. They follow the *Atharva Veda* and worship tombs of Muslim saints in Pirāna; they also observe Ramaḍān, repeat the *kalima* and bury their dead both with Hindu and Muslim prayers. This is an interesting illustration of the commixture of Hinduism and Islam, and is not restricted to western India. Other illustrations given by Hutton are the Nayitas (Malwa), the Kuvachandas (Sind), the Husaini Brahmans, the Malkānas (U.P.), the Bhagwānias or Satyadharma (Bengal) and the Chuhras (Punjab). J. D. M. Derrett, *Religion, Law and The State in India,* 49, n.1.

For the Meos, in particular, see *Census of India,* 1931, XXVII, 126; and R. V. Russell and Hira Lal, *Tribes and Castes of the Central Provinces* (Macmillan, 1916), IV, 233, s.v. 'Meo Mewāti'. It has been recently held that Mewātis are Muslims governed by Muhammadan law, and there is no custom amongst them excluding females from inheritance, *Hooriya* v. *Munna* A.I.R. (1956) Madh. Bh. 56. And for the Satpanthis, see Mātia Kunbis in the *Bombay Gazetteer,* Vol. 9, Part i, p. 167, and *Devchand* v. *Ghanashyam* (1935) 37 Bom. L.R. 417. The classic discussion on such communities will be found in M. Mujeeb, *The Indian Muslims* (London) 1967), 10 sqq.

The position, therefore, may be briefly stated as follows: (i) On conversion to Islam, Muhammadan law is applicable. (ii) But certain communities have retained customary laws to some extent, for example Khojas, Sunni Bohoras, and Molesālam Girāsias, and Moplahs in Madras and Malabar (*o*). (iii) The force of custom has to a large extent been cut down by the provisions of the Shariat Act, 1937. The main exceptions are, as we have seen, the devolution of agricultural land in communities governed by special custom, wills and charities.

Whenever the question of the applicability of custom arises, we have to distinguish between two questions: (i) Is the custom proved?—a question of fact; and (ii) Is it binding?—a question of law (*p*). The leading case on the subject of custom is *Abdul Hussein* v. *Sona Dero* (*q*). Before dealing with that case, we may consider the brief statement of Sir George Rankin on the validity of custom (*r*).

> In the cases and textbooks one may read of the essentials of a valid custom: negative conditions are that it must not be contrary to justice, equity and good conscience, nor declared void by competent authority nor contravene any express law. The positive conditions that a custom must be ancient, certain and invariable are, however, not always satisfied in any high degree where custom is relied upon to provide the general law, e.g. of succession, and not merely to engraft exceptions thereupon.

In *Abdul Hussein's Case* the litigation related to the estate of a Sindhi nobleman, Mir Hussein Ali Khan of Tālpur, who died without leaving issue or widow. The son of a half-brother contended that the deceased's sister and sister's son had no claim to the property, and that he alone was entitled to succeed, as there was a family custom whereby daughters were

(*o*) Customary law is applicable in Kashmir, the Punjab and Malabar as well, Mulla §§11, 11A, 172.

(*p*) Tyabji, 14 sqq.

(*q*) (1917) 45 I.A. 10; *Cases*, 94.

(*r*) The Rt Hon'ble Sir George Rankin, P.C. 'Custom and the Muslim Law in India', an address to the Grotius Society delivered on 21 June 1939, 28-9; *Transactions of the Grotius Society*, Vol. 25, 1940, 89, 116-17. This and Dr Ḥāmid Ali's *Custom and Law in Anglo-Muslim Jurisprudence* (Thacker, Calcutta, 1938) are the two most valuable discussions of custom as it affects Muslims in India; Tyabji, 17 sqq.

excluded by sons, and sisters by male paternal collaterals. The appellant's contention was that in this case custom overrode the plain provisions of Muhammadan law and that therefore the sister and sister's son should be excluded. Their lordships of the Privy Council held the custom not proved, and during the course of their judgment they laid down a number of propositions of law and made valuable observations regarding Muslim customs and their effects on society. Lord Buckmaster says that it is incumbent upon the plaintiff specifically to allege and to prove the custom (pp. 13, 14) and also that 'It is of the essence of special usages modifying the ordinary law of succession that they should be ancient and invariable' (p. 15).

In considering the effects of custom, the courts are warned that the evidence must be carefully sifted, for it often happens that even in families governed by Muhammadan law, women are denied their proper rights, and 'in many parts of the country it is unusual for Mahomedan ladies to insist on their unquestioned rights' (p. 17). It is further pointed out that in every case of this kind, although the plaintiff may be able to adduce a number of striking instances in support of his case, it receives a severe blow when prominent members of the families concerned deny that the custom exists (p. 19).

The factors regarding custom superseding the general Muhammadan law may now be summarized. First, the burden lies heavily upon the person who asserts (i) to plead the custom relied upon, and (ii) to prove clearly that he is governed by custom and not by the general law. Secondly, as to the proof of custom, (i) there is in law no presumption in favour of custom; (ii) the custom must be ancient and certain, and not opposed to public policy.

In regard to the reasonableness of the custom, an important rule was laid down by the Supreme Court in *Bhau Ram* v. *Baij Nath*. Wanchoo J., speaking for the majority on the bench, said that in considering whether a custom was reasonable or not, decisions given previously to the Constitution, and even earlier enactments, were not decisive. 'We have to judge the reasonableness of the law in the context of the fundamental rights which were for the first time conferred by the Constitution on the people of this country and which were not there when the courts might have considered the reasonableness of the custom, if any, in the context of things then prevalent' (*rr*).

Thirdly, as to the evidence of custom, (i) specific instances of its acceptance as law may be proved; (ii) such evidence may be supplemented by general evidence; (iii) previous decisions in which the custom has been accepted as binding are important pieces of evidence, but their reasoning may not be binding; (iv) the court must scrutinize the custom set up jealously and must be careful not to be misled by pitfalls due to unfamiliarity with social conditions (*s*).

As regards the quantum of proof, in *Asrar Ahmed* v. *Durgah Committee, Ajmer*, Lord Simonds said that a custom may be established in India by something far short of that which the law of England would require (*t*).

§4. Three Commercial Communities: Khojas, Bohoras, Memons

To understand the effects of custom upon the general law of the land, three commercial communities among Muslims require special attention. These are the two Shiite Ismaili communities, Khojas and Bohoras, and the Sunnite Hanafi community, the Memons. These three communities are to be found in many of the cities of India and Pakistan, but their stronghold is in the states of Maharashtra and Gujarat. Although numerically small (*u*), their importance in law is

(*rr*) *Bhau Ram* v. *Baij Nath* A.I.R. (162) S.C. 1472, 1480 (para. 4).

(*s*) *Abdul Hussein* v. *Bibi Sona Dero, Cases*, 94 sqq.

(*t*) (1946) 49 Bom. L.R. 235, 243.

(*u*) According to the Census of 1931, Vol. I, Part 2, 529, there were 212,752 Bohoras in India (Bombay, 118,952), and 135,574 Memons (Bombay, 42,958; Western Indian States, 78,758). The figures for Khojas are not available. In 1911, according to Russell and Hira Lal, *Tribes and Castes of Central India* (Macmillan, 1916), there were 127,215 Khojas in India. Unfortunately, such figures have been omitted in the censuses of 1951 and 1961.

due to the fact that as trading communities they are often involved in litigation and the claims are large.

(A) *Khojas*

The Khojas are Ismaili Shiites (*uu*) of the Nizarian Branch and we have already dealt with them briefly (*v*). The word *khōja* (strictly, *khwāja*) is a term of respect and means 'the honourable person'. (*w*) The history of their community was dealt with fully by Mr Justice Arnould in a memorable judgment, *Advocate-General* v. *Muhammad Husen Huseni*, generally known as the *Aga Khan Case* (*x*). Briefly, the Khojas were originally Hindus of the trading class, and they hailed from Sind and Cutch. Sind was conquered early by the Muslims and the trading communities were converted to Islam. The conversion on a large scale was mainly due to the efforts and personality of Pir Sadruddin, who lived some 500 years ago, and whose tomb is in Ootch, Kathiawar. According to the beliefs of the majority, Pir Sadruddin was a missionary sent to Sind by Shah Islam, one of the ancestors of His Highness the Aga Khan who is the head of the community in all religious matters and is called the 'Hāzar Imām'. (*y*) According to Khoja belief, the Hāzar Imām is a descendant of the

(*uu*) For a general account, see the author's article, 'The Ismā'īlīs' in *Religion in the Middle East*, ed. A. J. Arberry, I (Cambridge, 1969), 318-29.

(*v*) Introduction, pp. 41 sqq. A good account will be found in R. E. Enthoven, *Tribes and Castes of Bombay* (Bombay, 1920-2) II, 217, and in J. W. Hollister, *The Shī'a of India*, 306 sqq. For a historical account of early Ismailism, see M. G. S. Hodgson, *The Order of Assassins* ('s-Gravenhage, 1955), and S. C. Misra, *Muslim Communities in Gujarat* (Bombay, 1964) 54 sqq. or conditions prevailing among Indian Ismailis in Africa, see Hatim M. Amiji's article in *Islam in Africa*, edd. J. Kritzeck and W. H. Lewis (New York, 1969), 141, 145-55.

(*w*) Ameer Ali, II, 136, citing 12 Bom. H.C. Rep. 323 343.

(*x*) A very full summary of this important case will be found in Tyabji §502, ill. (2). The judgment was delivered on 12 November 1866, and is reported in (1866) 12 Bom. H.C.R. 323-63; *Cases*, 504-49. Modern accounts of their beliefs may be found in the *Ency. of Islam*, s.v. 'Ismā'īlīya' and 'Khōja', Ameer Ali, II, 135 sqq., follows Mr Justice Arnould, and the earlier judgment of Sir Erskine Perry, *Hirbae* v. *Sonabae* (1847) Perry's Oriental Cases 110.

(y) Indian Khoja pronunciation of *imām-e ḥāḍir* or *al-imām al-ḥāḍir*, as distinguished from the Ithna 'Asharī *imām-e ghā'ib*.

Prophet and is therefore entitled to absolute reverence; he is the final interpreter of religion.

The language of the Khojas is mostly Cutchi, and their chief religious book is the *Dasavatār* (z), in the Sindhi character and Cutchi language. Sir Erskine Perry referring to this book observes, 'Narayan, the interpreter, has procured me some translated passages, . . . which, as professing to give a history of the tenth incarnation in the person of their saint, Sadr Din, appears to be a strong combination of Hindu articles of faith and the tenets of Islam.'(*a*)

It was held in the *Aga Khan's Case* that the followers of the Aga Khan are not Sunnites; and later in 1909 it was held that they are not Shiites of the Ithnā 'Asharī school (*b*).

The original faith of the Ismaili Khojas was a hybrid between Hinduism and Islam. Gradually the community has come more and more under the influence of orthodox Islam; even the original Ismailis have been attracted by the simpler form of the faith, and some of them have seceded and have formed themselves into two groups. The larger of these professes the Shiite Ithnā 'Asharī faith; the smaller has adopted the Hanafi school. Therefore the Khojas now consist of three groups: (i) The majority are Ismailis, being followers of the Aga Khan; (ii) a smaller group professes the Shiite Ithnā 'Asharī faith; (iii) a still smaller group follows the Hanafi school of Sunnite law.

The legal position of the Khojas may be summed up as follows:

(z) This treatise exists in two versions, a Sindhi and a Gujarāti version. There is no scientific edition or translation, but extracts from the Gujarāti version have been translated by V. N. Hoda in his article 'Specimens of Satpanthi Literature', *Collectanea I* (Ismaili Society Series, Bombay, 1948), 112-15.

(*a*) Ameer Ali, II, 138, citing *Hirbae* v. *Sonabae* (1847) Perry's Oriental Cases 110. This opinion, however, is not well founded, for Mr Justice Arnould points out (12 Bom. H.C.R., p. 354) that the *Dasavatār* is a treatise of ten chapters dealing with ten *avatārs*. The first nine chapters deal with the nine incarnations of the Hindu God, Vishnu, and the tenth chapter deals with the incarnations of the 'Most Holy Ali'. See also the observations of Russell J. in *Haji Bibi's Case*, 11 Bom. L.R. 409, 431.

(*b*) *Haji Bibi* v. *H.H. Sir Sultan Mahomed Shah, the Aga Khan* (1908), 11 Bom. L.R. 409.

I. *Prior to 1937*, they were governed by the Hindu law of inheritance and succession, which they had retained by custom (*c*). Russell J. said picturesquely that 'The living Mahomedan by operation of law became a dead Hindu' (*d*)—an inaccurate and misleading dictum. They were, however, not governed by the Hindu law of joint family or partition (*e*), and in all other respects they were governed by Muhammadan law.

II. *After the Shariat Act, 1937*: (i) as to *intestate* succession, they are governed by Muhammadan law; (ii) as to *testamentary* succession, they still retain the right to will away the whole of their property (*f*); (iii) as to *agricultural land*, the customary law prevails.

In all other respects they are governed by Muhammadan law; and should a Khoja make a declaration under the Shariat Act, Sec. 3(1), he would be governed by the Muhammadan law even in respect of testamentary succession.

Khoja Wills. The will of a Khoja is to be construed according to Muhammadan law; although, prior to the Shariat Act, 1937, it used to be construed in accordance with Hindu law. Since the Shariat Act, a Khoja can still will away the whole of his property; but questions relating to the making or the revocation of a will, and to the validity of trusts and *wakfs* will be determined by the principles of Muhammadan law (*g*).

A Khoja, originally governed by the customary law of wills and inheritance, migrated to the former state of Hyderabad, where no such custom could be pleaded by a Muslim. Held by the Supreme Court, that in such a case he was not entitled to raise any custom of variance with Muhammadan law (*h*).

(*c*) Tyabji §2(8); Mulla §22.

(*d*) *Rashid* v. *Sherbanoo* (1904) 29 Bom. 85, 89.

(*e*) Tyabji, p. 9, citing *Jan Mahomed* v. *Datu* (1913) 38 Bom. 449, 550. Mulla §57.

(*f*) Tyabji §2(8); Mulla §24.

(*g*) *Ashrafalli Cassamalli* v. *Mahomedalli Rajaballi* (1945) 48 Bom. L.R. 642.

(*h*) (*Begum*) *Noorbanu* v. *Deputy Custodian General of Evacuee Property* A.I.R. (1965) S.C. 1937.

In *Nur Ali* v. *Malka Sultana*, a Pakistan decision (PLD 1961 (W.P.) Lahore 431), which may well become the leading case on the subject, it was held by a Division Bench of the Lahore High Court (Shabbir Ahmad and Sajjad Ahmad JJ.):

(1) that the followers of His Highness the Aga Khan, the *imām-i ḥāḍir* of the Ismaili Khojas, come from all sects including Hindus. A Hindu, although he had not embraced Islam, was a follower. The *Memoirs* of the late Aga Khan show that considerable liberty of religious profession was allowed among his followers. The mere fact that a Muslim was the follower of His Highness the Aga Khan (as *imām-e ḥāḍir*) would not establish conclusively that he was a Shiite by religion (Para. 10), and

(2) that Ismailis (followers of His Highness the Aga Khan) in the Punjab and the North-West Frontier Provinces were not necessarily governed by the Shiite law of succession.

The document known as *Dastūr-ul-Amal* lays down:

The ceremonies concerning Nikah (marriage contract) and mourning such as Goosal (strictly, *ghusl*, ritual washing of the corpse), offering the prayer over the corpse, etc., shall be solemnized by Moulvies belonging to Ehl-i-Sunnat Jamat. Any person acting contrary to this shall be punished by the Council (Para. 11).

And there is a religious direction of profound significance, both in law and in religion:

The ancient Kulma [i.e. the fundamental creed of Islam] 'Lā ilāha illallāh Muhammad-ur-Rasoolullah' shall be recited publicly among all Ismaili Jamats throughout the Punjab (loc. cit.).

It is further pointed out that Hanafi law was followed and practised by the community throughout (Para. 12), and therefore the presumption of law that Hanafi law governed them in India and Pakistan unless the contrary is established, was applicable in this case.

The decision is far-reaching and, it is submitted, well-founded in the circumstances. But now that the *Da'ā'im al-*

Islām of the Cadi Nu'mān, a textbook of law written during the time and at the behest of the Caliph-Imām al-Mu'izz li-dīni'l-lāh, has been edited and published in its entirety, it is submitted with confidence that the Fatimid law, in which elements of the Māliki and Shāfi'ī schools are to be found in abundance, should apply, and not the Hanafi system (*i*).

This doctrine is of prime importance, and the further development of the law will be watched with great interest by students of Muhammadan law as understood and applied in the sub-continent.

(B) *Bohoras*

The Bohoras are also Ismailis and they separated from the other groups during the Fatimid régime (*j*). The word *bohōra* means 'a merchant'. Bohoras are a distinct and flourishing trading community doing business in all parts of the world, but they are mostly established in Western India. They are divided into Dā'ūdīs, Sulaymānīs (*k*) and some smaller branches (*l*), and as a group, they are called 'Western' Ismailis to distinguish them from the 'Eastern' Ismailis, the Khojas.

The Bohoras are governed in all respects by Muhammadan law, but their law is still not well known, except for a brief manual. Their chief legal authority, the *Da'ā'im al-Islām* of Cadi Nu'mān has been edited and published by me (*m*). The two most important cases that give us an insight into their history and tenets are *Advocate-General of Bombay* v.

(*i*) A brief statement of the law will be found in the author's *Compendium of Fatimid Law*, op. cit.

(*j*) *Ency. of Islam*, rev. ed. (1960), I, 1254; R. E. Enthoven, *Tribes and Castes of Bombay*, I, 197; W. Ivanow, *Brief Survey of Ismailism* (Bombay, 1952); J. N. Hollister, *The Shī'a of India*, 246 sqq.

(*k*) According to Manfred W. Wenner, *Modern Yemen*, 1918-1960 (Baltimore, 1967), there are about 25,000 Sulaymānīs in the Yemen.

(*l*) Fyzee, *Ismaili Law of Wills* (Oxford University Press, 1933), 3-5. See Fyzee, *Compendium of Fat. Law*, op. cit.

(*m*) Dar El Mareef, Cairo, Vol. I, 1951; Vol. II, 1961; both volumes have been reprinted. Tyabji p. 4 and *passim; Burhanpur Dargah Case*, para. 27.

Yusufalli (*n*), and *Seth Tayabali* v. *Abdulhusein* (*o*). These judgments contain much that is interesting from the social and religious points of view but, purely as a matter of law, they establish the high position of the head of the community, the *Dā'ī'l-Muṭlaq*. The present religious head is the Mullaji Saheb of the Dā'ūdī Bohoras, who is recognized by the community as their *Dā'ī'l-Muṭlaq*. The *dā'ī* is an assistant of the Imām, the final religious head; but as the Imām is *mastūr*, 'hidden from sight', the *dā'ī* has large powers of interpreting religion. A peculiar belief of the community is that the Imām must always exist, and he must always have a *dā'ī* (*p*); but as the Imām is in seclusion (*q*), the *dā'ī* is entitled to the *mīthāq* (oath of allegiance), and is for all practical purposes the authoritative interpreter of religion and the leader of the community. The smaller groups, like the Sulaymānīs, have their own religious heads, but in essentials their beliefs are almost identical.

According to the beliefs of the Dā'ūdī Bohora community, the *Dā'ī* has the right to excommunicate a member of the community on religious grounds. In this important case their lordships of the Supreme Court made many interesting observations on religion, religious toleration, 'community', etc. The dissenting judgment of Sinha C.J. is stimulating and commendable, and is worthy of close study (*r*).

The importance of the Bohora community lies in the fact that, as traders, they often litigate, but their system of juris-

(*n*) (1921) 24 Bom. L. R. 1060. Summarized in Tyabji, p. 17, note (24). Known as the *Chandabhoy Gulla Case*.

(*o*) Generally known as the Burhanpur Dargah Case, being suit No. 25 of 1925 in the Court of the 1st Class Sub-Judge, Burhanpur, C.P. Judgment, dated 2 January 1931. On appeal, Appeal No. 52 of 1931, decided by F. H. Staples. I.C.S., Additional Judicial Commissioner. Central Provinces, on 10 November 1934. Both the judgments have been reprinted in Bombay. The Privy Council judgment in this appeal, *Hasanali and others* v. *Mansoorali and others*, will be found in (1947) 75 I.A. 1.

(*p*) Burhanpur Dargah Case, para. 27 sqq.

(*q*) The Imāms have been in seclusion so long that Mr Staples in his judgment holds that 'from the point of view of the law they must be held to be non-existent'. See his judgment, para. 23.

(*r*) *Sardar Syedna Taher Saifuddin* v. *State of Bombay* A.I.R. (1962) S.C. 853.

prudence is little known; and from the little that is known it seems to be akin to the Mālikī rather than the Shiite Ithnā 'Asharī school in several respects (*s*).

Sunni Bohoras. The Dā'ūdī Bohoras—and generally all Ismaili Bohoras—must be sharply distinguished from the Sunnite Bohoras of Gujarat (*t*), who, although they are descended from the same stock, are Sunnite by persuasion. Before the Shariat Act, Sunnite Bohoras were governed in matters of inheritance by the customary law, analogous to the Hindu law, and not by the *sharī'at*. This interesting community is an example of an orthodox Sunnite group, long governed by custom, which has now been made subject to its own religious laws by the operation of the Shariat Act (*u*).

(C) *Memons*

The word 'Memon' is probably a corruption of *mu'min*, a believer. The Memons, as a community, are divided into two groups, the Cutchi Memons and the Halai Memons. Halai Memons of Bombay are governed by Hanafi law in all respects (*v*). The Cutchi Memons, like the Khojas, are converts from a Hindu trading community, the Lohānās from Kathiawar, and mostly speak the Cutchi language. They are, however, strict adherents of the Sunnite creed and follow the Hanafi school (*w*). The Cutchi Memons had, until 1938,

(*s*) A good account of the history and religion of the Western Isma'īlīs will be found in Zāhid 'Alī, *Tārīkh-e Fātimiyyīn-e Miṣr* (Urdu), (Hyderabad, Deccan, 1948/1367); *Fat. Law*, Intr., xxviii sqq.; Kritzeck and Lewis (edd.), *Islam in Africa* (New York, 1969), 155-164.

(*t*) Tyabji p. 15; Mulla §26 fails to consider the force of the Shariat Act, 1937.

(*u*) In *Bai Asha* v. *Bai Biban* (1956) 59 Bom. L.R. 470, it has been held that Sunni Bohoras of the territory formerly known as the Baroda State are governed by the Hindu Law in matters of succession and inheritance. The decision appears to be doubtful, as the learned judge's attention was not drawn pointedly to the Shariat Act. It is submitted that Mulla in §26 of his work on Mahomedan Law has stated the law too widely, and this has misled the court.

(*v*) Mulla §25. But Halai Memons residing at Porbandar in Kathiawar used to be governed by customary law.

(*w*) See R. E. Enthoven, *Tribes and Castes of Bombay*, III, 53.

retained their own customary law, which was identical with Hindu law, in regard to succession and inheritance (*x*).

The legal position of the Cutchi Memons may now be summarized.

(i) Prior to the Cutchi Memon Act, 1920, the community was governed by the Hindu law of succession and inheritance.

(ii) By the Act of 1920, a Cutchi Memon could, by making a declaration, subject himself in all respects to the Muhammadan law of inheritance (that is, Hanafi law).

(iii) In 1937 came the Shariat Act, which made their position similar to that of the Khojas. As to *intestate* succession, they were in all respects governed by Hanafi law. As to *testamentary* succession, they retained their customary right to dispose of the whole of their property by will, unless a declaration was made in terms of Sec. 3, in which case they would be governed in all respects by Hanafi law, thus limiting their testamentary capacity to the bequeathable third.

(iv) By the Cutchi Memons Act, X of 1938, the option to make a declaration was taken away, and they were governed entirely by the Hanafi law, and the Act of 1920 was repealed by Sec. 4.

(v) The latest enactment dealing with Cutchi Memons is Act XXV of 1942. By this Act, Sec. 4 of the Cutchi Memons Act X of 1938 is repealed. The effect of this repeal is to remove from the Statute Book a section that is 'spent' and redundant, and not to create any new right, or to revive an old one.

The result is that today Cutchi Memons are governed by Hanafi law in all matters, including testamentary and intestate succession, the only exceptions being those specified in the Shariat Act.

Cutchi Memon wills. Formerly it used to be held that the will of a Cutchi Memon should be construed by the rules of Hindu law, but since the passing of the Shariat Act, 1937, it

(*x*) *Mulla* §§22. 23.

has been held that the will of a Cutchi Memon must be construed in accordance with Muhammadan law (y).

§5. Schools of Law—Principles of Interpretation

1. *Sunnite law.* The vast majority of Muslims in all parts of the world taken in the aggregate are Hanafi. The Hanafi school, although the oldest in time, is reputed to be the least archaic in outlook. It is the dominant school in India, Pakistan, Asia Minor, Palestine and Cyprus (*z*). In Egypt, while the majority are Shāfi'ī, the state code is Hanafi. In India, the Hanafi rite was introduced by the Mughal Emperors who were central Asian Turks, and the Turks, whether Osmanli or Seljuk, are mostly Hanafis (*a*).

Whenever a case arises in which the Muhammadan law is to be applied, it is for the judge to determine in each case the law of the school or sub-school which is applicable (*b*). The general principle is that it is highly undesirable 'to introduce purposeless distinctions between the law applicable in the case of one community, and that applicable in the case of another' (*c*). In *Bafatun* v. *Bilaiti Khanum* (*d*) it was observed that in India 'there is a presumption that the parties are Sunnis, to which the great majority of the Mahomedans of this country belong, as has been pointed out by Baillie, in the Introduction to his Digest of the Imameea Law'. But while this is so, the Shiite law is also the law of the land (*e*) and has been applied to Shiites for over a century since the decision of the Privy Council in *Rajah Deedar Hossein* v. *Ranee Zuhoor-oon Nissa* (*f*):

According to the true construction of this Regulation, in the absence of any judicial decisions or established practice limiting

(*y*) *Bayabai* v. *Bayabai* [1942] Bom. 847. See also the observations of Chagla J. in *Ashrafalli* v. *Mahomedalli* (1945) 48 Bom. L.R. 642, 646, a Khoja Case; *C. Mohammed Yunus* v. *Syed Unissa* [1962] 1 S.C.R. 67.

(*z*) Fitzgerald, 10.

(*a*) Wilson, 23.

(*b*) ibid., §16.

(*c*) Tyabji §14(2).

(*d*) (1903) 30 Cal. 683 686.

(*e*) *Aziz Bano* v. *Muhammad Ibrahim* (1925) 47 All. 823, 835.

(*f*) (1841) 2 M.I.A. 441; *Cases*, 490.

or controlling its meaning, the Mahomedan law of succession applicable to each sect ought to prevail as to litigants of that sect. It is not said that one uniform law should be adopted in all cases affecting Mahomedans, but that the Mahomedan law, whatever it is, shall be adopted. If each sect has its own rule according to the Mahomedan law, that rule should be followed with respect to litigants of that sect (*g*).

The usual practice in this sub-continent is to use the terms 'Sunni' law or 'Shia' law. Strictly speaking, this is inexact; by the former is meant the Hanafi law and by the latter, the Ithnā 'Asharī school of the Shī'a.

Although the majority of the Sunnites in India are Hanafis and ordinarily the Hanafi law is applicable (*h*), the Sunnite school is divided into four sub-schools, Hanafi, Mālikī, Shāfi'ī and Ḥanbalī, each of which is considered equally orthodox by the Sunnite jurists (*c*). Abdur Rahim, in a learned discussion, shows how far it is necessary for a Muslim to follow one particular school or sub-school (*j*). The equality is so firmly established that it is open to a follower of one school to adopt on a particular point of law the interpretation by the jurists of any other Sunnite school in preference to that of his own (*k*).

A Hanafi may freely become a Shāfi'ī and vice versa. So also, a Hanafi *kazi* can under certain circumstances adopt a rule of law based upon the interpretation of a different Sunnite school (*l*). In *Muhammad Ibrahim* v. *Gulam Ahmed* (*m*) it was laid down that a Hanafi woman on attaining majority can select a husband without reference to the wishes of her father or guardian. But a Shāfi'ī or Fatimid virgin cannot, whether before or after puberty, dispose of her hand without

(*g*) ibid., 477. See also the valuable observations of Ameer Ali, II, 23.

(*h*) *Akbarally* v. *Mahomedally* (1931) 34 Bom. L.R. 655.

(*i*) *LME*, I, 70.

(*j*) Abdur Raḥim, 172 sqq.

(*k*) ibid., 177. It is of interest to observe that the great scholar Shiblī Nu'mānī, although he was a Hanafi, adopted the Shāfi'ī school for a short while during a voyage to Europe, Sayyid Sulaymān, *Ḥayāt-e Shiblī* ɪ*Azam*-gadh, U.P., 1362/1943), I, 287-8; Ameer Ali, II, 23.

(*l*) Abdur Rahim, 181.

(*m*) (1864) 1 Bom. H.C.R. 236.

the consent of her father (*n*). A Shāfi'ī girl on attaining puberty became a Hanafi and got married as a Hanafi. It was held that a Muslim female of any one of the four Sunnite sects can elect at will to belong to whichever sect she pleases, and the legality of her subsequent acts will be tested by the tenets of the Imām whose follower she has become (*o*).

As regards the power of a judge to adopt a rule of law drawn from another school, Abdur Rahim states clearly that a Hanafi *kazi* may decide a case according to the Shāfi'ī law, if he prefers that view, or he may transfer the case to a Shāfi'ī *kazi*, if there is one available. For instance, a Hanafi *kazi*, following the views of another Sunnite school in preference to those of his own, may declare that divorce by a drunken person is not valid, or may uphold a marriage contracted without two witnesses (*p*). Although this rule is supported by a formidable array of authorities, later jurists have laid down that a *kazi* of the present day should restrict himself to the precepts of his own school (*q*). It will thus be observed that the ancient liberty of juristic interpretation has been gradually cut down, thus leading to a narrow outlook (*r*).

2. *Applicability*. The general position regarding the applicability of Muhammadan law may now be summarized:

(i) Where both the parties to a suit are Muslims and belong to the same school, the Muhammadan law of that school will apply (*s*).

(ii) Where the parties to a suit differ in religion or do not belong to the same school of Muhammadan law, the law of the defendant will apply. For example, if an Ithnā 'Asharī

(*n*) Such guardian is called *walī-e mujbir* (compelling guardian) *Fat. Law*, xxxv, §§52 sq.

(*o*) Wilson §14; Fitzgerald, 18.

(*p*) Abdur Rahim, 180-1. A recent illustration in India is the Dissolution of Muslim Marriages Act, VIII of 1939. This Act follows the law as laid down by Mālikī jurists, but is applicable to all Muslims, whatever the school to which they adhere.

(*q*) For example, Ruxton, *Maliki Law*, 274.

(*r*) It is this catholicism of Islam which is expressed in a saying of the Prophet. 'Diversity of opinion among my people is a mercy from God.' Fitzgerald, 17. Mahmassani, 98.

(*s*) Tyabji §11; *Cases*, xix.

husband sues his Hanafi wife for restitution of conjugal rights, the wife is entitled to the benefit of a defence valid only in Hanafi law (*s*).

(iii) Where a person in good faith changes his religion, or his school of law in Islam, ordinarily the personal law changes *with immediate effect* from the time of such conversion. For instance, if a Hindu embraces Islam, the Muhammadan law will apply from the date of such conversion (*t*).

(iv) Where a person who is a convert to a new faith, or has changed his school of law in Islam, dies, the law of succession applicable to the estate will be the law of the religion or the school which he professed at the time of his death. For example, a Muslim is converted to Christianity before his death. The Indian Succession Act, 1925, will apply. Or, a Hanafi becomes an Ithnā 'Asharī and then dies. The Ithnā 'Asharī Shiite law will apply (*u*).

3. *Shiite law.* The Shī'a are divided into innumerable groups, but the three chief schools of law are the Ithnā 'Asharī, Ismaili and Zaydī. There are no Zaydīs in India; they are to be found mostly in the Yemen, South Arabia. The Ithnā 'Asharī school, to which the largest number of Shiites belong, has a very large legal literature, but the *Sharā'i'al-Islām* (commonly, *Sharaya* and even *Suraya*) is the leading authority (*v*).

As regards Ismailis, their most important text is the *Da'ā'im al-Islām* (*w*) of Cadi Nu'mān, written in the time of Imām al-Mu'izz (fourth century A.H./tenth century A.D.), before the split between the Khojas (Nizarians) and Bohoras (Musta'lians). While, however, the Bohoras, being Ismailis, are undoubtedly governed by it, it is extremely doubtful if the Khojas, the Ismaili followers of the Aga Khan, would

(*s*) Tyabji §13; *Cases,* loc. cit.
(*t*) Ameer Ali, II, 148. *Farooq Leivers v. Adelaide Bridget* PLD 1958. (W.P.) Lahore 431, 436.
(*u*) Tyabji §638.
(*v*) *Aziz Bano* v. *Muhammad Ibrahim* (1925) 47 All. 823, per Sulaiman J.
(*w*) Literally, 'Pillars of Islam'.

accept it as authoritative, although on principle its binding force is undeniable. It was a textbook written at the behest of one of their own Imāms; its precepts have been followed, at least by one branch, for over a thousand years; but the Nizarians, since they left Egypt and went eastward, have lost touch with it, and ordinarily they are now governed by 'Shia' law—a vague term—which in India means the Ithnā 'Asharī law (*x*). Thus it would be more satisfactory to use the nomenclature 'Fatimid law' for the law of Muslims such as the Ismaili Bohoras, who for historical reasons are governed by the *Da'ā'im*, to distinguish it from the law applicable to Ismaili Khojas. The main provisions of the law applicable will be found in my *Compendium of Fatimid Law*.

We have seen that there exists a considerable degree of amity between the four sub-schools of the Sunnites. Unfortunately, for historical and doctrinal reasons, no such concord prevails among the minor groups of the Shī'a. It is almost certain than on a point of Ithnā 'Asharī law, no Shiite *mujtahid* would agree to abide by a rule drawn from the Fatimid or Zaydī school of jurisprudence, even if, under modern social conditions, the particular rule of his school would not lead to substantial justice.

4. *Rules of interpretation.* The basis of the Islamic law, as understood all over the world, is four-fold: *Koran, Sunna, Ijmā', Qiyās*. But it is unnecessary, and sometimes even improper and misleading, to go to the original sources themselves. The law has been studied, analysed, codified, and commented upon for fourteen centuries, and each country and each *madhhab* (school or sub-school) has its own appropriate and authoritative texts. Under these circumstances it is undesirable for the present-day courts to put their own construction on the Koran and *ḥadīth* where the opinions of text-writers are clear and definite.

As to the Koran, the courts should not

speculate on the mode in which the text quoted from the Koran

(*x*) Wilson, 34, following Ameer Ali.

. . . is to be reconciled with the law as laid down in the Hedaya and by the author of the passage quoted from Baillie's Imameea. . . . It would be wrong for the courts on a point of this kind to put their own construction on the Koran in opposition to the express ruling of commentators of such great antiquity and high authority (*y*).

Similarly, as to the precepts of the Prophet, the Privy Council has held that new rules must not now be deduced by the courts. The *locus classicus* on the subject is the judgment of Sir Arthur Wilson to be found in *Baker Ali* v. *Anjuman Ara* (*z*). It is a matter of some interest, however, that in *Abul Fata* v. *Russomoy*, by holding that family *wakfs* were void, their Lordships departed from the principles of the Muhammadan law of *wakf*, misapplied a rule of English law to the Muslim institution of *wakf*, and overruled a long line of Muslim jurists, both modern like Mr Justice Ameer Ali (*a*) and ancient, too numerous to mention. Poetic justice was, however, done when they themselves were overruled by an Act of the Indian legislature (*b*).

The danger of departing from the classical texts in a cavalier fashion was pointed out in a Madras decision:

We have, therefore, to administer without in any way circumventing or deviating from the original texts, the law, as promulgated by the Islamic Law-givers to suit the present-day conditions, and, in doing so, it has to be remembered that Courts are not at liberty to refuse to administer any portion of those tenets even though in certain respects they may not sound quite modern (*c*).

As to classical texts, Chagla J. (as he then was) has sounded a note of warning against following them slavishly:

Now there is no doubt that these ancient Muslim texts must be considered with the utmost respect. But it must also be

(*y*) *Aga Mahomed* v. *Koolsom Bee Bee* (1897) 24 I.A. 196, 203-4; *Cases*, 1.

(*z*) (1903) 30 I.A. 94, 111-12, cited in the Introduction, p. 50-1, above; *Cases*, 4.

(*a*) (1894) 22 I.A. 76, particularly 85-9; *Cases*, 388.

(*b*) Mussalman Wakf (Validating) Act, 1913.

(*c*) Per Govinda Menon and Ramaswami Gounder JJ. in *Veerankutty* v *Kutti Umma* [1956] Mad. 1004, 1009. For further rules of interpretation where the classical jurists differ, see below.

remembered at the same time that Muslim jurisprudence is not a static jurisprudence. It is a jurisprudence which has grown and developed with the times and the quotations from Muslim texts should be so applied as to suit modern circumstances and conditions. It is also dangerous to pick out illustrations wrenched from their context and apply them literally. Illustrations merely illustrate a principle and what the Court should try to do is to deduce the principle which underlies the illustration (*d*).

A difficulty, however, does arise when the judge is faced with a conflict of opinion among jurists of authority. Here we have the most fruitful source of error and both Abdur Rahim (*e*) and Tyabji (*f*) have shown why the law has sometimes not been correctly appreciated in Indian courts. Abdur Rahim deals with the so-called 'complexity, uncertainty and artificiality' of the Islamic legal system. Tyabji shows how the exposition of Islamic law in India suffers from unfamiliarity with the language of the texts and the social conditions when they came to be written, and the unwarranted assumption that the texts are confused, inconsistent or inaccurately expressed.

It is, however, impossible to deny that differences of opinion among the authorities are to be found on a number of questions. This is not in the least surprising if only two of the numerous factors favouring such divergencies are considered, apart altogether from discrepancies in the transmission of texts, imperfect recensions and inaccurate renderings.

The two factors are age and provenance. Three of the most authoritative texts in India are the *Hedaya*, the *Fatāwā ʻĀlamgīrī* and the *Sharā'iʻ al-Islām*. The first two are paramount authorities in Hanafi law, the *Sharā'iʻ* is the leading Ithnā ʻAsharī Shiite text. The *Hedaya* was translated by Hamilton (*g*) and is continuously cited by the Bench and the

(*d*) *Ashrafalli Cassamalli* v. *Mahomedalli Rajaballi* (1945) 48 Bom. L.R. 642, 652.

(*e*) *Muhammadan Jurisprudence*, 39-41.

(*f*) 3rd ed., §11c; 4th ed., §15.

(*g*) Trans. C. Hamilton, 4 volumes, 1791; 2nd ed., in one volume by S. G. Grady, London, 1870. On its value, see the remarks of Mahmood J. in 7 All. 775, 798, of Abdur Rahim in *Muhammadan Jurisprudence*, 41-2, of Ameer Ali, I, 335 and II, 561, of Wilson, 43-4, and of Aghnides, Preface, p. 5. See *Cases*, 270 (per Mr Ameer Ali).

bar. Baillie's *Digest,* Vol. I, is based on the *Fatāwā 'Ālamgīrī,* and Vol. II on the *Sharā'i'al-Islām* (*h*). Baille's renderings are considered by competent critics to be more successful than Hamilton's (*i*).

Considered chronologically, the *Hedaya* (strictly, *hidāya*) comes first. The author was Burhān al-dīn Marghīnānī who died in A.H. 593/A.D. 1197. He lived and wrote in Marghīnān, a small town in the district of Farghāna, in Russian Turkestan, to the east of Bukhārā. The *Hedaya* was a commentary by the author himself on a smaller work of his own, the *Bidāya.* The *Hedaya* and its author have achieved worldwide renown (*j*).

Next comes the *Sharā'i' al-Islām,* the leading text of Ithnā 'Asharī Shiite law. It was written by Najm al-dīn al-Hillī who died in A.H. 677/A.D. 1277. He lived mostly in Hilla, a small town in the district of Baghdad (*k*).

And lastly, the *Fatāwā 'Ālamgīrī.* It is a collection of *fatwās,* or the replies of jurisconsults to the questions addressed to them, composed by Shaykh Niẓām Burhānpūrī and four others under the orders of the Emperor Awrangzeb 'Ālamgīr during the eleventh century Hijri/seventeenth century A.D. The scene of their labours was, therefore, Delhi or the neighbouring districts (*l*).

It is hardly necessary to dilate upon the variations in economic conditions, social life and cultural values during these three periods in such widely divergent lands. A triangle drawn on the map of Asia with Samarkand, Baghdad and Delhi as its points is sufficient for our purposes. And, if in

(*h*) Neil B. E. Baillie, *Digest of Moohummudan Law,* Vol. I, 1st ed. 1865; 2nd ed. 1875; Vol. II, 1869.

(*i*) Abdur Rahim, 42.

(*j*) Aghnides, 180 (12); *Ency. of Islam,* III, 279. Hamilton's *Hedaya,* criticized by Mahmood J. in *Gobind Dayal's Case, Cases,* 449.

(*k*) Aghnides, 194. On its value, see Sulaiman J. in 47 All. 823, 828, 829.

(*l*) Aghnides, 186 (22). On the authorities of Muslim law in India the student is especially referred to Morley, *Administration of Justice,* pp. 241 sqq., a useful summary of which is to be found in Abdur Rahman, *Institutes of Mussalman Law* (Calcutta, 1907), pp. lv sqq.; also the exhaustive bibliographies in Schacht, *Introduction to Islamic Law* (Oxford, 1964).

addition it is remembered that printing was unknown, that copyists naturally made errors, that the law was expounded all over the world, and that not every cadi could be a finished scholar of Arabic—a language whose grammatical complexities and idiomatic subtleties are both bewildering and fascinating—the surprising thing is, not that there are differences, but that they are on such comparatively minor points. The Four Imāms and their disciples cast the law in an iron mould and gave it a stable pattern; and the labours of the later jurists remind one of the ancient story of old wine in new jars.

When the ancient authorities differ in their opinions what is the duty of the *Kazi*? (*m*). The earlier texts laid down precisely what his duties were. In modern times the word *kazi* has been rendered 'magistrate' by Hamilton, but in Muhammadan law there is no distinction between civil or criminal law. In the British system, the *kazi* means the Civil Court (*n*); and therefore it is for the judge to decide for himself which opinion he will follow and why.

Earlier decisions seem to lay down that in the case of Hanafi law, where the two disciples, Cadi Abū Yūsuf and Imām Muḥammad al-Shaybāni differed from their Master, the Great Imām (*al-aʿẓam*) Abū Ḥanīfa, the opinions of the disciples prevailed. There are also cases which go to show that under certain circumstances the opinion of one or

(*m*) The *Hedaya*, Chapter xx, is devoted to 'the Duties of the Kazee', Hamilton, 2nd ed., 334-52. Abdur Rahim has dealt with the duties very fully, see index, esp. 172 sqq.; and recently Émile Tyan, in his valuable *Histoire de l'Organization Judiciare en Pays d'Islam*, Vol. I (Paris, 1938), has dealt very fully with the *qāḍī*, particularly in ch. ii; Asaf A. A. Fyzee, 'The *Adab al-Qāḍī* in Islamic Law', *Malayan Law Review*, 1964, vol. 6, 406-16.

The spelling *Kazi* is Indian, *cadi* being usual in plain English, and *qāḍī* being preferred by the learned. Fitzgerald records six variations in spelling, p. vii, and one has sympathy with the delightful protest of Colonel T. E. Lawrence in his *Seven Pillars of Wisdom* with regard to the bewildering variety in spelling Muslim names.

(*n*) Tyabji §15 (com.) shows the distinction between the *qāḍi* of the Muhammadan law texts and the *kazi* who is a mere officiant. The P.C. dictum laying down that the place of the *kazi* has been taken by the Civil Court will be found in *Mahomed Ismail* v. *Ahtmed Moolla* (1916) 43 I.A. 127, 134.

other of the disciples is to prevail (*o*); but the correct view is that 'when Muslim jurists of authority have expressed dissenting opinions on the same question, the courts, presided over by the *kazi* (a civil court judge), have authority to adopt that view which, the presiding officer is of opinion, is, in the particular circumstances, most in accordance with justice'. (*p*)

The question of divergent authorities has been fully and authoritatively discussed by Sir Shah Muhammad Sulaiman C.J. in *Anis Begam* v. *Muhammad Istafa* (*q*).

Their Lordships of the Privy Council in the case of *Aga Mahomed Jaffer Bindanim* v. *Koolsom Beebee*, remarked: 'But it would be wrong for the courts on a point of this kind' (the right of the widow to inherit) 'to attempt to put their own construction on the Quran in opposition to the express ruling of commentators of such great antiquity and high authority' (as the *Hedaya* and the *Fatāwā 'Ālamgīrī*). It is the practice of the great commentators to state the difference of opinion which at one time prevailed on a particular point and then to add on which view is the *fatwā*, or which is the more correct or stronger view, or to use other expressions of like import. But where the learned commentators content themselves with a mere statement of the conflict of opinion without expressing any definite opinion of their own in favour of one or the other view and without saying anything about the consensus of opinion or the *fatwā* being in accordance with a particular view, they imply that the conflict of opinion was still continuing and that no unanimity or general concurrence had till then been obtained. This would have the effect of leaving the question open. The Qazi would then be free to choose whichever of the two opinions appears to him to be the sounder and better adapted to the conditions and the needs of the times (*r*).

In the case of the Shiite law, Sulaiman and Mukerji JJ

(*o*) Mulla §37; Wilson §15. The latter part of both these sections mentions the correct modern rule.

(*p*) Tyabji §15. This, however, is a somewhat wide statement; the correct position is that even among divergent authorities, one is supposed to be binding (*wa 'alayhi 'l-fatwā*, on which rests the decision), and in other schools and particularly outside India, the judge would not have so much discretion.

(*q*) (1933) 55 All. 743, 752-3; *Cases*, 18, 24-5. See also the observations of Tyabji J. in *Ebrahim Alibhai* v. *Bai Asi* (1933) 58 Bom. 254, esp. 259-60.

(*r*) See Waliullah J.'s remarks in *Mohammad Yasin* v. *Rahmat Ilahi* [1947] All. 520; A.I.R. (1947) All. 201 (F.B.) at pp. 207-8.

had previously held that the *Sharā'i'al-Islam* is the leading authority and also that 'where there are two opinions on a point of Muhammadan law, the court should accept only that opinion which is in consonance with justice, equity and good conscience'. (*s*)

While the question of divergent authorities is being discussed, it must never be overlooked that we are only discussing a case which is not covered by modern authority. A judge in an Indian or Pakistani court, it is hardly necessary to insist, cannot decide in opposition to a decision of the Privy Council, the Supreme Court, or to a series of decisions of the High Court which he represents, or to which he is subordinate; in such cases the doctrine of precedent applies (*t*).

Judicial discretion vested in the court can only be exercised where the authorities of *the same school* differ amongst themselves; the court is not entitled on the score of social justice to adopt a rule taken from another school of Islamic law. This course is for the legislature in a modern state and not for the judiciary (*u*).

(*s*) *Aziz Bano* v. *Muhammad Ibrahim* (1925) 47 All. 823, 848, citing Ameer Ali.

(*t*) Wilson §16, last part.

(*u*) Ruxton, *Maliki Law*, 274. See however an interesting case decided in Pakistan and mentioned in Noel J. Coulson, *Conflicts and Tensions in Islamic Jurisprudence* (Chicago, 1969), 105 sqq.

CHAPTER II

MARRIAGE

§6. Introduction

CONSIDERED juristically, marriage (*nikāḥ*) in Islam is a contract and not a sacrament. This statement is sometimes so stressed, however, that the real nature of marriage is obscured and it is overlooked that it has other important aspects as well. Before coming to the law proper, we shall consider the three aspects of marriage in Islamic law, which are necessary to understand the institution of marriage as a whole, namely, (i) Legal, (ii) Social, (iii) Religious.

I. *Legal aspect*. Juristically, it is a contract and not a sacrament. *Qua* contract, it has three characteristics: (i) there can be no marriage without consent; (ii) as in a contract, provision is made for its breach, to wit, the various kinds of dissolution by act of parties or by operation of law; (iii) the terms of a marriage contract are within legal limits capable of being altered to suit individual cases.

II. *Social aspect*. In its social aspect, three important factors must be remembered: (i) Islamic law gives to the woman a definitely high social status after marriage. (ii) Restrictions are placed upon the unlimited polygamy of pre-Islamic times, and a controlled polygamy is allowed. (iii)

The prophet, both by example and precept, encouraged the status of marriage. He positively enjoined marriage to all those who could afford it. And the well-known saying attributed to the Prophet. 'There is no monkery in Islam', expresses his attitude towards celibacy briefly but adequately (*a*).

III. *Religious aspect*. While considering the social and legal aspects, the aspect of religion is often neglected or misunderstood. First, let us consider the Koranic injunctions regarding marriage. Marriage is recognized in Islam as the basis of society. It is a contract, but it is also a sacred covenant. Temporary marriage is forbidden. Marriage as an institution leads to the uplift of man and is a means for the continuance of the human race. Spouses are strictly enjoined to honour and love each other. Secondly, the traditions of the Prophet follow the same lines. The Prophet was determined to raise the status of woman. He asked people to see their brides before marrying them (*b*), and taught that nobility of character is the best reason for marrying a woman (*c*). The Founder of Islam once delivered a sermon on marriage; and to this day it is repeated with certain variations at Muslim marriages; it contains practical wisdom and noble sentiments (*d*).

This aspect of Muslim marriage is very often overlooked. In discussing a question of the payment of dower Sir Shah Muhammad Sulaiman C.J. observes: 'It may not be out of place to mention here that Maulvi Samiullah collected some

(*a*) It would be out of place to refer fully to books on Islamic tradition, but when an elementary question arises, the student is recommended to consult Muhammad Ali, *Manual of Hadith* (Lahore, 1944) and A. J. Wensinck, *Handbook of Early Muhammadan Tradition* (Leiden, 1927). The former contains a handy selection of traditions from Bukhārī; the latter is a useful index of the whole body of authoritative traditions in Islam. Chapter xx on Marriage in the first book, and s.v. 'Marriage', p. 143, in the second are most revealing. In view of the recent work of Schacht, however, these traditions have to be viewed in an altogether different light.

(*b*) Muhammad Ali, *Manual*, 271, No. 7. *Fat. Law* §§25 sqq.

(*c*) Muhammad Ali, ibid., 272-3, No. 11. *Fat. Law* §10.

(*d*) Muhammad Ali, ibid., 274, No. 15. This may be compared with the Fatimid version, *Fat. Law* §32.

authorities showing that a marriage is not regarded as a mere civil contract, but as a *religious sacrament*.'(*e*)

Hence the saying that marriage partakes of the nature both of *'ibāda* (worship) and *mu'āmala* (worldly affairs).

§7. Definition of Marriage

Among the Arabs *nikāḥ*, 'marriage', is a wide term, comprising many different forms of sex relationship (*f*); but in Muhammadan law it has a very definite legal meaning. It is a contract for the legalization of intercourse and the procreation of children. Ameer Ali cites an ancient text defining its objects as follows: 'Marriage is an institution ordained for the protection of society, and in order that human beings may guard themselves from foulness and unchastity';(*g*) and Mahmood J. in the leading case of *Abdul Kadir* v. *Salima* (*h*) observes: 'Marriage among Muhammadans is not a sacrament, but purely a civil contract (*i*); and though solemnized generally with recitation of certain verses from the Kuran, yet the Muhammadan law does not positively prescribe any service peculiar to the occasion.' The objects, therefore, are the promotion of a normal family life and the legalization of children. It is to be distinguished from the modern notion of marriage (*j*) by the toleration of a modified form of polygamy.

For further details see Tyabji §21 and Wilson §17. One of the most valuable works on marriage is *Institutes of Mussalman Law*

(*e*) *Anis Begam* v. *Muhammad Istafa* (1933) 55 All. 743, 756, *Cases*, 18, 27. See also G. H. Stern, *Marriage in Early Islam* (Royal Asiatic Society, London, 1939), 104-8. On marriage generally, see the article on *Nikāḥ* by J. Schacht in *Ency. of Islam*, III, 912-14; Prof. Abū Zahrā in *LME*, I, 132 sqq. The most comprehensive treatment of the law of marriage according to the four Sunnite schools will be found in Jazīrī, *Kitāb al-fiqh 'alā'l-madhāhib al-arba'a* (2nd ed., Cairo, 1938), IV, 1-277.

(*f*) Robertson Smith, *Kinship and Marriage in Early Arabia* (London, 1907), 87.

(*g*) Ameer Ali, Students' 7th ed., 97. This definition is based on the Koran and Traditions.

(*h*) (1886) 8 All. 149, 154-5. *Cases*, 103, 108, citing Sircar.

(*i*) This must be read subject to what has been stated in the preceding discussion.

(*j*) Compare the dictum of Lord Penzance, quoted in the Introduction, p. 9 note (*w*). Fitzgerald, 34-7, has some interesting observations to make on the Muslim institution of *nikāḥ*.

by Nawab A. F. M. Abdur Rahman (Calcutta, 1907). It is a translation of the Egyptian Code of Hanafi law, but is to be considered an authority because the Hanafi law according to its foremost exponents is laid down with precision and accuracy.

§8. Form and Capacity

The legal incidents of marriage in Islam are remarkable for their extreme simplicity. 'Marriage may be constituted without any ceremonial';(*k*) there are no special rites, no proper officiants, no irksome formalities. The essential requirements are offer (*ījāb*) and acceptance (*qabūl*). Marriage is legally contracted by a declaration made by one contracting party being followed by a corresponding acceptance from the other *at the same meeting*. The declaration and acceptance may be made by the parties, or by their agents, if both are competent. In case of legal incompetency, like minority or unsoundness of mind, the guardians may validly enter into a contract of marriage on behalf of their wards (*l*).

As to the form, the following conditions are necessary: (1) declaration or offer (*ījāb*) on the part of the one; (2) acceptance (*qabūl*) by the other (or by guardians, as the case may be); (3) before sufficient witnesses (i.e. in Hanafi law, two; in Shiite law witnesses are not necessary) (*m*).

(4) The words must indicate with reasonable certainty that a marriage has been contracted. There must be no ambiguity, no question of an intention to marry, nor a mere promise to marry at some future time. 'As in other contracts, there must be *per verba de praesenti*—not *de futuro*. And as Arabic has only two tenses, the perfect and the aorist, ambiguity is avoided by the use of the perfect.'(*n*) In other words, verbally, the contract must be completed at one and the same time and place. Wilson observes that in order to distinguish an *actual contract* of marriage from a *mere promise* to marry, it is necessary that the words of proposal and acceptance should

(*k*) Fitzgerald, 38, citing 48 I.A. 114 per Mr Ameer Ali.
(*l*) Abdur Rahman, Art. 5; Tyabji §23; Mulla §252.
(*m*) *Abdul Kadir* v. *Salima* (1886) 8 All. at p. 155; *Cases*, 108; Abdur Rahman, Art 7.
(*n*) Fitzgerald, 38; *Hedaya*, 25-6.

be such as to show an intention to establish the conjugal relation *from the moment of acceptance* (italics are mine, Wilson §25). The usual form of proposal is 'I *have married* myself to you'; the acceptance being 'I *have consented*' (Baillie, 4, 5, 10, 14); not 'I *am marrying*' or '*will marry*', etc. Or an offer may be in the imperative 'Marry your daughter to me', and the father accepts in the perfect tense 'I *have* consented' (*Hedaya*, 26).

(5) The proposal and acceptance must both be expressed at one meeting; a proposal made at one meeting and an acceptance at another meeting do not constitute a valid marriage (*o*).

A mere betrothal does not create any rights in Muhammadan law (*p*).

The requirements of law in each marriage are to be distinguished from the ceremonies and customs that prevail. Ameer Ali has graphically described how marriages used to be celebrated in the past (*q*); and in dealing with the ceremonies Fitzgerald rightly mentions three in particular (*r*). (1) A marriage feast is generally given by the bridegroom; this is supposed to be almost a religious duty. (2) The presence of one or more *wakīls* (agents) to represent each side is customary. They settle the details of the treaty of marriage. (3) The *kazi* is ordinarily present. The *kazi* in India is the mere keeper of a marriage register. His function is purely evidentiary. It is a mistake to suppose that he joins the couple in marriage; the marriage takes effect by operation of law on the contract being completed between the parties.

The question of witnesses in a marriage arises often, and in order to understand what actually happens in a Muslim marriage in India reference may be made to *Mst. Ghulam Kubra* v. *Mohammad Shafi* (*s*). The description of a typical

(*o*) Abdur Rahman, Art. 6; Tyabji §§24, 30. A strange case is reported in Tyabji §26 (2).

(*p*) *Mst. Zainaba* v. *Abdul Rahman*, A.I.R. (1945) Peshawar 51.

(*q*) Ameer Ali, II, 555 (Appendix I).

(*r*) Fitzgerald, 38-9.

(*s*) A.I.R. (1940) Peshawar 2, 3. Reference may also be made to *Mst. Zainaba* v. *Abdul Rahman*, A.I.R. (1945) Peshawar 51.

marriage ceremony given in that case by Mir Ahmad J. is both instructive and interesting, for, with minor local variations, the matter is of everyday occurrence in India. He says:

According to Mahomedan law, it is absolutely necessary that the man or someone on his behalf and the woman or someone on her behalf should agree to the marriage at one meeting and the agreement should be witnessed by two adult witnesses. As women are in pardah in this part of the country it is customary to send a relation of the woman to her inside the house accompanied by two witnesses. The relation asks the girl within the hearing of the witnesses whether she authorizes him to agree to the marriage on her behalf for the dower money offered by the husband. He explains to her the detail (*sic*) of the dower proposed. When the girl says 'yes' or signifies her consent by some other method, the three persons come out. The future husband and those three persons are then placed before the Mullah. The Mullah asks the boy whether he offers to marry the girl on payment of the specified dower. He says 'yes'. Then the relation, who had gone inside, tells the Mullah that he is the agent of the girl. The Mullah asks him whether he agrees to the marriage on payment of the specified dower. The relation says 'yes'. The witnesses are present there so that if the Mullah has any doubt he should question them as to whether the relation is a duly authorized agent of the girl. Directly both sides have said 'yes' the Mullah reads the scriptures and the marriage is complete.

I have been at pains to describe the method which is usually adopted in this part of the country for effecting a marriage in order to show that the vague allegation that there were two witnesses of the nikah has no value and that it should be proved that the whole procedure has been gone through . . .

A very detailed study of marriage customs in India is by Cora Vreede de Stuers, 'Le mariage chez les musulmans de condition *Ashraf* dans l'Inde du Nord', *Orient* (Paris), No. 25, 1963, 35-7.

Capacity. Every Muslim of sound mind who has attained majority can enter into a contract of marriage. Majority is attained at puberty (*t*). The presumption is that a person attains majority at 15, but the *Hedaya* lays down that the

(*t*) The same is the rule in Ceylon, ***Abdul Cader*** v. ***Razik*** [1953] A.C. 285.

earliest period for a boy is 12 years and for a girl 9 years. The Privy Council in a Shiite case says that majority in the case of a girl is attained at the age of 9 (*u*).

The marriage of minors can be contracted only by their guardians. Such a marriage, although valid, is capable of being repudiated. A marriage entered into by a girl while she had not attained puberty was not a marriage in the eye of the law, and was therefore void (*v*). For this subject, see the chapter on Guardianship, §35, Guardianship in Marriage.

Option of Puberty. If a Muslim minor has been married during minority by a guardian, the minor has the right on attaining majority to repudiate such marriage. This is called *khiyār al-bulūgh*, the Option of Puberty. Such a minor may be given in marriage either (1) by the father or grandfather, or (2) by any other guardian. By the older law, a minor girl contracted in marriage by her father or grandfather could not exercise the option of puberty; this restriction has now been removed by statute (*w*). Such an option can only be exercised by the wife, if she files a substantive suit under the Act; it cannot be exercised by her in a suit by her husband for restitution of conjugal rights or in any other proceedings (*x*). But in Madhya Pradesh the view has been taken that the wife can exercise the option even in a suit filed by the husband for restitution (*y*).

In the case of a girl married during minority, she is entitled to a dissolution of her marriage if she proves the following facts. First, that she was given in marriage by her father or other guardian; secondly, that the marriage took place before she attained the age of 15; thirdly, that she repudiated the marriage before she attained the age of 18; and fourthly, that

(*u*) *Nawab Sadiq Ali Khan* v. *Jai Kishori* (1928) 30 Bom. L.R. 1346, 1351 (P.C.). This case is not reported in Indian Appeals. See also Tyabji §27; Mulla §251; Abdur Rahman, notes to Art. 47; *Fat. Law* §42.

(*v*) *Allah Diwaya* v. *Kammon Mai* PLD 1957 (W.P.) Lah. 651.

(*w*) Abdur Rahman, Arts. 44-50; Mulla §§272-4. See (*Mst.*) *Ghulam Sakina* v. *Falak Sher*, A.I.R. (1950) Lahore 45.

(*x*) *Sk. Shaib Ali* v. *Jinnatan Nahar* (1960) 64 C.W.N. 756.

(*y*) *Nizamuddin* v. *Huseni* A.I.R. (1960) M.P. 212.

the marriage has not been consummated (*z*). Consummation of marriage *before* the age of puberty does not deprive the wife of her option (*a*).

Clause (vii) of Sec. 2 of the Act fixes fifteen as the age of puberty without any opportunity of rebuttal. This clause does not speak of puberty at all, but only of an age, though in fact it deals with the option arising at puberty. And the only way it can be reasonably interpreted is that a woman who has before the age of fifteen years been given away in marriage by her guardian is allowed to repudiate her marriage for a period of three years *after* she attains the age of fifteen and *before* she attains the age of eighteen (*b*).

The husband, married during minority, has the same right to dissolve his marriage, but in his case there is no statutory period of time within which he must exercise his right. The option can be exercised on his attaining majority, and payment of dower or cohabitation implies ratification.

The right of repudiation is lost, first, on consummation. It has been held, however, that a wife's right is not determined by mere consummation if she was ignorant of her right (*c*). Secondly, the right is also lost in the case of a female if on attaining puberty and *on being informed of the right*, she does not repudiate the marriage within a reasonable time. By the statute, the wife must exercise the option before she attains the age of 18.

The mere exercise of the option to repudiate does not sever the marital tie. The repudiation must be confirmed by a court; until that time, the marriage subsists, and if one of the spouses dies, the other has the right to inherit from him or her.

The High Court of Lahore (West Pakistan) has decided that a court's decree is not necessary to sever the marital tie;

(*z*) Dissolution of Muslim Marriages Act, VIII of 1939, Section 2(vii). *Allah Diwaya* v. *Kammon Mai* PLD 1957 (W.P.) Lah. 651.

(*a*) *Behram Khan* v. *Akhtar Begum* PLD 1952 (W.P.) Lah. 548.

(*b*) *Daulan* v. *Dosa* PLD 1956 (W.P.) Lah. 712.

(*c*) Tyabji §78.

but the High Court of Madhya Pradesh has held that a decree of the court is necessary (*d*).

§9. Disabilities

There are seven main limitations to the unfettered capacity of a Muslim to marry any person of the opposite sex. The prohibition may be on the grounds of (1) Number, (2) Religion, (3) Relationship (consanguinity or affinity), (4) Fosterage, (5) Unlawful Conjunction, (6) *'idda*, or (7) Miscellaneous Prohibitions (*e*).

(1) *Number*

As to plurality of husbands or wives, the rule in Islamic law is that a Muslim man may marry any number of wives, not exceeding four; but a Muslim woman can marry only one husband (*f*). If a Muslim marries a fifth wife, such a marriage is not void, but irregular (*g*); whereas if a Muslim woman marries a second husband, she is liable for bigamy under Sec. 494, Indian Penal Code, the offspring of such a marriage are illegitimate and cannot be legitimated by any subsequent acknowledgement (*h*).

Sometimes a man having a wife, lawfully married according to the law of Islam, proceeds to England and desires to marry another wife, on the ground that the English law does not recognize a Muslim marriage, which is a polygamous union, and that, therefore, such a union would be valid according to English law. This question will be dealt with under the caption 'Foreign Marriages', in the next section.

(2) *Religion*

Difference of schools. Muslims belonging to different schools may intermarry freely with one another, and a mere difference of a school of law, such as Shiite or Sunnite, Hanafi

(*d*) Tyabji §74; Wilson §§18, 19; Mulla §275. *Muni* v. *Habib Khan* PLD 1956 (W.P.) Lahore 403.
(*e*) Tyabji §35; Wilson §31 sqq.
(*f*) Wilson §§31, 32, 33; Mulla §§255, 256; Abdur Rahman, Art. 19.
(*g*) Mulla §255.
(*h*) Wilson §33; Mulla §256.

or Shāfi'ī, is entirely immaterial (*i*). Each spouse retains his or her own status on marriage, and no rule of law compels the wife to adopt the husband's school; there is thus no mergence as in the law of domicile (*j*).

Difference of religion. A man in Hanafi law may marry a Muslim woman or a *kitābiyya*; but a Muslim woman cannot marry any one except a Muslim (*jj*). It is necessary to explain the terms *kitābī* and *kitābiyya*, the former of which refers to a man and the latter to a woman. A *kitābī* is a man believing in a revealed religion possessing a Divine Book (*k*). The words *kitābī* and *kitābiyya* have also been rendered 'scripturary'.(*l*) In India, it is a term applied only to Jews and to Christians, each of whom possesses a revealed Book (*kitāb*), but it really extends to the adherents of other religions also, for instance to Samaritans, Sabaeans (*m*), and, according to the Ithna 'Asharī and Fatimid Shiites, to the Zoroastrians as well (*n*). The question arose before the Privy Council, whether a Buddhist can be regarded as a scripturary or not. But when it was proposed to examine and discuss the tenets of Buddhism with a view to showing that Buddhists come under the same category as Jews and Christians, with whom Muslims could undoubtedly intermarry, their lordships declined to entertain that question in the circumstances of that case (*o*). Thus it remains an open question.

A Muslim, however, cannot marry an idolatress or a fire-worshipper; and a Muslim woman cannot even marry a *kitābī*, except in India under the Special Marriage Act, 1954.

The rule among the Shiites is stricter. A Shiite, whether male or female, cannot marry a non-Muslim in the *nikāḥ* (or

(*i*) *Aziz Bano* v. *Muhammad Ibrahim* (1925) 47 All. 823; Tyabji §§54, 55; Mulla §258; *Fat. Law* §§23, 147.

(*j*) Ameer Ali, II, 23, 459.

(*jj*) *Fat. Law* §148.

(*k*) Tyabji §54; Fitzgerald, 40; Mulla §259. A good discussion will be found in *ahl al-kitāb* by Goldziher in *Ency. of Islam*, I, 184.

(*l*) H. Lammens, *Islam: Beliefs and Institutions* (London, 1929), 23 and index.

(*m*) Fitzgerald, 40; Ameer Ali, II, 154.

(*n*) Baillie, II, 29, 40; *Fat. Law* §§149, 489.

(*o*) *Abdool Razack* v. *Aga Mahomed* (1893) 21 I.A. 56, 64-5.

permanent) form; but he can contract a *mut'a* (or temporary marriage) with a *kitābiyya* (including a fire-worshipper) (*p*). As the Fatimids hold that Zoroastrians (*majūs*) belong to the group designated as *ahl al-kitab*, a man belonging to that school can marry a Zoroastrian female lawfully though a Fatimid woman cannot lawfully marry a Zoroastrian man. (*pp*).

The question arises: What is the position if a marriage prohibited on the ground of religion does take place? Is it to be treated as entirely void (*bāṭil*) or merely irregular (*fāsid*)? Ameer Ali has argued eloquently that an examination of the law reveals a basic misconception in this branch. He is of opinion that 'A Muslim may, therefore, lawfully intermarry with a woman belonging to the Brahmo sect. Nor does there seem to be any reason why a marriage with a Hindu woman *whose idolatry is merely nominal* (italics mine) and who really believes in God should be unlawful. The Moghul Emperors of India frequently intermarried with Rajput (Hindu) ladies and the issue of such unions were regarded as legitimate and often succeeded to the imperial throne.'(*q*) He, therefore, proceeds to lay down that such unions are merely *irregular*, and not *void*. 'For example, when a Muhammadan marries a Hindoo woman, the marriage is only invalid (*irregular*, according to our nomenclature) and does not affect the legitimacy of the offspring, as the polytheistic woman may at any time adopt Islam which would at once remove the bar and validate the marriage.'(*r*) He shows that the rules as to difference of religion or apostasy were based on the principle of political safety. Infidelity implied hostility to the commonwealth of Islam and apostasy was tantamount to treason (*s*). These conditions no longer exist and he pleads for a more liberal view.

(*p*) Tyabji §56; Baillie, II, 29, 40.

(*pp*) *Fat. Law* §148.

(*q*) Ameer Ali, II, 154. Akbar married Jodhbai; *Cases*, 78.

(*r*) ibid., 282. (*s*) ibid., 16-17.

Whether the courts would, in view of the clear texts of law and Koranic provisions, accept such a broad view in all its implications is extremely doubtful, but Tyabji says, 'The present conditions of life conduce to marriages between persons of different religions and it is not unlikely that the legislature may step in and validate such marriages.'(*t*) This has now been done in India by the Special Marriage Act, 1954, where a civil marriage can take place.

The present position appears to be that the *nikāḥ* of a Muslim man with an idolater or fire-worshipper is irregular and not void (*u*). Mulla goes on to say, however, that the marriage of a Muslim woman with a non-Muslim is only irregular, not void. This is, it is submitted, an inaccurate statement of the law. The marriage of a Muslim woman with a non-Muslim is declared by the Koran to be *bāṭil*, void and not merely irregular (*v*). Thus it would seem that reform, in consonance with the view of Ameer Ali, can only be introduced by legislation.

Marriages with Christians and Jews. In India a Muslim can lawfully marry a Jewish or Christian woman according to the tenets of Muhammadan law. We must now consider each of these cases in greater detail.

If a Muslim marries a Jewess the union is valid according to Muhammadan law, but as all religions are equal before the law we have also to consider the Jewish law on the point; for obviously a complication would arise if such a union is valid according to the law applicable to one party but not according to the law applicable to the other. If the wife filed a suit against the husband, he could not deny the marriage, as the law of the defendant would be applicable. On the other hand, if the husband took action against her, and she denied the validity of the marriage, what would be the result? No such case seems to have occurred in India and we do not know of

(*t*) Tyabji §55 (note).

(*u*) Mulla §259.

(*v*) Kor. ii, 220. Abdur Rahman, Art. 122, lays down the rule correctly.

the Jewish law on the point. But it is submitted that in such a case the court would decide in accordance with the law of the defendant (*w*).

Marriages between Muslims and Christians have been fairly frequent and we must now consider them more fully. A Muslim woman cannot marry a Christian; such a union would be void (*x*); but a Muslim may marry a Christian woman in accordance with Muhammadan law. Such a marriage must in India be solemnized in accordance with the provisions of the Indian Christian Marriage Act, XV of 1872. The marriage of a Christian must take place in the presence of a marriage registrar, else it would be 'void'. Since a Muslim woman cannot lawfully marry a non-Muslim, she cannot be married to a Christian under the provisions of this Act (*y*).

Civil Marriage. It is necessary to add that the above discussion applies only in the case of *nikāḥ* according to Muhammadan law, and *not to a civil marriage* in India under the Special Marriage Act, 43 of 1954.

This Act provides for a marriage between any two persons, regardless of religion, provided that (a) neither party has a spouse living, (b) neither party is an idiot or a lunatic, (c) the male has completed the age of twenty-one years and the female the age of eighteen years, (d) the parties are not within the degrees of prohibited relationship, and (e) where the marriage is solemnized outside India, both parties are citizens of India and domiciled in India.

This Act provides, in Sec. 15-18, for the registration of other forms of marriage. Upon such registration, the most

(*w*) Recently a court in Palestine has decided that a Jewess had not the capacity to marry a Christian. Would not the same rule apply, by parity of reasoning, to the Jewish wife of a Muslim husband, in the case of a *nikāḥ*, as distinguished from a civil marriage? [1958] 74 *Law Quar. Rev.* 235. Apparently, the case of a 'limping' marriage has not been reported in the sub-continent.

(*x*) Abdur Rahman, ibid. It is submitted with great respect that the view that such marriages are merely irregular is not well-founded, see Tyabji §82; Wilson §39(1); Mulla §259(2). Kor. ii, 220 appears to be a mandatory prohibition; *Fat. Law* §148.

(*y*) Mulla, loc. cit., notes; Wilson §39(3).

important consequence for a Muslim is that succession to the property of such person and his issue is regulated by the Indian Succession Act, 39 of 1925. We shall discuss this question fully in the chapter on Administration, §76 below.

§10. Foreign Marriages

Difficult questions sometimes arise when a Muslim resident in India goes abroad and marries in some foreign country. Such a marriage may be valid according to the *lex loci celebrationis*, but not according to the *lex domicilii*. Or after a marriage, validly contracted, one or both of the parties may change their faith, and the marriage may be rendered void or irregular according to the personal law of one or both of the parties. These and allied questions have been dealt with by Ameer Ali (*z*) and by Fitzgerald (*a*), but a full discussion of such difficult matters is out of place in a brief text-book; moreover, with the changing social conditions, newer problems are arising almost daily, and we shall therefore confine our attention to some of the most important points that have actually arisen.

Macnaghten says that if a married Muslim were to marry again, the second wife being a European converted to Islam, such second marriage would be lawful (*b*). It is not mentioned that the marriage takes place in India; but presumably that is so, and there is no difficulty.

A Muslim, having a Muslim wife in India, proceeds to England, and there enters into a form of marriage with an English Christian woman. Is such a marriage valid? According to Muhammadan law, a man may marry a second wife who is a Christian. According to English law, bigamy is not lawful; but the Muslim marriage, it may be argued, being a potentially polygamous union and not recognized as such by English law, is not a marriage at all, hence the English

(*z*) Ameer Ali, II, 148 sqq.

(*a*) Fitzgerald, 84 sqq.

(*b*) *Principles*, 255, case VII.

marriage is valid. This argument would not prevail now in view of the latest cases.

In an old case the Nawab Nazim of Bengal, who had other wives living, went to England and married an Englishwoman in Muslim fashion in 1870. Later in 1875, he acknowledged the marriage and the children of the marriage. Still later in 1880, he purported to marry another English lady and thereupon the first English wife refused to live with him. Mr Justice Chitty held: 'The marriage was a Mahommedan and by consequence a polygamous marriage and not intended to be monogamous. Even if the ceremony were according to the Mahommedan law a marriage binding on the husband, yet still, according to English law, it was not a marriage binding on any spouse of English domicile, the reason being that it was not intended to be a marriage.'(*c*) He refrained from holding that the children of the union were illegitimate, for they had been recognized as legitimate by the father and by Government, and were legitimate by Muhammadan law; thus the curious result that the marriage was treated as invalid, but the children were held to be legitimate, at least for some purposes.

Recently, however, it has been held in two cases that if a Hindu having a lawfully married wife living in India goes through a form of marriage at a registry office in England with an Englishwoman, such a marriage is a nullity and the Englishwoman is entitled to a decree *nisi* (*d*). In the second case it was held that the domicil of the Hindu husband was immaterial and the result would be the same whether the husband's domicil was England or India (*e*). In both cases, Mr Justice Barnard held that the Hindu marriage, though

(*c*) *Re Ullee* (1885) Law Times Rep., N.S. 711, 712, affirmed in (1886) L.T.R., N.S. 286; *Cases*, 124. See also Ameer Ali, II, 173-5; and Tyabji, 50 sq.

(*d*) *Srini Vasan* v. *Srini Vasan* [1946] P. 67; [1945] 2 All. E.R. 21.

(*e*) *Baindail* v. *Baindail* [1945] 2 All. E.R. 374; affirmed on appeal [1946] P. 122. Discussed in a note by Prof. J. H. C. Morris, *Law Quar. Review* for 1946, 116-18.

potentially polygamous in character, was to be recognized as valid in English law; hence the second marriage was bigamous and amounted to a nullity.

If a Hindu marriage, potentially polygamous in character, has now been recognized for certain limited purposes as lawful by the English law, by a parity of reasoning it is impossible to deny the legality of a Muhammadan marriage. It is therefore submitted that the observations in *re Ullee* would now be treated as overruled; that the Muslim marriage, lawfully contracted in India, would be accorded recognition in some measure; and that the subsequent marriage before a registrar in England, entered into by a Muslim, would be treated as a nullity (*f*). In *Shahnaz* v. *Rizwan,* the parties were married in Hyderabad. Although the marriage was potentially polygamous, it was considered lawful by the law of England, and a contract for dower acquired (*ff*); and in another case, a wife from Pakistan was awarded maintenance at £6 per week by the Court of Appeal (*fff*).

An Indian Muslim (H) married a wife (W) at Hyderabad in 1958 according to the rites of Islam. Later H and W came to reside in England, where H had been residing since 1954. In 1959 W left H and later came away to India with her child. By the middle of 1961 H obtained a domicil of choice in England. In 1963 he presented a petition for divorce on the ground of W's desertion; W denied desertion; alleged cruelty, and further denied the court's jurisdiction on the ground that the marriage was polygamous. In 1964 H committed adultery, and W cross-prayed for dissolution on that ground: *Held* (1) that the court was precluded from exercising jurisdiction as the alleged desertion took place in 1959, at a time when a potentially polygamous union existed between the parties.

(*f*) See Ameer Ali's remarks, II, 171 and 178 (top). But such a case is to be distinguished from a case like *Risk* v. *Risk* [1950] 2 A.E.R. 973, which is discussed later.

(*ff*) [1964] 2 All E.R. 993. On this case see P. R. H. Webb, 'Polygamy and the Eddying Winds', *Intern. cnd Comp. Law Quar.*, 1965, 14, 273.

(*fff*) *Imam Din* v. *National Assistance Board* [1967] 2 W.L.R. 257.

(2) that H acquired English domicil by choice in 1961, and thus altered the nature of the union to a monogamous union;

(3) that for this reason the court had the power to exercise jurisdiction on the grounds of adultery committed by H in 1964, and therefore

(4) that the wife was entitled to a *decree nisi* (*ffff*).

The reason for discussing this important decision fully is that marriages between Indians and English women are increasing, and Indian wives are accompanying their Indian husbands who reside in England either temporarily, or permanently with change of the husband's domicil. Although such cases do not form part of Indian law, they are of interest to students who have to study both Muhammadan and International law, and to lawyers who may be required to advise on questions relating to the validity of marriage, contracts of dower, divorce, cruelty and desertion. Furthermore the judgment of Cummings-Bruce J. deals with the British case law exhaustively, and lays down several principles which should be widely known in India and Pakistan.

There is no doubt, however, that an unmarried Indian Muslim may contract a valid marriage with an Englishwoman before a registrar in England (*g*). A marriage between a Muslim and a non-Muslim woman, celebrated in a foreign country, is valid under Muhammadan law if it is performed in accordance with the *lex loci contractus* (*h*). But *aliter* if the Muslim is duly married in India and purports to marry in England a domiciled Englishwoman converted to Islam. A marriage was celebrated in England according to Muslim

(*ffff*) *Ali* v. *Ali* [1966] 1 All E.R. 664. This case was discussed by D. Tolstoy, 'Conversion of a Polygamous Union into a Monogamous Union', *Intern. and Comp. Law. Quar.*, 1968, 17, 721 and by J. H. C. Morris, ibid., 1014.

(*g*) *Rex v. Hammersmith* [1917] 1 K.B. 634; *Cases*, 131. There are recent cases where an unmarried Englishwoman contracted a marriage, valid according to Egyptian law, with an Egyptian Muslim in Egypt, *Risk* v. *Risk* [1950] 2 A.E.R. 973, and *Maher* v. *Maher* [1951] Probate 342, [1951] 2 A.E.R. 37. See note by S. V. Fitzgerald, *Law Quar. Review* for 1951, 171-2.

(*h*) *Ameer Ali*, II, 155, 156-7.

rites in a private house. The person who celebrated the marriage was indicted under Sec. 39 of the Marriage Act (now Sec. 75 of the Marriage Act, 1949) for unlawfully celebrating a marriage. The Muslim marriage contracted in India was 'recognized' despite the fact that it was potentially polygamous, and the second *nikāḥ* was declared unlawful according to the law of England (*i*).

R. v. *Rahman,* the above case, has however been overruled by the Court of Criminal Appeal in *R.* v. *Bham* where it was held that a 'Nichan' (obviously, *nikāḥ*), between a Muslim and an English girl who had adopted the Muslim faith in a private house, was potentially polygamous. As such, it was not a 'marriage within the meaning of English law, and there was no intention to effect an English marriage (*ii*).

To this rule, however, there are certain limitations. Suppose a Hindu wishes to marry a Muslim in India. The only way to legalize such a union would be to marry under the Special Marriage Act, 1954, and such unions are fairly common after the passing of the Act.

The law of polygamous marriages has been altered in England by the passing of two new Acts, the Recognition of Divorces and Legal Separations Act 1971 (Eliz. 1971, Chapter 53) and the Matrimonial Proceedings (Polygamous Marriages) Act 1972 (Eliz. 1972, Chapter 38), and D. Pearl has discussed the English law in a learned paper (*j*).

§11. Further Disabilities

(3) *Relationship*

(A) *Consanguinity.* The third bar to marriage is on the ground of blood relationship (*k*). A man is prohibited from

(*i*) *R.* v. *Rahman* [1949] A.E.R. 165.

(*ii*) *R.* v. *Bham* [1965] 3 All E. R. 124.

(*j*) 'Muslim Marriages in English Law', [1972A] C. L. J. 120-143. I am indebted to Mrs. D. Hinchcliffe (London) for sending me the two Acts.

(*k*) On the subject of such bars generally, see Robertson Smith, *Kinship and Marriage*, Chapter VI.

marrying (i) his mother or grandmother how high soever; (ii) his daughter or grand-daughter how low soever; (iii) his sister whether full, consanguine or uterine; (iv) his niece or great-niece how low soever; (v) his aunt or great-aunt how high soever, paternal or maternal.

A marriage with a woman prohibited by reason of blood relationship is totally void and the issue illegitimate (*l*).

(B) *Affinity*. A man is prohibited from marrying certain relations by affinity. These are (i) ascendants or descendants of his wife; and (ii) the wife of any ascendant or descendant. By way of exception, a man may marry the descendant of a wife with whom the marriage has not been consummated (*m*).

A marriage prohibited on the ground of affinity is generally declared to be void (*n*).

(4) *Fosterage*

Where the relationship of fosterage is established, Muhammadan law prohibits the marriage within certain limits. A man may not, for instance, marry his foster-mother, or her daughter, or his foster-sister. A marriage forbidden by reason of fosterage is void.

The rules as to fosterage are now to a large extent obsolete and no useful purpose would be served by giving details, which may be found in the textbooks (*o*).

(5) *Unlawful Conjunction*

A man is also forbidden to have two wives *at the same time*, so related to each other by consanguinity, affinity or fosterage, that they could not have lawfully intermarried with each other if they had been of different sexes (*p*). Thus a man

(*l*) Tyabji §36; Mulla §260; *Fat. Law* §105 sqq.

(*m*) Tyabji 37; Mulla §261.

(*n*) Abdur Rahman, Articles 21, 23; Mulla, loc cit.; Fitzgerald, 47. But see Tyabji §82, who shows that in the opinion of some jurists such a union is merely irregular. *Fat. Law* §108 sqq.

(*o*) Tyabji §41; Wilson §37; Mulla §262; *Fat. Law* §129 sq.

(*p*) Wilson §38; Tyabji §39; Mulla §263; *Fat. Law* §112 sqq.

cannot marry two sisters, or an aunt and her niece. Under Hanafi law, generally speaking, disregard of the bar of unlawful conjunction renders the marriage irregular but not void.

The most important case arising under this rule is the marriage of two sisters to one man. There is nothing to prevent a man from marrying his wife's sister after the death or divorce of his wife; but it is unlawful to marry two sisters at the same time, or to marry the sister of the wife during the wife's lifetime. The view of the Calcutta High Court, guided clearly by the Koranic provision (Kor. iv, 23): *And (it is forbidden unto you) that ye should have two sisters together*, was that such unions were void and the issue illegitimate (*q*); but the High Courts of Bombay, Madras and Lahore, and the Chief Court of Oudh have in recent decisions declared them to be merely irregular and the issue legitimate (*r*). It is evident that the later decisions have been influenced by the elaborate criticism of *Aizunnissa's Case* by Ameer Ali (*s*), and as they tend to legitimize the issue of such marriages, almost all the text writers favour them and the rule may now be said to be firmly established in India. It seems, however, necessary to insist that where a clear rule of law is found in the Koran, legislation and not 'elastic interpretation' is the proper remedy.

(6) *'Idda*

In Muhammadan law, when a marriage is dissolved by death or divorce, the woman is prohibited from marrying within a specified time. This period is called '*idda*[*t*]. 'The most approved definition of '*idda* is the term by the completion of which a new marriage is rendered lawful'.(*t*) It is a

(*q*) Wilson, 108; *Aizunnissa* v. *Karimunnissa* (1895) 23 Cal. 130; Abdur Rahman, Art. 133, gives full details of such cases.

(*r*) *Tajbi* v. *Mowla Khan* (1917)41 Bom. 485; Mulla §263; Tyabji §82. Such unions are clearly void in *Fatimid Law*, §121 (ii), (iii).

(*s*) Ameer Ali, II, 203, 328 sqq., 341 sqq.

(*t*) The *Hedaya* cited by Mahmood J. in *Re Din Muhammad* (1882) 5 All. 226, 231; Fitzgerald, 52; Tyabji §42; Wilson §31; Mulla §257. The Fatimid law declares a marriage during *'idda* as void, as distinguished from being merely irregular, *Fat. Law* §§254 sqq.

period of continence imposed on a woman on the termination of a marriage in the interests of certainty of paternity during which a woman is supposed to live a life of seclusion and to abstain from certain luxuries.

(A) The observance of *'idda* is necessary where cohabitation has taken place. Cohabitation may be lawful, as in the case of the consummation of marriage or unlawful, as in illicit intercourse. If pregnancy follows illicit intercourse, *'idda* must be observed (*u*).

(B) If consummation of marriage has taken place and the marriage is dissolved by divorce, the duration of *'idda* is three courses, or if the woman is pregnant, till delivery. If the marriage is dissolved by death, the period of *'idda* is four months and ten days or, if the woman is pregnant, till delivery, whichever is longer.

(C) If the marriage is not consummated, *'idda* has to be observed in the case of death, but not in the case of divorce (*v*).

Valid retirement (al-khalwat al-ṣaḥīḥa). The question of consummation is, therefore, of prime importance in the law relating to *'idda*. In certain cases 'valid retirement' has the same legal effect as consummation. When the husband and wife are alone together under circumstances which present no legal, moral or physical impediment to marital intercourse, they are said to be in 'valid retirement' or in *al-khalwat al-ṣaḥīḥa* (*w*). The *Radd al-Muḥtār* lays down that four conditions are necessary: (i) there must be actual privacy; (ii) there must not be any physical, (iii) moral, or (iv) legal bar (*x*). The *Fatāwā 'Ālamgīrī* (*y*) and the *Radd al-Muḥtār* (*z*) have laid

(*u*) Tyabji §42.

(*v*) Tyabji §§42 sqq.; Fitzgerald, 52-3; Mulla, loc. cit. The most detailed rules will be found in Abdur Rahman, Arts. 310-23.

(*w*) Ameer Ali, II, 322-5; Tyabji §81; Mulla, loc. cit.

(*x*) Ameer Ali, II, 323. (*y*) Baillie, I, 101. (*z*) Ameer Ali, III, 324-5.

down in precise terms the cases in which valid retirement is to be treated as having the same legal effects as actual consummation. In (i) the confirmation of *mahr*, (ii) the establishment of paternity, (iii) the observance of *'idda*, (iv) the wife's right of maintenance and residence during *'idda*, (v) the bar of marriage with the wife's sister, and (vi) the bar as to marrying four other wives beside her, valid retirement has the same effects as consummation. But mere valid retirement does not prevent marriage with the wife's daughter and, in the case of a triply divorced couple, remarriage between them is impossible unless the divorced wife is married to another husband, and duly divorced by the second husband after *actual* consummation.

In these two cases, actual consummation is necessary, valid retirement not being sufficient (*a*).

A marriage with a woman undergoing *'idda* is irregular, but not void. The Fatimids declare such marriages to be void (*b*).

(7) *Miscellaneous Prohibitions*

In addition to the regular prohibitions to marry, there are a few others, perhaps not quite so important, which must now be considered. These are the doctrine of equality (*kafā'a*), illicit intercourse and undue familiarity, pilgrimage and divorce. Some of them, as is obvious, are rules of prudence rather than mandatory provisions of law. The Muhammadan law texts abound in moral precepts in addition to strict provisions of law and Mr Justice Mahmood has pointed out the danger of confusing moral with legal obligations (*c*): 'One of the greatest difficulties in the administration of Muhammadan law, as indeed of all ancient systems, lies in distinguishing between *moral* from *legal* obligations.'

(*a*) Tyabji §81; Mulla, loc. cit. The Shiite law will be found in Tyabji.

(*b*) Tyabji §82; Mulla, loc. cit.; *Fat. Law* §§254 sqq.

(*c*) 7 All. at p. 805.

(A) *The doctrine of Equality in Marriage* (kafā'a). In spite of the equalizing character and democratic spirit of Islam, Arabian society could hardly be expected to act in full consonance with the Koranic dictum that *all Muslims are brothers* (*d*). It was, therefore, recognized by society that in order that a marriage may bear the character of a suitable union in law, the husband must be the equal of the woman in social status (*e*). There was no corresponding provision that the wife should be of an equal status with the husband, for by marriage he was assumed to raise her to his own position The Hanafis, accordingly, hold that equality (*kafā'a*) between the two parties is a necessary condition in marriage, and an ill-assorted union or a runaway marriage is, under certain circumstances, liable to be set aside by the court (*f*). In Hanafi law, the following factors must be considered for determining equality: (i) family, (ii) Islam, (iii) profession, (iv) freedom, (v) good character, (vi) means. The Shāfi'īs consider slightly different qualifications (*g*).

From the nature of the rules, however, it is obvious that *kafā'a* is not so much a legal prohibition, as a rule of worldly wisdom. In a Punjab case it was laid down that a disregard of the rules of equality does not render the marriage void *ab initio,* and that the court was not justified in dissolving the marriage (*h*). On the particular facts of the case, the decision may have been proper, but it is submitted that, as pointed out by Tyabji, in certain circumstances the court exercising the jurisdiction of the *kazi* has the power to annul such a marriage (*i*).

The true nature of the rule is that it is not an absolute prohibition to marry, but it allows the *kazi* to rescind the

(*d*) Kor. xlix, 10.

(*e*) The Prophet is reported to have recommended marriage with fit spouses: 'Marry your *equals*', Muhammad Ali, *Manual,* 272 (No. 10). *Fat. Law* §10.

(*f*) Ameer Ali, II, 364 sqq.; Abdur Rahman, Articles 52, 62-9; Fitzgerald, 54-6.

(*g*) Fitzgerald, 55.

(*h*) *Jamait Ali Shah* v. *Mir Muhammad* (1916) Punjab Record 371 (No. 119).

(*i*) Tyabji §79.

marriage (*faskh*) in certain cases of *mésalliance*. It may be likened to a voidable contract. The rule may be formulated as follows: Where a woman, being of age, contracts herself in marriage with a man who is not her equal (*ghayr kuf'*) without the consent of any of those male relations who would be entitled to be guardians of her marriage (*walī*) if she were a minor, the court, on the application of such relations, has the power to rescind the marriage (*j*). Ameer Ali illustrates this by saying that if a woman were to contract a runaway marriage with a servant of the family, the marriage would be annulled on the application of the *walī* (*k*). Thus the rules of equality in marriage are salutary rules of worldly wisdom which must be carefully considered by a *kazi* exercising his powers of *faskh* (annulment of marriage), and as such, should really be treated as considerations relating to that form of dissolution of marriage known as *faskh*. A great deal is left to the discretion of the *kazi*, depending upon the circumstances of each individual case.

(B) *Illicit intercourse and undue familiarity*. If a person has illicit intercourse with a woman or commits acts of 'undue familiarity', some of the woman's relations are forbidden to him, although he can marry the woman herself (*l*).

(C) *Pilgrimage*. In Ithnā 'Asharī and Shāfi'ī law a man who has come within the sacred precincts of the Ka'ba and put on the pilgrim's dress, may not enter into a contract of marriage while on the pilgrimage (*m*).

(D) *Divorce*. Divorce constitutes an important legal bar and will be fully considered in the section on Divorce. Briefly stated, the rule is that when a man divorces a woman, and the divorce is effective as a *triple ṭalāq*, remarriage between them is impossible unless the woman observes *'idda*, lawfully marries another husband, the second marriage is consummated, and the second husband lawfully and effectively

(*j*) ibid.
(*k*) It should be added that such rescission is at the discretion of the *kazi*, not by the compulsion of law. Ameer Ali, II, 368.
(*l*) Tyabji §38; *Fat. Law* §§107, 117-19. (*m*) ibid. §57; *Fat. Law* §123.

divorces her. Some important cases have occurred in India and they require careful consideration (*n*).

§12. Classification of Marriages

A marriage, according to Muhammadan law, may be either (1) Valid (*ṣaḥīḥ*), or (2) Void (*bāṭil*), or (3) Irregular (*fāsid*) (*o*).

(1) *Valid Marriage* (Ṣaḥīḥ)

A marriage which conforms in all respects with the law is termed *ṣaḥīḥ*, i.e. 'correct', in regard to legal requirements. For a marriage to be valid it is necessary that there should be no prohibition affecting the parties. Now, prohibitions may be either perpetual or temporary. If the prohibition is perpetual, the marriage is *void*; if temporary, the marriage is *irregular* (*p*).

(2) *Void Marriage* (Bāṭil)

A marriage which has no legal results is termed *bāṭil* or void. It is the semblance of marriage without the reality. A marriage forbidden by the rules of blood relationship, affinity or fosterage is void. The issue of such a union is illegitimate, and law knows no process whereby the union may be legalized (*q*). Similarly, a marriage with the wife of another, or remarriage with a divorced wife, when the legal bar still exists, is void (*r*).

A void marriage is an unlawful connexion which produces no mutual rights and obligations between the parties. For example, there is no right of dower, unless there has been consummation. The death of one of them does not entitle the other to inherit from the deceased. The illegality of such unions commences from the date when the contracts are entered into and the marriage is considered as totally non-existing in fact as well as in law (*s*).

(*n*) Tyabji §§48 sqq.; Wilson §78(6); Mulla §336(4), (5); *Fat. Law* §§205, 292 sqq.
(*o*) Mulla §253.
(*p*) Abdur Rahman, Arts. 20, 21.
(*q*) Mulla §§260-2, read with §264; Fitzgerald, 45-9.
(*r*) *Rashid Ahmad* v. *Anisa Khatun* (1931) 59 I.A. 21.
(*s*) Ameer Ali, II, 348.

(3) *Irregular Marriage* (Fāsid) (*t*)

A union between a man and a woman may be either lawful or unlawful. Unlawfulness may be either absolute or relative. If the unlawfulness is absolute, we have a void (*bāṭil*) marriage. If it is relative, we have an *irregular* (*fāsid*) marriage.

The following marriages have been considered irregular:

(i) A marriage without witnesses;
(ii) A marriage with a woman undergoing *'idda*;
(iii) A marriage prohibited by reason of difference of religion (*u*);
(iv) A marriage with two sisters, or contrary to the rules of unlawful conjunction (*v*);
(v) A marriage with a fifth wife (*w*).

The Ithnā 'Asharī and Fatimid schools of law do not recognize the distinction between void and irregular marriages. A marriage is, according to those systems, either valid or void; hence, the above-mentioned unions would be treated as void marriages (*x*).

We must now consider the effects of an irregular union. In considering these effects we shall observe that two principles emerge. As between the parties themselves, the irregular union is a flimsy tie, giving very few rights; but, as regards the issue, they are given full legal status.

As to Separation. It is the duty of the *kazi* to separate the spouses, but the union may be terminated also by either party at any time; neither divorce, nor the intervention of a court is necessary. One of them may say 'I have relinquished you',(*y*) and the unholy alliance ends.

(*t*) The fullest discussion of such marriages will be found in Ameer Ali, II, 328-64, read with 276-86; and in *Ata Mohammad* v. *Saiqul Bibi* (1911) 8 All. L.J. 953, per Karamat Husain J.

(*u*) That is, a Muslim marrying an idolatress; but not, it is submitted, the reverse case, see pp. 82-4 above.

(*v*) Wilson §39A; Mulla §263; Tyabji §82.

(*w*) Ameer Ali, II, 280; Mulla §264, read with §255.

(*x*) Tyabji §82(2); Mulla §264 (note); *Fat. Law* §§198 sqq.

(*y*) Tyabji §§83-5; Mulla §267.

As to Consummation. If there has been consummation the wife is entitled to dower, proper or specified, whichever is less, and she must observe *'idda* for three courses (*z*).

As to Inheritance. No rights of inheritance are created between the husband and the wife by an irregular marriage (*a*).

As to Issue. The issue are treated as legitimate and are entitled to a share of the inheritance (*b*).

The 'irregular marriage' of Islam is a connexion between a man and a woman which, though not amounting to a lawful marriage, confers the status of legitimacy on the children. In this respect it is similar to a Scottish or Canadian putative marriage (*c*). The logical separation of the question of the legitimacy of the child from that of the validity of the parents' marriage was also developed by canon law and has been accepted in English law. It was said by the Privy Council in a case dealing with a Chinese conjugal union that 'a court may do well to recollect that it is a possible jural conception that a child may be legitimate though its parents were not and could not be legitimately married'.(*d*)

Presumption of Marriage

Sometimes the question arises whether a man and a woman who have cohabited are validly married or not. Where there has been prolonged and continuous cohabitation as husband and wife, in the absence of direct proof a presumption arises that there was a valid marriage. Similarly, where a man acknowledges the woman as his wife, or the issue of the union as legitimate, a like presumption arises.

The presumption does not arise, however, where there is a legal prohibition, or where the conduct of the parties was

(*z*) Mulla, loc. cit.

(*a*) Ameer Ali, II, 348; Mulla §267(2)(iii) citing Baillie, I, 694, 710.

(*b*) Wilson §39A; Mulla, loc. cit.; Ameer Ali, II, 343 sqq., 349, 350.

(*c*) 'Polygamous Unions before the English Courts,' *The Law Times*, 5 May 1946, Vol. 201, 248-9.

(*d*) *Khoo Hooi Leong* v. *Khoo Hean Kwee* [1926] A.C. 529, 543, per Lord Phillimore; Ameer Ali, II, 176.

inconsistent with the relation of husband and wife (*e*). It has been held, for example, that cohabitation with a woman, admittedly a common prostitute, does not raise the presumption of marriage (*f*).

For a fuller discussion see Acknowledgement, §32, below.

§13. The Legal Effects of a Valid Marriage

In the leading case of *Abdul Kadir* v. *Salima*, Mahmood J. has discussed the legal effects of a Muslim marriage:

These authorities leave no doubt as to what constitutes marriage in law, and it follows that, the moment the legal contract is established, consequences flow from it naturally and imperatively as provided by the Muhammadan law. I have said enough as to the *nature* of the contract of marriage, and in describing its necessary legal effects I cannot do better than resort to the original text of the *Fatawa-i-Alamgiri*, which Mr Baillie has translated in the form of paraphrase, at page 13 of his digest, but which I shall translate here literally, adopting Mr Baillie's phraseology as far as possible: 'The legal effects of marriage are that it legalizes the enjoyment of either of them (husband and wife) with the other in the manner which in this matter is permitted by the law; and it subjects the wife to the power of restraint, that is, she becomes prohibited from going out and appearing in public; it renders her dower, maintenance, and raiment obligatory on him; and establishes on both sides the prohibitions of affinity and the rights of inheritance, and the obligatoriness of justness between the wives and their rights, and on her it imposes submission to him when summoned to the couch; and confers on him the power of correction when she is disobedient or rebellious, and enjoins upon him associating familiarly with her with kindness and courtesy. It renders unlawful the conjunction of two sisters (as wives) and of those who fall under the same category.'

That this conception of the mutual rights and obligations arising from marriage between the husband and wife bears in all main features close similarity to the Roman law and other European systems which are derived from that law, cannot, in my opinion, be doubted; and even regarding the power of correc-

(*e*) *Abdool Razack* v. *Aga Mahomed* (1893) 21 I.A. 56.

(*f*) *Ghazanfar* v. *Kaniz Fatima* (1910) 37 I.A. 105; *Mohd. Amin* v. *Vakil Ahmed* [1952] S.C.R. (India) 1133. For further cases see Tyabji §80; Mulla §268.

tion, the English law seems to resemble the Muhammadan, for even under the former 'the old authorities say the husband may beat his wife'; and if in modern times the rigour of the law has been mitigated, it is because in England, as in this country, the criminal law has happily stepped in to give to the wife personal security which the matrimonial law does not. To use the language of the Lords of the Privy Council in the case already cited: 'The Muhammadan law, on a question of what is legal cruelty between man and wife, would probably not differ materially from our own, of which one of the most recent expositions is the following: "There must be actual violence of such a character as to endanger personal health or safety, or there must be a reasonable apprehension of it."' 'The Court,' as Lord Stowell said in *Evans* v. *Evans*, 'has never been driven off this ground.'

Now the legal effects of marriage, as enumerated in the *Fatawa-i-Alamgiri*, come into operation as soon as the contract of marriage is completed by proposal and acceptance; their initiation is simultaneous, and there is no authority in the Muhammadan law for the proposition that any or all of them are dependent upon any condition precedent as to the payment of dower by the husband to the wife (*g*).

The legal effects of a valid marriage may now be summarized:

(1) Sexual intercourse becomes lawful and the children born of the union are legitimate;

(2) The wife becomes entitled to her dower (*mahr*);

(3) The wife becomes entitled to maintenance;

(4) The husband is entitled to restrain the wife's movements in a reasonable manner and to exercise marital authority;

(5) Mutual rights of inheritance are established;

(6) The prohibitions regarding marriage due to the rules of affinity come into operation;

(*g*) (1886) 8 All. 149, 155-7; *Cases*, 103, 108-10.

(7) The wife is not entitled to remarry after the death of her husband, or after the dissolution of her marriage, without observing *'idda*;

(8) Where there is an agreement between the parties, entered into either at the time of the marriage or subsequent to it, its stipulations will be enforced, in so far as they are not inconsistent with the provisions or the policy of the law (*h*);

(9) A woman does not change her status on marriage. She remains subject to her own pre-marital school of law. Neither the husband nor the wife acquires any interest in the property of the other by reason of marriage (*i*).

§14. *Mut'a* or Temporary Marriage

Introduction (*j*)

The word *mut'a* literally means 'enjoyment, use'; and in its legal context it may be rendered, according to Heffening, a 'marriage for pleasure'. It is a marriage for a fixed period for a certain reward paid to the woman. The institution of *mut'a* was fairly common in Arabia both before and at the time of the Prophet (*k*). It seems fairly certain that it was tolerated by the Prophet for some time, but all schools of law, except one, the Ithnā 'Asharī Shiite, are agreed that finally he declared such unions as unlawful.

The old Arabian custom of *mut'a* was justified as being useful in times of war and on travels; but even after the pro-

(*h*) This is the modern Indian rule, and slightly wider than the strict Hanafi, Shāfi'ī or Mālikī doctrine. As to agreements that the wife shall reside with her parents see Tyabji §31 and *Fat. Law* §91.

(*i*) The best summary of rights is in Tyabji §31, which I have adopted with slight modifications. Fuller discussions will be found in Ameer Ali, II, 405-32; Wilson §§40-50; Abdur Rahman, Art. 17.

(*j*) The best general account of *mut'a* is by Heffening in the *Ency. of Islam*, III, 774-6. See also Schacht, 266-7; Robertson Smith, *Kinship*, 82-3: Levy, *Social Structure*, 116 sqq.; Hollister, op. cit., 55-7.

(*k*) It is asserted that Kor. iv, 24 regulates and sanctions the practice of *mut'a*.

hibition, it persisted and was really suppressed and ruthlessly condemned by the Caliph Omar. It is probably for this reason among others that the Ithnā 'Asharī school retains the practice and considers it lawful. Some of the learned and the pious among the Shī'a who take *mut'a* wives unto themselves are wont to repeat the dictum of the theologian al-Ḥurr al-'Āmilī: 'The believer is only perfect when he has experienced a *mut'a*.'

The practice is not very common in India, and in Lucknow and other places where there is a Shiite population, ladies of the better classes do not contract *mut'a* marriages. In Persia and Iraq, *mut'a* generally descends to the level of legalized prostitution. There is a delightful description of the practice in Persia, where such unions are termed *ṣīghé*, in Morier's *Hajji Baba*.

Before coming to its legal incidents, it is well to remember that this interesting Arabian custom is forbidden by all schools, Sunnite as well as Shiite, including the Zaydī and the Fatimid schools (*l*), and that it is permitted only by the Ithnā 'Asharī Shiite authorities (*m*).

Legal Incidents

According to Ithnā 'Asharī Shiite law, a *mut'a* (or *ṣīghé*) is a marriage for a fixed period of time. It may be for a day, a month, a year or a term of years (*n*). The essentials of such a union are four: the form, the subject, the period, and the dower (*o*).

As regards the form, there must be a proper contract: declaration and acceptance are necessary.

As regards the 'subject', a man may contract a *mut'a* with a Muslim, Christian, Jewish or a fire-worshipping woman (*majūsiyya*), but not with the follower of any other

(*l*) The Khojas and Bohoras consider it unlawful, *Da'ā'im*, II, §§858, 859; (1931) 33 Bom. Law Rep. Jl., 30; Tyabji §34, notes; *Fat. Law* §§95-7.

(*m*) Ameer Ali, II, 317, 318, 398-404; Sircar, II, 373-82, is a good summary of the rules.

(*n*) Baillie, II, 42; Sircar, II, 373.

(*o*) Sircar, loc. cit.

religion (*p*). But a Shiite woman may not contract a *mut'a* with a non-Muslim. Relations prohibited by affinity are also unlawful in temporary marriage (*q*). A man may contract *mut'a* with any number of women (*r*).

As regards the term of *mut'a*, this must be specified; else a lifelong *mut'a* will be presumed if the original cohabitation commenced with a lawful *mut'a*. In *Shoharat Singh* v. *Mst. Jafri Bibi*, their lordships of the Privy Council held that where cohabitation of a man and a woman commenced with a *mut'a*, and there was no evidence as to the term of the marriage, the proper inference would, in default of evidence to the contrary, be that the *mut'a* continued during the whole period of cohabitation (*s*).

In a recent Hyderabad case it was held (i) that there is no difference between a *mut'a* for an unspecified period and a *mut'a* for life (report, p. 7); (ii) that a permanent *nikāḥ* marriage for life can be contracted by the use of the word *mut'a* also; (iii) that specification of the period for which a *mut'a* marriage is contracted alone makes a permanent marriage for life, a temporary *mut'a* marriage for the period specified; (iv) that where the specification of period is omitted, whether intentionally or inadvertently, a permanent *nikāḥ* marriage results, with all the legal incidents of a *nikāḥ* marriage, including the right of inheritance between the contracting parties, and (v) that where the period is for life, a *nikāḥ* marriage will result (*t*).

The learned judge in this case purports to follow the authority of the *Jawāhir al-Kalām*, an exhaustive commentary on the *Sharā'i' al-Islām*, by Shaykh Muḥammad Ḥasan al-Najafī, in six volumes. He says that it is of higher authority than the *Sharā'i' al-Islām*. In view of the remarks of

(*p*) Tyabji 34(3).
(*q*) Sircar, II, 375.
(*r*) Tyabji §34(4). Aboo Baseer reports from Imam Ja'far al-Ṣādiq: 'I inquired respecting women contracted in *moota*, whether their number was restricted to four. He replied, "No! nor to *seventy*."' Baillie, II, 345.
(*s*) (1914) 17 Bom. L.R. 13, 17; Mulla §269(4)(b).
(*t*) *Shahzada Qanum* v. *Fakher Jahan* A.I.R. (1953) Hyd. 6.

Mahmood J. in *Agha Ali* v. *Altaf Hasan* (1892) 14 All. 429, 450 and of Sulaiman J. (as he then was) in *Aziz Bano's Case* (1925) 47 All. 823, 828-9, it is difficult to accept the opinion of the learned judge. The view which he advocates may, in the circumstances prevailing in Hyderabad, have some justification; but in so far as it tends to obliterate the well-known distinction between a *mut'a* and a *nikāḥ*, it is respectfully submitted that the judgment requires reconsideration. The fixation of a period in the marriage contract destroys the concept of *nikāḥ* as understood in Islamic law (*u*). The mere omission to specify the period may result in a valid *mut'a* for life; but to equate a *mut'a* for life with a regular *nikāḥ* is a serious step, which *inter alia* fails to take into consideration the question of intention. Recent case law refuses to extend a life interest into an absolute gift, mainly on the ground of intention, and similarly, would not the real test be: What was the real intention of the parties, rather than the legal force of the words used, including the words omitted? Questions of maintenance, the possible number of such unions, inheritance, the observance of *'idda* after death, and other related questions would have to be carefully investigated before such broad generalizations can be accepted as good law.

A *mut'a* terminates by the efflux of time or by death. On the expiry of the term, no divorce is needed. During the period, the husband has no right to divorce the wife, but the husband may make a 'gift of the term' (*hiba-e muddat*) and thereby terminate the contract, without the wife's consent (*v*).

The dower (*mahr*) is a necessary condition of such a union. If it is not specified the agreement is void. Where the marriage is consummated, the wife is entitled to the whole amount; if not, to half the dower. In case the wife leaves the husband before the expiry of the term, the husband is entitled to deduct a proportionate part of the dower (*w*). On the expiry of the period, where there has been cohabitation, a short *'idda* of

(*u*) Prof. Muḥammad Abū Zahrā, 'Family Law' in *LME*, I, 132, 133.
(*v*) Tyabji §34(9); Mulla §269(4)(d).
(*w*) Tyabji 34(5); Mulla §269(4)(e).

two courses is prescribed; where, however, there has been no consummation, no *'idda* is necessary (*x*).

The issue of a *mut'a* union are legitimate and entitled to inherit. In the absence of a specific agreement, the husband or the wife does not inherit from the other, but if there is such a stipulation it will be effectual (*y*).

A *mut'a* wife is not entitled to maintenance, for, according to the *Sharā'i' al-Islām*, 'the name of a *wife* does not in reality apply to a woman contracted in *mut'a*'.(*z*)

§15. Judicial Proceedings

Questions relating to the maintenance of wives and the rules concerning guardianship will be found in the chapters on Maintenance and Guardianship, respectively.

1. *Restitution of Conjugal Rights*

Marriage confers important rights and entails corresponding obligations both on the husband and on the wife. Some of these rights are capable of being altered by an agreement freely entered into by the parties, but in the main the obligations arising out of marriage are laid down by the law.

An important obligation is 'consortium', which not only means living together, but implies a union of fortunes. A fundamental principle of matrimonial law is that one spouse is entitled to the society and comfort of the other (*a*). Thus where a wife, without lawful cause, refuses to live with her husband, the husband is entitled to sue for restitution of conjugal rights (*b*); and similarly the wife has the right to demand the fulfilment by the husband of his marital duties (*c*).

This right, however, is not absolute. The Koran enjoins husbands to retain their wives with kindness or to part with

(*x*) Tyabji §34(12-15).
(*y*) Sircar, II, 381; Tyabji §34(8).
(*z*) Baillie, II, 344; Wilson §441; Mulla §269(4)(f).
(*a*) Latey on *Divorce*, 12th ed. (1940), 166. The same is the principle of Muhammadan law, Ameer Ali, II, 422; Abdur Rahim, 333-4.
(*b*) Mulla §281; Tyabji §87.
(*c*) Abdur Rahim, 334.

them with an equal consideration (*d*). Whenever a case of this nature arises it is to be borne in mind that, as the Muslim husband is dominant in matrimonial matters, the court leans in favour of the wife and requires strict proof of all allegations necessary for matrimonial relief (*e*). The law, however, does recognize circumstances which would justify her in refusing to live with him.

There are a number of valid defences to a suit for restitution of conjugal rights, and we shall now consider some of the most important among them. The leading case on the subject is *Moonshee Buzloor Ruheem* v. *Shumsoonnissa Begum* (*f*). The relations between a Muslim husband and his wife were considered in broad terms and it was held that a suit for restitution of conjugal rights would lie in a civil court by a Muslim husband to enforce his marital rights; but if there were cruelty to a degree rendering it unsafe for her to return to his dominion, or if there were a gross failure on his part to perform the obligations imposed on him by the marriage contract, the court would be justified in refusing such relief (*g*). In *Anis Begum* v. *Muhammad Istafa* (*h*), it was laid down by Sulaiman C.J. that the courts in this country have a large discretion when a suit is brought for restitution of conjugal rights. It was established in this case that the husband was keeping a mistress in the same house with his wife, and that when quarrels ensued on that account he treated his wife cruelly. The court, while decreeing restitution, imposed certain conditions on the husband, namely, that unless he gave an undertaking not to keep any mistress in the house, a separate house should be provided for the wife, and two servants of her choice for her personal safety.

Actual violence, infringing the right to the safety of life, limb and health, or reasonable apprehension of such violence

(*d*) Kor. lxii, 2.
(*e*) *Abdul Rahiman* v. *Aminabai* (1935) 59 Bom. 426; Tyabji, 104.
(*f*) (1867) 11 M.I.A. 551; *Cases*, 281.
(*g*) Tyabji §215; Mulla §281(2).
(*h*) (1933) 55 All. 743; *Cases*, 18.

would be a good defence (*i*). Charges of immorality and adultery, and the heaping of insults also constitute cruelty (*j*). The dictum of the Judicial Committee that 'The Muhammadan law on a question of what is legal cruelty between man and wife would probably not differ materially from our own . . .' has been liberally construed by our courts, and the decree for restitution of conjugal rights is not permitted to be made an engine of cruelty. Similarly, where the marriage is irregular, or the marriage has been avoided by the lawful exercise of an option, or where the husband has been made an outcaste by his community (*jamāt*, strictly, *jamā'at*) the relief of restitution is refused (*k*).

The question of cruelty depends upon the facts alleged and proved. In an Allahabad case, a suit for restitution was filed by the husband. An unsigned letter, proved to have been written by the wife to her father, complaining of cruelty on the part of the husband, was taken into consideration and relief refused (*l*).

A husband's second marriage may, in certain circumstances, involve cruelty to the first wife, justifying her refusal to live with him. In *Itwari* v. *Asghari* (*m*) it has been laid down that in a suit for restitution of conjugal rights by a Muslim husband against the first wife after he has taken a second, if the court feels that the circumstances are such as to make it inequitable for the court to compel the first wife to live with him, it will refuse relief. Muslim law permits polygamy but does not encourage it, and the Koranic injunction (Kor. iv, 3) shows that in practice perfect equality of treatment on the part of the husband is, for all practical purposes, impossible of achievement. Hence, 'Muslim law as enforced

(*i*) Tyabji §§87, 215; *Asha Bibi* v. *Kadir Ibrahim* (1909) 33 Mad. 22, 25.

(*j*) *Husaini Begum* v. *Muhammad Rustam Ali Khan* (1906) 29 All. 222, 227.

(*k*) Tyabji, loc. cit.; Mulla §281(2), (5), (6).

(*l*) (*Mst.*) *Safia Begum* v. (*Syed*) *Zaheer Hasan Rizvi*, A.I.R. (1947) All. 16.

(*m*) A.I.R. (1960) All. 684; *Cases*, 188 (Italics, mine).

in India has considered polygamy as an institution *to be tolerated but not encouraged*' (p. 686).

As to cruelty, the judge quotes with approval the dictum of the Privy Council in *Moonshee Buzloor Ruheem's Case* (11 Moo. Ind. Ap. 551) and goes on to say:

> Indian law does not recognize various types of cruelty such as 'Muslim' cruelty, 'Christian' cruelty, 'Jewish' cruelty, and so on, and that the test of cruelty is based on the universal and humanitarian standards, that is to say, conduct of the husband which would cause such bodily or mental pain as to endanger the wife's safety or health . . . The onus today would be on the husband who takes a second wife to explain his action and prove that his taking a second wife involved no insult or cruelty to the first . . . and in the absence of cogent explanation *the Court will presume, under modern conditions, that the action of the husband in taking a second wife involved cruelty to the first*, and it would be inequitable for the Court to compel her against her wishes to live with such a husband (p. 687).

This strong judgment shows clearly that since the passing of the Dissolution of Muslim Marriages Act, 1939, the courts have leaned heavily in favour of the wife in all such cases, and restitution cannot be had by the husband unless the wife is clearly in the wrong.

2. *Enforcement of Lawful Agreements*

A Muslim wife is entitled at the time of marriage, or subsequently, to make a contract with her husband. Such a contract will be enforced by the courts if it is lawful and not opposed to the policy of law. A contract may lay down the terms upon which marital life is to be regulated. It may also provide for the dissolution of the marriage by the wife, without the intervention of the court (*n*).

Ameer Ali holds that the following stipulations would be enforceable at law: (i) That the husband shall not contract a second marriage during the existence or continuance of the

(*n*) Ameer Ali, II, 321-2; the writer's 'The Muslim Wife's Right of Dissolving her Marriage' in (1936) 38 Bom. Law Rep. Jl., 113, 120-3. See below §23, Delegated Divorce.

first. (We shall discuss this question more fully later.) (ii) That the husband shall not remove the wife from the conjugal domicile without her consent. (iii) That the husband shall not absent himself from the conjugal domicile beyond a certain specified time. (iv) That the husband and the wife shall live in a specified place. (v) That a certain portion of the dower shall be paid at once or within a stated period, and the remainder on the dissolution of the contract by death or divorce. (vi) That the husband shall pay the wife a fixed maintenance. (vii) That he shall maintain the children of the wife by a former husband. (viii) That he shall not prevent her from receiving the visits of her relations whenever she likes (*o*).

The commonest conditions relate to (i) the place of residence, (ii) the payment of periodical sums of money to the wife, and (iii) the restriction of the husband's right to marry a second wife. We shall confine our attention here to the first two cases; the third can conveniently be considered later, as it is usually coupled with the Muslim wife's right to divorce herself.

The deed of marriage is called the *kābīn-nāma* in India, and is generally kept with the wife or her relations. It contains the terms of the agreement between the parties and usually specifies the amount of the dower. The custom of handing it over to her dates from pre-Islamic times and is necessary for the protection of her interests (*p*).

(i) *Residence.* There is ample authority in early traditions for the broad proposition that conditions made at the time of marriage are sacred obligations and should not be disregarded (*q*). Thus, reasonable conditions regarding the wife's right of residing where she pleases may be enforced; but an agreement that the wife shall be at liberty to live permanently with her parents has been held to be void (*r*). It may, however,

(*o*) Ameer Ali, ibid.

(*p*) Ameer Ali, II, 322.

(*q*) Muhammad Ali, 273, No. 12; Wensinck, *Early Muhammadan Tradition,* 146; Tyabji §31(7).

(*r*) Wilson §56; Mulla §281(3). In Fatimid law, however, such a condition is valid, *Fat. Law* §91.

be observed that while this proposition appears to be well established in the courts of law, it is opposed to the views of both Ameer Ali (*s*) and Tyabji (*t*), and the only direct authority for it is Macnaghten (256, Case vii). Where a man marries a second wife and stipulates that the second wife shall be at liberty to live at her parent's house and that, in case of disagreement, a sum of Rs 30 per month shall be payable to her at her parental home, the court upheld both these conditions (*u*). A husband, who was already married to two wives, married a third wife and agreed with her that if he brought any of his first two wives to live with her in his house, she would be at liberty to divorce him. It was held in Assam that such a condition is valid and is not repugnant to Sec. 23 of the Contract Act (*v*).

It is difficult to state the law with precision when the decisions lay down a rule which is disapproved by eminent text writers, and some ancient legists, particularly of the Hanafi school, are not favourably inclined to allow freedom of contract in marriage; but the Indian law may be briefly summarized thus.

An agreement between man and wife designed to regulate marital relations is favoured by the law, as being in consonance with the Prophet's injunctions. Such an agreement may be made either at the time of marriage or thereafter. The courts will enforce it if it is reasonable, and not contrary to the provisions or the policy of the law. As the husband has the right in general to control the actions of the wife, the wife can make reasonable stipulations safeguarding her right to stay freely where she likes. But if the agreement provides that the wife shall have the absolute and unqualified right to reside permanently with her parents, the courts will hesitate to enforce such a stipulation as it would create moral, social and legal difficulties. For instance, it would be difficult for the

(*s*) Ameer Ali, II, 321, (b), (c), (d).
(*t*) Tyabji §31, comment, especially 60 sq.
(*u*) *Mst. Sakina* v. *Shamshad Khan*, A.I.R. (1936) Pesh. 195.
(*v*) *Saifuddin* v. *Soneka* (1954) 59 Cal. W.N. 139.

husband to exercise control over the wife's actions; consortium would not always be easy; the question of separate maintenance would arise; the guardianship of children would raise thorny problems; the adjustment of mutual rights and obligations would be difficult. As the husband, however, has preponderant authority in matters matrimonial, the courts, within reasonable limits, tend to lean in favour of the wife. Where some reason exists for supporting it, the courts would readily enforce an agreement which has been freely entered into by the parties. Thus a second wife, or a first wife when the husband remarries, may enforce the agreement to reside at her parent's home, and may even obtain maintenance, for such a condition could hardly be considered unreasonable.

A necessitous Hindu woman, Protima, became a convert to Islam and under the name of Begum Noorjahan married a Muslim, NH. At the time of the marriage there was an agreement that the husband would live in the wife's house, and that she would not be compelled to reside with him, at his place of residence with other relations. Such an agreement was held to be reasonable and valid, and the wife obtained a decree for maintenance, residing separately from her husband (*vv*).

Under the Shiite law, a stipulation that the husband shall not take away his wife from her own city is binding. According to the leading Fatimid authority, the *Da'ā'im al-Islām,* if a man marries a woman on the express condition that she should be permitted to reside amongst her own people or in a specified country, such a condition is lawful, for every condition is enforceable, unless it legalizes what is forbidden, or forbids what is permissible (*w*).

(ii) *Maintenance,* kharch-e pāndān. A Muslim wife is entitled to be maintained by her husband so long as she stays

(*vv*) *Nizamul Haque* v. *Begum Noorjahan* A.I.R. (1966) Cal. 465.

(*w*) Cadi Nu'mān, *Da'ā'im,* II §854; *Fat. Law* §91. A fairly exhaustive list of such actions will be found in the notes to Tyabji §§31, 87.

with him and is dutiful (*x*). In addition to maintenance, she is also entitled to receive certain sums at regular intervals if this is provided for in the marriage contract. These allowances are known by different names. *Kharch-e pāndān* is expense of the betel box, and hence pocket money; it is 'a personal allowance . . . to the wife customary among Mahomedan families of rank, specially in upper India, fixed either before or after the marriage, and varying according to the means and position of the parties . . .' Although there is some analogy between this allowance and the pin-money in the English system, it appears to stand on a different legal footing, arising from difference in social institutions. Pin-money, though meant for the personal expenses of the wife, has been described as 'a fund which she may be made to spend during the coverture by the intercession and advice and at the instance of the husband'. No such obligation exists with regard to *kharch-e pāndān* and the husband has no control over the allowance (*y*). Thus a father, who was a nobleman and landed proprietor, agreed at the time of the marriage of his minor son that he would pay the sum of Rs 500 per month in perpetuity to his son's wife. The wife was also a minor at the time of marriage. No conditions were attached to the payments, which were designated as *kharch-e pāndān*. The payments were to be made from the date of the 'reception' of the wife in her conjugal home (*z*), and his landed properties were charged with the payment of these monthly sums. In due course, the wife went to her husband's house and lived there for some years. Later, on account of differences, she left the conjugal home and sued for the amount due to her. It was held that she was entitled to recover the whole amount not-

(*x*) Tyabji §298 sqq.

(*y*) Per Mr Ameer Ali in *Khwaja Md. Khan* v. *Nawab Husaini Begum* (1910) 37 I.A. 152, 159.

(*z*) This is a common feature in certain Muslim families. The marriage takes place at a certain time, and the girl is sent to the husband's house some time later. The legal marriage is called *nikāḥ* or *shādī*; the 'reception' in the conjugal home is called *rukhṣatī*. The custom is due to various reasons, one of which is the fact that the wife is often below the age of puberty when the marriage takes place.

withstanding the fact that she was not a party to the agreement, for she was clearly entitled to proceed in equity to enforce her claim. Further, that, as there were no conditions attached to the payments, it was quite immaterial whether she stayed with her husband or not, provided there had been 'reception' in the husband's home and, as that had been proved, her claim could not be resisted (*a*).

A Muslim married a woman X in 1916; later he married another woman Y. As a consequence of the second marriage, he settled certain properties on X for her life, without any conditions. After some time differences arose and he divorced X and brought a suit claiming back the properties settled on her. It was held that as no conditions were attached to the settlement, X was entitled to enjoy the income of the properties settled on her for her lifetime, divorce or no divorce (*b*).

The allowances designated *mēwa khōrī* (lit., for eating fruit) *guzārā* (lit., subsistence allowance) and *kharch-e-pāndān* are similar in character (*c*).

The question whether a wife is entitled to separate maintenance or not will be discussed in the chapter on Maintenance.

Consequences of breach. The breach of a valid condition in a marriage contract does not necessarily give the wife the right to have the marriage dissolved unless such an option is expressly reserved. The result may be (1) that restitution may be refused to the husband; (2) that certain rights as to dower may arise; or (3) that the wife may have the right to divorce herself, or, in an extreme case, (4) that the marriage itself may be dissolved *ipso facto* (*d*).

(iii) *Future separation*. An agreement for future separa-

(*a*) *Khwaja Md. Khan* v. *Nawab Husaini Begum* (1910) 37 I.A. 152; Wilson §48A; Tyabji §298 (footnote 13), and elsewhere.

(*b*) *Mydeen Beevi* v. *Mydeen Rowther*, A.I.R. (1951) Mad. 992.

(*c*) Tyabji §§31 sq. contains the fullest discussion; Mulla §306.

(*d*) Tyabji, 64 (top), 66 sq.

tion between a Muslim husband and his wife is void as being against public policy (*e*).

(iv) *Jactitation*. Jactitation is a false pretence of being married to another. If a man or a woman falsely claims to be the husband or wife of another person, the proper remedy is to bring a suit for a declaration that the parties are not married. Such an action will lie between Muslims in India (*f*); and minority of the plaintiff does not bar such a suit (*ff*).

Similarly a suit can be brought by a wife for a declaration under Sec. 42 of the Specific Relief Act that she is the lawfully wedded wife of her husband. Where a second wife brings such a suit, the first wife may be properly joined as a party respondent in the suit, if she alleges collusion between her husband and the second wife (*g*).

(v) *Breach of promise to marry*. According to Muhammadan law, unless the contract of marriage is completed, no rights and obligations arise, and therefore a suit for damages for breach of promise to marry is strictly impossible. The only relief that can be asked for, if an engagement (Arabic, *khiṭba*; Hindustāni, *mangnī*) is broken, is the return of ornaments, clothes and money (*h*).

(vi) *Enticement, Persuasion*. If a person forcibly prevents, or persuades a wife to live apart from her husband, the husband can obtain damages against him (*i*). Similarly, a person who entices away the wife of a Muslim is also liable (*j*).

(vii) *Expulsion from caste*. The relief of restitution of conjugal rights may be refused to the husband where the wife complains that he has been expelled from the 'caste'. This peculiar decision—contrary to the entire spirit of Islam, but just and fair considering the particular circumstances of the

(*e*) Wilson §58A; Mulla §322.

(*f*) Baillie, I, 20; *Mir Azmat Ali* v. *Mahmud-ul-Nissa* (1897) 20 All. 96; Wilson §39B; Tyabji §90; Ameer Ali. II, 426.

(*ff*) *Abdullah Dar* v. *Mst. Noori*, A.I.R. (1964) Jam. and Kash. 60.

(*g*) *Razia Begum* v. *Anwar Begum* [1959] S.C.R. (India) 1111.

(*h*) Tyabji §90; Macnaghten, 250-2; Mulla §283.

(*i*) *Muhammad Ibrahim* v. *Gulam Ahmed* (1864) 1 Bom. H.C. Rep. 236.

(*j*) *Abdul Rahiman* v. *Aminabai* (1934) 59 Bom. 426; Tyabji §91; Mulla §284.

case—was given in a Bombay case and the parties belonged to the Khārwa community (*k*). This case is a significant illustration of Hindu influence on Muslim society in India.

(*k*) *Bai Jina* v. *Kharwa Jina* (1907) 31 Bom. 366.

CHAPTER III

DOWER (*MAHR*)

§16. Definition

PRIOR to Islam, two kinds of marital gifts were prevalent. In a certain type of marriage, the so-called *beena* marriage, where the husband visited the wife but did not bring her home, the wife was called *ṣadīqa* or female friend, and a gift given to the wife on marriage was called *ṣadāq*. 'In Islam *ṣadāq* simply means a dowry and is synonymous with *mahr*. But originally the two words were quite distinct: *ṣadāq* is a gift to the wife, and *mahr* to the parents of the wife.'(*a*) The latter term belongs to the marriage of dominion, which is known as the *baal* marriage, where the wife's people part with her and have to be compensated.

Now *mahr* in the *baal* form of marriage was used by the Prophet to ameliorate the position of the wife in Islam, and it was combined with *ṣadāq*, so that it became a settlement or a provision for the wife (*b*). In Islamic law, *mahr* belongs absolutely to the wife (*c*). Thus, historically speaking, the idea of sale is latent in the law of *mahr* (dower).

Mr Justice Mahmooḍ defines dower as follows: 'Dower, under the Muhammadan law, is a sum of money or other property promised by the husband to be paid or delivered to the wife in consideration of the marriage, and even where no dower is expressly fixed or mentioned at the marriage

(*a*) Robertson Smith, *Kinship,* 93.
(*b*) On *Mahr* generally, see *Ency. of Islam,* III, 137.
(*c*) Kor. iv, 4; Ameer Ali, II, 461-2; *Fat. Law* §70.

ceremony, the law confers the right of dower upon the wife.'(*d*) It is not 'consideration' in the modern sense of the term; but an obligation imposed by the law upon the husband as a mark of respect to the wife (*e*). This is made abundantly clear by the author of the *Hedaya* when he says: 'The payment of dower is enjoined by the law merely as *a token of respect* for its object (the woman), wherefore the mention of it is not absolutely essential to the validity of a marriage; and, for the same reason, a marriage is also valid, although the man were to engage in the contract on the special condition that there should be no dower.'(*f*)

There is no doubt that *mahr* was originally analogous to sale-price, but since the inception of Islam it is hardly correct to regard it as the price of connubial intercourse. If the authors of the Arabic text-books on Muhammadan law have compared it to price in the law of sale, it is simply because marriage is regarded as a civil contract in that system (*g*).

In pre-Islamic Arabia, *ṣadāq* was a gift to the wife; but *mahr* was paid to the wife's father, and could therefore be regarded as tantamount to sale-price. But when Islam insisted on its payment to the wife, it could no longer be regarded strictly as a sale (*h*). Thus Islam sought to make *mahr* into a real settlement in favour of the wife, a provision for a rainy day and, socially, it became a check on the capricious exercise by the husband of his almost unlimited power of divorce. A husband thinks twice before divorcing a wife when he knows that upon divorce the whole of the dower would be payable immediately.

The Muslim concept of dower has no reference to the price that under some systems of law was paid to the father of the bride when she was given in marriage. On the other hand, it is considered a debt with consideration (for submission of her

(*d*) *Abdul Kadir* v. *Salima* (1886) 8 All. 149, 157; *Cases,* 103, 110.
(*e*) Abdur Rahim, 334.
(*f*) Hamilton's *Hedaya*, 2nd ed. by Grady, 44, cited by Mahmood J. at 8 All. 157-8; *Cases,* loc. cit. (italics mine).
(*g*) loc. cit.; Tyabji, 108; Ameer Ali, II, 432-3.
(*h*) Robertson Smith, *Kinship*, 92-3, 111; Ameer Ali shows how the change was effected, II, 432-4, 461-3.

person by the wife). The result is that dower is purely in the nature of a marriage settlement and is for consideration. It is a claim arising out of contract by the husband and as such has preference to (*sic*) bequests and inheritance, but on no principle of Muhammadan law it can have priority over other contractual debts (*i*).

The best general observations on dower are those of Lord Parker of Waddington in *Hamira Bibi* v. *Zubaida Bibi* (*j*):

Dower is an essential incident under the Mussulman law to the status of marriage; to such an extent this is so that when it is unspecified at the time the marriage is contracted the law declares that it must be adjudged on definite principles. Regarded as a consideration foı the marriage, it is, in theory, payable before consummation; but the law allows its division into two parts, one of which is called 'prompt', payable before the wife can be called upon to enter the conjugal domicil; the other 'deferred', payable on the dissolution of the contract by the death of either of the parties or by divorce . . . But the dower ranks as a debt, and the wife is entitled, along with the other creditors, to have it satisfied on the death of the husband out of his estate. Her right, however, is no greater than that of any other unsecured creditor, except that if she lawfully obtains possession of the whole or part of his estate, to satisfy her claim with the rents and issues accruing therefrom, she is entitled to retain such possession until it is satisfied. This is called the widow's lien for dower, and this is the only creditor's lien of the Mussulman law which has received recognition in the British Indian Courts and at this Board.

Amount of Dower

The amount of *mahr* may either be fixed or not; if it is fixed, it cannot be a sum less than the minimum laid down by the law.

Minimum Dower

(i) Hanafi law—10 *dirhams*

(ii) Mālikī law—3 *dirhams*

(iii) Shāfi'ī law, and } No fixed minimum
(iv) Shiite law }

(*i*) Per Khaliluzzaman J. in *Kapore Chand* v. *Kadar Unnissa* [1950] S.C.R. 747, 751.

(*j*) (1916) 43 I.A. 294, 300-1; *Cases*, 145, 149; also cited in *Syed Sabir Husain* v. *Farzand Hasan* (1937) 65 I.A. 119, 127.

A *dirham* (Persian, *diram*, a word derived from the Greek) is the name of a silver coin 2·97 grammes in weight (*k*), and is usually valued at 3-4 annas or 20-25 paise. Ten *dirhams* have been valued at 6*s*. 8*d*. and three *dirhams* at 2*s*. (*l*). In India, it has been held that the value of ten *dirhams* is something between Rs 3 and 4 (*m*). Thus it will be seen that the minimum dower fixed by the law can hardly be deemed to be an adequate provision for the wife. In fact, it would be a mistake to lay too great a stress upon the monetary value of the minimum dower. It is said that in the case of an extremely poor man, the Prophet requested him to teach the Koran to his wife, and this was considered by the Lawgiver to be an adequate requital of the husband's obligation (*n*).

Among the Muslims of India two distinct tendencies are to be found in society. In some cases, as in the Sulaymānī Bohoras, the dower is Rs 40, it being considered a point of honour not to stipulate for a sum higher than the minimum fixed by the Prophet for his favourite daughter Fāṭima, the wife of Ali, namely 500 *dirhams* (*o*). Among certain other communities, there are dowers of anything between a hundred and a thousand rupees; Ameer Ali mentions amounts between four to forty thousand rupees. An altogether different tendency is to be found in Uttar Pradesh, and also to some extent in Hyderabad, Deccan, where the absurd rule appears to be that the nobler the family, the higher the *mahr*, regardless of the husband's ability to pay or capacity to earn. In one case known to the writer a middle-class man agreed to the sum of eleven lacs of *ashrafīs* (or gold mohurs, originally

(*k*) *Ency. of Islam,* I, 978; according to Wilson's *Glossary,* 'a silver coin 45-50 grains in weight, rather heavier than six pence'. For Islamic weights and measures, see W. Hinz, *Islamische Masse und Gewichte* (Leiden, 1955); Ch. Issawi, *Economic History of the Middle East* (Chicago, 1966), App. 1, 517; S. D. Goitein, *A Medieval Society,* Vol. I, *Economic Foundations* (University of California, 1967), 359.

(*l*) Fitzgerald, 63.

(*m*) *Asma Bibi* v. *Abdul Samad* (1909) 32 All. 167; Tyabji §95; Wilson §41 contains a learned discussion on the value of a *dirham* on the footing of the purchasing power of the silver contained in the coin.

(*n*) Ameer Ali, II, 440; *Da'ā'i m,*II §828.

(*o*) Cadi Nu'mān, *Da'ā'im,* II §822; *Fat. Law* §73; Ameer Ali, II, 437

15-20 rupees each) as dower. This sum, even in these days of astronomical figures, would give serious cause for anxiety to any young bridegroom (*p*).

§17. Classification of Dower

We have seen that dower is payable whether the sum has been fixed or not, Ali said: 'There can be no marriage without *mahr*' (*pp*). Thus, dower may, first of all, be either specified or not specified. In the latter case, it is called *mahr al-mithl*, Proper Dower, or to be strictly literal, 'the dower of the like'. The meaning of this expression will appear shortly. If the dower has been specified, then the question may be whether it is prompt (*mu'ajjal*) or deferred (*muwajjal*, strictly *mu'ajjal*).

Thus we have two kinds of dower in Islam:

(A) Specified Dower (*al-mahr al-musammā*); and

(B) Unspecified Dower, or Proper Dower (*mahr al mithl*).

Specified Dower may again be divided into—

(I) Prompt—*mu'ajjal* (معجّل), and

(II) Deferred—*mu'ajjal* (مؤجّل).

In (A) and (B) the question before the court is the amount payable; in (I) and (II) the question is the time when payment has to be made.

(A) *Specified Dower* (al-mahru al-musammā) (*q*)

Usually the *mahr* is fixed at the time of marriage and the *kazi* performing the ceremony enters the amount in the register; or else there may be a regular contract called *kābīn-nāma*, with numerous conditions (*r*). The sum may be fixed either at the time of marriage or later, and a father's contract on behalf of a minor son is binding on the minor (*s*).

(*p*) Indian conditions are discussed by Ameer Ali, II, 434-5.
(*pp*) *Fat. Law* §§69 sqq.
(*q*) Also called *mahr al-'aqd*, Fitzgerald, 65 sq.; Ameer Ali, II, 432-9; Wilson §42; Tyabji §95; Mulla §286.
(*r*) Tyabji, §98, com. See Appendix B.
(*s*) Mulla §288.

Where a father stipulates on behalf of his minor son, in Hanafi law, the father is not personally liable for the *mahr*; but *aliter* in Ithnā 'Asharī law. In *Syed Sabir Husain* v. *Farzand Hasan*, a Shiite father had made himself surety for the payment of the *mahr* of his minor son. Thereafter he died, and it was held that the estate of the deceased was liable for the payment of his son's *mahr*. Accordingly each heir was made responsible for a portion of the wife's claim in proportion to the share received by the particular heir on distribution from the estate of the deceased. The heirs were, however, liable only to the extent of the assets received by them from the deceased, and not personally (*t*).

Where the amount has been specified, the husband will be compelled to pay the whole of it, however excessive it may seem to the court, having regard to the husband's means; but in Oudh, only a reasonable amount will be decreed, if the court deems the amount to be excessive or fictitious (*u*).

(B) *Unspecifid Dower* (mahr al-mithl) (*v*)

The obligation to pay dower is a legal responsibility on the part of the husband and is not dependent upon any contract between the parties; in other words, if marriage, then dower (*w*). Where the dower is specified, any amount, however excessive, may be stipulated for. But what are the principles upon which the amount of dower is to be determined where no agreement exists?

The customary or proper dower of a woman is to be fixed with reference to the social position of her father's family and her own personal qualifications. The social position of the husband and his means are of little account. The *Hedaya*

(*t*) (1937) 65 I.A. 119.

(*u*) Tyabji §95(2); Oudh Laws Act, 1876. See Mulla §286, comment. This is called 'fictitious dower', Ameer Ali, II, 435-6. Sometimes for the purpose of 'glorification' a larger *mahr* is announced, but the real *mahr* is smaller. Such a *mahr* for the purposes of 'show' is known as *sum'a*, Ameer Ali, II, 465.

(*v*) Ameer Ali calls it the 'customary' dower, II, 436 sq.; Fitzgerald, 66; Abdur Rahman, Articles 76, 78; Wilson §42; Tyabji §97; Mulla §289.

(*w*) This has been emphasized by the Privy Council in *Syed Sabir Husain's Case* (1937) 65 I.A. 119, 127; *Fat. Law* §69.

lays down the important rule that her 'age, beauty, fortune, understanding and virtue' must be taken into consideration (*x*). Islamic marriage, therefore, safeguards the rights of a wife and attempts to ensure her an economic status consonant with her own social standing. Historically speaking, and on the analogy of sale, it is permissible to ask with Fitzgerald: 'What have the circumstances of a purchaser to do with the intrinsic value of the thing he buys?'(*y*) The answer is that the Indian courts no longer consider marriage as a form of sale or barter, and do not proceed upon the analogy that dower is the price of consortium.

In fixing the amount of the proper dower, regard is to be had to the amount fixed in the case of the other female members of the wife's family. '*Mahr* is an essential incident under the Mussalman law to the status of marriage; to such an extent that is so that when it is unspecified at the time the marriage is contracted the law declares that it must be adjudged on definite principles'.(*z*) The main consideration is the social position of the bride's father's family, and the court will consider the dowers fixed upon her female paternal relations, such as sisters or paternal aunts who are considered to be her equals (*a*).

The Prophet once allowed the marriage of an indigent person for a silver ring; and on another occasion, merely on the condition that the husband should teach the Koran to his wife (*aa*). In Hanafi law, where the specified dower is less than 10 *dirhams*, the wife is entitled only to the minimum, namely 10 *dirhams*, and in Ithnā 'Asharī law, the proper dower can never exceed 500 *dirhams*, the dower fixed for the Prophet's daughter Fāṭima (*b*). Thus, among the Shiites there are three kinds of *mahr:* (i) *mahr-e sunnat,* the dower supported by tradition, i.e. 500 *dirhams*; (ii) *mahr-e mithl,* 'the

(*x*) Ameer Ali cites this well-known passage, II, 437 (note 1).
(*y*) Fitzgerald, 66.
(*z*) (1916) 43 I.A. 294, 300, cited in (1937) 65 I.A., 127.
(*a*) Ameer Ali, II, 436; Tyabji §97 *Fat. Law* §§78 sq.
(*aa*) *Fat. Law* §75 (II).
(*b*) Tyabji §97 (2) and (3).

dower of the like', or the dower of an equal, which is the technical name for proper or unspecified dower; and (iii) *mahr-e musammā,* the specified dower (*c*).

Prompt (mu'ajjal) *and Deferred* (mu'ajjal) *Dower*

When the dower is specified, the question arises: At what times and in what proportions is the amount payable? Here two somewhat puzzling terms are used and it is necessary to distinguish carefully between them. The technical term for 'prompt' dower is *mu'ajjal* (معجّل). It is derived from a root meaning 'to hasten, to precede'. The term *mu'ajjal,* therefore, means 'that which has been hastened or given a priority in point of time'. The term *mu'ajjal* (مؤجّل), however, means 'delayed, deferred', and comes from a root which means 'to delay or postpone'. Written in the original Arabic there would be no cause for confusion, but in the usual English forms of spelling the words often puzzle those who are not familiar with the Arabic tongue.

Prompt dower is payable immediately after the marriage, if demanded by the wife; while deferred dower is payable on the dissolution of the marriage or on the happening of a specified event (*d*). When dower is fixed, it is usual to split it into two equal parts and to stipulate that one shall be paid at once or on demand, and the other on the death of the husband or divorce or the happening of some specified event. But a difficulty arises when it is not settled whether the dower is prompt or deferred.

In Ithnā 'Asharī law the presumption is that the whole of the dower is prompt (*e*); but in Hanafi law the position is different. The whole of the dower may be promptly awarded (*f*); but a recent Full Bench decision lays down first, that where the *kābīn-nāma* is silent on the question, the usage of

(*c*) Ameer Ali, II, 437-8.

(*d*) Tyabji §98 Ameer Ali, II, 441-2; Wilson §46; Mulla §§289A, 290.

(*e*) Ameer Ali, II 442; Tyabji §123; as to different schools, Fitzgerald, 66-8.

(*f*) Per Mahmood J. in *Abdul Kadir* v. *Salima* (1886) 8 All. 149, 158; *Husseinkhan* v. *Gulab Khatum* (sic) (1911) 35 Bom. 386; Tyabji, loc. cit.

the wife's family is the main consideration; and secondly, that in the absence of proof of custom, the presumption is that one-half is prompt, and the other half deferred, and the proportion may be changed to suit particular cases (*g*).

§18. Increase or Decrease of Dower

The husband may at any time after marriage increase the dower (*h*). Likewise, the wife may remit the dower, wholly or partially (*i*); and a Muslim girl who has attained puberty is competent to relinquish her *mahr*, although she may not have attained majority (18 years) within the meaning of the Indian Majority Act (*j*). The remission of the *mahr* by a wife is called *hibat al-mahr* or *hiba-e mahr*.

It has, however, been held in Karachi that in certain cases remission of dower cannot be upheld. For instance, if a wife feels that the husband is increasingly showing indifference to her and the only possible way to retain the affection of her husband is to give up her claim for *mahr* and forgoes her claim by executing a document, she is not a free agent and it may be against justice and equity to hold that she is bound by the terms of the deed (*k*).

§19. Enforcement of Dower

The claim of the wife or widow for the unpaid portion of *mahr* is an unsecured debt due to her from her husband or his estate, respectively. It ranks rateably with unsecured debts, and is an actionable claim (*l*). During her lifetime the wife can recover the debt herself from the estate of the deceased husband. If she predeceases the husband, the heirs of the wife, including the husband, become entitled to her dower (*m*). A lady, whose *mahr* was Rs 50,000, received from her husband

(*g*) Wilson §46; Tyabji §123(2), (3); Ameer Ali, II, 443; Mulla §290.
(*h*) Tyabji §99; Mulla §287; Ameer Ali, II, 462.
(*i*) Tyabji §100; Mulla §291; Baillie, I, 553; Wilson §47A.
(*j*) *Qasim Husain* v. *Bibi Kaniz* (1932) 54 All. 806.
(*k*) *Shah Bano* v. *Iftekhar Muhammed* PLD 1956 (W.P.) Kar. 363.
(*l*) Tyabji §105. For English law, see [1965] *L.R.* 12, noting on *Shahnaz* v. *Rizwan* [1964] 3 W.L.R. 759; [1964] 2 All. E.R. 993.
(*m*) Ameer Ali, II, 449.

during his lifetime sums of money in the aggregate exceeding the *mahr* settled on her. The largest of such payments was Rs 3,000. There was no evidence that these payments were intended by the husband to satisfy the dower debt. The question arose whether these payments satisfied the husband's obligation. The Judicial Committee held that such payments were not to be treated as having been made in satisfaction of the dower debt (*n*).

If a husband refuses to pay prompt dower, the guardian of a minor wife has the right to refuse to allow her to be sent to the husband's house; and similarly, the wife may refuse the husband his conjugal rights, provided no consummation has taken place. The wife is under Muhammadan law entitled to refuse herself to her husband until the prompt dower is paid; and if in such circumstances she happens to reside apart from him, the husband is bound to maintain her (*o*).

This right of refusing herself is, however, lost on consummation (*p*). Thus if the husband files a suit for restitution of conjugal rights before cohabitation, non-payment of prompt dower is a complete defence; but after cohabitation, the proper course for the court is to pass a decree for restitution conditional on payment of prompt dower. This was laid down in the leading case of *Anis Begam* v. *Muhammad Istafa Wali Khan* (*q*).

The non-payment of deferred dower by its very nature cannot confer any such right of refusal on the wife. The right to enforce payment arises only on death, divorce or the happening of a specified event (*r*).

(*n*) *Mohammad Sadiq* v. *Fakhr Jahan* (1931) 59 I.A. 19. As regards Limitation, see Mulla §292.

(*o*) *Nur-ud-din Ahmad* v. *Masuda Khanam* PLD 1957 Dacca 242; *Muhammadi* v. *Jamiluddin* PLD 1960 Karachi 663.

(*p*) Tyabji §108; Wilson §48; Mulla §293. In Lahore it has been held that consummation does not deprive the wife of her right to refuse conjugal relations if the prompt dower is not paid, *Rahim Jan* v. *Muhammad*, PLD 1955 Lahore 122; *per contra, Rabia Khatoon* v. *Mukhtar Ahmad* A.I.R. (1966) All. 548, which, it is submitted is the correct view.

(*q*) (1933) 55 All. 743; *Cases*, 18. This case is of great importance as Sulaiman C.J. has carefully considered and criticized certain dicta of Mahmood J. in the leading case of *Abdul Kadir* v. *Salima* (1886) 8 All. 149; *Cases*, 103.

(*r*) Tyabji §109.

The dower ranks as a debt and the widow is entitled, along with the other creditors of her deceased husband, to have it satisfied out of his estate. Her right, however, is the right of an unsecured creditor; she is not entitled to a charge on the husband's property, unless there be an agreement. The Supreme Court of India has laid down (i) that the widow has no priority over other creditors, but (ii) that *mahr* as a debt has priority over the other heirs' claims (*s*). And the heirs of the deceased are not personally liable to pay the dower; they are liable rateably to the extent of the share of the inheritance which comes to their hands (*t*).

§20. The Widow's Right of Retention

Muhammadan law gives to the widow, whose dower has remained unpaid, a very special right to enforce her demand. This is known as 'the widow's right of retention'. A widow lawfully in possession of her deceased husband's estate is entitled to retain such possession until her dower debt is satisfied (*u*). Her right is not in the nature of a regular charge, mortgage or a lien (*uu*); it is in essence a *personal* right as against heirs and creditors to enforce her rights (*v*); and it is a right to *retain, not to obtain*, possession of her husband's estate. Once she loses possession of her husband's estate, she loses her special right and is in no better position than an unsecured creditor (*w*).

The nature of this right was discussed by their lordships of the Privy Council in *Maina Bibi* v. *Chaudhri Vakil Ahmad* (*x*). One Muinuddin died in 1890 possessed of immovable property leaving him surviving his widow Maina Bibi, who

(*s*) They have specially approved of the law as stated by Tyabji in his 3rd ed. (1940), without mentioning the paragraphs specifically, *Kapore Chand* v. *Kadar Unnissa* [1950] S.C.R. 747.

(*t*) Tyabji §105B; Mulla §296.

(*u*) Ameer Ali, II, 451; Tyabji §110; Mulla §§294 sqq. *Mirvahedalli* v. *Rashidbeg*, A.I.R. (1951) Bom. 22.

(*uu*) *Zaibunnissa* v. *Nazim Hasan* A.I.R. (1962) All. 197.

(*v*) Ameer Ali, II, 452.

(*w*) Tyabji §110, notes 5 and 6; Mulla, §§296 sqq. *Zaibunnissa* v. *Nazim Hasan* (above).

(*x*) (1924) 52 I.A. 145; *Cases*, 151.

entered into possession. In 1902 some of the heirs filed a suit to recover possession of their share of the property. The widow pleaded that the estate was a gift to her, or alternatively that she was entitled to possession until her dower was paid. In 1903 the trial judge made a decree for possession in favour of the plaintiffs on condition that the plaintiffs paid a certain sum by way of dower and interest to the widow within six months. This sum was not paid, however, and the widow remained in possession. In 1907 Maina Bibi purported to make a gift of the whole of her property to certain persons. The original plaintiffs challenged this gift and the Privy Council held that the widow had no power to make a gift of the properties, and could not convey the share of the heirs to the donees. Their lordships, in discussing the nature of a widow's right of retention, said that 'the possession of the property being once peaceably and lawfully acquired, the right of the widow to retain it till her dower-debt is paid is conferred upon her by Mahomedan Law' (p. 150). They further said that it is not exactly a lien (p. 150), nor a mortgage, usufructuary or other. 'The widow who holds possession of her husband's property until she has been paid her dower has no estate or interest in the property as has a mortgagee under an ordinary mortgage' (p. 151). Thus, in essence, it is a personal right given by Muhammadan law to safeguard the position of the widow (*y*).

The Supreme Court (India) has laid down that a Muslim widow in possession of her husband's estate in lieu of her claims for dower, whether with the consent of the heirs or otherwise, is not entitled to priority as against his unsecured creditors (*z*).

There is a conflict of opinion whether in order to retain possession the consent, express or implied, of the husband or his heirs is necessary. Some judges are of opinion that

(*y*) The Patna High Court has adopted this view, ***Abdul Samad*** v. ***Alimuddin*** (1943) 22 Pat. 750.

(*z*) *Kapore Chand* v. *Kadar Unnissa* [1950] S.C.R. 747.

such consent is necessary; others, that it is not. It is submitted, with great respect, that on first principles, having regard to the nature of the right, the consent of the husband or his heirs is immaterial. Muhammadan law casts a special obligation on every debtor to pay his debt, and the right of the widow for her dower is a debt for which the widow has a good safeguard. Thus, the question of consent appears to be immaterial (*a*).

The right of retention does not confer on the widow any title to the property. Her rights are twofold: one, as heir of the deceased, and two, as widow entitled to her dower and, if necessary, to retain possession of the estate until her *mahr* has been paid. The right to hold possession must, therefore, be sharply distinguished from her right as an heir (*b*). The widow, in these circumstances, has the right to have the property administered, her just debts satisfied and her share of the inheritance ascertained and paid. She has no right to alienate the property by sale, mortgage, gift or otherwise (*c*), and if she attempts to do so, she loses her right of retention; but the widow may assign her right of *mahr* (*d*).

There are two other major questions on which the law is still unsettled. Can the widow *transfer* her right of retention? And is this right of retention *heritable*? In *Maina Bibi* v. *Chaudhri Vakil Ahmad* (*e*) their lordships expressed a doubt whether a widow could transfer the dower debt or the right to retain the estate until the *mahr* was paid. Following that case there has been much conflict of judicial opinion on the questions as to the heritability and transferability of this right (*f*). The Mysore and Allahabad High Courts have decided that the right is both heritable and transferable (*g*); but the Patna High Court has held that the widow's is a personal

(*a*) See the observations of Tyabji in §110, notes 8 and 18.

(*b*) Mulla §§298, 304.

(*c*) Tyabji §120; Mulla §301.

(*d*) Tyabji §111.

(*e*) (1924) 52 I.A. 145, 159.

(*f*) For the conflicting cases see Mulla §302 and Tyabji, loc. cit.

(*g*) *Hussain* v. *Rahim Khan* A.I.R. (1954) Mysore 24; *Zaibunnissa* v. *Nazim Hasan* A.I.R. (1962) All. 197.

right, and not a lien, and as such, it is not transferable (*h*). Although there is a conflict of opinion, in view of *Kapore Chand's Case*, the balance of authority seems to be in favour of the Patna view.

(*h*) *Zobair Ahmad* v. *Jainandan Prasad* A.I.R. (1960) Pat. 147.

CHAPTER IV

DISSOLUTION OF MARRIAGE

§21. Introductory

It has been pointed out by several authorities that prior to Islam divorce among the ancient Arabs was easy and of frequent occurrence (*a*), and that this tendency has persisted to some extent in Islamic law. But to take a fair and balanced view, it must be observed that the Prophet showed his dislike to it in no uncertain terms. He is reported to have said that 'with Allah, the most detestable of all things permitted is divorce'. (*b*) Cadi Nu'mān records an instance where Ali refused to divorce one of his four wives in order to marry another; and he told the people of Kūfa not to give their daughters in marriage to Imām Ḥasan (his own son), for he was in the habit of marrying and divorcing a large number of women, a course of action which Ali disapproved (*c*). Ameer Ali says:

> The reforms of Mohammed marked a new departure in the history of Eastern legislation. He restrained the power of divorce possessed by the husbands; he gave to the women the right of obtaining a separation on reasonable grounds; and towards the end of his life he went so far as practically to forbid its exercise by the men without the intervention of arbiters or a judge. He

(*a*) *Ency. of Islam,* III, 636; Ameer Ali, II, 471-2; see also the observations of Robertson Smith, *Kinship,* 83 sqq; *Fat. Law* §199.

(*b*) Muhammad Ali, *Manual,* 284, No. 1; Tyabji, 143; Fitzgerald, 73; in Ameer Ali, II, 472, note 2, by the exclusion of the initial word *abghaḍ,* the text makes no sense.

(*c*) Cadi Nu'mān, *Da'ā'im,* II §979; *Fat. Law* §200.

pronounced '*talak* to be the most detestable before the Almighty God of all permitted things', for it prevented conjugal happiness and interfered with the proper bringing-up of children. The permission, therefore, in the Koran, though it gave a certain countenance to the old customs, has to be read with the light of the Lawgiver's own words. When it is borne in mind how intimately law and religion are connected in the Islamic system, it will be easy to understand the bearing of the words on the institution of divorce (*d*).

In considering the institution of divorce glib generalizations are somewhat dangerous. Some years ago, in writing on the subject, I ventured to observe:

It is sometimes suggested that the greatest defect of the Islamic system is the absolute power given to the husband to divorce his wife without cause. Dower to some extent restricts the use of this power. But experience shows that greater suffering is engendered by the husband's withholding divorce than by his irresponsible exercise of this right. Under such conditions the power to release herself is the surest safeguard for the wife. No system of law can produce marital happiness, but humane laws may at least alleviate suffering. And when marital life is wrecked, the home utterly broken up by misunderstanding, jealousy, cruelty or infidelity, what greater boon can a wife have than the power to secure her liberty? The unfortunate position of the women of India is due to the fact that women, being illiterate, are ignorant of their rights; and men, being callous, choose to remain ignorant (*e*).

This view is shared by a modern author who says:

Few will disagree with the passage from Lord Westbury's speech in *Shaw* v. *Gould* (1868, L.R., 3 H.L., 55), in which he said: 'Marriage is the very foundation of civil society, and no part of the laws and institutions of a country can be of more vital importance to its subjects than those which regulate the manner and conditions of forming, and, if necessary, of dissolving, the marriage contract.'

If this is true, and it seems to be more true now when so many of the other props of civilization have been weakened, it follows

(*d*) Ameer Ali, II, 472.

(*e*) 'The Muslim Wife's Right of Dissolving her Marriage' in (1936) 38 Bom. Law Rep., Jl. 113, 123. This article has recently been cited by a Division Bench of the Kerala High Court, A.I.R. (1959) Kerala 151, 153.

that any legal doctrine which may operate to render uncertain the status of divorced persons, and which may, therefore, prejudice the stability of a later marriage by either party, is a social evil that calls for the intervention of the law reformer. Divorce, since it disintegrates the family unity, is, of course, a social evil in itself, but it is a necessary evil. It is better to wreck the unity of the family than to wreck the future happiness of the parties by binding them to a companionship that has become odious. Membership of a family founded on antagonism can bring little profit even to the children, but though divorce is unavoidable, we can at least do our best to ensure that there is no uncertainty in the status of the members of the family after the decree absolute (*f*).

The law of divorce, whatever its utility during the past, was so interpreted, at least in the Hanafi school, that it had become a one-sided engine of oppression in the hands of the husband. And almost everywhere, Muslims are making efforts to bring the law in accord with modern ideas of social justice.

For a comprehensive treatment of the law of *ṭalāq* according to the four Sunnite schools see Jazīrī, *Kitāb al'-Fiqh 'alā'l-Madhāhibi'l-Arba'a,* IV, 278-end (Cairo, 1938, 2nd ed.).

See also the observation of a celebrated physician Ibn al-Nafīs who disapproves of polyandry but not polygamy, and would like to give the wife the right to claim divorce, *The Theologicus Autodidactus of Ibn al-Nafīs*, ed. M. Meyerhof and J. Schacht (Oxford, 1968), 61 sqq.

For modern reforms in the Middle East, see Anderson and Coulson, op. cit.; for Iran, Doreen Hinchcliffe, 'The Iranian Family Protection Act', *Inter. and Comp. Law Quar.*, 1968, 17, 516-21; and for Singapore, see the articles of Mrs. S. Siraj, 'The Shariah Court of Singapore and its Control of the Divorce Rate', 5 *Malaya Law Review*, 1963, 148, and subsequent volumes.

§22. Classification

The early European authors like Juynboll classified the different forms of dissolution as follows (*g*):

(*f*) Prof. G. C. Cheshire, 'The International Validity of Divorces' (1945), 61 *Law Quar. Rev.* 352.

(*g*) Th. W. Juynboll, *Handbuch des islamischen Gesetzes* (Leiden-Leipzig, 1910), 229 and following him a modern author, E. Neufeld, *Ancient Hebrew Marriage Laws* (London, 1944), 180, note 8. Also, per Cornelius C.J. in *Sayeeda Khanum* v. *Muhammad Sami* PLD 1952 Lah. 113, 128 (F.B.).

(i) By the husband without the intervention of the court;
(ii) By common consent without the intervention of the court;
(iii) By decree of the court on the application of either party.

This classification does not take into consideration the fact that marriage in Islam is absolutely dissolved by the death of either spouse, and hence the following classification is proposed: (A) By the Death of Spouse; (B) By the Act of Parties; (C) By Judicial Process.

(A) *By the Death of Spouse.*

(B) *By the Act of Parties—*

I. *By the Husband:*

(1) *Ṭalāq* (Repudiation).
(2) *Īlā'* (Vow of Continence).
(3) *Ẓihār* (Injurious Assimilation).

II. *By the Wife:*

Ṭalāq-e Tafwīḍ (see (1) above, Delegated Divorce).

III. *By Common Consent:*

(4) *Khul'* (Redemption).
(5) *Mubāra'a* (Mutual Freeing).

(C) *By Judicial Process—*

(6) *Li'ān* (Mutual Imprecation).
(7) *Faskh* (Judicial Rescission).

We must now proceed to consider each of these forms in some detail.

§23. Forms of Dissolution

A. By the Death of Spouse

The death of the husband or the wife operates in law as a dissolution of marriage (*h*). When the wife dies, the husband may remarry immediately, but the widow has to wait for a certain period before she can remarry. This period is called *'idda*[*t*], and the *'idda* of death is four months and ten days

(*h*) Tyabji §98, com.; §124, note 3.

from the death of her husband, and if on the expiration of this period she is pregnant, until she is delivered of the child (*i*).

B. By the Act of Parties

I. *BY THE HUSBAND*

(1) *Ṭalāq (Repudiation)*

The word *ṭalāq* is usually rendered as 'repudiation';(*j*) it comes from a root (*ṭallaqa*) which means 'to release (an animal) from a tether'; whence, to repudiate the wife, or free her from the bondage of marriage. In law, it signifies the absolute power which the husband possesses of divorcing his wife at all times (*k*); for, 'The matrimonial law of the Mahomedans, like that of every ancient community, favours the stronger sex' (*kk*).

A Muslim husband of sound mind may divorce his wife whenever he so desires without assigning any cause (*l*). Such a proceeding, although abominable, is nevertheless lawful (*m*). The divorce operates from the time of the pronouncement of *ṭalāq*. The presence of the wife is not necessary, nor need notice be given to her (*n*). In Hanafi law, no special form is necessary; whereas Ithnā 'Asharī law insists on a strict formula being used (*o*). The words used must indicate a clear and unambiguous intention to dissolve the marriage. They may be express (*ṣarīḥ*), e.g. 'Thou art divorced', or 'I have *divorced* thee', or 'I divorce *X* for ever and render her *ḥarām* for me',(*p*) in which case no proof of intention is necessary.

(*i*) Tyabji §§42 sqq.; Wilson §31.

(*j*) Fitzgerald, 73; Baillie, I, 205; Tyabji §124; *Fat. Law* §198 sqq.

(*k*) A good account of *ṭalāq* will be found in *Ency. of Islam,* III, 636-40 by J. Schacht. See also the valuable observations of Tyabji in §118 and notes; a good summary of the law will be found in §119. Wilson §60; *Fat. Law* §198.

(*kk*) Sir James Colville in *Moonshee Buzloor Ruheem* v. *Shumsoonnissa Begum.* (1867) 11 *Moore's Indian Appeals* 551; *Cases,* 281, 296; and Mayne, cited by Tyabji, 163.

(*l*) Fitzgerald, 73; Mulla §308.

(*m*) Ameer Ali, II, 471-3.

(*n*) *Mohd. Shamsuddin* v. *Noor Jahan* A.I.R. (1955) Hyd. 144; *Lalan Bibi* v. *Muhammad Ashfaq* PLD 1951 Lahore 467.

(*o*) Tyabji §§125 sq.

(*p*) *Rashid Ahmad* v. *Anisa Khatun* (1931) 59 I.A. 21, 26.

But if the words are ambiguous (*kināya*), the intention must be proved. For instance, 'Thou art my cousin, the daughter of my uncle, if thou goest' or 'I give up all relations and would have no connexion of any sort with you'.(*q*)

In Ithnā 'Asharī law, a strict adherence to certain forms is essential. The pronouncement of *ṭalāq*, in the Arabic tongue, must be uttered orally in the presence and hearing of two male witnesses who are Muslims of approved probity. In the estimation of the jurists of the Ithnā 'Asharī school marriage is an approved and divorce a hated practice; therefore, they insist upon a strict adherence to forms as evidence of the clear intention (*r*).

The pronouncement of *ṭalāq* may be either revocable or irrevocable. As the Prophet of Islam did not favour the institution of *ṭalāq*, the revocable forms of *ṭalāq* are considered as the 'approved', and the irrevocable forms are treated as the 'disapproved' forms. A revocable pronouncement of divorce gives a *locus pœnitentiae* to the man; but an irrevocable pronouncement leads to an undesirable result without a chance to reconsider the question. If this principle is kept in mind, the terminology is easily understood (*s*). The forms of *ṭalāq* may be classified as follows:

I. *Ṭalāq al-Sunna* (i.e. in conformity with the dictates of the Prophet):

1. *Aḥsan* (the *most* approved).
2. *Ḥasan* (approved).

II. *Ṭalāq al-Bid'a* (i.e. of innovation; therefore not approved):

3. Three declarations (the so-called triple divorce) at *one* time; or
4. One irrevocable declaration (generally in writing) (*t*).

(*q*) Tyabji, loc. cit.; Mulla §310.

(*r*) Tyabji §127; Mulla, loc. cit.; *Fat. Law* §201.

(*s*) Tyabji §128; Abdur Rahim, 336; Ameer Ali, II, 475-6. A very clear statement of the different kinds of repudiation will be found in Abdur Rahman, *Institutes*, Arts. 226 sqq.

(*t*) Tyabji §§141 sqq., and see chart, page 151; Wilson §61; Mulla §§311 sqq.

I. *Ṭalāq al-Sunna* (*Approved Forms*)

1. *Aḥsan Form* (*u*). The *aḥsan* (or most approved) form consists of one single pronouncement in a period of *ṭuhr* (purity, i.e. when the woman is free from her menstrual courses), followed by abstinence from sexual intercourse during that period of sexual purity (*ṭuhr*) as well as during the the whole of the *'idda.* If any such intercourse takes place during the periods mentioned, the divorce is void and of no effect in Ithnā 'Asharī and Fatimid Law (*uu*). It is the mode or procedure which seems to have been approved by the Prophet at the beginning of his ministry, and is consequently regarded as the regular or proper and orthodox form of divorce (*v*).

Where the parties have been away from each other for a long time (*w*), or where the wife is old and beyond the age of menstruation, the condition of *ṭuhr* is unnecessary (*x*).

A pronouncement made in the *aḥsan* form is revocable during *'idda.* This period is three months from the date of the declaration or, if the woman is pregnant, until delivery. The husband may revoke the divorce at any time during the *'idda.* Such revocation may be by express words or by conduct. Resumption of conjugal intercourse is a clear case of revocation. For instance, *H* pronounces a single revocable *ṭalāq* against his wife and then says, 'I have retained thee,' or cohabits with her. The divorce is revoked under Hanafi as well as Ithnā 'Asharī law (*y*).

After the expiration of the *'idda* the divorce becomes irrevocable (*z*).

A Muslim wife, after divorce, is entitled to maintenance

(*u*) Tyabji §136; Mulla, loc. cit.

(*uu*) Baillie, II, p. 111; *Da'ā'im,* II §§985, 986, 1000; *Fat. Law* §§202, 203, 206 (ii).

(*v*) *Sheikh Fazlur Rahman* v. *Mst. Aisha* (1929) 8 Patna 690, 695, citing Ameer Ali, II, 474.

(*w*) Nu'mān, *Da'ā'im,* II §1002 (p. 264); *Fat. Law* §212.

(*x*) *Chandbi Badesha* v. *Badesha Balwant* (1960) 62 Bom. L.R. 866.

(*y*) Tyabji §§156 sq.

(*z*) Mulla §312.

during the *'idda*, and so also her child, in certain circumstances (*a*).

2. *Ḥasan Form* (*b*). The *ḥasan* is also an approved form, but less approved than the first, *aḥsan*. It consists of three successive pronouncements during three consecutive periods of purity (*ṭuhr*). Each of these pronouncements should have been made at a time when no intercourse has taken place during that particular period of purity.

The *ḥasan* form of *ṭalāq* requires some explanation and a concrete illustration should suffice. (i) The husband (*H*) pronounces *ṭalāq* on his wife (*W*) *for the first time* during a period when *W* is free from her menstrual courses. The husband and wife had not come together during this period of purity. This is the *first ṭalāq*. (ii) *H* resumes cohabitation or revokes this first *ṭalāq* in this period of purity. Thereafter, in the following period of purity, at a time when no intercourse has taken place, *H* pronounces the *second ṭalāq*. (iii) This *ṭalāq* is again revoked by express words or by conduct, and the third period of purity is entered into. In this period, no intercourse having taken place, *H for the third time* pronounces the formula of divorce. This third pronouncement operates in law as a final and irrevocable dissolution of the marital tie. The marriage is dissolved; sexual intercourse becomes unlawful; *'idda* becomes incumbent; remarriage between the parties becomes impossible unless *W* lawfully marries another husband, and that other husband lawfully divorces her after the marriage has been *actually* consummated (c).

Thus it is clear that in these two forms there is a chance for the parties to be reconciled by the intervention of friends or otherwise. They are, therefore, the 'approved' forms and are recognized both by Sunnite and Shiite law. The Ithnā 'Asharī and the Fatimid schools, however, do not recognize

(*a*) *Mohd. Shamsuddin* v. *Noor Jahan* A.I.R. (1955) Hyd. 144.
(*b*) Tyabji §146; Mulla §311.
(*c*) See the explanation in Tyabji §144.

the remaining two forms and thus preserve the ancient conventions of the times of the Lawgiver (*cc*).

The first or *aḥsan* form is 'most approved' because the husband behaves in a gentlemanly manner and does not treat the wife as a chattel. The second is a form in which the Prophet tried to put an end to a barbarous pre-Islamic practice. This practice was to divorce a wife and take her back several times in order to ill-treat her. The Prophet, by the rule of the irrevocability of the *third* pronouncement, indicated clearly that such a practice could not be continued indefinitely. Thus if a husband really wished to take the wife back, he should do so; if not, the third pronouncement, after two reconciliations, would operate as a final bar (*d*). These rules of law follow the spirit of the Koranic injunction: *Then, when they have reached their term, take them back in kindness or part from them in kindness* (*e*).

II. *Ṭalāq al-Bid'a* (*Disapproved Forms*)

3. *The triple declaration.* In this form three pronouncements are made in a single *ṭuhr*, either in *one* sentence, e.g. 'I divorce thee triply or thrice', or in three sentences, 'I divorce thee, I divorce thee, I divorce thee.' Such a *ṭalāq* is lawful, although sinful, in Hanafi law; but in Ithnā 'Asharī and the Fatimid laws it is not permissible (*f*). This is called *al-ṭalāq al-bā'in,* irrevocable divorce.

4. *The single, irrevocable declaration.* Another form of the disapproved divorce is a single, irrevocable pronouncement made either during the period of *ṭuhr* or even otherwise (*g*). This form is also called *al-ṭalāq al-bā'in* (also called *talak-e-bā'in,* or *bā'in talak*), and may be given in writing. Such a

(*cc*) *Fat. Law* §§201 sqq.

(*d*) A clear statement of this Arabian practice will be found in Abdur Rahim, 10. See also Fitzgerald, 75.

(*e*) Kor. lxv, 2. Explained fully by Tyabji §148, com.

(*f*) Cadi Nu'mān, *Da'ā'im,* II §978; *Fat. Law* §204 (i); 206 (iv); Tyabji §148; Mulla §311.

(*g*) *Sheikh Fazlur Rahman* v. *Mst. Aisha* (1929) 8 Patna 690; Tyabji §147; Mulla, loc. cit.

'bill of divorcement' comes into operation immediately and severs the marital tie (*h*). This form is not recognized by the Ithnā 'Asharī or the Fatimid school (*i*).

A full discussion of these four forms will be found in Tyabji (*j*) where he points out that by a deplorable development of the Hanafi law the sinful or abominable forms (*ṭalāq al-bid'a,* Nos. 3 and 4) have become the most common for 'Men have always moulded the law of marriage so as to be most agreeable to themselves'.(*k*)

It may, in passing, be mentioned that *ṭalāq* pronounced during the menstrual period is a form of *bid'a,* recognized in certain cases by the Hanafi rite, but not in Fatimid or Ithnā 'Asharī law (*l*).

Divorce, When Effective

In the *aḥsan* form, the divorce is effective on the expiration of the *'idda*. In the *ḥasan* form, the divorce is effective on the third pronouncement. In the *ṭalāq al-bid'a,* the divorce is effective from the moment of pronouncement or the execution of the writing of divorce (*ṭalāq-nāma*) (*m*).

Legal Effects of Divorce

(i) Where the divorce has become irrevocable, marital intercourse becomes unlawful between the couple; but they may remarry, unless there have been more than *two* pronouncements.

(ii) Where there has been a triple divorce, remarriage can only take place under certain stringent conditions to be hereinafter mentioned (see below, *Reconciliation and Remarriage*).

(iii) If the husband or the wife dies during the period of

(*h*) Mulla §313; for a strange and very unfair application of the strict rule, see *Mohammad Ali* v. *Fareedunnisa Begam,* A.I.R. (1970) A.P. 298.

(*i*) Cadi Nu'mān, *Da'ā'im*, II §986, etc.

(*j*) Tyabji §148, com.

(*k*) Tyabji p. 163, citing Mayne, *Hindu Law;* and see p. 150 (*kk*), above.

(*l*) *Sheikh Fazlur* v. (*Mst.*) *Aisha* (1929) 8 Patna 690; *Fat. Law* §§202, 203, 205 (i), 206 (i).

(*m*) Mulla §313; Wilson §§61, 63.

'idda following upon a revocable pronouncement of divorce, each is entitled to inherit from the other.

(iv) If the pronouncement of divorce was irrevocable (*ṭalāq al-bid'a* or *ṭalāq-e bā'in*), neither of them can inherit from the other (*n*).

(v) The wife becomes entitled to maintenance during the *'idda* of divorce; but not during the *'idda* of death (see §37, below).

As to the Shiite law in death-illness, see Tyabji, pp. 160-64; *Sharā'i'*, III (Beirut, 1930/1295), 58-9; Baillie, II, 122; *Fat. Law* §§336, 374, 379.

Ṭalāq under Compulsion or under the Influence of Intoxication

By a peculiar rule of Hanafi law, as distinguished from the Fatimid, Ithnā 'Asharī or Shāfi'ī law, a divorce pronounced under compulsion or under the influence of intoxication is valid and effective (*o*).

This extraordinary rule has been discussed by several writers, and perhaps its only usefulness is mentioned by Fitzgerald who points out that in Turkey under the Sultans, by a well-understood convention, a wife who wished to be rid of a dissolute husband would go before the *kazi* with two irreproachable witnesses and depose that he had divorced her when drunk, an allegation which he would not be in a position to deny (*p*). Apart from this saving grace, the rule appears to be absurd and unjust, and should be abolished. One way to deal with it is suggested by Ameer Ali and Abdur Rahim, namely, that in such cases the court should, on grounds of equity, apply the Shāfi'ī, and not their own law, where the parties happen to be Hanafis (*q*). The proper remedy, it is submitted, is to do away with it by statute.

(*n*) Tyabji §160(2).

(*o*) Cadi Nu'mān, *Da'ā'im*, II §1008. Ameer Ali, II, 478 sqq.; Wilson §64; Tyabji §130; Mulla §315.

(*p*) Fitzgerald, 73.

(*q*) See Ameer Ali, II, 414-17, particularly the last lines of p. 416 and the top of p. 417. This very illustration will be found in Abdur Rahim, p. 181 (top).

Reconciliation and Remarriage

The procedure for reconciliation or remarriage may now be briefly indicated.

(i) When there have been one or two declarations in the approved forms, a reconciliation can take place *during 'idda*, without a regular remarriage. The reconciliation may be by a formal revocation of *ṭalāq* or by resumption of marital life.

(ii) Where there have been one or two declarations in the approved forms, *and the period of 'idda has expired*, a mere reconciliation is not enough. A regular remarriage is necessary and possible.

(iii) Where there have been *three declarations*, amounting to an irrevocable *ṭalāq*, the remarriage of the couple is only possible if the following course is adopted; otherwise the second marriage is irregular (*r*). In case no second marriage takes place, the union is void and the offspring of such union are illegitimate (*s*).

(a) The wife should observe *'idda.*

(b) After observing *'idda,* the wife should be lawfully married to another husband.

(c) Such intervening marriage must be *actually* consummated.

(d) The second husband must pronounce divorce.

(e) The wife should observe *'idda* after this divorce.

(f) After the expiry of *'idda*, a remarriage can lawfully take place between the couple (*t*).

It has been explained that this rule 'did away with a great engine of oppression in the hands of the pre-Islamic Arabs, who could keep their wives in a species of perpetual bondage, pretending to take them back after repeated divorces, merely for the purpose of preventing the wives from remarrying and from seeking the then much-needed protection of a husband'. (*u*)

(*r*) Mulla §336(5).

(*s*) See illustration in note (*v*) below.

(*t*) The clearest statement will be found in Abdur Rahman, *Institutes*, Arts. 247, 248; see also Ameer Ali, II, 497; Tyabji 159, read with §48. For *Fat. Law*, see §§292 sqq.

(*u*) Tyabji, p. 84.

A strict adherence to the rule, however, sometimes spells hardship, as in the Privy Council decision, *Rashid Ahmad v. Anisa Khatun* (*v*). One Ghiyasuddin pronounced a triple repudiation on his wife Anisa Khatun in the presence of witnesses, the wife being absent. Four days later he executed a deed of divorce which stated that the three divorces were given in the abominable form. There was no remarriage between the parties, nor was there any proof of an intermediate marriage. The couple afterwards lived together and five children were born. Ghiyasuddin treated Anisa as his wife and the children as legitimate. It was held that as the words of divorce were clear and effectual, there was an irrevocable divorce. There being no intermediate marriage, the bar to remarriage was not removed. In these circumstances, the acknowledgement of legitimacy was of no avail, and the five children born after the triple divorce were held to be illegitimate.

The decision appears to be harsh, but it is difficult to see how, in the existing state of the law, it could have been otherwise. There was no proof of the remarriage of Ghiyasuddin with Anisa Khatun. If, however, even without an intervening marriage, remarriage had been established, the children would have been held to be legitimate, since the remarriage would have been by law merely irregular and not void (*w*).

Ṭalāq-e tafwīḍ (*Delegated Divorce*) (*x*)

The husband in Muhammadan law has the power to delegate his own right of pronouncing divorce to some third person or to the wife herself. A stipulation that, under certain specified conditions, the wife can pronounce divorce upon herself has been held to be valid, provided first, that the option is not absolute and unconditional and secondly, that

(*v*) (1931) 59 I.A. 21.

(*w*) Mulla §336(5) citing Baillie, 151.

(*x*) Generally, see *LME*, I, 147; Schacht, *Esquisse*, says that it enforces monogamy, 71. For an Indian form in common use, see Appendix C, below.

the conditions are reasonable and not opposed to public policy (*y*). É. Tyan mentions the interesting case of Salmā bint 'Āmir al-Najjārī who never married unless the husband promised her the right to divorce herself (*yy*). The traditional classification of the forms of *tafwīḍ* (generally mis-spelt *tafweez*) is threefold: (i) *ikhtiyār* (choice); (ii) *amr bi-yad* ('the affair is in your hands'); (iii) *mashī'a* ('at your pleasure'); but the technical differences meant to be indicated by these apparently synonymous expressions are not of great practical value in countries where the Arabic language is not used (*z*).

An antenuptial agreement by a Muslim husband in a *kābīn-nāma* that he would pay separate maintenance to his wife in case of disagreement and that the wife should have the power to divorce herself in case of failure to pay maintenance for a certain period is not opposed to public policy and is enforceable under the Muhammadan law. The wife exercising her powers under the agreement must establish that the conditions entitling her to exercise the power have been fulfilled (*a*).

This form of delegated divorce is perhaps the most potent weapon in the hands of a Muslim wife to obtain her freedom without the intervention of any court and is now beginning to be fairly common in India (*b*). An agreement by which the husband authorizes the wife to divorce herself from him in the event of his marrying a second wife without her consent has been repeatedly held to be both valid and irrevocable (*c*). In such cases, the mere happening of the contingency is not sufficient; the wife must clearly establish first, that the events entitling her to exercise her option have occurred, and secondly, that she has actually exercised her option (*d*).

(*y*) Ameer Ali, II, 321, 322, 495 sqq.; Tyabji §§132 sqq.; Fitzgerald, 77; Wilson §66; Mulla §314; Abdur Rahman, Arts. 260-5.

(*yy*) *Inst. de droit Pub. Musulman,* I (Paris, 1954), 18.

(*z*) Wilson §66; Ameer Ali, II, 495.

(*a*) *Buffatan Bibi* v. *Sk. Abdul Salim* A.I.R. (1950) Cal. 304.

(*b*) Further details and references will be found in 'The Muslim Wife's Right of Dissolving her Marriage' (1936) 38 Bom. Law Rep., Jl., 113, 120-1.

(*c*) Mulla, loc. cit.

(*d*) *Mirjan Ali* v. (*Mst.*) *Maimuna Bibi* A.I.R. (1949) Assam 14; *Buffatan Bibi* v. *Sk. Abdul Salim* A.I.R. (1950) Cal. 304.

Tyabji has pointed out that the breach of a valid condition in a marriage contract does not necessarily give the wife a right to have the marriage dissolved, and he has discussed exhaustively the problems that commonly arise in India (*e*).

Contingent and conditional divorces are very rare in India, see Tyabji §150; Fitzgerald (*ṭalāq-e ta'līq*), 77; Mulla §309. Also §15 above, and Appendix C, below.

Ṭalāq, Where Conflict of Laws

We have seen that a Muslim can marry a *kitābiyya*, that is a Jewish or a Christian woman; but a Muslim woman cannot marry a Jew or a Christian. Now a Muslim may marry according to the *sharī'at*, in which case the marriage is a *nikāḥ*; or he may marry in some other form which is laid down by the law. A *nikāḥ* can be dissolved by *ṭalāq*, but a marriage in another form cannot be dissolved by a mere *ṭalāq*.

In India, however, where *one* of the parties is a Christian, a marriage is lawful only if it is solemnized under the provisions of the Indian Christian Marriage Act, XV of 1872, or the Special Marriage Act, 1954. A marriage solemnized in any other form is void (*f*).

The position with regard to the Jews cannot be stated with certainty as there is no case-law on the subject. But a marriage in the *nikāḥ* form between a Muslim and a Jewess is, according to Muhammadan law, perfectly valid; and apparently, a *nikāḥ* of this character can be dissolved by *ṭalāq*.

A marriage between a Muslim and a non-*kitābiyya* would be governed in India by the Special Marriage Act, 1954. Divorce in the *ṭalāq* form is not possible in such cases and the provisions of the Act would apply.

A civil marriage solemnized at a Registrar's office in London between a Muslim domiciled in India, and an

(*e*) These discussions are far too detailed for an elementary treatise, and deal *inter alia* with an agreement not to marry a second wife, and an agreement to enable the wife to reside where she pleases, Tyabji §31(9), com.

(*f*) Sec. 4 of the Act; Wilson §39(3).

Englishwoman domiciled in England, cannot be dissolved by the husband handing to the wife 'a writing of divorcement' (*ṭalāq-nāma*), although in Muhammadan law it would be an appropriate mode of dissolving a marriage in the *nikāḥ* form (*g*). But if the wife thereafter comes out to India and formally embraces Islam, she is subject to Muhammadan law, and the marriage can be dissolved by *ṭalāq*. In *Khambatta* v. *Khambatta*, the petitioner, a Christian woman domiciled in Scotland, married a Muslim, domiciled in India, in Scotland, according to the requirements of Scots law. After the marriage, the parties came to stay permanently in India and the petitioner embraced Islam. Sometime afterwards the husband pronounced *ṭalāq* and divorced his wife. The petitioner thereupon obtained a declaration that she was no longer the wife of the Muslim husband and later married a Parsi. In divorce proceedings between the petitioner and the Parsi husband a preliminary point arose whether the first marriage was dissolved by the pronouncement of *ṭalāq*, and it was held that, in the circumstances, the divorce by *ṭalāq* was valid (*h*).

But, where a marriage is solemnized under the Special Marriage Act, 1872, and the husband subsequently embraces Islam, it cannot be dissolved in Muslim fashion by *ṭalāq* (*i*).

In a recent Pakistan case, it has been held that although according to the *sharī'at* it is possible for the husband, upon conversion to Islam, to divorce his Christian wife, the existing statutory law renders such a course unlawful. The conclusion appears to be sound, but the argument in some of its ramifications requires simplification and reconsideration. It is

(*g*) *Rex* v. *Hammersmith* [1917] 1 K.B. 634, *Cases*, 131, fol. in *Maher* v. *Maher* [1951] Probate 342, an Egyptian case; Mulla §316. An interesting Jewish case is *Har-Shefi* v. *Har-Shefi* [1953] 2 W.R. 690.

(*h*) (1933) 36 Bom. L.R. 11, on appeal (1934) 36 Bom. L.R. 1021 and (1934) 59 Bom. 278. This decision has been criticized by Edgeley J. in *Noor Jehan* v. *Eugene Tiscenko* (1940) 45 C.W.N. 1047, 1062-5; [1942] 2 Cal. 165. See also Tyabji §§199 sq.

(*i*) *Andal Vaidyanathan* v. *Abdul Allam* [1947] Mad. 175.

submitted that *Skinner* v. *Orde* and *Rex* v. *Hammersmith* could have been used to greater advantage (*j*).

(2) *Īlā'* and (3) *Ẓihār*

Although these two forms of divorce are mentioned in the Shariat Act, 1937, Sec. 2, they are very rare in India and of no practical importance. In *īlā'* the husband swears not to have intercourse with the wife and abstains for four months or more. The husband may revoke the oath by resumption of marital life. After the expiry of the period of four months, in Hanafi law the marriage is dissolved without legal process; but *aliter* in Ithnā 'Asharī and Shāfi'ī law, where legal proceedings are necessary (*k*). This form is obsolete in India and apparently there is no case-law on the subject (*l*).

In *ẓihār* the husband swears that to him the wife is like 'the back of his mother'. If he intends to revoke this declaration, he has to pay money by way of expiation, or fast for a certain period. After the oath has been taken, the wife has the right to go to the court and obtain divorce or restitution of conjugal rights on expiation.

This is an archaic form of oath and dates from pre-Islamic Arabia. '*Ẓihār*,' says Tyabji, 'has hardly any significance so far as the law courts in India are concerned. The words do not come naturally to Indian Muslims. A person, wishing deliberately to give his wife a cause of action for restitution of conjugal rights in India, would probably adopt an easier, more usual, and better understood mode of doing so.'(*m*)

II. *BY THE WIFE*

See *Ṭalāq-e tafwīḍ* (delegated divorce), p. 158 sqq. above.

(*j*) *Farooq Leivers* v. *Adelaide Bridget* PLD 1958 (W.P.) Lahore 431. The headnote in this case is misleading and should be used with caution.

(*k*) Tyabji §§164 sqq., 191 sqq.; Mulla §317. It is a great pity that this form has been revived by the Shariat Act, 1937, although in practice it is so well and truly buried as to be past resuscitation. *Fat. Law* §§232-34.

(*l*) A case of *īlā'* was unsuccessfully raised in *Bibi Rehana* v. *Iqtidar Uddin* [1943] All. 295.

(*m*) Tyabji, p. 184. Generally, see Tyabji §§191 sqq.; Mulla §318.

§24. Divorce by Common Consent

III. *BY COMMON CONSENT*

(4) *Khul'* and (5) *Mubāra'a* (*n*)

Dissolution of marriage by the common consent of the spouses is a peculiar feature of Islamic law. Prior to Islam the wife had practically no right to ask for divorce; it was the Koranic legislation which provided for this form of relief (*o*). The *Fatāwā 'Ālamgīrī* lays down that 'when married parties disagree and are apprehensive that they cannot observe the bounds prescribed by the divine laws, that is, cannot perform the duties imposed on them by the conjugal relationship, the woman can release herself from the tie by giving up some property in return in consideration of which the husband is to give her a *khula*, and when they have done this a *talak-ul-bain* would take place'.(*p*)

It is of interest to observe that the Special Marriage Act (43 of 1954), provides for a form of divorce by the common consent of the spouses, Sec. 28.

The two essential conditions are: (i) common consent of the husband and wife, and, as a rule, (ii) some *'iwaḍ* (return, consideration) passing from the wife to the husband (*q*). If the desire to separate emanates from the wife, it is called *khul'*; but if the divorce is effected by mutual aversion (and consent), it is known as *mubāra'a[t]*. The word *khul'* (*r*) means literally 'to take off clothes' and thence, 'to lay down one's authority over a wife'; and the word *mubāra'a* denotes the act of 'freeing one another mutually'. In the case of *khul'*, the wife begs to be released and the husband agrees for a certain consideration, which is usually a part or the whole of the *mahr*; while in

(*n*) Ameer Ali, II, 506 sqq.; Abdur Rahman, Arts. 273-97; Wilson §§69 sqq.; Tyabji §§168 sqq.; Fitzgerald, 78-9; Mulla §§319-20; *Fat. Law* §§226 sqq.

(*o*) Kor. ii, 229; R. Smith, however, in his *Kinship*, says that *khul'* was known even before Islam, 112 sqq.

(*p*) Cited by Ameer Ali, II, 506.

(*q*) Fitzgerald, 78.

(*r*) Loosely and popularly spelt *khoola* or *khula*, and even *khala*.

mubāra'a apparently both are happy at the prospect of being rid of each other.

One of the earliest instances raising a case of *khul'* is *Moonshee Buzul-ul-Raheem* v. *Luteefut-oon-Nissa* (*s*), where their lordships of the Privy Council say:

> It appears that by the Mahomedan law divorce may be made in either of two forms: *Talak* or *Khoola*.
>
> A divorce by *Talak* is the mere arbitrary act of the husband, who may repudiate his wife at his own pleasure, with or without cause. But if he adopts that course he is liable to repay her dowry, or *dyn-mohr*, and, as it seems, to give up any jewels or paraphernalia belonging to her.
>
> A divorce by *Khoola* is a divorce with the consent, and at the instance of the wife, in which she gives or agrees to give a consideration to the husband for her release from the marriage tie. In such a case the terms of the bargain are a matter of arrangement between the husband and wife, and the wife may, as the consideration, release her *dyn-mohr* and other rights, or make any other agreement for the benefit of the husband.

The law of *khul'* and *mubāra'a* has, within the course of the last few years, assumed a great deal of importance in India.

(A) *Form*

According to Hanafi law, the husband proposes dissolution, and the wife accepts it at the same meeting. The proposal and acceptance need not be in any particular form. The contract itself dissolves the marriage and operates as a single *ṭalāq-e bā'in*, and its operation is not postponed until the execution of the *khul'-nāma* (document of release) (*t*). In Ithnā 'Asharī law, as is to be expected, certain forms are to be strictly followed and witnesses are required.

(B) *Consideration*

As a general rule, in *khul'* the wife makes some compensation to the husband or gives up a portion of her *mahr*; but

(*s*) (1861) 8 Moo. I.A. 379, 395, *Cases*, 159, 167 sq.
(*t*) *Moonshee Buzul's Case;* Tyabji §169; Mulla §319.

this is not absolutely necessary. The Egyptian code of Hanafi law, Art. 275, based upon the classical authorities, lays down: 'A *khul'* repudiation can validly take place before or after consummation of the marriage, and *without payment of compensation by the wife.*'(*u*) The true position is that once common consent is proved and the dissolution has been effected, the question of releasing the *mahr* or making compensation is a question of fact to be determined with reference to each particular case, and there is no general presumption that the husband has been released of his obligation to pay dower (*v*).

Tyabji has shown that jurists of authority differ on this question:

(i) Abū Ḥanīfa holds that, in the absence of agreement, *mahr* is deemed to be relinquished by the wife both by *khul'* and by *mubāra'a*;

(ii) Abū Yūsuf lays down that *mahr* is deemed to be relinquished by *mubāra'a*, but not by *khul'*; and

(iii) Imām Muḥammad holds that *mahr* is deemed to be relinquished neither by *khul'*, nor by *mubāra'a* (*w*).

Where the Hanafi jurists of authority differ, it is the duty of the court to consider the matter for itself and to arrive at a just decision. The whole procedure of *khul'* and *mubāra'a* depends upon consent and understanding, and it is submitted that the court would not be justified in making a presumption one way or the other. Each case is to be determined with reference to its facts; and where there is no agreement as to consideration, it would be proper for the court to award the *mahr*, or part of it, to the wife, if it is just and convenient to do so, but not otherwise.

(*u*) Abdur Rahman, p. 159, Art. 275. The following article lays down that the husband can renounce the wife by *khul'* by paying compensation *of a greater amount* than dower.

(*v*) It is submitted that in Wilson §71 and Mulla §320 the law is unduly stretched in favour of the husband.

(*w*) Tyabji §173 and comment, where an exhaustive discussion will be found.

(C) *Legal Effects*

Khul' and *mubāra'a* operate as a single, irrevocable divorce. Therefore, marital life cannot be resumed by mere reconciliation; a formal remarriage is necessary.

In either case, *'idda* is incumbent on the wife, and in the absence of agreement to the contrary, the wife and her children do not lose the rights of maintenance during the period (*x*).

§25. *C. Dissolution by Judicial Process*

(6) *Li'ān (Mutual Imprecation)*

Divorce by mutual imprecation is mentioned in the Koran (*y*) and is supported by the traditions of the Prophet. It is reported that a man from the Anṣār accused his wife of adultery. The Prophet thereupon asked them both to take an oath; then he ordered them to be separated from each other (*z*).

The law of Islam punishes the offence of adultery (*zinā*) severely, and so it takes a serious view of an imputation of unchastity against a married woman. If a husband accused his wife of infidelity, he was liable to punishment for defaming his wife (*qadhf*) unless he proved his allegation. If there was no proof forthcoming, the procedure of *li'ān* was adopted (*a*).

(*x*) Tyabji §§171 sqq.; Mulla §§319-20.

(*y*) Kor. xxiv, 6-9. See *Shorter Ency. of Islam* (Leiden, 1953), 1569, s.v., *Li'ān. Fat. Law* §§235 sqq.

(*z*) Muhammad Ali, *Manual*, 290, No. 11 (Bukhārī). On *li'ān* generally, see *Ghulam Bhik* v. *Hussain Begum* PLD 1957 (W.P.) Lahore 998. The learned judges in this case have been pleased to make many interesting observations and indulge in *obiter dicta* involving matters of Arabic scholarship, *ḥadīth* criticism, and even to express opinions on a treatise which cannot be treated as an authority in a Court of Record. Their lordships have strayed a fair distance from the strait and narrow path chalked out by the Judicial Committee of the Privy Council in the tradition of the common law and equity; and, with the greatest respect, it may be pointed out that such judicial valour in highly technical spheres may have serious consequences in the development of sound judicial canons of judgment in the sub-continent, *vide*, Cardozo, *The Nature of the Judicial Process.*

(*a*) A brief but adequate account of *li'ān* will be found in Fitzgerald, 82-3.

The procedure of *li'ān* may be described briefly as follows. A husband accuses his wife of adultery, but is unable to prove the allegation. The wife in such cases is entitled to file a suit for dissolution of marriage. It is to be observed that a mere allegation or oath, in the form of an anathema, does not dissolve the marriage. A *kazi* must intervene; in Indian law, a regular suit has to be filed.

At the hearing of the suit, the husband has two alternatives: (i) he may formally retract the charge. If this is done at or before the commencement of the hearing (but not after the close of the evidence or the end of the trial), the wife is not entitled to a dissolution. (ii) The husband may, however, not retract and, if he persists in his attitude, he is called upon to make oaths. This was followed by similar oaths of innocency made by the wife. The four oaths are tantamount to the evidence of *four eye witnesses* required for the proof of adultery in Islam (*aa*). After these mutual imprecations, the judge pronounces that the marriage is dissolved (*b*).

The High Court of Bombay has laid down that three conditions are necessary for a valid retractation: (1) The husband must admit that he has made a charge of adultery against the wife; (2) he must admit that the charge was false, and (3) he must make the retraction before the end of the trial (*c*); but, even after the passing of the Dissolution of Muslim Marriages Act, VIII of 1939, the husband's retractation non-suits the aggrieved wife (*d*).

The essence of *li'ān* is the persistence by the husband in

(*aa*) *Fat. Law* §§235, 237.

(*b*) The ancient oaths are picturesque and may be of interest both to students and to lawyers. According to the *Fatāwā 'Ālamgīrī* (Baillie, I, 338), the judge begins with the husband who swears four times as follows: 'I attest, by God, that I was a speaker of truth when I cast at her the charge of adultery,' and the fifth time he says: 'The curse of God be upon him (i.e. refers to himself) if he was a liar when he cast at her the charge of adultery.' Then follows the wife and she swears four times: 'I attest, by God, that he is a liar in the charge of adultery that he cast upon me,' and says on the fifth occasion: 'The wrath of God be upon me if he be a true speaker in the charge of adultery which he has cast upon me.'

(*c*) *Mahomedali Mahomed* v. *Hazrabai* [1955] Bom. 464.

(*d*) *Tufail Ahmad* v. *Jamila Khatun* A.I.R. (1962) All. 570.

an unproved allegation of unchastity on the part of the wife. If the infidelity is proved, the wife's action for dissolution fails (*e*).

§26. Judicial Rescission

(7) *Faskh*

Dissolution of Muslim Marriages Act, 1939

The word *faskh* means annulment or abrogation. It comes from a root which means 'to annul (a deed)' or 'to rescind (a bargain)' Hence it refers to the power of the Muslim *kazi* to annul a marriage on the application of the wife. It may be defined as 'The dissolution or rescission of the contract of marriage by judicial decree' (*f*). This is known as *taḥkīm* in Fatimid law (*ff*).

The Koranic basis of the law will be found in the fourth chapter, dealing with wives (*g*). There it is laid down that men are in charge of the affairs of women and should deal fairly with them. Women are likewise asked to be obedient to men, but if they do not behave themselves, men may *admonish them, banish them to beds apart, and scourge them. And if ye fear a breach between them twain (the man and wife), appoint an arbiter from his folk and an arbiter from her folk. If they desire amendment Allah will make them of one mind* (*h*).

The law of *faskh* is founded upon this Koranic injunction and traditions of the Prophet like the one cited by Ameer Ali, 'The power of the Kazi or judge to pronounce a divorce is founded on the express words of the Prophet: "If a woman be prejudiced by a marriage, let it be broken off." '(*i*)

The classical jurists, however, differed in their opinions and in the course of centuries the schools of Islamic law held

(*e*) Tyabji §§197 sqq.; Mulla §333.

(*f*) Fitzgerald, 79; Tyabji §§211 sq.; Ameer Ali, II, 519 sqq.

(*ff*) *Fat. Law* §§218 sqq.

(*g*) Kor. iv, 34-5. (*h*) Verse 35.

(*i*) Ameer Ali, II, 519 (citing Bukhārī).

widely divergent views regarding the interpretation of the basic texts. While it was conceded that it was possible for the wife to obtain dissolution, the schools could not agree either as to the grounds of dissolution or as to the procedure to be followed. Elsewhere it has been shown, on a comparison of the different schools, that in this respect the Mālikī school is most favourable to women; the Shāfi'ī and Ḥanbalī come next; the Hanafi, Ithnā 'Asharī and Fatimid are the least favourable to them (*j*). These matters are only of academic interest now, for the Dissolution of Muslim Marriages Act, VIII of 1939, is applicable to all Muslims in India, regardless of the school or sub-school to which they belong.

Prior to the passing of this Act the courts, following the Hanafi interpretation of the law, had denied to Muslim women the rights of dissolution available to them under the *sharī'at*. After a great deal of public agitation Qazi Muhammad Ahmad Kazmi introduced a bill in the central legislature on 17 April 1936. Ultimately, the bill was passed by the Assembly with suitable modifications and became law on 17 March 1939, as the Dissolution of Muslim Marriages Act, VIII of 1939, and ever since it has been hailed as one of the most progressive enactments passed by the legislature within recent years. It achieved two objects: it restored to Muslim wives an important right accorded to them by the *sharī'at*, and it treated all Muslims alike. For once differences in the minutiæ of the law were not allowed to assume the importance of regular exceptions. The Act, therefore, applies to every Muslim, to whatever school of law he belongs.

The statement of objects and reasons says (*k*):

There is no provision in the Hanafi Code of Muslim Law enabling a married Muslim woman to obtain a decree from the Courts dissolving her marriage in case the husband neglects to maintain her, makes her life miserable by deserting or persistently

(*j*) 'The Muslim Wife's Right of Dissolving her Marriage' in (1936) 38 Bom. Law Rep., Jl., 113, 115. This article has been cited with approval by a Division Bench of the Kerala High Court in *Kunju Ismail* v. *Md. Kadeja Umma* A.I.R. (1959) Kerala 151, 153.

(*k*) *Gazette of India*, Part V, 1938, p. 36.

maltreating her or certain other circumstances. The absence of such a provision has entailed unspeakable misery to innumerable Muslim women in British India. The Hanafi Jurists, however, have clearly laid down that in cases in which the application of Hanafi Law causes hardship, it is permissible to apply the provisions of the 'Maliki, Shafi'i or Hambali Law'. Acting on this principle the Ulemas have issued fatwas to the effect that in cases enumerated in clause 3, Part A of this Bill, a married Muslim woman may obtain a decree dissolving her marriage. A lucid exposition of this principle can be found in the book called 'Heelat-un-Najeza' published by Maulana Ashraf Ali Sahib who has made an exhaustive study of the provisions of Maliki Law which under the circumstances prevailing in India may be applied to such cases. This has been approved by a large number of Ulemas who put their seals of approval on the book.

As the Courts are sure to hesitate to apply the Maliki Law to the case of a Muslim woman, legislation recognizing and enforcing the above-mentioned principle is called for in order to relieve the sufferings of countless Muslim women (*l*).

The text of the Act will be found in Appendix B.

Retrospective Effect

It is a general principle that no statute shall be given a retrospective effect unless the language plainly requires such construction. The question has arisen whether Sec. 4 of the Act can be said to be retrospective in its application. Considering the three cases that have arisen in the Lahore High Court, it would appear that having regard to the language used in Sec. 4, it was not intended to interfere with rights acquired under the existing law (*m*).

Sec. 2 lays down that even a single ground mentioned in the Act is sufficient for a married woman to obtain a dissolution of her marriage. Dissolution may be obtained on any of the following grounds.

(*l*) As to applying the Mālikī law in a case where the parties are Hanafis, see *al-Ḥīlat al-Nājiza* by Mawlānā Ashraf 'Alī Thānawī (Deoband, 1355, 1936), 2-3; Abdur Rahim, 180-1; Ameer Ali, II, 416, 521, 525, 534 (Shāfi'ī law); 'The Muslim Wife's Right of Dissolving her Marriage' (1936) 38 Bom. Law Rep., Jl., 113, 116.

(*m*) Mulla §323, com., states the law accurately.

(1) *Missing husband*. The wife is entitled to obtain a decree for the dissolution of her marriage if the whereabouts of the husband have not been known for a period of four years; but a decree passed on this ground will not take effect for a period of six months from the date of such decree, and if the husband appears either in person or through an authorized agent within that period and satisfies the court that he is prepared to perform his conjugal duties, the court must set aside the decree. In such a suit—

(i) the names and addresses of the persons who would have been the heirs of the husband under Muslim law if he had died on the date of the filing of the plaint shall be stated in the plaint,

(ii) notice of the suit shall be served on such persons,

(iii) such persons shall have the right to be heard in the suit.

The paternal uncle and brother of the husband, if any, must be cited as party even if he or they are not heirs (*n*).

(2) *Failure to maintain*. If the husband has neglected or has failed to provide for the wife's maintenance for a period of two years (*o*). Sec. 2(*ii*) has been the cause of a difference of judicial opinion. In *Fazal Mahmud* v. *Ummatur Rahim* (*p*), a Peshawar case, it was held that the section does not abrogate the general principles of Muhammadan law; therefore, before a husband can be said to have neglected or failed to provide maintenance, it must be shown that the husband was under a legal duty to provide such maintenance. Where the wife refuses to reside with her husband or fails to discharge her marital obligations, without any reasonable cause, she cannot claim maintenance, and therefore she is not entitled to divorce. This case has been followed in Bombay (*q*).

But the Sind High Court has taken a different view. In

(*n*) Sec. 2(*i*) read with proviso (*b*), and Sec. 3 of the Act. The rules as to a missing person (*mafqūd*) will be found in Ameer Ali, II, 92-6, especially 93 (as to husband). The four-year rule is known both to Mālikī and Shāfi'ī law.

(*o*) Mulla §325.

(*p*) A.I.R. (1949) Peshawar 7.

(*q*) *Bai Fatma* v. *Mumna Miranji* [1957] Bom. 453.

(Mst.) Nur Bibi v. *Pir Bux* (*r*), it was laid down that where a husband has failed to provide maintenance for his wife for a period of two years immediately preceding the suit, the wife would be entitled to a dissolution of her marriage under Sec. 2(*ii*) of the Act, in spite of the fact that on account of her conduct in refusing to live with her husband, she would not have been entitled to enforce any claim for maintenance against the husband in respect of the period during which the husband has failed to maintain her.

The above case has been followed recently in Kerala where it was held that the conduct of the wife is not material to the issue (*rr*). V. R. Krishna Iyer J. says:

> . . . I hold that a Muslim woman, under Sec. 2 (*ii*) of the Act, can sue for dissolution on the score that she has not as a fact been maintained, *even if there is cause for it*,—the voice of the law, echoing public policy is often that of the realist, not of the moralist (p. 270. Italics, mine).

This is an interesting case, but in so far as it lays down that the wife's conduct is not material, it is with respect open to serious doubt. Is it the opinion of the judge that the wife, after a few days of consortium, as in this case, and without any evidence of the conduct or behaviour of the husband, may go away from the matrimonial home, and after two years, sue for divorce under Sec. 2(*ii*)? Stated thus, the proposition seems open to serious doubt. The phrase 'failure to maintain' under the Act clearly envisages a proper inquiry into the conduct both of the husband and of the wife.

The true rule appears to be (i) that the failure to maintain under the statute need not be wilful; mere inability due, for instance, to poverty or even other causes, is sufficient, but (ii) that, the wife, wilfully refusing to stay with the husband, would be out of court if she proceeded under the section. In Shāfi'ī law, apart from 'inability to maintain', as such,

(*r*) A.I.R. (1950) Sind 8.

(*rr*) *Yousuf* v. *Sowramma* A.I.R. (1971) Ker. 261.

'neglect or failure to maintain' is a good ground for the wife to dissolve her marriage (*s*).

A full discussion of the husband's obligation to maintain will be found in Chapter VII on Maintenance.

(3) *Imprisonment of husband*. If the husband is sentenced to imprisonment for a period of seven years or more. No decree can be passed until the sentence has become final (*t*).

(4) *Failure to perform marital obligations*. If the husband fails to perform, without reasonable cause, his marital obligations for a period of three years (*u*).

It is difficult to give an exhaustive list of the husband's obligations arising on marriage, but a general survey will be found in Ameer Ali, II, 405-22, and Tyabji §31; and the most exact formulation of duties in Abdur Rahman, *Institutes*, Arts. 150-216.

(5) *Impotence*. It must be proved that the husband was impotent at the time of marriage, and that he continues to be so; but before passing a decree on this ground, the court is bound, on application by the husband, but not otherwise, to make an order requiring the husband to satisfy the court within a period of one year from the date of such order that he has ceased to be impotent. If the husband satisfies the court, within a year, that he is no longer impotent, no decree can be passed (*v*).

The statute has changed the law relating to the impotence of the husband. The older law may be summarized as follows: (i) The husband must be proved to have been impotent at the time of marriage. (ii) The wife must not have known it at the time. (iii) The impotence must have continued till the time of the suit. No suit could be filed if the wife knew that the

(*s*) *Kunju Ismail* v. *Md. Kadeja Umma* A.I.R. (1959) Kerala 151. The puzzling thing in this case is that at p. 152 of the report it is stated that the parties belong to the 'Shia sect of Muslims', and yet the decision is according to Shāfi'ī law. It is presumed that 'Shia' is a misprint for 'Shāfi'ī', which is the common school in South India.

(*t*) Sec. 2(*iii*) read with proviso (*a*).

(*u*) Sec. 2(*iv*).

(*v*) Sec. 2(*v*) read with proviso (*c*).

husband was impotent at the time of marriage, nor if the marriage had been consummated even once. In these circumstances the suit would be adjourned for a year to ascertain whether the impotence continued. After this probationary year, if the incapacity of the husband continued, the marriage would be dissolved (*w*).

The two chief differences are, first, that the ignorance of the wife regarding the impotency of the husband need not be proved. She can obtain a divorce even if she knew of it; and, secondly, that the adjournment of the case for one year is not essential. It is only on the application of the husband that an adjournment may be obtained. If no such application is made, the decree dissolving the marriage can be passed without delay. Thirdly, under the statute, the onus is thrown on the husband to prove that he is free from the physical defect of impotence (*x*).

(6) *Insanity, leprosy, venereal disease.* If the husband (i) has been insane for a period of two years, or (ii) is suffering from leprosy or (iii) a virulent venereal disease (*y*).

(7) *Option of puberty.* If the marriage has been performed by the father or grandfather and the wife was under the age of 15, the wife has the option of repudiating the marriage until she attains the age of 18, provided the marriage has not been consummated (*z*). In some cases, a wider view of the law was current, but the Calcutta High Court has laid down that the Dissolution of Muslim Marriages Act, 1939, is applicable only to suits for dissolution of marriage by a Muslim wife, and not in other cases. Therefore, the view that the distinction between the effect, validity or repudiation of marriage by exercising the 'option of puberty' between the two classes, namely, cases of father and grandfather and of other persons, acting as guardians in marriage, has been

(*w*) Wilson §73; Mulla §328.

(*x*) The question of potency is to be determined with reference to the wife; general proof of potency is not enough, *Muhammad Ibrahim* v. *Altafan* (1925) 47 All. 243.

(*y*) Sec. 2(*vi*).

(*z*) Sec. 2(*vii*).

nullified by the said Act, is not a correct view of the law (*a*).

A fuller treatment of the law on this point will be found in the chapter on Marriage, §8—Form and Capacity, p. 94 above.

(8) *Cruelty*. If the husband treats the wife with cruelty, which means that he—

(i) habitually assaults her or makes her life miserable by cruelty or bad conduct even if such conduct does not amount to physical ill-treatment;

Even before this statutory provision, cruelty (*b*) was considered a sufficient ground for dissolving the marriage at the suit of the wife, but mere incompatibility of temperament was not regarded as a good ground (*c*).

(ii) or associates with women of evil repute or leads an infamous life;

This clause apparently implies a conduct amounting to gross immorality or leading a shameful life. Apparently, a stray act of immorality or faithlessness would not be a sufficient cause.

(iii) or attempts to force her to lead an immoral life;

(iv) or disposes of her property or prevents her from exercising her legal rights over it;

(v) or obstructs her in the observance of her religious profession or practice;

(vi) or if he, having more wives than one, does not treat her equitably in accordance with the Koranic injunctions (*d*).

With the making of this statutory provision a number of *sharīʿat* rules for the equal treatment of wives are likely

(*a*) *Sk. Shaib Ali* v. *Jinnatan Nahar* (1960) 64 Cal. W.W. 756.

(*b*) *Kadir* v. *Koleman Bibi* (1935) 62 Cal. 1088; see a full discussion in 'The Muslim Wife's Right of Dissolving her Marriage' (1936) 38 Bom. Law Rep., Jl., 113.

(*c*) *Mustafa Begam* v. *Mirza Kazim Raza Khan* (1932) 8 Lucknow 204; Mulla §§331, 332. On the changing concept of 'cruelty', see above, §15.

(*d*) Sec. 2(*viii*), clauses (*a*) to (*f*).

to be brought up for consideration in courts of law. The *fiqh* books contain numerous injunctions of this character, and a brief but interesting set of rules based mostly on the *Radd al-Muḥtār* will be found in Abdur Rahman, *Institutes*, Arts. 150-9.

(9) *Any other ground under Shariat*. A Muslim wife is entitled, in addition to the above grounds, to sue for dissolution of her marriage on any other ground which is recognized as valid under Islamic law (*e*).

After giving a fairly complete list of the grounds upon which a Muslim wife may obtain a judicial divorce, the Act proceeds to lay down a residuary provision in order that the wife may not lose the benefit of any other ground which may have escaped the attention of the legislature. In addition to the grounds mentioned in this Act, reference may be made also to Sec. 2 of the Shariat Act, 1937, which mentions *ṭalāq* (whence, *ṭalāq-e tafwīḍ*, delegated divorce), *īlā'*, *ẓihār*, *li'ān*, *khul'*, and *mubāra'a*.

Incompatibility of temperament, dislike or ill-will, is not a sufficient ground under the Muhammadan law for obtaining a dissolution. In a learned and exhaustive judgment *Sayeeda Khanam* v. *Muhammad Sami* (*f*), Cornelius C.J. has discussed this question authoritatively and dealt with the nature of incompatibility (120 sq.); divorce and *khul'* (122-3); meaning of *shiqāq*, citing Kor. iv. 34, 35, 128, 130 (125-7); how the arbiters should act, and how the great Imāms differ (Mālik-Awzā'ī *versus* Abū Ḥanīfa-Shāfi'ī-Aḥmad b. Ḥanbal), and why the Full Bench agrees with the latter (128-32).

A later Full Bench decision of the same High Court carries the law farther in the same direction. In *Balqis Fatima* v. *Najm-ul-Ikram Qureshi* (*g*), in which the facts were strongly in favour of the wife, the Mālikī view that in a fit case the arbitrators (*ḥakams*) had the power to dissolve the marriage

(*e*) Sec. 2(*ix*).
(*f*) PLD 1952 (W.P.) Lahore 113, F.B.; *Cases*, 169.
(*g*) PLD 1959 (W.P.) Lahore 566.

was adopted and the law moulded more in consonance with the spirit of the Koran, as interpreted in modern times.

After examining the various interpretations of the Koran and traditions the court came to the conclusion that 'the only reasonable inference from the use of the word is that the *ḥakam* has the power to separate' (para. 18). But such power is to be sparingly exercised, and 'It is only if the judge apprehends that the limits of God will not be observed, that is, in their relations to one another, the spouses will not obey God, that a harmonious married state, as envisaged by Islam, will not be possible that he will grant a dissolution' (para. 42).

The question referred to the Full Bench was:

'Whether under Muslim law the wife is entitled to *khula* as of right?'

The Full Bench rightly interpreted this to mean:

'Is the wife entitled to dissolution of marriage on restoration of what she has received from the husband in consideration of marriage?' and their answer was as follows:

'The answer to the question referred to is that the wife is entitled to a dissolution of marriage on restoration of what she received in consideration of marriage if the judge apprehends that parties will not observe the limits of God.'

While the husband has the unfettered power to divorce the wife, the wife can only do so if she comes to the court and proves to its satisfaction that the further continuance of the marriage is improper (paras. 44 and 45).

The facts in this case were eminently favourable to the wife: the parties had litigated for over five years, the husband had prosecuted the father and brother of the wife, the husband had accused the brother's wife of an amorous connexion between himself and her, the marriage was as good as broken up completely, and it is satisfactory to observe that the courts in Pakistan have decided to ameliorate the lot of the wife in terms of the teaching of the Mālikī school.

§27. Change of Religion

(10) *Apostasy, conversion* (*h*). We must now consider the effect of change of religion on the status of marriage. This subject has assumed great importance in modern India. A Muslim may renounce Islam, and this is known as apostasy (*ridda*); or a non-Muslim may embrace Islam and this is called conversion. According to the general principles of Muhammadan law, a person who embraces Islam is immediately governed by Islamic law (*i*). But a man who renounces Islam suffers greatly under civil as well as criminal law. Islamic polity declares apostasy a treasonable offence; an apostate (*murtadd*), if a man, is in extreme cases liable to suffer the death penalty; if a woman, to suffer imprisonment. Ameer Ali explains:

> There is hardly any religious system which does not regard secession from the established religion of the State as tantamount to treason, or does not visit the culprit with punishment of the severest character. So late as the close of the eighteenth century of the Christian era, the Christian churches in Western Europe condemned 'heretics' to the stake or the gallows; no distinction was made on the score of sex or age. Even when the growing conscience of the people led to the relaxation of the penalty of death, renunciation of the particular communion to which the seceder belonged, was attended with forfeiture of civil rights and exposure to social ostracism and obloquy.
>
> The peculiar and difficult circumstances under which the Church of Islam came into existence made 'apostasy' a danger to the State; the abandonment of Islam was tantamount to the renunciation of allegiance to the Islamic Commonwealth; it was nothing short of treason. The law consequently prescribed the death-penalty for the offence but not at the stake, nor by drowning or hanging. The extreme penalty was, however, reserved only for the adult male *murtadd*, the traitor-apostate, and that only when he was a Moslem born. A woman, a youth, a man who had adopted Islam under compulsion, a young man whose parents were not Moslems and a number of other persons similarly circumstanced, were exempt from the death-penalty.

(*h*) For early history, Schacht, 276-7. For a discussion of Malayan law, useful even to us in India, see (Mrs.) M. Siraj, 'The Legal Effect of Conversion to Islam,' 7 *Malaya L. Rev.* (1965), 95-112.

(*i*) Ameer Ali, II, 148.

When a woman abandoned Islam, she was to be imprisoned until she returned to the Faith (*j*).

In order to understand the principles underlying the body of rules relating to the matrimonial status of persons renouncing or embracing Islam, we shall consider four classes of cases. First, a Muslim husband may become an apostate; secondly, a Muslim wife may renounce Islam; these are the two commonest forms of apostasy. Thirdly, a non-Muslim husband or, fourthly, a non-Muslim wife, may embrace Islam; these are the two commonest cases of conversion.

(A) **Husband renounces Islam.** The first question that often arises in cases of this kind is: Has there been on the part of the party concerned 'an act of apostasy'? The Lahore High Court has held that a formal declaration is sufficient, and a genuine conversion to some other religion need not be proved (*k*). Apostasy may be either express, as 'I hereby renounce Islam', or 'I do not believe in God and the Prophet Muhammad'; or it may be by conduct, for instance by using grossly disrespectful or abusive language towards the Prophet. Conversion to another faith is also tantamount to apostasy.

A Muslim husband who renounces Islam is an apostate and as such his marriage with his Muslim wife is dissolved *ipso facto* (*l*).

Ameer Ali is of the view that when a Muslim married couple abandon Islam and adopt another faith, their marriage is not dissolved but remains intact (*m*).

(B) **Wife renounces Islam.** The present law on the subject may be stated in the form of two propositions: (i) The mere renunciation of Islam by a Muslim wife does not *by itself* dissolve her marriage. (ii) The above rule does not apply to a woman converted to Islam from some other faith who re-embraces *her former faith*. For instance, *W*, a Christian

(*j*) Ameer Ali, II, 388; and also pp. 392-3.
(*k*) *Mst. Resham Bibi* v. *Khuda Bakhsha* (1937) 19 Lah. 277.
(*l*) Tyabji §200; Wilson §78A; Ameer Ali, II, 390; Mulla §321 (3) and (5), *Fat. Law* §§151(i), 156.
(*m*) Ameer Ali, II, 394.

woman, embraces Islam and marries *H*, a Muslim husband. She then commits an act of apostasy in the eye of the *sharī'at* and re-embraces Christianity. In this case, the marriage of *W* with *H* is dissolved (*n*).

According to the older law, as laid down by the classical jurists of Islam, apostasy on the part of the wife operated as an immediate and absolute dissolution of marriage (*o*). But in India this rule was used for the purpose of dissolving a marriage which had grown irksome to the wife, as there was no other way open to her to get rid of her husband. Now that the Dissolution of Muslim Marriages Act, 1939, gives a remedy, the statute provides that apostasy by itself does not dissolve the marriage, unless it be that a women re-embraces her former faith.

(C) **Husband embraces Islam.** According to Islamic law conversion to Islam on the part of a man following a scriptural religion, such as Judaism or Christianity, does not dissolve his marriage with a woman belonging to his old creed. The rule, however, is different if the couple belong to a non-scriptural faith. In that case the Muslim husband could not lawfully retain a non-*kitābiyya* wife; wherefore, Islam was to be 'offered' to her and, on her refusal, a decree for dissolution was to be passed (*p*). These rules, however, cannot be applied in a modern state where 'all religions are equal in the eye of the law' (*q*) and where 'the court, judicially administering the law, cannot say that one religion is better than another' (*r*). In this branch of jurisprudence, where men and women often

(*n*) Dissolution of Muslim Marriages Act, 1939, Sec. 4.

(*o*) *Amin Beg* v. *Saman* (1910) 33 All. 90 (Conversion to Christianity); *Mst. Resham Bibi* v. *Khuda Bakhsha*, op. cit., (apostasy *simpliciter*, wife says she has no religion); Mulla §321; Tyabji §200. Ameer Ali held the view that if a wife becomes a Jew or a Christian this rule should not be applied in its strictness. This view (Ameer Ali, II, 384, 390, 391) was not accepted by the courts, but social events have moved so fast since that the new Act in effect goes a long way towards upholding his reasoning.

(*p*) Ameer Ali, II, 384, 387; *Fat. Law* §§151 sqq.

(*q*) *O'Hanlon* v. *Loque* [1906] 1 Irish Reports 247, 260.

(*r*) Per Maclean C.J. in *Mookoond Lal* v. *Nobodip Chunder* (1898) 25 Cal. 881, 885.

try to twist and mould the rules of law to suit their own selfish ends, the words of Blagden J. must always be kept in view:

British India as a whole, is neither governed by Hindu, Mahomedan, Sikh, Parsi, Christian, Jewish or any other law, except a law imposed by Great Britain under which Hindus, Mahomedans, Sikhs, Parsis and others enjoy equal rights and the utmost possible freedom of religious observance, consistent in every case with the rights of other people. I have to decide this case according to the law as it is, and there seems, in principle, no adequate ground for holding that in this case Mahomedan Law is applicable to a non-Mahomedan (*s*).

These principles enunciated by an English judge in a British Indian court would apply equally in India and Pakistan (*t*).

A non-Muslim, lawfully married in accordance with his own law, cannot by a mere conversion to Islam dissolve his own marriage (*u*). Thus, if a Christian, lawfully married to a Christian woman, were to declare himself a convert to Islam and marry a Muslim woman in Muslim fashion, the second marriage would be, in the judgment of the Privy Council, of doubtful validity (*v*); but *aliter*, if there had been a *bona fide* conversion of *both* parties to the Islamic faith. In *Skinner* v. *Skinner*, Lord Watson observes:

One of the many peculiar features of this suit arises from the circumstance that, in the case of spouses resident in India, their personal status, and what is frequently termed the status of the marriage, is not solely dependent upon domicil, but involves the element of religious creed. Whether a change of religion, made *honestly* after marriage with the *assent of both spouses*, without any intent to commit a fraud upon the law, will have the effect of altering rights incidental to the marriage, such as that of divorce, is a question of importance and, it may be, of nicety (*w*).

Recently, however, it has been held in Calcutta that a married Christian domiciled in India, after his conversion to

(*s*) *Robaba Khanum* v. *Khodadad Bomanji Irani* (1946) 48 Bom. L.R. 864, 869. See also *Skinner* v. *Orde*, cited at p. 63, note (*i*) above.

(*t*) Constitution of India, Art. 25.

(*u*) Tyabji §199, applied and adopted in *Keolapati* v. *Harnam Singh* (1936) 12 Luck. 568, 581.

(*v*) *Skinner* v. *Orde* (1871) 14 M.I.A. 309, 324, *Cases*, 254, 257.

(*w*) *Skinner* v. *Skinner* (1897) 25 I.A. 34, 41 (italics mine); Ameer Ali, II, 386-7; Wilson, 84-5. Compare the observations of Lord Upjohn in a P.C. case from Ceylon at p. 64 above.

Islam, is governed by Muhammadan law, and is entitled, during the subsistence of his marriage with his former Christian wife, to contract a valid marriage with another woman according to Muhammadan rites (*x*). This decision appears to overlook the important principle that a previous marriage in accordance with one scheme of personal law cannot be destroyed by the mere adoption of another faith by *one* of the spouses. It is also in conflict with the opinions of Ameer Ali (*y*), Tyabji (*z*), Wilson (*a*) and Fitzgerald (*b*), and it is submitted that it is erroneous (*c*).

(D) **Wife embraces Islam.** The conversion of a non-Muslim wife to Islam does not *ipso facto* dissolve her marriage with her husband, and the ancient procedure of 'offering Islam' to the husband and, on his refusal, obtaining a dissolution of marriage, as laid down in the texts (*d*), cannot be followed in India. It has been held that by this procedure, neither a Hindu (*e*), nor a Christian (*f*), nor a Jewish (*g*), nor an Irani Zoroastrian wife (*h*) can get rid of her husband.

But *aliter* in Pakistan. Baqar Shah, a Muslim residing in

(*x*) *John Jiban* v. *Abinash Chandra* [1939] 2 Cal. 12.

(*y*) Ameer Ali, II, 384, 387. (*z*) Tyabji §199.

(*a*) Wilson §11(*d*). (*b*) Fitzgerald, 85.

(*c*) *Farooq Leivers* v. *Adelaide Bridget* PLD 1958 (W.P.) Lahore 431 (para. 10). The head-note is very confused and the judgment, with respect, full of irrelevancies.

(*d*) Ameer Ali, II, 385, 387; *Fat. Law* §151; *Ahmad Bux* v. *Smt. Nathoo* AIR (1969) All. 75.

(*e*) *Rakeya Bibi* v. *Anil Kumar Mukherji* [1948] 2 Cal. 119. The decision of the Calcutta High Court *Mst. Ayesha Bibi* v. *Subodh Ch. Chakravarty* (1945) 49 C.W.N. 439, it is submitted with respect, is not good law; see ibid., 745.

(*f*) *Noor Jehan* v. *Eugene Tischenko* [1942] 2 Cal. 165. In this case, there was an additional difficulty, namely, that the plaintiff was a Russian woman married in Berlin. Later, the plaintiff came to India, embraced Islam and called upon her husband to accept her newly adopted religion. The husband refused. Thereupon she filed this suit for a declaration that her marriage with the defendant stood dissolved. The court refused the declaration.

(*g*) *Sayeda Khatoon* v. *M. Obadiah* (1945) 49 C.W.N. 745, expressly dissenting from *Mst. Ayesha Bibi* v. *Subodh Chandra Chakravarty* (1945) 49 C.W.N. 439.

(*h*) *Robaba Khanum* v. *Khodadad Bomanji Irani* (1946) 48 Bom. L.R. 864. The name Robaba has been mis-spelt 'Robasa' in the Bombay Law Reporter; the original judgment contains the correct name, see [1948] Bom. 223.

British India, married Said Begum, a Muslim by birth. Later he married a second wife Madad Bi, a Hindu woman converted to Islam who had a Hindu husband living. There were no court proceedings declaring that Madad Bi's marriage with her Hindu husband had been duly dissolved, this being impossible under the older Hindu law. Baqar Shah died leaving offspring by both the wives. The question arose whether the issue of Madad Bi were legitimate. It was held *inter alia* that, immediately upon the conversion of Madad Bi to Islam, her marriage with her Hindu husband was dissolved and her marriage to Baqar Shah was lawful; wherefore her children by him were legitimate (*i*).

For reasons which have been sufficiently discussed, it is respectfully submitted that the reasoning in this case is unsound and the decision erroneous.

A considered decision on the point is a Bombay case decided by Blagden J. in December 1945, and confirmed by a Division Bench on appeal (*j*). Robaba, an Iranian woman, Zoroastrian by religion, who was domiciled in India, was married to Khodadad in Persia according to Zoroastrian rites. Two sons were born of the union. She embraced Islam and 'offered Islam' to her Zoroastrian husband. On his refusal, she filed a suit for a declaration that her marriage in the circumstances stood dissolved. It was held that a Zoroastrian (or Christian) wife cannot do away with her marriage by a mere profession of Islam. Blagden J., in this case, expressly dissents from a decision of the Calcutta High Court, *Mst. Ayesha Bibi* v. *Subodh Ch. Chakravarty* (*k*), the case of a Hindu woman, and agrees with the later decision of the same High Court in the case of a Jewish lady, *Sayeda Khatoon* v. *M. Obadiah* (*l*). It is submitted with respect that the decision in *Robaba's case* is correct.

(*i*) *Faiz Ali Shah* v. *Ghulam Akbar Shah* PLD 1952 'Azad' Jammu and Kashmir 32.

(*j*) *Robaba Khanum* v. *Khodadad Bomanji Irani* (1946) 48 Bom. L.R. 864.

(*k*) (1945) 49 C.W.N. 439.

(*l*) (1945) 49 C.W.N. 745.

In conclusion, a few general observations may be made.

When a court of law has to decide a case involving change of marital status due to conversion or apostasy, it must never be overlooked that since the rules were formulated in Islamic jurisprudence, social conditions have changed so completely that a blind adherence to some of the rules, torn out of their proper context, would lead neither to justice nor to a fair appraisal of the system under which they were promulgated (*m*). This has been pointed out forcibly by Ameer Ali, a leading modern authority on Muhammadan law. He says:

> The British Indian Courts in their adherence to the strict letter of the ancient doctrine have, it is submitted, missed the spirit of the enunciation; and have, accordingly, treated in the case of a wife as a privilege what was intended to be a punishment. By the interpretation put on the rule, a Musulman woman is thus enabled to obtain by a simple abjuration of Islam a dissolution of the marriage-tie which had become irksome. *The enforcement of the Musulman Law in its entirety regarding apostates has become impossible under existing conditions* in most countries inhabited by Moslems. A husband abandoning Islam cannot be punished by death; nor a woman abjuring the Faith can be liable to incarceration. Shortly stated, *apostasy has ceased*, especially in these countries, *to be a State offence*. It is absurd and contrary to the principles of justice that one part of the rule should be enforced whilst the other should be ignored.
>
> The legal position of the married parties one of whom abandons Islam must therefore be determined on principles of the Musulman Law other than those relating to apostasy. For example, it is the general rule that a non-Moslem cannot contract a valid marriage with a Moslemah; according to the majority of lawyers it is an illegal union. Consequently, when a Moslem husband abandons Islam, his connection with his wife becomes an illegal or at any rate an invalid connection. And the woman, accordingly, on the expiration of her *'iddat*, can marry someone else (*n*).

The second observation to be made is regarding the party who brings a suit. In all such cases the court is entitled to

(*m*) A good account of the rules of Islamic law has been given by Heffening, s.v. *'Murtadd'*, in *Ency. of Islam*, III, 736-8.

(*n*) Ameer Ali, II, 393 (italics mine).

ask: Who is the person that seeks relief? If the husband changes his religion, it is understandable that the wife should complain and sue for dissolution; and vice versa. But is it right and just that one spouse should declare himself or herself a convert and then ask the court to declare the marriage dissolved? The result would be that by these means a party to a marriage would be able to evade the legal obligations of a marriage entered into at a prior time and in accordance with a different system of personal law.

The third matter for serious consideration would be: Can one spouse by changing his (or her) religion alter the status of another person who has not changed his faith? A man may be, and is, permitted to change his religion at his own choice, but why should such an act be allowed completely to alter the legal status of another person who has not changed his religion?

These are some of the difficult legal and social problems raised by the law in modern society; and while it has so far been found impossible to formulate a law of marriage and divorce which would be satisfactory in all respects, it is urged that in holding the balance equally between conflicting principles, it is our duty also to examine the social and historical background before deciding a purely legal question (*o*).

(11) *Dower*. Sec. 5 of the Dissolution of Muslim Marriages Act, 1939, lays down that a dissolution obtained under the Act by a Muslim woman does not affect her rights of dower.

(12) *Procedure*. A suit by a Muslim woman under the provisions of the Dissolution of Muslim Marriages Act, 1939, can now be filed under the Civil Procedure Code, 1908, in the court of the lowest jurisdiction competent to try it.

This is the effect of the repeal of the Shariat Act, Sec. 5, by the Dissolution of Muslim Marriages Act, Sec. 6. For an explanation, see above, Chapter One §1 (last part).

(*o*) See the judgment in *Rakeya Bibi* v. *Anil Kumar Mukherji* [1948] 2 Cal. 119. For early history, see Schacht, 276-7.

§28. Effects of Dissolution

(1) *Matrimonial intercourse.* After the dissolution is effective, matrimonial intercourse between the parties becomes unlawful. Nevertheless, the parties may, in certain circumstances, lawfully remarry.

(2) *Remarriage, reconciliation.* A divorced couple cannot always remarry. For a full discussion of how reconciliation or remarriage can take place, see above, *Ṭalāq,* §23.

(3) *Fresh marriage.*

(i) Where the marriage was *consummated*, the wife has to wait till the expiration of her *'idda* in order to be able to remarry.

The husband, if he has four wives, must wait until the completion of the divorced wife's *'idda.*

(ii) Where the marriage was *not consummated*, the parties can marry immediately, without waiting for the expiry of the *'idda.*

(4) *Dower.* If the marriage was consummated, the whole dower is immediately due; if not, half the dower is payable.

(5) *Maintenance.* The husband has to provide maintenance to the wife during *'idda.*

In a suit for maintenance, where a divorce has taken place earlier, but has come to the knowledge of the divorced wife later, the wife cannot be saddled with the knowledge of such divorce until the later date (*oo*).

(6) *Inheritance.* So long as the divorce is revocable one spouse can inherit from the other; but when the divorce becomes irrevocable, the rights of inheritance terminate *inter se.*

This is a very brief statement of the rules; a further discussion will be found under the different headings of the various chapters (*p*).

(*oo*) *Enamul Haque* v. *Taimunnissa* A.I.R. (1967) Pat. 344.
(*p*) Tyabji §159 sqq.; Mulla §336; *Fat. Law* §§198 sqq., 276-81.

§29. Miscellaneous Rules

(i) *Divorce proceedings in England, where there is a foreign Muslim marriage.* An Englishwoman, domiciled in England, who marries a Muslim in a foreign country in the *nikāḥ* form cannot ask an English court for a decree of nullity. The marriage being a potentially polygamous one, the wife is not entitled to an adjudication in accordance with the Matrimonial law of England, *Risk* v. *Risk* [1950] 2 A.E.R. 973, discussed in *Law Quar. Rev.* for 1951, 171-2.

Another interesting case is *Maher* v. *Maher* [1951] Probate 342, in which an Englishwoman petitioned for a dissolution of her marriage celebrated in England with an Egyptian of English domicile. Her husband deserted her, returned to Egypt and pronounced *ṭalāq*, the *ṭalāq-nāma* being handed over to the wife by the Egyptian Embassy in England. Barnard J. held that the *ṭalāq* pronounced in Egypt did not dissolve the marriage, and granted the wife a divorce on the ground of desertion.

See generally, Cheshire, *Private International Law*, 6th ed. (Oxford, 1961), pp. 302 sqq., and 402 sqq.; *Russ* v. *Russ*, *The Times* (London), 2 February 1962, p. 3; 'Polygamous Marriage in the Light of English Law', by J. C. Arnold, *Quarterly Review*, April 1962 and §10 above.

(ii) *Costs in divorce proceedings.* The rule of English law whereby the husband is *prima facie* liable for the wife's costs is not applicable in Muhammadan law, *A* v. *B* (1896) 21 Bom. 77; Mulla §335.

(*iii*) *Suit by wife under 18.* In Muhammadan law a woman of sixteen can sue for divorce, without a guardian, by virtue of Sec. 2(*a*) of the Indian Majority Act, 1875; *Ahmed Suleman* v. *Bai Fatma* (1930) 32 Bom. L.R. 1372; *Hanufa Bibi* v *Moksed Ali* (1960) 64 Cal. W.N. 786.

(iv) *Gift* (mut'a) *to divorced wife on divorce—Fatimid Law.* The Fatimid law lays down very specifically that on divorce, and apart altogether from the payment of *mahr*, the husband shall make a gift (called *mut'a*, and to be distinguished from the term used for temporary marriage in Ithnā 'Asharī law) to the divorced wife. This payment is to compensate her for loss of consortium, and is based on the text of the Koran, ii, 236. Unfortunately however this rule is not known in India and it is submitted that it should be enforced on the parties governed by this school of law, *Fatimid Law* §§286-91.

CHAPTER V

PARENTAGE AND LEGITIMACY

§30. Legitimation, Legitimacy
§31. Presumptions
§32. Acknowledgement

§30. Legitimation, Legitimacy

In the Muhammadan, as in other systems of law, parentage involves certain rights and obligations. The relation between a father and his child is called paternity; the relation between a mother and her child is called maternity (*a*).

By and large, there are two modes of filiation known to the law: as a rule, the law treats the natural father as the father of the child; sometimes, however, adoption leads to the result that someone who is not the father acquires rights similar to those of the father. Adoption is not recognized in Islam (*b*), as it was disapproved by the Koran (*c*). In addition to natural filiation, the first form, another is also known, namely, acknowledgement of paternity. The peculiarity of Muhammadan law is that in certain cases where it is doubtful whether a person is the child of another, the acknowledgement of the father confers on the child the status of legitimacy.

In considering these and allied questions, the distinction between the *status* of legitimacy and the *process* of legitimation must be kept in mind. 'Legitimacy is a status which results from certain facts. Legitimation is a proceeding which creates a status which did not exist before. In the proper sense there is no legitimation under the Muhammadan law.'(*d*) In Muhammadan law such an acknowledgement is a declaration

(*a*) Wilson §79; Tyabji §§217 sqq.
(*b*) Mahmood J. in *Muhammad Allahdad* v. *Muhammad Ismail* (1888) 10 All. 289, 341; Cases, 199; Wilson §80; Tyabji §228.
(*c*) The Koranic passages in Tyabji, loc. cit.; Ameer Ali, II, 218.
(*d*) *Habibur Rahman* v. *Altaf Ali* (1921) 48 I.A. 114, 120; *Cases*, 251; Cheshire, *Private Internationol Law*, 6th ed. (Oxford, 1961), 427.

of legitimacy, and not a legitimation (*e*). 'No statement made by one man that another (proved to be illegitimate) is his son can make that other legitimate, but where no proof of that kind has been given such a statement or acknowledgement is substantive evidence that the person so acknowledged is the legitimate son of the person who makes the statement provided his legitimacy be possible.'(*f*) Legitimation *per subsequens matrimonium* is not known to Muhammadan law (*g*).

Parentage is therefore established in Islam in one of *two* ways and there is no third: (i) by birth during a regular or irregular (but not void) marriage, or (ii) by acknowledgement, in certain circumstances.

§31. Presumptions

In order to understand the present law on the subject, we must first state briefly the rules regarding the presumption of legitimacy according to Muhammadan law, and then note how far they have been altered by legislation (*h*). Islamic law ordains that—

1. A child born within six months of the marriage is illegitimate, unless the father acknowledges it.
2. A child born after six months of the marriage is legitimate, unless the father disclaims it.
3. A child born after the termination of marriage is legitimate if born—

   within 10 lunar months—in Shiite law;
   within 2 lunar years—in Hanafi law; and
   within 4 lunar years—in Shāfi'ī or Mālikī law (*i*).

The reasons for such divergent periods are not difficult to

(*e*) Tyabji §225, com.

(*f*) *Sadik Husain* v. *Hashim Ali* (1916) 43 I.A. 212, 234; *Cases*, 247; also per Straight J. in *Muhammad Allahdad* v. *Muhammad Ismail, Cases*, 216.

(*g*) F. A. Mann, 'Legitimation and Adoption in Private International Law', *Law Quar. Rev.* for 1941, 112; Cheshire, loc. cit.

(*h*) Baillie, I, 392-3, 396-7.

(*i*) Tyabji §219, where the author says rightly that at present these periods are repealed in India. Ameer Ali, II, 191-2.

understand. In the first instance, we have to take into consideration the imperfect knowledge of gestation and pregnancy prevalent in early times. Baillie thinks that in laying down such long periods, the Sunnite doctors had in view those abnormal conditions which 'sometimes perplex the most skilful of the medical faculty in Europe'.(*j*) The second reason is humane sentiment. If a woman gave birth to an illegitimate child, not only would the child be excluded from inheritance, but the woman herself would be punishable for the offence of *zinā* (*k*). Thus Ameer Ali cites the views of two European jurists, D'Ohsson and Sautarya, who are of opinion that the ancient jurists 'were actuated by sentiments of humanity, and not any indifference to the laws of nature, their chief desire being to prevent an abuse of the provisions of the law regarding divorce and the disavowal of children'.(*l*)

The present rule on the subject is to be found in the conclusive presumption raised in Sec. 112, Indian Evidence Act. The rule may be shortly stated as follows: A child born during the continuance of a valid marriage, or within 280 days after its dissolution, the mother remaining unmarried, is *conclusively* presumed to be legitimate, unless there was no access when he could have been begotten. The question whether Sec. 112, Indian Evidence Act, supersedes the rules of Muhammadan law was left open in the leading case of *Muhammad Allahdad* v. *Muhammad Ismail* by Mahmood J. (*m*), but since that time the trend of modern decisions is to regard this as purely a question of the law of evidence governed by Sec. 112, Indian Evidence Act, even with regard to Muslims (*n*). If, however, the marriage is held to be irregular, difficult questions may arise.

(*j*) Ameer Ali, II, 191, note 4.

(*k*) *Zinā* in Islam is the generic name for illicit intercourse, the chief forms whereof are adultery and fornication.

(*l*) Ameer Ali, loc. cit.

(*m*) (1888) 10 All. 289, 339.

(*n*) The clearest exposition of this view will be found in Tyabji §§219 sqq.; Mulla §340, com.

§32. Acknowledgement

Acknowledgement (*iqrār*) of paternity takes place in Islam as follows: (1) where the paternity of a child is not known or established beyond a doubt (*o*); and (2) it is not proved that the claimant is the offspring of *zinā* (illicit intercourse); and (3) the circumstances are such that they do not rebut the presumption of paternity, an acknowledgement of paternity by the father is possible and effective.

We shall now discuss each of these three incidents (*p*).

(1) *Unknown Paternity*

The rule as to acknowledgement of legitimacy arises only if the paternity of the child is not certain. To use the terminology of the Indian Evidence Act, the paternity of the child must neither be 'proved' nor 'disproved', but it should be 'not proved'.(*q*)

The leading case on the subject is *Muhammad Allahdad* v. *Muhammad Ismail* (*r*). *A*, claiming to be the eldest son of *G*, brought a suit against *I* and his three sisters for his rights in certain villages. *I* and his three sisters were born to Moti Begum after her marriage to *G*; but *A* was born to her at a time unknown. Nothing was known or proved as to who the father of *A* was, it being certain that the mother was Moti Begum. *G*, during his lifetime, had acknowledged *A* as his legitimate son. It was held (i) that there was no proof of the paternity of *A*, (ii) that there was no legal impediment to the marriage of *G* with Moti Begum, and (iii) that it was not proved that *A* was the offspring of *zinā* (illicit intercourse), or that he was the natural son of *G* born *before* his marriage with Moti Begum. Therefore *A* had the status of an acknowledged

(*o*) 'Paternity does not admit of positive proof, because the connection of a child with its father is secret. But it may be established by the word of the father himself . . .' Ameer Ali, II, 190-1, citing *Fatāwā 'Ālamgīrī.*

(*p*) Fitzgerald, 92.

(*q*) *Roshanbi* v. *Suleman* (1944) 46 Bom. L.R. 328, where a good summary of the law will be found.

(*r*) (1888) 10 All. 289; *Cases*, 199. The leading judgment is that of Mahmood J., pp. 324-43. The opinion of Straight J. (pp. 300-21) is also important as it contains texts.

son of *G* and as such had the right to inherit *G*'s property with *I* and his sisters.

The Muhammadan law of acknowledgement of parentage with its legitimating effect has no reference whatsoever to cases in which the illegitimacy of the child is proved and established, either by reason of a lawful union between the parents of the child being impossible (as in the case of an incestuous intercourse or an adulterous connection), or by reason of marriage necessary to render the child legitimate being *disproved*. The doctrine relates only to cases where either the fact of the marriage itself or the exact time of its occurrence with reference to the legitimacy of the acknowledged child is *not proved* in the sense of the law as distinguished from disproved. In other words, the doctrine applies only to cases of uncertainty as to legitimacy, and in such cases acknowledgement has its effect, but that effect always proceeds upon the assumption of a lawful union between the parents of the acknowledged child (*s*).

(2) *Must not be Illegitimate*

An illegitimate son cannot be 'acknowledged' as legitimate, for there is no such thing as 'legitimation' in Islam. Mahmood J. points out that the legitimation of an illegitimate son is possible in Roman and Scots law, but

. . . no analogy exists between the principles upon which those rules proceed and those upon which the Muhammadan rule of the acknowledgement of parentage is founded. Putting the matter shortly, the former two systems proceed upon the principle of legitimating children whose illegitimacy is proved and admitted, whilst the Muhammadan law relates only to cases of uncertainty and proceeds upon the assumption that the acknowledged child is not only the offspring of the acknowledger by blood, but also the issue of a lawful union between the acknowledger and the mother of the child (*t*).

In *Sadik Husain* v. *Hashim Ali* (*u*), the Judicial Committee of the Privy Council held that an acknowledgement by a

(*s*) Per Mahmood J., 10 All. at pp. 334-5. This doctrine is now well established, Tyabji §225; Mulla §§342-4.

(*t*) 10 All. at p. 341.

(*u*) (1916) 43 I.A. 212; *Cases*, 238.

Muslim that a person is his son is substantive evidence that the person is his legitimate son. Statements made by a member of a Muslim family, in this case the widow of the alleged father, that a person is a son, or an heir, are evidence merely of family repute of legitimacy.

(3) *Nothing to rebut Presumption*

First, the ages of the parties must be such as to be in consonance with the presumption of paternity; secondly, marriage must be possible between the father and mother; thirdly, the person acknowledged must not be the offspring of *zinā* (illicit intercourse); and fourthly, there must not have been a disclaimer or repudiation on the part of the person acknowledged (*v*).

An important decision on legitimacy is *Habibur Rahman Chawdhury* v. *Altaf Ali Chawdhury* (*w*). *H*, the son of a Jewess, Mozelle Cohen, claiming to be the legitimate son of Nawab Sobhan of Bogra, filed a suit against *A* and others, for a share of inheritance. *A* was the daughter's son of the deceased Nawab. *H* affirmed that Mozelle was married to the Nawab, and that, in any event, the Nawab had acknowledged him as his son on many occasions. It was held that neither a marriage nor a proper acknowledgement was proved, and the plaintiff failed. Lord Dunedin, in delivering the judgment of the Board, said:

> Before discussing the subject, it is as well at once to lay down with precision the difference between legitimacy and legitimation. Legitimacy is a *status* which results from certain facts. Legitimation is a *proceeding* which *creates a status which did not exist before*. In the proper sense there is *no legitimation under the Mohammedan law*. Examples of it may be found in other systems. The adoption of the Roman and the Hindu law affected legitimacy. The same was done under the Canon law and the Scotch law in respect of what is known as legitimation per subsequens matrimonium (*x*). By the Mohammedan law a son to be legitimate

(*v*) Wilson §85; Tyabji, loc. cit.
(*w*) (1921) 48 I.A. 114; *Cases*, 247.
(*x*) See F. A. Mann, op. cit.

must be the offspring of a man and his wife or of a man and his slave; any other offspring is the offspring of zina, that is, illicit connection, and cannot be legitimate. The term 'wife' necessarily connotes marriage; but, as marriage may be constituted without any ceremonial, the existence of a marriage in any particular case may be an open question. Direct proof may be available, but if there be no such, indirect proof may suffice. Now one of the ways of indirect proof is by an acknowledgement of legitimacy in favour of a son. This acknowledgement must be not merely of sonship, but must be made in such a way that it shows that the acknowledger meant to accept the other not only as his son, but as his legitimate son. It must not be impossible upon the face of it: i.e. it must not be made when the ages are such that it is impossible in nature for the acknowledger to be the father of the acknowledgee, or when the mother spoken to in an acknowledgement, being the wife of another, or within prohibited degrees of the acknowledger, it would be apparent that the issue would be the issue of adultery or incest. The acknowledgement may be repudiated by the acknowledgee. But if none of these objections occur, then the acknowledgement has more than a mere evidential value. It raises a presumption of marriage—a presumption which may be taken advantage of either by a wife-claimant or a son-claimant. Being, however, a presumption of fact, and not juris et de jure, it is, like every other presumption of fact, capable of being set aside by contrary proof. The result is that a claimant son who has in his favour a good acknowledgement of legitimacy is in this position: The marriage will be held proved and his legitimacy established unless the marriage is disproved. Until the claimant establishes his acknowledgement the onus is on him to prove a marriage. Once he establishes an acknowledgement, the onus is on those who deny a marriage to negative it in fact (*y*).

The acknowledgement may be either express, or implied by conduct (*z*). It must be a statement or conduct intended to have legal effect; a mere casual admission is not enough. A prolonged cohabitation in the nature of concubinage, inconsistent with the relation of husband and wife, is not sufficient (*a*); nor can such a presumption arise in the case of a

(*y*) 48 I.A. 114, 120-1, italics mine; *Cases*, 251 sq.

(*z*) Wilson §86; Tyabji §225(5); Mulla §343; *Mohd. Amin* v. *Vakil Ahmed* [1952] S.C.R. (India) 1133.

(*a*) *Abdool Razack* v. *Aga Mahomed* (1893) 21 I.A. 56.

common prostitute (*b*). A clear repudiation by the father would also destroy the force of an implied acknowledgement (*c*).

Effects. The acknowledgement of the children has the legal effect of the acknowledgement of the wife as well; for the acknowledgement of a man is valid with regard to five persons —his father, mother, child, wife and *mawlā* (a freed slave) (*d*). A valid acknowledgement gives rights of inheritance to the children, the parents and the wife. An acknowledgement once made is not revocable (*e*).

(*b*) *Ghazanfar Ali Khan* v. *Mst. Kaniz Fatima* (1910) 37 I.A. 105.

(*c*) *Habibur Rahman* v. *Altaf Ali* (supra); as to the way in which paternity can be disclaimed, see Tyabji §§222-24.

(*d*) Baillie, I, 407; *Mst. Bashiran* v. *Mohammad Husain* [1941] Luck. 615.

(*e*) Wilson §87; Tyabji §223; Mulla §346.

CHAPTER VI

GUARDIANSHIP

§33. Guardianship of the Person
§34. Guardianship of Property
§35. Guardianship in Marriage

GUARDIANSHIP (*wilāya*) may be (i) of the person, (ii) of property, and (iii) in marriage (*a*). In the first instance there is guardianship of the person. Guardians of property, as such, are rarely appointed in Islamic law; an executor (*waṣī*) is the guardian of property. Guardianship in marriage is a species of *wilāya*, and a marriage guardian is called *walī* (*b*).

§33. Guardianship of the Person

In Indian law, three periods of guardianship of minors have to be considered. A minor is (i) a person under 15, in Muhammadan law, (ii) a person under 18, under the Indian Majority Act (*c*), and (iii) a person under 21, who has a guardian appointed by the court, or who is under the superintendence of the Court of Wards (*d*).

In India, broadly speaking, a minor is a person who has not completed the age of eighteen years. In Muhammadan law, minors between the ages of 15 and 18 can act independently of any guardian in marriage, dower and divorce. For instance, a Muslim wife of 16 may sue for divorce without the intervention of a guardian (*e*).

All applications for the appointment of a guardian of the person, or of the property, or of both, of a minor must be made under the provisions of the Guardians and Wards Act, VIII of 1890. The court will, if necessary, make the order

(*a*) Wilson §90.
(*b*) Tyabji §235.
(*c*) Section 3; Guardians and Wards Act, 1890, Section 4, Clause i.
(*d*) Ameer Ali, II, 535-6; Tyabji §231; Mulla §348.
(*e*) See §29 (iii) above; *Ahmed Suleman* v. *Bai Fatima* (1930) 55 Bom. 160; Tyabji and Mulla, loc. cit.

consistently with the welfare of the minor. In making such order the court shall be guided (i) by what, consistently with the law to which the minor is subject, is for the welfare of the minor; (ii) by the age, sex and religion of the minor, by the character and capacity of the proposed guardian, and the wishes of a deceased parent; and (iii) by the preference of the minor himself, if sufficiently old to form a preference (*f*).

Mother. The custody of an infant child belongs to the mother; this right is known as *ḥiḍāna* (*ff*). The mother is entitled

in *Hanafi law*—

to the custody of her male child till the age of 7 years, and

of her female child till puberty;

and in *Ithnā ʻAsharī law*—

to the custody of her male child till the age of 2 years, and

of her female child till the age of 7 years (*g*).

'The mother is, of all persons, the best entitled to the custody of her infant child during marriage and after separation from her husband, unless she be an apostate, or wicked, or unworthy to be trusted.'(*h*)

Although the mother has the custody of a child of tender years, this does not imply that the father has no rights whatever. The nature and extent of the mother's right of custody were considered by the Privy Council in *Imambandi* v. *Mutsaddi*, and it was said:

It is perfectly clear that under Mahomedan Law the mother is entitled only to the custody of the person of her minor child up to a certain age according to the sex of the child. But, she is not

(*f*) Mulla §§349-51 gives the substance of the Act.

(*ff*) Classical, *ḥaḍāna;* legal, *ḥiḍ-*; loosely spelt in India *hizanut*, from the Persianized form, *Ency. of Islam*, III (rev. ed.), 16, *per* de Bellefonds.

(*g*) Tyabji §238; Mulla §352. Some Hanafi texts mention other ages as well: but this is the rule in India. *Fat. Law* §§279-80.

(*h*) Baillie, I, 435. For a discussion of the rights of the mother, see *Atia Waris* v. *Sultan Ahmad* PLD 1959 (W.P.) Lahore 205.

the natural guardian; the father alone, or, if he be dead, his executor (under the Sunni law) is the legal guardian (*i*).

Thus, where the father and mother are living together, their child must stay with them and the husband cannot take the child away with him; nor can the mother take it away without the permission of the father, even during the period when she is entitled to the custody of the child. Where the child is in the custody of one of its parents, the other is not to be prevented from seeing and visiting it. The father's supervision over the child continues in spite of the child being under the care of female relations, for it is the father who has to maintain the child (*j*).

Disqualifications. A minor cannot act as a guardian, except in the case of his own wife or child. If one of the parents is a non-Muslim, the other is entitled to the custody of the child.

Incidents. As regards the mother or a female guardian, marriage to a person not related to the child within the prohibited degrees is a bar to guardianship; so also, immorality or adultery, or neglect to take proper care of the child. 'A person is not worthy to be trusted who is continually going out and leaving the child hungry' (*k*). The ancient doctor would obviously have frowned upon a modern society mother who goes out for bridge (or social service) in the morning, has lunch with a friend and comes home late in the evening after a dance at the club.

A mother does not lose the custody of her infant children merely because she is no longer the wife of her former husband (*l*); but where she marries a second husband, the custody of such children normally belongs to her former husband, especially where he is otherwise a fit and proper person to be appointed a guardian of the person of his

(*i*) (1918) 45 I.A. 73, 83; *Cases*, 264.
(*j*) Tyabji §238, com.
(*k*) Baillie, I, 435.
(*l*) *Rashida Begum* v. *Shahab Din* PLD 1960 (W.P.) Lahore 1142, a curious case where, it may be pointed out with deference, the judge has introduced irrelevant considerations regarding the Koran and traditions; the only portion which need be perused is §§1-3 and 40-1.

children (*m*); and even a step-cousin can be preferred by the court (*mm*).

On account of disputes relating to the properties belonging to the petitioner, Zynab, she and her husband, Mohammad Ghouse, resided separately in the city of Madras. There were four children of the marriage, three daughters and one son, the youngest child. Their ages were seven, five, three and one year and ten months, respectively. For some time Ghouse married a second wife, but the marriage was dissolved by *khul'*. All the children resided with the mother, Zynab, but one day the husband came and forcibly took away two of the children, a girl aged five and the boy, aged one year and ten months. Zynab thereupon preferred a petition under the Guardians and Wards Act for the custody of her two children. It was held that she was entitled to the custody of her children and the fact that she stayed separately from her husband was not a disqualification (*n*).

Other relations. Failing the mother (by absence or disqualification), the following female relations are entitled to custody in order of priority: (i) mother's mother, how high soever; (ii) father's mother, how high soever; and (iii) full sister and other female relations including aunts (*o*). A female relation of a minor, on marrying a stranger, does not suffer from an absolute disqualification. She only loses her preferential right, and where there is no other suitable person, she may be appointed a guardian by the court in the last resort (*p*).

Failing the mother and female relations, the following

(*m*) *Mir Mohamed Bahauddin* v. *Mujee Bunnissa Begum* A.I.R. (1952) Mad. 280; Mulla §§352, 354. Custody must however be distinguished from guardianship, and if for any reason the mother is deprived of custody, the right to custody revives, and till the child attains the prescribed age, the custody belongs to the mother's mother. Tyabji §252; Baillie, I, 431, 436.

(*mm*) *Mohd. Amin* v. (*Mst.*) *Ateeka Banu* A.I.R. (1963) Jam. and Kash. 82.

(*n*) *Zynab Bi* v. *Mohammad Ghouse* A.I.R. (1952) Mad. 284.

(*o*) For details see Tyabji §239; Wilson §107.

(*p*) (*Mst.*) *Johara Khatun* v. *Amina Bibi* (1957) 62 Cal. W.N. 357.

male relations are entitled to the custody of a Muslim child in order of priority: (i) the father; (ii) nearest paternal grandfather; (iii) full brother; (iv) consanguine brother and other paternal relations (*q*). The custody goes to the nearest male paternal relative, reckoning proximity in the same order as for inheritance (*r*).

The father and, failing the father, the paternal relatives mentioned above are entitled to the custody of boys over seven and unmarried girls above the age of puberty.

The husband of a wife who has not attained puberty is not entitled to the custody of his wife in preference to the wife's mother (*s*).

Sex. The general principle is that no male is entitled to the custody of a female minor unless he is related to her by consanguinity within the prohibited degrees; in addition, profligacy is a disqualification (*t*).

Illegitimate child. Macnaghten says:

> A bastard belongs legally speaking to neither of its parents, and it is in every sense of the word *filius nullius*; but for the purpose of securing its due nourishment and support, it should, until it has attained the age of seven years, be left in charge of the mother. After that age it may make its own election with which of the parents it will reside, or it may live apart from them altogether (*u*).

Gohar Begam was a singing woman in the keeping of one Trivedi, a Hindu. She was the unmarried Muslim mother of a natural daughter, Anjum, acknowledged by Trivedi as his daughter. Anjum was sent to stay with a friend of her mother, Nazma Begam, who later refused to part with her claiming that she had great affection for the child and had sufficient

(*q*) Tyabji §§239 sqq.; Mulla §355.
(*r*) Wilson §109; Mulla, loc. cit. If the child is a female the guardianship goes to the nearest male paternal relative *within the prohibited degrees*, Tyabji §254. As to Shiite law, Tyabji 245 sqq.
(*s*) Tyabji §250; Mulla §356.
(*t*) Tyabji §254; Mulla §355.
(*u*) Macnaghten, 298-9 (Case XLV). Mulla §358 is too brief and does does not give accurately the substance of what Macnaghten says. *Fat. Law* §361.

means to look after Anjum. It was held by the Supreme Court that the mother of an illegitimate daughter is in Muhammadan law entitled to its custody; that the refusal to restore the child to its mother was illegal detention within the meaning of Sec. 491, Criminal Procedure Code; that a dispute as to the paternity of the child was irrelevant for the purpose of the application; that before making the order for custody the court will consider the welfare of the child; that the fact that a person has a remedy under the Guardians and Wards Act is no justification for denying him the remedy under Sec. 491 of the Criminal Procedure Code; that it is well established in England that in issuing a writ of *habeas corpus* a court has power in the case of an infant to direct its custody to be placed with a certain person; and that the Supreme Court will interfere with the discretionary powers of the High Court if the discretion was not judicially exercised.

The order of the High Court of Bombay was reversed and Anjum was handed over to her mother, Gohar Begam (*v*).

§34. Guardianship of Property

Legal guardians. In Sunnite law, the father is the guardian of the minor's property; failing him, in order of priority, the following are entitled: (i) the father's executor; (ii) the father's father; (iii) the paternal grandfather's executor (*w*). These are the legal guardians of the property of the minor. It must be emphasized that the substantive law of Islam does not recognize any other relatives, such as the mother, the uncle or brother, as legal guardians, but they may be appointed by the court (*x*).

(*v*) *Gohar Begam* v. *Suggi alias Nazma Begam* [1960] 1 S.C.R. (India) 597; *Cases*, 275.

(*w*) The Hanafi texts distinguish the powers of the father from those of any other guardian, and subdivide fathers according to their powers of judgment. It is unnecessary to go into these details in a work of an elementary character.

(*x*) *Imambandi* v. *Mutsaddi* (1918) 45 I.A. 73, 84; *Cases*, 260, 266; Tyabji §259; Wilson §112; Mulla §359.

Guardians appointed by the court. Failing the above, the court is entitled to appoint a guardian; and in the exercise of its judgment it may appoint the mother or some other person as such guardian, for a woman is under no disqualification to be so appointed (*y*).

De facto guardian. A person, not being a legal guardian or clothed with the authority of a guardian by the court, may place himself in the position of a guardian by intermeddling with the property of the minor. Such a person is called a *de facto* guardian, as distinguished from the *de jure* guardians who are, as we have seen above, (i) the legal guardians and (ii) guardians appointed by the court. Such *de facto* guardians are merely custodians of the person or the property of the minor, and have no rights but only obligations. Neither the mother, nor the brother, nor the uncle can, without the authority of the court, deal with the property of a minor (*z*).

The minor may be the owner of immovable or movable property. As to—

(A) ***Immovable Property***

(i) The *legal* guardian cannot sell the immovable property of the minor except where he can obtain double its value; or where it is necessary for the maintenance of the minor; or where there are debts and legacies to be paid, and there are no other means; or where the expenses of the property exceed the income; or where the property is falling into decay (*a*). (ii) A guardian appointed by the court has no power to sell or mortgage without the permission of the court. A wrongful disposal contrary to the provisions of the Guardians and Wards Act, 1890, is voidable (*b*). Nor can a guardian pur-

(*y*) Tyabji §§259, 261; Mulla §360; (*Mst.*) *Johara Khatun* v. *Amina Bibi* (1957) 62 Cal. W.N. 357.

(*z*) Tyabji §261; *Musali Khan* v. *Nazir Ahmad* PLD 1952 (W.P.) Peshawar 1.

(*a*) Macnaghten cited by the Privy Council, see Tyabji §274 com.; Mulla §362.

(*b*) Mulla §363. The most exhaustive discussion of the powers of guardians appointed by the court will be found in Tyabji §§265 sqq.

chase property on behalf of the minor (*c*). (iii) A *de facto* guardian has no power to sell the property of a minor; such a sale is a nullity (*d*). A *de facto* guardian cannot refer disputes relating to immovable property to arbitration (*e*); nor can a Muslim mother, who has no authority to act as a guardian of the property of the minor, refer matters to arbitration, without leave of court, and without getting herself appointed as a legal guardian (*f*).

The leading case on the subject is *Imambandi* v. *Mutsaddi* (*g*). One Ismail Ali Khan died in March 1906, possessed of considerable landed property. He left three widows, *A*, *B* and Zohra, and several children by each widow. Zohra had two children, a son and a daughter. In June 1906, Zohra conveyed for Rs10,000 the shares of herself and her children to certain purchasers. The purchasers applied for mutation of names in the local registers, and the two widows *A* and *B*, and their children, opposed them. The purchasers from Zohra filed a suit claiming that Zohra was the acknowledged wife and her children the legitimate children of Ismail Ali Khan and that Zohra, acting on her own and her children's behalf, could lawfully alienate the property. It was held by the Privy Council that the mother had no power to alienate the property, for she was not the legal guardian.

Mr Ameer Ali, in delivering the judgment of the Board, lays down that the mother in Muhammadan law is only entitled to the custody of a minor and is not the natural guardian. The father is the legal guardian (*h*). Speaking of *de facto* guardians, he says, 'It is difficult to see how the situation of an unauthorized guardian is bettered by describing him as a "de facto" guardian. He may, by his de facto guardianship, assume important responsibilities in relation

(*c*) Tyabji §274.
(*d*) Mulla §364; *Jamadar Mian* v. *Amir Hassan* A.I.R. (1957) Pat. 213; *Musali Khan* v. *Nazir Ahmad* PLD 1952 (W.P.) Peshawar 1.
(*e*) *Mohammad Ejaz* v. *Md. Iftikhar* (1931) 59 I.A. 92.
(*f*) *Johara Bibi* v. *Mohammad Sadak* A.I.R. (1951) Mad. 997.
(*g*) (1918) 45 I.A. 73; *Cases*, 260.
(*h*) ibid p. 83.

to the minor's property, but he cannot thereby clothe himself with legal power to sell it.' (*i*) The judgment then proceeds to lay down who are the legal guardians in the absence of the father, and the important distinction which the *Hedaya* makes between dealing with the immovable and the movable property of the minor (*j*). Curiously enough, one who intermeddled with the property of another was known by the term 'fazuli' (or *fazoolee*, strictly *fuḍūlī*) in early times, and yet is known by the undeservedly dignified title of *de facto* guardian in modern law (*k*). Summing up, he says:

> For the foregoing considerations their Lordships are of opinion that under the Mahomedan law a person who has charge of the person or property of a minor without being his legal guardian, and who may, therefore, be conveniently called a 'de facto guardian', has no power to convey to another any right or interest in immovable property which the transferee can enforce against the infant; nor can such transferee, if let into possession of the property under such unauthorized transfer, resist an action in ejectment on behalf of the infant as a trespasser. It follows that, being himself without title, he cannot seek to recover property in the possession of another equally without title (*l*).

Mother as de facto *guardian.* In *Venkama Naidu* v. *S. V. Chisty* (*m*), the minor's father, together with other co-sharers, created a mortgage on the suit properties. Later after the father's death, the mother, as guardian of the minor, and other co-sharers, executed a sale-deed. It was held (1) that the sale-deed executed by the mother was void and inoperative under the Muhammadan law, but (2) that where a Muslim minor seeks to recover property sold by his unauthorized guardian professing to act on his behalf, he seeks an adjudication that the sale is void and without such a declaration he cannot obtain the property; (3) that in such cases, the maxim that 'he who seeks equity must do equity' clearly applies,

(*i*) ibid., p. 84, quoting an earlier judgment of Lord Robson.
(*j*) (1918) 45 I.A. 73, 84-5.
(*k*) ibid., p. 87.
(*l*) ibid., pp. 92-3.
(*m*) A.I.R. (1951) Mad. 399.

and the court has power under Sec. 41 of the Specific Relief Act to award compensation if the justice of the case so requires.

The same High Court (Madras) has held that while the alienation by a mother of immovable property of a minor is void, where there is a joint sale of property held by the minor in common with other major heirs, the sale is valid so far as the shares of the major heirs is concerned (*mm*).

But the Patna High Court has taken a different view. In *Kharag Narain* v. *Hamida Khatoon* (*n*), it was held that since such a deed was void, no compensation need be paid by the minor, and no discretion need be exercised under Sec. 41 of the Specific Relief Act.

A different set of circumstances arose in Nagpur. It was affirmed that a Muslim mother is not the legal guardian capable of dealing with the property of her minor children. But a Muslim mother, if she is appointed a *guardian ad litem*, is not required to obtain permission of the District Judge under Sec. 29 of the Guardians and Wards Act for transferring the property of the minor in order to settle amicably a dispute before the court. All that she has to do is to obtain the permission of the court itself. The Collector is not such a court, but he has certain powers of the court conferred on him. If therefore the matter fell within the jurisdiction of the Collector and was decided by him, the permission thus granted would also be for the larger purposes of the compromise. The sale, being not merely by a *de facto* guardian, but by a *guardian ad litem*, with the consent and approval of the Collector, was held to be binding on the minor (*o*).

Similarly, the brother has no such right. A Muslim died leaving a will, there being four grandsons who were brothers. There was nothing in the will to show that any of the brothers was to act as a guardian for the others during their minority.

(*mm*) *Maimunnissa Bibi* v. *Abudul Jabbar* A.I.R. (1966) Mad. 470.

(*n*) A.I.R. (1955) Patna 475; see also *Md. Zāfir* v. *Amiruddin* A.I.R. (1963) Pat. 108.

(*o*) *Babu Gyanu* v. *Mohammad Sardar* A.I.R. (1955) Nag. 192.

It was held that the three eldest brothers, not being legally entitled to act in the absence of testamentary appointment, had no power to sell their minor brother's property for the purpose of satisfying a mortgage debt (*p*).

Purchase of immovable property. The guardian of a minor has no right to make an agreement for the purchase of immovable property on behalf of the minor; such an agreement is void by Indian law (*q*).

A Full Bench of the Hyderabad High Court has considered the question: 'Whether a minor who has agreed to purchase property through his guardian can bring a suit for specific performance of the contract.' The majority M. S. Alikhan and Siddiqi J.J. answered the question as follows:

'No', but if the guardian is a *de jure* guardian and competent to bind the minor by his contract, and the contract is for the benefit of the minor, then 'yes'.

Deshpande J., however, dissented and made a distinction between a contract for sale and a contract for purchase of property. The former, according to him, may be legal in certain circumstances; but the latter, not. In view of the difference of opinion, it is difficult to state the law with certainty. But, with respect, it is submitted that in view of the Privy Council decision, the minority judgment appears to be preferable (*r*).

(B) *Movable Property*

A legal guardian of the property of a minor has the power to sell or charge the movable property of the minor for the minor's necessities (*s*), such as food, clothing and nursing; and a *de facto* guardian has similar rights (*t*). But a guardian appointed by the court has larger powers. He has, however,

(*p*) *Mata Din* v. *Ahmad Ali* (1911) 39 I.A. 49; *Mohd. Amin* v. *Vakil Ahmed* [1952] S.C.R. 1133.

(*q*) *Mir Sarwarjan* v. *Fakhruddin* (1912) 39 I.A. 1; Mulla §365; Tyabji §274.

(*r*) *Amir Ahmmad* v. *Meer Nizam Ali* A.I.R. (1952) Hyd. 120.

(*s*) For necessities in English law, see *Anson on Contracts*, 18th ed., 126.

(*t*) *Imambandi's case*.

to deal with the property of the minor as carefully as would a man of ordinary prudence if it were his own (*u*).

Termination of Guardianship

No person is entitled to the custody of a child after it has attained puberty. Puberty is the age of majority in Islam, and in the absence of evidence it is attained at the age of 15 (*v*). No person is entitled to the custody of a virgin after she has attained puberty and discretion (*w*); if she is married, she is then capable of being taken to the house of the husband. Hence, guardianship in Islam terminates at puberty.

A guardian appointed by the court may for sufficient reason be removed or he may resign. In a fit case the court is entitled to appoint a person other than the legal guardian if the legal guardian is, in the opinion of the court, unfit for the responsibility of guardianship (*x*).

§35. Guardianship in Marriage

'Marriage,' the Prophet is reported to have said, 'is committed to the paternal kindred,' and relations stand in the same order in point of authority to contract minors in marriage as they do in point of inheritance (*y*). Ameer Ali shows that *wilāyat al-ijbār* or *patria postestas* is not a peculiarity of Islamic law. The distinguishing feature of Islamic jurisprudence is that it empowers a father to impose the status of marriage on his minor children. This power of imposition is called *jabr*; the abstract right of guardianship *wilāyat* (or *wilāya*), and the guardian so empowered is known as *walī*. The right in varying forms was recognized both by the pre-Islamic Arabs and Jews; and under the Muhammadan law of all schools, the father has the power to give his children

(*u*) Guardians and Wards Act, 1908, Sec. 27. A full discussion of the powers of guardians will be found in Wilson §§113 sqq.; Tyabji, pp. 244 sqq. and Mulla §§366-8.

(*v*) Tyabji §280. (*w*) Tyabji §281. (*x*) Tyabji §§282 sqq.

(*y*) Wilson §93, comment, based on the *Hedaya* and *Fatāwā 'Ālamgīrī*. See generally, Wilson §§90-96A; Ameer Ali, II, 234 sqq.; Tyabji §§63 sqq.; *Fat. Law* §§52 sqq.

of both sexes in marriage without their consent, until they reach the age of puberty—known as *bulūgh* (z).

We have seen above that guardianship may be of the person or of property; in both these cases, guardians can be appointed by the court in certain circumstances. It is to be noted, however, that in respect of marriage guardianship, no one can be appointed by the court. It is the substantive law itself that declares who, for the purposes of marriage, possesses the *patria potestas*; the court cannot appoint a *walī* for marriage although, in some cases, the *kazi* himself could act as a marriage guardian (*a*).

A minor can only be given in marriage by a marriage guardian (*walī*); minority, in the absence of specific proof, terminates at the age of 15 (*b*). A guardian must be (i) a person who has attained puberty, (ii) of sound mind, and (iii) a Muslim (*c*). It is extremely doubtful if a non-Muslim can be a guardian for the marriage of a Muslim girl (*d*).

The following persons are entitled, in order of priority, to act as guardians in marriage: (i) the father (*e*), (ii) father's father, h.h.s., (iii) the brother and other collaterals according to the priorities in the laws of inheritance (i.e. *'aṣabāt*, Agnatic Heirs), (iv) the mother and maternal relations, and finally (v) the ruling authority, that is, the *kazi* or the court (*f*).

In Fatimid law, where the father and the grandfather of a virgin coexist, the grandfather has the prior right (*ff*).

A minor was married with the consent of a remoter relation, but without the consent of a nearer one who was the proper legal guardian. The consent of the legal guardian was not obtained, nor was the marriage ratified by him. *Held*, that such a marriage was void, and even consummation could not remove the taint of its total invalidity (*fff*).

(*z*) Ameer Ali, II, 234-5.
(*a*) Tyabji §65; Ameer Ali, II, 243.
(*b*) Ameer Ali, II, 235; Wilson §§91, 92; Mulla §§270, 271.
(*c*) Tyabji §64. (*d*) Wilson §95; Tyabji, loc. cit., com., Mulla §271.
(*e*) Tyabji §65.
(*f*) Ameer Ali, II, 242-3; Tyabji, loc. cit.; Wilson §93; Mulla §271.
(*ff*) *Fat. Law* §§57 (ii), 64, 65.
(*fff*) *Ayub Hasan* v. *Akhtari* A.I.R. (1963) All. 525.

A judge, however, cannot marry the girl to himself, for it would be a marriage without a guardian. In his personal concerns he is a mere subject and the guardianship devolves on the person above him, that is the *walī*. 'Nay, the Caliph himself is no more than a subject in things that regard himself.'(*g*) This appears to be a salutary safeguard against the unlimited powers of an amorous or dishonest *kazi*.

A person, if married during minority, has, on attaining majority, the right to terminate the marriage by exercising the 'option of puberty'(*h*); if he is still unmarried, guardianship terminates, and such person has the absolute right to contract a lawful marriage. This rule applies both to men and to women, but there is a difference of opinion on the point regarding women.

The right of *jabr* in general terminates on the attainment of puberty. The Hanafis and Ithnā 'Asharī Shiites hold that the right of *jabr*, in the case of males as in that of females, continues only until they have arrived at the age of puberty. After that age a Hanafi or an Ithnā 'Asharī female can marry without a guardian. The Mālikīs, Shāfi'īs and Fatimid Shiites, on the other hand, hold that *jabr* continues in the case of females until they are married and emancipated from parental control (*i*). Hence, a Mālikī, Shāfi'ī, or a Dā'ūdī or Sulaymānī Bohora virgin who has attained majority cannot marry without a guardian and her only remedy is, as in the case of *Muhammad Ibrahim* v. *Gulam Ahmed* (*j*), to change over to the Hanafi school and marry according to its tenets.

As to marriage guardians in other schools, see Tyabji §68; and 'Marriage of Minors' in (1936) 38 Bombay Law Reporter, Journal 41-3; and among the Dā'ūdī and Sulaymānī Bohoras, see *Da'ā'im*, II §807 sq.; and *Fat. Law* §§52-68. For a Shāfi'ī case, see *K. Abubukker* v. *V. Marakkar* A.I.R. (1970) Ker. 277.

(*g*) Ameer Ali, II, 243.

(*h*) See above, pp. 94 and 174.

(*i*) Ameer Ali, II, 236; Wilson §392, p. 419.

(*j*) (1864) Bom. H.C.R., O.C.J., 236, discussed fully in Ameer Ali, II, 239. See above, pp. 93-96.

CHAPTER VII

MAINTENANCE

§36. Maintenance Defined
§37. Obligations Arising on Marriage
§38. Obligations Arising out of Blood Relationship

§36. Maintenance Defined

THE first difficulty we encounter in this, as in some other branches of the law, is that the ancient lawyers do not observe the modern distinction between a legal and a moral obligation. Therefore it is not always easy to say what is legally enforceable and what is merely an ethical recommendation (*a*).

Maintenance is called *nafaqa*, and it 'comprehends food, raiment and lodging, though in common parlance, it is limited to the first. There are three causes for which it is incumbent on one person to maintain another—marriage, relationship and property.'(*b*)

The highest obligations arise on marriage; the maintenance of the wife and children is a primary obligation.

The second class of obligations arise when a certain person has 'means' and another is 'indigent'. The test appears to be: 'Are you prevented by Islamic law from accepting alms?' If you are, you are possessed of means; otherwise you are indigent. For instance, in one case, according to the *Fatāwā 'Ālamgīrī*, the possession of a surplus of 200 *dirhams* (60-80 rupees) over a man's necessities was deemed sufficient to prevent him from begging and to include him in the class which is designated as being possessed of 'means'.(*c*)

§37. Obligations Arising in Marriage

(A) *Wife's Right*

According to the ordinary sequence of natural events, the wife comes first. The wife is entitled to maintenance from

(*a*)Tyabji §287, com. (*b*)Baillie, I, 441.
(*c*) Baillie, I, 465; Tyabji §287, esp. p. 255.

her husband although she may have the means to maintain herself, and although her husband may be without means (*d*). The *Durr al-Mukhtār* lays down that the wife is the *aṣl* (root) and the child is the *far‘* (branch), wherefore her priority is established (*e*).

The husband's duty to maintain commences when the wife attains puberty and not before; provided always that she is obedient and allows him free access at all lawful times (*f*). If a wife deserts her husband, she loses her right to maintenance (*ff*). In addition to the legal obligation to maintain there may be stipulations in the marriage contract which may render the husband liable to make a special allowance to the wife. Such allowances are called *kharch-e pāndān, guzārā, mēwa khorī*, etc. (*g*). For example, a husband may have a lawful agreement with the first wife that, on his marrying a second wife, the first wife may reside with her parents and obtain a regular allowance; or similarly, an agreement with a second wife to allow her to reside in her parents' house and to pay her maintenance (*h*).

An agreement for future separation, however, and for the payment of maintenance in such an event is void as against public policy (*i*).

Polygamy is only permissive in Islam. It is *not* the fundamental right of a Muslim to have four wives; therefore it cannot be said that any provision of law in favour of monogamy involves a violation of Art. 25 of the Constitution. The Shariat Act, 1937, does not affect the provisions of Sec. 488, Criminal Procedure Code. Hence, a Muslim wife who resides separately from her husband on his contracting a second marriage, is not disentitled from claiming her statutory right of maintenance under the Criminal Procedure Code (*j*).

(*d*) Tyabji §289(1)(*c*); Fitzgerald, 95; Wilson §53; *Fat. Law* §170 sqq.
(*e*) Tyabji §312; *Fat. Law* §§195-97.
(*f*) Tyabji §298; Mulla §277. (*ff*) *Fat. Law* §174.
(*g*) See §15 1.(ii) above; Tyabji §298,(4); Mulla §280.
(*h*) Mulla, loc. cit.
(*i*) *Bai Fatma* v. *Alimahomed* (1913) 37 Bom. 280.
(*j*) *Badruddin* v. *Aisha Begum* (1957) All. L.J. 300; *Itwari* v. *Asghari, Cases*, 188, 192 (9).

A Muslim wife has a just ground for refusal to live with her husband and she can claim separate maintenance against him where he has taken a second wife or keeps a mistress. This is an independent statutary right, under Sec. 488 of the Code of Criminal Procedure, and is not affected by any provision of the wife's personal law (*k*).

Right to sue. If a husband refuses to pay maintenance, the wife is entitled to sue for it. Her right may be based on the substantive law or she may sue under the Code of Criminal Procedure, 1908, Sec. 488 (as amended by Act XXVI of 1955), in which case the court cannot order the husband to pay more than a sum of Rs 500 per month (*l*). But the wife is not entitled to past maintenance, except under Shiite and Shāfi'ī law, or where there is a distinct agreement (*m*). In fixing the sum by way of maintenance, the *Hedaya* and *Fatāwā 'Ālamgīrī* lay down the rule that the judge in exercising his discretion should consider the rank and the circumstances of both the spouses, a rule which appears to be eminently fair and just (*n*).

Duration of right. The wife's right to maintenance commences on divorce, or when *she comes to know* of the divorce, and ceases on the death of her husband, for her right of inheritance supervenes. The widow is therefore not entitled to maintenance during the *'idda* of death. It is otherwise in the case of divorce, where she is entitled to maintenance ducing *'idda* (*o*). A widow is not one of the *ayāl* (*oo*) which means 'wife, children, and other dependants'(*p*).

Failure to Maintain, Desertion. Under the Dissolution of Muslim Marriages Act, 1939, Sec. 2(ii), a wife is entitled to dissolution if the husband has failed or neglected to provide maintenance for a period of two years. The older

(*k*) *Sarwari* v. *Shafi Mohammad* [1957] 1 All. 255.
(*l*) Tyabji §298; Mulla §278.
(*m*) Tyabji §311.
(*n*) Tyabji §299.
(*o*) Tyabji §§302 sq.; *Mohd. Shamsuddin* v. *Noor Johan* A.I.R. (1955) Hyd. 144; Mulla §279; *Chandbi* v. *Badesha* (1960) 62 Bom. L. R. 866; *Fat. Law* §§177 sqq.
(*oo*) Loose spelling of *'iyāl,* sing. *'ā'ila*, which means 'family'.
(*p*) *Rashidunnissa* v. *Ata Rassol* A.I.R. (1958) All. 67, 73.

rule, however, was different. In Hanafi law neither inability, nor refusal, nor neglect to maintain were sufficient grounds, but the schools of Imām Mālik and Imām Shāfi'ī considered these as proper grounds for granting dissolution (*q*).

For further details see Ameer Ali, II, 405 sqq., Tyabji §§298 sqq. and §26, above.

(B) *Children and Descendants*

A father is bound to maintain his sons until they attain puberty (*r*), and his daughters until they are married. He is also responsible for the upkeep of his widowed or divorced daughter. The father is not bound to provide separate maintenance for a minor son who refuses to live with him without reasonable cause (*s*); nor is an unmarried daughter entitled to separate maintenance unless the circumstances are such as to justify her in staying away (*t*). But the father's obligation is not lessened by the child being in the *ḥiḍāna* (custody) of the mother. An adult son need not be maintained unless he is infirm.

If the father is poor, the mother is bound to maintain the children. And, failing her, it is the duty of the paternal grandfather (*u*). Thus grandchildren and other lineal descendants also possess rights of maintenance.

(C) *Daughter-in-law*

A father-in-law is under no obligation to maintain his widowed daughter-in-law (*v*).

(*q*) Fitzgerald, 95; Ameer Ali, II, 413 sqq., recommended that the Shāfi'ī rule be applied in the case of Hanafis.

(*r*) Wilson was of the opinion that a father was bound to maintain his sons till the age of 18. Mulla took a contrary view and said that his obligation ceases when the son completes the age of 15. This question has so far not been settled by judicial authority, Wilson §§140, 142; Mulla §370; *Fat. Law* §§182 sqq.

(*s*) *Dinsab Kasimsab* v. *Mahmad Husen* (1944) 47 Bom. L.R. 345.

(*t*) *Bayabai* v. *Esmail* [1941] Bom. 643.

(*u*) Fitzgerald, 96; Mulla §370; Tyabji §§315 sqq.

(*v*) *Mahomed Abdul Aziz* v. *Khairunnissa Abdul Gani* (1948) 52 Bom. L.R. 133.

(D) *Illegitimate Child*

A father is not bound to maintain an illegitimate child; but in the Hanafi school the mother is bound to support her natural son or daughter. The Code of Criminal Procedure, Sec. 488 (as amended by Act XXVI of 1955), provides that the putative father of an illegitimate child can be ordered to pay a sum not exceeding Rs 500 per month by way of maintenance (*w*).

The natural daughter of a Muslim father and a Harijan lady is not entitled to claim maintenance from the putative father or the assets left by him, apart from any statutory rights which she may possess. In this respect there was agreement between the principles of Hindu and Muhammadan law. The case law was fully considered, and it was further held that whatever may be the moral or ethical obligation of the putative father, the daughter's right was not judicially enforceable (*x*).

§38. Obligations Arising out of Blood Relationship

(1) *Ascendants*. A person in easy circumstances is bound to maintain his indigent parents, and also his grandparents, paternal as well as maternal (*y*).

(2) *Other relations*. The general principle is laid down in the *Fatāwā 'Ālamgīrī*:

> Every relative *within the prohibited degrees* is entitled to maintenance, provided that, if a male, he is either a child and poor, or, if adult, that he is infirm or blind and poor, and if a female, that she is poor whether a child or adult. The liability of a person to maintain these relatives is *in proportion to his share in their inheritance*, not (of course) his actual share, for no one can have any share in the inheritance of another till after his death, but his capacity to inherit (*z*).

(*w*) Tyabji §289(2).

(*x*) *Pavitri* v. *Katheesumma* A.I.R. (1959) Kerala 319.

(*y*) Tyabji §§290 sq.; Wilson §150; Mulla §§371, 372; *Fat. Law* §§185-87.

(*z*) Baillie, I, 467, italics mine; Mulla §373; *Fat. Law* §196.

The main ground of liability is therefore the capacity to inherit; but there is an important distinction to be borne in mind. Poor or not, a man is bound to maintain his wife and children; but distant relatives are only to be maintained if they are poor and he himself is 'in easy circumstances'.(*a*)

Apparently the wife need *never* maintain the husband (*b*).

(*a*) For collaterals see Tyabji §335. Relations by affinity need not be maintained, Tyabji §344.

(*b*) The only direct authority known to me is mentioned in *Fat. Law* §195.

CHAPTER VIII

GIFTS

§39. Policy, Definition

A MAN may lawfully make a gift of his property to another during his lifetime; or he may give it away to someone after his death by will. The first is called a disposition *inter vivos*; the second, a testamentary disposition. Muhammadan law permits both kinds of transfers; but while a disposition *inter vivos* is unfettered as to quantum, a testamentary disposition is limited to one-third of the net estate. Muhammadan law allows a man to give away the whole of his property during his lifetime; but only one-third of it can be bequeathed by will.

The policy of the Mahomedan law appears to be to prevent a testator interfering by will with the course of the devolution of property according to law among his heirs, although he may give a specified portion, as much as a third, to a stranger. But it also appears that a holder of property may, to a certain extent, defeat the policy of the law by giving in his lifetime the whole or any part of his property to one of his sons, provided he complies with certain forms (*a*).

The English term 'gift' is much wider than the Islamic word *hiba*, and the two must not be confused (*b*). The term 'gift' is generic and is applied to a large group of transfers. The word *hiba*, however, is a narrow and well-defined legal

(*a*) *Ranee Khujooroonissa* v. *Mst. Roushun Jehan* (1876) 3 I.A. 291, 307; *Cases*, 302, 308. See the illuminating discussion in Ameer Ali, I, 33 sq.
(*b*) Tyabji §347, com.

concept. *Hiba* is the *immediate and unqualified transfer of the corpus of the property without any return.* The *Durr al-Mukhtār* defines *hiba* as 'the transfer of the right of the property in the substance (*tamlīk al-'ayn*) by one person to another without return (*'iwaḍ*)'.(*c*) 'To make a person the owner of the substance of a thing (*tamlīk al-'ayn*) without consideration is a *hiba* (gift), while to make him the owner of the profits only (*tamlīk al-manāfi'*) without consideration is an *'āriya*.'(*d*)

§40. How Gifts are made—Incidents

The three essentials of a gift are: (i) *declaration* of the gift by the donor (*ījāb*); (ii) *acceptance* of the gift by the donee (*qabūl*); (iii) delivery of *possession* (*qabḍa*) (*e*). Their lordships of the Privy Council have adopted and approved of the following passage in Ameer Ali which lays down the three conditions necessary for a valid gift (*f*): '(1) Manifestation of the wish to give on the part of the donor. (2) The acceptance of the donee, either impliedly or expressly. (3) The taking possession of the subject-matter of the gift by the donee, either actually or constructively.'(*g*)

The first condition involves the question of intention; the second, the consent of the donee; the third is a peculiarity of Islamic law and will be considered separately below. Where there is no real intention to make a gift, the gift fails; there may be, for example, sham gifts, colourable or *benami* transactions. All these must be distinguished from gifts which are legally and properly constituted (*h*).

Fatimid Law. In the Fatimid law, however, following the Mālikī school, a gift is complete and effective *on its acceptance* by the donee, and delivery of possession is not necessary as in Hanafi law, *Da'ā'im* II §1216; *Fat. Law* §302.

(*c*) Ameer Ali, I, 40.
(*d*) ibid., I, 35, citing *Muhammad Faiz Ahmad Khan* v. *Ghulam Ahmad Khan* (1881) 3 All. 490, 492, the leading case on the subject.
(*e*) Ameer Ali, I, 41; Fitzgerald, 201; Tyabji §348; Mulla §149.
(*f*) Ameer Ali, I, 41, based on *Hedaya*, 482; and Baillie, I, 515.
(*g*) *Mohammad Abdul Ghani* v. *Fakhr Jahan Begum* (1922) 49 I.A. 195. 209: *Amjad Khan* v. *Ashraf Khan* (1929) 56 I.A. 213, 218-19.
(*h*) Illustrations will be found in Tyabji §349.

Oral Gifts, Writing, Registration

Writing is not essential to the validity of any gift; in Muhammadan law a gift can be made validly by word of mouth (*i*). 'It is firmly settled that under the Muhammadan law, a gift of immovable properties can be made verbally without recourse to a written document.'(*j*) Sec. 129 of the Transfer of Property Act lays down that Chapter VII of the Act, dealing with gifts, does not apply to gifts made under Muhammadan law. Thus the validity of gifts made by Muslims is to be tested solely by Muhammadan law (*k*).

We must now consider the question of registration. A gift may be made either orally or in writing. In the case of an oral gift, if the conditions necessary in Muhammadan law are all strictly followed, the gift is complete and valid. Thus, *A* makes a declaration of gift of a landed property to *B* in the presence of a large gathering. *B* accepts the gift and *A* hands over the possession of the property then and there to *B*. Here the gift is complete, and no question of writing, much less of registration, arises (*l*).

In order, however, to have proper evidence of the transaction, the gift may be made in writing. Now a writing may be of two kinds: (i) it may merely recite the fact of a *prior gift*; such a writing need not be registered (*m*). On the other hand, (ii) it may itself be the *instrument of gift*; such a writing in certain circumstances requires registration. In the illustration given above, any of the numerous persons present could testify to the gift; but if, instead, there is a declaration, acceptance and delivery of possession, coupled with a formal instrument of gift, it must be registered. Registration is therefore necessary where there is an instrument of gift of immovable property situate in a place where any of the acts

(*i*) Tyabji §350; Mulla §147.
(*j*) Tyabji, p. 298, citing a Calcutta decision.
(*k*) Mulla, loc. cit., com., *Maniran* v. *Mohd. Ishaque* A.I.R. (1963) Pat. 229.
(*l*) The P.C. have upheld an oral gift in *Kamarunnissa Bibi* v. *Hussaini Bibi* (1880) 3 All. 266.
(*m*) *Nasib Ali* v. *Wajed Ali* A.I.R. (1927) Cal. 197.

relating to registration is in force (*n*). Registration, however, by itself, without the other necessary conditions, is not sufficient. For instance, if *A* executes a deed of gift of a piece of land in favour of *B*, and the deed is duly registered, but possession is not delivered to *B*, the gift is incomplete and is therefore void (*o*).

A Muslim in Bihar cannot make an oral gift of an occupancy in contravention of the Bihar Tenancy Act; for, the general rules of Muhammadan law must be deemed to be displaced by the particular provisions of a statute (*p*).

See also *Bye Mukasa* (gifts from husband to wife in lieu of dower), §50.

Gifts with Conditions

In *hiba* the immediate and absolute ownership in the *substance* or *corpus* of a thing is transferred to a donee; hence, where a *hiba* is purported to be made with conditions or restrictions annexed as to its use or disposal, the conditions and restrictions are void and the *hiba* is valid (*q*). The *Fatāwā 'Ālamgīrī* says:

> All 'our' masters are agreed that when one has made a gift and stipulated for a condition that is *fāsid*, or invalid, the gift is valid and the condition void. . . It is a general rule with regard to all contracts which require seisin, such as gift and pledge, that they are not invalidated by vitiating conditions (*r*).

For example (i) *D* makes a *hiba* of a house for the residence of the donee and his heirs, generation after generation, declaring that if the donee sells or mortgages it the donor or his heirs will have a claim on the house, but not otherwise. The donee takes an absolute estate both in Hanafi and in Ithnā 'Asharī law (*s*). (ii) *D* makes a *hiba* on condition that he has an option of cancelling the *hiba* within three days. The *hiba*

(*n*) Tyabji §350.
(*o*) Mulla §§147, 150; Wilson §302.
(*p*) *Bibi Sharifan* v. *Sheikh Salahuddin* A.I.R. (1960) Pat. 297.
(*q*) Tyabji §351.
(*r*) Baillie, I, 546-7.
(*s*) Tyabji, loc. cit., ill. (1).

is valid, and the option void (*t*). (iii) *A* makes a gift of Government promissory notes to *B* on condition that *B* should return one-fourth part of the notes to *A* after a month. The condition relates to a return of part of the corpus. The condition is void and the gift is valid (*u*). (iv) *A* makes a *hiba* of certain property to *B*. The deed of gift lays down the condition that *B* shall not transfer the property. The restraint against alienation is void and *B* takes the property absolutely (*v*).

Some of the earlier decisions of the Indian High Courts had laid down that a life interest is nothing but a gift coupled with a condition, and the tendency was to hold that the gifts were valid and the conditions void. But the modern trend is otherwise, and we shall discuss this fully below, §47—Life Interests.

Future, Conditional and Contingent Gifts

A declaration purporting to transfer certain property by way of *hiba* to the donee at a future time or contingently on the happening of a certain event is void (*w*). The simplest examples are of gifts *in futuro*. *A* makes a gift to *B* of 'the fruit that may be produced by *A*'s palm tree this year';(*x*) or a husband executes a deed purporting to give to his wife and her heirs in perpetuity an annuity of Rs 4,000 out of the future income of certain villages; both of these are bad. In the latter case, Farran J. said, 'The law is express on the subject. A gift cannot be made of anything to be produced *in futuro* although the means of its production may be in the possession of the donor.' The most important factor is that 'the subject of the gift must be actually in existence at the time of the donation', for Muhammadan law insists on physical delivery of possession wherever it is possible (*y*).

(*t*) Tyabji, §351, ill. (4).
(*u*) Mulla §164, ill. (*b*).
(*v*) Mulla, ibid., ill. (*d*).
(*w*) Tyabji §352; Wilson §314; Mulla §§162, 163.
(*x*) Mulla §162, ill. (*a*).
(*y*) Wilson §314; Mulla §162, ill. (*b*).

The general rule is that conditional or contingent gifts are not valid. The expressions 'conditional' and 'contingent' are somewhat ambiguous and require elucidation. A *conditional* gift is a gift depending on the fulfilment of some condition by the donee. For instance, a man may say to *X*, 'If you help me in this affair, I shall give you my house.' The gift takes place, if at all, in the case of *X* rendering help, but not otherwise. Such a gift is void in Muhammadan law.

A *contingent* gift is a gift to take effect on the happening of a contingency; and a contingency is a possibility, a chance, an event which may or may not occur. The word 'contingent' when applied to a use, remainder, devise, bequest or other legal right or interest, implies that no present interest exists, and that whether such right or interest will ever exist depends upon a future uncertain event (*z*). A gift by a Shiite to *A* for life and, in the event of the death of *A* without leaving male issue, to *B*, is, so far as *B* is concerned, a contingent gift and therefore void (*a*). A classical example of a contingent gift is *ruqba*. *D* says: 'My mansion is thy *ruqba*,' that is, 'If you die, it is mine; if I die, it is yours.' Strictly, this is a contingent gift, depending on the donee surviving the doner, and is void (*b*).

Such a gift (*ruqba*) would be valid in Fatimid law, *Fat. Law* §307.

Gift of Insurance Policy

The Insurance Act, IV of 1938, makes a statutory provision whereby any person can, in certain circumstances, assign his policy, his personal law notwithstanding. Sec. 38 deals with the assignment and transfer of insurance policies. The transfer or assignment can be made by endorsement. Such assignment is complete and effectual on the execution of the endorsement, but the insurer has to be given notice.

The commonest form of assignment is by the husband to the wife. To take a simple illustration, a Muslim husband,

(*z*) Shumaker and Longsdorf, *Cyclopedic Law Dictionary* (Chicago, 1940), 239.

(*a*) Mulla §163.

(*b*) How in certain ways it can be construed as a valid transfer is discussed by Tyabji §351, ill. (6).

H, insures himself and assigns his policy to his wife, *W*, with the condition that if *W* predeceases *H*, the assignment will be inoperative, and the interest in it will in that event revert to *H*. This transaction can be looked at from two points of view. It may be considered as creating a valid contractual obligation between the insurer and the assured (*c*); or else it may be regarded as a gift by a Muslim vitiated by a contingency, and therefore invalid under Muhammadan law. It is possible to urge that such an assignment creates no rights *in praesenti*; that the interest of *W* arises only on the contingency that she survives her husband, but not otherwise. Or, it may also be argued that it is a valid gift with a condition annexed; hence the condition is void and the gift valid. It has been held that a conditional assignment of a life policy made by a Muslim prior to 1938 is to be considered a contingent gift, the gift being absolute and the condition void (*d*).

To do away with all these difficulties the Insurance Act, 1938, Sec. 38(7), lays down:

'Notwithstanding any law or custom having the force of law to the contrary, an assignment in favour of a person made with the condition that it shall be inoperative or that the interest shall pass to some other person on the happening of a specified event during the lifetime of the person whose life is insured, and an assignment in favour of the survivor or survivors of a number of persons, shall be valid.'

Thus, a husband assigned policies of insurance to his wife by a valid endorsement on the condition 'that in the event of my said wife predeceasing me, this assignment shall become null and void', and it was held that under the Act such an assignment was perfectly valid (*e*).

In addition to this, the commonest form, two other kinds of assignments can be made. First, *H* may assign his policy to *W*, on the condition that if *W* dies in *H*'s lifetime, the

(*c*) Tyabji §455 has forcefully argued that the matter is outside the pale of Muhammadan law, and such transactions are valid.

(*d*) In *re Khyrunnissa Begum* A.I.R. (1955) Mad. 459.

(*e*) *Sadiq Ali* v. *Zahida Begum* [1939] All. 957. Mulla §144, com.

interest in the policy shall go to *X*; or secondly, *H* may validly assign his policy to *X*, *Y* and *Z*, or the survivor or survivors of them in equal proportions (*f*).

§41. Who can make Gifts—Capacity

Every Muslim who has attained majority and is of sound mind can make a gift (*g*). A woman has the same right to make a gift as a man, and marriage does not entail any disabilities (*h*). The ordinary presumption is that a person making a gift understands what he is doing; but if the donor is a woman designated as *pardanashin*, the presumption does not arise. The suspicion of the court is aroused and the court extends to the woman the same protection that a court of Chancery would to the weak, the ignorant and the infirm. In such circumstances, in order to show that the gift was free from the effects of undue influence, it is necessary for the donee to satisfy the court that the act was the free act of the woman. For this purpose, the proof of independent outside advice is the usual mode of discharging the burden on the donee (*i*).

A *pardanashin* Bohora lady was brought from Nagpur to Burhanpur on the false pretext that her sister's husband was ill. After a fit of hysteria, she was made to affix her signature on a deed of gift, without affording her the opportunity of independent advice. The lady signed the document believing that it was to take effect only after her death. Held, that the

(*f*) Tyabji §§359 and 455. See generally, In *re Khyrunnissa Begum* A.I.R. (1955) Mad. 459.

(*g*) Tyabji §363; Mulla §139.

(*h*) Tyabji §364; Ameer Ali, I, 53. Ameer Ali lays down four conditions: (1) majority, (2) understanding, (3) freedom, and (4) ownership of the property. The third condition need not be considered, because there is no slavery in India now; the fourth condition is self-evident. In modern law no one can make a gift of someone else's property.

(*i*) The Privy Council has given numerous decisions on the position of a *pardanashin* lady; a useful selection will be found in Tyabji §366. Also the observations of Debabrata Mookerjee J. in *Sonia Parapini* v. *Sk. Moula Baksha* [1956] 2 Cal. 579, 583.

transaction was not a voluntary one and the deed was void (*j*). In another case, the deed was upheld. A deed executed by a *pardanashin* lady stands in a peculiar position. The dispositions made must be substantially understood by the donor; the document must be the expression of the will of the maker of the gift. The court must be satisfied that the deed was explained to, and understood by, her. In the Tamil districts of Madras, the Muslims do not observe *parda* with the same rigidity as in some other parts, and thus the gift was held to be valid (*k*).

The exercise of undue influence and its true import was explained in a case from Rajasthan, and the presumption rebutted even where the donor was illiterate, and aged 61 (*kk*).

Gifts may also be made during death-illness, or *mard al-mawt*. This will be considered separately later; see §80 below.

§42. Object (donee)

A gift can be made to any person. In the case of a minor or a lunatic, possession must be handed over to the legal guardian (*l*). A donor *D* desires to make a gift of an immovable property to *M*, a minor. *D* must hand over the possession of the property to *M*'s father, the legal guardian. If possession is handed over to *M*'s brother, or *M*'s mother, the gift fails (*m*).

A gift can be made validly to an heir presumptive; but it is abominable, though not unlawful, to prefer one child to another (*n*); but in the Fatimid school it is permissible to discriminate between the children and give larger gifts to some of them. This rule is based on the practice of such respected

(*j*) *Hussaina Bai* v. *Zohra Bai* A.I.R. (1960) Mad. Pr. 60.

(*k*) *Kairum Bi* v. *Mariam Bi* A.I.R. (1960) Mad. 447.

(*kk*) *Mahboob Khan v. Abdul Rahim* A.I.R. (1964) Raj. 250.

(*l*) Tyabji §413; Mulla §156; Wilson §304.

(*m*) Illustrations will be found in Tyabji, loc. cit.

(*n*) Tyabji §364(2).

Imāms as 'Alī, Ḥusayn b. 'Alī, Muḥammad al-Bāqir and Ja'far al-Ṣādiq (*nn*).

A *hiba*, being the absolute transfer of all rights in property, cannot be made to an unborn person as there is no one to take possession of his interest. But limited interests and usufructs stand on a different footing; they can be created in favour of a person not in being at the time of the grant, provided he is in being when his interest opens out. Thus, if a life interest is granted to *A*, and thereafter to *B*, it is sufficient if *B* is in being at the death of *A* (*o*).

Gifts may be made validly to mosques and charitable institutions like schools. Such gifts are treated as *ṣadaqa* (*p*).

§43. Subject (what property can be given)

For the purpose of the law of gifts, Muhammadan law does not distinguish between ancestral or self-acquired property, realty or personalty, movable or immovable property (*q*). The idea of property, *māl*, is simple; all forms of property over which dominion can be exercised are proper subjects of gift. 'Anything over which dominion or the right of property may be exercised, or anything which can be reduced into possession or which exists as a specific entity or as an enforceable right, or anything, in fact, which comes within the meaning of the word *māl*, may form the subject of gift.' *Choses in action* and incorporeal rights may form the subject of gift equally with corporeal property. 'A debt,' says the *Kifāya*, 'considered with reference to the prospect of payment is *māl* or corporeal property (so much so that *zakāt* is obligatory on it); and it is susceptible of *tamlīk*.'(*r*) Thus actionable claims

(*nn*) *Fat. Law* §301.

(*o*) Illustrations will be found in Tyabji §373; Mulla §141. This is the general principle; a fuller discussion of this topic will be found below when we consider life interests in §47.

(*p*) Tyabji §371.

(*q*) See observations of Sir John Beaumont in *Sardar Nawazish Ali Khan* v. *Sardar Ali Raza Khan* (1948) 75 I.A. 62, 77, 79; *Cases*, 342.

(*r*) Which means, *making owner*. Ameer Ali, I, 64.

and incorporeal property, no less than corporeal property, can be gifted away (*s*).

Equity of redemption. A Muslim mortgagor can make a valid gift of his equity of redemption even if the mortgagee is at the time in possession (*t*).

Spes successionis. We have seen that a future or contingent interest cannot be made the subject-matter of a valid gift; nor can the expectation of succeeding to the estate of a living person (*u*).

Advancement, Joint account. Where a Muslim died leaving deposits in the joint names of himself and his daughter, payable to either or survivor, such deposits did not constitute a gift in the nature of advancement to the daughter in the absence of proof of specific intention. There is a widespread practice in India to make transfers *benāmī*, without the slightest intention to transfer the beneficial interest; hence, the burden of proving the intention of an advancement is on the person who asserts it, though, in the case of close relatives, very little evidence is enough to establish the claim (*v*).

Tenancy-in-common, Joint-tenancy. English law, as we have seen, has had considerable influence in modifying certain applications—if not principles—of Muhammadan law in India. As conveyances of property in larger towns are often in English, the question arises whether, by gift or otherwise, a tenancy-in-common and a joint-tenancy can be created.

It has been held in Bombay that where a gift is made to two persons jointly, without specifying their individual shares, the donors took as tenants-in-common; for the court leans heavily

(*s*) Mulla §144; Wilson §306; *Mohideen* v. *Madras State* [1957] Mad. 893, 901.

(*t*) It is unnecessary in an elementary work to show how Ameer Ali's opinion (see Vol. I, 70 sqq.) has ultimately prevailed in the courts. Wilson §307; Tyabji §381; Mulla §145.

(*u*) Tyabji §382.

(*v*) *Mujtabai Begum* v. *Mahbub Rehman* A.I.R. (1959) Madh. Prad. 359, 364. The law of *benānī* transfers in India was fully discussed by Mallick J. in *Nur-al-Hasan* v. *Amir Hasan* A.I.R. (1962) Cal. 569.

against a joint-tenancy (*w*). But in another case, not involving a gift, the same High Court has laid down that there is nothing in Muhammadan law against the creation of a joint-tenancy, with benefit of survivorship (*x*). It would, therefore, seem that both a tenancy-in-common and a joint-tenancy can be created by appropriate means.

Property held adversely to the donor. A valid gift cannot be made of property held adversely to the donor, because possession cannot be delivered. Such a gift can only be validated, first, by obtaining and delivering physical possession or secondly, by doing everything possible in order to enable the donee to obtain possession (*y*).

X by deed makes a gift of certain lands to *Y*. The lands are in the possession of *Z* and are held adversely to *X*. *X* during his lifetime never obtains possession of the lands. After *X*'s death *Y* sues *Z* to recover possession. The suit must fail, for the gift was never completed by delivery of possession (*z*).

But in certain circumstances the admission of *X* may validate the gift. For instance, *X* makes a gift of immovable property in favour of *Y*. At the time of the gift the property is in the possession of *Z* who claims it adversely to *X*. *Y* sues *Z* to recover possession of the property from him, joining *X* as a party defendant. *X by his written statement admits Y's claim*. *Z* contends that the gift is void, for at the time of the gift *Z* was in possession and no possession was ever given to *Y*. In such a case the gift is valid, for the donor has done everything in his power to complete the gift (*a*).

CORPUS, USUFRUCT. In Muhammadan law there is a clear distinction between a gift of the corpus or substance (*'ayn*) and the gift of the usufruct or the fruits (*manāfi'*) of the property. This distinction, forcefully emphasized by Tyabji,

(*w*) *Mahamad Yusuf* v. *Hasina Yusuf* (1946) 49 Bom L.R. 561; Tyabji §362.

(*x*) *Mahomed Jusub* v. *Fatmabai Jusub* (1946) 49 Bom. L.R. 505.

(*y*) Mulla §146.

(*z*) Mulla, ibid., ill. (*a*).

(*a*) Mulla ibid., ill. (*b*), based on *Mahomed Buksh* v. *Hosseini Bibi* (1888) 15 I.A. 81.

is now accepted by the Privy Council (*b*). The '*ayn*, variously called the substance, or the corpus, or the thing itself, can be given away, and this is called *hiba*. For instance, a man may give away a piece of land or a house or an animal or jewellery. Or, he may give away the *manāfi'* (lit., profits) and these are the produce, fruits, usufruct, or use. This is not *hiba*, but '*āriya*, in its various forms.

The distinction is important when we come to discuss the recent cases regarding life interests, and in this connexion the following remarks of Tyabji must be borne in mind (*c*):

> *Hiba* does not mean the same as 'simple gifts'. Gift is a wide term, applicable to all transfers without consideration: *hiba* is much narrower. The connotation of *hiba* includes within its scope only transfers (without consideration) of the full ownership of determinate objects—of the '*ayn*: s. 347. Hence once a person makes a *hiba*, the property passes out of his control: he cannot exercise any further control over it. He cannot lay down how property, which he has placed beyond his own control, shall be utilized. He cannot provide for a succession of transfers commencing with a *hiba*, because by the first transfer he parts with all his power and control over the subject of transfer. From this it does not follow that in no way can interests limited in duration be created. Subject to what is stated below, such interests can, under the principles of Muslim law, be created by grants of the usufruct for successive periods: under a grant of the usufruct for life the same rights may be given to the grantee as are enjoyed by a life tenant.

Muhammadan law, as it is now received in Indian courts, allows gifts of rights in property not amounting to full ownership. The most important of these is a life interest, which will be considered separately, but the following gifts are considered valid: (i) the right to collect a specified share of the rents of undivided land, (ii) shares in villages under attachment by the Collector for arrears of revenue; (iii) rights in zamindari lands, and a number of others (*d*).

(*b*) *Sardar Nawazish Ali Khan* v. *Sardar Ali Raza Khan* (1948) 75 I.A. 62, 77; *Cases*, 342.

(*c*) Tyabji, p. 333-34. Tyabji had the distinction of being cited by the Privy Council in *Nawazish Ali Khan's Case* in his own lifetime.

(*d*) Tyabji §§376, 379.

Power of Appointment. X, an Ithnā 'Asharī Shiite, bequeathed his property to *A, B* and *C* successively for life, and then provided as follows: 'The last devisee shall have the power to nominate as his successor any one whom he might consider fit from amongst the descendants of each of the three successors.' It was held by the Privy Council that such powers of appointment were unknown to the Muhammadan law, although they had been imported into the Hindu law as administered in India (*e*).

§44. Delivery of Possession

When Necessary

In order to understand the Islamic principle of delivery of possession (*f*) in a gift, it is necessary to remember that 'a gift cannot be implied. It must be express and unequivocal, and the intention of the donor must be demonstrated by his *entire relinquishment* of the thing given.'(*g*) It is for this reason that the Prophet is reported to have said that a gift is not valid without seisin (*h*). Delivery of possession is therefore an essential characteristic of the Islamic law of gifts, for in early times it was a clear and tangible proof that the ownership of the donor had ended and the ownership of the donee had been perfected and could not be questioned. Therefore 'the taking possession of the subject-matter of the gift by the donee, either *actually* or *constructively*' is necessary to complete a gift (*i*).

It is important to observe that the question whether possession was delivered or not is relevant only between the

(*e*) *Sardar Nawazish Ali Khan* v. *Sardar Ali Raza Khan* (above).

(*f*) Possession is called *qabḍa*, and the delivery of possession, *taqbīḍ*, in Islamic law.

(*g*) Macnaghten, 51, No. 8.

(*h*) Tyabji 4th ed., 370, citing *Hedaya*, 482, col. ii.

(*i*) Ameer Ali, I, 41, adopted in *Mohammad Abdul Ghani* v. *Fakhr Jahan Begam* (1922) 49 I.A. 195, 209. The law of possession was fully discussed recently by Hidayatullah J. in *Katheessa Umma* v. *Pathakkalan Narayanath* A.I.R. (1964) S.C. 275. See also *Gulab* v. *Khaleq* [1964] 1 W.R. 47, (P.C.-E. Africa), and *Ibrahim Bivi* v. *K. M. M. Pakkir Mohideen* A.I.R. (1970) Mad. 17, in which this edition was cited.

settlor and the donee, and those claiming under him; a stranger cannot raise the issue where otherwise the gift is lawful (*j*). Delivery of possession, however, is not necessary in Fatimid law, applicable both to the Dā'ūdī and Sulaymānī Bohoras (*jj*).

Registration—of a deed of gift, without delivery of possession, is not enough. Where *A* executes a deed of gift of a dwelling-house belonging to him in favour of *B*, and the deed is registered but possession is not delivered to *B*, the gift fails (*k*).

A gift, in order to be valid, must be made in accordance with the rules of Muhammadan law even where it is evidenced by writing,

> unless all the essential forms are observed, it is not valid according to law. That being so, a deed of gift executed by a Mahomedan is not the instrument affecting, creating or making the gift, but a mere piece of evidence . . .

and as such, *strictly*, it need not be registered according to Indian law (*l*).

Possession, however, may be either actual or constructive. We shall deal with constructive possession a little later.

Actual (*m*) possession must be delivered both of movable and of immovable property. As to movable property, the term usually applied is *'aṭiyya* or *hadiyya*, rather than *hiba*. Money, jewels, clothes and all tangible movable property must be actually transferred to the donee (*n*); a mere entry in a book of account, without any evidence of actual transfer, is not sufficient (*o*). First, in the case of immovable property

(*j*) *Kairum Bi* v. *Mariam Bi* A.I.R. (1960) Mad. 447, 452, following an earlier dictum of Bose J. (Nagpur).

(*jj*) *Fat. Law*, page xxxvi, §302.

(*k*) Mulla §150(2); *Noor Jahan Begum* v. *Muftkhar Dad Khan* A.I.R. (1970) All. 170.

(*l*) per Suhrawardy J., in *Nasib Ali* v. *Wajed Ali* A.I.R. (1927) Cal. 197; *Ghulam Hassan* v. *Sarfaraz Khan* PLD 1956 Sup. Court (Pak.) 309.

(*m*) Or *khāṣ*, as it is called in Indian courts.

(*n*) Wilson §301; Tyabji §402.

(*o*) Tyabji §403.

which is in the exclusive possession of the donor, it is necessary that the donor should physically depart from the premises, and hand over possession formally to the donee, and that the donee should accept such possession. If a person lives in a house and purports to make a gift by saying to the donee 'take possession' or 'I have delivered possession', and no overt act of tender and acceptance of possession takes place, there is no gift (*p*).

Or secondly, the property may be in the possession of tenants. In this case it is sufficient if the donor requires the tenants to attorn to the donee (*q*). If a house is in the possession of tenants, the landlord may give notice to them that the property has been gifted and that in future the rents should be paid to the donee (*r*).

In the case of an equity of redemption, a gift of the equity may be made validly by the mortgagor giving to the mortgagee a proper notice that the ownership in the property has been transferred to the donee, subject to the rights of the mortgagee. In such a case, physical possession need not, because it cannot, be transferred (*s*).

Where the property is in the possession of a trespasser, a mere declaration and acceptance of the gift is not sufficient; there must be either delivery of possession, 'or some overt act by the donor to put it in the power of the donee to obtain possession' (*t*).

When Not Necessary

The general principle is that possession must be handed over; to this rule there are certain qualifications and exceptions which we shall now proceed to consider.

Transfer of possession is not necessary (1) where the donor and the donee reside in the same house; (2) where the gift is

(*p*) Tyabji 404, ill.; Mulla §152. (*q*) Tyabji §405.

(*r*) Cases in Mulla §152(2).

(*s*) Tyabji §407; Wilson §307 gives the history of the controversy; Mulla §145.

(*t*) *Maqbool Alam* v. *Mst. Khodaija* A.I.R. (1966) S.C. 1194, 1197.

from the husband to the wife or vice versa; (3) where the father or the mother makes a gift to a child (*u*); (4) where a guardian makes a gift to the ward; or (5) where a gift is made to a bailee in possession; or (6) where the Fatimid law is applicable (*uu*).

(1) *Residence in the same house.* Where the donor and the donee reside in the same house, the donor can complete the gift without physical transfer of possession; but there must be the unequivocal manifestation by the donor of an intention to transfer exclusive possession to the donee (*v*). A Muslim lady, who had brought up her nephew as her son, executed a deed of gift, in favour of the nephew, of a house in which they were both residing at the time of the gift. The donor never departed from the house physically, nor was the house formally handed over to the donee, but the property was transferred, and the rents were recovered, in his name. It was held that the gift was valid, although there was no physical delivery of possession (*w*).

If, however, certain important steps for divesting ownership were not taken, then the court is entitled to presume that the gift was not complete. For example, a Muslim lady and her nephew resided in a house which belonged to the lady. The lady executed a deed of gift in favour of her nephew. There was no formal delivery of possession; no mutation of names was effected; the nephew continued to live in the house with his aunt; the deed was not delivered to the nephew; the aunt continued to pay the municipal taxes. In these circumstances, it was held that there was no valid gift (*x*).

(2) *Husband to wife.* Where a married couple live in a house which belongs to the husband, the husband may make

(*u*) (*Mst.*) *Natho* v. *Hadayat Begum* [1948] Lahore 197.

(*uu*) *Fat. Law* §302.

(*v*) The leading case on the subject is *Ibhram* v. *Suleman* (1884) 9 Bom. 146. Tyabji §412; Mulla §152(3).

(*w*) *Humera Bibi* v. *Najm-un-Nissa* (1905) 28 All. 147; *Muhammad Yusuf Rowther* v. *Muhammad Yusuf Rowther* A.I.R. (1958) Mad. 527; *Ibrahim Bivi* v. *K. M. M. Pakkir Mohideen* A.I.R. (1970) Mad. 17.

(*x*) *Qamar-ud-din* v. *Mst. Hassan Jan* (1934) 16 Lah. 629.

a gift of the house to the wife, without physical delivery of possession. A strict adherence to formalities would necessitate (i) that the husband and wife should leave the premises; (ii) that the husband should formally hand over vacant possession to the wife; (iii) that the wife should accept such possession and enter into the house as an undisputed monarch. Such a *tamāshā* (y) is not required by the law.

The same rule is applicable in the case of a wife making a gift to the husband (z). The leading case on the subject is *Amina Bibi* v. *Khatija Bibi* (a). There, a husband had made a gift of his house and certain outhouses to his wife. He had made over the keys to the wife, left the house for a few days, to show clearly that possession had been delivered, but had returned afterwards and lived with her till his death. It was held that the gift was valid.

If a gift has been made by the husband to the wife, and the wife's name has been duly entered into the public registers as proprietor, the fact that the husband continues to live in the house or to receive the rents after the gift does not militate against the validity of the gift. The presumption in this case is that the husband acts as the agent of the wife (b). Furthermore, if the deed of gift declares that the husband delivered possession to the wife and the deed is handed over to her and is in her possession, even mutation of names is not necessary (c).

Where a gift was made by a husband to his minor wife by a registered deed, and possession handed over to the minor wife's mother, it was held by the Supreme Court (India) that the gift was valid (cc).

(y) A Hindustani word which may in this context be rendered as 'farce'.

(z) Ameer Ali, I, 115 sqq.; Tyabji §419; Mulla §153.

(a) (1864) 1 Bom. H.C.R. 157. See the discussion of this case in Ameer Ali, I, 115 sqq., who considers the judgment of Sausse C.J. as 'one of the most valuable decisions concerning the question of possession'.

(b) *Ma Mi* v. *Kallander Ammal* (1926) 54 I.A. 23.

(c) *Mohammad Sadiq* v. *Fakhr Jahan* (1931) 59 I.A. 1, 13.

(cc) (*Valia Peedikakkandi*) *Katheessa Umma* v. *Pathakkalan Narayanath* A.I.R. (1964) S.C. 275. The law of possession was fully discussed and laid down.

(3) *Father or Mother to child*; (4) *Guardian to ward*. Where a father or mother makes a gift of immovable property to their minor child, no physical transfer of possession is necessary. The same is the rule between guardian and ward. One reason for the rule is that this would involve the absurdity of the owner of the property (parent) handing over possession to himself as guardian of the child (*d*). In *Ameeroonissa* v. *Abedoonissa,* the Judicial Committee of the Privy Council stated that 'where there is, on the part of the father or other guardian, a real and *bona fide* intention to make a gift, the law will be satisfied without change of possession, and will presume the subsequent holding of the property to be on behalf of the minor'.(*e*) Where, for instance, the gift is made to an infant by a person other than the father or guardian, the gift is rendered complete by the seisin of the father of the infant (*f*).

The real basis of the exception is that delivery of possession is excused only when the legal guardianship of the minor vests in the donor. Thus a gift by a grandfather to his grandson would not be within the exception where the father is alive and has not been relieved of his legal guardianship. A decision of the Privy Council makes this perfectly clear (*g*). One Abdul Rasul had a daughter, Rahimatbai, and she was married to Shaffi. Shaffi had two sons, and Shaffi, his wife and children used to reside with Abdul Rasul. Abdul Rasul made a gift of his landed property to his two grandsons, but no mutation of names was effected; possession was not given to Shaffi, as guardian of his two sons, and Abdul Rasul continued in general management of the property. In these circumstances, the Privy Council held that the exception with regard to delivery of possession in the case of the gift from a

(*d*) Tyabji §417; Wilson §303; Ameer Ali, I, 113, 123; Mulla §155.

(*e*) (1847) 2 I.A. 87, 104; discussed fully in Ameer Ali, I, 113 sqq. and 123 sqq.

(*f*) Ameer Ali, I, 124; Mulla §156.

(*g*) *Musa Miya* v. *Kadar Bux* (1928) 55 I.A. 171. For Pakistan see *Ghulam Hassan* v. *Sarfaraz Khan* PLD 1956 S.C. (Pak.) 309.

father to his minor son should be construed strictly. It does not extend to a gift by a grandfather to his minor grandsons, if their father is alive and has not been deprived of his guardianship, even though the minors have always lived with their grandfather and have been brought up and maintained by him.

On the other hand, where a grandfather makes a gift to his grandchildren, and the father had knowledge of the gift, and also that the income of the movable property was used for the benefit of the minors, the gift was held to be valid (*gg*).

Nor can a mother, who is not a legal guardian, accept such a gift on behalf of her minor children, from their grandfather (*h*). But in Ceylon the *rule* is different, and the Judicial Committee of the Privy Council were in agreement with the Supreme Court of Ceylon, who reached the conclusion that under the Muslim law as received in Ceylon, and in the circumstances of the particular case (where a *fidei commissum* as known to Roman-Dutch law was created), the mother had the necessary authority to accept the gift (*i*).

(5) *Gift to donee in possession.* Where the subject of the gift is in the possession of the donee at the time of the making of the gift, the gift is completed on acceptance, and delivery of possession is unnecessary (*j*). The *Fatāwā ʻĀlamgīrī* says that if the subject of the gift is in the hands of the donee, either as a deposit or *ʻāriya* (commodate loan), or trust (*amāna*), the gift is completed by acceptance, and formal delivery of possession is not necessary; similarly, property in the hands of a tenant, usurper or pledgee (*k*). A piece of cloth is deposited with *R*, who says to the owner, 'Give it to me.' The owner says, 'I have given it to thee.' This is a valid gift (*l*). But if the owner of a house wishes to make a gift of it to his

(*gg*) *Qhamarunnissa* v. *Fathima* A.I.R. (1968) Mad. 367.
(*h*) *Abdul Rehman* v. *Mishrimal Shrimal* [1959] Bom. 1649.
(*i*) *Noorul Muheetha* v. *Sittie Rafeeka Leyaudeen* [1953] A.C. 320.
(*j*) Tyabji §§397, 417(3); Mulla §157.
(*k*) Baillie, I, 522.
(*l*) Tyabji §397, ill.

rent-collector, some overt act of transfer of possession is necessary; for the rent-collector is not in possession of the house; he is merely an agent and, although he may have certain rights, he is not in possession of the property (*m*).

Constructive Possession

Possession in law may be either actual or constructive. Constructive (or symbolical) possession means not actual, but by construction of law; 'that which amounts, in view of the law, to an act, although the act itself is not performed';(*n*) for instance, constructive fraud, constructive notice, constructive crime, constructive possession.

Muhammadan law rightly understood does not insist on delivery of *physical* possession in every case. In the case of chattels and land, or corporeal property generally, actual delivery of possession is necessary. But in the case of incorporeal property and actionable claims, where the property is not susceptible of physical possession, the donor must do everything in his power to show a clear intention of transferring the property effectively to the donee and of relinquishing entirely his own dominion over the property (*o*).

A makes a gift to *B* of a Government promissory note according to the tenor of which the right to receive payment of the sum therein specified and interest passes by delivery and endorsement. The gift is complete as soon as the note has been endorsed and delivered to the donee (*p*). *A* makes a gift to *B* of his zamindari rights. The gift may be completed by mutation of names (*q*).

A hands over to his wife a receipt passed to him by a bank

(*m*) Mulla §157, ill. (*b*).

(*n*) Shumaker and Longsdorf, *Cyclopedic Law Dictionary* (Chicago, 1940).

(*o*) Wilson §306; Tyabji §§395, 407-10; Mulla §§ 148-50, 154; *Kairum Bi* v. *Mariam Bi* A.I.R. (1960) Mad. 447.

(*p*) *Nawab Umjad Ally Khan* v. *Mst. Mohumdee Begum* (1867) 11 M.I.A. 517; *Cases*, 337.

(*q*) Wilson §306, ill. (*a*); Mulla §154, ill. (*b*).

in respect of money deposited by him with the bank and says 'after taking a bath, I shall go to the bank and transfer the papers to your name'. The receipt contains in the margin the words 'not transferable'. *A* dies before the transfer. The gift fails (*r*).

In *Jamil-un-Nissa* v. *Muhammad Zia*, the donor was one of the co-sharers in a village. He was in exclusive possession of a piece of open land, and he executed a deed of gift whereby he made a gift of the land to another co-sharer in the village, and declared in the deed that he had delivered possession to the donee. It was held that there was sufficient delivery of possession to the donee to complete the gift. Sir Shah Muhammad Sulaiman C.J. observed:

> . . . although in order to make the gift complete, delivery of possession is necessary under the Muhammadan law, actual possession is not necessary. All that is required is that steps should be taken to place the donee in a position to take possession effectively and invest her with authority for that purpose. Actual possession is not necessary where the property gifted is not capable of being possessed physically (*s*).

As Balakrishna Aiyar J. says:

> The rules of Mahomedan law do not require that to make a gift valid the donor must have physical possession of the property and must hand over that physical possession to the donee. It is enough if he has got legal possession of the property and transfers to the donee such possession as the matter is susceptible of (*ss*).

In regard to symbolical possession, the handing over of the keys of a house may, in appropriate circumstances, be regarded as sufficient (*t*).

(6) *Where Fatimid Law applicable*. Cadi Nu'mān lays down in the *Da'ā'im* that 'A gift (*hiba*) is valid on its *acceptance* by the donee, whether possession is delivered to him or not,

(*r*) Wilson §306, ill. (c).

(*s*) [1937] All. 609, 612-13.

(*ss*) *Kairum Bi* v. *Mariam Bi* A.I.R. (1960) Mad. 447, 450.

(*t*) Tyabji §410, citing an obiter of Sausse C.J.

and whether the property is divided by metes and bounds or nɔt.' This rule is so far not known in India, but, it is submitted that it applies to Dā'ūdī and Sulaymānī Bohoras (*tt*).

§45. *Mushā‘*

The word *mushā‘* means an 'undivided part' (Baillie) or share, a common building or land (*u*). The general rule is laid down in the *Hedaya*: 'A gift of a part of a thing which is capable of division is not valid unless the said part is divided off and separated from the property of the donor; but a gift of an indivisible thing is valid.'(*v*) An undivided share may be capable of division or otherwise; if it is divisible, then an undivided part cannot form the subject of gift; if it is not divisible, an undivided part can form the subject of gift (*w*).

In Fatimid law, such gifts are vaild on acceptance, and property can be transferred without dividing it by metes and bounds (*ww*).

I. *Property Indivisible*

The gift of an undivided share in property which does not admit of partition is valid (*x*). An undefined share in a small house or a small bath are mentioned as cases of *mushā‘*, a gift of which would be valid (*y*). *A*, who owns a house, makes a gift to *B* of the house and of the right to use a staircase used by him jointly with the owner of an adjoining house. The gift of *A*'s undivided share in the use of the staircase is not capable of division; therefore it is valid (*z*).

(*tt*) *Fat. Law*, Introduction, p. xxxvi, §§302, 304 (*hiba, mushā‘*); §321 (*ṣadaqa*).

(*u*) Tyabji §385 explains the root meaning as being 'confusion'; Ameer Ali, I, 96; Mulla §158.

(*v*) *Hedaya*, 483.

(*w*) Tyabji shows how there is no inherent objection to such gifts, but the objection relates to the doctrine of possession, Tyabji, loc. cit.

(*ww*) *Fat. Law, supra*.

(*x*) Wilson §309; Tyabji §385, expl. i, Mulla §159.

(*y*) Wilson §309.

(*z*) *Kasim Husain* v. *Sharif-un-Nissa* (1883) 5 All. 285.

II. *Property Divisible*

The gift of an undivided share in any property capable of division is, with certain exceptions, incomplete and irregular (*fāsid*), although it can be rendered valid by subsequent separation and delivery of possession (*a*). This is the rule in Hanafi law; but in Shāfi'ī and Ithnā 'Asharī law the gift of *mushā*' is valid provided the donor withdraws his dominion over the property and permits the donee to exercise control (*b*).

Before coming to the illustrations, it is necessary to observe that the spirit of modern law is opposed to this clog on the free transfer of property. In *Sheikh Muhummad Mumtaz* v. *Zubaida Jan* (*c*), Sir Barnes Peacock observes:

> The authorities relating to gifts of mushaa have been collected and commented upon with great ability by *Syed Ameer Ali* in his *Tagore* Lectures of 1884. Their Lordships do not refer to those lectures as an authority, but the authorities referred to shew that possession taken under an invalid gift of mushaa transfers the property according to the doctrines of both the Shiah and Soonee schools, see pages 79 and 85. The doctrine relating to the invalidity of gifts of mushaa is *wholly unadapted to a progressive state of society, and ought to be confined within the strictest rules* (*d*).

For instance, *A*, a partner in a firm, makes a gift of his share of the partnership assets to *B*. The gift is not valid unless the share is divided off and handed over to *B* (*e*). But, where *A* makes a gift of her undivided share in certain lands to *B*, and the share is not divided off at the time of the gift but is subsequently separated and possession thereof is delivered to *B*, the gift although irregular (*fāsid*) in its inception, is deemed valid by subsequent delivery of possession (*f*).

(*a*) Wilson §308; Tyabji §§385; 392; Mulla §160.

(*b*) Tyabji §385, expl. ii; Mulla, loc. cit., note on Shiite law.

(*c*) (1889) 16 I.A. 205, 215.

(*d*) The italics are mine.

(*e*) Mulla, loc. cit., ill. (*e*).

(*f*) *Sheikh Muhummad Mumtaz* v. *Zubaida Jan, supra.*

The rule regarding *mushā'* is not only confined within the strictest limits, but is cut down by numerous exceptions (*g*).

Exception 1. Gift to Co-heir

The rule does not apply where one co-heir makes a gift to another (*h*). A Muslim woman died leaving a mother, a son, and a daughter. The mother made a gift of her unrealized one-sixth share jointly to the deceased's son and daughter. The gift was upheld by the Privy Council (*i*).

Exception 2. Co-sharers in Undivided Land or Zamindari

Ameer Ali has shown that the doctrine of *mushā'* was applicable only to small plots of land, and not to specific shares in large landed properties, like zamindaris in India (*j*). The modern rule is that in this case the rule as to *mushā'* does not apply (*k*). Thus, if *A* and *B* are co-sharers in a zamindari, each having a well-defined share in the rents of undivided land, and *A* makes a gift of his share to *B*, there being no regular partition of the zamindari, the gift is valid.

Exception 3. Gift to Two or More Persons

Although the texts and cases are not always easy to reconcile, it may now be stated with some confidence that if the shares of the donees are clearly and distinctly specified, a gift to two or more persons jointly is valid, notwithstanding that the donor has not divided the property by metes and bounds, and handed over the specific shares to each donee (*l*). Thus, *X* makes a gift of a house to *A* and *B* in equal shares as tenants-in-common. The property is not divided off and,

(*g*) Like the rule in *Rylands* v. *Fletcher*.

(*h*) Wilson §310; Tyabji §§388-90; Mulla §160(1).

(*i*) *Mahomed Buksh* v. *Hosseini Bibi* (1888) 15 I.A. 81; *Azizi* v. *Sona* A.I.R. (1962) Jam. and Kash. 4.

(*j*) Ameer Ali, I, 91 sqq.

(*k*) Wilson §311; Mulla §160, exc. (2). As to an occupancy under the Bihar Tenancy Act, see *Bibi Sharifan* v. *Sheikh Salahuddin* A.I.R. (1960) Pat. 297.

(*l*) Ameer, Ali, I, 98; Wilson §312; Tyabji §§385 (ill. 7) and 390.

although their shares are clearly defined, possession of their specific shares is not given to *A* and *B*. The tenants are given clear notice that the properties have been given away to *A* and *B*, to whom rent is to be paid. The Bombay, Calcutta and Nagpur High Courts have held that such a gift is valid (*m*). In such cases the donees take as tenants-in-common.

A *pardanashin* lady by deed gave the whole of her undivided share in her deceased son's estate, to which she became entitled as his heir along with others, to her daughter and daughter's husband jointly. The real reason of the rule of *mushā'* is to avoid confusion; where there is no likelihood of confusion, the rule cannot be invoked. Joint owners may thus continue to hold the property jointly, without partition, if it is convenient for them, and the doctrine of *mushā'* does not apply in such cases (*n*).

Exception 4. Freehold Property in a Commercial Town, or

Exception 5. Shares in a Land Company

A owns a house in Rangoon. He makes a gift of one-third of his house to *B*. The property being situated in a large commercial town, the gift is valid (*o*). Similarly, in the same case it was held that shares in a land company are not subject to the rule regarding *mushā'* because 'it would be inconsistent with that decision (*Mumtaz Ahmad* v. *Zubaida Jan*, 16 I.A. 205, 215) to apply a doctrine, which in its origin applied to very different subjects of property, to shares in companies and freehold property in a great commercial town'.(*p*)

Exception 6. Periodical payments in the nature of life-grants

Where property is transferred absolutely to certain donees, and it is stipulated that they shall make certain periodical

(*m*) *Ebrahim Alibhai* v. *Bai Asi* (1933) 58 Bom. 254; followed in *Golam Gous* v. *Roujan* (1945) 50 C.W.N. 81 and in *Mahamad Yasuf* v. *Hasina Yasuf* (1946) 49 Bom. L.R. 561; see also *Kalu Beg* v. *Gulzar Beg* [1946] Nagpur 510.

(*n*) *Kairum Bi* v. *Mariam Bi* A.I.R. (1960) Mad. 447; [1960] Mad. 785.

(*o*) *Ibrahim Goolam Ariff* v. *Saiboo* (1907) 34 I.A. 167.

(*p*) ibid., 178.

payments out of the recurring income of the property, such payments do not attract the law of *mushā'*, which in Indian law is to be limited strictly in its application (*q*).

Devices against Doctrine of Mushā'

It must always be remembered that the doctrine of *mushā'* only renders the gift *fāsid* (irregular) but not *bāṭil* (void); and it is therefore possible to employ a device in order to get over it (*r*). Ameer Ali quotes *the Radd al-Muḥtār* as laying down that:

'A gift of a moiety of a house (which would otherwise be bad for *mushā'*) may validly be effected in this way (according to the *Bazazia*), that is, the donor should sell it first at a fixed price, and then absolve the debtor of the debt, that is, the price.'(*s*)

§46. Gift Through the Medium of a Trust

The conception of the trust (*amāna*) apart from gift was well known in Islam, although Islamic law differs in several respects from the modern law (*t*). There is, therefore, no inherent objection to the introduction of the machinery of a trust for effectuating a gift. A gift can be made validly through the medium of a trust. If the gift is *inter vivos*, possession must be handed over to the trustees, else the gift fails (*u*). A Shiite (Ithnā 'Asharī) executes a deed purporting to transfer certain immovable properties to trustees for the benefit of his wife and children. The deed is duly executed by the settlor and registered. The properties are not transferred to the names

(*q*) *Mohideen* v. *Madras State* [1957] Mad. 893, 901.

(*r*) Ameer Ali, I, 105, 106.

(*s*) ibid., 106. This dictum has been followed in an Allahabad case, *Ahmadi Begum* v. *Abdul Aziz* (1927) 49 All. 503.

(*t*) Tyabji §399, comment, citing Mr. Ameer Ali in *Vidya Varuthi* v. *Balusami Ayyar* (1921) 48 I.A. 302, 308.

(*u*) Tyabji, loc. cit.; Mulla §§151, 165; *Sadik Husain* v. *Hashim Ali* (1916) 43 I.A. 212, 221, 231; *Cases*, 238.

of the trustees, nor is possession handed over to them. Such a gift through the medium of a trust fails (*v*).

In a Bombay case Badruddin Tyabji J. said,

It was argued that trusts being unknown in the Mahomedan law, English law must be applied. The proposition came to me as a great surprise, because I am not aware that trusts are unknown in the Mahomedan law. In fact if any system of law enforces and recognizes them it is the Mahomedan law. We find ramifications of trusts throughout almost every branch of Mahomedan law.

He then goes on to explain that delivery of possession is necessary in such a case (*w*). The learned judge's opinion is entirely in accord with Fatimid law, by which he himself was governed (*ww*).

Recently a Madras Bench has pointed out that trusts can be supported on the grounds of religion:

The basic duty of true Muslims to honour the obligation they have undertaken was pointed out by the Holy Prophet himself. In *Tavakalbhai* v. *Imatiyaj Begum* (*x*) the learned judges extracted the passage from the Koran—

It is of no avail that ye turn your faces (in prayer) towards the East and the West, but righteousness is in . . . those who perform their engagements in which they have engaged . . . these are the true and these are the pious (*y*).

Nothing can be effectuated, contrary to the general law of gifts, by employing the machinery of a trust; for instance, a gift for an immoral purpose, or a gift which is void under Muhammadan law, cannot be validated by the introduction of a trust (*z*).

§47. Life Interests

'Estate' is a term of art in English law and has a definite meaning in its technical sense. A 'life estate' implies the

(*v*) *Sadik Husain* v. *Hashim Ali* (supra).
(*w*) *Moosabhai* v. *Yacoobbhai* (1904) 29 Bom. 267, 275, discussed in Ameer Ali, I, 122.
(*ww*) *Fat. Law* §§348 sqq.
(*x*) (1916) 41 Bom. 372, 376, citing Tyabji's *Muhammadan Law* in its third year of publication, §408. The 1st ed. was published in 1913.
(*y*) *Mohideen v. Madras State* [1957] Mad. 893, 903.
(*z*) Mulla §151.

transfer of the corpus of the property to a certain person with certain limitations as to its use and alienation. In this technical sense of the term, a life *estate* is now declared by the Privy Council (*Sardar Nawazish Ali Khan's Case*) to be unknown to Muhammadan law as administered in India; but life interests are well known and can be created in the following ways:

I. By Family *Wakfs* (*wakf 'alā'l-awlād*);
II. — Wills (*waṣiyyat bi'l-manāfi'*);
III. — the Rule in *Nawab Umjad Ally Khan's Case* (1867) 11 M.I.A. 517; *Cases*, 337;
IV. — the law of Gifts as explained in *Amjad Khan* v. *Ashraf Khan* (1929) 56 I.A. 213; *Cases*, 342;
V. — *Sardar Nawazish Ali Khan's Case* (1948) 75 I.A. 62, *Cases*, 342; and
VI. — *Anjuman Ara Begum* v. *Nawab Asif Kader* [1955] 2 Cal. 109; *Cases*, 357; and
VII. — Family Settlements (*tawrīth*).

We shall deal with each of these cases briefly, paying special attention to the last three, for the first two will be dealt with fully in the chapters on *Wakfs* and Wills, respectively.

Before coming to the law of gifts in this respect, it is necessary to remind ourselves of the difference between the corpus (*'ayn*) and the usufruct (*manāfi'*) of property according to Muhammadan law (*a*), where both the corpus and the usufruct can be the subjects of gift (*b*).

The *'ayn* is the substance of a thing, e.g. a plot of land, a house, a camel or a book. This is also called 'corpus' in modern text-books in India. *Manāfi'* (singular, *manfa'a*) is literally the profits or the produce. It means, not the thing itself, but its use, benefit, produce or profits. For instance,

(*a*) Tyabji has discussed this question exhaustively, see §§375, 376, 426, 458, 461. For a brief discussion see above §43, Subject (what property can be given).

(*b*) Tyabji §375. The Privy Council has accepted the reasoning of Tyabji §459, and cited it with approval in *Sardar Nawazish Ali Khan's Case* (1948) 75 I.A. 62, 79. This has been adopted finally in India, see *Anjuman Ara's Case* [1955] 2 Cal. 109, where all the previous cases have been discussed.

the right to reside in a house, the right to fish in a stream, the right to take the produce of a garden, the recurring income of a partnership or dividends on shares or interest on Government loans or stock.

The main distinction is this: with the right to take the produce is intimately connected the notion of time or duration; so that you may transfer the *manāfi'*, usufruct, for a specified time, but not the corpus. If the corpus is transferred, in Islamic jurisprudence, there can be no question of a time limit; it is the absolute transfer of ownership and is therefore for an indeterminate duration or, in ordinary parlance, for ever.

Now *hiba* in Muhammadan law is a transfer of the corpus; hence the rule in the texts that when *hiba* has been made, you cannot cut it down by a condition repugnant (*c*). The well-known tradition of the Prophet as regards *'umrā* (*d*) is an illustration. According to the traditionist Bukhārī, it is related on the authority of Jābir that the Prophet decided in the matter of *'umrā* that it is for him *to whom it has been gifted* (*e*). Now if the text is looked at, it contains the words *li-man wuhhibat lahu*, that is, to whom it has been made *hiba*. The expression used is the verbal form of a root-word from which is derived the noun *hiba*, gift of the corpus.

The Prophet therefore says nothing more than this: 'When you have made an *absolute gift* of a house, you cannot cut it down by conditions repugnant to it; you cannot restrict the use of the property to the lifetime of a man in such a case.'

Therefore, according to Muhammadan law as received in India, you can make a gift of the corpus; this is called *hiba*. Or you may make a gift of the usufruct; this can be done by the rules as to *'āriya*, *waṣiyyat bi'l-manāfi'*, *tawrīth* and in various other ways. A life interest may therefore be considered as *a transfer of the usufruct for a well-defined*

(*c*) Ameer Ali, I, 134; Wilson §313; Mulla §§138, 164.

(*d*) Very commonly mis-spelt *amree*.

(*e*) Muhammad Ali, *Manual of Hadith*, 330, No. 13.

period (*f*), and Sir John Beaumont has declared such interests to be valid in all schools of Muhammadan law in *Sardar Nawazish Ali Khan's Case*, where he says:

> Limited interests have long been recognized under Shia law. The object of 'Habs' is 'the empowering of a person to receive the profit or usufruct of a thing with a reservation of the owner's right of property in it. . . I have bestowed on thee this mansion . . . for thy life or my life or for a fixed period' is binding by seisin on the part of the donee. (Bail: II 226.) See also *Banoo Begum* v. *Mir Abed Ali* (*g*). Their Lordships think that there is no difference between the several Schools of Muslim law in their fundamental conception of property and ownership. A limited interest takes effect out of the usufruct under any of the schools. Their Lordships feel no doubt that in dealing with a gift under Muslim law, the first duty of the court is to construe the gift. If it is a gift of the corpus, then any condition which derogates from absolute dominion over the subject of the gift will be rejected as repugnant; but if on construction the gift is held to be one of limited interest the gift can take effect out of the usufruct, leaving the ownership of the corpus unaffected except to the extent to which its enjoyment is postponed for the duration of the limited interest (*h*).

I. *Wakfs*

First, as to *wakfs*, it is clear that if *A* makes a *wakf* of his property for the benefit of his children and descendants (*wakf 'ala'l-awlād*), and on the extinction of the line of his lineal descendants, to a school, the children and descendants, generation after generation, take life interests (*i*).

(*f*) Perhaps the best and fullest discussion of the cases and texts will be found in *Amjad Khan* v. *Ashraf Khan* A.I.R. (1925) Oudh 568. This contains a fuller report of this important case than the other two reports, (1929) 4 Lucknow 305, and (1929) 56 I.A. 213, containing the Privy Council decision, which are much shorter than the original judgment of Mr Wazir Hasan A.J.C.

(*g*) (1907) I.L.R. 32 B. 172, 179.

(*h*) (1948) 75 I.A. 62, 79; *Cases*, 342. Two recent Indian decisions have followed and adopted this reasoning, *Anjuman Ara's Case* [1955] 2 Cal. 109 (Ithnā 'Asharī Shiites), and *Shaik Mastan Bi* v. *Shaik Bikari Sahab* (Hanafi Sunnites) A.I.R. (1958) Andh. Prad. 751.

(*i*) See the Chapter on *Wakf*.

II. *Wills*

As to wills, the Lucknow High Court has in two considered judgments held that a life interest can be created by will. Thus, if a life interest is given by will to *A* for life, and thereafter to *B*, the life interest in favour of *A* is valid (*j*). Life interests created by wills are also upheld in Calcutta (*k*).

A recent Calcutta decision raises two important questions: the extent of testamentary power and the consent of heirs. In *Anarali* v. *Omar Ali* (*l*), it was held that while the creation of a life interest is not repugnant to Muhammadan law, a Muslim cannot, under cover of the law relating to life-grants, dispose of more than one-third of his estate. The interposition of a life interest in a certain estate will be deemed to be a bequest of the entire property for a certain period to the exclusion of other heirs, and as such, it cannot be valid unless the heirs have consented to it. In Hanafi law, consent to be effective must be given *after* the death of the testator, and may be proved (i) by acquiescence or (ii) by consent given *before* the death of the testator and *not revoked* after it. The second proposition appears to be open to doubt, for in a Muslim family it is possible for the *pater familias* to browbeat the future heirs by his personal influence; and the rule in Hanafi law is formulated precisely to render ineffective such doubtful consent under moral pressure, if not legal duress. It is submitted that this part of the judgment requires further examination.

But where upon the true construction of the deed the court comes to the conclusion that the gift is a transfer of the corpus, and not merely of the usufruct, the gift is valid and the conditions void. A testator bequeathed all his

(*j*) This is now clear, it is submitted, after *Sardar Nawazish Ali Khan's Case*. *Naziruddin* v. *Khairat Ali* (1937) 13 Luck. 713; *Faqir Mohammad* v. *Hasan Khan* (1940) 16 Luck. 93.

(*k*) *Anarali* v. *Omar Ali* A.I.R. (1951) Cal. 7.

(*l*) ibid.

property (1) to his three sons, X, Y, and Z, with full powers of alienation, (2) to his grandson (by a predeceased son), W, without any power of transfer, and (3) provided that the male issue of W shall have the right to own the property absolutely and to sell or transfer it. (4) He also left a certain property to his widow N, for her life, without power of alienation. Held that, on a proper construction of the deed, W was the owner of the corpus and not merely of the usufruct, and therefore all limitations in derogation of his rights, such as the incapacity to transfer the property, were void. The case further illustrates the rule that the first problem before the court is the proper interpretation of the terms of the grant. If the court comes to the conclusion that the settlor intended to convey the corpus and not merely the usufruct, then, in accordance with the well-known rule of Muhammadan law, the gift will take effect and the condition will be held to be void (*m*).

III. *Rule in Nawab Umjad Ally Khan's Case* (*n*)

The facts of this leading case may be simplified as follows. *A* transfers and endorses Government promissory notes to the name of his son *B*, and delivers them to *B*. Thus *A* retains no dominion over the corpus of the property; but stipulates that *B* should pay the recurring income to *A* during *A*'s lifetime. Their lordships of the Privy Council held both the gift and the condition to be valid.

The decision lays down, first, that there must be an absolute and valid transfer of the corpus. If the condition had related to the return of a part of the corpus, the gift would have been valid and the condition void. Secondly, that a stipulation for obtaining the right to the recurring produce during his lifetime does not invalidate the gift. It is to be

(*m*) *Siddiq Ahmad* v. *Vilayat Ahmad* A.I.R. (1952) All. 1.

(*n*) (1867) 11 M.I.A. 517; *Cases*, 337; Ameer Ali, I, 136 sqq.; Tyabji §395, ill. (3); Wilson §315.

supported as an agreement raising a trust and constituting a valid obligation. This is explained as follows:

> It remains to be considered whether a real transfer of property by a donor in his lifetime under the Mahommedan Law, reserving not the dominion over the corpus of the property, nor any share of dominion over the corpus, but simply stipulating for and obtaining the right to the recurring produce during his lifetime is an incomplete gift by the Mahommedan Law. The text of the *Hedaya* seems to include the very proposition and to negative it. The thing to be returned is not identical but something different, see *Hedaya*, 'Gifts', Vol. III, Book XXX, p. 294, where the objection being raised that a participation of property in the thing given invalidates a gift, the answer is, 'The donor is subjected to a participation in a thing which is not the subject of his grant, namely, the use (of the whole indivisible article) for his gift related to the substance of the article, not to the use of it.' Again, if the agreement for the reservation of the interest to the father for his life be treated as a repugnant condition, repugnant to the whole enjoyment by the donee, here the Mahommedan Law defeats not the grant but the condition; *Hedaya*, 'Gifts', Vol. III, Book XXX, p. 307. But as this arrangement between the father and the son is founded on a valid consideration, the son's undertaking is valid and could be enforced against him in the Courts of India as an agreement raising a trust and constituting a valid obligation to make a return of the proceeds during the time stipulated. The contention of the parties therefore is not found to violate any provision of the *Hedaya*, and the transfer is complete (*o*).

In *Nawab Umjad Ally Khan's Case* the parties were Shiites, but the Privy Council did not proceed to decide the case on the assumption that the Shiite law was, as is well known now, different from the Hanafi law, inasmuch as it is more favourable to the creation of life interests. Fifty-six years later, the same principle was applied to a case in which the parties were governed by Sunnite law, *Mohammad Abdul Ghani* v. *Fakhr Jahan Begam* (*p*), and the principle of these

(*o*) 11 M.I.A. 517, 547-8.

(*p*) (1922) 49 I.A. 195.

cases has been extended considerably by recent decisions of the Indian High Courts (*q*).

A Madras decision illustrates the rule. One Salia Sahib was the owner of an estate known as 'Bevuhalli Mitta'. He executed a deed of gift whereby he gave away the corpus of the estate to his two sons, Azizullah and Inayatullah, and stipulated that out of the recurring income of the estate, the two sons should pay a sum of Rs 500 per year to himself for life, and the sum of Rs 350 per annum to his daughter Amirunnissa for her life, and thereafter to her heirs and successors in perpetuity. The obligation to pay this sum was to be a charge on the income of the estate.

Salia Sahib the settlor died in 1909. 'Bevuhalli Mitta' was acquired by Government in 1951 and the heirs of Amirunnissa, who had died in 1950, claimed under the settlement. It was held (1) that the corpus (*'ayn*) of the estate was gifted away to the two sons, and part of the usufruct (*manāfi'*) was given away in perpetuity to the daughter; (2) that the terms of the deed made it clear that the settlor was giving away a part of her inheritance to his daughter Amirunnissa in perpetuity; (3) that there was a clear distinction in Muhammadan law between corpus and usufruct, and that both the gifts, of the corpus to the sons, and of the usufruct to daughter, were valid; (4) that the doctrine of *mushā'* could not be extended to a grant of usufruct, and (5) that the validity of the obligation imposed upon the donees to pay a yearly sum in perpetuity could be supported on the principle of trust.

Throughout this learned judgment Rajagopalan and Rajagopala Ayyangar JJ. cited Tyabji (especially 3rd ed., §§366 A sqq. and 382) with approval and adopted his reasoning (*r*).

(*q*) Mulla §165.

(*r*) *Mohideen* v. *Madras State* [1957] Madras 893. See also *Veerunkutty* v. *Kutti Umma* [1956] Mad. 1004, where a settlor gave away his properties to his grandson, and reserved for himself only a life interest in the properties, without power of alienation or charge.

IV. *Rule in Amjad Khan* v. *Ashraf Khan* (*s*)

The Judicial Committee of the Privy Council in an early decision *Humeeda* v. *Budlun* (*t*) observed that 'the creation of (such) a life estate does not seem to be consistent with Mahomedan usage and there ought to be clear proof of so unusual a transaction'. Twenty years later, in *Abdul Gafur* v. *Nizamudin* (*u*), their lordships referred to 'life rents' as 'a kind of estate which does not appear to be known to Mahomedan law'. Following these decisions the courts and the text-writers expressed themselves in language which clearly showed that a life interest was nothing more than a gift with a condition, and the condition being repugnant to the gift, the condition was void and the gift was good. Thus, it was held that if *A* gave to *B* a life interest in a certain property, *B* took it absolutely (*v*).

Tyabji, however, had always maintained (i) that in Muhammadan law, corpus is to be distinguished from use; (ii) that the early texts speak of *hiba*, that is the transfer of the corpus, and (iii) that a life interest, being a transfer of the use, and not of the corpus, is valid (*w*). This view has in the main been accepted by the Judicial Committee in *Sardar Nawazish Ali Khan's Case*, which we shall discuss shortly. This case, read with *Amjad Khan's Case*, has now been followed in two important decisions, in India *Anjuman Ara Begum* v. *Nawab Asif Kader* [1955] 2 Cal. 109, and *Shaik*

(*s*) There are three reports of this case. The fullest report of the decision of a division bench of the Judicial Commissioner's Court at Oudh is A.I.R. (1925) Oudh 568-91, in which Ashworth A.J.C. and Wazir Hasan A.J.C. arrived at different conclusions. The Privy Council decision will be found in (1929) 56 I.A. 213 and in (1929) 4 Luck. 305; the latter, containing a substantial portion of the judgment of Mr Wazir Hasan A.J.C., is the fuller report.

(*t*) (1872) 17 W.R. 525.

(*u*) (1892) 19 I.A. 170.

(*v*) *Nizamudin* v. *Abdul Gafur* (1888) 13 Bom. 264; *Abdoola* v. *Mahomed* (1905) 7 Bom. L.R. 306. This view will be found in Ameer Ali. I, 140; Students' ed. (7th), p. 143, Art. 21; Wilson §313; Mulla §55.

(*w*) Tyabji, 2nd ed., 1919, §§443-4, esp. pp. 498 sqq.; in the 3rd ed., 1940, §§443-4, some matter had been excluded in view of the very full discussion by Wazir Hasan A.J.C.

Mastan Bi v. *Shaik Bikari Sahab* A.I.R. (1958) Andhra Pradesh 751.

Tyabji's view, advanced in the 2nd ed. of his *Principles of Muhammadan Law* (1919), was substantially adopted and judicially recognized by Wazir Hasan A.J.C., in his judgment in *Amjad Khan* v. *Ashraf Khan* (*x*). The Judicial Committee did not accept the whole of the reasoning of Wazir Hasan A.J.C., but arrived at the same conclusion. We must therefore turn to this important decision and examine it very carefully.

A Hanafi husband, Ghulam Murtaza Khan, executed a deed whereby he made a gift without consideration of his entire property to his wife, Mst. Waziran. He divided the property which was worth Rs 15,000 into two parts, one-third and two-thirds. Waziran was to remain in possession of the one-third with full power to alienate, and as to the rest, namely the two-thirds, she had no power to alienate it, but she was to remain in possession for her lifetime. After her death, 'the entire property', that is the two-thirds as well as any portion of the one-third remaining undisposed of, was to revert to Ghulam Murtaza's collaterals.

After the death of Ghulam Murtaza and of Waziran, the wife's brother claimed the whole property. He contended that the intention was to make a gift of the whole property itself subject to a restrictive condition, and that under Muhammadan law the gift was valid, but the condition void. His claim was opposed by the husband's collaterals.

The matter came up before a division bench consisting of Mr Ashworth and Mr Wazir Hasan, Additional Judicial Commissioners. Mr Ashworth held (*y*) that Muhammadan law permits the separation of corpus and use, for in *'āriya* the complete rights of an owner may be analysed as (i) the

(*x*) (1929) 4 Luck. 305, 306-29; A.I.R. (1925) Oudh 568, 577-91. A careful comparison of Tyabji, 2nd ed., 1919, with the Oudh report will show the extent of the debt which the judgment of Wazir Hasan A.J.C., owed to the well-known textbook.

(*y*) A.I.R. (1925) Oudh 568-77.

right to the corpus, (ii) the right to the use, and (iii) the right to revoke the use. On an examination of the texts and the cases, it appears that a man may *retain* but cannot *transfer* a life interest; and a life interest can only be created by transferring the corpus and retaining or reserving the use. A gift of a life interest is a gift of the whole interest, coupled with an invalid condition; this is not permitted in Muhammadan law and Tyabji's argument is not tenable in view of the texts. The proper remedy is legislation, and not 'by the courts under fiction of exposition' (p. 574).

He therefore came to the conclusion that Mst. Waziran took, if at all, an absolute interest. But he also held on the evidence that the gift was not perfected by delivery of possession, and hence it was void. In the result, the husband's collaterals succeeded.

Mr Wazir Hasan, however, took a different view (*z*). He begins his judgment by asking: Is a court compelled to hold that where a life interest is granted, Muhammadan law requires that it should be enlarged into an absolute estate? He considers the texts and Privy Council decisions and arrives at the following conclusions:

(1) Proof of the intention to create a life interest is permissible.

(2) Giving an interest in a certain property is different from, and is not the same thing as, the gift of the corpus.

(3) Such an interest may be supported on the basis of a trust resulting from an agreement for valuable consideration.

(4) Where the manifest intention of the donor is to give the corpus of and the absolute interest in the property gifted to one person and such gift is accompanied with a reservation of a limited estate in the same property in favour of another, both the gift and the reservation are valid.

(*z*) ibid., 568, 577-91, and (1929) 4 Luck. 305, 306-29.

(5) No rule of the Muhammadan law is propounded to the effect that where the donor in a transaction of a simple gift merely creates a life interest in the property gifted in the donee and reserves the reversion to his heirs at law, the donee of the life interest takes the absolute estate (*a*).

Therefore he held that the deed created a life interest in favour of Mst. Waziran and that the life interest was valid. As, however, at the date of the suit Mst. Waziran had died, her interest had ended, and her heirs took no interest. Thus, although for entirely different reasons, he arrived at the same conclusion as Mr Ashworth.

The Judicial Committee '*basing their decision on the terms of the deed*' were 'of opinion that the conclusion arrived at by the learned Judicial Commissioner, Mr Wazir Hasan, on this part of the case is correct, and that Musammat Waziran acquired merely a life interest in the property under the deed of January 17, 1905, together with a power of alienation over one-third of the property'.(*b*) Therefore they adopted the construction of the deed proposed by Mr Wazir Hasan.

Secondly, their lordships *expressed no opinion* as to the validity in Muhammadan law of a life interest:

. . . because in view of the construction of the deed which their Lordships have adopted, the plaintiff appellant is on the horns of a dilemma. If the interest acquired by Musammat Waziran was of a life-estate only, and if such an interest can be acquired under Muhammadan law by way of a gift, that interest came to an end on the death of Musammat Waziran, and the plaintiff claiming as heir has no title to the property. On the other hand if, as argued on behalf of the plaintiff, under the Hanafi law such a limited interest as a life estate could not be transferred to Musammat Waziran by way of gift *inter vivos*, then Musammat Waziran acquired no interest in the property under the deed of January 17, 1905, and the plaintiff, claiming as her heir, can have no title to the property (*c*).

(*a*) 4 Luck. at pp. 315-16. (*b*) 56 I.A. at p. 220.
(*c*) 56 I.A. at pp. 221-2.

The decision therefore laid down two propositions: (i) that a life interest CANNOT BE ENLARGED into an absolute interest, and (ii) that the validity of a life interest by the law of gifts WAS AN OPEN QUESTION.

Following *Amjad Khan* v. *Ashraf Khan*, the modern tendency is to favour the validity of life interests. The Bombay and Nagpur High Courts have upheld the validity of the gift of a life interest (*d*), and the Chief Court of Oudh has held that the bequest of a life interest is valid (*e*). We shall deal fully with the two latest decisions of the High Courts of Calcutta and Andhra Pradesh after dealing with *Sardar Nawazish Ali Khan's Case*, and show that life interests are now fully established in Hanafi no less than in Ithnā 'Asharī law, and the gap between Sunnites and Shiites has been narrowed down considerably.

V. *Sardar Nawazish Ali Khan's Case* (1948) 75 I.A. 62; *Cases*, 342.

The main question in this appeal was whether a power of appointment given to a life tenant was valid according to the Shiite Ithnā 'Asharī law, and it is submitted that, strictly speaking, the rule laid down in this case may be formulated as follows:

Where a Muslim testator bequeaths his property to *A*, *B* and *C* successively for life, and then provides that the last surviving devisee should have the power to nominate his successor from among the descendants of the three life tenants, such a power was not known to any school of Muhammadan law as administered in India and was therefore void.

In view of the full discussion of this case in *Anjuman Ara's Case* (see below), and its inclusion in my *Cases*, it is unnecessary to give details.

(*d*) *Bai Saroobai* v. *Hussein Somji* [1936] Bom. 18 and 38 Bom. L.R. 903; *Mst. Subhanbi* v. *Mst. Umraobi* A.I.R. (1936) Nagpur 113.

(*e*) *Naziruddin* v. *Khairat Ali* (1937) 13 Luck. 713; *Faqir Mohammad* v. *Hasan Khan* (1940) 16 Luck. 93. See also Abdur Rahman, *Institutes*, Art. 439.

Where, however, a Muslim executes a deed and attempts to limit the succession to *male heirs only* by creating successive life interests, and thus to create a line of succession unknown to Muhammadan law, the deed is bad (*f*).

VI. *Anjuman Ara Begum* v. *Nawab Asif Kader*

The most important recent decision on life-grants is *Anjuman Ara Begum* v. *Nawab Asif Kader* [1955] 2 Calcutta 109; *Cases*, 357, and with a detailed analysis of this case we shall arrive at a fair comprehension of the complicated law of life interests applicable to Muslims in India.

The Nawab Nazim of Bengal, an Ithnā 'Asharī Shiite, had seven daughters. He made a trust whereby he settled a sum of Rs 20,000 on each daughter, so that Rs 5,000 were to be paid to each on marriage, and the remaining Rs 15,000 invested in Government securities in the name of the trustees (which in this case was the Government itself) for the benefit of each daughter, and finally, the remainder to the Nawab's residuary heir absolutely. A suit was filed by the Nawab's residuary heir as plaintiff against some of the daughters and the Government, claiming the securities together with the accumulated interest. It was held that the life-grant in favour of the daughters was valid, and that the Government notes reverted absolutely to the heir according to Muhammadan law.

The judgment of the divisional bench was delivered by Mr Justice P. N. Mookerjee, and is the most exhaustive pronouncement dealing with limited interests in Muhammadan law; it is therefore proposed to give a fairly detailed analysis of his lordship's decision. The lower court held (1) that the daughters were entitled to the money absolutely, the condition being void, but (2) that a usage had been proved that in the family of the Nawab Nazim women could not own the *Niẓāmat* property absolutely but were entitled only to the usufruct. P. N. Mookerjee J., delivering the judg-

(*f*) *Imam Saheb* v. *Ameer Saheb* A.I.R. (1955) Mad. 621.

ment of the divisional bench, laid down that in *Amjad Khan* v. *Ashraf Khan,* read with *Sardar Nawazish Ali Khan's Case,* 'the validity of life-grants in Muhammadan Law was also, in general, affirmed and expressly recognized' (p. 120). He held, following *Amjad Khan's Case*, that

(i) if the life-grants were valid, they ended with the death of the daughters;

(ii) if not, they were totally void; and in any case,

(iii) life-grants *could not be enlarged* into absolute estates.

Regard being had to the two Privy Council decisions, the dissenting opinions of Rangnekar J. in *Rasul Bibi* v. *Yusuf Azam* and *Bai Saroobai* v. *Hussein Somjee* were no longer good law, and the authority of earlier decisions can no longer be invoked (p. 121). In the view of the bench, in *Nawazish Ali Khan's Case,* the Judicial Committee clearly approved the judgment of Wazir Hasan A.J.C. (p. 122), which is, as we have seen, based very closely on Tyabji, 2nd ed., 1919.

The learned judge distinguishes between *corpus* and usufruct as follows (pp. 122-4):

> To appreciate the true legal position it is necessary to remember that 'life-estate', that is, life-grant of a property which is usually called a life-estate is not regarded in Muhammadan Law as an estate or interest in the '*corpus*'. That law recognizes only one kind of estate, namely, full ownership in the '*corpus*'. The '*corpus*' means the 'article', 'the thing' or 'the substance'. It is distinct from the usufruct which means the 'use' of the 'article' or the produce of the 'thing'. A gift of the *corpus* connotes and comprehends the entire bundle of rights in 'the thing' or 'the substance', in other words, full rights over the 'article' or complete dominion over 'the substance'. The test is this complete dominion over 'the substance'. That dominion is absolute and indivisible. It permits no slicing and tolerates no obstacle or restriction. Grant of full dominion over the '*corpus*' may, however, be accompanied by a gift of the use or usufruct to another, that is, a condition or limitation as regards the 'usufruct',

and both the grant and the condition will be valid. Limited interests—short of complete ownership—may also be created but not in the form of a gift of the '*corpus*' subject to a condition affecting the same—'the thing' or 'the substance'. Any such interest—whether limited 'in point of quality or in point of duration'—is in Muhammadan Law, different from the 'corpus' and takes effect out of the 'usufruct'.

In the Muhammadan Law, therefore, as already stated, there is a clear distinction between the '*corpus*' or 'the substance' and the 'usufruct'. Over the '*corpus*' that law recognizes only absolute, complete and indivisible ownership and there it countenances no detraction or limitation. In the 'usufruct' however, limited interests can be created and the limitation may well be in point of time or duration, *e.g.*, for life or for a fixed period. Limited interests are thus recognized in Muhammadan Law—though not in the *corpus* but only in the usufruct—and where the grant is of a limited character—but not a grant of the *corpus* subject to condition—it takes effect out of the usufruct and is not regarded as a grant of the *corpus* at all but only as a grant of or in the usufruct. A grant of the *corpus* must be absolute and any condition or restriction derogatory to the grant and affecting the '*corpus*' must be disregarded and if a limited grant is sought to be made by such a device it leads to the same result, namely, that the condition or restriction is swept aside and the grant takes effect as an absolute grant, that being the only grant which can be made of the corpus. A grant of the *corpus* may, however, be validly made, accompanied by conditions or restrictions, relating to the usufruct, and it takes effect subject to those conditions: (*vide, Nawab Umjad Ally Khan* v. *Musammat Mohumdee Begum* (*g*), which though a *Shiâ* case, states the general Muhammadan Law on the point, as explained in *Mohammad Abdul Ghani* v. *Fakhr Jahan Begum* (*h*), a case under the *Sunni* or *Hânâfi* (*i*) law . . .

. . . we hold, therefore, that the question of validity of life-grants, with which we are here concerned, must be answered in affirmative.

His lordship then proceeds to discuss and distinguish the three Privy Council decisions *Musammat Humeeda* v.

(*g*) (1867) 11 Moore's In. Ap. 517; *Cases*, 337.

(*h*) (1922) 49 I.A. 195, 209.

(*i*) *Sic*, a misprint. Submitted with respect, the word is *Ḥanafī*, not *Ḥānāfi*.

Budlun, Abdul Wahid Khan v. *Musammat Nuran Bibi* and *Abdul Gafur* v. *Nizamudin* (pp. 125-7). And, finally, he concludes this part of his judgment with these words (p. 128):

In the light of what we have stated so far the true approach when a Muhammadan grant falls for consideration is first to construe the deed as a whole, bearing in mind that life-grants are not very familiar in Muhammadan Law. If, upon such construction, the grant is held to be an absolute grant, no further question arises. If, however, the grant is found to be a limited grant, the direct or the immediate subject-matter of the gift has to be ascertained. If it is the 'corpus', as explained above, any restrictive condition, affecting the same, will be invalid and the grant will have effect as an absolute grant. If, on the other hand, the direct or the immediate subject-matter of the grant be the limited interest and not the '*corpus*', the grant takes effect out of the usufruct as a valid limited grant. In this view of the matter we hold that the disputed life-grants in the present case were valid as such and did not enlarge into any absolute grant in favour of the grantees (*j*).

A recent decision from Andhra Pradesh adopts the same reasoning and carries the law farther in the direction of the recognition of life interests. A Hanafi Muslim transferred certain immovable properties in the following manner:

I have, on account of my affection for you, conveyed to you under *dakhal* (the following property) . . . belonging to me, and created rights to you in the property now [*sic*] itself. Till my life-time, I shall retain the property covered by the *dakhal* in my possession and enjoy the produce thereof. After my life-time, you and your heirs shall take possession of the . . . property and enjoy the produce thereof. After my life-time, you and your heirs shall take possession of the . . . property and enjoy the same from your son to grandson and so on in succession with absolute power of disposition by way of gift, sale, etc.

It was held (1) that a Hanafi Muslim cannot without consideration convey the ownership of the property with limita-

(*j*) *Anjuman Ara Begum* v. *Nawab Asif Kadar Sir Syed Wasif Ali Meerza*, op. cit. This leading case was decided in 1953, and, apart from this official report, apparently it is not reported elsewhere. His lordship, or the printer, has used *four* different spellings for the word 'Muhammadan', and I have ventured to reduce them to a pedestrian regularity, departing from the practice of so great a genius as T. E. Lawrence.

tions for the life of the donor; but (2) that when the absolute ownership is conveyed to X, and only the enjoyment of the property is reserved to Y, the limitation does not apply and both gifts are valid. Limitation therefore in the *enjoyment* of property is permissible, but not in the *ownership* itself; and (3) that there is a clear distinction between *hiba* (gift of the corpus) and *'āriyat* (gift of the usufruct), and an *'āriyat* for life is legal and permissible in the Hanafi law. A feature of the judgment is the fairly exhaustive examination of the case law and a full consideration of the recent Privy Council decisions (*k*).

Anjuman Ara's Case, decided in 1953 (Calcutta), dealt with Ithnā 'Asharī law, and *Mastan Bi's Case,* decided in 1958 (Andhra Pradesh), laid down the law for Hanafis; and it may safely be asserted that since the Calcutta decision, there is no doubt whatever of the validity of life-grants, both by will and by deed, in Muhammadan law as received and interpreted in India, regardless of the school to which the parties belong. It is needless to add that such limited interests are always subject to the basic norms governing the law of Islam.

It will thus be seen that the law relating to life interests is now much clearer than before; but difficulties and doubts still remain, and it is submitted that, Tyabji having cleared the ground and shown that there is nothing in it inherently opposed to the principles of Islamic jurisprudence, legislation should now be introduced to remove some of the cobwebs which still surround the law regarding limited interests. A matter of such extreme practical importance ought not to be allowed to remain in a state of uncertainty. In particular, it is essential that on two points the law should be laid down with unmistakable precision—first, What are the kinds of property that can be transferred for life and secondly, What are the limits within which life interests may be created?

(*k*) *Shaik Mastan Bi* v. *Shaik Bikari Sahab* A.I.R. (1958) Andhra Pradesh 751.

In view of the two decisions of the Calcutta and Andhra Pradesh High Courts, the position may be clear to an acute lawyer; but for the public at large, a short enactment is preferable, and it is hoped that appropriate legislation will soon be undertaken both in India and in Pakistan.

Shiite law of life interests. What we have discussed so far is the law applicable to the persons governed by the Hanafi school of Sunnite law. We must now turn to the Ithnā 'Asharī and the Fatimid law on the subject (*l*).

Both the Ithnā 'Asharī and Fatimid schools of Shiite law recognize limited interests to a larger extent. The commonest forms are:

(i) *'Umrā*, a life grant; the grant of the use or usufruct for life.

(ii) *Suknā*, the right to reside in a house for life.

(iii) *Ruqbā*, the right to take the usufruct for a certain period depending on a contingency (*m*).

Thus it is clear that by Shiite law life interests may be validly created (*n*). It was formerly thought that the Ithnā 'Asharī school permitted the creation of vested remainders as well; but since *Sardar Nawazish Ali Khan's Case*, the earlier decisions must be treated as overruled.

The chief rules for the creation of a life interest may now be stated. The grantor must deliver possession of the property to the life tenant (*o*). The grantee must be in existence at the time of the grant. This rule applies only to the first grantee; where there are successive life grants, the succeeding grantees should be in existence when their interests open out (*p*). Everything of which a *wakf* can be made may be the subject of the grant of a limited interest. The essential condition is that the

(*l*) Ameer Ali, I, 142 sqq.; Tyabji §§463 sqq.; *Fat. Law* §307.

(*m*) Ameer Ali, I, 143; *Fat. Law* §307 (iii).

(*n*) *Banoo Begum* v. *Mir Abed Ali* (1907) 32 Bom. 172, which contains a number of texts referred to in 75 I.A. at p. 79.

(*o*) Tyabji §465.

(*p*) ibid., §466; *Gulamhusein Sajan* v. *Fakirmahomed Sajan* (1946) 48 Bom. L.R. 733.

property must admit of use without being consumed (*q*). A life-grant made for a purpose other than religious, or for an indeterminate period, is revocable at the wish of the grantor, and is determined at any rate at the death of the grantor (*r*); unless the remainder is disposed of, it reverts to the donor (*s*).

The latest decision on life-grants is *Anjuman Ara's Case*, which has been fully discussed above.

Vested remainders. In *Abdul Wahid Khan* v. *Mst. Nuran Bibi* (1885) 12 I.A. 91, the Privy Council held that a vested remainder was not known to Muhammadan law; and this appears to be the generally accepted view as regards the Hanafi law, despite *Umes Chander Sircar* v. *Mst. Zahoor Fatima* (1889) 17 I.A. 201 (*t*). On the other hand, Tyabji is of the opinion, consistently with his views on the question of life interests, that there is no reason why it should not be held valid (*u*). The question is not free from difficulty, but after *Sardar Nawazish Ali Khan's Case*, a true vested remainder, as understood in the common law of England, would, it is submitted, be difficult to justify; for

> . . . though the same terms may be used in English and Muslim law, *to describe much the same things*, the two systems of law are based on quite different conceptions of ownership . . . No doubt where the use of a house is given to a man for his life he may, not inaptly, be termed a tenant for life, and *the owner of the house, waiting to enjoy it until the termination of the limited interest*, may be said, *not inaccurately*, to possess *a vested remainder* (*v*).

The case of *Anjuman Ara Begum* v. *Nawab Asif Kader* does not discuss the creation or the validity of vested remainders (*w*).

For Shāfi'ī law, see *Mahomed Ibrahim* v. *Abdul Latiff* (*x*).

(*q*) Ibid., §467.

(*r*) Ibid., §468.

(*s*) ibid., §472.

(*t*) Mulla §§55, sq.

(*u*) Tyabji §§382, 450 sqq.

(*v*) 75 I.A. at p. 78; *Cases*, 342, 350. The italics are mine.

(*w*) [1955] 2 Cal. 109, esp. 122-8; *Cases*, 357.

(*x*) (1913) 37 Bom. 447.

VII. *Family Settlements.*

Where there is a *bona fide* dispute between certain parties (*y*), they may arrive at a compromise, and such an arrangement may be in the nature of a *tawrīth*; but a later decision has held that a regular dispute is unnecessary, provided that the parties have arrived at a settlement *bona fide* to avoid disputes in future (*z*). 'The arrangement contained in the compromise would be called by the Mahomedan lawyers "a tauris", (*a*) or "making some stranger an heir", and cannot be regarded as creating a present or vested interest.' (*b*) In *Muhammad Raza* v. *Abbas Bandi Bibi*, Sir George Lowndes said, 'It must be remembered in this connection that family arrangements are specially favoured in Courts of Equity.' (*c*)

A family arrangement is an agreement settling disputes between the parties and a transaction for a consideration, and there is no doubt whatever that a life interest may be created by such an agreement (*d*).

The relinquishment of a contingent right of inheritance by a Muslim heir is generally void under the Muhammadan law; but if it is supported by consideration, and forms part of a valid family settlement it is perfectly valid (*e*).

§48. Revocability

A tradition of the Prophet Muhammad shows that he was entirely against the revocation of gifts (*f*); and this is under-

(*y*) *Amjad Khan* v. *Ashraf Khan,* A.I.R. (1925) Oudh 568, 569, 591.

(*z*) *Kochunni Kochu* v. *Kunju Pillai* A.I.R. (1956) Trav-Co. 217, 219. See also *Allah Rabbul Almin* v. *Hasnain Ahmad* A.I.R. (1952) All. 1011, where Mushtaq Ahmad J. held that for a family settlement a *bona fide* dispute must exist between the parties, but the other judge, Desai J., said that a regular dispute was unnecessary, provided that the parties were settling a vexed question of succession.

(*a*) The word *tawrīth* is loosely spelt *tauris* by many writers.

(*b*) *Abdul Wahid* v. *Mst. Nuran Bibi* (1885) 12 I.A. 91, 101; Tyabji, 3rd ed., p. 512.

(*c*) (1932) 59 I.A. 236, 246.

(*d*) Ameer Ali, II, 36-8. For illustrations of family arrangements see Tyabji §382, and Mulla §55(2).

(*e*) *Kochunni Kochu* v. *Kunju Pillai* A.I.R. (1956) Trav.-Cochin 217.

(*f*) This forceful tradition, hardly mentionable at the dinner table, will be found in Muhammad Ali, *Manual,* 330, No. 12. The same sentiment will be found in the *Da'ā'im*, *Fat. Law* §324.

standable, for in early times as nowadays the making of mutual gifts improves the relations between men and leads to cordiality and affection (*g*). In Hanafi law, although the revocation of a gift is abominable from the moral point of view, it is nevertheless legal in certain cases (*h*), and in this respect it resembles the equally reprehensible institution of *ṭalāq*.

According to Muhammadan law all voluntary transactions are revocable, hence revocability is a characteristic of the law of gifts (*i*). Not every gift, however, is revocable, and the texts contain long lists of gifts which, once perfected by delivery, are irrevocable (*j*). The revocation of a completed gift is in Hanafi law possible only by the intervention of a court of law or by the consent of the donee; a mere declaration on the part of the donor is not enough, except in Ithnā 'Asharī and Shāfi'ī law (*k*).

Before coming to the exceptional cases—and the exceptions almost outnumber the cases within the rule—the revocation of a completed gift must be distinguished from an inchoate gift. For instance, *A* makes a gift of a house to *B* and *B* accepts the gift; but *before* delivery of possession *A* changes his mind; this is an inchoate or incomplete gift; and if no further steps are taken by *A* in pursuance of the original intention, the gift does not take effect. It is best not to call this a revocation at all; we shall restrict the term 'revocation' to completed gifts. It follows that no order of the court is necessary for the 'revocation' of an inchoate gift (*l*).

This illustration does not apply in a case governed by Fatimid law, where delivery of possession is not necessary (*m*).

(*g*) *Muhammad Ali*, ibid., 326, No. 2; *Fat. Law*, pp. 72, 73.

(*h*) Ameer Ali, I, 150; Baillie, I, 533.

(*i*) Tyabji §437.

(*j*) Baillie, I, 534 sqq.

(*k*) Ameer Ali, I, 155; Wilson §316; Tyabji §440; Mulla §167.

(*l*) Ameer Ali, loc. cit.; Mulla, loc. cit.

(*m*) See §44, above.

The following gifts are irrevocable (*n*):

1. When a gift is made to a person who is so closely related by consanguinity that if the parties differed in sex, a marriage between them would be unlawful (*o*).
2. By a wife to the husband or by the husband to a wife.
3. When the donor or donee dies.
4. When the thing given is lost or destroyed.
5. When the thing given has been transferred by the donee by gift, sale or otherwise.
6. When the thing has increased in value, whatever be the cause of such increase.
7. When the donor has accepted a return (*'iwaḍ*) for the gift.
8. Where the motive for the gift is religious or spiritual, for in this case the gift amounts to *ṣadaqa*.

§49. *Hiba, 'Āriya, Ṣadaqa, Wakf, Ḥabs*

I. *Hiba*

In considering the law of gifts, it is well to remember, as has been pointed out before, that the English word 'gift' is generic and must not be confused with the technical term of Islamic law, *hiba*. *Hiba* is the absolute gift of the corpus (*'ayn*) of the property without any return. We must now contrast it with some other kinds of gifts. Tyabji has given a convenient list of such related legal concepts (*p*); and it is proposed to deal with the following terms in this section, *'āriya*, *ṣadaqa*, *wakf* and *ḥabs*, and to deal with return gifts and gifts with stipulations in the next.

(*n*) Ameer Ali, I, 156 sqq.; Wilson §316; Tyabji §§441 sqq.; Mulla, loc. cit.; Abdur Rahman, *Institutes*, Articles 450-64.

(*o*) Case of brothers, *Tajju Khan* v. *Mazhar Khan* A.I.R. (1952) All. 614.

(*p*) Tyabji §376, com.

II. *'Āriya*

'Āriya is to transfer the right to enjoy the use or profits without any return (*q*). According to the *Durr al-Mukhtār*, 'to make a person the owner of the substance of a thing without consideration is a *hiba* (gift), while to make him *the owner of the profits only* without consideration is an *'āriya* or *commodatum*'.(*r*) In the classical definition of the *Hedaya* and the *'Ālamgīrī*, it is 'the giving (*tamlīk*) of the usufruct (*manāfi'*) without any return'.(*s*) For instance, 'I have lent this thing to you', or 'I have given you the use of this garment or house', or 'my house is your residence'.

In *hiba* the transferee acquires the right to the property itself; in *'āriya*, he only obtains the use or beneficial enjoyment for a limited time, and the property does not pass to him.

The chief incidents of this form of gift are, first, that the period for which the gift is made may or may not be specified; and secondly, that it is revocable at will.

The law of *'āriya* has been somewhat neglected in India, but since the passing of the Shariat Act, 1937, it is likely to assume greater importance (*t*).

III. *Ṣadaqa*

The word *ṣadaqa* in the widest sense means a pious or charitable act; 'a smile in the neighbour's face is *ṣadaqa*; to help the weary is *ṣadaqa*'. But in Muhammadan law it means a gift made with the object of obtaining merit in the eyes of

(*q*) Popularly mis-spelt '*Areeat*'. Ameer Ali, I, 34-9, discusses the leading case on the subject, *Muhammad Faiz Ahmad Khan* v. *Ghulam Ahmad Khan* (1881) 3 All. 490 (or 8 In. Ap. 25), and at pp. 747-9, gives a translation from the *Fatāwā 'Ālamgīrī*. Tyabji §458; Mulla §170. *Fat. Law* §§339 sqq

(*r*) Ameer Ali, I, 35.

(*s*) *tamlīk al-manāfi' bi-ghayri 'iwaḍ*, Tyabji, loc. cit., and (1933) 10 Bom. Law Journal, 351, 353, 'The Book of *'Āriya*'.

(*t*) The fullest modern discussion of *'āriya* will be found in Tyabji, loc. cit., and a literal translation by the present writer of the Book of *'Āriya* in *Fatāwā 'Ālamgīrī* will be found in (1933) 10 Bom. Law Journal, 351-5.

God (*u*). The motive of *hiba* is secular; the motive of *ṣadaqa* is religious.

Delivery of possession is necessary in *ṣadaqa*; but it is doubtful if the rule against *mushā*ʿ applies to it in its strictness. Thus, if a man were to give 10 *dirhams* to two poor men, according to Abū Ḥanīfa, the gift by way of *ṣadaqa* is perfectly valid (*v*).

In Fatimid law a charitable gift is valid and effective on acceptance by the donee, and delivery of possession is unnecessary (*w*).

In the legal texts of Islamic law the term *ṣadaqa* clearly applied both to *wakfs* (permanent foundations) and to ordinary gifts (where the substance is consumed) (*x*); but in modern usage it is best to keep the two terms distinct, applying *ṣadaqa* to gifts which are consumed in use and *wakf* to permanent foundations. If *A* gives Rs 10,000 for purchasing books for the poor, it would be *ṣadaqa*; but if the same sum is invested in some permanent form and a *wakf* made for purchasing books for the poor from its income, it would be a *wakf*.

Fatimid Law. It is a remarkable feature of this school that *wakf* and *ṣadaqa* do not appear to be distinguished in the texts, and no separate treatment of *wakf* will be found, *Fat. Law* §§320 ff.

IV. *Wakf*

Wakf is a permanent foundation for a religious or pious object; the corpus belongs to God and cannot be consumed. The similarity between *ṣadaqa* and *wakf* is that in both the motive is religious. But while the term *ṣadaqa* could in certain cases be applied to a *wakf* as well, it is best to restrict *ṣadaqa* to a charity the substance whereof is consumed (*y*).

(*u*) Ameer Ali, I, 213 sqq.; Tyabji §452; Mulla §171; Fitzgerald, 202, gives the East African law.
(*v*) Baillie, I, 554; *Hedaya*, 485 (cols. i-ii); Tyabji, loc. cit.
(*w*) *Fat. Law* §321.
(*x*) Ameer Ali, I, 215 sqq.; Tyabji §474 and notes.
(*y*) For details, see Chapter IX on *Wakf*.

V. *Ḥabs*

The word *ḥabs* is an infinitive meaning 'to prevent or restrain'(*z*) and is therefore synonymous with *waḳf* (*a*).

Some authorities in India, for instance Ameer Ali (*b*) and Tyabji (*c*), however, use the term *ḥabs* as if it is to be restricted to limited estates at Shiite law of a secular character. This is hardly justifiable and the eminent authors have apparently been misled by Baillie (*d*); for in the *Sharā'i'* and other authoritative Shiite texts no evidence of such a use will be found (*dd*).

§50. *Hiba bi'l-'iwaḍ, Hiba bi-sharṭi'l-'iwaḍ*

A *hiba-bi'l-'iwaḍ* (*h-i*) is in reality a transaction consisting of two separate and distinct parts, a *hiba* (original gift by the donor to the donee) and an *'iwaḍ* (return gift by the donee to the donor) (*e*). The term means 'gift with return'. The gift and the return gift are separate and distinct acts, and where both are completed, the transaction is called *h-i*. For example, *A*

(*z*) Heffening in *Ency. of Islam*, IV, 1096, s.v. *'waḳf'*.

(*a*) The process whereby *waḳf* or *ḥabs* is made is called *taḥbīs* or *tasbīl*, and the property so endowed is called *mawḳūf*, *maḥbūs* or *ḥabīs*. Now *waḳf* is also used as a noun and means an endowment (plural, *wuḳūf*, *awḳāf*); and similarly, the word *ḥabs*, pl. *ḥubus*, although strictly the latter is the plural of *ḥabīs*.

Among the Mālikīs, and in Morocco, Algeria and Tunis, the common name of such endowments is *ḥabīs* (plural, *ḥubus*), whence in French legal language we have *habous*, for instance, the famous work of Clavel, *Droit Musulman: Wakf ou Habous*, Cairo, 2 vols., 1896. All this goes to show that the infinitives *waḳf* and *ḥabs* are synonyms, but the endowments themselves are called *waḳf* (plural, *awḳāf*, *wuḳūf*) or *ḥabīs* and *ḥabs* (plural, *ḥubus*), and in French usage, *habous*; Th. W. Juynboll, *Handbuch des Islāmischen Gesetzes* (1910), 277, note 1.

(*b*) Ameer Ali, I, 142, esp. 143, read with 179 sqq.

(*c*) Tyabji, 4th ed., p. 473, notes 17 and 18.

(*d*) Baillie, II, 226, has 'hoobs', which is an unusual form. It should be *ḥabs* (infinitive). The last para. on p. 227, is a rendering of the text of the *Sharā'i'* (Calcutta ed.), p. 241 (last 6 lines), and a perusal of the text makes it clear that the author is speaking of *pious endowments*, p. 227, note 7, read *ḥabasa, yaḥbisu ḥabs* (not *hubusu*, from *hoobs*, which is placing the cart before the horse).

(*dd*) *Fat. Law* §§ 329 sqq.

(*e*) Commonly mis-spelt, *iwaz*, *ewaz*. In the remarks that follow I propose to use the abbreviations *h-i* and *h-s-i* for the above two terms, respectively.

makes a gift of a horse to *B*, and later *B* makes a gift of a camel to *A*. If *B* says that the camel is given as and by way of a return or exchange, then both the gifts are irrevocable. The law requires that all the formalities of the law of *hiba* should be strictly followed in each of the two gifts (*f*). Mahmood J. says:

The fundamental conception of a *h-i* in Muhammadan law is that it is a transaction made (*g*) of two separate acts of donation, that is, it is a transaction made up of mutual or reciprocal gifts between two persons, each of whom is alternately the donor of one gift and the donee of the other (*h*).

Indian Form

Baillie, however, mentions that there is an Indian form of *h-i* (*i*):

But in the *h-i* of India, there is only one act; the *'iwaḍ* or exchange being involved in the contract of gift as its direct consideration . . . The transaction which goes by the name of *h-i* in India is, therefore, in reality not a proper *h-i* of either kind, but a sale, and has all the incidents of the latter contract.

Hence (i) delivery of possession is not necessary in this case, and (ii) an undivided share in property capable of division (*mushā'*) may be lawfully transferred. The Indian form is therefore to be distinguished from the ancient and classical form of *h-i*.

The Indian form has created a number of difficulties which have been discussed by Tyabji who justly says that 'the popular misapplication of technical terms of law (*j*) cannot affect the law as laid down in texts which are expressed in precise language',(*k*) and by other writers (*l*). Nevertheless

(*f*) Tyabji §§424, 426; Wilson, 324; Abdur Rahim, 303; Abdur Rahman, *Institutes*, Art. 457.

(*g*) *Sic*, perhaps 'up' has been omitted by the printer.

(*h*) *Rahim Bakhsh* v. *Muhammad Hasan* (1888) 11 All. 1, 5; see also *Kulsum Bibi* v. *Bashir Ahmad* [1936] All. 285.

(*i*) I, 122-3.

(*j*) Referring to Baillie and Macnaghten.

(*k*) *Tyabji*, §424, p. 401.

(*l*) Ameer Ali, I, 158 sqq., esp. 162; Wilson, 324; Mulla §168.

the 'misapplication' is now so well established in India that Mr Ameer Ali in delivering the judgment of the Judicial Committee in *Hitendra Singh* v. *Maharaja of Darbhanga* says, 'Under the Mahomedan law a transfer by way of a hiba-bil-ewaz is *treated as a sale and not a gift*.'(*m*) This statement is likely to be misunderstood and it is necessary to restrict it to the *Indian form* mentioned by Baillie and Macnaghten, and not to the *ancient form* of the classical jurists.

An illustration of the Indian form is *Muhammad Faiz Ahmad Khan* v. *Ghulam Ahmad Khan* (*n*). *A* and *B*, two Muslim brothers, were owners of certain villages held by them as tenants-in-common. *A* died leaving him surviving his brother *B* and a widow *W*. Some time after *A*'s death, *B* executed a deed whereby he granted two of the villages to *W*. Two days after the date of the grant, but as part of the same transaction, *W* executed a writing whereby in consideration of the grant to her of the two villages she gave up her claim to her husband's estate in favour of *B*. The transaction was called a *h-i*, and was held to be valid despite the fact that possession was not delivered.

In Muhammadan law a *h-i*, as distinguished from *hiba*, is a gift for consideration. There is no authority for the proposition that the *'iwaḍ* (return, consideration) should be in the form of money. The promise to marry has been recognized as a good consideration; and this is particularly so where, as in Islamic law, marriage is defined as a civil contract. Therefore where the plaintiff agreed to marry the defendant's son there was sufficient consideration for the defendant to make a settlement in favour of the plaintiff (*o*).

An Ithna 'Asharī Muslim, *HA*, made a gift of immovable property by deed to *S*, a Hindu, to compensate him for the good services rendered by the father of *S* to *HA*. Later *HA* revoked the gift by selling the property to *B* and *N*. *S* there-

(*m*) (1928) 55 I.A. 197, 204-5 (italics mine).

(*n*) (1881) 3 All. 490.

(*o*) *Tajunnisa Bibi* v. *Rahmath Bibi* [1959] Mad. 630.

upon filed a suit claiming the property. Held (1) that the gift was a *hiba* and not an *h-i*; (2) that the Ithnā 'Asharī Shiite law applied; (3) that a decree was not necessary for evoking such a gift; and (4) that the revocation of the gift was valid. It is submitted with respect that some of the observations of Singh J. regarding past services not being a proper *'iwaḍ*, require reconsideration, and the decision cannot be deemed to be of unquestionable authority (*oo*).

Bye mukasa (*bay' al-muqāsāt*)

A curious form of *h-i* in India is what is called *bye mukasa*. This is a transfer of property by the husband to the wife in lieu of *mahr*, and an agreement by the wife not to claim dower (*p*). It is in Indian law a sale and the formalities of the law of gift, such as possession for instance, need not be followed strictly; but registration is necessary where immovable property is concerned, and such a gift cannot be made orally (*q*).

Hiba bi-sharṭi'l-'iwaḍ

When a gift (*hiba*) is made with a stipulation (*sharṭ*) for a return (*'iwaḍ*), the transaction as a whole is called *h-s-i* (*r*). The return stipulated for, may or may not be specified.

The main distinction is that in *h-i* a voluntary gift is followed by a voluntary return; in the *h-s-i*, the gift itself is made with a stipulation. The distinction between a *h-i* and *h-s-i* in their inception is, first, that the intention to make an *'iwaḍ* is an afterthought in *h-i*, whereas in *h-s-i* 'the two (gift and return) go hand in hand, not one before the other'; and, secondly, that the return is in contemplation by both parties in *h-s-i* (*s*).

(*oo*) *Someshwar* v. *Barket Ullah* A.I.R. (1963) All. 469.

(*p*) See Macnaghten, 216 sqq.; Baillie, I, 123-5; Ameer Ali, I, 174.

(*q*) *Ghulam Abbas* v. (*Mst.*) *Razia* A.I.R. (1951) All. 86, F.B.; followed in *Masum Vali Saheb* v. *Illuri Modin Saheb* A.I.R. (1952) Mad. 671.

(*r*) Ameer Ali, I, 158 sqq.; Tyabji §425; Mulla §169.

(*s*) Tyabji, loc. cit., com.

The kinds of property that can be given away by way of *hiba* can also be given by way of return gift (*'iwaḍ*) (*t*); and the return gift must be made with all the formalities necessary for a *hiba* (*u*).

After the gift and the return have been completed by delivery of possession, neither of them can be revoked (*v*). For example, *D* makes a gift of a house to *S* and puts him in possession. Thereafter *S* gives *D* a horse as an *'iwaḍ*, and *D* accepts it. Later, *D* purports to sell the house to *T*. The sale has no effect (*w*).

(*t*) ibid., §426.

(*u*) ibid., 427.

(*v*) ibid., §433

(*w*) loc. cit., com. For further details see Tyabji §§434 sqq., and his chart on p. 290.

CHAPTER IX

WAKF

§51. Introduction (a)

THE law of *wakf* is, according to Ameer Ali, the most important branch of Muhammadan law, for it is 'interwoven with the entire religious life and social economy' of Muslims (*b*). It is also the most difficult branch; the literature of the institution of *wakf* is vast; there are conflicting decisions; the texts differ amongst themselves widely, and this is not surprising: the social, economic and cultural life of the people in countries such as North Africa, Nigeria, Egypt, Turkey, Arabia, Palestine, Persia, Central Asia, Pakistan, India, and the Far East differs so widely that such divergences are only to be expected. Moreover, in all Muslim countries vast funds, properties and agricultural lands are dedicated as *wakfs*: hence it is necessary to give a brief general account of *wakf* before dealing with the law (*c*).

The word *waḳf* literally means 'detention';(*d*) but in Islamic law it means (i) state lands which are inalienable, used for charitable purposes; and (ii) pious endowments. In India generally we are concerned with the second meaning, and *wakf* is thus a pious endowment which is inalienable

(*a*) The best short account of the institution of *waḳf* is by Heffening in *Ency. of Islam,* IV, 1096-1103, and it is the basis of my remarks. On the purely legal aspects, the most exhaustive is Ameer Ali, I, 192-567 and 754-94.

(*b*) Ameer Ali, I, 193.

(*c*) In addition to the sources mentioned, see also Tyabji, p. 492 sqq., and Fitzgerald, 207.

(*d*) Pl. *awḳāf, wuḳūf*; usually spelt *waqf*, which I prefer; a synonym is *ḥabīs*, pl. *ḥubus*, and rarely, *ḥabs*, pl. *aḥbās* (North Africa), whence 'habous', in French. The common Indian spelling is used by me.

and therefore supposed to be perpetual although, in actual practice, this quality of perpetuity is cut down by several limitations.

It is tolerably certain that prior to Islam there were no *wakfs* in Arabia. The earliest *wakf* mentioned by the legal authorities is that of 'Umar the Second Caliph, and as it is made the basis of the law it is best to give a full account of it as related by the traditionist Bukhārī (*e*):

> Ibn Omar reported, 'Omar ibn al-Khaṭṭāb got land in Khaybar; so he came to the Prophet, peace and blessings of Allah be on him, to consult him about it. He said, "O Messenger of Allah! I have got land in Khaybar than which I have never obtained more valuable property; what dost thou advise about it?" He said: "If thou likest, make the property itself to remain inalienable, and give (the profit from) it in charity." '
>
> So Omar made it a charity on the condition that it shall not be sold, or given away as a gift, or inherited, and made it a charity among the needy and the relatives and to set free slaves and in the way of Allah and for the travellers and to entertain guests; there being no blame on him who managed it if he ate out of it and made (others) eat, not accumulating wealth thereby (*f*).

This appears to be the first reported instance, but it is fairly certain that many other lands and properties were dedicated by the close associates and followers of the Prophet, and hence the saying attributed to the Founder of Islam, 'Tie up the substance and give awav the fruits' (*ḥabbis al-aṣl wa sabbil al-thamara*) (*g*). 'Umar's *wakf* was at a place called Khaybar; later palm-gardens, fields and landed properties were similarly dedicated, and an instance of the dedication of a riding camel is also recorded.

(*e*) The tradition has come down to us in various forms in many of the authoritative texts, see *Ency. of Islam.* A short account of first principles will be found in Shāfi'ī, *Umm*, III, 281-3.

(*f*) Muhammad Ali, *Manual*, 331-2, No. 14, cited for convenience of reference. The tradition is reported in slightly varying forms by Bukhārī, Muslim, Abū Dā'ūd, Tirmidhī, Nasā'ī, Ibn Māja, Ibn Sa'd, and Imām Aḥmad b. Ḥanbal, Wensinck, *Handbook of Early Muhammadan Tradition*, 245.

(*g*) Ameer Ali, I, 497; Baillie, II, 212; Sircar, II, 463.

The *Da'ā'im al-Islām*, the primary authority in Fatimid law, gives details of *wakfs* made by the Prophet, Ali and Fatima (*gg*).

In the early days there was much uncertainty about the law. Abū Ḥanīfa held, for instance, that the founder's right of ownership continued even after the completion of a *wakf*, while Imām Shāfi'ī, the founder of another Sunnite school, and Abū Yūsuf, disciple of Abū Ḥanīfa, maintained the opposite view. It was only in the second century after the Flight, that a body of rules based on consensus (*ijmā'*) is to be found, which may be said to constitute the basis of all future laws.

The origin of *wakf* is to be sought in the strongly marked impulse to charitable deeds which is characteristic of Islam. In addition to this the Arabs found in most conquered lands endowments for churches, monasteries, orphanages and poorhouses. These endowments were of Byzantine origin and were under the direct supervision of the Bishops. The impulse to endow property 'in the way of God' (*li-wajhi'l-lāh, fī sabīli'l-lāh*) increased gradually, and in the centuries that followed, shops, warehouses, stables, baths, mills, bakeries, soap and paper works, looms, agricultural establishments such as gardens, farms and even villages came to be endowed by way of *wakf*. The commonest objects were to pay the mosque staffs and to endow schools and hospitals.

The importance of the institution will be better understood if we take into consideration the enormous extent of *wakf* land—or, the possessions of the DEAD HAND—in the various countries of Islam (*h*). In the Turkey of 1925, three-fourths of the arable land, estimated at 50,000,000 Turkish pounds, was endowed as *wakf*. At the end of the nineteenth century, one-half of the cultivable land in Algiers was dedicated. Similarly, in Tunis one-third, and in Egypt one-eighth, of the cultivated soil was 'in the ownership of God'. But it was already realized by the beginning of the twentieth century, first by France

(*gg*) *Fat. Law* §§331 sqq.

(*h*) A picturesque rendering of 'mortmain', for which see the legal dictionaries and the *Shorter Oxford English Dictionary*.

and later in Turkey and Egypt, that the possession of the Dead Hand spelled ruin. The institution of *wakf* was in some respects a handicap to the natural growth and development of a healthy national economy.

In 1830, the French Government took over the *habous* in Algiers, and later on in Morocco. Elsewhere Government control was made more stringent. In 1924 the Turkish republic abolished the Ministry of Wakfs and it was taken over by a general directory, or by the secular state administration, as we would call it. In Egypt it was Muhammad Ali who first confiscated all agricultural *wakfs* and compensated the beneficiaries and in 1924 the Wakf Ministry came directly under the control of parliament (*i*). Although in Russia *wakfs* existed in Muslim districts for centuries, soon after the revolution such endowments were confiscated and declared state property.

We must now consider briefly the advantages and disadvantages of the institution. The religious motive of *wakf* is the origin of the legal fiction that *wakf* property belongs to Almighty God; the economic ruin that it brings about is indicated by the significant phrase 'The Dead Hand'. *Wakf* to some extent ameliorates poverty, but it has also its dark side. When a father provides a certain income for his children and descendants, the impulse to seek education and the initiative to improve their lot gradually decrease. Charitable aid often keeps people away from industry, and lethargy breeds degeneration. Furthermore, some people who desire fame by making foundations and endowments obtain property by shady means, amounting even to extortion and exploitation. Agricultural land deteriorates in the course of time; no one is concerned with keeping it in good trim; the yield lessens, and even perpetual leases come to be recognized. In India, instances of the mismanagement of *wakfs*, of the worthlessness of *mutawallīs* (managers), and of the destruction of

(*i*) In September 1952 it was reported in the press that, following the coup of General Najīb, certain kinds of *wakfs* had been abolished in Egypt.

wakf property have often come before the courts. Considering all these matters, it can by no means be said that the institution of *wakf* as a whole has been an unmixed blessing to the community.

If we examine the conditions relating to *wakfs* in Muslim countries in general, and in India in particular, two general tendencies will appear with unmistakable clarity. First, everywhere there is a tendency towards greater state control; and secondly, there is probably a move in the direction of reduction of *wakfs*, and particularly of personal and family *wakfs*. As illustrative of the former, we have the numerous Wakf Acts all over India; of the latter, it is impossible to be certain, but people are beginning to realize the disadvantages of tying up property in perpetuity, where succeeding generations obtain successively smaller fractions of the income, part of which—if not the whole—is often squandered in vexatious and frivolous litigation, and duly 'absorbed' by unscrupulous lawyers. Speaking for myself, and in the light of actual experience, it is unfortunate that the opinion of Lord Hobhouse in *Abul Fata's Case* did not prevail in India, although it is contrary to the law laid down by ancient authorities.

§52. Definition

The word *waḳf* means, as we have already seen, 'detention'. We must now consider it juristically, and for this purpose we shall first discuss Abū Ḥanīfa's view, historically the earliest; secondly, the view of his disciples Cadi Abū Yūsuf and Imām Muḥammad; thirdly, the definition in the Shiite text, *Sharā'i' al-Islām*; and lastly, the definition in the Wakf Act, 1913.

(1) *Abū Ḥanīfa*

According to the Imām Abū Ḥanīfa, *wakf* is 'the tying-up of the substance of a property in the ownership of the *wāḳif* (*j*)

(*j*) The word *wāḳif* means the founder of a *wakf*.

and the devotion of its usufruct, amounting to an *'āriya*, or commodate loan, for some charitable purpose'.(*k*)

The two elements to be noted are that the right of the owner continues and that the usufruct is to be devoted to some charitable or pious purpose.

(2) *The Two Disciples*

According to the two disciples of Abū Ḥanīfa—Cadi Abū Yūsuf and Imām Muḥammad—*wakf* is

. . . the tying-up of the substance of a thing under the rule of the property of Almighty God, so that the proprietary right of the *wāḳif* becomes extinguished and is transferred to Almighty God for any purpose by which its profits may be applied to the benefit of His creatures (*l*).

This is an important definition and as it was accepted substantially by the later Hanafi jurists, it must be carefully analysed. The three elements are: (i) the ownership of God, whence perpetuity and irrevocability; (ii) the extinction of the founder's right; (iii) the benefit to mankind. This difference between the Imām and his two disciples is extremely important for other purposes as well, and in this case the view of the disciples prevailed in the succeeding centuries (*m*).

(3) *The Shiite View*

The *Sharā'i' al-Islām* defines *wakf* as follows: 'A contract, the fruit or effect of which is to tie up the original of a thing and to leave its usufruct free.'(*n*)

The chief points in this definition are (i) the immobilization of the corpus and (ii) the use of the income or profits for certain purposes. The definition does not state clearly to whom the corpus belongs (*o*).

(*k*) Ameer Ali, I, 336, citing *Hedaya,* 231; Baillie, I, 557-8. Hamilton's unnecessary restriction is pointed out by Baillie, who is 'our best translator', Fitzgerald, 234. Tyabji §474, com.; Wilson §317; Abdur Rahim 303-4.

(*l*) Ameer Ali, I, 336; Baillie, I, 559-60; Tyabji, loc. cit.

(*m*) Ameer Ali, I, 337.

(*n*) Baillie, II, 211; Ameer Ali, I, 497; Sircar,II, 463.

(*o*) Tyabji says that, according to Shiite authorities, the corpus belongs to the beneficiaries, Tyabji §474, p. 494, n. 15.

The *Da'ā'im* says that Ali made an endowment of landed property in Medina; Imām Ḥasan, and after him Imām Ḥusayn were to be the *mutawallis*, and both of them were given the right to maintain themselves from the income of the *wafk* (*oo*).

(4) *The Wakf Act, 1913*

'Wakf means the permanent dedication by a person professing the Mussulman faith of any property for any purpose recognized by the Mussulman Law as religious, pious or charitable.' (Sec. 2(1).)

The Privy Council has held that the above definition is for the purposes of the Act and not necessarily exhaustive (*p*). Hence it is necessary to consider briefly the three dominant characteristics of a *wakf*. In the first instance, the motive must be religious; a merely secular motive would render the dedication a gift or a trust, but not a *wakf* (*q*). Secondly, it is a permanent endowment; a pious gift which is not a permanent foundation may be a *ṣadaqa*, but cannot in law be termed a *wakf*. And lastly, the usufruct is to be utilized for the good of mankind.

The real nature of *wakf* can be well understood by contrasting it with the notion of trust in modern law (*r*). Mr Ameer Ali in delivering the judgment of the Judicial Committee in *Vidya Varuthi* v. *Balusami Ayyar* says (*s*):

> The conception of a trust apart from a gift was introduced in India with the establishment of Moslem rule. And it is for this reason that in many documents of later times in parts of the country where Mahommedan influence has been predominant, such as Upper India and the Carnatic, the expression wakf is used to express dedication.
>
> But the Mahommedan law relating to trusts differs fundamentally from the English law. It owes its origin to a rule laid

(*oo*) *Fat. Law* §332.

(*p*) *Ma Mi* v. *Kallander Ammal* (No. 1) (1926) 54 I.A. 23, 27.

(*q*) Tyabji p. 495.

(*r*) ibid., pp. 497 sqq.

(*s*) (1921) 8 I.A. 302, 312; *Cases*, 379, 384.

down by the Prophet of Islam; and means 'the tying up of property in the ownership of God the Almighty and the devotion of the profits for the benefit of human beings'. When once it is declared that a particular property is wakf, or any such expression is used as implies wakf, or the tenor of the document shows, as in the case of *Jewun Doss Sahoo* v. *Shah Kubeer-ood-din* (1840) 2 M.I.A. 390, that a dedication to pious or charitable purposes is meant, the right of the wakif is extinguished and the ownership is transferred to the Almighty. The donor may name any meritorious object as the recipient of the benefit. The manager of the wakf is the mutawalli, the governor, superintendent, or curator.

The essentials of *wakf* may now be summarized. The motive in *wakf* is always religious; in trust, it is generally temporal; this is the first characteristic.

Secondly, *wakf* is a foundation endowed in perpetuity (*t*). In the eye of the law the property belongs to God, and as such, the dedication is both permanent and irrevocable. The property itself is 'detained' or, to use the expressive language of French lawyers, it is 'immobilized' and no further transfers can be effected (*u*). In a trust, permanency is not an essential condition; a trust of property for the benefit of *A* and thereafter absolutely to *B* is a valid trust terminable on the death of *A*. In Islamic law, a *wakf* is not terminable; it is God's property and should be as permanent as human ingenuity can make it. Permanency is ensured by the legal fiction that the property is transferred to the ownership of Almighty God.

Thirdly, in a trust, the settlor himself can lawfully take an interest; but in a *wakf*, except in the case of the Hanafis, a *wāḳif* is not entitled to take any benefit in the *wakf* property.

Fourthly, it is now established beyond any possibility of doubt that any property capable of being endowed in perpetuity can be the subject-matter of *wakf*. There is in this respect no distinction between a *wakf* and a trust.

And fifthly, as to the administration, a trustee differs widely from a *mutawallī*. A *mutawallī* is merely a 'procurator',

(*t*) Ameer Ali, I, 195; Mulla §174. (*u*) Fitzgerald, 206.

manager or superintendent, 'the property is not vested in him and he is not a "trustee" in the technical sense'.(*v*)

§53. Classification

It is proposed here to make a few brief observations regarding the essential nature of *wakf* as a legal institution. The first observation is that a *wakf* is a religious or pious endowment, and although it often provides for charities and charitable institutions, it should not be confused with a 'charity' or a 'charitable trust' as understood in English law. The classification of *wakfs* by the Muslim jurists makes this abundantly clear.

According to Ameer Ali, *wakfs* may be divided into three classes (*w*):

(i) In favour of the rich and the poor *alike*.
(ii) In favour of the rich and *then* for the poor.
(iii) In favour of the poor *alone*.

The first class of *wakfs* would comprise what might be termed in modern law public trusts of a charitable or beneficial character; for example, schools or hospitals open to all persons. The second class would include family *wakfs* in favour of a settlor's family, the ultimate benefit of which goes to the poor. The third class would comprise endowments for giving food, clothing or medical relief to the needy alone.

Another classification would be to divide *wakfs* into three classes: *public*, *quasi-public* and *private*.

Essentials of a wakf. A *wakf*, however, must be a permanent endowment; it cannot be contingent, or revocable. Secondly, writing is not necessary to create it; an oral dedication is deemed to be sufficient in certain circumstances, and

(*v*) *Vidya Varuthi's Case*, 48 I.A. at p. 312; *Cases*, op. cit. The best discussions on the difference between a trust and *wakf* will be found in *Muhammad Rustam Ali* v. *Mushtaq Husain* (1920) 47 I.A. 224; *Vidya Varuthi* v. *Balusami* (1921) 48 I.A. 302; and *Zain Yar Jung* v. *Director of Endowments* A.I.R. (1963) S.C. 985. A good summary will be found in Tyabji, pp. 497 sqq.

(*w*) Ameer Ali, I, 193.

the use of the word '*wakf*' is not necessary (*x*). Thirdly, a *wakf* may also be validly constituted by long user (*y*); on this ground a number of mosques and graveyards have been declared *wakfs*. Fourthly, a *wakf* can be made by a will, as also in *marḍ al-mawt,* but such *wakfs* cannot comprise more than one-third of the settlor's property (*z*).

§54. *Wāḳif*—Who can make a *waḳf*?

Any Muslim who has attained majority and is of sound mind can make a *wakf* (*a*). Ameer Ali points out that, according to the classical jurists of Islam, even non-Muslims could make *wakfs* (*b*); and his view has prevailed in Nagpur and Patna, where it has been held that non-Muslims can validly make public wakfs, 'but the law requires that the objects for which the dedication is made should be lawful according to the creed of the dedicator as well as the Islamic doctrines' (*c*).

Neither a minor, nor a guardian on behalf of the minor, can make a *wakf*, and such a *wakf*, even if purported to be made, is void (*d*). And finally, a *wakf* cannot be made for an illegal object, for example, to delay or defeat creditors (*e*).

§55. Completion

(A) A dedication by way of *wakf* is complete, according to Abū Yūsuf, by the mere declaration. Neither delivery of

(*x*) Tyabji §475; Mulla §183.

(*y*) Tyabji, loc. cit.; Mulla §188.

(*z*) Ameer Ali mentions Qāḍī Khān's classification of *wakfs* in this respect: (1) made in health; (2) made during mortal disease (*marḍ al-mawt*); (3) made by will; Ameer Ali, I, 212. Tyabji §§476 sq.; Mulla §§184-5.

(*a*) Baillie, I, 560; Tyabji §478; Mulla §182.

(*b*) Ameer Ali, I, 200; Tyabji, pp. 508, 570.

(*c*) *Motishah* v. *Abdul Gaffar* A.I.R. (1956) Nag. 38, 42; (*Mst.*) *Mundaria* v. *Shyam Sundar* A.I.R. (1963) Patna 98, which laid down that a Hindu could not dedicate an *imāmbāra*, which was a private, as distinguished from a public, *wakf*; see below §61(6).

(*d*) *Commissioner of Wakfs* v. *Mohammad Moshin* (1953) 58 Cal. W.N. 252.

(*e*) Tyabji 479. See below §58 (A).

possession, nor appointment of *mutawallīs* is essential. This view has been adopted by most of the High Courts in India (*f*).

(B) According to Imām Muḥammad, however, a *wakf* is not complete unless (i) there is a declaration, coupled with (ii) appointment of *mutawallīs*, and (iii) delivery of possession (*g*). The doctrine of Imām Muḥammad is not followed in India. Delivery of possession, however, is unnecessary where the *wāḳif* constitutes himself the *mutawallī*.

(C) The Shiite Ithnā 'Asharī law is similar to the view of Imām Muḥammad and insists on delivery of possession. Baillie says, 'The contract is not rendered obligatory except by giving possession (i.e. act of *wāḳif*).'(*h*).

Registration. A *wakf-nāma*, by which immovable property of the value of Rs 100 or more is dedicated by way of *wakf*, requires to be registered under the Indian Registration Act, 1908 (*i*).

This point appears to be implied in *Muhammad Rustam Ali* v. *Mushtaq Husain*. As the head-note of the case in 47 Indian Appeals is somewhat misleading, we shall briefly consider the facts. Nawab Azmat Ali Khan made a *wakf* of his property and executed a document, called the *wakf-nāma*, on 25 August 1908, whereby he appointed himself as *mutawallī* of the *wakf* property. This document, the *wakf-nāma*, was duly registered. Two and a half months later, on 9 November 1908 he executed another document, called 'the trusteenama', and this document was not registered. By this trusteenama he appointed additional *mutawallīs* of the *wakf* and gave further directions. It was held by the Judicial Com-

(*f*) *Mohammad Yasin v. Rahmat Ilahi* [1947] All. 520, F.B.; *Mohd. Sabir Ali v. Tahir Ali*, A.I.R. (1957) All. 94; Ameer Ali, I, 231, 237; Tyabji §481; Mulla §186. *Garib Das* v. *M. A. Hamid* A.I.R. (1970) S.C. 1035.

(*g*) *Hedaya*, 233; Baillie, I, 559; Tyabji and Mulla, loc. cit. Tyabji has sought to reconcile the views of Abū Yūsuf and Imām Muḥammad, §481, com., esp. p. 515 sqq.

(*h*) Baillie, II, 212.

(*i*) See Section 17(1)(*b*); *Muhammad Rustam Ali* v. *Mushtaq Husain* (1920) 47 I.A. 224; Mulla §187.

mittee that this 'trusteenama' did not require registration, as there is no analogy between a 'trustee', in the sense of the English Common law, and a *mutawallī*. Property vests in a trustee, but a *mutawallī* is a mere superintendent; and 'the further use of the term "trustee" is apt to mislead until this distinction is borne in mind'.(*j*)

Hence it is clear that a document which creates a *wakf*, extinguishes the property of the settlor or *wāḳif*, and thus requires registration; but a document which merely transfers the right of the *mutawallī* in the *wakf*, does not create or assign property, and does not require to be registered.

Long user. Where land has for long been used as a *wakf*, proof of express dedication is not necessary, and the legal dedication will be inferred. The Indian courts have often upheld the *wakf* of mosques and graveyards on this ground (*k*).

A wakf normally requires express dedication, but if land has been used from time immemorial for a religious purpose, then the land is by user *wakf*, although there is no evidence of an express dedication. Where, to an original mosque, which is proved to be *wakf* property, an area is added by the *mutawallis* by way of construction of rooms and this area is used by the public for religious purposes along with the old mosque, then if the area has been made into a separately demarcated compact unit for a single purpose, namely collective and individual worship in the mosque, it must be regarded as one unit and treated as such. The whole becomes dedicated property by user (*l*).

One Haidar Bakhsh, belonging originally to a wealthy Hindu family, adopted Islam in A.D. 1794, and remained on good terms with his Hindu brother Munna Lal and his descendants. In 1813 he built a mosque and an *imāmbāra*, and planted a grove called Imam Bagh. These were in a com-

(*j*) 47 I.A. at p. 232.

(*k*) Tyabji §475, ills. 6, 7 and 8. Mulla §188.

(*l*) *Mohammad Shah* v. *Fasihuddin Ansari* A.I.R. (1956) S.C.R. 713.

pound containing residential houses in one of which Haidar Bakhsh lived. Thenceforward the mosque was used for worship and the *imāmbāra* for burial of *tazias* in accord with the Shiite faith. The Privy Council held that the *wakf* was established, and Lord Uthwatt delivering the judgment of the Board said:

> There is no evidence that Haidar Bakhsh ever executed a wakfnama and no direct evidence of any oral dedication by him. But if the proper inference from the history of the matter, the dealings with the properties, the litigation that has affected it and the admissions and assertions made by the respondent's predecessors-in-title is that Haidar Bakhsh purchased the villages in the names of Maiku Lal and *Bahadur* Lal on the expressed footing that they were to be an endowment of an existing wakf consisting of the mosque, grove and imambara, their Lordships do not doubt that all the requirements of the Shia law necessary to the valid creation of a wakf attaching to the villages were satisfied (*m*).

And in *Jawaharbeg* v. *Abdul Aziz,* the court, adopting the same principles, came to the conclusion that, on the evidence and the surrounding circumstances, the *wakf* was not established (*n*).

§56. Incidents

(1) *Perpetuity*

Perpetuity is an essential characteristic of a *wakf*; a *wakf* for a limited period is not recognized by law. The Wakf Act, 1913, lays down that (i) in a *wakf*, the dedication must be 'permanent' (Sec. 2(1)), and (ii) in the case of *wakf 'alā'l-awlād* (family *wakfs*), the ultimate benefit must be 'expressly or impliedly reserved for the poor or for any other purpose recognized by the Mussalman law as a religious, pious or charitable purpose of a permanent character' (Sec. 3, proviso). Thus even in the case of a family *wakf*, the foundation would continue to function for the benefit of humanity

(*m*) *Mazhar Husain* v. *Adiya Saran* A.I.R. (1948) P.C. 42, 43.

(*n*) A.I.R. (1956) Nagpur 257.

(*o*). For instance, Ibrahim says, 'This house of mine is a *wakf* for the poor for one month or twenty years.' The *wakf* is void *ab initio*. If a *wakf-nāma* contains a condition that in the case of mismanagement the property should be divided among the heirs of the settlor, the intended dedication is void (*p*).

A question sometimes arises whether, on a proper construction of the terms of the document, the dedication is to be deemed permanent or not. Ameer Ali points out that, in accordance with the view of the early jurists, once a particular property is dedicated by way of *wakf*, the right of the *wāḳif* (founder) is extinguished for ever, and therefore, where appropriate and technical words are used, it is unnecessary to say that the dedication is permanent. For instance, where the legal terms of *waḳf* or *mawḳūfa* (in relation to the property) are used, permanence will be presumed as a matter of law, and the ultimate benefit will go to the poor, though unnamed (*q*).

In view of the terms of the proviso to Sec. 3, this question assumes importance. What is the meaning of the word 'impliedly'? Is it intended to give effect to the opinion of Abū Yūsuf, as adopted by Ameer Ali, so that the mere use of the word *wakf* is sufficient to import an ultimate and permanent gift to charity? The answer is that it is doubtful, for the recent authorities in India seem to lay down that some clearer indication is necessary (*r*); but in Madras it has been held recently that unless there are indications to the contrary, the use of the term *wakf* may by itself be taken to imply an ultimate dedication for the poor or for other unfailing charitable objects (*s*). And this appears to be the correct view.

(*o*) Wilson §317. In the comment he points out that the Mālikī jurists consider a temporary *wakf* valid. See also §323B; Tyabji §483; Mulla §174.

(*p*) Mulla, loc. cit.

(*q*) Ameer Ali, I, 232-4; followed in *Syed Ahmad* v. *Julaiha Bibi* [1947] Mad. 480 and *Thanga Mayil* v. *Fathima* [1960] Mad. 481.

(*r*) *Abdul Gafur* v. *Nizamudin* (1892) 19 I.A. 170; *Ghulam Mohammad* v. *Ghulam Husain* (1931) 59 I.A. 74; Mulla §197, note (3).

(*s*) *Syed Ahmad* v. *Julaiha Bibi* [1947] Mad. 480.

(2) *Irrevocability*

A *wakf*, once it is validly constituted, is irrevocable (*t*). A testamentary *wakf* operates only from the death of the testator, and there is nothing to prevent a man from revoking his will and making another. Such a revocation is not the revocation of a *wakf*, but only the revocation of a will (*u*).

If a condition is inserted in a deed of *wakf*, that the *waḳif* reserves to himself the power of revoking the *wakf*, the *wakf* is void *ab initio*. Two settlors, Ahmed and Sulaiman, purported to create a *wakf* by a deed which contained a clause enabling one of them by deed wholly to alter the trusts declared by the deed and by the same deed or by will or codicil to declare new trusts concerning the trust premises. It was held that the power of revocation reserved in favour of the settlors rendered the whole deed void (*v*); for, as Beaumont C.J. points out, 'It is impossible to contemplate property transferred to Almighty God subject to a condition enforceable in the temporal courts for recovering that property for the benefit of the settlor.'(*w*)

But a *wāḳif* may at the time of dedication reserve to himself the power to alter the beneficiaries either by adding to their number or excluding some. In a *wakf-nāma* the *wāḳif* reserved to himself certain powers in the following terms:

'If during my life-time, I so desire, I shall be competent to rescind or alter by a fresh *wakf-nāma* the provisions as to the appointment of the *mutawalli* and other rules and procedure . . .' It was held that the words of reservation did not imply the power of revocation of the *wakf*, but only to the mutation of the *mutawallis* (*x*). Power to amend the *wakf*

(*t*) *Hedaya*, 234, Baillie, I, 565; Tyabji §484.

(*u*) Mulla §189(1).

(*v*) *Abdul Satar* v. *Advocate General of Bombay* (1932) 35 Bom. L.R. 18. followed in *Abdeally Hyderbhai* v. *Advocate General of Bombay* (1946) 48 Bom. L.R. 631.

(*w*) 35 Bom. L.R. at p. 25 *Fat. Law* §335.

(*x*) *North Sylhet Local Board* v. *Gaznafar Ali* (1949) 54 Cal. W N., D.R.53.

after completion may be reserved; but not the absolute power to change the objects of the *wakf* (y).

(3) *Inalienability*

As a *wakf* is a permanent endowment, perpetuity is ensured by the doctrine that *wakf* property belongs to God and cannot be alienated by human beings for their own purposes. Hence the rule of law that *wakf* property is not alienable (z).

Although *wakf* property cannot be sold, transferred or encumbered, in a fit case the *mutawallī* may apply to the court, and for the protection or the better management of the *wakf*, he may sell or grant leases with the court's express permission (*a*). The prohibition to sell must not be confused with a mere variation of investments, and the courts have often consented readily to allow an alteration in the form of investment (*b*).

Lost Grant. Where certain persons have for long peaceably enjoyed certain property as tenants, the facts that the lands once belonged to a *wakf* and that the necessary permission to alienate is not forthcoming, are not sufficient grounds to displace the tenants' rights. In a Bengal case (*c*), the *mutawallī* of an ancient *wakf* sued the defendants for possession of land. An imperial *sanad* of the Emperor Shāh 'Ālam, granted in 1772, appointing a *mutawallī*, prohibited the grant of permanent tenancies. The defendants, however, proved that they had been tenants for over seventy years at an unchanged rent, and the tenancy was treated as heritable property. In such circumstances, the doctrine of a 'lost grant' was applied by the Judicial Committee, and it was presumed that the *kazi* (or court) had, at some time unknown, granted a lawful

(*y*) *Rashidunnissa* v. *Ata Rasool* A.I.R. (1958) All. 67, 72.

(*z*) Tyabji §484; Mulla §§193, 194.

(*a*) This will be discussed more fully when we come to the powers of the *mutawallī*, Mulla §§207-9.

(*b*) Tyabji §486.

(*c*) *Mahammad Mazaffar* v. *Jabeda Khatun* (1930) 57 I.A. 125.

permission to create the tenancy. Lord Sumner, in delivering the judgment of the Board, said:

> The presumption of an origin in some lawful title, which the courts have so often readily made in order to support possessory rights, long and quietly enjoyed, where no actual proof of title is forthcoming is one which is not a mere branch of the law of evidence. It is resorted to because of the failure of actual evidence (*d*).

(4) *Contingency*

A dedication purported to be made subject to a contingency is void (*e*). A Muslim wife conveys her property to her husband upon trust to maintain herself and her children out of the income, and to hand over the property to the children on their attaining majority and, in the event of her death without leaving issue, to devote the income to certain religious purposes. The dedication is subject to a contingency, namely the settlor's death, without leaving children, and thus it is void (*f*).

(5) *Application of Income*

Where a *wakf* is constituted by the execution of a document, the income of the *wakf* property is to be applied according to the terms laid down in the *wakf-nāma*. In general, however, it may be said that the income of the *wakf* property is to be applied for the following purposes:

(i) the maintenance and repair of *wakf* property;
(ii) the specified objects of the *wakf*;
(iii) the incidental expenses necessary for carrying out the specified objects; and finally,
(iv) the benefit of the poor (*g*).

(*d*) ibid., p. 130.

(*e*) Tyabji §482; Wilson §319.

(*f*) Mulla §191; *Pathukutti* v. *Avathalakutti* (1888) 13 Mad. 66; *Commissioner of Wakfs, W. Bengal* v. (*Hazi*) *Rashid Ali* A.I.R. (1958) Cal. 413.

(*g*) Tyabji §487.

§57. Subject: The kind of property which may be dedicated as wakf (*h*)

When the institution of *wakf* came into being, the oldest known *wakfs* were of a reasonably permanent character and consisted of lands, fields or gardens. But very soon thereafter, jurists of all shades of opinion were agreed that, in addition to immovable property, some other kinds of property could also be dedicated. For instance, working cattle and implements of husbandry (*i*); Korans for reading in mosques (*j*); other movables not necessarily consumed in their use (*k*); war horses, camels and swords (*l*); and a chest of money for loans to the poor (*m*).

It was at one time thought that nothing but land and immovable property could be dedicated by way of *wakf*; and the Calcutta High Court decided in 1905 that *wakf* of shares in a joint stock company was not valid (*n*); but this decision was subjected to severe criticism and can no longer be regarded as laying down the correct rule (*o*).

Abdur Rahim lays down that the property dedicated must possess two characteristics: (i) it must be *māl*, tangible property, and (ii) it must be capable of being used without being consumed (*p*). Subject to this, there are no further restrictions; and recent decisions have emphasized that the terms of the Wakf Act, 1913, Sec. 2(1), where the expression 'any property' is used, are wide enough to include almost every species of property. Thus, Government promissory notes (*q*), cash (*r*), rights of a grove holder (*s*), and offerings

(*h*) A full discussion of the texts will be found in Ameer Ali, I, 246-72; Abdur Rahim, 307-8.

(*i*) Wilson §318(1).

(*j*) ibid., §318(2).

(*k*) ibid., §318(3).

(*l*) Abdur Rahim, 307.

(*m*) Fitzgerald, 214.

(*n*) *Kulsom Bibee* v. *Golam Hossein* (1905) 10 C.W.N. 449.

(*o*) Ameer Ali, I, 247 sqq., 257 sqq.; Abdur Rahim, 307; Tyabji §495; Wilson §318, notes.

(*p*) Abdur Rahim, 307.

(*q*) *Mohammad Sadiq* v. *Fakhr Jahan* (1931) 59 I.A. 1, 17-18.

(*r*) *Abdulsakur* v. *Abubakkar* (1929) 54 Bom. 358, 369-70.

(*s*) *Amir Ahmad* v. *Muhammad Ejaz Husain* (1935) 58 All. 464.

on a shrine (*t*) may be validly dedicated. On the other hand, a usufructuary mortgagee cannot make a valid *wakf* of his rights (*u*); nor can a dower debt, which may or may not be paid to the widow, be dedicated (*v*); nor a simple money decree, which may or may not be realized from the debtors (*w*).

It is submitted that in view of the expression 'any property' used in the Act, it is desirable to take a wider view of the law. There is no reason why 'any property' may not include forms of property, expendable or consumable in themselves, but capable of being converted into more or less permanent investments bringing in a regular income. On this analogy, a usufructuary mortgagee or the holder of a money decree could sell his interest and invest the proceeds in a profitable form.

The property dedicated must be in the ownership of the *wāḳif*; it must also be in his possession (*x*). For example, *A* bequeaths certain land to *B*, who purports to dedicate it in *A*'s lifetime. Later *A* dies. The *wakf* is not valid.

A *mushā*' (or an undivided part in property) may be validly dedicated as a *wakf* (*xx*), but *aliter* if the property is to be used for a mosque or a burial ground (*y*). Nor if the *mushā*' is a share in leasehold property (*yy*). This was the opinion of Cadi Abū Yūsuf and it is generally approved in India, although Imām Muḥammad held otherwise. Thus, one of several heirs of a deceased Muslim may make a *wakf* of his undivided share in the inheritance for a school or a hospital, but not for a mosque or a burial ground.

(*t*) Tyabji §498. A comprehensive modern list will be found in Tyabji §§495 sq.

(*u*) *Mst. Rahiman v. Mst. Baqridan* (1935) 11 Luck. 735.

(*v*) *Nosh Ali* v. *Shams-un-Nissa Bibi* [1938] All. 322.

(*w*) *Ghulam Mohiuddin* v. *Abdul Rashid* [1947] All. 334.

(*x*) Tyabji §496; Mulla §176.

(*xx*) *Fat. Law* §320 (iii).

(*y*) Tyabji §497; Mulla §177.

(*yy*) *Mst. Peeran* v. *Hafiz Mohammad* A.I.R. (1966) All. 201.

Pakistan. The Lahore High Court has decided in a well-considered and exhaustive judgment that a fund collected for a religious foundation, but not yet used for the purchase of property for the purpose of the endowment, is to be regarded as a duly constituted *wakf, Abdul Hamid* v. *Fateh Muhammad* PLD 1958 (W.P.) Lahore 824.

Property which cannot be dedicated

The subject of a *wakf* must be clearly defined. *X* says, 'Let a horse or a mansion be dedicated as *wakf*.' The dedication is void for uncertainty (*z*). A *wakf* cannot be made of the rights of a usufructuary mortgagee; nor of a dower debt, which may or may not be paid; nor of a simple money decree; nor will a *wakf* be upheld which is in fraud of the rights of certain heirs (*a*).

Talukdari property, governed by the Oudh and Estates Act (I of 1869), cannot be dedicated as *wakf 'alā'l-awlād* (*aa*); nor can a mere leasehold (*aaa*).

§58. Objects: The purposes for which and the persons for whom a wakf can be created

The subject may be conveniently divided into three parts: (A) For what purposes? (B) For whom? (C) Family *wakf* (*wakf 'alā'l-awlād*).

Before beginning a discussion of the subject proper, it is well to remember that in this context two words are often used promiscuously which occasionally cause confusion. The word 'purpose' is clear enough (*b*); but the word 'object' has two meanings. The word is used as a synonym of the word 'purpose', for instance the objects of a company, or the objects of a club; but it may also be used for the persons who benefit by a legal transaction, for example the objects of a power, or the objects of a trust or settlement.

(*z*) Tyabji §499.
(*a*) Mulla §§175, 176.
(*aa*) *Mohd. Ismail* v. *Sabir Ali* A.I.R. (1962) S.C. 1722.
(*aaa*) *Mst. Peeran* v. *Hafiz Mohammad* A.I.R. (1966) All. 201.
(*b*) Compare Indian Trusts Acts, Secs. 4 and 6.

In the discussion which follows an attempt has been made to keep these two meanings clearly in view.

(A) *For what purposes?*

The real purpose of making a *wakf* is to acquire merit in the eyes of the Lord; all other purposes are subsidiary. Therefore every purpose considered by the Muhammadan law as 'religious, pious or charitable'(*c*) would be considered valid. Ameer Ali explains this clearly by saying that a *pious* act may be a smile in a neighbour's face or help to the weary; but in Islamic law 'it means an offering or gift made with the object of obtaining the approval of the Almighty or a reward in the next world'.(*d*) The test is: What has the *sharī'a* to say about it? You may make a *wakf* validly for a school or a hospital or a mosque; but you cannot legally dedicate a gambling-house, or a wine-shop, or a shop for the sale of ham and bacon. Wilson gives the following representative list: mosques and provisions for *imāms*; colleges and provisions for teachers; aqueducts, bridges, caravanserais; distribution of alms to the poor; and assistance to enable poor persons to perform the pilgrimage to Mecca (*e*).

What is Religion?

The question sometimes arises as to what, in essence, is a matter of religion; and the Supreme Court has held that 'A religion is not merely an opinion, doctrine or belief. It has its outward expression in acts as well', and '*Religious practices* or performances of acts in pursuance of religious belief are as much a part of religion as faith or belief in particular doctrines' (*f*). Explaining this further, in another case Gajendragadkar J. (as he then was) said 'a religion may not

(*c*) Wakf Act, 1913, Sec. 2(1).

(*d*) Ameer Ali, I, 213 sqq.; *Fat. Law* §331.

(*e*) Wilson §322 (citing *Hedava*, 240); further illustrations will be found in Tyabji 501; Mulla §178; and Fitzerald, 209; *Fat. Law* §330 (ii).

(*f*) *Ratilal Panachand* v. *State of Bombay* [1954] S.C.R. (India) 1055, 1064, 1065. The italics are mine.

only lay down a code of rules for its followers to accept, it might prescribe rituals and observances, ceremonies and modes of worship which are regarded as integral parts of religion, and these forms and observances might extend to matters of food and dress'. But these 'must be regarded by the said religion as *its essential and integral part* . . .' and he sounded a note of warning that they do not include 'superstitious beliefs' and 'extraneous and unnecessary accretions to religion itself' (*ff*).

The ultimate object of a *wakf*, however, is the benefit of the poor. 'In every wakf the benefaction of which is bestowed upon any individual or upon one's descendants, the charity is continued, upon their extinction, expressly or by implication of law to the general poor.'(*g*) According to Qudūrī, cited in the *Hedaya*, 'though the poor be not named in a wakf, yet they will take on failure of the objects named.'(*h*)

Uncertainty

The purposes of a *wakf* are not always indicated with reasonable certainty; on this point we have an interesting divergence of view between modern authorities and the ancient doctors.

The modern view is that the purposes of a trust must be indicated with reasonable certainty; if they are not, the trust fails. Applying this doctrine, a number of *wakfs* have been held to be void (*i*). The view of the ancient jurists, however, was different. According to them, once a man made a *wakf*, *even without designating clearly the purpose for which the income was to be applied*; it was nevertheless a lawful dedication (*j*). This question therefore requires a full discussion (*k*).

(*ff*) *Durgah Committee, Ajmer* v. *Syed Hussain Ali* [1962] 1 S.C.R. (India), 383, 411 sq. (italics mine.)

(*g*) Wilson, 6th ed., 354, footnote, citing Ameer Ali J. in *Bikani Mia's Case* (1892) 20 Cal. 116, 157. See also Ameer Ali, I, 273, 275.

(*h*) Ameer Ali, I, 339; *Fat. Law* §332. Cf. Matt. xxvi, 11; John xxii, 8.

(*i*) Mulla §179

(*j*) Ameer Ali, I, 218 sqq., 414; Tyabji §502.

(*k*) The question is discussed fully in Tyabji §502, com.; Ameer Ali, I, 218 sqq., 414; Wilson, 6th ed., 354.

The ancient legists said. 'The primary question is, "Has the *wāḳif* made a *wakf*?" Is so, we cannot possibly take upon ourselves the responsibility of denying him the opportunity to acquire religious merit accruing to him from the endowment. We shall hold the *wakf* to be valid; and we shall use if necessary the income or the fruits of the property for the good of the poor, for they are always the ultimate beneficiaries in *wakfs*.'

The modern jurists say: 'No *wakf* can be said to be validly constituted unless the objects are stated with reasonable certainty. How can you have a trust or a *wakf* when an essential pillar of the structure is missing? Without the "three certainties", as laid down by Lord Langdale (*l*), no trust or *wakf* is possible.'

The Indian text-writers and judges are not unanimous on the point. In *Morice* v. *Bishop of Durham* (*m*), a leading case on charities in England, it was laid down that a bequest for 'such objects of benevolence or liberality as the executor should most approve of' was too vague and uncertain to be enforced. Adopting this principle, it was held by the Privy Council in *Runchordas* v. *Parvatibai* (*n*), that a Hindu bequest which directed the trustees to act 'in such manner as they think proper for preserving my name, so that my money might always be used for some good *dharam* (religious or charitable purpose) after my death and by which good might be done to me (in a future state?)' was void for uncertainty. Following this decision there was a tendency among the Indian High Courts to hold that a *wakf* for 'good objects' in general was void for uncertainty (*o*). This opinion was supported by Wilson and by Mulla (*p*).

(*l*) Snell, *Equity*, 22nd ed., 80; *Knight* v. *Knight* (1840) 3 Beaven 148, 173.

(*m*) (1805) 10 Vesey 522.

(*n*) (1899) 26 I.A. 71; 23 Bom. 725.

(*o*) Mulla, §174.

(*p*) Wilson, 6th ed., §322, and particularly note 2, where he criticizes Ameer Ali; Mulla §179 sqq.

Ameer Ali, on the other hand, was of the opinion that the principle of *Morice* v. *Bishop of Durham* was not applicable to the law of *wakfs* (*q*); Tyabji agreed with him, and answered the criticism of Wilson in a learned note (*r*).

In these circumstances a conflict of decisions was inevitable and some curious results of juristic interpretation may be found in the Indian Law Reports. In an early Bombay case, *Gangbai* v. *Thavar* (*s*), the will of a Khoja written in the English language was construed and it was decided that a gift of a fund 'to be disposed of in charity as my executor shall think right' was a valid charitable bequest; but where the will is in the native language, and the word *dharm* or *daram* [sic] is used, the word is vague and uncertain, not comprehended in the word 'charity' as understood in the English language, and the court will not uphold the trust or legacy. In 1929, however, in a Cutchi Memon case, Mirza J. held that the expression 'religious ceremonies (*dharmakriya*) in connexion with my death' was perfectly clear and free from ambiguity (*t*). The law in Bombay appears to lay down that if a Khoja uses the word *dharam* in his native language, the courts cannot comprehend its meaning; if, on the other hand, a Cutchi Memon, using the same language, employs the expression *dhạrmakriya,* the meaning becomes crystal clear.

The matter, however, does not rest there. In *Mariambi* v. *Fatmabi* (*u*), a single judge of the Bombay High Court held that a bequest for *khairāt* was void for uncertainty; while the expression *umūr-i-khair* was absolutely clear to a Division Bench in Allahabad (*v*). Consistently with the latter decision, the Allahabad view now is that the significance of the word *khairāt,* at any rate in the United Provinces (now

(*q*) Ameer Ali, I, 218 sqq., and 414.

(*r*) Tyabji §502, com.

(*s*) (1863) 1 Bom. H.C.R., O.C. 71.

(*t*) *Abdulsakur* v. *Abubakkar* (1929) 54 Bom. 358.

(*u*) (1928) 31 Bom. L.R. 135.

(*v*) *Mukarram Ali* v. *Anjuman-un-Nissa* (1922) 45 All. 152.

the state of Uttar Pradesh) corresponds with the technical meaning of the word 'charity', as understood in English law (*w*).

If it is provided that after the provisions made for the founder's family are completed, the ultimate benefit was to go to any *kār khayr* (good purposes) as determined by the *ulema* of the city, with the recommendation that as far as possible the poor, the orphans and the widows among the *wāḳif's* relations should be given preference, it was held that the ultimate benefit was not defined with sufficient certainty and therefore the *wakf* was bad.

The words 'maintenance' and 'support' were defined and distinguished: the former generally means lodging, boarding, clothing and other necessaries of life; whereas the latter has a wider import and means not only maintenance, but also includes other expenses relating to the convenience of the beneficiary (*x*).

Despite the conflict of opinion on the subject, the latest tendency appears to be to agree with the views of Ameer Ali and Tyabji and to hold that—

(1) Once it is clear that there is a *bona fide* intention on the part of the *wāḳif* to create a *wakf*, and divest himself completely of the property, there is a good *wakf* which will not be allowed to fail. A valid *wakf* may thus be constituted: (i) where the objects are not specified at all, or (ii) where the objects fail as being impracticable, or (iii) where the objects are partly valid and partly not valid. In cases (i) and (ii), the *cy près* doctrine may be applied (*y*); and in case (iii) the valid objects may be acepted by the court and the others rejected

(2) The poor, by necessary implication, constitute the ultimate beneficiaries of every *wakf*.

(*w*) *Muhammad Yusuf* v. *Azimuddin* [1941] All. 443. The Lahore High Court upheld a *wakf* for *mazhabi aur khairati kam*, *Mohammad Afzal* v. *Din Mohammad* [1946] Lah. 300.

(*x*) *Faqir Mohammad* v. *Abda Khatoon* A.I.R. (1952) All. 127; [1952] 2 All. 806, an important case.

(*y*) On the *cy près* doctrine, see *Mahammad Hashim* v. *Iffat Ara* [1947] 2 Cal. 16, and Mulla §181.

(3) A Hindu endowment to *dharam* must be distinguished from a Muslim endowment by way of *wakf*.

This view was put forward in an exhaustive judgment by Hatim Tyabji J. in *Haji Ishak* v. *Faiz Muhammad* (*z*), and while there are conflicting decisions on the point (*a*), it is submitted that, having regard to the ancient texts and general notions of Muhammadan law, it is the correct view (*b*).

Illegal wakfs

A *wakf* cannot be made for an illegal object (*c*); nor to defeat or delay creditors (*d*). Where, however, the *wakf* is partly lawful and partly unlawful, the court will separate the two and enforce the valid portion (*e*).

A Nawab of the Ithnā 'Asharī Shiite persuasion, who was in greatly involved circumstances, created two *wakfs* without making any provision for the payment of debts. It was held that as the *wakfs* were intended clearly to delay or defeat the creditors, they were void (*f*).

(B) *For Whom?—the Beneficiaries*

The first question which arises is: Is poverty a necessary condition for obtaining benefit from a *wakf*? According to Muhammadan law, *wakfs* may be made (i) for the affluent and the indigent *alike*; or (ii) for the affluent and *thereafter* for the indigent; or (iii) for the indigent *alone* (*g*). The law does not insist that a man must necessarily be proved to be

(*z*) [1943] Karachi 166, A.I.R. (1943) Sind 134. The judgment is valuable despite minor slips.

(*a*) See especially the Full Bench decision, *Mst. Ahmadi Begam* v. *Mst. Badrunnisa* (1940) 15 Luck. 586.

(*b*) See also *Mohammad Afzal* v. *Din Mohammad* [1946] Lah. 300; and *Syed Ahmad* v. *Julaiha Bivi* [1947] Mad. 480; *Mohd. Sabir Ali* v. *Tahir Ali* A.I.R. (1957) All. 94.

(*c*) Baillie, I, 560; Mulla §178, com. (B).

(*d*) Tyabji §479.

(*e*) Wilson §323A.

(*f*) (*Mst.*) *Bibi Kubra* v. *Jainandan Prasad* A.I.R. (1955) Pat. 270.

(*g*) Ameer Ali, I, 193, 275.

poor before he can take the benefit of a *wakf*. Poverty is one of the many qualities that are recognized as being capable of attracting the benefit of a *wakf*, but it is by no means a *sine qua non*. Therefore, all persons, regardless of considerations of wealth, are entitled to come in as beneficiaries. Nevertheless, it is perfectly correct to say that when all other purposes fail, the relief of the poor is the ultimate purpose of every *wakf* (*h*).

Thus it is clear that the objects of a *wakf* may be different from the objects of a charitable trust as understood in English law.

As regards relationship—

(1) the *wāḳif* (but *only* in Hanafi law), or
(2) the family and descendants of the *wāḳif*, or
(3) unrelated persons,

are all capable of enjoying the benefits of a *wakf*.

The *wāḳif* (or founder) is not entitled to take any benefit after the dedication, except under the Hanafi law. While the Ithnā 'Asharī law does not allow such a reservation in favour of the settlor, the Hanafi jurists permit him to take the whole of the usufruct for his own life or for a lesser period, or to provide for the payment of his own debts (*i*).

An Ithnā 'Asharī woman provided in a dedication that she should be the first *mutawallī* and have a remuneration of Rs 1,500 a year, and that succeeding *mutawallīs* should have Rs 360. The total income of the *wakf* properties was Rs 19,000. It was held by the Judicial Committee that such a reservation in favour of the settlor rendered the *wakf* wholly void (*j*) The Fatimid rule appears to be identical (*jj*).

This difference between the schools is a striking one and

(*h*) Ameer Ali, I, 273, 275 and specially 339, where *Qudūrī* is cited in the *Hedaya;* and Ameer Ali, I, 414, cited in (1943) Karachi 166, 189.

(*i*) Ameer Ali, I, 281 sqq.; Tyabji §507; Mulla §192; Wakf Act, 1913. Sec. 3(*b*).

(*j*) *Abadi Begum* v. *Kaniz Zainab* (1926) 54 I.A. 33; Tyabji §507, ill. (5).

(*jj*) *Fat. Law* §335.

calls for an explanation (*k*). One explanation appears to be that Imām Abū Ḥanīfa held that the *wāḳif*'s interest in the dedicated properties continued in some measure even after a valid dedication by way of *wakf*. Hence, there was no difficulty in allowing him to share with others the usufruct of the property. The two disciples, on the other hand, were of the opinion that the property, once it had been validly dedicated, became the property of God. Imām Muḥammad and the Ithnā 'Asharī authorities insist that possession should be handed over to the trustees before the dedication is complete. Consistently with this view, the Ithnā 'Asharī and the other Sunnite Schools hold that the *wāḳif*, having relinquished his property in favour of God, cannot be permitted to take any benefit from it (*l*).

Non-Muslim. A non-Muslim is entitled to take the benefit of a *wakf*, provided that he is not an alien enemy (*m*).

§59. Family Endowments

(C) Wakf 'alā'l-awlād (*Family Wakfs*)

The law on the subject of *wakfs* in favour of descendants may be divided conveniently into two parts: the law *before*, and the law *after*, the Wakf Act, 1913.

I. *The law before the Wakf Act, 1913*

The leading case on the subject is *Abul Fata Mahomed Ishak* v. *Russomoy Dhur Chowdhry* (*n*). Briefly the facts were that two Muslim brothers made a *wakf* whereby they themselves were to be the first *mutawallīs* of the *wakf*. The entire benefit of the *wakf* was to go to their children in the first instance and their descendants from generation to generation, until the total extinction of the family. There-

(*k*) Ameer Ali, I, 281 sqq., mentions other reasons as well.

(*l*) For another explanation, see Tyabji §376, com.

(*m*) Ameer Ali, I, 276, 288-9.

(*n*) (1894) 22 I.A. 76; *Cases*. 388. Criticized by Ameer Ali, I, 295 sqq.; see Tyabji, §501, p. 548, ill. 8; Mulla §196, ill. (*d*).

after the income of the *wakf* was to be applied for the benefit of widows, orphans, beggars and the poor. The judge of first instance held that the *wakf* was valid; on appeal, the High Court reversed the decision; on further appeal, the Privy Council upheld the High Court.

The decision of the Judicial Committee is short, but contains passages which are so often cited that the student is urged to read the latter half of the judgment of Lord Hobhouse carefully (22 I.A., 86-9; *Cases*, 394-96).

The result of this decision was that if the gifts to charity were substantial, not illusory, the *wakfs* were valid; but where the *wakfs* were founded for 'the aggrandizement of a family', or where the gifts to charity were illusory or merely nominal, the *wakfs* were declared to be void (*y*).

This case created a storm in the country; it was deemed to go against the fundamental notions of Islamic law; it was refuted with a wealth of learning by Ameer Ali in his well-known work on *Mahommedan Law* (*z*); a number of Muslim divines, headed by the late 'Allāma Shiblī Nu'mānī, protested against it and wrote forceful pamphlets (*a*); and finally the legislature stepped in by passing the Mussalman Wakf Validating Act, 1913 (*b*).

It is, however, interesting to observe that in *Fatuma binti Mohamed* v. *Mohamed bin Salim* [1952] A.C.1, an appeal from Kenya, the Judicial Committee followed their own decision in *Abul Fata Mahomed's Case*, rather than *Bikani Mia's Case*, which is designated as the leading case on the subject. Lord Simonds in his judgment says that their lordships' decision is binding everywhere as a precedent, unless it is altered by statute as in India (*c*).

(*y*) Tyabji §500, Wilson §323; Mulla §196.

(*z*) Vol. I, pp. 273-379 and 754-94.

(*a*) Sayyid Sulaymān Nadwī, *Ḥayāt-e Shiblī*, i, 536 sqq.

(*b*) A very valuable discussion of the texts and cases will be found in Wilson, 6th edition, App. B, pp. 483-97.

(*c*) Criticized by J. N. D. Anderson in his *Islamic Law in Africa* (London, 1954), App. D., p. 340.

II. *The law after the Wakf Act, 1913*

According to the ancient texts, *wakfs* for the support of a man's descendants and family were considered to be proper and lawful. The Prophet is reported to have said that 'When a Muslim bestows on his family and kindred, hoping for reward in the next world, it becomes alms, although he has not given to the poor, but to his family and children.'(*d*) What in the estimation of the English lawyers would be a pernicious perpetuity, calculated to aggrandize the family of the founder, is according to the *sharīʿat* the best of charities. It is therefore not surprising that the Judicial Committee went against the weight of ancient authority by *ijmāʿ*. Ameer Ali, whose work is very exhaustive on all matters relating to pious foundations, has dealt so fully with this question that any further discussion seems entirely superfluous (*e*). The position may be summed up in his own words:

> From the promulgation of Islam up to the present day there has been an absolute consensus of opinion regarding the validity of *wakfs* on one's children, kindred and neighbours. Practical lawyers, experienced judges, high officers of every sect and school under Mussulman sovereigns are all in unison on this point. There are minor differences, viz. whether a *wakf* can be created for one's self, whether the unfailing object should be designated, whether the property should be partitioned or not, whether consignment is necessary or not; but so far as the validity of a *wakf* constituting one's family or children the recipients of the benefaction, in whole or in part, is concerned, there is absolutely no difference. A *wakf* is a permanent benefaction for the good of God's creatures: the *wāḳif* may bestow the usufruct, but not the property, upon whomsoever he chooses and in whatever manner he likes, only it must endure for ever. If he bestows the usufruct in the first instance upon those whose maintenance is obligatory on him, or if he gives it to his descendants so long as they exist to prevent their falling into indigence, it is a pious act, —more pious, according to the Prophet, than giving to the general

(*d*) Ameer Ali, I, 300-10; *Fat. Law* §§331 sqq.

(*e*) In addition to the passages from his learned work on Muhammadan law already referred to, attention is also drawn to his judgment in *Bikani Mia's Case* (1892) 20 Cal. 116, 132-77, which is the leading case on the subject, see [1952] A.C.1.

body of the poor. He laid down that one's family and descendants are fitting objects of charity, and that to bestow on them and to provide for their future subsistence is more pious and obtains greater 'reward' than to bestow on the indigent stranger. And this is insisted upon so strongly that when a *wakf* is made for the *indigent* or *poor* generally, the proceeds of the endowment is applied to relieve the wants of the endower's children and descendants and kindred in the first place (see Baillie's Dig., 2nd ed., p. 593). When a *wakf* is created constituting the family or descendants of the *wakf* [*sic*, for *wāḳif*] the recipients of the charity so long as they exist, the poor are expressly or impliedly brought in *not* for the purpose of making the *wakf* charitable (for the support of the family and descendants is a part and parcel of the charitable purpose for which the dedication is made), but simply to impart permanency to the endowment. When the *wāḳif's* descendants fail, it *must* come to the poor. So it is an enduring benefaction—an act of *'ibādat* or worship, to use the language of the *Jawāhir-ul-Kalām*,—an act by which *kurbat* or 'nearness' is obtained to the Deity, according to the *Bahr-ur-Raik* (*f*).

The Wakf Act, 1913, purported to restore the law of the *sharī'at* in India and to overrule the law as laid down by the Privy Council. It is therefore necessary to consider its provisions in some detail.

The text of the Act is as follows (*g*):

Act No. VI of 1913

[*7th March, 1913.*]

An Act to declare the rights of Mussalmans to make settlements of property by way of 'wakf' in favour of their families, children and descendants.

WHEREAS doubts have arisen regarding the validity of wakfs created by persons professing the Mussalman faith in favour of themselves, their families, children and descendants and ultimately for the benefit of the poor or for other religious, pious or charitable purposes; and whereas it is expedient to remove such doubts; It is hereby enacted as follows:—

(*f*) *Bikani Mia's Case*, 20 Cal. at pp. 145-6.
(*g*) *Unrepealed Central Acts* (1950), VI, 238-9.

1. (*1*) This Act may be called the Mussalman Wakf Validating Act, 1913. Short title and extent

(*2*) It extends to the whole of British India.

2. In this Act, unless there is anything repugnant in the subject or context,— Definitions

(*1*) 'Wakf' means the permanent dedication by a person professing the Mussalman faith of any property for any purpose recognized by the Mussalman law as religious, pious or charitable.

(*2*) 'Hanafi Mussalman' means a follower of the Mussalman faith who conforms to the tenets and doctrines of the Hanafi school of Mussalman law.

3. It shall be lawful for any person professing the Mussalman faith to create a wakf which in all other respects is in accordance with the provisions of Mussalman law, for the following among other purposes:— Power of Mussalmans to create certain wakfs

(*a*) for the maintenance and support wholly or partially of his family, children or descendants, and

(*b*) where the person creating a wakf is a Hanafi Mussalman, also for his own maintenance and support during his lifetime or for the payment of his debts out of the rents and profits of the property dedicated:

Provided that the ultimate benefit is in such cases expressly or impliedly reserved for the poor or for any other purpose recognized by the Mussalman law as a religious, pious or charitable purpose of a permanent character.

4. No such wakf shall be deemed to be invalid merely because the benefit reserved therein for the poor or other religious, pious or charitable purpose of a permanent nature is postponed until after the extinction of the family, children or descendants of the person creating the *wakf*. Wakfs not to be invalid by reason of remoteness or benefit to poor, etc.

5. Nothing in this Act shall affect any custom or usage whether local or prevalent among Mussalmans of any particular class or sect. Saving o[f] local an[d] sectarian custom

(1) *Definition of* Wakf, *Section 2(1)*

The definition, as we have already observed (*h*), is not exhaustive (*i*); it is only for the purposes of the Act. The incidents mentioned are: (i) permanency of the endowment, (ii) its creation by a Muslim, (iii) of '*any property*', and (iv) for 'any purpose recognized by the Mussalman law as religious, pious or charitable'.(*j*)

It would be entirely out of place in a student's text-book to give a complete list of the objects which the courts have considered either as lawful or as unlawful; but reference should be made to a Bombay decision in which Chagla J. held that the payment of marriage expenses is not charity according to Muhammadan law, nor is a bequest to feed the members of the settlor's community on the anniversary of his death. In this case it was further provided in the trust deed that Rs 300 a year was to be paid to Sayyids and Fakirs; and it was held that while payments to Fakirs—

> not indeed professional beggars but treating that expression to mean the 'poor'—would be justifiable, it was doubtful if payment to 'Sayyids' would be a good charitable gift, the reason being that after fourteen centuries it was not easy to determine clearly whether a person really belonged to the class described as 'members of the Prophet's family'.(*k*)

(2) *Family Settlements, Section 3(a)*

The section says that a *wakf* for the maintenance and support wholly or partially of the settlor's 'family, children or

(*h*) See §52, above.

(*i*) *Ma Mi* v. *Kallander Ammal* (1926) 54 I.A. 23, 27.

(*j*) For lists of lawful and unlawful purposes see Mulla §178; Tyabji §501.

(*k*) *Abdul Karim* v. *Rahimabai* (1946) 48 Bom. L.R. 67. Descendants of the Prophet are usually called *sharīfs* in other countries. See *Ency. of Islam*, s.v. '*Sharif*'.

descendants' is lawful. The main question is: What is the meaning of the word 'family'?—the expressions 'children' and 'descendants' not admitting of any doubt (*l*). It has been held in Bombay that the word 'family' in Sec. 3(*a*) of the Mussalman Wakf Validating Act of 1913 includes: (i) all those persons residing in the same house as the settlor and dependent upon him for maintenance, and (ii) all those connected with the settlor through a common progenitor or by ties of common lineage. A *wakf*, however, in favour of utter strangers is not valid (*m*). In this particular case a nephew (sister's son, residing in the settlor's house) was considered to be within the term 'family'. A similar view was taken by the Lahore High Court, and it was later held that the kindred (*aqārib*) and their descendants are not included within the meaning of the expression 'family' as used in the Wakf Act, 1913. It is to be observed that the Bombay decision was not cited before their lordships A. Rashid and Ram Lall JJ. in this case (*n*).

This restrictive meaning of the word 'family' has not been accepted in Allahabad, where it has been held that the word 'family' in Sec. 3(*a*) of the Mussalman Wakf Validating Act is not restricted only to those persons residing in the house of the settlor for whose maintenance he was responsible, but was intended to be used in its broad popular sense, namely persons descended from one common progenitor and having a common lineage, e.g. nephews of the settlor and their descendants were included in the term, irrespective of whether they lived in the settlor's house or whether the settlor was responsible for their maintenance (*o*). Even the step daughter of the settlor's sister, bred, brought up and

(*l*) Mulla §197, note (1).

(*m*) *Ismail Haji Arat* v. *Umar Abdulla* [1942] Bom. 441, (1941) 44 Bom. L.R. 256.

(*n*) *Mohammad Afzal* v. *Din Mohammad* (1945) 27 Lah. 300, 354-6.

(*o*) *Muhammad Azam* v. *Hamid Shah* [1946] All. 575. The word *ayāl* (strictly *'iyāl*, sing. *'ā'ila*). 'family' is discussed fully in *Rashidunnissa* v. *Ata Rasool* A.I.R. (1958) All. 67, 69, 73, by Srivastava J.

married by him, was considered as falling within the definition, but not her descendants (*oo*).

The Madras High Court has gone still further (*p*). Technically the word 'family' may mean 'all the persons who live in a household', and include parents, children and servants; and boarders.

He then goes on to say:

> Popularly, however, the term indicates persons descended from one common progenitor and having a common lineage. It will take in both agnates and cognates, and relations by blood or marriage. The nephews of the settlor are in this sense the members of his family. Similarly daughters-in-law, the son of a half-brother or the son of a half-sister . . . (*q*).

The whole question is not free from difficulty, and it is submitted that for understanding the true import of the word 'family', a deeper examination of the original texts of authority is necessary, and recourse only to English or modern law is not conclusive (*r*).

Words and phrases such as *farzand*, *awlād*, *bā farzandān*, *naslan ba'd naslin*, *baṭnan ba'd baṭnin*, have a technical meaning and were recently reconsidered in Calcutta (*s*).

(3) *Reservation for Settlor, Section 3(b)*

The clause does not lay down any new rule of law; in the Hanafi school, it was always considered well established that the settlor was entitled during his lifetime to 'eat out' of the property endowed as *wakf* (*t*).

(*oo*) *Abdul Qavi* v. *Asaf Ali* A.I.R. (1962) All. 364.

(*p*) *Asha Bibi* v. *Nabissa Sahib* A.I.R. (1957) Mad. 583.

(*q*) ibid., 587.

(*r*) It is submitted with deference, that the first category laid down by Chagla J. (as he then was) is too wide, as it may conceivably include illegitimate children and maternal relations. Tyabji §501, p. 551, n. 10, says that the word 'family' used in its broad sense would include relatives more or less dependent on the settlor. See 'Family' in R. Burrows, *Words and Phrases* (London, 1943), II, 281.

(*s*) *Mahammad Eshaque* v. (*Mst.*) *Maimuna Bibi* [1949] 1 Cal. 333.

(*t*) Ameer Ali I, 281-6. Cases will be found in Mulla §192. Tyabji explains how the benefit in a *wakf* is a disposition of the usufruct §376, esp. pp. 376 sqq.

Reservation of income for life in favour of the settlor is permissible, but not the creation of successive life interests (*u*).

The question arises whether a Hanafi settlor's interest in the *wakf* is a true life interest, and in a Bombay case it has been held that, under the Act, a Hanafi is not permitted to reserve for his absolute use during his lifetime the whole of the income of the *wakf*. He is only entitled to reserve the income for his own maintenance and support. The distinction is explained by Chagla J. as follows:

> Now a reservation of a life interest in the income of a trust property is a very different thing from securing to himself for his own maintenance and support the income of the trust property. The difference in law between these two provisions is clear and of considerable importance. If what he had reserved to himself was for his own maintenance, that would not be transferable as property under the Transfer of Property Act, nor could it be attachable under the provisions of the Civil Procedure Code. Whereas if he had reserved for himself a life interest, that particular provision would not attract to itself the provisions of Section 6 of the Transfer of Property Act and Section 60 of the Civil Procedure Code with regard to non-transferability and non-liability to attachment contained in the provisions of the two sections (*v*).

In *Mohd. Sabir Ali* v. *Tahir Ali* (*w*), it was held that the creation of a life interest in the whole of the property for the maintenance of the *wāķif* was valid, following *Faqir Md.* v. *Mst. Abda Khatoon* A.I.R. (1952) All. 127 (F.B.), contrary to the decision of Chagla J. in a Bombay case (*x*). *Mohd. Sabir Ali's Case* is a decision relating to wills and life-estates in a *talukdari* governed by the Oudh Estates Act, which is an independent code by itself, a further discussion whereof is beyond the scope of this book.

(*u*) *Rashidunnissa* v. *Ata Rasool* A.I.R. (1958) All. 67.

(*v*) *Abdul Karim* v. *Rahimabai* (1946) 48 Bom. L.R. 67, 72.

(*w*) A.I.R. (1957) All. 94, 101.

(*x*) *Abdul Karim* v. *Rahimabai* A.I.R. (1946) Bom. 342; (1946) 48 Bom. L.R. 67.

(4) *Ultimate Benefit, Section 3, proviso*

Even in a family *wakf*, the ultimate benefit must always be reserved for the poor; and such a reservation may be either express or implied. The exact force of the word 'impliedly', used in this clause, has been repeatedly discussed in the Courts in India, as the ancient jurists are not unanimous on the point.

According to the author of the *Hedaya*, there are two opinions concerning this question (*y*). The Imām Abū Ḥanīfa and his younger disciple, Imām Muḥammad al-Shaybānī, held that the ultimate objects of the *wakf* must be clearly specified, else the *wakf* fails. On the other hand, Cadi Abū Yūsuf held that the ultimate benefit may be implied in favour of the poor. For instance, if a man were to say, 'I have appropriated this property to Zayd,' that is, 'I give this property by way of *wakf* to Zayd,' the *wakf* is completely constituted, and the income will go to the poor after the death of Zayd, although they are not named. The *Fatāwā 'Ālamgīrī* leans towards this opinion (*z*). The question is not free from doubt, but the recent tendency is to hold that even if the document is absolutely silent as regards the ultimate objects, the very use of the word 'wakf' is a sufficient indication (*a*).

(5) *Remoteness, Section 4*

This clause specifically repeals the view taken in *Abul Fata's Case* which was reaffirmed by the Privy Council in *Fatuma* v. *Mohamed* [1952] A.C.1 (Kenya, East Africa).

(6) *Custom, Section 5*

This clause saves local custom; but in view of the Shariat Act, 1937, its application is extremely limited.

(*y*) *Hedaya*, 234; Tyabji §§500 sq.; Mulla §197, note 3.

(*z*) Baillie, I, 566.

(*a*) See particularly *Syed Ahmad* v. *Julaiha Bivi* [1947] Mad. 480, and *Mahammad Hashim* v. *Iffat Ara* [1947] 2 Cal. 16. Also a Shāfi'ī case, where it was held that there was no dedication to charity at all, *Salah* v. *Husain* A.I.R. (1955) Hyd. 229.

(*b*) (1922) 49 I.A. 153.

(7) *Retrospective Effect, Act XXXII of 1930*

In *Khajeh Solehman* v. *Salimullah Bahadur* (*b*), it was held by the Privy Council that the Mussalman Wakf Validating Act, 1913, was not retrospective, and therefore did not apply to *wakfs* created prior to 7 March 1913. By the Mussalman Wakf Validating Act, XXXII of 1930, which came into force on 25 July 1930, the Wakf Act of 1913 was made retrospective and made applicable to *wakfs* created before 7 March 1913.

(8) *Benefit of* Wakf *among Descendants*

Where a *wakf* is made for the benefit of the settlor's descendants, and no rules are laid down as to the distribution of the shares in the succeeding generations, the descendants take *per stirpes* and not *per capita*, males and females taking equally, contrary to the general rules of inheritance (*c*).

Fatimid Law

Here there is a striking divergence between the Hanafi and Fatimid legists. The Fatimid rule is that where no provision has been made by the settlor, a male shall take the share of two females (as in the law of inheritance); but a provision whereby the *wāḳif* provides equally for males and females among his progeny, is permissible and valid (*cc*).

§60. Administration

(1) *Mutawallī*
(2) Competence
(3) Appointment and removal
(4) Powers of alienation
(5) Statutory control

(1) Mutawallī, Tawliyat

A *mutawallī*, as we have seen, is not a trustee, but a manager or superintendent of property. The *wakf* property does not vest in him; it belongs to the Almighty and is in very deed 'God's Acre'(*d*). The *mutawallī* is not the owner of

(*c*) Macnaghten, 341, 342; Ameer Ali, I, 361; Wilson §§324, 325; Tyabji §§545 sq. Mulla §200.

(*cc*) *Fat. Law* §§337 sq.

(*d*) Per Lord Sumner in *Abdur Rahim* v. *Narayan Das* (1922) 50 I.A. 84, 90

the property, but merely the servant of God, managing the property for the good of His creatures (*e*). His rights and duties are analogous to those of a trustee, but there are important differences; and his 'trusteeship' is known as *tawliyat*. Apart from legal responsibilities, the performance of his obligations is a moral and religious duty, and a disregard of such duties is morally and ethically reprehensible.

Powers (*f*). It is the duty of the *mutawallī* to do everything that is necessary and reasonable to protect and administer the *wakf* property (*g*); and he may, as a trustee, employ agents and servants to perform the ministerial acts necessary to carry out the duties of his office (*h*). In general, he is not allowed to sell, mortgage or lease the *wakf* property, unless he obtains the permission of the court and the civil court, inheriting the jurisdiction of the *kazi*, has general powers of controlling the actions of a *mutawallī* (*i*).

A Full Bench decision of the Allahabad High Court has laid down that it is not open to a *wāḳif* to amend the *wakf* deed itself by changing its provisions and, if by the second deed he has attempted to change the character of the *wakf*, and that portion is not separable from the portion relating to the change of the *mutawallī*, then the second deed must be held to be wholly bad (*j*).

Statutory provision has now been made in the various states of India and in Pakistan to regulate and supervise public charities under which particulars of the dedication and annual accounts are to be filed and made available to members of the public (*jj*).

(*e*) *Vidya Varuthi* v. *Balusami Ayyar* (1921) 48 I.A. 302; *Cases*, 379; *Abdur Rahim* v. *Narayan Das* (1922) 50 I.A. 84; *Saadat Kamel Hanum* v. *Attorney-General for Palestine* [1939] A.C. 508, A.I.R. (1939) Privy Council 185, 189. Tyabji §527; Mulla §202.

(*f*) Ameer Ali, I, 441 sqq.

(*g*) Tyabji §529.

(*h*) ibid., §531.

(*i*) ibid., §538.

(*j*) *Khalil Ahamad* v. *Malka Mehar Nigar Begum* A.I.R. (1954) All. 362 (F.B.).

(*jj*) For details, which are unnecessary in an elementary textbook, see Tyabji §530; and Saxena, *Muslim Law*, 4th ed. (Lucknow, 1963), 608 sqq. and 644 sqq.

(2) *Competence*

It may be said generally that every sane adult is entitled to be a *mutawallī*, unless there is a specific bar. It is well settled that the following can legally act as *mutawallīs*: (i) the founder himself (*wāḳif*); (ii) his children; (iii) women; (iv) non-Muslims; (v) Sunnites in a Shiite *wakf* and vice versa (*k*).

Minority and unsoundness of mind are positive disqualifications; in Pakistan it has been held that a minor can be appointed a *mutawallī*, if the office is declared to be hereditary (*l*). And as regards women, their lordships of the Privy Council have ruled that sex is no bar in cases where no religious duties have to be performed (*m*); but *aliter*, if religious duties or spiritual functions are part of the duties of a *mutawallī*, and in such cases, a female or a non-Muslim cannot act as a *sajjāda-nashīn, khaṭīb, mujāwar* of a *dargāh*, or an *imām* of a mosque (*n*).

(3) *Appointment of* Mutawallī (*o*)

Where a dedication to *wakf* is purported to be made, but no *mutawallī* is designated, the jurists of authority differ as to the legal results. (i) Imām Abū Ḥanīfa and Imām Muḥammad held that, under Hanafi law, the dedication failed. (ii) On the other hand, Cadi Abū Yūsuf was of opinion that the dedication was lawful and the *wāḳif* became the *mutawallī*. (iii) The Shiite jurists took the view that the dedication was effective and the beneficiaries were entitled to administer the *wakf* (*p*).

It is usual for the founder in a deed of *wakf* to lay down rules for succession to the office of *mutawallī*; but if no such rules have been framed (i) the *wāḳif* possesses during his lifetime the power to designate his successor. In certain cases,

(*k*) Mulla §203.

(*l*) *Muhammad Bakhtiyar* v. *Bashir Ahmad* PLD 1957 (W.P.) Lah. 803.

(*m*) *Shahar Banoo* v. *Aga Mahomed* (1906) 34 I.A. 46, 53.

(*n*) Mulla, §203. Tyabji in §510 gives a number of apt illustrations.

(*o*) Generally, Ameer Ali, I, 447 sqq.; Mulla §204.

(*p*) Tyabji §511(2).

such a nomination may be made by a *wāḳif* even on his death-bed (*q*); (ii) after the death of the *wāḳif*, his executor is entitled to appoint the *mutawallī*; and (iii) failing the *wāḳif* and his executor, the court is entitled to make the appointment (*r*). The District Judge as 'the Principal Court' of original jurisdiction has, by virtue of his powers as a *kazi*, a general power of appointing a *mutawallī* when there is a vacancy in the office, in a summary proceeding (*s*). (iv) The fourth way is appointment, in certain circumstances, by the congregation (*t*).

It is not open to a settlor to change the character of the wakf while laying down new rules for the appointment of *mutawallīs* (*u*).

The court's discretion in Islamic law is very wide, and may be said to be analogous to the powers of the Chancery court superintending a trustee's actions. Mr Ameer Ali, in delivering the judgment of the Privy Council in *Mahomed Ismail* v. *Ahmed Moolla* cites an ancient authority as laying down that 'were the wakif (the founder) to make a condition that the King or Kazi should not interfere in the management of the wakf, still the Kazi will have his superintendence over it, for his supervision is above everything'. He goes on to explain this in a well-known passage:

> The Mussulman law, like the English law, draws a wide distinction between public and private trusts. Generally speaking, in case of a wakf or trust created for specific individuals or a determinate body of individuals, the *Kazi, whose place in the British Indian system is taken by the Civil Court*, has in carrying the trust into execution to give effect so far as possible to the expressed wishes of the founder. With respect, however, to public, religious or charitable trusts, of which a public mosque is a common and well-known example, the Kazi's discretion is very wide. He may not depart from the intentions of the founder or

(*q*) Tyabji §512; Mulla §205.

(*r*) Tyabji, loc. cit.; Mulla §204(2).

(*s*) *Abdul Awal* v. *Abdul Monaem* PLD 1960 Dacca 90.

(*t*) *Khagum Khan* v. *Mohamed Ali* A.I.R. (1955) Andhra Prad. 209.

(*u*) *Khalil Ahamad* v. *Malka Mehar Nigar Begum* A.I.R. (1954) All. 362, F.B.

from any rule fixed by him as to the objects of the benefaction; but as regards management which must be governed by circumstances he has complete discretion. He may defer to the wishes of the founder so far as they are comformable to changed conditions and circumstances, but his primary duty is to consider the interests of the general body of the public for whose benefit the trust is created. He may in his judicial discretion vary any rule of management which he may find either not practicable or not in the best interests of the institution (*v*).

In this case the Privy Council declared that a certain section of the worshippers in a mosque had a greater right to manage and act as trustees, and the appointment of trustees was left to a committee which was to act under the general guidance of the court (*w*).

The office of a *mutawallī* is not hereditary, and if a custom to that effect were set up, it would have to be proved strictly (*x*). In appointing a *mutawallī,* other things being equal, the court would show a preference towards a member of the founder's family; but this is a matter within the discretion of the court, and not a matter of right for the relative concerned (*y*).

In *Shahar Banoo's Case*, the Privy Council decided that there is no legal prohibition against a woman holding a *mutawallīship*, when the trust, by its nature, involves no spiritual duties which a woman could not discharge, in person or by deputy. But in this case, the appellant Shahar Banoo, a daughter of the founder, had not an absolute right to be appointed as a *mutawallī*, for she had forsaken the Shiite faith and had become a Bābī, and as such, could not be enthusiastic about the observances of her former faith; wherefore, a well-known member of the Shiite community, not a lineal descendant, was preferred as a *mutawallī* (*z*).

Removal of Mutawallī. Once a *mutawallī* has been duly

(*v*) (1916) 43 I.A. 134; *Cases,* 397, 402 sq. Italics mine.
(*w*) See also Ameer Ali, I, 479, 480.
(*x*) Tyabji §512(3); Mulla §206.
(*y*) *Asha Bibi* v. *Nabissa Sahib* A.I.R. (1957) Mad. 583.
(*z*) *Shahar Banoo* v. *Aga Mahomed* (1906) 35 I.A. 46.

appointed, the *wāḳif* has no power to remove him from the office (*a*). The court, however, can in a fit case remove a *mutawallī* and appoint another in his place. On proof of misfeasance, breach of trust, insolvency, or on the *mutawallī* claiming adversely to the *wakf*, a court has the right to remove him.

A *mutawallī* has no right to transfer the office to another, but he may appoint deputies or agents to assist him in the administration of the *wakf* (*b*). The *wāḳif*, however, who is himself the first *mutawallī*, can resign his office during his own lifetime and appoint another *mutawallī* (*c*).

An illiterate *pardanashin* woman purported to transfer her *mutawalliship* to a person who stood in a fiduciary capacity to her. It was held, first, that the onus was heavily on persons who set up such a deed to prove that the mind of the lady went with the deed, that this onus was not discharged and that the transfer was void. Secondly, where the deed itself does not lay down rules for the transfer of the *tawliyat*, and the transfer has been purported to be made to a person not in the direct line of succession, such a transfer cannot be set up and must fail (*d*).

The Privy Council has decided an important point regarding the office of *tawliyat* held jointly by several *mutawallīs*. *A*, *B* and *C* were appointed joint *mutawallīs* of a certain *wakf*. No direction was given regarding the succession of the *mutawallīs*, and no custom or usage was proved. *A* died during the lifetime of *B* and *C*, leaving a will whereby he appointed *X* as *mutawallī* after him. It was held that such appointment was not valid, for the office of *mutawallīship* (*tawliyat*) was one and indivisible, and on the death of *A*, it passed by survivorship to *B* and *C* (*e*).

(*a*) *Siddiq Ahmed* v. *Syed Ahmed* (1945) 49 C.W.N. 311; *Mian Jan* v. *Fakir Mohammad* PLD 1960 (W.P.) Karachi 420.

(*b*) Tyabji §§521, 529, 531; Mulla §214; *Abdul Kayum* v. *Alibhai* A.I.R. (1963) S.C. 309.

(*c*) *Ali Asghar* v. *Fariduddin Hasan* [1946] All. 661; Tyabji §522.

(*d*) *Abdul Mannan* v. *Mutwali of Janebali* A.I.R. (1956) Cal. 584.

(*e*) (*Haji*) *Abdul Razaq* v. (*Sheikh*) *Ali Bakhsha* (1948) 75 I.A. 172; Mulla §205A.

A Full Bench of the Allahabad High Court has laid down that the provisions of the Indian Trusts Act do not apply to a *wakf 'alā'l-awlād*, and the removal of a *mutawallī* can be effected only by means of a regular suit and not in summary proceedings started upon a mere application (*f*).

Remuneration. The remuneration of a *mutawallī* may be provided for by the founder. If no provision is made for the remuneration of the *mutawallī,* the court may fix a sum not exceeding one-tenth of the income of the *wakf* as such remuneration (*g*).

(4) *Powers of Alienation, Charge, and Lease* (*h*)

A *mutawallī* has no right to sell or mortgage *wakf* property without the permission of the court, but the *wakf-nāma* may expressly empower him to do so (*i*).

A *mutawallī* has no power to grant a lease of *wakf* property, if it be agricultural, for a term exceeding three years, and, if non-agricultural, for a term exceeding one year; provided that he may be expressly authorized to do so by the *wakf-nāma*, or that where he has no such authority, he may obtain the permission of the court (*j*).

Where, however, certain persons have peaceably and for long enjoyed the benefits of a lease, contrary to the express provisions of an ancient *sanad*, the doctrine of 'a lost grant' will be invoked in their favour and the court will make a presumption in favour of a legal origin of the lease (*k*).

The law of limitation applies to *wakfs,* and *wakf* property may sometimes be lost by adverse possession (*l*); but a suit

(*f*) *Muhammad Ali* v. *Ahmad Ali* [1945] All. 818, F.B.

(*g*) Tyabji §§523, 524, 526; Mulla §211; *Fat. Law* §332.

(*h*) See generally, Ameer Ali, I, 471 sqq.

(*i*) Tyabji §559; Mulla §207.

(*j*) Ameer Ali, I, 477; Tyabji §533; Mulla §208.

(*k*) *Mahammad Mazaffar* v. *Jabeda Khatun* (1930) 57 I.A. 125. This case has been distinguished in *Sundaramurthi Nainar* v. *Chhotti Bibi* [1943] Mad. 61.

(*l*) Tyabji §528; Mulla §217

against a *mutawallī* or against his legal representatives or assigns (except for valuable consideration) is, by the present law, not barred by the lapse of any length of time (*m*).

(5) *Statutory Control*

Since 1923 a number of Acts have been passed by the Central and State Legislatures regulating the administration of *wakfs*. The most important of these is the Mussalman Wakf Act, 1923 (XLII of 1923), which was passed for making provision for the better management of *wakf* property and for ensuring the keeping and publication of proper accounts. The chief provisions are that *mutawallīs* are bound to furnish the District Court with a statement containing a description and particulars of *wakf* property; that *mutawallīs* are bound to file proper accounts of the administration of the *wakf* property, and that any person may require the *mutawallī* to furnish further information.

The Mussalman Wakf Act, 1923, which does not apply to family *wakfs*, has been modified to suit local conditions in several states of India: (i) in Bengal, it has been replaced by the Bengal Wakf Act, 1934 (Act XIII of 1934); (ii) in Bombay, it has been modified by the Mussalman Wakf (Bombay Amendment) Act XVIII of 1935; and (iii) in Uttar Pradesh, the United Provinces Muslim Wakfs Act, XIII of 1936, replaces the Act of 1923.

Another important Act is the Wakfs Act, 1954 (XXIX of 1954) to provide for the better administration and supervision of *wakfs*; details will be found in Mulla and Tyabji, but it may be mentioned that it has been extended only to some and not all the States in India.

In addition to the Wakf Acts, there are a number of enactments which deal with private and charitable endowments in India and the law on the subject may be found in Tyabji §§510 sqq.; and a useful list of statutory provisions will be found in Mulla §212, 212A, 225 and Saksena, *Muslim Law*, 4th ed. (Lucknow, 1963), 644 sqq.

(*m*) Mulla §216.

§61. Mosques and Other Institutions

(1) Mosque
(2) *Takia*
(3) *Khānqāh*
(4) *Cemetery*
(5) *Dargāh*
(6) *Imāmbāra*
(7) *Kazi*

(1) **Mosque** (*n*)

Dedication. To consecrate a mosque, it is not sufficient merely to construct it: (i) the building must be separated from the other property of the owner, (ii) a way must be provided to the mosque, and (iii) either public prayers must be said or possession must be delivered to the *mutawallīs* (*o*). In Ithnā 'Asharī law, the dedication is complete where a formal declaration has been made and prayers have been said.

Where a mosque has been validly dedicated, the right of the *wāḳif* in the property is entirely extinguished (*p*).

Reservation for locality or school. The right to offer prayers in a mosque (as in a temple) is a legal right, for the disturbance of which a Muslim is entitled to relief at law. Where it was found that a certain ceremony, known as 'chandakundam' was celebrated in a mosque in Kerala and accompanied with music from times immemorial, it was decreed that the ceremonies should so be conducted as not to disturb the five obligatory prayers each day, and the times for such prayers were fixed with precision (*q*).

Once a mosque is validly consecrated, a reservation in favour of the people of a particular locality is deemed to be bad and it will be open to all persons (*r*). Similarly, a mosque cannot be restricted to the followers of a particular school or *madhhab*; if the dedication is complete, the restriction is bad and it will be open to all Muslims, whatever their school or

(*n*) The *masjid* is an important educational and religious institution in Islam, for which see the masterly article of Pedersen and others in *Ency. of Islam, 'Masdjid'*, III, 313. Tyabji §§550-52; Wilson §§347; Mulla §218.

(*o*) Tyabji, loc. cit.; Ameer Ali, I, 393 sqq.

(*p*) Ameer Ali, I, 393; Tyabji §551.

(*q*) *Pathananithitta Majilissae Islamia* v. *Nagoor Meeran Sheik Muhammad* A.I.R. (1963) Ker. 49.

(*r*) Tyabji §550; Mulla §218.

sub-school (*s*). The law, however, will not tolerate any deliberate disturbance in the prayers of a congregation (*t*). Ameer Ali says:

> A mosque does not belong to any particular sect. It is open to all Mussulmans to go in and offer their adoration to the Almighty. Suppose a Hanafi erects a mosque; the Shafeis, the Malikis and the Hanbalis may pray there equally with the members of the Hanafi sect. Nor is there any objection to a Shiah going and praying there according to his own ritual. The Hanafi *mutwalli* cannot prevent any person, so long as he is the worshipper of God, and does not interrupt or disturb the worship of others from coming and offering his adoration to the Almighty. This view of the law was given effect to in the case of *Ata-Ullah* v. *Azim-Ullah* (1889, I.L.R., 12 All. 494) where the Allahabad High Court held that a mosque, being dedicated to God, is for the use of all Mahomedans, and cannot be lawfully appropriated to the use of any particular sect (*u*).

Mohammad Wasi v. *Bachchan Sahib* [1955] 2 Allahabad 128, A.I.R. (1955) Allahabad 68

The leading case on the subject is a decision of the Allahabad High Court, consisting of three judges sitting at the Lucknow division. It is designated 'Full Bench' in the official Series and 'Special Bench' in the All-India Reporter. It was decided on 8 November 1955 and was the subject of wide comment in the press.

Some Hanafi Muslims of the town of Mahmoodabad (U.P.) in their representative capacity filed a suit against their Shiite (Ithnā 'Asharī) co-religionists to restrain them permanently from certain ceremonies which they were performing within the precincts of the mosque. An important group of Sunnites refused to associate themselves with the plaintiffs and were impleaded as party defendants. It appears that the

(*s*) *Queen Empress* v. *Ramzan* (1885) 7 All, 461 (F.B.), especially the opinion of Mahmood J. at p. 465; *Ata-Ullah* v. *Azim-Ullah* (1889) 12 All. 494 (F.B.); *Jangu* v. *Ahmad Ullah* (1889) 13 All. 419 (F.B.); in this case Mahmood J. discusses a number of texts: *Fuzul Karim* v. *Haji Mowla Buksh* (1891) 18 I.A. 59.

(*t*) Ameer Ali, I, 400.

(*u*) ibid., 399.

mosque was built by a Hanafi, and the forms of prayer prevalent in it were at all material times in accord with the Hanafi ritual. Gradually the Shiites also began performing other ceremonies known as *gahwārā* and *tāziadārī*, in connexion with the martyrdom of Imām Ḥusayn, the Prophet's grandson and the tragic hero of the massacre of Karbala. The Hanafis objected and filed a suit to restrain the Shiites from practices which were abhorrent to them. The suit was dismissed by the lower court, and in view of its importance to the community, it was referred to a bench of three judges. The Full Bench upheld the decision of the lower court and dismissed the suit. The Full Bench laid down (p. 145 sq.):

(1) that a mosque is dedicated for the purpose that any Muslim belonging to any sect can go and say prayers therein;

(2) that it cannot be reserved for Muslims of any particular denomination or sect;

(3) that no one can claim to have the form of congregational prayer usually said in a mosque altered to suit him;

(4) that even though the congregational prayers are said in a mosque in a particular form any Muslim belonging to any other sect can go into a mosque and say his prayers at the back of the congregation in the manner followed by him so long as he does not do anything *mala fide* to disturb the others (*v*);

(5) that the object of the dedication can neither be altered nor the beneficiaries limited or changed, and

(6) that a Muslim will have a cause of action if he is deprived of his right to say prayers in a mosque or is prevented from doing so.

Malik C.J. approved the principles laid down by Tyabji J. in *Akbarally Adamji Peerbhoy* v. *Mahomedally Adamji Peerbhoy* (*w*) and went on to say (p. 139):

In a country like India, where people are free to follow their own faith, according to their own belief, the policy of live and let live must govern the relationship between followers of various religions or sects, so long as it does not conflict against (*x*) the

(*v*) This can be seen daily in the great Umayyad Mosque of Damascus, where a Christian saint is also buried and the Muslim devotees offer a prayer at his shrine as well.

(*w*) A.I.R. (1932) Bom. 365, 362, (1931) 34 Bom. L.R. 655.

(*x*) [*sic*] Seems a misprint for 'with'.

rules of public morality or decency. It is not open to a member of a particular sect to claim that the others should not follow their faith according to their belief because it offends against his susceptibilities. We had recently a case from Amethi in which the Muslims had objected to the blowing of conch-shells on the ground that it was intimately connected with idol worship which was repugnant to Muslim sentiment. [See *Shaikh Ahmad Ali* v. *Babu Ram*, 1954 A.W.R. 525.] It appears to us, therefore, that the only way of ensuring peace and religious freedom to all would be by laying down that the practices followed peacefully and without objection for years at a place of worship should not be disturbed on the ground that it was being objected to by some people because they claimed that it was repugnant to the true tenets of their faith (*y*).

The Hanafis were in control and management of a certain mosque since 1915. The *Ahl-e Ḥadīth* (Sunnites) used also to pray separately in the same mosque. Two groups of Sunnites can offer prayers peacefully in the same place of worship; but while every Muslim is entitled to pray in a mosque—which is the House of God—not every sect has an inherent right to form a separate congregation and offer prayers; and as the relations between the two groups were strained, it was not possible to allow the *Ahl-e Ḥadīth* to pray as a separate congregation with the Hanafis at the same time (*z*).

Whether a mosque is a juristic person. In a Lahore decision (*a*) it was held that a mosque was a juristic person, and could sue and be sued, but in the *Masjid Shahid Ganj Case* (*b*), it was decided by the Privy Council that suits cannot be brought by or against mosques, for they are not 'artificial' persons in the eye of the law. However, they left the question open, whether a mosque could for any purpose be regarded as a 'juristic' person. In view of the importance of this case, we shall deal with it fully later.

(*y*) Reminds one in some ways of the reasoning in *Beatty* v. *Gillbanks* (1882) 9 Q.B.D. 308.

(*z*) *Haji Mohd. Sayeed* v. *Abdul Ghafoor* A.I.R. (1955) All. 688.

(*a*) *Maula Buksh.* v. *Hafiz-ud-din*, A.I.R. (1926) Lah. 372.

(*b*) (1940) 67 I.A. 251.

Loudspeakers. A distinction must be drawn between religious *faith* and religious *practices* (*c*). What the State protects is faith, not all actions purporting to be done in the name of religion. If religious practices run counter to public order, morality or health, then such practices must give way to the public weal. For these reasons, the Muslims have no inherent right to use loudspeakers in their mosques, and the Commissioner of Police, in his discretion, has the right to stop the use of loudspeakers for worship in mosques (*d*). The judgment of Mr Justice Sinha is, with deference, a model of lucidity and felicity. He contrasts the 'romantic sound of the early morning muezzin' with the raucous music produced by loudspeakers (not only in India, but all over the Middle East) and says that such a noisy fanfare is neither artistic nor necessary.

(2) **Takia** (*e*)

A *takia* is, literally, a resting-place; hence it may be a tomb or a burial ground (*f*).

A takia is a place where a fakir or dervish (a person who abjures the world and becomes an humble servitor of God) resides before his pious life and teachings attract public notice, and before disciples gather round him, and a place is constructed for their lodgement (*Mohiuddin* v. *Sayiduddin*, 1893, I.L.R. 20 Cal. 810, 822). A takia is recognised by law as a religious institution, and a grant or endowment to it is a valid wakf or public trust for a religious purpose (*g*).

The real idea is that sanctity is attached to a place wherein a saintly man, having taken refuge from the world, has taught spiritual truths all his life, and has finally died and lies buried.

(*c*) A distinction which has been emphasized by the Supreme Court (India) in *Durgah Committee, Ajmer* v. *Syed Hussain Ali*, see §58(A) above, 'What is religion?'

(*d*) *Masud Alam* v. *Commissioner of Police* (Calcutta) (1955) 59 Cal. W.N. 293.

(*e*) Tyabji §505, esp. p. 573. Mulla §222.

(*f*) *Hussain Shah* v. *Gul Muhammad* (1924) 6 Lah. 140; *Baqar Khan* v. *Babu Raghoindra Pratap* (1934) 9 Luck. 568.

(*g*) *Maule Shah* v. *Ghane Shah* (1938) 40 Bom. L.R. 1071. 1072 (P.C.).

Not every *takia* is necessarily a *wakf*, but some may become so by long user (*h*), or by endowment (*i*).

(3) **Khānqāh, Sajjādanashīn** (*j*)

A *khānqāh* (Persian, caravanserai) is a Muslim monastery or religious institution, where dervishes and other seekers after truth congregate for religious instruction and devotional exercises (*k*). It is a Muslim institution analogous in many respects to a *maṭh* where religious instruction is given according to the Hindu faith (*l*). A *khānqāh* is founded by a holy man, in the place where his esoteric teaching acquires a certain fame and sanctity. After his death, if he is buried there, as often happens, the place may also be called his *takia*, abode or resting-place (*m*).

Personal grants, however, must be distinguished from such *wakfs*, which may be constituted either by endowments or by long user. A *sanad* of Shah Jahan, dated 1651, granted a village and other land in *inam* to one Syed Hasan, 'settled and conferred manifestly, and knowingly for means of subsistence of the children of the said Syed Hasan . . . that they may engage themselves in praying for this ever-enduring Government'; it was held that this grant did not constitute a *wakf*, that the property was not descendible *per stirpes*, nor would the grant be forfeited or avoided by neglect to pray for the said Government, nor by its downfall (*n*).

A typical case of *wakf* by long user is the Multan shrine of Māi Pāk Dāman. A lady, Māi Pāk Dāman, was revered as a saint, and her body was buried in a shrine near Multan. Later, Muslims began to bury their dead in the waste land

(*h*) *Chhutkao* v. *Gambhir Mal* (1931) 6 Luck. 452.

(*i*) *Maule Shah* v. *Ghane Shah* (1938) 40 Bom. L.R. 1071.

(*j*) Tyabji §474(10); Mulla §220. Much useful information is collected by Ramaswami J. in *Syed Shah Abdul Latif* v. *Mohammad Lebbai* (1958) 2 Mad. L.J. 199.

(*k*) Tyabji, loc. cit.

(*l*) *Vidya Varuthi* v. *Balusami Ayyar* (1921) 48 I.A. 302, 312 *Cases*, 379.

(*m*) *Hussain Shah* v. *Gul Muhammad* (1924) 6 Lah. 140, 148-9.

(*n*) Tyabji 475, ill. (4).

about her tomb, because of the desire to be buried near the body of a saint. For hundreds of years the land about her tomb was used as a burial ground. In 1858 a representative public meeting of the Muslims was held to consider the question of Muslim graveyards for the city. The graveyard of Māi Pāk Dāman was one of the four resolved to be kept open. Though there was no direct proof of dedication as *wakf*, the High Court and the Privy Council concluded that long before 1858 it had become *wakf* by long user (*o*).

The religious head of a *khānqāh* is called a *sajjādanashīn* (literally, one who sits at the head of a prayer-carpet). He is essentially a spiritual preceptor; he may—and generally is—the *mutawallī* of *wakf* property (*p*), and so, the secular office of a *mutawallī* must be distinguished from the spiritual status of a *sajjādanashīn*.

The special feature of the office of a *sajjādanashīn* is that the original founder has the right to nominate his successor, who in turn enjoys the same right. Thus a chain of preceptors (called a *silsila*) comes into being, and the followers, known as *murīds*, pay homage not only to the founder but also to the whole line, including the present link, called *pīr* or *murshid*. Theoretically the most illustrious disciple is to be installed as heir apparent, but, according to custom, in the majority of cases the office becomes hereditary. In one case the *sajjādanashīn* was found to be so worthless that he was removed from the *mutawallīship*, but was allowed to retain the spiritual office (*sajjādanashīnī*) which was considered to be hereditary (*q*).

(4) **Cemetery** (*qabristān*) (*r*)

A Hindu brought a suit for declaration of his title to and possession of a plot of land against the Muslims in a certain

(*o*) Tyabji, loc. cit., ill. (6).

(*p*) Tyabji §475, ill. (*b*).

(*q*) *Syed Shah Muhammad Kazim* v. *Syed Abi Saghir* (1931) 11 Patna 288, 346-7, a very interesting and important case. Other illustrations will be found in Tyabji, §475; see also *Ghulam Mohammad* v. *Abdul Rashid* (1933) 14 Lah. 558.

(*r*) Also known popularly as *maqbara* and *kabrastān*.

village. The defendants pleaded that the land was *wakf*, being used as a burial ground from time immemorial. Held, that the case fell to be decided, not on the principles of Muhammadan law, but on the ground of justice, equity and good conscience, which means rules of English law and equity so far as they are applicable to conditions prevailing in India.

And the plaintiff (Hindu) had proved his right and was entitled to a declaration. Their lordships further cited the following passage from an earlier case with approval:

> The Mohammedan law is not the law of British India. It is only the law so far as the laws of India have directed it to be observed. We are not bound by all the rules of the Mohammadan law which are in force under Mohammadan Governments nor by the law as laid down by the Fatwa [*sic*] Alumgiri, the digest of Mohammadan law, prepared under the Emperor *Aurangzeb Alumgir*. We are bound by Regulation 4 of 1793, except so far as that law has been modified by Regulation 7 of 1832 (*s*).

A cemetery is a consecrated ground and is not a private property; whether it is a burial ground or not depends upon the number of persons buried there or evidence of dedication derived from the testimony of witnesses or reputation.

A cemetery once created continues to be so even though there remain no traces of the dead, not even the bones. If the land has been used as a burial ground for a long time, it becomes *wakf* by long user, although there is no evidence of an express dedication (*t*).

(5) Dargāh (*u*)

In Persian and Urdu, the word *dargāh* means a threshold. In India it is a term applied to a shrine or the tomb of a Muslim saint; and is therefore a place of resort and prayer (*v*).

(*s*) *Ramzan Momin* v. *Dasrath Raut*, A.I.R. (1953) Patna 138.

(*t*) *Motishah* v. *Abdul Gaffar*, A.I.R. (1956) Nag. 38; *Mohd. Kasam* v. *Abdul Gafoor* A.I.R. (1964) Mad. Prad. 227.

(*u*) Tyabji §513, com.; *Syed Shah Abdul Latif* v. *Mohammad Lebbai* (1958) 2 Mad. L.J. 199.

(*v*) In Kashmir it is generally called a *ziyārat*, abbreviated form of *ziyāratgāh* (place of visit).

A Bombay decision discusses the law relating to *dargāhs* exhaustively (*w*). The origin of *dargāh* is discussed, and it is laid down that a *dargāh* is a respectful term applied to the shrine of a Muslim saint in India. In spite of the Prophet's disapproval of building tombs, great reverence is paid all over the sub-continent to such tombs. The word *dargāh* often includes a group of buildings of which the tomb is the nucleus.

A *mujāwar* is a servant of a Muslim shrine or mosque (*x*). The claim of a *mujāwar* to act as an intermediary or intercessor between God and man is opposed to Islamic teaching (*y*), for the office of *mujāwar* as an integral part of a *dargāh* is not known to Muhammadan law, and unless there is long user, the claim to the office by hereditary succession cannot be recognized. The institutions known as *takias*, *dargāhs* and *khānqāhs* are closely related and possess many similar features, in which the strict principles of *sharī'at* are often fused with, and give way to, immemorial custom. If a saintly man dies, his tomb is a *dargāh*; and in some instances, it may assume the importance of a *takia* or *khānqāh* (*z*).

Dargah Khwaja Saheb. An interesting case dealing with the most famous Sufi shrine in India, popularly known as *Dargah Khwaja Saheb, Ajmer,* is the one decided by the Supreme Court of India, *The Durgah Committee, Ajmer* v. *Syed Hussain Ali* [1962] 1 S.C.R. 383. Except for a clarification regarding religion and its proper observances, not many legal points were decided. But, as the case is of interest to the Muslim community, the following points may be noted: history, pp. 392-5; "denominations", 411; "religion" and its integral parts, 411-13. The impugned sections of the Durgah Khwaja Saheb Act (XXXVI of 1955) were held to be *intra vires.*

(6) **Imāmbāra** (*a*)

An *imāmbāra* is a private tenement set apart by a member of the Ithnā 'Asharī Shiite faith for the performance of

(*w*) *Mahomed Oosman* v. *Essak Salemahomed* [1938] Bom. 184.
(*x*) [1938] Bom. at p. 200. (*y*) ibid., p. 202.
(*z*) Further details may be found in Ameer Ali, I, 443.
(*a*) Tyabji §474 (12) and index; Mulla §223; Wilson, 6th ed., 386.

certain ceremonies at Muḥarram and other times; it is not a public place of worship like a mosque. It is a private, as distinguished from a public endowment and a Hindu cannot create one (*b*).

(7) **Kazi** (*c*)

The word *qāḍī* is in India usually spelt 'kazi', and this misspelling is so common that it must now be given recognition as correct by popular approval (*d*). The Prophet and the early Caliphs decided many matters in person, but later since the time of the Umayyads came the *qāḍīs*, who were judges charged with deciding all questions, civil as well as criminal, in accordance with the sacred law. The *qāḍī* was therefore a 'religious' judge working under the guidance of the *sharī'at*. Since in Islam, religion and law are confluent streams, the qualifications necessary for appointment were that he should be a Muslim, of blameless life, and thoroughly learned in the law. Each district was required to have a competent *qāḍī*; and every competent person was bound to act as a *qāḍī*, if duly appointed. The procedure in his courts was laid down by the law, and his judgment was decisive, there being ordinarily no appeal from it.

Although this ideal was kept in view, 'the bad *qāḍī*' is a well-known figure in the history of Islam. The great Imām Abū Ḥanīfa refused to act as a *qāḍī* because of the moral difficulties of having to please the secular authority (*e*).

An interesting sidelight on the character of the *qāḍī*, his duties, his behaviour and his independence, is afforded by one single example of the instructions given to him. Omar the

(*b*) *Mst. Mundaria* v. *Shyam Sundar* A.I.R. (1963) Pat. 93.

(*c*) The institution of *qāḍī* is of great importance in Islam, see *Ency. of Islam,* II, 606-7 by Juynboll: and Émile Tyan, *Histoire de l'Organisation Judiciaire en Pays d'Islam* (Paris, 1938), Vol. I, Chapter 2, on the *Qāḍī*. É. Tyan, *LME,* I, 236 sqq., esp. 236-41; *Maẓālim,* ibid., 263; *Shurṭa,* ibid., 274. Also, the author's article 'The *Adab al-Qāḍī* in Islamic Law', *Malayan L. Rev.,* Vol. 6 (1946, 406-16.

(*d*) In English the usual form is *cadi;* but Fitzgerald mentions six spellings, among which are *al-kali* (not to be confused with the Hindu Goddess Kali) and *kathi,* p. vii; Tyabji §15 sq.

(*e*) Shibli, *Sirat al-Nu'mān* (Azamgadh, 1936), 50-1.

Great, second Caliph of Islam, in his instructions to *qāḍis*, laid down that the *qāḍī* should first follow the principles of the Koran, and then the practice of the Prophet. Every person, high or low, rich or poor, should be treated with equality. The forms of procedure should be properly followed and proper evidence obtained before a decision was given. Lawful compromises should be encouraged. Even after judgment, if the *qāḍī* felt that an error had crept in, he should not stand on his dignity, but should review his judgment, for 'it is better to retract than to persist in injustice'.

Use your intelligence about matters that perplex you, to which neither law nor practice seems to apply; study the theory of analogy, then compare things, and adopt that judgment which is most pleasing to God and most in conformity with justice, so far as you can see (*f*).

If there were different schools (*madhāhib*) of Muslims within the state, as far as possible the state appointed a *qāḍī* for each of such schools. An important point of distinction between the *sharī'at* courts in Muslim lands and the Indian courts is this: in Islamic countries it is the *madhhab* (school) of the *qāḍī* which determines the principles of law to be administered in his court; whereas in India, the religion and school of the litigant is taken into consideration. For instance, in Egypt, whatever the law of the parties, the Hanafi law will generally be applied to Muslims in personal matters; but in India the law of the parties—Hanafi, Shāfi'ī, Ithnā 'Asharī or Fatimid Ismā'īlī—will be applicable. In addition to the general rules of law the textbooks contain chapters on the 'Duties of the *Qāḍī*' which remind us, in many instances, of the rules laid down by Chancery judges for the guidance of courts of Equity (*g*).

It was this officer, the *qāḍī* of the texts of Islamic jurisprudence, which the Judicial Committee of the Privy Council had in view when they laid down that in India the place of

(*f*) The author's *A Modern Approach to Islam* (Bombay, 1963), 37 sqq.

(*g*) For example, *Hedaya*, Book XX, 334 sqq. and the author's 'The *Adab al-Qāḍī in Islamic Law*', op. cit.

the 'Kazi' had been taken by the Civil Court (*h*). But in India the term 'Kazi' is also applied to certain petty religious officiants and the two classes of *kazis* must be sharply distinguished. There are enactments regulating their appointment and rights (*i*), and it has been held that the Muhammadan law does not recognize the office of *kazi* as hereditary (*j*).

§62. Miscellaneous Points

I. The Masjid Shahid Ganj Case (*k*)

Within recent years the *Shahid Ganj Mosque Case* was, in every sense of the term, a *cause célèbre*, and it is proposed to give briefly the facts and the law laid down by the Privy Council.

A structure which had been built as a mosque in Lahore was dedicated in 1722, but from about 1762 the building and adjacent land were in the occupation and possession of the Sikhs. In 1849, at the time of the British annexation, the mosque building and the property which had been dedicated therewith were in the possession of certain Sikhs, Mahants of a Sikh shrine (gurdwara), and the mosque building was used by the custodians of the Sikh institution. In 1927, by notification made pursuant to the Sikh Gurdwaras Act (Punjab Act VIII of 1925), the old mosque building and land adjacent thereto were included as belonging to the Sikh Gurdwara. Litigation was brought before the Sikh Gurdwaras Tribunal in 1928 'on behalf of the Muhammadans', who claimed that the land and property had been dedicated for a mosque and did not belong to the Gurdwara. The Tribunal held that the claim failed by reason of adverse possession and previous decisions, and in the result, the property and build-

(*h*) *Mahomed Ismail* v. *Ahmed Moolla* (1916) 43 I.A. 127, 134.

(*i*) Tyabji §§15 sq.

(*j*) Mulla §221. As to Mullagiri lands, see *Mohd. Isak* v. *Najaruddin* A.I.R. (1962) Mysore 253.

(*k*) *Masjid Shahid Ganj* v. *Shiromani Gurdwara Parbandhak Committee, Amritsar* (1940) 67 I.A. 251.

ing were given into the custody of the defendants, and on 7 July 1935 the building was suddenly demolished by or with the connivance of its Sikh custodians under the influence of communal ill-feeling.

The suit out of which the appeal arose was brought by eighteen plaintiffs, the first being the mosque itself, in the sense of the site and building, suing by a next friend, and the other plaintiffs, including minors and women, were persons who claimed that they had a right to worship in the mosque. The suit was brought against the Shiromani Gurdwara Parbandhak Committee and the Committee of Management for the notified Sikh Gurdwaras at Lahore, who were in possession of the disputed property, and was *inter alia* for a declaration that the building was a mosque in which the plaintiffs and all followers of Islam had a right to worship, and for a mandatory injunction to reconstruct the building.

Three important principles were laid down in this case by the Privy Council:

(1) As to limitation—'The rules of limitation which apply to a suit are the rules in force at the date of the institution of the suit, limitation being a matter of procedure' (*l*). The Indian Limitation Act applies to mosques in India.

(2) As to juristic personality of mosques—the Privy Council held that in the present case it was not necessary to decide whether in any circumstances, or for any purpose, an Islamic institution could be regarded in law as a 'juristic person'; but it was sufficient to 'hold that suits cannot competently be brought by or against such institutions as artificial persons in the British Indian Courts' (*m*).

(3) As to the ascertainment of Muhammadan law—Muhammadan law is the law of the land, and not a foreign system. 'It is therefore the duty of the courts themselves to interpret the law of the land and to apply it and not to depend upon the opinion of witnesses howsoever learned they

(*l*) 67 I.A. 251, 262.
(*m*) ibid., 265, 266.

may be.' The Privy Council adopted with approval these observations of Sulaiman J. in *Aziz Bano* v. *Muhammad Ibrahim* (*n*).

II. *Suit for Obtaining a Declaration that Certain Property is* Wakf

A suit for a declaration that certain property belongs to a *wakf* can be brought by Muslims interested in the *wakf* without the sanction of the Advocate-General. The provisions of Sec. 92 of the Civil Procedure Code, 1908, do not apply to such a suit; for, that section applies only to suits claiming any of the reliefs specified in it (*o*).

III. *Construction* of Wakf-nāma

The deed of *wakf* must be construed in accordance with the intention of the *wāḳif*, and the canons of construction are laid down in detail by the authorities of Islamic jurisprudence, see Tyabji §§539 sqq.

(*n*) 47 All. 823, 835 cited at 67 I.A., p. 260.

(*o*) *Abdur Hahim* v. *Mahomed Barkat Ali* (1927) 55 I.A. 96; Tyabji §556; Mulla §195.

CHAPTER X

PRE-EMPTION

§63. Origin, Application, Definition

THE history of pre-emption in India has been given by Sir John Edge in *Digambar Singh* v. *Ahmad Said Khan*:

Pre-emption in village communities in British India had its origin in the Mahomedan law as to pre-emption, and was apparently unknown in India before the time of the Moghul rulers. In the course of time customs of pre-emption grew up or were adopted among village communities. In some cases the sharers in a village adopted or followed the rules of the Mahomedan law of pre-emption, and in such cases the custom of the village follows the rules of the Mahomedan law of pre-emption. In other cases, where a custom of pre-emption exists, each village community has a custom of pre-emption which varies from the Mahomedan law of pre-emption and is peculiar to the village in its provisions and its incidents. A custom of pre-emption was doubtless in all cases the result of agreement amongst the shareholders of the particular village, and may have been adopted in modern times and in villages which were first constituted in modern times. Rights of pre-emption have in some provinces been given by Acts of the Indian Legislature. Rights of pre-emption have also been created by contract between the sharers in a village. But in all cases the object is as far as possible to prevent strangers to a village from becoming sharers in the village. Rights of pre-emption when they exist are valuable rights, and when they depend upon a custom or upon a contract, the custom or the contract, as the case may be, must, if disputed, be proved (*a*).

Mahmood J. observes in *Gobind Dayal's Case:*

The law of pre-emption is essentially a part of Muhammadan jurisprudence. It was introduced into India by Muhammadan

(*a*) (1914) 42 I.A. 10, 18.

Judges who were bound to administer the Muhammadan law. Under their administration it became, and remained for centuries, the common law of the country, and was applied universally both to Muhammadans and Hindus, because in this respect the Muhammadan law makes no distinction between persons of different races or creeds. 'A Musalman and a *Zimmee* being equally affected by principles on which *shafa* or right of pre-emption is established, and equally concerned in its operation, are therefore on an equal footing in all cases regarding the privilege of *shafa*.' (Hamilton's *Hedaya*, Vol. III, p. 592.) What was the effect of this? In course of time, pre-emption became adopted by the Hindus as a custom (*b*).

The law of pre-emption is based clearly upon the texts of Islamic law, and while there seem to be foreign elements in it (*c*), it is a well-established doctrine in India. It was adopted by Islam, in general, to prevent the introduction of a stranger among co-sharers and neighbours, likely to cause both inconvenience and vexation (*d*).

In *Gobind Dayal* v. *Inayatullah*, Mahmood J. defined pre-emption (*shuf'a*) as:

> . . . a right which the owner of certain immoveable property possesses, as such, for the quiet enjoyment of that immoveable property, to obtain, *in substitution for the buyer*, proprietary possession of certain other immoveable property, not his own, on such terms as those on which such latter immoveable property is sold to another person (*e*).

Three things are, therefore, requisite: (i) the pre-emptor must be the *owner* of immovable property; (ii) there must be a *sale* of certain property, not his own; (iii) the pre-emptor must stand in a certain *relationship* to the vendor in respect of the property sold. If these conditions are satisfied, he has the right to be substituted for the purchaser.

(*b*) (1885) 7 All. at p. 790; *Cases*, 429, 439-40.

(*c*) Roman and Germanic, per Holloway J., in *Ibrahim Saib* v. *Muni Mir* (1870) 6 Mad. H.C.R. 26, 30-1.

(*d*) Ameer Ali, I, 712. For a general discussion, see *Sayeeduddin Ahmed* v. *Iunus Mia* PLD 1960 Dacca 416 (*milk, mālik* discussed at p. 419 sqq.).

(*e*) (1885) 7 All. 775, 799; *Cases* at p. 448. The italics are mine. The word *shuf'a* is often mis-spelt *shafa, shuffa* and *shoofa*.

In *Bishan Singh* v. *Khazan Singh*, Subba Row J. has summarized in the Supreme Court the main rules of pre-emption in India:

To summarize: (1) The right of pre-emption is not a right to the thing sold but a right to the offer of a thing about to be sold. This right is called the primary or inherent right. (2) The pre-emptor has a secondary right or a remedial right to follow the thing sold. (3) It is a right of substitution but not of re-purchase, i.e. the pre-emptor takes the entire bargain and steps into the shoes of the original vendee. (4) It is a right to acquire the whole of the property sold and not a share of the property sold. (5) Preference being the essence of the right, the plaintiff must have a superior right to that of the vendee or the person substituted in his place. (6) The right being a very weak right, it can be defeated by all legitimate methods, such as the vendee allowing the claimant of a superior or equal right being substituted in his place (*f*).

§64. *Gobind Dayal's Case*

This is the leading case on the subject and, as several important points were discussed and decided therein, it is perhaps best to give a summary of the judgment of Mahmood J. which is considered to be one of the most authoritative expositions of the law of pre-emption (*g*).

The pre-emptor and the vendor were Muslims, and the vendees (purchasers) were Hindus. The question was whether, in such a case, the right of pre-emption could be enforced against a non-Muslim. The court of first instance held that such a right could not be enforced against a non-Muslim vendee. The lower appellate court reversed the decree, and the defendants appealed to the High Court. The appeal came up for hearing before Straight and Mahmood JJ., who referred the following question to the Full Bench:

'In a case of pre-emption, where the pre-emptor and the

(*f*) A.I.R. (1958) S.C. 838, 841, a very important judgment which, although dealing with the Punjab Pre-emption Act, 1913, makes general observations of an illuminating character.

(*g*) *Gobind Dayal* v. *Inayatullah* (1885) 7 All. 775; *Cases*, 429. The judgment of Mahmood J. will be found at pp. 776-814, and the references in brackets are to the pages in I.L.R., 7 Allahabad.

vendor are Muslims and the vendee a non-Muslim, is the Muhammadan law of pre-emption to be applied to the matter, in advertence to the terms of Section 24 of Act VI of 1871?'

The Full Bench consisted of Sir W. Comer Petheram C.J., Oldfield, Brodhurst, Mahmood and Duthoit JJ. The judgment of the Full Bench was delivered by Mahmood J., with whom all the judges agreed.

The case raised two questions: (i) Whether Sec. 24 of the Bengal Civil Court Act (VI of 1871) rendered it imperative on the courts to administer the Muhammadan law in cases of this nature; (ii) What was the Muhammadan law of pre-emption on this point?

Mahmood J. deals with the early history of the law culminating in Sec. 24 of Act VI of 1871, and raises the question 'whether pre-emption is "a religious usage or institution"' within the meaning of the section (p. 779).

In Hindu and Muhammadan laws, religion is closely blended with law (781). Pre-emption is clearly connected with the Muhammadan law of inheritance (782); it would therefore be inconsistent to apply the Muhammadan law of inheritance, and not pre-emption. He then deals with three matters: first, the history of the law of pre-emption, secondly, the manner in which it has been administered in the British courts, and thirdly, the Islamic texts upon which his conclusions are founded (785). Despite the opinion of Sir William Macnaghten, pre-emption as a rule of law was unknown among Hindus (785-90). The law of pre-emption is essentially a part of Muhammadan jurisprudence. It was introduced into India by Muhammadan judges who were bound to administer the Muhammadan law. It thus became for centuries the common law of the country and was applied universally both to Muhammadans and Hindus (790). In the course of time, Hindus adopted pre-emption as a custom.

If all parties are Muslims, no problem arises, but the question is whether the law of pre-emption should be administered where only the vendee is a Hindu (790-1).

(i) If all parties are Muslims, Muhammadan law applies.

(ii) If all parties are Hindus, Muhammadan law does not apply.

(iii) If the vendor and the vendee are Hindus, but the pre-emptor is a Muslim, there is no pre-emption.

(iv) If the pre-emptor is a Hindu, and the vendor and the vendee are Muslims, there is no pre-emption.

(v) If the vendee is a Muslim, and the pre-emptor and the vendor are Hindus, there is no pre-emption.

(vi) If the vendor is a Muslim, and the pre-emptor and the vendee are Hindus, there is no pre-emption.

This is so because now Muhammadan law is a personal law, and not the common law of the land (793), and the rights and obligations must be reciprocal (793).

(vii) The last instance is where the pre-emptor and the vendor are Muslims, but the vendee is a Hindu (796).

Mahmood J. differs from the decision of Mitter J. in *Kudratulla's Case*, and holds that the right of pre-emption arises.

The most important case till then was *Sheikh Kudratulla* v. *Mahini Mohan Shaha* (1869) 4 Bengal L.R. 134, where it was held by a majority of the Full Bench of the Calcutta High Court that a Hindu purchaser is not bound by the Muhammadan law of pre-emption in favour of a Muslim coparcener, nor is he bound by the law of pre-emption on the ground of vicinage. And this, because the right of pre-emption possessed by a Muslim does not depend on any defect of title on the part of his Muslim coparcener, but upon a rule of Muhammadan law, which is not binding on the court, nor on any purchaser other than a Muslim (791).

Mitter J. held that pre-emption is *a right of repurchase* not from the vendor, but from the vendee. Two propositions were laid down: (i) That the right of pre-emption under the Muhammadan law does not exist before actual sale (798), and (ii) that a sale, in respect of which pre-emption can be claimed, passes full ownership to the vendee, and does not involve any defect of title. From these the conclusion was drawn that it was 'a mere right of repurchase, not from the vendor, but from the vendee'.

Mahmood J. then discusses the nature of the right. The law of pre-emption 'creates what I may call a legal servitude running with the land'.(800) He translates a passage of the *Hedaya* and shows that that high authority lays down that sale is not the cause of pre-emption. The real cause is the situation of the properties in question. The right to enforce the pre-emptor's right comes into being after the sale, which clearly shows the intention to dispose of the property. The right exists independently of and antecedent to the sale (801).

'The object of the right is to prevent the intrusion, not of all purchasers in general, but only of such as are objectionable from the pre-emptor's point of view.'(803) Any action by the pre-emptor before actual sale is premature. The rule of pre-emption is a qualified disability on the part of the vendor (805).

He then explains the traditions of the Prophet that it is morally objectionable, although not legally unlawful, to sell a property without offering it to the pre-emptor (805-7).

The right of pre-emption is *not* a right to repurchase from the vendee, but it is *a right of substitution*, entitling the pre-emptor to stand in the shoes of the purchaser (809) (*h*). After a few other considerations, he points out that the right of pre-emption cannot be said to be merely a restriction on the free transfer of property, and even in a country like Germany, a similar right (*retractrecht*) was enforceable (814).

As to the nature of the right, it has been held in Calcutta (*i*) and Bombay (*j*) that the right of pre-emption is *a right of repurchase* from the buyer; Mahmood J., however, held that

(*h*) This passage is cited with approval by the Supreme Court in *Bishan Singh* v. *Khazan Singh* A.I.R. (1958) S.C. 838, 840, where Mahmood J.'s judgment is rightly raised to the rank of a classic.

(*i*) *Kudratulla's Case* (1869) 4 Bengal L.R. 134.

(*j*) *Hamedmiya* v. *Benjamin* (1928) 53 Bom. 525; but see *Dashrathlal Chhaganlal* v. *Bai Dhondubai* (1940) 43 Bom. L.R. 581, 592.

it was *a right of substitution* (*k*), and therefore an incident of property, likening it to a servitude running with the land. This reasoning has been accepted by the Patna High Court (*l*), and in a recent Full Bench decision of the Bombay High Court, Sir John Beaumont C.J., agreeing with Mahmood J., came to the conclusion that the right of pre-emption was originally, under Muhammadan law, a right attached to the land (*m*). As this reasoning is adopted by the Supreme Court of India, it is submitted that the question is no longer open to doubt.

Full ownership. The right of pre-emption arises only when there is full ownership in the property, not, when a lessor interest such as a leasehold is sold (*mm*).

Application (*n*)

(1) The law of pre-emption is applied to Muslims throughout India as a matter of justice, equity and good conscience, except in the State of Madras (now Tamil Nadu), where it is considered as opposed to justice, equity and good conscience (*o*).

(2) By custom, the law of pre-emption is applied also to Hindus in certain localities, for instance in Bihar, in Sylhet, and in certain portions of Gujarat (*p*).

(3) By Statute, the law of pre-emption is applied in the

(*k*) A view accepted by the Supreme Court in *Bishan Singh* v. *Khazan Singh*, as shown above.

(*l*) Saksena, *Muslim Law as Administered in India* (2nd ed., 1938), 530-1.

(*m*) *Dashrathlal Chhaganlal* v. *Bai Dhondubai* (1940) 43 Bom. L.R. 581, 592.

(*mm*) *Munni Lal* v. *Bishwanath Prasad* A.I.R. (1968) S.C. 450.

(*n*) Tyabji §5. Saksena, *Muslim Law*, 4th ed. (Lucknow, 1963) is particularly exhaustive on questions concerning pre-emption, see Ch. XII, p. 737 sqq.

(*o*) *Ibrahim Saib* v. *Muni Mir* (1870) 6 Mad. H.C. Rep. 26; Mulla §227. This divergence of view reminds one of the story of the Chancellor's foot in Equity.

(*p*) Tyabji §566; Mulla §229; as to Ahmedabad, see *Dashrathlal Chhaganlal* v. *Bai Dhondubal* (1940) 43 Bom. L.R. 581, and Bihar, see *Sonabashi Kuer* v. *Ramdeo Singh* A.I.R. (1951) Pat. 521.

Punjab, the former North-West Frontier Province and Oudh, both to Hindus and to Muslims (*q*).

(4) Rights of pre-emption may also arise in certain cases by contract (*r*).

Previous to the recent decision of the Supreme Court, *Bhau Ram* v. *Baij Nath*, there was considerable difference of opinion in India whether the law of pre-emption was constitutional or not, regard being had to Art. 19 (1) (*f*). The Supreme Court has now decided that the law of pre-emption creates a restriction on the fundamental right guaranteed under the Constitution; but custom prevails in some cases.

When considering the reasonableness of any custom creating such right both previous decisions and enactments are relevant, but the crucial test as laid down by a majority of their lordships of the Supreme Court in *Bhau Ram* v. *Baij Nath* (*s*) is this:

> We have to judge the reasonableness of the law in the context of fundamental rights which were for the first time conferred by the Constitution on the people of this country and which were not there when the Court might have been considering the reasonableness of the custom, if any, in the context of things then prevalent (para. 4).
>
> The reasonableness of a custom is, however, not a constant factor and what is reasonable at one stage of the progress of society may not be so at another (para. 7).

Accordingly it was held (i) that *vicinage* was no ground for pre-emption; but

(ii) the right of a *co-sharer* was a reasonable ground; or

(iii) the right of a participator in certain appendages such as a of a person having a *common entrance* to the property; or

(iv) where there was a *common staircase*.

This case decided factually upon the validity or otherwise of certain clauses in statutes relating to the Rewa State,

(*q*) Tyabji, loc. cit.; Mulla §228.

(*r*) Mulla §230.

(*s*) A.I.R. (1962) S.C. 1476. See also J. D. M. Derrett, 'The Supreme Court and Pre-emption' (1963) 65 Bom. L. R., Jl., 1.

Punjab and Berar; but, the principles enunciated in it will apply necessarily in all suits after the decision (*t*).

Shiite Law

Where some of the parties are Shiite, the courts have laid down precisely what law is applicable: Mulla §§248, 249, and see *Pasha Begum* v. *Syed Shabber Hasan* A.I.R. (1956) Hyd. 1 (F.B.), fully discussed below. For Fatimid Law, see *Da'ā'im,* II §§265 sqq.

§65. Who can Pre-empt, and When?

(A) *Who can Pre-empt?* (*u*) I. *Hanafi Law*

Three classes of persons are entitled in Hanafi law to exercise the right of pre-emption: (i) *shafī'-e sharīk,* (ii) *shafī'-e khalīṭ,* (iii) *shafī'-e jār.*

(i) *Shafī'-e sharīk,* i.e. a co-sharer in the property. A co-sharer (*sharīk*) is an owner of an undivided share in the property. There must be full ownership in the land pre-empted, and therefore the right to pre-empt does not arise on the sale of a leasehold interest in the land (*v*). For instance, Daud and Ibrahim are the two sons of Ahmad, and as such are joint owners of a landed property. If Daud sells his portion of the land to *X* or Ibrahim to *Y*, Ibrahim or Daud, respectively, have the right to pre-empt. But there must be a sale of the land, and not merely the transfer of a lease (see above, §64, note *mm*).

Such a right is constitutional and can be exercised (§64 above).

(ii) *Shafī'-e khalīṭ,* i.e. a participator in immunities and appendages. This expression means a person who is entitled to such easements as a right of way, or discharge of water.

Some of these rights have been declared to be constitutional by the Supreme Court (India), *supra.*

(*t*) Mulla §231.

(*u*) Tyabji 607 sqq.; Mulla §231.

(*v*) Mulla, loc. cit.

(iii) *Shafī'-e jār,* i.e. the neighbour, the owner of an adjoining property.

The right of vicinage has been declared unconstitutional by the Supreme Court (India), as we have seen above.

The two classes of pre-emptors take in the order specified above; the first class excludes the second (*x*).

Pre-emptors of the same class are in Hanafi law entitled to pre-empt in equal proportions, notwithstanding that they are owners of unequal shares. Under Shāfi'ī law, however, the right of a pre-emptor is proportionate to his share in the property (*y*).

As between pre-emptors of the same class no distinction is made. Thus, if *X* is a participator in appendages (*khalīṭ*) and *also* a neighbour (*jār*), and *Y* is only a participator (*khalīṭ*), *X* has no priority over *Y*. Similarly a co-sharer who is a neighbour, has no priority over a co-sharer who is *not* a neighbour (*z*).

Wakf and pre-emption

The *wāḳif* has no right to pre-empt on behalf of the *wakf* property (*a*); nor can God, as the ultimate Sovereign and Owner of property, claim pre-emption on behalf of the foundation.

> The conception of God being impleaded as a party in a claim before a Qazi is so foreign to Muslim religion and Muslim jurisprudence . . . that Muslim jurists have nowhere discussed whether a suit . . . can be filed on behalf of God Almighty . . . In the Islamic system God alone has supreme legislative power and he promulgates His laws on this earth from time to time through His messengers (*rusul*) and prophets (*anbiyā*). It is contrary to the principles of that system that God should figure as a party litigant, either as plaintiff or defendant (*b*).

(*x*) Tyabji §619.
(*y*) Tyabji 621, and ill. (1).
(*z*) Tyabji §619; Muhammadan law does not recognize degrees of nearness in the same class, although the nearness may be recognized by custom, *Syed Haji Imambakhsh* v. *Mir Muhammadali Khan*, A.I.R. (1946) Sind 55.
(*a*) *Girraj Kunwar* v. *Irfan Ali* A.I.R. (1952) All. 686.
(*b*) ibid., 688, per Malik C.J.

A *wakf* estate is therefore not entitled to claim the right of pre-emption in the case of a sale of adjoining property (*c*).

II. *Shāfi'ī Law*

The Shāfi'ī school is stricter than the Hanafi and permits only a co-sharer to exercise the right of pre-emption (*d*).

III. *Ithnā 'Asharī Shiite Law*

The Shiite system goes a step further, and restricts the right of pre-emption to cases where there are only *two co-sharers* in the property. The right of a participator or a neighbour is not recognized, nor can pre-emption be claimed where there are more than two co-owners (*e*).

A woman is not precluded by reason of her sex from exercising her right of pre-emption, even if she is entitled to a widow's share of inheritance; but a woman, entitled only to maintenance, cannot exercise the right of pre-emption (*f*).

IV. *Fatimid Law*

The *Da'ā'im* does not recognize a neighbour's right to pre-empt, II §265 and details will be found in the later articles. This subject has not been dealt with by me in the *Compendium,* as being of diminishing importance in India.

(B) *When Does the Right Arise?* (*g*)

The right of pre-emption arises only on sale or barter, that is exchange of property for property; it does not arise either on a transfer without consideration, or on a transfer by operation of law. It is not necessary, however, that the land sold should be actually separated or divided by metes and bounds (*h*).

If sale alone gives rise to the right of pre-emption, how are we to determine the exact point of time when the sale may be

(*c*) ibid., 691.
(*d*) Tyabji §607(2).
(*e*) loc. cit., (3).
(*f*) Mulla, loc. cit.
(*g*) Tyabji §§576 sqq.; Mulla §232.
(*h*) Tyabji, loc. cit.

said to be complete? Are we to determine the question in accordance with the Muhammadan notions of sale (*bay'*)? Or are we to consider the Indian law on the subject? Or is there a third criterion?

An Allahabad decision seems to lay down that the question whether a sale is complete must be determined by applying the Muhammadan law; and, if a complete sale is effected under that law, as where the price is paid and possession is delivered, the right of pre-emption will arise, although the sale is not complete under the Transfer of Property Act (*i*). On the other hand some judges have opined that the right of pre-emption does not arise until after registration, as required by the statutory law of India (*j*).

A recent decision of the Supreme Court deals with this aspect. *P* executed a sale-deed of a house on January 31, 1946, in favour of *D*, and presented it for registration on the *same* day. On hearing of the sale, *RS* made a *ṭalab-e muwāthaba* (the first demand) on February 2. The deed was copied out in the Registrar's books on February 9. *RS* filed a suit for pre-emption. *D* resisted the suit on the ground that the sale was completed only on February 9, and not earlier; therefore the demand was made prematurely. Held by a majority (three to two) that the demand was made prematurely and must fail (*k*).

The principle previously accepted by the courts that the intention of the parties should be the guiding principle to determine when the sale was deemed to be complete (*l*), was apparently abandoned in this case.

With great respect, the majority opinion appears to be harsh and technical, and its only justification seems to be the prevailing view of the Supreme Court that all transactions involving pre-emption are discriminatory as offending a

(*i*) *Begam* v. *Muhammad Yakub* (1894) 16 All. 344, F.B.

(*j*) See the cases cited in Mulla §232.

(*k*) *Ram Saran* v. (*Mst.*) *Domini Kuer* [1962] 2 S.C.R. 474.

(*l*) *Sitaram Bhaurao* v. *Jiual Hasan* (1921) 48 I.A. 475.

fundamental right guaranteed under the Constitution. Juristically a more satisfactory view appears to have been taken recently in Pakistan (*m*), but as this case has not been seen by me, it is not possible to comment upon it.

Transfer in lieu of mahr (*n*). Where a husband transfers landed property to the wife in lieu of her unpaid dower, the question arises whether such a transaction is a sale or a barter, which would give rise to a right of pre-emption. The Allahabad High Court, guided by the opinion of Mahmood J. (*o*), had held that, inasmuch as such a transfer is in satisfaction of a previous obligation, it is one for consideration and should be regarded as a 'sale', thus giving rise to the right of pre-emption.

On the other hand, the Chief Court of Oudh, adopting the reasoning of Ameer Ali (*p*), came to the conclusion that the transaction should be regarded as a *hiba bi'l-'iwaḍ*—a gift of the property by the husband to the wife, coupled with a gift by the wife to the husband of her dower debt—and that the right of pre-emption does not arise (*q*).

In spite of the matchless reasoning of Mahmood J., it is submitted with deference that the Lucknow view appears to be more in consonance with justice.

§66. Conflict of Laws

Religion of buyer, seller and pre-emptor. Where the parties to a transaction which gives rise to a case of pre-emption are governed by different personal laws, it is necessary to lay down the principles upon which the court would act. In India, all religions are treated with equality, and therefore in this branch of the law *the principle of reciprocity* should be logically applied. Hence, on general principles, it would

(*m*) Mulla, pp. 235-7; §232, com.

(*n*) Wilson §369; Tyabji §576; Mulla, loc. cit.

(*o*) In *Fida Ali* v. *Muzaffar Ali* (1882) 5 All. 65, a Shiite case.

(*p*) Ameer Ali, i, 713, esp. footnote (6).

(*q*) *Bashir Ahmad* v. *Mst. Zubaida Khatun* (1925) 1 Luck. 83, followed by other decisions, see Mulla, loc. cit.

be unfair to apply the law of pre-emption and to create rights in favour of persons who would not be subject to corresponding obligations (*r*).

(1) The seller and the pre-emptor must necessarily be Muslims (*s*). The vendor should be a Muslim; for there is no reason why the Muhammadan law of pre-emption should be applied to a vendor who is a non-Muslim. The pre-emptor should also be a Muslim; the reason being that as a Muslim, if he subsequently wishes to sell the property, he will be obliged to offer it to his Muslim neighbours or co-owners. If, however, the right of pre-emption is recognized in favour of a non-Muslim, he may take advantage of it as a pre-emptor; but would not be subject to a similar obligation.

(2) As regards the purchaser, there is a conflict of opinion. According to the Allahabad and Patna decisions, the purchaser need not be a Muslim; while, according to the Calcutta and Bombay view, the purchaser should also be a Muslim (*t*).

(3) As between Sunnites and Shiites, if a Shiite sues a Sunnite for pre-emption, the Shiite, which is the narrower law, will be applied; thus a neighbour, being a Shiite, will have no right to pre-empt from a Sunnite vendor (*u*).

A Hyderabad case illustrates the principles to be followed in determining suits where one of the parties is a Sunnite and the other a Shiite (*v*). One Abdur Rahman (Hanafi) sold a house to Pasha Begum (also Hanafi). Thereupon Syed Shabber Hasan (Twelver Shiite) filed a suit for pre-emption. The question arose whether the Hanafi or the Ithnā 'Asharī law was to apply. The two questions referred to the Full Bench were formulated as follows:

(*r*) One of the earliest discussions of the subject is by Mahmood J., see p. 336 sqq. above, based on his remarks in 7 Allahabad at p. 793. This appears to be the guiding principle in recent decisions such as *Pasha Begum* v. *Syed Shabber Hasan* A.I.R. (1956) Hyd. 1 (F.B.).

(*s*) Wilson §357; Tyabji 572; Mulla §234.

(*t*) Mulla, loc. cit.

(*u*) Mulla §§248, 249.

(*v*) *Pasha Begum* v. *Syed Shabber Hasan* A.I.R. (1956) Hyd. 1, Full Bench (five judges).

(1) Whether all suits of pre-emption are to be decided according to the rules of Hanafi law irrespective of the fact that the parties belong to different persuasions? and

(2) In case it is held that the personal law of other sects has the force of law then by what law the suit would be governed if the person claiming is a Shiite and the defendant a Sunnite or vice versa.

The bench consisted of five judges. The majority held that the law of pre-emption in Hyderabad is neither statutory, nor customary, nor territorial, nor yet 'the Common Law' (p. 2b). The true principle was that Hindu and Muhammadan laws were applied as personal laws to Hindus and Muslims, respectively (3a). The law of pre-emption has been declared to be a personal law by the Supreme Court (3b), and if the parties are Muslims no question arises and the Muhammadan law will apply.

As the personal law of each party would apply, what happens if the pre-emptor is of the Shiite school and the vendor of the Sunnite faith? The following scheme was adopted:

(i) If both the parties belong to one and the same school. the rules of that particular school apply.

(ii) If the vendor is a Shiite and the pre-emptor a Sunnite, then as the Shiite law does not recognize the right of pre-emption on the ground of vicinage, applying the principle of reciprocity, the pre-emptor does not succeed; and similarly

(iii) Where the vendor is a Sunnite and the pre-emptor a Shiite, again, for want of reciprocity, the pre-emptor must fail.

It will be recalled that this reasoning is the one put forward by Mahmood J. in the leading case of *Gobind Dayal* v. *Inayatullah*, and the majority cited it with approval and adopted the principle of reciprocity as being in consonance with justice and equity.

§67. The Necessary Formalities

According to the *Hedaya* 'the right of *shuf'a* is but a feeble right, as it is the disseizing another of his property merely in order to prevent apprehended inconveniences'.(*x*) For this reason, the law considers certain formalities as imperative (*y*).

The Muhammadan law of pre-emption is a law of technicality, and the existence of the right depends upon the full and complete observance of formalities. It is a ritual. If the ritual be defective, the *Djinn* will not emerge from his bottle. Unless the words are 'open sesame' the door will not open. If the ceremonies are in any way incomplete or erroneous, the right of *shaffa* does not take form, but remains unsubstantial. It is right that it should be so, because the doctrine involves an interference with one of the fundamental human rights, the right of freedom of contract (*z*).

The Three Demands

No person is entitled to pre-empt unless he takes the proper steps at the proper time, and conforms strictly to the necessary formalities. These formalities or ceremonies are known as the Three Demands.

(1) *The First Demand*, ṭalab-e muwāthaba (*a*). The pre-emptor must assert his claim immediately on hearing of the sale, but not before. Witnesses are not necessary, as in the second demand; nor is any particular form essential. 'I have demanded or do demand pre-emption' is enough (*b*). The courts enforce this formality strictly; and any unreasonable delay will be construed as an election not to pre-empt. A delay of twelve hours was, in one case, considered too long; and in another, the right of pre-emption was denied to a man who, on hearing of a sale, entered his house, opened a chest and took out a sum of money (probably to tender the money

(*x*) *Hedaya*, 550, left column.

(*y*) Wilson §375; Tyabji §§591 sqq.; Mulla §236.

(*z*) *C. S. Tiwari* v. *R. P. Dubey* (1949) 28 Pat. 861, 871—so Meredith J., felicitously.

(*a*) Literally, 'the demand of jumping'. The idea is of a person jumping from his seat, as though startled by news of the sale, Wilson, 406, foot-note. The word is loosely spelt *mowasibat* (Wilson) or *muathibat* (Tyabji).

(*b*) Tyabji §§581 sqq.

to the buyer), and then made the first demand (*ṭalab-e muwāthaba*) (*c*). The principle is that the law requires extreme promptness and any laxity will be fatal to the pre-emptor's claim.

(2) *The Second Demand,* ṭalab-e ishhād (*d*). The pre-emptor must, with the least practicable delay, make a second demand. He must (i) refer to his first demand (*e*); (ii) do so in the presence of two witnesses; and (iii) do so in the presence of either the vendor (if he is in possession), or the purchaser, or on the premises. This is also known as *ṭalab-e taqrīr,* the demand of confirmation (*f*).

A common form of the demand is: the pre-emptor says, 'Such a person has bought such a house of which I am the pre-emptor (*shafī*'). I have already claimed my privilege of pre-emption (*shuf'a*) and now I again claim it: be ye witnesses thereof.'(*g*) The property must be clearly specified by the pre-emptor (*h*).

If the pre-emptor is at a distance and cannot be personally present, the second demand may be made by an agent, or even by a letter (*i*). An omission by the agent will bind the pre-emptor. Tender of the price is not necessary, provided that he offers to pay the agreed price; and if that price appears to be fictitious, then such price as the court fixes (*j*). If there are several purchasers, the demand must be made to all of them, unless it is made on the premises, or in the presence of the vendor (*k*). If, however, the demand is made to some only of the purchasers, the pre-emptor can claim his rights as against these purchasers only, and not as against the others.

Sometimes, the first two demands may be combined. If, at

(*c*) Mulla, loc. cit.; Tyabji, loc. cit.

(*d*) Or *istishhād*; literally, the demand which is witnessed, Tyabji §583.

(*e*) This is an absolute necessity, without which the demand is void, *C. S. Tiwari* v. *R. P. Dubey* (1949) 28 Pat. 861.

(*f*) Tyabji, loc. cit.

(*g*) *Hedaya,* 551.

(*h*) *Fakir Shaikh* v. *Syed Ali Shaikh* A.I.R. (1955) Cal. 349.

(*i*) Wilson §377; Mulla §236, explanation II.

(*j*) Wilson §§378, 379.

(*k*) Mulla §236, explanation IV.

the time of the first demand, the pre-emptor has an opportunity of invoking witnesses in the presence of the vendor or purchaser, or on the premises, to attest the *ṭalab-e muwāthaba*, the first demand, and witnesses are actually present to testify to this formality, the requirements of both demands are satisfield. This, however, is the only case where the first two demands can be combined lawfully (*l*).

It is not necessary for the pre-emptor to enter the house and make a demand. It is enough if he goes near the house and, touching the walls, makes the demand. This would be a sufficient compliance with the legal requirements of the second demand (*m*).

(3) *The Third Demand*. The third demand is not really a demand, but taking legal action, and is not always necessary; it is only when his claim is not conceded that the pre-emptor enforces his right by bringing a suit. Such an action is called *ṭalab-e tamlīk* or *ṭalab-e khuṣūmat* (the demand of possession, or the demand where there is a dispute) (*n*). The suit must be brought within one year of the purchaser taking possession of the property, if it is corporeal; or within one year of the registration of the instrument of sale, if incorporeal (*o*).

In a suit or claim for pre-emption, the whole of the interest must be claimed; a claim to a part of the estate sold is not sufficient (*p*).

A transfer of property, after the proper demands, does not affect the right of the pre-emptor (*q*).

§68. Right When Lost

The right of pre-emption may be lost by acquiescence, death or release (*r*).

(*l*) Mulla §236, com. (4).

(*m*) (*Mst.*) *Nanhi Nabbi* v. (*Mst.*) *Bunyadi Begum* A.I.R. (1954) All. 87.

(*n*) Wilson §375(3).

(*o*) Limitation Act, Art. 10.

(*p*) Mulla §245

(*q*) ibid. §237; a good summary of the law as to the demands will be found in Tyabji, pp. 658 sqq.

(*r*) ibid. §§595 sqq.; Mulla §§240 sqq.

(1) *Acquiescence or Waiver.* The most ordinary form of acquiescence is to omit to take the necessary formalities. *S* sells land to *B*. *P*, who has a right to pre-empt, on receiving information of the sale omits, without sufficient cause, to claim his right immediately; or makes an offer of the house to *B*; or agrees to cultivate the land with *B*. In each of these cases *P* will be deemed to have acquiesced in the sale and to have lost his right to pre-empt (*s*).

(2) *Death.* The right to pre-empt is extinguished if the pre-emptor dies after the first two demands, but before filing a suit (*t*). The right is extinguished if death occurs during the pendency of a suit, and the action cannot be continued by his legal representatives (*u*). Under Ithnā 'Asharī and Shāfi'ī law, the right descends to the heirs proportionately.

(3) *Release.* The right may be destroyed if there is a release for consideration to be paid to the pre-emptor (*v*); the right, however, is not lost if there has been a refusal on the part of the pre-emptor to buy before the actual sale, nor by an unwillingness to make an offer to purchase the property after notice that the property was for sale (*w*).

§69. Subject of Pre-emption

It is reported that the Prophet said that there was no *shuf'a* except in a mansion or a garden (*x*), whence the law lays down that landed property alone (*y*), including houses and gardens, can be subject to the law of pre-emption (*z*). If the property consists of a share in a village or a large estate, a mere neighbour cannot claim pre-emption (*a*); but a co-sharer can, and probably also a participator in appendages.

(*s*) Tyabji, loc. cit., ill. 1; see also §§597 sqq.
(*t*) ibid., §596.
(*u*) Mulla §239, Tyabji, loc. cit. *Mohammad Ismail* v. *Abdul Rashid* [1956] 1 All. 143 (F.B.), A.I.R. (1956) All. 1.
(*v*) Tyabji §600.
(*w*) Mulla §§242, 243.
(*x*) Tyabji §605, com.
(*y*) Arabic *'aqār*, pl. *'aqārāt*.
(*z*) Tyabji §§605 sqq.; Wilson §359.
(*a*) Tyabji and Wilson, loc. cit.

In Shāfi'ī law property which is incapable of division cannot be the subject of pre-emption; and some Shiite authorities would allow pre-emption to be exercised even in the case of movables (*b*).

To take a few familiar illustrations, movables cannot be the subject of pre-emption, but trees or buildings, when transferred with the land on which they stand, or a dwelling-house sold for occupation, without the ownership of the site, may be the subject of pre-emption (*c*).

Pre-emption must be claimed of the whole of the estate; if the pre-emptor is one of many, he can claim his rateable share and tender the money. If several distinct properties are sold by one contract, the pre-emptor may exercise his right in respect of any one or some of them, and not necessarily in respect of them all (*d*). The right of a plaintiff pre-emptor is not lost if in a suit to enforce his right, he joins with him a stranger (*e*).

This has been explained fully by Mahmood J. in *Sheobharos Rai* v. *Jiach Rai* (*f*). The principle underlying the denial of the right of pre-emption, except as to the whole of the property sold, is that by breaking up the bargain the pre-emptor would be at liberty to take the best portion of the property and leave the worst part of it with the purchaser. The rule applies only to those transactions which, while contained in one deed, cannot be broken up or separated. It should be limited to such transactions, and cannot be applied where the shares are separately specified.

§70. Legal Effects of Pre-emption

On the claim of pre-emption being enforced, the pre-emptor stands in all respects in the shoes of the buyer, and

(*b*) Tyabji, loc. cit.

(*c*) ibid. §605, ill. (1).

(*d*) ibid. 606.

(*e*) *Raja* v. *Hussain* PLD 1957 (W.P.) Lahore 52, criticizing Mulla §241, on a point of great practical importance.

(*f*) (1886) 8 All. 462, 465-6; Tyabji, p. 675.

takes the property subject to prior equities (*g*). If the sale has already been completed in its entirety, the original buyer becomes the new vendor, and the pre-emptor the new purchaser. The original buyer is entitled to receive or retain the rents and mesne profits between the date of sale to himself and the date of the transfer to the pre-emptor (*h*).

S agrees to sell to *B* land which is mortgaged to *M* for Rs 50. *P* enforces his claim for pre-emption and takes possession of the land. *P* is liable to pay to *M* the mortgage debt, whether he had notice of it or not (*i*).

The principle is that the pre-emptor takes the property from the buyer and not from the seller; therefore the buyer must always be made a party to the suit. Whether the seller is to be made a party or not depends upon the possession of the property; if the seller is in possession at the date of the suit, he is a necessary party; if, on the other hand, the buyer is in possession, the original vendor need not be joined (*j*).

The ownership in the land is transferred to the pre-emptor only when possession is given to him; and the pre-emptor may refuse to take possession unless an order of the court is obtained. The decree of the court should preferably contain clear directions regarding the date when payment is to be made, the exact extent of the property, costs, etc. (*k*).

The pre-emptor's rights are not affected by any attempted disposition of the property by the purchaser, nor by the purchaser's death (*l*). After the completion of the contract of sale, alterations in the terms of the sale, if any, do not affect the pre-emptor (*m*).

§71. Devices for Evading Pre-emption

Evasions and devices were not unknown in Jewish and canon law, and legal fictions played a considerable part in

(*g*) Tyabji §§623 sqq.
(*h*) ibid. §623.
(*i*) loc. cit. ill. (1).
(*j*) Tyabji, loc. cit., com.
(*k*) ibid. §624.
(*l*) ibid. §625.
(*m*) ibid. §552. As to improvements in, and deterioration of, the land see §§627 sqq.

Roman law (*mm*). The ancient Islamic authorities are not agreed whether recourse can be had to devices (*n*) for evading pre-emption (*o*), Imām Muḥammad considering such devices abominable and Abū Yūsuf taking the contrary view. The textbooks give many illustrations of the so-called 'devices', but it is doubtful if they can be treated as permissible in India, and Wilson mentions only one which may conceivably be capable of achieving its object. The right of a neighbour, though not that of a co-sharer or a participator, may be defeated by the vendor reserving to himself a strip of land, however narrow, so that his land does not actually adjoin the land sold (*p*).

Although Tyabji mentions a number of other devices (*q*), it is well to remember the words of Mahmood J. when he says:

> And, speaking generally, I may say that if it is once conceded that the technicalities of the Muhammadan law of contract, procedure or evidence are not binding upon us, it will be found that no 'tricks or artifices' can defeat the pre-emptive right in our Courts. Such devices are held to be '*abominable*' even where the technicalities of Muhammadan adjective law might give them some plausible effect; and this is the prevalent doctrine, notwithstanding the opinion of Kazi Abu Yusuf . . .(*r*).

It is therefore well-established that a modern court, as a court of equity, would be loath to countenance any device which interferes with the right of pre-emption.

(*mm*) Schacht, *Introduction*, 79.

(*n*) Arabic *ḥīla*, plural *ḥiyal*.

(*o*) Tyabji §635; Mulla §247.

(*p*) Wilson §391. This question cannot arise in India after *Ram Saran* v. *Mst. Domini Kuer*, cited above.

(*q*) Tyabji §635.

(*r*) *Gobind Dayal* v. *Inayatullah* (1885) 7 All. 775, 814; *Cases*, 429, 461. Why *ḥiyal* were used, *LME*, I, 78 and 107.

CHAPTER XI

WILLS AND GIFTS MADE IN DEATH-ILLNESS

§72. Introductory
§73. Form of Will
§74. Capacity of Testator
§75. What may be Bequeathed
§76. Effect of Registration under the Special Marriage Act, 1954
§77. Who can Take
§78. Revocation of Wills
§79. Interpretation
§80. Death-bed Gifts
§81. Miscellaneous

§72. Introductory

To understand the rules of the Muhammadan law of wills and legacies fully, it is of the utmost importance to appreciate the effects of two divergent tendencies to be found in Islam. In pre-Islamic times, a man had an almost unlimited power of disposing of his property; but as the Koran laid down clear and specific rules for the distribution of the inheritance, it was thought undesirable for man to interfere with God's ordinances. Hence, it is true to say that Muhammadan sentiment is in most cases opposed to the disposition of property by will (*a*).

On the other hand, Bukhārī reports a tradition laying down that a Muslim who possesses property should not sleep even for two nights unless he has made a written will (*b*). This tradition points in reality to another tendency, to wit, that it is ethically incumbent upon a man to make moral exhortations and give spiritual directions to his close relatives, and incidentally, to indicate within the limits laid down by the law what should be done regarding his property. Illustrations of wills which are mainly ethical may be found in abundance in ancient literature (*c*), and therefore we may

(*a*) Fitzgerald, 167; *Fat. Law* §369, 373.

(*b*) Muhammad Ali, *Manual of Hadith* (Lahore, 1944), 334, No. 1; a similar tradition is to be found in the Fatimid text, *Da'ā'im al-Islām,* II §1291; see the author's *Ismaili Law of Wills* (Oxford University Press, 133), (text) 29, No. 2, and (translation) 63, No. 2 and *Fat. Law* §§367 sqq.

(*c*) An illustration will be found in *Ismaili Law of Wills*, §9, (text) 34 sqq., and (translation) 67 sqq. This is the well-known Testament of Ali in the *Da'ā'im,* II, see Chapter ii in my *A Modern Approach to Islam* (Bombay, 1963), 46-50.

consider the meaning of the word *waṣiyya*, which is commonly used in this connexion.

Waṣiyya means a will, whether oral or written, but it has also other meanings: it may signify a moral exhortation, a specific legacy or the capacity of the executor, executorship (*d*). A document embodying the will is called *waṣiyyat-nāma*. It is thus not difficult to reconcile the dual insistence on moral exhortation as well as legal rectitude.

The object of making a will is well explained by M. Sautayra, a jurist quoted by Ameer Ali:

> A will from the Mussulman's point of view is a divine institution, since its exercise is regulated by the Koran. It offers to the testator the means of correcting to a certain extent the law of succession, and of enabling some of those relatives who are excluded from inheritance to obtain a share in his goods, and of recognizing the services rendered to him by a stranger, or the devotion to him in his last moments. At the same time the Prophet has declared that the power should not be exercised to the injury of the lawful heirs (*e*).

The nucleus of the law of wills is, by common consent, to be found in a tradition of the Prophet, reported by Bukhārī (*f*):

> Sa'd ibn Abī Waqqās said: 'The Messenger of God used to visit me at Mecca, in the year of the Farewell pilgrimage, on account of (my) illness which had become very severe. So I said, "My illness has become very severe and I have much property and there is none to inherit from me but a daughter, shall I then bequeath two-thirds of my property as a charity?" He said, "No." I said, "Half?" He said, "No." Then he said: "*Bequeath one-third* and one-third is much, for if thou leavest thy heirs free from want, it is better than that thou leavest them in want, begging of (other) people; and thou dost not spend anything seeking thereby the pleasure of Allah but thou art rewarded for it, even for that which thou puttest into the mouth of thy wife." '

Thus the policy of the Muhammadan law is to permit a man to give away the whole of his property by gift *inter*

(*d*) Fyzee, *Ismaili Law of Wills*, 8.
(*e*) Ameer Ali, I, 569.
(*f*) Muhammad Ali, *Manual of Hadith* (Lahore, 1944), 334-5, No. 2. See also Ameer Ali, loc. cit.; Tyabji §672, com. p. 765 sq.; Fitzgerald, 167.

vivos, but to prevent him, except for one-third of his estate, from interfering by will with the course of the devolution of property according to the laws of inheritance (*g*). It is uncertain how the limit of one-third was fixed, but it has been suggested that Roman law may have influenced this decision (*h*).

It is pertinent to observe how the fetters around the testamentary power have been removed gradually: in some systems of antiquity, like the Hindu law, wills were considered with disfavour (*i*); in Islam the testamentary capacity was limited to the extent of the bequeathable third; in modern law, a man is permitted to dispose of the whole of his property by will.

In Islam the power of making wills was grudgingly conceded, and in this connexion the following extract from the *Hedaya* is most illuminating:

> Wills are lawful, on a favourable construction. Analogy would suggest that they are unlawful; because a bequest signifies an endowment with a thing in a way which occasions such endowment to be referred to a time when the property has become void in the proprietor (the testator); and as an endowment with reference to a future period (as if a person were to say to another, 'I constitute you proprietor of this article on the morrow') is unlawful supposing even that the donor's property in the article still continues to exist at that time, it follows that the suspension of the deed to a period when the property is null and void (as at the decease of the party) is unlawful *a fortiori*. The reasons, however, for a more favourable construction in this particular are two-fold. First, there is an indispensable necessity that men should have the power of making bequest; for man, from the delusion of his hopes, is improvident and deficient in practice; but when sickness invades him he becomes alarmed, and afraid of death. At that period, therefore, he stands in need of compensating for his deficiencies by means of his property, and this in such a manner that if he should die of that illness, his objects, namely, compensation for his deficiencies and merit in a future state, may be obtained; or, on the other hand, if he should recover, that he may apply the said property to his wants; and as

(*g*) Ameer Ali, I, 33. See *Cases*, 308; and §39, above.
(*h*) Saksena, *Muslim Law* (Abridged ed., 1938), 366
(*i*) Mayne, *Hindu Law*, 10th ed. (Madras, 1938), 876.

these objects are attainable by giving validity to wills, they are therefore ordained to be lawful. And to the objection, 'If the right of property in the proprietor become extinct at his death, how can his act of endowment become valid?' it is replied, 'His right of property is accounted to endure at that time from necessity, in the same manner as holds with respect to executing the funeral rites, or discharging the debts of the dead.'(*j*)

The testamentary capacity of a Muslim is cut down by two principal limitations: as to quantum, he *cannot bequeath more than one-third of his net estate*; and as to the legatees, he *cannot bequeath to his own heirs*. We shall deal with both of these matters more fully below.

The will of a Muslim is governed in India, subject to the provisions of the Indian Succession Act, 1925, by the Muhammadan law (*k*).

§73. Form of Will (*l*)

Muhammadan law does not prescribe any particular form for the making of wills. The will of a Muslim need not be in writing: an oral will is perfectly valid; but in the majority of cases wills are, for obvious reasons, in writing, for 'he who rests his title on so uncertain a foundation as the spoken words of a man, since deceased, is bound to allege, as well as to prove, with the utmost precision, the words on which he relies, with every circumstance of time and place'(*m*). If the will is in writing it need not be signed; and if signed, it need not be attested. So long as the intention of the testator is reasonably clear, the testament takes full effect. A letter written by the testator shortly before his death, and containing directions concerning the disposition of his property, was considered to constitute a valid will (*n*).

Even a gesture, if the intention is sufficiently manifest, is

(*j*) Wilson, 6th ed., 304-5, citing *Hedaya*, 670.
(*k*) Tyabji §666.
(*l*) ibid., §689; Mulla §116.
(*m*) *Baboo Beer Pertab* v. *Maharajah Rajender Pertab* (1867) 12 M.I.A. 1, 28.
(*n*) Mulla, loc. cit., com.

enough; thus the *Fatāwā 'Ālamgīrī* says: 'A sick man makes a bequest, and being unable to speak from weakness gives a nod with his head, and it is known that he comprehends what he is about—if his meaning be understood, and he dies without regaining the power of speech, the bequest is lawful.'(*o*) A similar decision is recorded in the *Da'ā'im al-Islām* of Cadi Nu'mān, an ancient Fatimid text, where the Imāms Ḥasan and Ḥusayn jointly upheld the will by gestures of a lady named Umāma, a grand-daughter of the Prophet (*p*).

The will of a Muslim need not be attested, for the verse in the Koran regarding witnesses is considered merely as a recommendation and is not mandatory (*q*).

§74. Capacity of Testator (*r*)

Every Muslim who is sane and rational is entitled to make a will. The testator must also be a major. Under Islamic law majority is attained at puberty, and the presumption is that a Muslim attains majority on the completion of the fifteenth year. In India, however, under the provisions of the Indian Majority Act, majority, for the purpose of making a will, is attained at eighteen and not at fifteen (*s*).

A will procured by undue influence, coercion or fraud will not be upheld, and the courts take great care in admitting the will of a *pardanashin* woman (*t*).

In Shiite law, a will made by a person after wounding himself or taking poison, with a view to committing suicide, is invalid; but *aliter*, if he makes a will and then commits suicide (*u*).

By will a Muslim cannot dispose of more than one-third

(*o*) Baillie, I, 652 cited in Tyabji §689, com.

(*p*) The author's *Ismaili Law of Wills* (Oxford University Press, 1933), §35; *Fat. Law* §385 (ii). Cf. Indian Evidence Act, Section 119.

(*q*) Koran, v, 106, as explained in Tyabji, loc. cit.

(*r*) Tyabji §§667 sqq.; Mulla §115.

(*s*) Tyabji, loc. cit., com.; Mulla §115; the Shiite rule of 10 years is abrogated in India, Tyabji, loc. cit.

(*t*) Tyabji §668.

(*u*) As was the case in *Mazhar Husein* v. *Bodha Bibi* (1898) 21 All. 91.

of his net estate; nor can he bequeath to an heir (*v*). And it is unlawful to make a bequest to benefit an object opposed to Islam as a religion (*w*). Where (i) a Muslim leaves to a stranger by will a house exceeding in value the bequeathable third, and the heirs do not consent to it; or (ii) a Hanafi or a Dā'ūdī Bohora makes a bequest to an heir and the heirs do not consent to it; or (iii) a Muslim makes a will for building a Hindu temple, or a Jewish synagogue, or a Christian church (*x*), the bequests would be void.

§75. What can be Bequeathed?—The Bequeathable Third

No Muslim can bequeath more than one-third of the residue of his estate, after the payment of debts and other charges. When a Muslim dies, as we shall see more fully in the chapter on Administration, his debts and funeral expenses are to be paid first; thereafter, out of the residue only one-third can be disposed of by will. To take a concrete illustration, Omar dies leaving Rs 3,500 as his gross assets. His funeral costs Rs 100 and his debts amount to Rs 400; the balance is Rs 3,000. Hence the bequeathable third amounts to Rs 1,000, and he cannot dispose of more than this amount by will (*y*).

The subject of the bequest must be in existence *at the time of the testator's death*; it is not necessary that it should be in existence at the time of the making of the will (*z*). The bequest may consist of the corpus of the thing, or its usufruct (*waṣiyyat bi'l-manāfi'*); and the usufruct may be given to one person and the corpus to another (*b*).

For instance, the service of a slave, or the right to occupy a house during a future period of time, or to take the rents or future produce, or usufruct for a limited time, or for the

(*v*) Tyabji §669 (a) and (b); this will be dealt with more fully later.
(*w*) loc. cit., (c).
(*x*) ibid., §672, ill. (3).
(*y*) The bequeathable third is defined in Tyabji §665(3); Mulla §118.
(*z*) Tyabji §675; Mulla §122, 123.
(*b*) Tyabji, loc. cit.; Wilson §277.

lifetime of a legatee, may be validly bequeathed (*c*). The High Courts of Calcutta and Allahabad and the Chief Court of Oudh have held that the bequest of a life interest is valid according to Muhammadan law, provided it does not offend the rule of the bequeathable third. For instance, if a life-grant is bequeathed of the whole of a testator's landed property, such a life interest can only be valid if the interest bequeathed is no more than a third of the total estate (*d*).

Consent of heirs. If the bequests exceed the bequeathable third, they do not take effect without the consent of heirs. Such consent must be obtained *after* the death of the testator in Hanafi law; whereas, in Ithnā 'Asharī or Fatimid law, it may be obtained either *before* or *after* the testator's death (*e*).

If *A* bequeaths a life interest to an heir *B*, and thereafter the remainder to *C*, a non-heir, the bequest to *C* will fail if the life-estate to *B* is invalid for want of the consent of heirs (*f*).

Abatement of legacies. Where the bequests taken in the aggregate exceed the bequeathable third and the heirs do not consent, in Hanafi law, the bequests abate rateably. Now bequests may, for the purposes of rateable reduction, be divided into bequests for pious purposes and bequests for secular purposes. As a general class, bequests for pious purposes are decreased proportionately to bequests for secular purposes, and do not have precedence over them.

But bequests for *pious purposes* are themselves divided into three classes: (i) *farā'iḍ* (obligatory charities); (ii) *wājibāt* (recommended, but not obligatory); (iii) *nawāfil* (voluntary and pious, but not recommended). An illustration of class (i) is a bequest for the performance of *ḥajj* on behalf of the deceased; of class (ii) is a bequest for charity on the day of breaking the fast; of class (iii) is building a bridge or an inn.

(*c*) Tyabji, loc. cit.

(*d*) See §47 (II), above; *Anarali* v. *Omar Ali* A.I.R. (1951) Cal. 7; *Siddiq Ahmad* v. *Vilayat Ahmad* A.I.R. (1952) All. 1.

(*e*) Tyabji §§671 sq.; Mulla §118; Baillie, II, 233; *Anarali* v. *Omar Ali* A.I.R. (1951) Cal. 7; as to Fatimid law, see *Ismaili Law of Wills*, 25, 26; *Fat. Law* §§369 (ii), 384.

(*f*) *Amina Khatun* v. *Siddiqur Rahman* PLD 1960 Dacca 647.

Bequests of the first class take precedence over those of the second; and bequests of the second class take precedence over those of the third.

To take a concrete illustration—a Hanafi testator leaves Rs 3,000 jointly to *A* and *B* and Rs 3,000 for pious purposes designated by him. The bequeathable third amounts to Rs 4,000; hence Rs 2,000 will be allotted to the secular bequests and Rs 2,000 to the pious ones. Out of the sum of Rs 2,000, *A* and *B* will each receive Rs 1,000. As to the sum of Rs 2,000 available for pious bequests, regard shall be had to the rules laid down above, and bequests for *farā'iḍ* will take precedence over, and may even exclude, those for *wājibāt*; and bequests for *wājibāt* will likewise have priority over those for *nawāfil* (*g*).

Ithnā 'Asharī law. The Ithnā 'Asharī law does not accept the principle of rateable reduction. The rule of that school is that, of several bequests, the first in time prevails, until the bequeathable third is exhausted; and for the purposes of this rule, where several bequests are to be found in a will, priority is determined by the order in which they are mentioned. For instance, if a testator leaves 1/3 of his estate to *A*, 1/4 to *B* and 1/6 to *C*, and the heirs refuse their consent to these bequests, *A* will take 1/3 of the estate, and *B* and *C* will take nothing; but if instead of 1/3, 1/12 had been left to *A*, then *A* would take 1/12, and *B* would take 1/4, but *C* who is mentioned last would get nothing, as the legal third is exhausted between *A* and *B* (*h*).

There is, however, an exception to this rule. If a man bequeaths one-third of his estate to two different persons in the same will, the later bequest prevails. For instance, a testator by will gives one-third of his estate to Salīm and later he says that one-third be given to Zayd; Zayd will get the one-third to the exclusion of Salīm (*i*).

(*g*) Tyabji §678; Mulla §119; *Fat. Law* §371.

(*h*) Mulla, loc. cit.

(*i*) The Hanafi rule is different, Tyabji §678(2)(b).

In the absence of heirs, and as against the right of the state to take by escheat, the testator may will away the whole of his property *(j)*.

As to future, conditional and contingent bequests, the law treats them on a footing of equality with gifts, and unless there is special provision the rules applicable are similar *(k)*. It is to be observed that usufructuary wills must have been fairly common in early times, for the *Fatāwā 'Ālamgīrī* devotes a special chapter to the subject *(l)*.

A Muslim cannot bequeath a power of appointment, which is a peculiar feature of English law and unknown to Muhammadan law *(m)*.

§76. Effect of Registration under the Special Marriage Act, 1954

We have seen that a Muslim cannot bequeath more than one-third of his property; but if he registers *his existing marriage* under the provisions of the Special Marriage Act, 1954, he has all the powers of a testator under the Indian Succession Act, 1925. It is therefore necessary to deal briefly with the Registration of Marriages under the Special Marriage Act, 1954 *(mm)*.

Chapter III deals with the Registration of Marriages; it consists of four sections, Secs. 15-18.

Sec. 15 lays down that *any marriage* celebrated either *before* or *after* the commencement of the Act, other than marriages under the Special Marriage Act, 1872, or the Special Marriage Act, 1954, may be registered by a Marriage Officer. The following conditions are necessary:

(a) A ceremony of marriage has been performed between the parties and they have been living as husband and wife ever since;

(j) Tyabji §671. He also explains the case where a testator, who dies leaving a husband or a wife, bequeaths the whole of his or her property by will to a stranger. In Fatimid law, the property would probably escheat, provided no heir or spouse survives, §389. *(k)* Mulla §§122 sqq.

(l) Baillie, I, 663-72. As to bequests of life interests, see §47. above.

(m) *Sardar Nawazish Ali's Case*, see §47 (V), above.

(mm) Tyabji §§641, com., 664, 698(2).

(b) neither party has at the time of registration more than one spouse living;

(c) neither party is a lunatic or an idiot;

(d) the parties have completed the age 21 years;

(e) the parties are not within the prohibited degrees of relationship.

There is a proviso which saves marriages performed in accordance with custom or usage having the force of law in certain special cases.

(f) The parties have been residing within the district of the Marriage Officer for a period of not less than 30 days preceding the date on which the application for registration has been made.

Under Sec. 16 the Marriage Officer, on receipt of the application signed by either party, shall give public notice and allow 30 days for receiving any objections. After hearing the objections within the period, he shall register the marriage and issue a certificate.

Sec. 17 provides for appeals which may be made within one month.

Sec. 18 is the most important one and lays down that if a marriage is duly registered under the provisions of this Act, the marriage shall be deemed, *as from the date of the entry*, to be a marriage solemnized under the Act, and the children born after such registration be legitimate.

It is therefore clear that by such registration a person does not cease to be a Muslim, and is governed for all purposes by the Muhammadan law except as specifically laid down under the Act. *A fortiori* it can be argued that it is a doctrine clearly received by the law in India that a Muslim who, in obedience to the law of the land, deviates in some respects only from the law as laid down in the Koran, does not necessarily abjure Islam and does not lose any of his civil rights. This view is one of the most potent influences creating the atmosphere of social reform among the Muslims in

India, and a number of educated Muslims are registering their marriages in the bigger cities.

The text of Chapter III, Secs. 15-18, will be found in Appendix C.

An important point of practice should be noted. A Muslim whose marriage is solemnized or registered under the Special Marriage Act, 1954, is governed by the exception made by Sec. 213 (2) of the Indian Succession Act, 1925, and therefore, Sec. 213 (1) of the said Act does not apply. Accordingly, a probate is unnecessary and a Succession Certificate can be granted under Sec. 370 of the Indian Succession Act (*n*).

§77. Who can Take?—The Legatee

A bequest can be made by a Muslim in favour of any person capable of holding property, the religion of the legatee being immaterial (*o*); a bequest can also be made to an institution or for a religious or charitable object which is not opposed to Islam (*p*).

According to the strict letter of the law, the legatee must be in existence *at the time of the bequest*, and not merely at the time of the testator's death (*q*); but how far this is applicable in India is somewhat doubtful. The general rule of modern law is that a will speaks from the death of the testator; this is the view taken in a Bombay decision, and recommended by Tyabji (*r*). A bequest to a person not in existence at the testator's death is clearly void; but a bequest can validly be made to a child conceived so long as it is born within six months from the date of the will (*s*). Here again, a modern court would probably extend the rule to include a legatee born within the normal span of gestation after the

(*n*) Re *Dr Alma Latifi: Nasima Latifi* (1961) 63 Bom. L.R. 940.
(*o*) Wilson §278; *Fat. Law* §380.
(*p*) Tyabji §586; Fitzgerald, 169.
(*q*) Tyabji, loc. cit.
(*r*) *Abdul Cadur* v. *C. A. Turner* (1884) 9 Bom. 158, 163; Mulla §120.
(*s*) Wilson §276; Tyabji, loc. cit.; Fitzgerald, 170.

death of the testator. The latest view appears to be that Muhammadan law contains two rules regarding the existence of the legatee: (1) that he must be in existence at the time of the *making of the will*, either actually or presumably (that is, within six months of the making of the will) and (2) that he must be alive at the time of the *death of the testator* (*t*).

Bequests to heirs. One of the most important limitations to the testamentary capacity of a Muslim is the maxim: No bequest to an heir. This is based upon a sentence in the Prophet's Last Sermon on the day of the Farewell Pilgrimage. He is reported to have said that God had given to every one his due, therefore there shall be no bequest to one who is entitled to inherit (*u*): Thus, we have the rule applicable to all the Sunnite schools and the Fatimid school, that a bequest to an heir is not valid unless the heirs consent to it (*v*). Such consent, as we have seen above, must in Hanafi law be obtained after the testator's death; but in Ithnā 'Asharī and the Fatimid law, the time when the consent is obtained is immaterial; it may be obtained either before or after the death of the testator.

The reason for this rule is well explained in a Fatimid authority, the *Da'ā'im al-Islām* of the Cadi Nu'mān. The argument is: 'If a bequest were permissible to the heir, verily a greater portion than that which has been fixed by God would be bequeathable to him. And he who bequeaths to his heir, verily belittles the decision of God concerning the heir and acts in contravention of His Book . . . and he who acts contrary to the Book of Allah . . . acts unlawfully.'(*w*)

The one school which does not adopt this reasoning is the Ithnā 'Asharī among the Shiites (*x*). Basing themselves on a

(*t*) *Channo Bi* v. *Muhammad Riaz* PLD 1956 (W.P.) Lahore 786.

(*u*) Muhammad Ali, *Manual of Hadith*, 336, No. 3; *Fat. Law* §373.

(*v*) *Da'ā'im*, II §§1305-7. Tyabji §§669 sqq.; Mulla §117.

(*w*) *Da'ā'im*, II §1305; the author's Ismaili Law of Wills (Oxford University Press, 1933), §19, p. 82. A full discussion of this point will be found in 'Bequests to Heirs: Shia Ismaili law', (1929) 31 Bom. L.R., Jl., 84-7. *Fat. Law*, loc. cit.

(*x*) Ameer Ali, I, 592; Wilson §478; Tyabji §672.

Koranic text (*y*), they hold that so long as the legacy does not infringe the one-third rule and is otherwise lawful, the fact that the legatee is an heir is immaterial. A simple illustration will explain this. Ali dies leaving three sons, Muhammad, Hasan and Husayn. His net estate amounts to Rs 9,000. Ali leaves by his will the sum of Rs 3,000 to his son Husayn. In Ithnā 'Asharī law, Husayn will receive the sum of Rs 5,000, Rs 3,000 as a legacy and Rs 2,000 as his share of the inheritance; while Muhammad and Hasan will receive Rs 2,000 each. The Sunnites and those who are governed by the Fatimid law, the Dā'ūdī and Sulaymānī Bohoras for instance, hold that the bequest in favour of Husayn is void, and each son will receive Rs 3,000.

Manslayer. The rule of law is that he who kills another cannot take a legacy from the deceased; in Hanafi law this provision is applied with great severity, and the manslayer is excluded whether the homicide is intentional or not. In Ithnā 'Asharī law, the more logical view is taken and only intentional homicide leads to exclusion, but the Fatimids have apparently adopted the Hanafi role (*z*).

A bequest for a charitable purpose is perfectly valid (*a*). The express or implied acceptance of the legatee is necessary before the legal title in the bequest is transferred to him; and the legatee has the right to disclaim (*b*).

If the legatee predeceases the testator, the legacy in Hanafi law lapses; but *aliter* in Shiite law, where, if the legatee dies leaving heirs, the legacy would pass to them; if there are no heirs, the legacy lapses (*c*). This is one more illustration of the curious divergence in the law relating to wills and bequests between the Sunnite and Shiite systems (*d*).

(*y*) Kor., ii, 180; see Tyabii, §672, com.

(*z*) Tyabji §682; Wilson §478A; Fitzgerald, 170; *Fat. Law* §446.

(*a*) Tyabji §683.

(*b*) ibid., §684.

(*c*) ibid., §685; Mulla §121.

(*d*) There is no thorough examination of the problem why the Ithnā 'Asharī system differs on so many points from the Hanafi law; but some valuable observations will be found in Tyabji, comment to §672.

§78. Revocation of Wills (*e*)

A testator may, at any time, revoke a bequest either expressly or impliedly. The bequest of a house is revoked impliedly, if, after making the will, the testator sells it or makes a gift of it to someone else.

In regard to additions, if the testator makes an addition to the subject of the bequest of such a nature that the subject of the bequest cannot be delivered without the addition, the bequest is revoked (*f*). But in such cases the paramount consideration is the real intention of the testator, and no hard and fast rules of interpretation can be laid down.

Where a testator makes a will, and by a subsequent will gives the same property to someone else, the prior bequest is revoked; but where, in the same will, the same thing is given to two different persons, the property will be shared equally by both (*g*).

Among the Fatimids a will can be revoked or altered both in health and in disease (*gg*).

§79. Interpretation of Wills (*h*)

A Muslim will must be construed primarily in accordance with the rules laid down in the Muhammadan law, bearing in mind the social conditions that prevail, the language employed and the surrounding circumstances.

A will speaks, as in modern law, from the date of the death of the testator (*i*). The court will, as far as possible, give effect to the intention of the testator (*j*). Where there is an ambiguous will, the heirs may be asked to interpret it. For

(*e*) Tyabji §696; Mulla §§ 128-30; *Fat. Law* §379.

(*f*) Tyabji loc. cit. (4). Chagla J. has criticized the broad statement of the law in para. 129 of Mulla's *Mahomedan Law*, and has laid down that the real question in each case is the intention of the testator, *Ashrafalli Cassamalli* v. *Mahomedalli Rajaballi* (1945) 48 Bom. L.R. 642, 651-3.

(*g*) Tyabji, loc. cit., Mulla §130.

(*gg*) *Fat. Law* §379.

(*h*) Wilson §§287-90A; Tyabji §§690 sqq.

(*i*) Wilson §387; Tyabji 691.

(*j*) ibid., §690.

instance, *T* says in his will that 'a trifle may be given to *L*'; the heirs may lawfully give something to him (*k*).

On the failure of a prior bequest, there may be either an acceleration of the later bequest, or an avoidance of it. *T* bequeaths certain property to *L* for his life and 'from and immediately after *L*'s decease' to *LA*. In this case there is no specific intention that *LA* is to take nothing till after the death of *L*; and if the testator simply revokes the bequest to *L*, the estate of *LA* would be accelerated. On the other hand, if *T* purports to give life interests in more than one-third of his property to his heirs, and thereafter to charity, and the heirs do not consent to such a disposition, both the bequests fail, and no question of acceleration arises (*l*).

Where a bequest is made of a thing or an article, and the thing or article does not exist at the time of the testator's death, it is for the court to decide whether the bequest fails or whether there is an intention to purchase and give the article out of the general assets (*m*).

Where a testator bequeaths a specified fraction of goods which are homogeneous, the fraction is to be calculated on the basis of the goods or articles owned *at the time of the bequest*, and not at the time of death. For instance, a testator bequeaths 'a fourth of my goats', possessing forty goats at the time of making the will. He dies leaving twenty goats. The legatee is entitled to ten goats, provided that the entire value of the testator's net assets is at least three times that of the ten goats (*n*).

Where, however, the goods or articles are not homogeneous, the fraction is to be calculated on the basis of the goods or articles owned *at the time of the testator's death*. Thus, a testator bequeaths 'a fourth of my clothes'. If the clothes are of different kinds, and some of them are destroyed or disposed of after the date of the bequest, the legatee will

(*k*) ibid., §692.
(*l*) Tyabji §693 and illustrations.
(*m*) For illustration see Wilson §288; Tyabji §694.
(*n*) Wilson §289.

only have a fourth of those that exist at the testator's death (*o*).

§80. Gifts Made during Death-illness (*mard al-mawt*) (*p*)

Buckley L.J. once described a *donatio mortis causa* as a gift of an amphibious nature; not exactly a gift, nor exactly a legacy, but partaking of the nature of both (*q*). It is impossible to describe a Muslim gift during mortal disease in terms more apt, for in Muhammadan law such a gift is governed by rules deduced from a combination of two branches of the law, the law of gifts and the law of wills.

Marḍ al-mawt

The term *marḍ al-mawt* means 'the disease of death', or 'the disease which causes death'. Not every disease, although it is serious and of long standing, can be so regarded; it must be a malady causing the apprehension of death, and it must also be the cause of death.

In order to constitute a *marḍ al-mawt*, the following conditions are necessary:

(i) The illness must cause the death of the deceased.
(ii) The illness must cause apprehension of death in the mind of the deceased.
(iii) There must be some external *indicia* of a serious illness (*r*).

Whether the disease is a *marḍ al-mawt* or not, is a question of fact and the usual questions which arise are: (1) Was the donor suffering at the time of the gift from a disease which was the immediate cause of his death? (2) Was the disease of such a nature or character as to induce in the person suffering,

(*o*) ibid., §290; Tyabji §695.

(*p*) Wilson §§284-6; Tyabji §691, read with §367; Mulla §§135-7; Fitzgerald, 173. For general observations see *Safi Ullah* v. *Ghulam Abbas*, PLD 1956 Lah. 191; *Fat. Law* §§374 sq.

(*q*) *Re Beaumont, Beaumont* v. *Ewbank* [1902] 1 Ch. 889, 892.

(*r*) Tyabji §367, com.; Mulla §135, com.

the belief that death would be caused thereby, or to engender in him the apprehension of death? (3) Was the illness such as to incapacitate him from the pursuit of his ordinary avocations or standing up for prayers—a circumstance which might create in the mind of the sufferer an apprehension of death? (4) Had the illness continued for such a length of time as to remove or lessen the apprehension of immediate fatality or to accustom the sufferer to the malady? (*s*).

A gift in death-illness takes place only when the donor dies; should the donor live after making the gift, the sole question would be whether there has been a valid gift or not.

The question of apprehension is of extreme importance; it is essential that the gift should 'be made under pressure of the sense of the imminence of death'.(*t*) In a Bombay decision it was emphasized that the crucial test of *marḍ al-mawt* is the subjective apprehension of death in the mind of the donor; and this is to be distinguished from the apprehension caused in the minds of others (*u*).

The characteristics of such an illness cannot be specified with exactitude; the *Hedaya* lays down that a malady is of 'long continuance' if it has lasted a year, in which case it cannot be regarded as a *marḍ al-mawt*, for the patient has become familiarized to the disease. This, however, is not a hard and fast rule, and the question must be determined by the court upon the evidence in each case (*v*).

The Fatimid authorities lay down the salutary rule that for a healthy man it is prudent to make a will; but, for a man who is ill, it is obligatory (*vv*).

Essential Conditions

(1) A gift made during death-illness is subject to all the conditions and formalities necessary to constitute a gift *inter*

(*s*) *Hassarat Bibi* v. *Golam Jaffar* (1898) 3 C.W.N. 57 cited in 34 I.A. at p. 169. For Fatimid law, see the interesting note to §336 in *Fat. Law*.

(*t*) *Ibrahim Goolam Ariff* v. *Saiboo* (1907) 34 I.A. 167, 177.

(*u*) *Safia Begum* v. *Abdul Rajak* (1944) 47 Bom. L.R. 381, 384.

(*v*) Tyabji §367; Mulla §135, com.; *Fat. Law* §336, note.

(*vv*) *Fat. Law* §367 (end).

vivos. If, for instance, a gift is purported to be made and such possession as is required by the law is not delivered, the gift fails (*w*).

(2) In addition, a gift made during *marḍ al-mawt* is subject to all the restrictions laid down in the law of wills: hence (i) not more than the bequeathable third can be given, and (ii) no such gift can be made to an heir, unless the other heirs consent to it. On both these points, the differences between the Sunnite and Shiite systems must be carefully noted (*x*).

Acknowledgement of Debts (*y*)

The Muhammadan law, in general, attaches considerable importance to an acknowledgement of legal liability if made deliberately. The root idea is similar to that of estoppel: that a man's deliberate and formal statement is binding on him. Fitzgerald cites an East African case in which a Muslim judge laid down the principle as follows:

> It is a maxim of Muhammadan law that when once a party to a suit has deliberately and intentionally made a declaration or an admission he cannot afterwards retract it and profit by it. Such declaration or admission is binding on his heirs and would debar them from suing to recover property sold to a third party in accordance with such declaration or admission, even though the heirs were in ignorance of its having been made (*z*).

The law is based upon the ethical obligation compelling a man to pay off his debts before he departs from this life. The traditions of the Prophet emphasize this in unmistakable terms. It is reported, for instance, that when a bier was brought to the Prophet and he was told that the deceased had died in debt, he refused to conduct the funeral service personally until someone undertook the payment of the debt (*a*).

An acknowledgement of liability may be made 'in health'

(*w*) Mulla §136.

(*x*) Tyabji §§639, 697, ills. As to consent of heirs, see §§74, 75, 77 above.

(*y*) A good discussion will be found in Fitzgerald, 175-8. *Fat. Law* §§375-78.

(*z*) Fitzgerald, 28.

(*a*) Muhammad Ali, *Manual of Hadith*, 317, No. 2.

or 'in disease'. When the testator acknowledges a debt on his death-bed and there is no other proof of the debt, it ranks in regard to priority, under Hanafi law, midway between a debt and a legacy. Accordingly, ordinary debts must be paid first. then the acknowledged liabilities, and finally legacies. An acknowledgement is of no effect if it is made in favour of an heir, save in Ithnā 'Asharī law; on the other hand, it may even be valid against the whole, and not merely to the extent of one-third, of the estate (*b*). An acknowledgement made in health takes precedence of an acknowledgement made in illness (*c*).

The acknowledgement may be (i) of a definite sum; or (ii) that certain property does not belong to the deceased, but is a deposit; or (iii) that someone has paid a debt owed to the acknowledger. The dangers of a fictitious acknowledgement are well pointed out by Fitzgerald, and the first duty of the court would be to see that the law of acknowledgement is not used as an engine of fraud or fraudulent preference (*d*).

§81. Miscellaneous Rules

(1) *Probate not necessary*. Under the provisions of the Indian Succession Act, 1925, the will of a Muslim may be admitted in evidence even though probate has not been obtained, Mulla §131. And the same is the rule where the marriage is registered under the Special Marriage Act, 1954, see §76 above. A Muslim whose *existing marriage* is registered need not take out probate, and a Succession Certificate can be granted (*e*).

(2) *Vesting of estate*. The estate of the deceased vests in the executor as from the death of the testator, Mulla §131.

(*b*) Fitzgerald, 176(*f*); Tyabji §639, com.

(*c*) Mulla §137.

(*d*) Fitzgerald, 175. Further details may be found in Abdur Rahman. *Institutes*, Arts. 494-505.

(*e*) Re *Dr Alma Latifi* (1961) 63 Bom. L.R. 940.

(3) *Letters of Administration not necessary.* Except as regards debts due to the estate of the deceased, letters of administration are not necessary in the case of a Muslim, Mulla §132.

(4) *Non-Muslim executor.* A Muslim may lawfully appoint a non-Muslim as an executor in India, Mulla §133, but see Tyabji §647(3).

A fuller discussion of these and allied topics will be found in the next chapter on The Administration of Estates.

CHAPTER XII

THE ADMINISTRATION OF ESTATES

§82. First Principles
§83. *Jafri Begam's Case*
§84. Administration of the Estate
§85. Power of Alienation
§86. Creditor's Suits
§87. Statutory Law

§82. First Principles (*a*)

'OUR learned in the law (to whom God be merciful!) say: "There belong to the property of a person deceased four successive duties *to be performed by the magistrate*: first, his funeral ceremony and burial without superfluity of expence [*sic*], yet without deficiency; next, the discharge of his just debts from the whole of his remaining effects; then, the payment of his legacies out of a third of what remains after his debts are paid; and, lastly, the distribution of the residue among his successors, according to the Divine Book, to the Traditions, and to the Assent of the Learned." '(*b*) The duty of administering an estate, according to the law of Islam, lay on the state, acting through the cadi who was both judge and magistrate, possessing civil as well as criminal jurisdiction. Hence it is correct to say that administration, as understood in modern law, involving necessarily the recognition of an executor or the appointment of an administrator, was unknown to Islamic jurisprudence.

Mahmood J. says that the *jus representationis* is entirely foreign to the Muhammadan law of inheritance (*c*). Fitzgerald takes the same view and shows the difficulties involved in not recognizing any person as standing completely in the shoes of the dead man (*d*).

Thus, strictly speaking, there was no administration in the law of Islam; administration was introduced into the fabric

(*a*) See generally, *LME*, I, 160 and *Schacht, Introduction*, Chap. 23.
(*b*) *al-Sirājiyyah*, translated by A. Rumsey (Calcutta, 1890), 2nd ed., pp. 11-12. The same is the rule laid down in the *Da'ā'im, Fat. Law* §453.
(*c*) *Jafri Begam's Case* (1885) 7 All. 822, 834; *Cases*, 464.
(*d*) Fitzgerald, 161-5. See also Mulla §40, com.

of Muhammadan law by the reception of the English concept of administration and later by the enabling provisions of the Probate and Administration Act, 1881 (*e*). According to the general principles of Islamic jurisprudence there was no administration, but a *mere distribution* of the estate, by the state if not by the heirs themselves, in accordance with the principles laid down in the *Sirājiyyah*. The estate did not vest in the cadi; it vested, subject to certain obligations, in the heirs from the moment of the death of the deceased. The notional process may be compared with conversion in equity, the physical distribution taking place much later than the apportionment in the eye of the law.

It is as though the estate were a round cake, which from a distance seems entire; but as each heir approaches the table, the cake is found to be carefully cut up and divided proportionately; and all that remains to be done is to hand over to him his particular piece.

§83. Vesting of Inheritance—Rule in *Jafri Begam's Case*

It is now necessary to consider the fundamental principles of Muhammadan law relating to the administration of estates as they were laid down by Mahmood J. in *Jafri Begam's Case* (*f*). One Ali Muhammad Khan died in 1878, leaving him surviving his father, mother, widow, two sons, three daughters (Jafri Begam, being the youngest) and a brother, Amir Muhammad Khan. Abdur Rahman, the husband of Jafri Begam, brought a suit and obtained a decree against the widow, two sons and three daughters for a debt due by the deceased. In execution of the decree a portion of the village belonging to the deceased was sold and purchased by Abdur Rahman himself. Later Amir Muhammad Khan, the brother, brought a suit against the widow, two sons and three daughters

(*e*) An interesting case, pointed out to me by Prof. G. W. Bartholomew (University of Singapore), is *Campbell* v. *Delaney* (1863) Marshall, 509, where the position of a Muslim heir was determined by reference to *Williams on Executors*.

(*f*) *Jafri Begam* v. *Amir Muhammad Khan* (1885) 7 All. 822; *Cases*, 464.

to recover his share of the estate, as he was not a party to the previous suit. The case was referred to a Full Bench and the judgment of Mahmood J. deals with the law on the subject exhaustively.

Three propositions were laid down:

Rule I. When a Muslim dies leaving debts unpaid, his estate devolves immediately on his heirs, and such devolution is not suspended till or contingent upon the payment of debts.

Rule II. A decree for a debt passed against such of the heirs as are in possession of the estate does not bind the other heirs.

Rule III. If one of the heirs, who was out of possession and who was not a party to the proceedings, brings a suit against the decree-holder for the recovery of his share of the estate, he must pay his proportionate share of the debt before recovering possession of his share of the inheritance.

It may safely be asserted that the whole of the present Indian law on the subject revolves round the rules laid down in this case, which was cited with approval by Sir George Rankin in *Kazim Ali Khan* v. *Sadiq Ali Khan* (*g*).

In regard to Rules I and II,

> Muhammadan heirs are independent owners of their specific shares, and if they take their shares subject to the charge of the debts of the deceased, their liability is in proportion to the extent of their shares. And once this is conceded, the maxim *res inter alios acta alteri nocere non debet* would apply without any such qualifications as might possibly be made in the case of Hindu co-heirs in a joint family. Now, putting aside questions of fraud or collusion between the creditors of the deceased and the heirs in possession, it may well be that such heir, though defending the suit, is incompetent to contest the claim, or, by reason of not being acquainted with the facts of the case, or not possessing evidence, cannot properly resist the claim. There seems no reason why, in such a case, those should be bound by the decree who

(*g*) (1938) 65 I.A. 219, 232.

were not parties to the litigation, and had no opportunity of defending themselves against the creditors' claim by putting forward their own case (*h*).

Rule I is, however, considerably affected by the paramount duty in Islam to pay debts, and Kayani J. says

. . . the theory that the property of a deceased Muslim vests in his heirs immediately after his death is considerably tempered (*i*) by the injunction that the heir is entitled only to the residue after the payment of a legacy or debt, and since the payment of debts and legacies necessarily involves the administration of the estate, such administration is implied in the very words of the Holy Quran and of authentic texts like the *Sirājiyyah* (*j*).

In the above case, one *S*, a Muslim, died in 1913 leaving considerable property, movable and immovable. This property was inherited by the plaintiff Razia Begum, her brothers and one sister, and her mother. The management was in the hands of the brothers who paid to the plaintiff her share till 1944, but failed to do so thereafter. She therefore filed a suit for the administration of the estate and for the rendition of accounts. It was held by the division bench that the suit was maintainable, Cornelius J. holding that as *S* had died as far back as 1913 (the proceedings were commenced by Razia Begum in 1948), it was preferable to regard the suit as one for the administration of a *quasi* trust rather than for the administration of the estate of the deceased Shaikh Danishmand Suqrat (*k*).

Joint family property. The heirs succeed to the estate as tenants-in-common in specific shares. The Hindu law of joint family is foreign to the Islamic jurisprudence, and the fact that the heirs live together in a common household, or that one of them manages the property to the exclusion of others, is not sufficient to create property rights in favour of the members of the family living in commensality (*kk*). But there are

(*h*) per Mahmood J. in 7 All. at p. 843. Tyabji §642; Mulla §41.
(*i*) The text has 'tampered', which is presumably a misprint.
(*j*) *Mahbub Alam* v. *Razia Begum* A.I.R. (1950) Lahore 12, 16 (para. 21).
(*k*) ibid., 19 (para. 34).
(*kk*) *Md. Zafir* v. *Amiruddin* A.I.R. (1963) Pat. 108.

qualifications, for example, if during the continuance of the family, properties are acquired in the name of the managing member of the family, and it is proved that they are possessed by all the members jointly, the presumption arises that they are properties of the family and not the separate property of the member in whose name they stand (*l*).

§84. Administration of the Estate

In India the estate of a deceased Muslim is administered under the provisions of the Indian Succession Act, 1925 (*m*). The law applicable to the estate of a deceased Muslim is the Sunnite or the Shiite law according to the rite he professed *at the time of his death*. If a Muslim changes his school during the course of his life, the test will be: What was he at the time of his death? This would be a question of fact, and accordingly the particular school of law would apply (*n*). If however he registers his marriage under the Special Marriage Act, 1954, his personal law would be ousted and the Succession Act applies, §76, above.

We have seen above how the estate of a deceased Muslim was to be administered according to the Hanafi text, *Sirājiyyah* (*o*); but in India, the Indian Succession Act replaces the Islamic rules and we have the following scheme laid down. The payments to be made are, in order of priority:

(1) Funeral expenses and death-bed charges;
(2) Expenses of obtaining probate or letters of administration;
(3) Wages for services rendered to the deceased within three months of his death by a labourer or servant;
(4) Debts, according to their priorities;

(*l*) *C. K. Setty* v. *Abdul Khadar* A.I.R. (1956) Mysore 14. See Tyabji, p. 202.

(*m*) For the earlier law, see Tyabji §§646 sqq., and Mulla, p. 29.

(*n*) Tyabji §638.

(*o*) Cited in §82, above.

(5) Legacies, not exceeding one-third of the residue (called the net estate), after all the above payments have been made (*p*).

Vesting of Estate

The executor or administrator of a deceased Muslim is his legal representative for all purposes, and the property of the deceased vests in him as such (*q*). It is his duty to collect the assets, discharge the debts, pay the legacies and distribute the estate amongst the heirs.

The executor, when he has realized the estate, is a 'bare' trustee for the heirs as to two-thirds of the estate, and an 'active' trustee as to one-third for the purposes of the will. This is so because a Muslim cannot by will dispose of more than one-third of his net estate, and the remaining two-thirds must devolve on the heirs according to the principles of the law of inheritance (*r*).

The terms 'bare' trustee and 'active' trustee require some explanation. A 'bare' trustee is a person to whose office no duties were originally attached, or who, although such duties were originally attached, would on requisition of his beneficiaries be compellable in equity to convey the estate to them, or to some other person by their direction (*s*). The bare trustee may be compared to a 'simple' trustee.

The term 'active' trustee is applied to a person who has duties to perform; and he may be compared to a 'special' trustee (*t*).

In Muhammadan law the term *waṣī* means an executor; *waṣiyyat* is a will or testament, and *waṣiyyat-nāma*, a written will.

(*p*) Indian Succession Act, 1925, Secs. 320-3 and 325; Tyabji, loc. cit.; Mulla §39. The parallelism between the ancient Fatimid and the modern Indian law is ramarkable, *Fat. Law* §453.

(*q*) Indian Succession Act, Sec. 211; Tyabji §640; Mulla §40.

(*r*) Tyabji §641, com.; Mulla §40.

(*s*) Tyabji §§641, 644.

(*t*) Hanbury, *Modern Equity* (4th ed., 1946), 115-16.

Where, however, no executor has been appointed by the testator, or no administrator has been appointed by the court, the whole of the estate of the deceased, or so much of it as has been left undisposed of by will, devolves upon the heirs in specific shares at the moment of his death. Such devolution is not suspended until the payment of his debts, if any. The devolution is subject (i) to the payment of debts, in proportion to the share of each heir and (ii) to the payment of legacies (*u*).

Evacuee property. Where a Muslim against whom proceedings are commenced under the Administration of Evacuee Property Act, 1950, for declaring him an evacuee, and his properties evacuee properties, dies during the pendency of the proceedings, he cannot, be declared an evacuee after his death; and his properties, which on his death, vest in his heirs under Muhammadan law, cannot be declared evacuee properties (*v*).

Representation, How Far Necessary

Where a Muslim dies leaving a will it is not necessary for the executor to obtain probate of the will to establish his right; nor are letters of administration necessary where there is no will (*w*). Representation, however, is necessary when it is sought to recover a debt due to the deceased (*x*); and no court will pass a decree in favour of the estate of a deceased person without such forensic recognition.

When there is no executor or administrator, the heirs themselves become the legal representatives and administer the estate (*y*).

(*u*) Tyabji §642; Mulla §41, based principally on *Jafri Begam's Case*. A very clear statement of the law relating to executors and administrators will be found in Tyabji, pp. 707 sq.

(*v*) *Ebrahim Aboobaker* v. *Tek Chand Dolwani* [1953] S.C.R. (India) 691.

(*w*) Mulla §40, notes; Tyabji §646. The same is the rule when the marriage is registered under the provisions of the Special Marriage Act, §76 above.

(*x*) Mulla §48; Tyabji §§646, 651.

(*y*) *Jafri Begam's Case*, 7 All. at p. 842.

Religion of Executor

According to the ancient texts a non-Muslim could not be appointed an executor of the will of a Muslim; but the courts in India have held that religion is no bar and a Muslim may appoint a non-Muslim as an executor (*a*).

§85. Power of Alienation by Heir

Any heir may, even before the distribution of the estate, transfer his own share and pass a good title to a *bona fide* transferee for value, notwithstanding any debts remaining unpaid by the deceased. This follows from Rule I in *Jafri Begam's Case* (*b*).

A Muslim dies leaving a widow and a son. A large sum of money is due to the widow for her dower. Dower is a debt, but the widow is not a secured creditor of the estate of her deceased husband. The son mortgages his share of the estate to *M* for Rs 4,800, without paying the dower debt. After the mortgage the widow obtains a decree against the son, who is in possession of the estate, for her dower debt, and attaches the son's share in execution of the decree. The mortgagee, *M*, thereafter obtains a decree against the son on the mortgage for sale of the son's share. The share is sold in execution of the decree and is purchased by *P*. It was held (i) that before the suit was instituted by the widow, the son had the right to dispose of his share of the inheritance, and (ii) that *P* was entitled to recover the son's share free from the attachment and that the widow could not follow the property into the hands of *P*, the execution purchaser (*c*).

Selling the share of an heir in execution of a decree passed against him at the suit of a creditor amounts to a valid 'transfer', and will pass a good title to the execution purchaser if he has had no notice. A Muslim dies leaving two sisters as his only heirs. After his death, *C, a creditor of the*

(*a*) Mulla §133; Tyabji §647(3).
(*b*) Tyabji §658; Mulla §42(1).
(*c*) Facts simplified from *Bazayet Hossein* v. *Dooli Chund* (1878) 5 I.A. 211. See Tyabji, loc. cit., ill. (2); Mulla §42, ill. (*c*); Fitzgerald, 162.

deceased, obtains a decree against the sisters for his debt. Subsequently *a creditor of the sisters* obtains a decree against them for his debt, and the property of the deceased come to their hands is sold in execution of the decree to *P*. In this case *C* is not entitled to attach the property in the hands of *P* in execution of his decree (*d*).

If the share transferred by an heir is a share in immovable property forming part of the estate of the deceased, and the transfer is made during the pendency of a suit by the widow of the deceased for her dower, wherein a decree is subsequently passed creating a charge on the estate for the dower debt, the transferee will take the share of the heir subject to the charge so created; but the transferee will not be affected if the widow's decree is a simple money decree.

A Muslim died leaving three widows and a son. He left considerable property, movable and immovable. After his death, the widows brought a suit against the son, who was in possession of the whole estate, for administration of the estate of the deceased, and for payment of the dower debt. A decree was passed in the suit directing the son to render an account of the properties of the deceased which had come to his hands, and providing for the payment of the dower debt out of the deceased's property. Thus, this was not a mere money decree; it was a charge created on the properties for the dower debt. Thereafter the widows applied for execution of the decree. Pending execution—which is the same as *pendente lite*—the son mortgaged his own share to *M*. *M* sued the son on the mortgage, and obtained a decree for the sale of the son's share mortgaged to him. The share was sold to *P* in execution of the decree, and *P* had notice of the decree in favour of the widows. The Privy Council held that *P*, in the circumstances, took the share subject to the prior decree in favour of the widows (*e*); the case would have been different if the mortgage had been effected *before the decree*.

(*d*) Mulla §42, ill. (*b*).
(*e*) loc. cit., illustration (*c*), based on *Mahomed Wajid* v. *Bazayet Hossein* (1878) 5 I.A. 211, 223-4; see generally Tyabji §§658 sqq.

One of several heirs of a deceased Muslim, though he may be in possession of the whole of the estate of the deceased, has no power to alienate the share of his co-heirs, not even to pay off the debts of the deceased. Such a transfer affects only his own share, and does not affect the rights of the other heirs and creditors. This was laid down in the leading case of *Abdul Majeeth* v. *Krishnamachariar* (*f*).

In this case one Muhammad Hamid died in 1909, being heavily involved in debt. In 1910 his widow, acting on her own, alienated the suit property. In 1912 a creditor filed an administration suit. The question arose in the suit:

When *one* of the co-heirs of a deceased Muslim, in possession of the *whole* estate of the deceased or *any part* of it, sells property in his possession forming part of the estate for the discharge of the debts of the deceased, is such sale binding on the *other* co-heirs or creditors of the deceased, and if so, to what extent?

The answer given by Abdur Rahim J., in delivering the opinion of the Full Bench, was in the negative, and his reasoning follows from *Jafri Begam's Case*, Rule II, in particular. He says:

On the death of a Muhammadan, the inheritance vests in his heirs according to their respective shares, although in the administration of the estate the funeral expenses, debts and legacies must be paid first and it is only the residue that is available for distribution among the heirs. It is not correct to say that the devolution of the estate on the heirs does not take place or is postponed until the funeral expenses and the debts and legacies have been paid. This is evident from the following facts: if an heir designated by the law dies after the death of the propositus, his share descends on his own heirs and does not lapse to the general estate. Each heir is entitled to the income that has accrued since the testator's death, in proportion to his share, and he can transfer his share by sale or gift, subject, it may be, as to the latter form of disposition, to such restrictions as are imposed by the doctrine of *Musha*.

The theory of Muhammadan jurisprudence, on which the right of succession and inheritance is based, is that *even after death, the deceased's rights in his properties still inhere in him*, to the

(*f*) (1916) 40 Mad. 243, F.B.; *Cases*, 485, approved by the Privy Council in *Jan Muhammad* v. *Karam Chand* (1947) 49 Bom. L.R. 577.

extent necessary for meeting the funeral charges and the legal obligations and liabilities incurred in his lifetime and also for carrying out his wishes, as expressed in his last will and testament, within the limits laid down by the law. A deceased person is classed among *persons of defective capacity* and his rights and obligations are considered not merely with reference to matters pertaining to this world but also with respect to his spiritual concerns. The payment of his funeral expenses and debts is described as his last need. And as for testamentary bequests, it is stated that, according to strict juristic theory, they should not be lawful at all but have been sanctioned in order that the testator might make up for his shortcomings in life by making gifts to deserving objects (*g*).

§86: Creditors' Suits: Recovery of Debts

A creditor may join all the heirs of a deceased person for recovering his debt; in such a case no difficulties arise. Difficulties, however, do arise when a suit is filed and a decree obtained against only some, but not all the heirs. Hard cases make bad law; and the disregard of the principles in *Jafri Begam's Case* occasionally produce a certain amount of confusion, especially in regard to Rules II and III.

Proceeding logically, the first principle to be borne in mind is that each heir is liable for the debts of the deceased in proportion to the share he receives of the inheritance, and no more. For instance, a Muslim dies leaving three heirs, who divide the estate amongst themselves in accordance with their rights. A creditor of the deceased sues two of the heirs but not the third; the two heirs sued will each be liable to pay a part of the debt proportionate to his own share of the inheritance, and they will not be made to pay the whole of the debt, either jointly or severally (*h*).

It follows therefore that if the estate is represented by an executor or administrator the suit must be filed against him; and where there is no personal representative the suit must be filed against the whole body of the heirs.

(*g*) 40 Mad. at pp. 253-4 (italics mine); *Cases*, 486.
(*h*) Tyabji §657; Mulla §43.

A complexity arises where a decree is passed against only some, but not all the heirs, and here there is a conflict of opinion between the High Courts. The earlier Calcutta view appears to be that where a creditor sues some, but not all the heirs, the suit may in certain circumstances be treated as an administration suit, and a decree be passed so as to bind the shares of the parties who were not on the record.

On the other hand, the Allahabad view is that *a decree for a debt due by the deceased, passed against some but not all of the heirs, does not bind the other heirs*; and it is immaterial in such a case, whether the defendants were in possession of the whole or part of the estate. The reason is that each heir, according to Islamic notions, is the owner of a specific and well-definded share of the inheritance, which devolves on him at the moment of the death of the deceased.

There is no need, in an elementary work, to go into the case law, but the later decisions of the Bombay and Nagpur High Courts concur with the Allahabad view, which, it is submitted, is the correct and logical one (*i*), following as it does Rule II in *Jafri Begam's Case*.

Finally, no single heir of a deceased Muslim, whether he is in possession of the whole or part of the deceased's estate, has any right to dispose of the shares of his co-heirs, for the payment of the debts of the deceased. Such a disposition or alienation affects his own share only (*j*).

§87. Statutory Law

In addition to the broad principles stated above, there is a considerable body of statute law applicable in cases relating to administration, for which reference should be made to Wilson §§164-207, Tyabji §§646-50 and Mulla §50.

(*i*) The detailed case law will be found in Tyabji §§657 sq.; Mulla §46.

(*j*) Tyabji §658 sqq.; Mulla §47, based principally on *Abdul Majeeth's Case*, approved by the Privy Council in *Jan Muhammad* v. *Karam Chand* (1947) 49 Bom. L.R. 577.

CHAPTER XIII

THE SUNNITE LAW OF INHERITANCE

§88. General Principles: Dual Basis of the Law

MUSLIM jurists gave a great deal of importance to the laws of inheritance (*farā'iḍ*), and they were never tired of repeating the saying of the Prophet: Learn the laws of inheritance, and teach them to the people; for they are one half of useful knowledge (*a*); and modern authors have admired the system for its utility and formal excellence.

Macnaghten says:

In these provisions we find ample attention paid to the interests of all those whom nature places in the first rank of our affections; and indeed it is difficult to conceive any system containing rules more strictly just and equitable (*b*).

And Tyabji adds:

The Muslim law of inheritance has always been admired for its completeness as well as the success with which it has achieved the ambitious aim of providing not merely for the selection of a single individual or homogeneous group of individuals, on whom the estate of the deceased should devolve by universal succession, but for adjusting the competitive claims of all the nearest relations. As to the excellence of the system in a formal sense, Sir William Jones said: 'I am strongly disposed to believe that no possible question could occur on the Muhammadan law of succession which might not be rapidly and correctly answered.'(*c*)

The Islamic law of inheritance is often considered an arbitrary scheme based upon the whims of a Semitic deity. This is a superficial view. On a critical examination of the

(*a*) *Sirājiyyah*, tr. A. Rumsey (Calcutta, 1890), 2nd ed., Preface and p. 11, Introduction; Tyabji, p. 801, note 4; Anderson and Coulson, op. cit. 77.
(*b*) Macnaghten, Preliminary Remarks, p. v.
(*c*) Tyabji §698, com.

fabric of the law, it will be found that the law consists of two distinct elements: the customs of ancient Arabia and the rules laid down by the Koran and the Founder of Islam. The Koranic reform came as a superstructure upon the ancient tribal law; it corrected many of the social and economic inequalities then prevalent; and thus it is another illustration of the profound truth that the Koran is to be likened to 'an amending act', rather than an exhaustive code (*d*).

By the spirit of reform inculcated by the Prophet, the ingenuity of jurists and the force of circumstances, the two distinct elements were welded together into a coherent and living organism; and yet, to borrow a phrase from equity, while the two streams flow in one channel, their waters do not mix, and it is possible, even after centuries, to distinguish between them. It is therefore essential to try to understand these two systems, before analysing the existing structure of the law.

Taking a broad view, the Islamic scheme of inheritance discloses three peculiarities: (i) the Koran gives specific shares to certain individuals; (ii) the residue goes to agnatic heirs, and failing them to uterine heirs; (iii) bequests are limited to one-third of the estate. The fundamental principles of the Muhammadan law of inheritance are well explained by that master mind, Mahmood J., in the leading case on pre-emption, *Gobind Dayal* v. *Inayatullah*:

I may observe that pre-emption is closely connected with the Muhammadan law of inheritance. That law was founded by the Prophet upon republican principles, at a time when the modern democratic conception of equality and division of property was unknown even in the most advanced countries of Europe. It provides that, upon the death of an owner, his property is to be divided into numerous fractions, according to extremely rigid rules, so rigid as to practically exclude all power of testamentary disposition, and to prevent any diversion of the property made even with the consent of the heirs, unless that consent is given

(*d*) Tyabji, 3rd ed. Introduction, p. 4. The editor of the 4th ed. has unfortunately omitted this classic phrase in the new introduction. For general principles, see *LME*, I, 161 sqq.

after the owner's death, when the reason is, not that the testator had power to defeat the law of inheritance, but that the heirs, having become owners of the property, could deal with it as they liked, and could therefore ratify the act of their ancestor. No Muhammadan is allowed to make a will in favour of any of his heirs, and a bequest to a stranger is allowed only to the extent of one-third of the property (*e*).

Recent Reforms. Although satisfactory in its own day, the law of inheritance in Islam has been found wanting in certain particulars in modern times, and efforts are being made almost everywhere in the Islamic world to introduce judicious alterations. Strictly, this subject is outside the scope of this book, but since the question of reform arises in India and Pakistan from time to time, the following articles may be consulted: J. Schacht, *Introduction to Islamic Law*, Ch. 23, read with Ch. 15 and the Bibliography; J. N. D. Anderson, 'Recent Reforms in the Islamic Law of Inheritance', *International and Comparative Law Quarterly* (London), April 1965, 349; J. N. D. Anderson and N. J. Coulson, 'Islamic Law in Contemporary Cultural Change', *Saeculum*, xviii, 1967, pp. 77 sqq., and A. A. A. Fyzee, 'The Reform of Muslim Personal Law in India', *Quest* (Bombay) Vol. 8, 1970; pp. 369-403, also published separately; Nachiketa, Bombay, 1971.

(A) *Principles of pre-Islamic Law*

The principles of the pre-Islamic customary law may be summarized as follows (*f*):

(1) The nearest male agnate or agnates (*'aṣabāt*) succeeded.

(2) Females and cognates were excluded.

(3) Descendants were preferred to ascendants, and ascendants to collaterals.

(4) Where the agnates were equally distant, the estate was divided *per capita*.

These principles should be borne in mind; for it will be found that among heirs belonging to Class II of the Sunnite school, the Agnatic Heirs (*'aṣabāt*), the same tendencies are still at work. The Hanafi law, to a certain extent, retains the principles of the ancient tribal law.

(*e*) (1885) 7 All. at pp. 782-3; *Cases*, 429, 436.
(*f*) Tyabji §699.

(B) *Principles of Islamic Law*

The main reforms introduced by Islam may be stated briefly as follows (*g*).

(1) The husband or wife was made an heir.

(2) Females and cognates were made competent to inherit.

(3) Parents and ascendants were given the right to inherit even when there were male descendants.

(4) As a general rule, a female was given one half the share of a male.

The Hanafi interpretation of the Koran, as expounded in the leading text, the *Sirājiyyah*, and as followed in India, has been carefully analysed by Tyabji (*h*), and we shall give below its chief features. The Ithnā 'Asharī scheme will be dealt with at a later stage.

The newly-created heir, as a close relative of the deceased, and often related even more closely than the customary heir, is assigned a specific fraction of the estate, called *sahm* (share). Such an heir is a member of the first class of heirs, the *aṣḥāb al-farā'iḍ* or KORANIC HEIRS. The earlier text-writers following Macnaghten called them 'Sharers'.(*i*)

The newly-created heirs were mostly females; but where a female was equal to the customary heir in proximity to the deceased, the Islamic law gave her half the share of the male; for example, if a daughter co-existed with the son, or a sister with a brother, the female obtained one share and the male two shares.

In the Hanafi scheme generally, specific fractions were given to the Koranic Heirs; and the rest of the property went to the tribal heirs.

In the actual application of the law, seven additional principles must be remembered.

(*g*) ibid., §§701 sqq., and pp. 802 sqq.

(*h*) Tyabji §702.

(*i*) W. H. Macnaghten, *Principles and Precedents of Moohummudan Law* (Calcutta, 1825), p. xi.

(1) *Nature of Property* (māl)

No distinction is made in Muhammadan law between movable or immovable property, joint or separate property (as in Hindu law), realty or personalty (as in English law). The doctrine of survivorship is not known to Muhammadan law; the share of each Muslim heir is definite and known before actual partition. Therefore rules relating to partial partition as applicable to a Hindu coparcenary are not applicable to Muslims (*j*). The concept of property, *māl*, is simple; it comprises all forms of property, and includes both corpus (*'ayn*) and usufruct (*manāfi'*) (*k*).

(2) *Birth-right, Spes successionis*

Islamic law does not recognize a birth-right; nor has a *spes successionis* any value. Rights of inheritance arise only on the death of a certain person (*l*). Hence, the question of the devolution of inheritance rests entirely upon the exact point of time when the person through whom the heir claims died—the order of deaths being the sole guide (*m*).

(3) *Relinquishment of Share, Release*

The relinquishment of a contingent right of inheritance (itself a nullity in law), by a Muslim heir is generally void in Muhammadan law (*n*); but if it is supported by good, and not necessarily valuable, consideration, and forms part of a valid family settlement, it is perfectly valid (*o*).

(*j*) *Khazir Bhat* v. *Ahmad Dar* A.I.R. (1960) Jammu and Kashmir 57.

(*k*) *Sardar Nawazish Ali Khan's Case*, see above, §47(v), and Mulla §51.

(*l*) Tyabji §706(8); Mulla §§53, 54; see the observations of Imam J. in *Razia Begum* v. *Anwar Begum* [1958] S.C.R. (India) 1111, 1137.

(*m*) per Mahmood J., 7 All. at p. 834; *Cases*, 436.

(*n*) *Abdul Kafoor* v. *Abdul Razack* (1958) II M.L.J. 492.

(*o*) *Kochunni Kochu* v. *Kunju Pillai* A.I.R. (1956) Trav.-Cochin 217; *Qamar Din* v. *Aisha Bi* PLD 1956 (W.P.) Lahore 795; Ameer Ali, II, 36-7.

(4) *Representation*

The princple of 'representation' is not recognized. We shall deal with this fully later on, but, to take a simple case, *A* dies leaving a son, *B*, and a predeceased son's son, *C*. The rule is that the nearer excludes the more remote and, there being no 'representation', *C* is entirely excluded by *B*, and *B* is the sole heir, both according to the Sunnite as well as the Shiite law (*p*). Macnaghten has explained this as follows: The son of a person deceased shall not represent such person, *if he died before his father*. He shall not stand in the same place as the deceased would have done had he been living, but shall be excluded from the inheritance if he have a paternal uncle. For instance, *A*, *B*, and *C*, are grandfather, father, and son. The father *B* dies in the lifetime of the grandfather *A*. In this case, the son *C* shall not take *jure representationis*, but the estate will go to the other sons of *A* (*q*). The distinguished author has pointed out the hardship of the rule:

> The only rule which bears on the face of it any appearance of hardship, is that by which the right of representation is taken away, and which declares that a son, whose father is dead, shall not inherit the estate of his grandfather together with his uncles. It certainly seems to be a harsh rule, and is at variance with the English, the Roman, and the Hindoo Laws. The Moohummudan doctors assign as a reason for denying the right of representation, that a person has not even an inchoate right to the property of his ancestor, until the death of such ancestor, and that, consequently, there can be no claim through a deceased person, in whom no right could by possibility have been vested (*r*).

Many modern writers, including Anderson (*s*), have

(*p*) Tyabji §704 and com.; Mulla §93.

(*q*) Adopted by Mahmood J. in 7 All. at p. 834; *Cases*, 436. For modern illustrations see Mulla §52.

(*r*) Preliminary Remarks, viii, in his *Principles and Precendents of Moohummudan Law*, Calcutta, 1825, a work of the highest standing.

(*s*) J. N. D. Anderson, *Islamic Law in the Modern World*, 78. A general disquisition on Family Law (*al-aḥwāl al-shakhṣiyya*) will be found in Muḥammad Abū Zahra, *LME*, I, 132, *in* 'Family Law'. Of exceptional value is also the paper of J. Schacht, 'Islamic Law in Contemporary States,' *American Journal of Comparative Law*, 1959, 133-47 and Anderson and Coulson, op. cit., 83 sq.

confirmed the unsatisfactory nature of this particular excluder, which, whatever its excellence in times past, is no longer considered just by the majority of thinking Muslims, and happily Pakistan has followed several Middle Eastern countries in abolishing it altogether. There are indications that dissatisfaction against it is gathering strength even in India and it is hoped that early legislation will put an end to this inequitable rule. The Muslim Family Law Ordinance 1961, Sec. 4, abolishes it effectively in Pakistan: see Appendix E, below.

(5) *Rights of Females*

Males and females have equal rights over property. For example, a Muslim dies leaving a son and a daughter. The estate will be divided into three equal portions, the son obtaining two, and the daughter one. The daughter does *not*, however, *by reason of her sex, suffer from any disability* to deal with her share of the property. She is the absolute master of her inheritance. The same rule applies to a widow or a mother. There is no such thing as a widow's estate, as in Hindu law, or the disabilities of a wife, as in the older English common law.

(6) A *line of succession* unknown to Muhammadan law cannot be created. A Muslim *JS* executed a deed of settlement whereby he gave all his properties to his son *MS*, and directed that he and his heirs should give a certain quantity of rice to his two daughters Kulsumbi and Jainabi, and after them absolutely to their *male* children. It was held that in so far as the dispositions could be regarded as an attempt to limit the succession to male heirs, and thus to create a line of succession unknown to Muhammadan law, the deed was bad (*t*).

(7) *Treaty between two sovereign powers.*

An important reservation to this rule, rarely mentioned in the leading textbooks, is that where a grant of pensions is

(*t*) *Imam Saheb* v. *Ameer Sahib* A.I.R. (1955) Mad. 621.

made in perpetuity, although invalid by the principles of Muhammadan law as understood and applied in India, it takes effect under a treaty between two sovereign powers, *Nawab Sultan Mariam Begum* v. *Nawab Saheb Mirza* (1889) 16 I.A. 175; see *Cases,* pp. x, xxvii, 493.

(8) The *registration of an existing marriage,* no less than its original celebration, under the provisions of the Special Marriage Act, 1954, *ousts the personal law* relating to succession, without affecting otherwise the legal or religious status of a Muslim. See §76, above.

§89. Competence to Inherit—Principles of Exclusion

Every person, including a child in the womb provided it is born alive (*u*), is entitled to inherit, unless there is a specific rule of exclusion.

Exclusion may be either imperfect or perfect. *Imperfect* exclusion means exclusion from one share and admission to another. For example, a sister by herself is a Koranic Heir; but by the co-existence of a brother, she may be excluded as a Koranic Heir and admitted as an Agnatic Heir.

As to *perfect* exclusion, there are two sets of persons who inherit: (i) the *primary* heirs, who are never excluded, they are the husband or the wife, the father and the mother, the son and the daughter; these heirs exclude others on occasion, but are themselves never excluded; (ii) all the *other* heirs, each of whom may be excluded by some one else. For example, the brother is an heir; but he may be excluded either by the son or by the father (*v*).

The term 'perfect' exclusion applies to cases where although a person is related to the propositus and is otherwise entitled to inherit, there is some legal cause which excludes him, and the most important of these, in Muhammadan law, are difference of religion, homicide, slavery and illegitimacy (*w*).

(*u*) Tyabji §706.
(*v*) *Sirājiyyah,* 27-8.
(*w*) Ameer Ali, II, 86-92.

Religion

Exclusion may be on the ground of religion. In the ancient Islamic law a non-Muslim could not inherit from a Muslim; but in India this rule does not apply (*x*). A mere difference of religion, due to apostasy or otherwise, does not operate as a legal bar. But a Hindu, who is converted to Islam and *dies a Muslim*, is governed by Muhammadan law; consequently in such a case, where Muslim heirs have taken their shares of inheritance, Hindu collaterals cannot claim the property by virtue of the Caste Disabilities Removal Act, 1850. For the law of succession in the case of a Hindu or a Muslim depends upon his own personal law (*y*).

A Hindu woman was converted to Islam and married a Muslim. The husband died in 1939, and the wife in 1947. She died intestate; leaving considerable property. There were no children of the marriage. The wife's brother, a Hindu, applied for letters of administration and claimed her property as brother. It was held that Muhammadan law applied, and as the claimant was a non-Muslim, he was not entitled to succeed (*z*).

Homicide

In Hanafi law, one who causes the death of another, either intentionally or unintentionally, cannot inherit from the deceased. In Ithnā 'Asharī law, only intentional homicide operates as a bar (*a*).

For the Ithnā 'Asharī and Fatimid Shiite law, see §100, Miscellaneous Points, (6), below.

Status

(1) *Slavery*. A slave in Islamic law is not entitled to inherit from a free man. This law, however, is now obsolete in India (*b*).

(*x*) Tyabji §706(7); Ameer Ali (Students' 7th ed., 1925, the last work from the illustrious author's pen), 66-7. *Fat. Law* §§442 sqq.

(*y*) *Mitar Sen* v. *Maqbul Hasan* (1930) 57 I.A. 313.

(*z*) *K. P. Chandrashekharappa* v. *Govt. of Mysore* A.I.R. (1955) Mysore 26.

(*a*) Tyabji 706(6); Mulla §58; Ameer Ali (Students' 7th ed.), 67-8.

(*b*) Ameer Ali, op. cit., 68; Tyabji §7.

(2) *Illegitimacy*. The bastard, in Hanafi law, cannot inherit from the father; but he (or she) may inherit from the mother. A Hanafi woman dies leaving a husband and an illegitimate son of her sister. The husband takes one half, and the other half goes to the illegitimate son of the sister, as he is related to the deceased through his mother (*c*).

Except as stated above, natural relationship is not recognized in Muhammadan law as affording a right to inherit. Mst. Qadri had two sons by Saadat; one illegitimate, Rahmatullah, the other legitimate, Muhammad Yakub. It was held that Muhammad Yakub and Rahmatullah were not related to each other as uterine brothers (*d*).

Moosan Moopan, a Kerala Muslim, kept Kalliani, a *harijan* woman, as a concubine. The plaintiff Pavitri was a daughter born of the union, and claimed maintenance after her father's death. It was held that the natural daughter of a Muslim father begotten upon a Hindu female was not entitled to maintenance either under the principles of Muhammadan law, or on 'general principles' of justice, equity and good conscience (*e*).

Neither unchastity nor insanity are treated as bars (*g*); but an alien enemy is excluded (*h*).

For the Ithnā 'Asharī and Fatimid Shiite Law, see §100, below.

(3) *Sex*. Daughters are sometimes excluded by custom or by statute; in such cases the shares of the other heirs are to be calculated as if the daughters did not exist (*i*).

(*c*) *Bafatun* v. *Bilaiti Khanum* (1903) 30 Cal. 683; Tyabji §606(2); Mulla §85.

(*d*) *Rahmatullah* v. *Maqsood Ahmad* [1950] All. 713.

(*e*) *Pavitri* v. *Katheesumma* A.I.R. (1959) Kerala 319.

(*g*) Ameer Ali (Students' 7th ed.), 69.

(*h*) Wilson §268.

(*i*) Mulla §§59 and 60, citing the Watan Act, 1886 (Bombay), and the Oudh Estates Act, 1869, dealing with Talukdars. These are special statutes and of limited application.

§90. Classes of Heirs

The Hanafi jurists divide heirs into seven classes, the three Principal and the four Subsidiary Classes.

(A) *The three Principal Classes* (*j*):

I Koranic Heirs—*dhawū'l-furūḍ* (called Sharers);
II Agnatic Heirs—*'aṣabāt* (called Residuaries);
III Uterine Heirs—*dhawū'l-arḥām* (called Distant Kindred).

(B) *The four Subsidiary Classes* (*k*):

IV The Successor by Contract;
V The Acknowledged Kinsman;
VI The Sole Legatee;
VII The State, by Escheat.

According to Hanafi law the property of the deceased goes, in the first instance, to the Koranic Heirs, Class I. If the estate is not exhausted by them, or failing them, it goes to the Agnatic Heirs, Class II. And finally, in the absence of heirs of Class I and Class II, the property is distributed among the Uterine Heirs, Class III.

These three principal classes of heirs together comprise all the blood relations of the deceased, whether they are agnates or cognates, and one relation by marriage, namely, the husband or the wife. The subsidiary heirs succeed only by way of exception.

General Considerations. (A) The Principal Heirs

Class I, Koranic Heirs. The Koran, as is well known, deals very exhaustively with the law relating to inheritance (*l*), and the first class of heirs consists of certain close relations of the deceased to whom a specific share (called *sahm*) is allotted in the Koran.

(*j*) Ameer Ali, II, 48; Tyabji 710; Mulla §61.

(*k*) Tyabji §§726-29; Mulla §80-2.

(*l*) Tyabji makes very valuable observations in his comment to §698; Wilson, 59-64, and appendix D, pp. 500 sqq.

The term 'sharers' is not a happy one and does not convey either the literal meaning of the Arabic original or its deeper significance, and therefore the term 'Koranic Heirs' is proposed. The expressions *aṣḥāb al-farā'iḍ* or *dhawū'l-furūḍ* mean 'possessors of obligatory shares'; and the law of inheritance is generally called *'ilm al-farā'iḍ* (*m*). The English rendering 'sharers' comes to us from the days of Sir William Jones who published a translation of the *Sirājiyyah* in 1792 (*n*). Macnaghten also uses the same expression (*o*). Perhaps its only justification is its age; otherwise it is time to put it in the lumber-room of obsolete terms, which no longer enlighten but befog our vision. To be fair to the older scholars, it is necessary to observe that the term is derived from the exact fractional 'shares' (Arabic, *sahm*, pl. *sihām*) fixed by the Holy Book. These fractions are six in number, to wit, 1/2, 1/4, 1/8, 2/3, 1/3, and 1/6; the persons to whom the shares are allotted are 'sharers', and as the fractional shares are specified in the Koran, they are in the highest sense 'obligatory', that is *farīḍa* (*p*).

As the shares are fixed by the Koran, Class I takes precedence of the other two classes; but the fundamental principle should not be overlooked. The rule must not be conceived as creating a preferential class of heirs which takes the bulk of the property. On a careful analysis of the usual cases, it will be found that the rule may be explained thus—take the whole of the property; from it take a *slice, according to the dictates of the Koran*; and let the *residue*, being in most cases the *bulk* of the property, *go to the tribal heirs*, the '*aṣabāt*, usually called the Residuaries.

(*m*) Robertson Smith, *Kinship*, 65; Juynboll, *Handbuch des islāmischen Gesetzes* (Leiden-Leipzig, 1910), 237 sqq.

(*n*) The full name is *al-Sirājiyyah* of Shaykh Sirāj al-dīn al-Sajāwandī; see A. Rumsey, *Sirājiyyah*, 2nd ed., Calcutta, 1890, which is a reprint of Sir William Jones's translation. The text and translation of the *Sirājiyyah* will be found in an exhaustive modern work on inheritance by M. U. S. Jung, *The Muslim Law of Inheritance*, Allahabad, 1934, 314 pages, with numerous diagrams.

(*o*) Macnaghten, Preliminary Remarks, xi.

(*p*) Pl. *farā'iḍ*. The word *farḍ* means 'ordinance, demanding compulsory obedience'; its plural is *furūḍ*. *Sirājiyyah*, 14.

The first class, Koranic Heirs, consists mainly of females, with a few exceptions. The reason is that the bulk of the property, in the majority of cases, is sought to be kept intact for the second class of heirs who are all males. For instance, a man dies leaving a widow and a son. The widow is a Koranic Heir and she gets 1/8 of the estate, while the son, a tribal heir, takes the remaining 7/8. This is an illuminating example of how Koranic reform affected Arabian custom.

Class II, Agnatic Heirs. The second class of heirs is called *'aṣabāt*, a term which may be rendered as 'near male agnates', and the term 'Agnatic Heirs' is adopted in preference to the somewhat misleading word 'Residuaries'. The term 'residuary' implies that a fractional share is to be taken out of the estate and the remaining portion is to be left to this class of heirs. This is taking a merely mechanical view of the scheme; in reality, *the Agnatic Heirs were the principal heirs before Islam*; *they continue to remain in Sunnite law the principal heirs, provided always that the claims of near relations mentioned in the Koran, the Koranic Heirs, are satisfied* by giving to each of them a specified portion, the *farīḍa*, plural *farā'iḍ*. The son, the father (in certain cases), the brother, the paternal uncle and the nephew are all in this important class, and in a majority of cases the residue forms the bulk of the estate.

Class I is given precedence owing to the respect paid to the Koran; else, the rule may be reversed and stated: Keep the *bulk* of the property for the Agnatic Heirs (*'aṣabāt*), the persons whose rights were always recognized by tribal law, and respect the Koranic provisions by giving *specific shares* to the persons mentioned in the Koran (*dhawū'l-furūḍ*).

Robertson Smith shows that the right of inheritance lay with the *ḥayy*, the family, as a whole; and when there were no near heirs, the estate was taken by those male relations who were called *'aṣabāt*, a word which primarily means 'those who go to battle together and have a common blood-feud'.(*q*) Therefore it is clear that 'Agnatic Heirs', that is heirs through

(*q*) *Kinship*, 85; Tyabji §705(13).

the male line, is a better designation than 'Residuaries'. If the class called *'aṣabāt* in Muhammadan law is examined, it will be found to contain (i) all male agnates, and (ii) four specified female agnates (daughter, son's daughter how low soever, full sister, consanguine sister), a Koranic innovation.

Class III, Uterine Heirs. The third class is usually called 'Distant Kindred'; this term is also a relic of the past and unsatisfactory, and richly deserves to be discarded. In the Muhammadan law applicable to the Hanafi school the *dhawū'l-arḥām* represent (i) all cognates, male or female, and (ii) all female agnates, with the four exceptions stated above.

The word *raḥm* or *raḥim* means 'womb', but it is also the most general Arabic word for kinship or blood relationship; the term *dhawū'l-arḥām* would therefore signify 'possessors of kinship, or kindred'.(*r*) Now blood relations may either be 'near', that is male agnates, those who are of the tribal group and bound to fight for the tribe; these are the *'aṣabāt*. Or they may be more 'distant', relatively speaking, because they belong to different family groups (*ḥayy*); these are the *dhawū'l-arḥām*, possessors of kinship. A sister or a daughter may be married in a different family group (*ḥayy*); her children may thus become 'distant',(*s*) inasmuch as there is no direct obligation to defend the group from aggression.

In trying to explain the unsatisfactory term 'distant kindred', we have seen that they are either cognates or female agnates. According to the *Sirājiyyah*, 'A distant kinsman is every relation, who is neither a sharer nor a residuary'.(*t*) The *dhawū'l-arḥām* of the Sunnite law may therefore be appropriately designated *Uterine Heirs* (*u*).

Conclusion. The scheme of inheritance which emerges from this analysis may now be summed up. The most ancient and

(*r*) *arḥām* is the plural of *raḥm*. See generally Robertson Smith, *Kinship*, 32, 37, 117.

(*s*) Fitzgerald, 131, considers the term 'distant kindred' inappropriate. Tyabji calls it a 'misleading translation' §710(3), note 5.

(*t*) *Sirājiyyah*, 44-5; Tyabji §717; Wilson §239.

(*u*) Following Ameer Ali (ii, 48) who calls them 'Uterine Relations'.

most important class of Sunnite heirs is Class II, *'aṣabāt*. Unless the deceased leaves a number of Koranic Heirs, the bulk of the property goes to them. But in deference to the Koranic injunctions, we take slices of the estate and give them to Koranic Heirs, the residue being divided among Agnatic Heirs. If there are no Agnatic or Koranic Heirs, the property goes to Uterine Heirs, subject always to the Koranic rights of the husband or wife; for, if the Koran itself gives shares to females, why should the cognates and female relations be excluded from inheritance? (*v*).

(B) THE SUBSIDIARY HEIRS

If no member of the three principal classes of heirs exists the deceased's estate goes to the subsidiary heirs, among whom each class excludes the next.

Class IV, Successor by Contract. The first of the subsidiary classes, Class IV in the general scheme of Hanafi law, is the Successor by Contract. Succession by contract arises in two ways: (i) by emancipation and (ii) by friendship. The first, called *walā' al-'itq*, arises as follows. If a man emancipates his slave, the master can inherit from the slave, but the slave cannot inherit from the master (*w*). This kind of *walā'* has become obsolete in India since the Slavery Act, 1843.

The second form is called *walā' al-muwālāt*. Here, for example, Hasan contracts with Ibrahim, a stranger, that if Hasan dies Ibrahim shall inherit from him on the condition that Ibrahim shall pay any fine or ransom (called *diya*) that may be payable by Hasan. The relationship is called *walā'*; the agreement, *muwālāt*, and the successor by contract, the *mawlā*. This rule is merely of antiquarian interest, because compensation for criminal offences (*diya*) is not payable in India (*x*).

(*v*) Robertson Smith, *Kinship*, 177, makes valuable remarks generally on mother-kinship.

(*w*) *Hedaya*, 513.

(*x*) *Hedaya*, 517; Robertson Smith, 55 sqq.; Wilson §262; Tyabji 726; Mulla §80.

Class V, The Acknowledged Kinsman. The acknowledged kinsman is a person of unknown descent in whose favour the deceased has made an acknowledgement of kinship, not through himself, but through another. Consequently, a man may acknowledge another as his brother (descendant of father), or uncle (descendant of grandfather), but not as his son (*y*).

Class VI, Universal Legatee. In default of all the above, a testator is empowered to bequeath the whole of his estate to any person, who is known as 'the Universal Legatee'. The rule of the one-third applies only where there are heirs; if no heir exists the whole of the property of the deceased can be willed away (*z*).

Class VII, Escheat. The state is the ultimate heir. In ancient Islamic law the property would go to the *bayt al-māl,* the Public Treasury; but in modern India it would escheat to the lawfully established secular state (*a*).

Further Reading. A grasp of first principles is essential for mastering the laws of inheritance, and it is suggested that the student should read Abdur Rahim, *Muhammadan Jurisprudence,* 346-50; Wilson, 6th ed., 59-64; and Tyabji, §698 and comments before memorizing the details that follow.

The following will also be found useful, Schacht, *Introduction,* Ch. 23; Abū Zahrā, 'Family Law', Ch. vi, in *Law in the Middle East,* I, Ed. M. Khadduri and H. J. Liebesny (Washington, D.C., 1955); and Anderson and Coulson, op. cit.

§91. Class I, Koranic Heirs (aṣḥāb al-farā'iḍ)

We must now proceed to a detailed examination of the

(*y*) Wilson §263; Tyabji §727; Mulla §81; *Fat. Law* §452.

(*z*) Wilson §264; Tyabji 728; Mulla §82.

(*a*) Ameer Ali suggests that the government established by law in India is not entitled to the property of Muslims by escheat, II, 145-7, as such property is to be used only for the benefit of Muslims. It is doubtful if this opinion is sound. See generally, Wilson §265; Tyabji §729; Mulla §83; *Fat. Law* §451.

principal heirs, beginning with the Koranic Heirs (*aṣḥāb al-farā'iḍ*).

According to Hanafi law the following twelve relations constitute Class I, the Koranic Heirs (*b*):

(A) *Heirs by Affinity*

1. Husband (h).
2. Wife (w).

(B) *Blood Relations*

3. Father (f).
4. True Grandfather, how high soever (ff, h.h.s.).
5. Mother (m).
6. True Grandmother, how high soever (mm, h.h.s.).
7. Daughter (d).
8. Son's Daughter, how low soever (sd, h.l.s.).
9. Full Sister (fs).
10. Consanguine Sister (cs).
11. Uterine Brother (ub).
12. Uterine Sister (us).

It will be noticed that of these twelve, eight are females. A few terms may be explained briefly before considering each heir.

1. An *agnate* is a person related to the deceased through male links only; for example, the son's son or the son's daughter, the father or the father's father.

2. A *cognate* is a person related to the deceased through one or more female links; for example, the daughter's son or the daughter's daughter, the mother's father or the father's mother's father (*c*).

(*b*) Tyabji §§710 sqq.; Mulla §§63 sqq.

(*c*) For this and the following definitions see Wilson §218; Tyabji 705; Mulla §62.

3. A *true grandfather* means a male ancestor between whom and the deceased no female intervenes; for instance, the father's father, the father's father's father and his father, how high soever.

4. A *false grandfather* means a male ancestor between whom and the deceased a female intervenes; for example, the mother's father and the mother's mother's father.

5. A *true grandmother* means a female ancestor between whom and the deceased no false grandfather intervenes; for example, the father's mother, the mother's mother, the father's mother's mother, etc.

6. A *false grandmother* means a female ancestor between whom and the deceased a false grandfather intervenes; for instance, the mother's father's mother (*e*).

7. A *son's son, how low soever* is a male agnate in the descending line; for example, a son's son, a son's son's son, and so on.

8. A *son's daughter, how low soever* is a female agnate in the descending line; for example, a son's daughter, a son's son's daughter, and the daughter of a son how low soever.

The student is now referred to the TABLE OF KORANIC HEIRS *facing this page which gives the main provisions of the law in tabular form, and is based on the works of* Wilson, Tyabji *and* Mulla (*f*).

In dealing with each heir, the method adopted below is this. First, a few general observations are made; secondly, the cases that commonly occur in practice are fully explained; and thirdly, unnecessary details are omitted, so that the cases of common occurrence in everyday life are embedded in the students' memory.

(*e*) These terms are somewhat quaint and puzzling, and ought to be carefully mastered; Tyabji §705, note 7, calls them 'misleading', although they are commonly used.

(*f*) Of particular importance are the general observations made by Tyabji in §710, com.

TABLE OF KORANIC HEIRS, CLASS I, SUNNITE (HANAFI) LAW

Heir	Share of: One	Share of: Two or more Collectively	Entirely excluded by	Affected by	How affected
1 Husband	1/4		**None**	Where no child or child of son h.l.s.	Share increased to 1/2.
2 Wife ...	1/8	1/8	**None**	Where no child or child of son h.l.s.	Share increased to 1/4.
3 Father	1/6		**None**	Where no child or child of son h.l.s.	Made Agnatic Heir.
4 True Grandfather ...	1/6		Father, nearer true grandfather.	Where no child or child of son h.l.s.	Made Agnatic Heir.
5 Mother	1/6		**None**	Where (1) no child, (2) no child of son h.l.s., (3) *one* brother *or* sister, (4) husband or wife co-exist *with* father.	Share increased to 1/3 of whole estate in cases (1) to (3): and 1/3 of the *residue after* deducting husband or wife's share in case (4).
6 Grandmother h.h.s. (*Maternal*) ...	1/6	1/6	Mother, nearer maternal or paternal grandmother.	None.	
(*Paternal*) ...			Mother, *nearer* maternal or paternal grandmother, father, *nearer* true grandfather.	None.	
7 Daughter	1/2	2/3	**None**	Existence of son	Made Agnatic Heir.
8 Son's Daughter ...	1/2	2/3	Son, *more* than one daughter, higher son's son, *more* than one higher son's daughter.	Existence of (1) *only* one daughter, (2) *only* one higher son's daughter, (3) equal son's son.	Share reduced to 1/6 in cases (1) and (2): made residuary in case (3).
9 Full Sister	1/2	2/3	Son, son h.l.s., father, true grandfather.	Existence of full brother ...	Made Agnatic Heir.
10 Consanguine Sister ...	1/2	2/3	Son, son h.l.s., father, true grandfather, full brother, *more* than one full sister.	(1) Existence of *only* one full sister. (2) Existence of consanguine brother.	(1) Share reduced to 1/6: (2) Made Agnatic Heir.
11 Uterine Brother } 12 Uterine Sister }	1/6	1/3	{ Child, child of a son h.l.s., father, true grandfather.	None.	

NOTE (1).—In distributing the estate of a deceased Sunnite (Hanafi) Muslim we have first to see whether there exist any of the Koranic Heirs mentioned in Col. 1; then to see that they are not entirely excluded by the persons mentioned in Col. 3; then to assign to them the shares mentioned in Col. 2; unless their shares are affected by the persons mentioned in Col. 4; in which case to assign to them the shares mentioned in Col. 5.

NOTE (2).—The table is *not* a complete statement of the law; for that reference must be made elsewhere in this book.

Facing p. 404.

Koranic Heirs

Relations by Marriage

(1) *Husband,* **(2)** *Wife*

The surviving spouse *always* inherits, and the husband or wife is the only heir by affinity which is made a primary heir by the Koran. In pre-Islamic times they were entirely excluded (*g*).

If a woman dies leaving children or agnatic descendants, the husband is entitled to 1/4 of the net estate, that is after payment of the funeral expenses, debts and legacies. If there are no children, the husband obtains 1/2 of the net estate.

The fractional shares mentioned in the succeeding pages refer to *the net estate*, and not to the gross assets, as explained above.

The wife inherits 1/8 if there are children, and 1/4 if there are none. In case of plurality of wives, they share the 1/8 or 1/4 equally between them.

Illustrations. The surviving relations are—

(i) Husband and father.	h. =	1/2 (as Koranic Heir)
	f. =	1/2 (as Agnatic Heir)
(ii) Widow and children.	w. =	1/8 (as Koranic Heir)
	Children =	7/8 (as Agnatic Heirs).

Even from these simple illustrations it will be observed that rules of inheritance in the first two classes are closely intertwined, and the law relating to Koranic Heirs can be fully understood only when we have a proper acquaintance with the law concerning Agnatic Heirs and vice versa.

Where the only heir surviving is the spouse, he or she takes the whole estate; for details, see §92, end; §93, The Rule of al-Jabarī, C, p. 424 below.

(*g*) For details, Tyabji §§710 sq.; Wilson §§210, 211: Mulla §63, ills. (a) to (c).

BLOOD RELATIONS

(3) *Father,* (4) *True Grandfather, h.h.s.*

The father always inherits, but the grandfather is excluded by the father, and the grandfather, h.h.s. by a lower grandfather, or the father.

Case 1. The father, with children, takes 1/6; the residue 5/6 goes to the children, the sons taking double the share of the daughters.

Case 2. If there are no children or agnatic descendants, the father or true grandfather, h.h.s., takes as an Agnatic Heir.

Case 3. Where the surviving relations are the father and the mother, m. = 1/3, and f. = 2/3 as Agnatic Heir (*h*).

Case 4. Father, daughter.

d. = 1/2 (as Koranic Heir)
f.—1/6 (as Koranic Heir) *plus*
1/3 (as Agnatic Heir)
= 1/2.

Here the father inherits in *two different capacities* at the same time. In the case of a daughter or a sister, she may inherit either as heir of Class I, or Class II, but she cannot inherit in both capacities simultaneously. The father, as we shall see later, inherits (i) as a Koranic Heir, for instance where there are sons, when he takes 1/6, the 5/6 going to the sons; or (ii) as an Agnatic Heir, where there are no children or agnatic descendants; or (iii) in *both capacities* at the same time, where there are only daughters or son's daughters, h.l.s., as in the above case (*i*).

The true grandfather, in the absence of the father, inherits in all these capacities; except where he co-exists with the mother, as in Mother, Case 4 (iii), p. 408. In this case he

(*h*) Mulla §63, ill. (d); §65, ill. (o).
(*i*) ibid., §65, case no. 3.

does not reduce the share of the mother from 1/3 of the estate to 1/3 of the residue left after deducting the husband's or the wife's share. This will be understood after we have studied the mother's case fully (*j*).

(5) *Mother,* (6) *True Grandmother, h.h.s.*

The mother always inherits, but the true grandmother inherits only in certain cases. The maternal true grandmother is excluded by the mother, or by a nearer true grandmother, paternal or maternal.

The paternal true grandmother is excluded by the father, or the mother, or a nearer true grandmother, paternal or maternal, or a nearer true grandfather.

Case 1. The mother takes 1/3 where there are no children, and 1/6 when there are children. For instance,

(i) m. = 1/6, as Koranic Heir.

2 s. and 1 d. = 5/6 (2/6, 2/6, 1/6) as Agnatic Heirs.

Or, (ii) mother and brother.

m. = 1/3 (as Koranic Heir)

b. = 2/3 (as Agnatic Heir).

Case 2. Mother, father. See Case 3, p. 406, above.

Case 3. Mother, two or more brothers, or two or more sisters, or one brother *and* one sister.

Here the mother's share is reduced to 1/6, as Koranic Heir, and the remaining 5/6 goes to the brothers and sisters as Agnatic Heirs. If, however, there is only *one* brother or *one* sister, the mother takes 1/3.

Case 4. Mother, father, husband *or* wife.

(i) h. = 1/2

m. = 1/6 (= 1/3 of 1/2)

f. = 1/3 (as Agnatic Heir).

(*j*) For details, Wilson §§216, 228, 229; Tyabji §§710 sq.; Mulla §§63 and 65, 3. Father, and 4. True grandfather, h.h.s. See also *LME*, I, 171.

As there are no children, ordinarily we should allot to the mother 1/3; but in that case the mother's share would be greater than that of the father. The father is both a Koranic as well as a tribal heir; his rights have to be respected. He is also a male. Therefore the Koranic ordinance of the 1/3 share is applied to the *residue*, after deducting the husband's share, and not to the whole estate.

(ii) w. = 1/4
m. = 1/4 (= 1/3 of 3/4)
f. = 1/2 (as Agnatic Heir).

The reasoning is the same and no further explanation is necessary (*k*).

The above two decisions were those of the Caliph Omar and have not been accepted by the Shīʿa.

(iii) h. = 1/2
m. = 1/3
ff. = 1/6 (as Agnatic Heir).

The mother takes 1/3 as the father's father does not reduce the share of the mother.

For the similar case of widow, mother and father's father, the shares would be 1/4, 1/3 and 5/12 (as Agnatic Heir), respectively (*l*).

(7) *Daughter,* **(8)** *Son's Daughter, h.l.s.*

The daughter is a primary heir; she always inherits in one of two capacities. A single daughter, or two or more daughters, without a son, inherit as Koranic Heirs, Class I. If the daughter (or daughters) co-exists with a son (or sons), she inherits as an Agnatic Heir, Class II. The son's daughter inherits only where there is no daughter (see Case 5).

(*k*) Mulla §63, ills. (h) and (j).

(*l*) Mulla §63, ills. (i) and (k). For true grandfather and true grandmother, see Mulla §63, ill. (1), onwards. For details, Tyabji, loc. cit.; Wilson §§214-18.

Case 1. A single daughter takes 1/2; two or more daughters take 2/3. For instance, father, mother, 2 daughters. Father = 1/6; mother = 1/6; 2 daughters = 2/3 (equally, 1/3 each).

Case 2. A daughter (or daughters), co-existing with a son (or sons), becomes an heir of Class II, *'aṣabāt.* This will be clearer when we come to Agnatic Heirs, but, to take a simple case, say 2 sons and 3 daughters.

2 s. = 4/7 (2/7 each)
3 d. = 3/7 (1/7 each).

Case 3. Daughter, sister. If there is one daughter and a sister, the daughter takes her Koranic share, and the sister takes the remaining 1/2 as an Agnatic Heir. Similarly, where there are 2 sisters and 2 daughters, the daughters have precedence. They take 2/3 as Koranic Heirs, and the residue goes to the sisters.

Case 4. Daughter, father. Here the father takes in *two different capacities* at the same time. Thus:

d. = 1/2
f.—1/6 (as Koranic Heir)
plus 1/3 (as Agnatic Heir)
= 1/2.

See (3) Father, Case 4 (p. 406).

Case 5. (i) Where there is no son or daughter, the son's daughter takes 1/2 by herself, and if there be more than one, 2/3, provided no son's son co-exists with them.

(ii) If, however, there is a son's daughter and a son's son's daughter, they take 2/3 between them and the division is as follows:

sd. = 1/2 (Koranic Share)
ssd. = 1/6 (so that the total comes to 2/3, the Koranic share of 2 daughters).

Illustrations

(1) Father, mother, 3 son's daughters.

f. = 1/6 (as Koranic Heir)
m. = 1/6 (as Koranic Heir)
3 sd. = 2/3 (each taking 2/9).

(2) Father, mother, daughter, 4 son's daughters.

f. = 1/6 (as Koranic Heir)
m. = 1/6 Do.
d. = 1/2 Do.
4 sd. = 1/6 (each taking 1/24, and with the daughter's share, making up the Koranic 2/3).

(3) Father, mother, 2 son's daughters, son's son's daughter.

f. = 1/6 (as Koranic Heir)
m. = 1/6 Do.
2 sd. = 2/3
ssd.—excluded by *two* sd. (but *not* by *one*, see below).

(4) Father, mother, son's daughter, son's son's daughter.

f. = 1/6 (as Koranic Heir)
m. = 1/6 Do.
sd. = 1/2 }
ssd. = 1/6 } = 2/3 { (Koranic share of two or more daughters) (*m*).

(9) *Full Sister,* **(10)** *Consanguine Sister*

The full sister is not a primary heir; she is excluded by (i) son, (ii) son's son, h.l.s., (iii) father, or (iv) true

(*m*) Mulla §63, ills. (r), (s), (t), (u). For details see Tyabji, loc. cit.; Wilson §§212, 213; Mulla §§63, 65.

grandfather. It is to be noticed that male agnates in the descending and the ascending lines exclude her as a collateral. With the full brother, and, in certain cases, with the daughter, she becomes a residuary.

The consanguine sister is excluded by a full brother or *two* full sisters, and by all the four relations who exclude a full sister. With the consanguine brother, the consanguine sister becomes a residuary. With a *single* full sister, she takes a specified share (see Case 2, below).

Case 1. Husband = 1/2; sister = 1/2; but husband and two sisters, husband = 1/2; two sisters = 2/3. This raises an anomaly, and we shall discuss this below (*'awl,* §§92, 100, c).

Case 2. Full sister, consanguine sister.

fs. = 1/2

cs. = 1/6, together making up the Koranic share of 2/3, as in the case of sd. and ssd.

But if there were *two* full sisters, the consanguine sister would be excluded.

Case 3. The full sister and consanguine sister co-existing with the full brother or consanguine sister, respectively, inherit collectively as Agnatic Heirs, the brother taking a double share.

Case 4. Full sister, daughter. Here the daughter has precedence; she takes as a Koranic Heir, the sister becoming in each case an Agnatic Heir, thus:

(i) daughter, sister—d. = 1/2, s. = 1/2

(ii) 2 daughters, 1 sister—2 d. = 2/3, s. = 1/3

(iii) 1 daughter, 2 sisters—d. = 1/2, 2 s. = 1/2 (1/4 each) (*n*).

(*n*) For a good illustration of succession among collaterals, see *Abdul Karim* v. *Amat-ul-Habib* (1922) 3 Lahore 397. For details see Tyabji, loc. cit., 623; Wilson §§219, 220; Mulla §63, ills. (v), (w), (x).

(11) *Uterine Brother,* **(12)** *Uterine Sister*

Three points to be noted are: (A) The uterine brother (or sister) is not a primary heir. He is excluded by (i) child, (ii) child of son, h.l.s., (iii) father, or (iv) true grandfather. (B) The full brother (or sister), however, does not exclude the uterine brother (or sister). And (C) the uterine brother and the uterine sister have *equal* shares, that is, if there is *one* uterine brother or one uterine sister, he or she takes 1/6. Where, however, there are two uterine brothers, or two uterine sisters, or one uterine brother and one uterine sister, in each of these cases they take 1/3 between them, brother and sister sharing *equally*. Another such case is that of the mother and the father, co-existing with other relations, and each taking a Koranic share.

Illustrations

(1) Mother = 1/6
2 full sisters = 2/3 (each taking 1/3)
consanguine sister—(excluded by two full sisters)
uterine sister (or brother) = 1/6.

(2) 2 Full sisters (or consanguine sisters) = 2/3 (each taking 1/3)
2 uterine sisters (or brothers) = 1/3 (1/6 each).

(3) Full sister = 1/2
2 consanguine sisters = 1/6 (each taking 1/12)
uterine brother }
uterine sister } = 1/3 (1/6 each) (*o*).

Among the remarkable cases mentioned by the early authorities is a decision of the Caliph Omar in the following case, called the *Ḥimāriyya.* A woman died leaving her husband, mother, two uterine sisters, and one full brother. The decision was as follows:

(*o*) Mulla and Tyabji, loc. cit.; Wilson §221; Fitzgerald, 135-6.

h. = 1/2 }
m. = 1/6 } The Koranic shares exhaust the estate.
2 us. = 1/3 }
fb.—entirely excluded.

This decision is generally adopted by the Hanafi school, but there are divergent opinions, and the problem is one of the very few where the courts may some day have to create a precedent (*p*).

Illegitimacy is a bar to inheritance between uterine brothers. If two sons are born to a woman, one legitimate, the other not, they are not related as uterine brothers so as to inherit from each other (*q*).

The word *kalāla*, used in the Koran and in works on succession, means collaterals in general, 'distant kindred' being a misleading rendering. The *kalāla*, as a rule, inherit only after descendants and ascendants (*r*).

Rules of Exclusion

We have now concluded a brief survey of the principal rules of inheritance concerning the class called Koranic Heirs, according to the Hanafi school of Sunnite law. These rules will become clearer if we take a few selected cases of exclusion.

If we consider the list of Koranic Heirs, we find that the husband and the wife are primary heirs; they cannot be excluded by anyone. But a feature of their rights is that they themselves exclude no one. The share of the spouses is fixed by law; if they exist they reduce the residue which may be taken by the Agnatic or Uterine heirs; but they do not exclude, either wholly or partially, any heir.

Next, we come to the father and the true grandfather. The father excludes the higher agnatic ascendants, and also the male collaterals, like the uncle, the brother and the nephew; similarly, the nearer true grandfather excludes the more

(*p*) Wilson §221; Fitzgerald, 135-6; Tyabji §714, ill. 23.
(*q*) *Rahmatullah* v. *Maqsood Ahmad* [1950] All. 713.
(*r*) Tyabji §698, n. 32; Fitzgerald, 131.

remote. These points will become clear when we come to the second class of heirs, *'aṣabāt*. In other cases the father does not affect the share of any Koranic Heir, except the sisters (full, consanguine or uterine), all of whom he excludes; and we may take a few illustrations. (1) Wife, father, brother. Brother excluded. (2) Husband, father, brother's son. Brother's son excluded. (3) Father, full sister, consanguine sister, uterine sister. The sisters excluded.

Then comes the mother and the true grandmother, h.h.s. The mother excludes the grandmother, and the nearer grandmother excludes the more remote. The mother's share is affected by the presence of (i) children or (ii) two or more brothers or sisters. Her share is also greatly affected by the existence of the husband (or wife) *and* the father (see Mother, Case 4, p. 407).

In the case of the daughter, she is a primary heir. She partially excludes lower son's daughters, but *one* daughter or son's daughter does not entirely exclude a lower son's daughter. For example:

(1) One daughter, one son's daughter. d. = 1/2, sd. = 1/6.

(2) Son's daughter, son's son's daughter. sd. = 1/2, ssd. = 1/6. The shares in both the above cases together total 2/3, the Koranic share of two daughters.

Two son's daughters will, however, exclude a *lower* son's daughter: (3) father, mother, two son's daughters, three son's sons' daughters. The 3 ssd. are excluded: f. = 1/6, m. = 1/6, 2 sd. = 2/3.

Finally we come to the sisters. Here there are some interesting cases.

(1) One full sister does not exclude the consanguine sister. fs. = 1/2, cs. = 1/6—taking together 2/3, the Koranic share of two sisters or two daughters.

(2) Two full sisters, however, exclude the consanguine sister. Two full sisters, one consanguine sister; the cs. is excluded.

The uterine brother or sister is *not* excluded by the full or consanguine brother or sister. For instance:

(1) Mother, two full sisters, consanguine sister, uterine sister. Consanguine sister excluded by two full sisters (*s*).

(2) Full brother, full sister, consanguine sister. cs. excluded.

(3) Full brother, consanguine brother, consanguine sister. cb. and cs. excluded.

(4) Full sister, consanguine sister, uterine sister. fs. = 1/2; cs. = 1/6; us. = 1/6. The total is 5/6. Therefore, by *radd* = 3/5, 1/5, 1/5.

We must now try to understand the principle: '*A person, though excluded himself, may exclude others.*'(*t*) Let us take the following cases:

(1) Mother, father, 2 sisters. The two sisters are excluded by the father; and yet, they reduce the share of the mother to 1/6. Thus m. = 1/6, f. = 5/6 (as Agnatic Heir); 2 s.—entirely excluded. This is a case of *partial* exclusion of the mother.

(2) Mother, brother (f., c., or u.), sister (f., c., or u.), father.
m. = 1/6 (because there is a brother *and* a sister).
b.—excluded by father.
s.—excluded by father.
f. = 5/6 (as Agnatic Heir).

Here again the brother and the sister, although *entirely* excluded from inheritance, *partially* exclude the mother, and reduce her share to 1/6, instead of 1/3 (*u*).

(3) Father's mother, mother's mother's mother, father.
fm.—excluded by father.
mmm.—excluded by fm., a nearer true grandmother.
f.—takes the whole property as Agnatic Heir.

Here fm., herself entirely excluded, excludes mmm.(*v*)

(*s*) See Uterine Brother and Sister, ill. (1) p. 412 above.
(*t*) *Sirājiyyah,* 28; Mulla §63, ill. (e).
(*u*) Mulla §63, ill. (g).
(*v*) ibid., ill. (q).

§92. Anomalous Cases: *'awl, radd*

Since fractional shares are allotted to the Koranic Heirs, there are three possibilities: that the fractions taken together may be (i) equal to unity, or (ii) more than unity, or (iii) less than unity. We shall consider each of these cases and see how the problem is solved in the latter two.

(i) *Equal to unity.* The surviving relations are father, mother and 2 daughters. Therefore f. = 1/6, m. = 1/6, 2d. = 2/3, and these fractions amount exactly to unity (*w*). Or, to take another example, father, father's father, mother, mother's mother, 2 daughters, son's daughter. Here—

f. = 1/6 (as Koranic Heir, because there are two daughters)
ff.—excluded by f.
m. = 1/6 (as there are daughters)
mm.—excluded by m.
2 d. = 2/3 (as Koranic Heirs)
sd.—excluded by two daughters (*x*).

Such cases occur but rarely. The commonest cases are those in which there are both Koranic and Agnatic Heirs, so that after allotting the fractional shares amongst the members of Class I, the residue is shared by members of Class II, and no difficulty arises.

(ii) *More than unity* (*'awl*). A real anomaly arises, however, when the fractions allotted to the Koranic Heirs amount to more than unity. To take a simple example, husband = 1/2; 2 full sisters = 2/3. The total of these fractions, reducing them to a common denominator, 3/6 + 4/6 = 7/6. This is an anomaly and has to be resolved. The solution is (a) *increase* the denominator to make it equal to the sum of the numerators, and (b) allow the individual numerators to remain, thus proportionately decreasing the share of each heir. The artificial inflation of the denominator is called *'awl*, literally.

(*w*) *Sirājiyyah*, 33.
(*x*) Mulla §63, ill. (a).

'increase'; but its real effect is *the proportionate reduction of the share.*

Applying this rule we have—h.=½=3/6; and 2s.=2/3=4/6.
Therefore reduce to 3/7 and 4/7, respectively.

We may take two simple illustrations:

(1)	husband	—1/2 = 3/6 reduced to 3/8	
	2 full sisters	—2/3 = 4/6 reduced to 4/8	
	mother	—1/6 = 1/6 reduced to 1/8	
		8/6	8/8
(2)	widow	—1/4 = 3/12 reduced to 3/15	
	2 full sisters	—2/3 = 8/12 reduced to 8/15	
	uterine sister	—1/6 = 2/12 reduced to 2/15	
	mother	—1/6 = 2/12 reduced to 2/15	
		15/12	15/15

It is unnecessary to multiply instances which can be found in abundance in the text-books (*y*).

(*iii*) *Less than unity* (*radd*). The third case is where the sum total of the fractions is less than unity, and there are no heirs of Class II to take the residue. Here the residue *returns* to the Koranic Heirs in proportion to their shares. This is called Return, *radd*.

The three rules of the doctrine of *radd* are:

(1) The residue returns in proportion to the share.

(2) The husband or the wife is not entitled to the return so long as there is a Koranic Heir (Class I) or a Uterine Heir (Class III).

(3) If there is no other surviving heir, the residue returns to the husband or the wife in India; this rule is, however, contrary to the strict letter of the *sharī'at*, whereby the residue would escheat to the State, the spouse being entitled only to the Koranic Share (*yy*).

(*y*) *Sirājiyyah,* 29-30, 33: Fitzgerald, 116; Wilson §222; Mulla §64; Tyabji §§710(1), read with 711.

(*yy*) If the husband is the sole surviving heir, and he belongs to the class known as Distant Kindred (Uterine Heir), he takes his wife's property in both capacities, *Mazirannessa* v. *K. G. Kibria,* A.I.R. (1970) Cal. 387.

We shall take an illustration for each rule. As to (1), mother and daughter.

m. = 1/6, d. = 1/2; 1/6 + 3/6 = 2/3: there remains 1/3 which 'returns'.

The rule in such a case is to reduce the fractional shares to a common denominator, and to decrease the denominator of these shares to make it equal to the sum of the numerators. In the present illustration the original shares, reduced to a common denominator, are 1/6 and 3/6. The total of the numerators is 1 + 3 = 4. The ultimate shares will therefore be 1/4 and 3/4 respectively.

As to (2), husband = 1/4
daughter = 3/4 (1/2 as sharer, 1/4 by return).

Or

wife = 1/4
sister (f. or c.) = 3/4 (1/2 as sharer, 1/4 by return).

In these cases the husband or the wife does not take the return. Similarly, husband = 1/2
daughter's son = 1/2.

The daughter's son belongs to Class III, Uterine Heir, and yet prevents the husband from taking the return.

As to (3), a Muslim dies leaving a widow as his sole heir. She takes 1/4 as her Koranic share and the residue 3/4 by return; the residue does not escheat to the State in India. *A fortiori*, the husband would be similarly entitled (z).

§93. Class II, Agnatic Heirs *('aṣabāt)*

Classification of Agnatic Heirs

The Agnatic Heirs entitled to succeed are classified by the *Sirājiyyah* as follows:

Males:— Group I. The Agnate in his *own* right— (*'aṣaba bi-nafsihi*);

(z) *Mir Isub* v. *Isab* (1920) 44 Bom., 947. For details see *Sirājiyyah*, 37; Mulla §66; Tyabji §716; Wilson §238, where a delightful Persian story illustrating the principle of Return is narrated.

Females:— { Group II. The Agnate in the right of *another* —(*'aṣaba bi-ghayrihi*);
Group III. The Agnate *with* another— (*'aṣaba ma'a ghayrihi*) (*a*).

The first group comprises *all male agnates*; this is the largest and most important class; it includes the son, the son's son, the father, the brother, the paternal uncle and his son, and so forth. These in pre-Islamic law were the most important heirs; they retain, to a large extent, in Hanafi law their primacy, influence and power.

The second group contains *four* specified *female* agnates, when they co-exist with male relatives of the same degree namely, (1) daughter (with son);

(2) son's daughter, h.l.s. (with *equal* son's son, h.l.s.);
(3) full sister (with full brother); and
(4) consanguine sister (with consanguine brother).

It must be noted here that (1) daughter and (2) son's daughter, h.l.s. are female agnates in the descending line; and every female agnate co-existing with an equal male agnate is included in this group. While the full and the consanguine sister are *persona designata*, their descendants are *not* included in the class *'aṣabāt*, for they are not agnates. Such descendants, being cognates, are included in the *dhawū'l-arḥām*, Class III.

The third group comprises the two anomalous cases of the full sister and the consanguine sister, when they inherit with daughters or son's daughters. If a man dies, leaving a daughter and a full sister, it is possible simply to allot 1/2 of the estate to each of them under the Koranic injunctions. But supposing we have two daughters and one sister, or one daughter and two sisters, or two daughters and two sisters, what are the principles of distribution? In these cases, as the Koranic shares sum up to more than unity, who is to be preferred and

(*a*) *Sirājiyyah*, 23-4; Ameer Ali, II, 51.

why? Here the daughter is preferred as a *descendant* to the sister who is a *collateral*; thus we place the daughter in Class I, and allot to her the Koranic share, and we give the residue to the sister as a member of Class II. Hence the curious expression 'with another'.(*b*)

To sum up, **Group I** consists of a limitless number of blood relations who are **all male agnates.** They constitute the most important class; in reality, these are *the tribal heirs of pre-Islamic Arabia.* **Group II** consists of **four female agnates** when they co-exist with males equal in degree. **Group III** consists of the **two anomalous cases of sisters,** full and consanguine, when they survive with daughters and there are no other nearer heirs.

We are now in a position to analyse the principles underlying the classification of male Agnatic Heirs, *'aṣabāt*, which is as follows:

A. Descendants, B. Ascendants and C. Collaterals, or as the *Sirājiyyah* lays down—

A. The 'offspring of the deceased', meaning sons and lineal descendants in the male line (*Descendants*).

B. His 'root', that is his father, father's father and so on in the male line ascending (*Ascendants*).

C. The 'offspring of his father', that is his brothers, full and consanguine, and their lineal descendants in the male line (*Collaterals*).

CC. The 'offspring of his true grandfather, how high soever'. that is paternal uncles and remoter relations, provided that they are lineal male descendants, however remote, of lineal male ascendants, however remote. The groups C. and CC. constitute together the class designated as Collaterals.

(*b*) Perhaps 'in spite of' would be an even better rendering of the original Arabic. See above §91, Daughter, Case 3 (p. 409); Sister, Case 4 (p. 411).

On careful examination this will be found to be an exhaustive classification of all the male agnates of the deceased (*c*).

This movement of the inheritance can be remembered by the rule: FIRST, THE DESCENDANTS; NEXT, THE ASCENDANTS; AND FINALLY, THE COLLATERALS. The rule is illustrated by the diagram which faces p. 422.

Priorities. The heirs may now be arranged and priority determined as follows (*d*).

AGNATIC HEIRS

GROUP I DESCENDANTS

1. Son.

♀ Daughter, with son.

2. Son's son, how low soever.

♀ (i) Son's daughter (with son's son) takes as a daughter, the son taking a double portion.

(ii) Son's daughter (with *lower* son's son) takes as an Agnatic Heir, provided she cannot inherit as a Koranic Heir.

Illustration. Two daughters, son's daughter, son's son's son. 2 d. = 2/3 (as Koranic Heirs); sd. = 1/3 of 1/3 = 1/9; and sss. = 2/3 of 1/3 = 2/9, as Agnatic Heirs.

There are two daughters, therefore the sd. cannot inherit as a Koranic Heir. Hence, she is relegated to Class II, with the lower male descendant, the son's son's son (*e*).

(iii) Where (a) there are two or more daughters, and (b) the son's daughter, h.l.s. takes as an Agnatic Heir *with* a lower son's son, and (c) there are son's daughters, h.l.s. *equal* in degree to the lower son's

(*c*) *Sirājiyyah*, 23-5; Ameer Ali, II, 52; Wilson §§224 sqq.; Tyabji §§712 sq.; Mulla §65.

(*d*) Wilson, 6th ed., 281; Tyabji, loc. cit.

(*e*) Mulla §65, ill. (k).

son, the higher and the lower son's daughters share equally, as if they were all of the same grade, the sons taking a double share.

Illustration. 2 daughters = 2/3 (Koranic share)

Son's son's son	= 2/4 of 1/3 = 1/6	As Agnatic Heirs (*f*).
Son's son's daughter	= 1/4 of 1/3 = 1/12	
Son's daughter	= 1/4 of 1/3 = 1/12	

Group II Ascendants

3. **Father** may inherit (i) as Koranic Heir, (ii) as Agnatic Heir, or (iii) *in both capacities* at the same time.
4. **True grandfather, how high soever.**

Group III Collaterals

(A) *Descendants of the Father*

5. **Full brother.**

♀ Full sister, with full brother, takes in the proportion of 1 to 2.

6. ♀ **Full sister.** Where there is no brother, the full sister takes as a residuary with (i) a daughter or daughters, (ii) one son's daughter or son's daughters, h.l.s., or (iii) one daughter *and* one son's daughter, h.l.s.(*g*).

Thus the full sister inherits (i) as Koranic Heir, (ii) as an Agnatic Heir, with the brother, and (iii) as an Agnatic Heir, with daughters and son's daughters, h.l.s.

Illustration:	daughter	= 1/2 (as Koranic Heir)
	son's daughter	= 1/6 (as Koranic Heir)
	husband	= 1/4 (as Koranic Heir)
	full sister	= 1/12 (Agnatic Heir, as above).

7. **Consanguine brother.**

♀ Consanguine sister, with consanguine brother, takes in the proportion of 1 to 2.

(*f*) loc. cit., ill. (m).

(*g*) loc. cit., ills. (r) to (x). A very good discussion of the daughter's and sister's claims of inheritance will be found in Tyabji §714.

DIAGRAM OF CLASS II. AGNATIC HEIRS ('AṢABĀT)

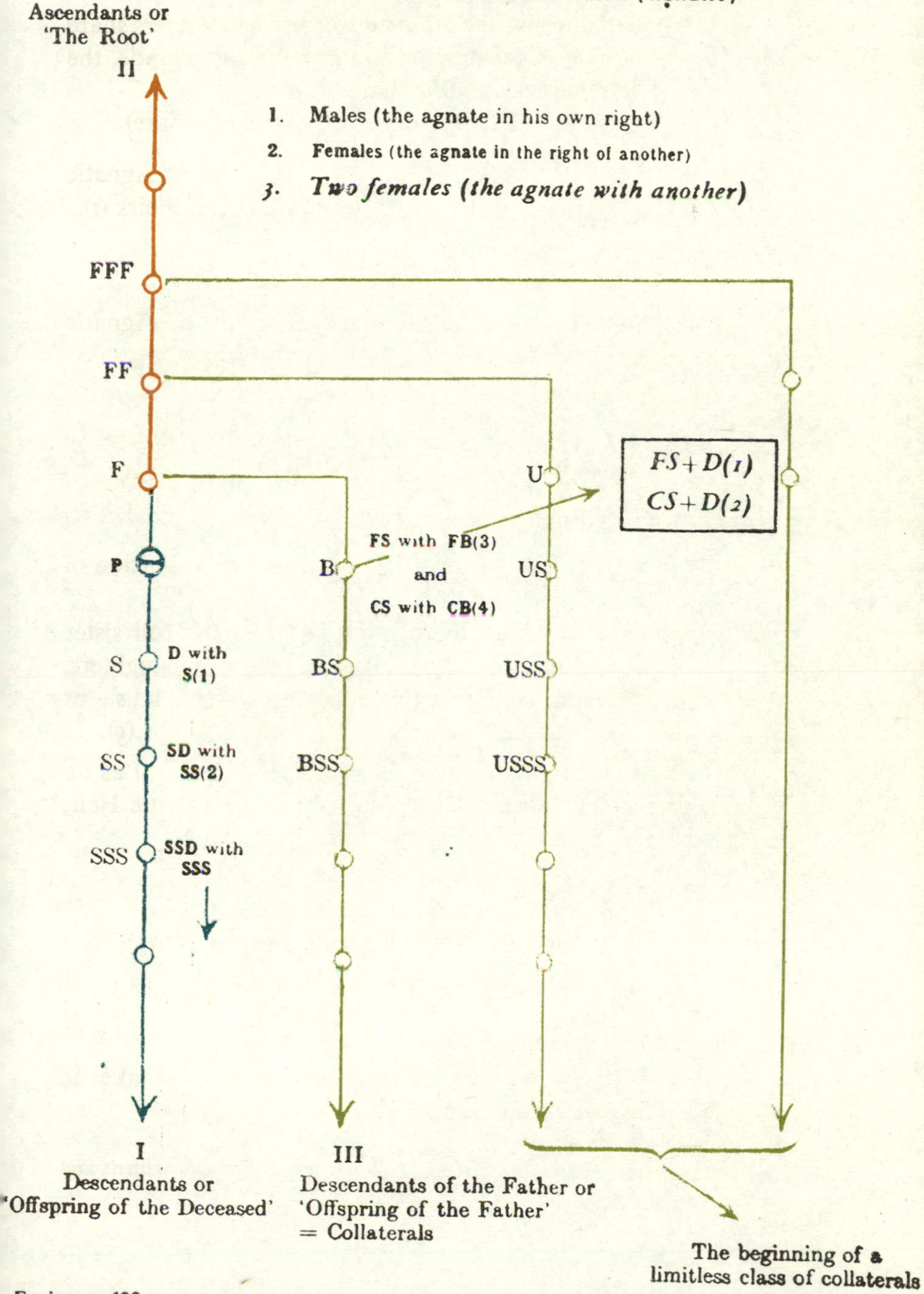
Ascendants or
'The Root'
II
1. Males (the agnate in his own right)
2. Females (the agnate in the right of another)
3. Two females (the agnate with another)
FFF
FF
F
P
S
SS
SSS
D with
S(1)
SD with
SS(2)
SSD with
SSS
U
FS+D(1)
CS+D(2)
FS with FB(3)
and
CS with CB(4)
B
US
BS
USS
BSS
USSS
I
Descendants or
'Offspring of the Deceased'
III
Descendants of the Father or
'Offspring of the Father'
= Collaterals
The beginning of a
limitless class of collaterals

8. ♀ **Consanguine sister.** When there is no consanguine brother, the consanguine sister takes the residue with (i) a daughter or daughters, or (ii) one son's daughter *or* son's daughters, h.l.s., or (iii) one daughter *and* one son's daughter, h.l.s.

   Once again we must note that the d., sd.h.l.s., fs. and cs. are the only *four female* agnates in Class II. The rest are *all* males.

9. **Full brother's son.**

10. **Consanguine brother's son,** and then remoter descendants.

(B) *Descendants of true Grandfather*

11. Full paternal uncle.

12. Consanguine paternal uncle.

13. Full paternal uncle's son.

14. Consanguine paternal uncle's son, and remoter descendants.

(C) *Descendants of true Grandfathers, h.h.s.*, in like order, *ad infinitum* in the order given in Tyabji §712; Wilson, 6th ed., 281; and Mulla §65, read with the table at 65A.

Principles of Distribution and Exclusion

1. Agnatic Heirs (*'aṣabāt*) succeed only where there are no Koranic Heirs (*aṣḥāb al-farā'iḍ*), or where, after assigning the shares to the said heirs, a residue is left. A man dies leaving two sons and a daughter; these are all heirs of Class II, the daughter entering the class of Agnatic Heirs as she co-exists with sons. The estate will therefore be divided into 5 shares, 2 shares whereof will be taken by each of the sons, and 1 share by the daughter. Or, to take another simple illustration, where

the surviving relations are a widow, a son and a daughter, the widow takes 1/8, and the residue 7/8 will be divided into three portions, and two of these will be taken by the son—$2/3 \times 7/8 = 7/12$, and one will be taken by the daughter—$1/3 \times 7/8 = 7/24$.

2. (i) In the four cases where a female enters this class (*'aṣabāt bi-ghayrihi*), to wit daughter with son, son's daughter, h.l.s. with equal son's son, h.l.s., full sister with full brother, and consanguine sister with consanguine brother, the female heir takes one-half the share of the male. For example, a man dies leaving two sons and three daughters, or two full brothers and three full sisters; the estate in each case will be divided into 10 shares, out of which the son (or brother) will take 2 shares each, and the daughter (or sister) 1 share each.

   (ii) As to the two unusual cases of *'aṣabāt ma'a ghayrihi*, where the female enters the second class 'with others', the cases have been sufficiently explained in the daughters' and sisters' cases, above.

3. **Rule of al-Jabarī.** The simplest way to remember priorities is to memorize *The Rule of al-Jabarī:*

Preference is given—

A. first, to the *order*;

B. next, to the *degree*; and

C. lastly, to the *strength of the blood tie* (*h*).

A. *First—Order*

A son and a father are both removed in the first degree from the propositus; but the son, as an Agnatic Heir, is superior, as he belongs to the order of descendants. The son, therefore, *qua* agnate excludes the father, who still has an independent Koranic share (*farḍ, farīḍa*) by which he gets 1/6.

(*h*) Fitzgerald, 118-19; Anderson and Coulson, op. cit., 78.

The three 'orders' are: (i) Descendants; (ii) Ascendants; (iii) Collaterals. This shows the close kinship between the principles of the Hanafi law relating to *'aṣabāt*, and the ancient tribal law (*i*).

B. *Next—Degree*

This means that the Hanafi system does not recognize the right of representation; and also that the nearer in degree rigorously excludes the more remote. *P* dies leaving one son and the son of a predeceased son; the former takes everything, the latter nothing. On this point, the Hanafi (Sunnite) and the Ithnā 'Asharī (Shiite) schools are at one.

Similarly, in the line of ascendants, the father excludes the father's father, and a paternal uncle excludes a paternal uncle's son.

The *Sirājiyyah* explains this principle of exclusion in two rules. The first is: 'Whosoever is related to the deceased *through any person* shall not inherit while that person is living.'(*j*) This is the case of simple exclusion. Thus a son excludes *his own* son, the grandson; and a father excludes a brother or a sister. But uterine brothers and sisters are *not* excluded by the mother. For a full explanation see Tyabji, §§712-14 and Mulla §65, pp. 69-7.

The second limb of the rule is the text of the *Sirājiyyah*: 'The nearest of blood must take.'(*k*) *P* dies leaving Ali, a son, and Muhammad, the son of Husayn, a predeceased son.

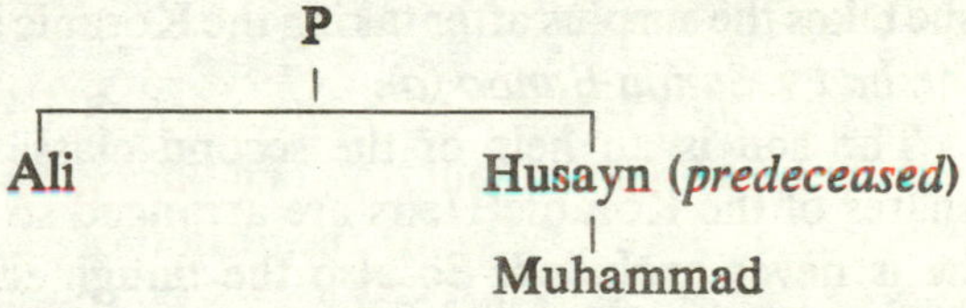

Ali excludes Muhammad, in all the schools (*l*). This is the

(*i*) The same rule is laid down in Tyabji §§712 sq.; Wilson §225 sqq. and *Sirājiyyah*, 23-5.
(*j*) *Sirājiyyah*, 27.
(*k*) *Sirājiyyah*, 27-8.
(*l*) For details and application, see Tyabji, loc. cit. and Mulla §65.

direct negation of representation. But *aliter* in Pakistan, The Muslim Family Laws Ordinance, VIII of 1961, dated 2 March 1961 (came into operation 15 July 1961). See Appendix E, below.

C. *Lastly—Strength of the Blood Tie*

If the order and degree are equal, the full blood is to be preferred. A full brother excludes a consanguine brother; but the latter will exclude a full brother's son (*m*).

The foundation for the rule is a tradition of the Prophet quoted by the *Sirājiyyah*: 'Surely, kinsmen by the same father and mother shall inherit before kinsmen of the same father only.'(*n*).

Primary heirs. From a consideration of the rules regarding Koranic and Agnatic Heirs, it will be seen that the following are the five primary heirs according to all schools of Islamic law—(1) **Husband** or **Wife**, (2) **Son**, (3) **Daughter**, (4) **Father**, (5) **Mother** (*o*). They are never excluded by any heir, although they may exclude others (*p*). We shall briefly recapitulate the rights of the primary heirs.

The husband and the wife are the only heirs by affinity in any class. They had no rights in pre-Islamic times; they were therefore made Koranic Heirs, their portion was unalterably fixed and they could not share in the Return (*radd*). This strict rule of the *sharī'at* has now been relaxed in India, and where the sole surviving heir is the husband or the wife he or she takes the surplus after taking the Koranic share, *Mahomed Arshad* v. *Sajida Banoo* (*q*).

The son is an heir of the second class, *'aṣabāt*, but the shares of the Koranic Heirs are arranged so ingeniously that he is never excluded. So also the daughter. She is either a Koranic Heir with a fixed portion or, when surviving with

(*m*) Tyabji §713(4) (*c*).
(*n*) *Sirājiyyah*, 24.
(*o*) *Sirājiyyah*, 27; Mulla §§65 sq.
(*p*) The primary heirs have also their substitutes, Mulla, loc. cit.
(*q*) (1878) 3 Cal. 702, and Mulla §66, with numerous illustrations.

the son, she shares the residue with him in the proportion of one to two.

Lastly we come to the father and mother. The mother's case has been dealt with fully above; she is always a member of Class I, and she gets a larger share if there are no children, or if there is one brother or one sister only.

The father's case is somewhat anomalous and we may briefly recapitulate what has been said before. *First*, the father may exist with the son. According to tribal law the father as an ascendant would be excluded by the son, *qua* descendant. So the Koran gives him a share, and he takes 1/6, the residue going to the son.

Secondly, in the case of both the parents surviving and there being no children, according to the older law in default of descendants the whole estate would go to the father, the mother being entirely excluded. In Islamic law, however, the mother is an heir of Class I, and she obtains 1/3, and the residue 2/3 goes to the father. If there are children, in addition to parents, the father and the mother each get 1/6, and the residue is divided amongst the children, a double share being taken by each son.

Thirdly, an anomaly arises where there is a daughter and the father. It will be seen from the above discussion that in the case of certain relations they may only inherit in *one* of two different capacities; the daughter and the son's daughter, h.l.s., the full sister and the consanguine sister, each of these relations inherits either as a Koranic or as an Agnatic Heir. None of them inherits both as an heir of Class I and an heir of Class II. So also the father, in all cases except one, inherits either as a Koranic or as an Agnatic Heir. The only exception is where the surviving relations are *the daughter* and *the father*.

Here we are faced with this difficulty. Before the advent of Islam the father entirely excluded the daughter. But the Koran lays down that 1/2 of the estate is to be given to the daughter; and as there is a child, the father's Koranic share is reduced to 1/6. What is to happen to the residue, namely, 1/3 of the estate? The daughter, as it is, gets a larger share; if the residue is divided proportionately or equally, the daughter's share would still be larger than that of the father. To obviate this difficulty, the remaining 1/3 is allotted to the father as an heir of Class II, *'aṣabāt*; thus the shares are d. = 1/2; f. = 1/2 (1/6 as Koranic Heir + 1/3 as Agnatic Heir). This is the only case of an heir inheriting in *two different capacities at the same time* (*r*).

Some authors use the expression 'double capacity'.(*s*) The expression as used in the context does not cause any special difficulty, but it is not altogether a happy one. One specific misunderstanding, in particular, must be guarded against; it may be said, somewhat loosely, that the daughter, the sister (full as well as consanguine) and the father inherit in a 'double capacity'; meaning thereby, *in one of two different capacities*, either as a Koranic Heir or an Agnatic Heir. This is true; but the case of the father is peculiar; he is the only heir who, in a certain case, inherits in *two different capacities at the same time*. Hence, the expression 'double capacity' is to be avoided, as it may lead to serious misunderstanding.

The case of the true grandfather is a somewhat complicated one, and a full discussion has been omitted as being unsuitable for a students' text-book; for details see *Sirājiyyah*, 70; Wilson §§229-30; Tyabji §§715 sq. and *Law in the Middle East*, I, 171.

§94. Class III, Uterine Heirs *(dhawū'l-arḥām)*

'A distant kinsman is every *relation*, who is neither a sharer (Koranic Heir) nor a residuary (Agnatic Heir)'—so, the *Sirājiyyah* (*t*). The expression *dhawū'l-arḥām* means 'kindred', and *raḥm* (pl. *arḥām*) in this context cannot be rendered as 'womb'. Now, who are the blood relations that

(*r*) Mulla §65, illustration (p).
(*s*) Mulla, 13th ed., 69; now happily given up.
(*t*) 44-5.

are neither Koranic nor Agnatic Heirs? Obviously *female agnates*, and *cognates*, male or female. The Koran mentions a certain number of relations and allocates a share (*sahm, farīḍa*) to each of them; this constitutes the first class, consisting of the spouses and certain close relations, mostly females. In the second class we have all the tribal heirs, the *'aṣabāt*; the two principles of pre-Islamic law still retained are (i) that they are all *males* (*u*), and (ii) that they are all *agnates*. After this enumeration, it may be asked, Who remain? The answer is: (i) female agnates (*v*), and (ii) cognates, male or female (*w*). These two groups together constitute Class III of the Sunnite Heirs, so aptly designated by Ameer Ali as 'Uterine Relations'.(*x*)

The rules may be briefly stated as follows: (i) where there are no Koranic or Agnatic Heirs, the estate is divided among Uterine heirs; (ii) where there is a husband or wife and Uterine heirs, the surviving spouse will take his or her Koranic share and the residue of the estate will be divided among Uterine Heirs (*xx*).

Classification of Uterine Heirs

The classification of this class is analogous to that of the previous class: Group I, Descendants; Group II, Ascendants; Group III, Collaterals. Therefore the order of priority is (*y*):

GROUP I, DESCENDANTS

1. Daughter's children and their descendants.
2. Children of son's daughters, h.l.s., and their descendants, *ad infinitum*.

GROUP II, ASCENDANTS

1. False grandfathers, h.h.s.
2. False grandmothers, h.h.s

(*u*) Except the four females, daughter, son's daughter, h.l.s., full sister and consanguine sister.

(*v*) Except the above four.

(*w*) Tyabji §717.

(*x*) Ameer Ali, II, 57.

(*xx*) Mulla §67; *Ali Saheb* v. *Hajra Begaum* A.I.R. (1968) Mysore 357—widow, 1/4; 2 daughter's daughters, 3/8 each.

(*y*) Ameer Ali, II, 57; Wilson §240; Tyabji §718; Mulla §68.

GROUP III, COLLATERALS

(A) Descendants of Parents.

1. Full brother's daughters and their descendants.
2. Consanguine brother's daughters and their descendants.
3. Uterine brother's children and their descendants and remote relations as in Tyabji §718, Table, Nos. 9 onwards; Mulla §68, Class III.

(B) Descendants of Grandparents (true as well as false).

1. Full paternal aunt and her descendants.
2. Consanguine paternal aunt and her descendants.
3. Uterine paternal uncles and aunts and their descendants (z).
4. Full paternal uncle's daughters and their descendants.
5. Consanguine paternal uncle's daughters and their descendants.
6. Uterine paternal uncle's children and their descendants;

and *remoter relations* as in Tyabji, loc. cit., Nos. 15 onwards and Mulla §68, Class IV, read with §§75 sq.

It will be observed that collaterals are usually grouped in a different manner; Group III(A) is considered as Class III, and Group III(B) is called Class IV by Wilson (§240), and following him, by Mulla (§68). But it is submitted that the above classification, following as it does the principles of ancient Arabian law, is more scientific. The so-called Classes III and IV are sub-classes of a large genus, collaterals; and it is therefore best to define Group III as a limitless class of cognates (and female agnates), descended from parents and higher ascendants, and therefore sub-groups III(A) and III(B) are indeed only two of the limitless branches of a large tree. The student must bear in mind that there are

(z) The order is correctly stated in Tyabji §718.

not 'four' classes, but *innumerable branches* of Group III, collaterals.

A careful examination of *'aṣabāt* (Class II) and *dhawū'l-arḥām* (Class III) will reveal clearly that *between them they exhaust all possibilities of blood relationship to the deceased.*

It may be mentioned that the classification of Uterine Heirs in the *Sirājiyyah* (pp. 44-6) is not exhaustive. Wilson points out that the fourth class (corresponding to Group III(B) in our scheme) consists exclusively of children of grandparents, 'but inasmuch as the same work shows clearly that remoter blood relations may inherit as Distant Kindred, and therefore, must be included in the same class, I have ventured to disregard this limitation'.(*a*) This opinion is now regarded as correct (*b*), and accordingly a fuller classification is to be found in the modern text-books.

Principles of Distribution and Exclusion

Class III of the Sunnite heirs, the *dhawū'l-arḥām*, is a vast and complicated class, and it is therefore proposed to confine our discussion to a few salient principles and typical examples. In particular, Groups III(A) and (B) will be discussed with extreme brevity; and the reason is that the ordinary student should not be expected to digest anything more than what the illustrious author of the *Sirājiyyah* offers (*c*).

Rule 1. Members belonging to Class III succeed only in the absence of members of Class I and Class II. They also succeed if the only surviving heir of Class I is the husband or widow of the deceased. The Uterine Heirs are divided into three groups: (I) descendants, (II) ascendants, (III) collaterals; group (I) excludes group (II), and group (II) excludes group (III).

(*a*) §240, comment.

(*b*) Ameer Ali, II, 58; *Abdul Serang* v. *Putee Bibi* (1902) 29 Cal. 738. Mulla follows Wilson.

(*c*) A comparison between the authorities is interesting: the *Sirājiyyah* deals with the Uterine Heirs in 14 very small pages (45-58); Sircar (1873) in 36 pages (139-74); Tyabji in 18 pages (843-60); Wilson in 14 pages 281-94); Mulla in 22 pages (74-96). The most exhaustive treatment will be found in Sircar, Tyabji and Mulla.

Rule 2. Among descendants priority is determined by the application of the following two fundamental rules:

(i) The nearer in degree excludes the more remote. For example, a daughter's son or a daughter's daughter inherits in preference to a son's daughter's son. The first two are two degrees removed, and the last is three degrees removed from the deceased, and he is therefore excluded. In Pakistan this rule must be read subject to the Muslim Family Laws Ordinance, 1961 (*d*).

(ii) Where the degrees are equal, the children of Koranic Heirs and Agnatic Heirs are preferred to those of Uterine Heirs. For instance, a son's daughter's son, being the child of a Koranic Heir—the son's daughter—is preferred to the daughter's daughter's son, who is the son of a Uterine Heir (*e*).

Order of priority

1. Daughter's children.
2. Son's daughter's children.
3. Daughter's grandchildren.
4. Son's son's daughter's children and remoter heirs.

Of the above groups, each entirely excludes the group which follows (*f*).

Having determined on these principles who the heirs are, we proceed to the allotment of shares; and the following simple rules are to be noted.

Allotment of Shares (*ff*)

GROUP I, DESCENDANTS

Rule 1. If the intermediate ancestors *do not differ* in their sexes, the estate is divided among the heirs *per capita*, the males taking a double share. For example, (1) daughter's son = 2/3, daughter's daughter = 1/3. (2) Two sons of a daughter *A*, and one daughter of a daughter *B*. ds. = 2/5; ds. = 2/5; dd. = 1/5.

(*d*) Appendix E, below. Tyabji §§706(11), 714.
(*e*) Tyabji 717 sq; Mulla §69. (*f*) Tyabji, loc. cit.; Mulla §70.
(*ff*) Subject to the right of the surviving spouse, if any.

Rule 2. If the intermediate ancestors *differ* in their sexes, the distribution will take place according to the following rules (*g*).

(i) *Two claimants, two lines of descent*

The simplest case is where there are only two claimants, the one claiming through one line of ancestors and the other claiming through another line. A Muslim, Ibrāhīm, dies leaving a daughter's son's daughter, Fāṭima, and a daughter's daughter's son, Yūnus.

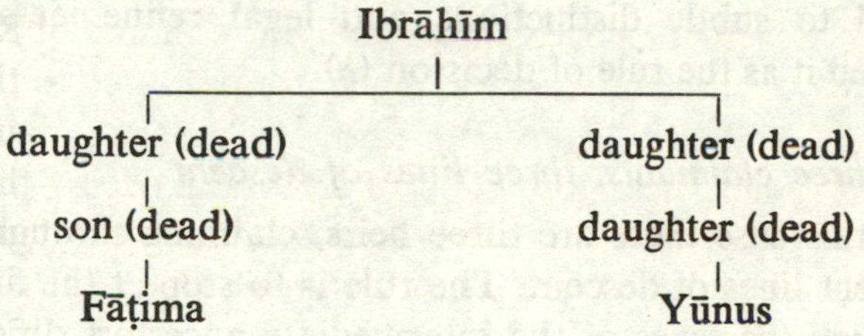

Here the following two points are to be noted; to begin with, both the heirs, Fāṭima and Yūnus, are three degrees removed; therefore, they are both entitled to succeed. The next question is the allotment of shares. Here two conceivable methods may be followed: (A) we may consider them as lineal descendants *simpliciter*, differing only in sex, and allot to Yūnus 2/3 and to Fāṭima 1/3, following the usual rule of distribution in Islam. This is the *scheme of the Cadi Abū Yūsuf*. His view was to disregard the sex of the intermediate ancestors and to allocate the shares on the basis of sex, male and female taking in the proportion of two to one.

This rule, simple as it is, is not followed in India.

(B) The second mode of distribution would be to pause at each degree where the sexes differ. In our case, the sexes do not differ in the first generation, and so there is no difficulty; but in the second generation, there is a son and a daughter. Allot to Fāṭima's *father* 2 shares, and allot to the

(*g*) On the allotment of shares among the Uterine Heirs of this group, a very clear and logical statement of the rules will be found in Mulla §71.

mother of Yūnus 1 share. Thus, Fāṭima would obtain 2 shares, and Yūnus 1 share.

This is the rule followed in India. It is the opinion accepted by al-Sajāwandī, the author of *Sirājiyyah,* who adopted the Doctrine of Imām Muḥammad al-Shaybānī, the younger disciple of Abū Ḥanīfa, in preference to that of the senior disciple, the Cadi Abū Yūsuf. The doctrine of Imām Muḥammad is unfortunately much more complex for the man in the street and causes needless difficulty to students; it is therefore not surprising that lawyers, habitually accustomed to subtle distinctions and legal refinements, have adopted it as the rule of decision (*h*).

(ii) *Three claimants, three lines of descent*

In this case there are three heirs, claiming through three different lines of descent. The rule is to stop at the first line in which the sexes of the intermediate ancestors differ, and to assign to each male ancestor a double portion. But the individual share of each ancestor does not descend to his or her descendants as in the preceding case, but the collective share of all the male ancestors will be divided among all the descendants claiming through them, and the collective share of all the female ancestors will be divided among their descendants. In these two groups the division will be in accordance with the rule of a double share to the male. For example—

A Muslim dies leaving a dsd., a dds., and a ddd., as shown below:

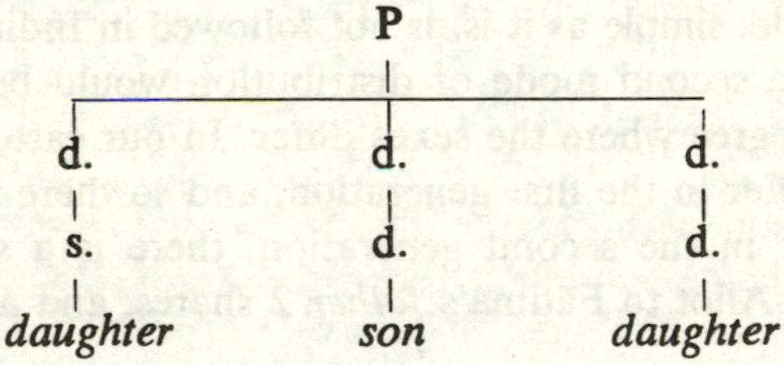

(*h*) *wa 'alayhi'l-fatwā*, as the Arabs have it.

In this case, *two steps* are to be taken: (i) the notional collection of shares; and (ii) the actual distribution. The ancestors differ in sex in the second line of descent, therefore—

ds. = 1/2
dd. = 1/4 } Collective share of females = 1/2.
dd. = 1/4 }

Now comes the second step. The daughter's son stands alone and his share descends to his daughter. The collective share of the two daughter's daughters is equal to a moiety of the estate, and it will be distributed among their descendants, male and female taking in the proportion of 2 to 1. Thus—

dds.—$2/3 \times 1/2 = 1/3$
ddd.—$1/3 \times 1/2 = 1/6$.

Hence the final result is dsd. = 1/2
dds. = 1/3
ddd. = 1/6.

According to the scheme of Abū Yūsuf, the division would be— dds. = 1/2
dsd. = 1/4
ddd. = 1/4 (*i*).

(iii) *More than two claimants, two lines*

A more complicated case must now be considered, and it may be illustrated by the following genealogical tree:

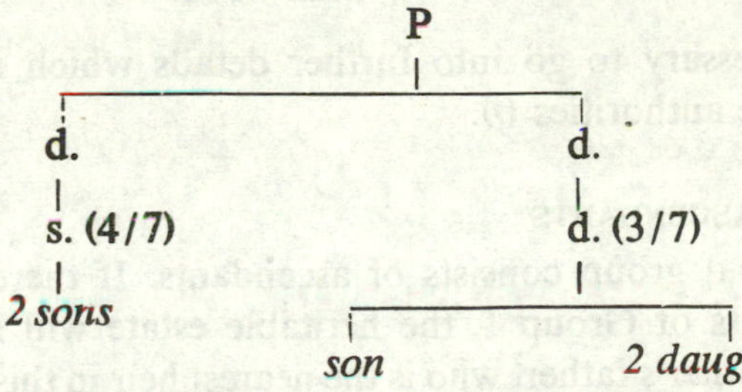

Here the ancestors differ in the second generation. The peculiarity in the case above is that the daughter's son will count as *two males* because he has two surviving heirs, and the

(*i*) For further cases, see Tyabji §720; Mulla §71.

daughter's daughter will count as *three females* because three of her descendants are among the surviving heirs. Thus we have—

ds. = 4/7

dd. = 3/7.

The 4/7 of ds. will go to his two sons equally so that each dss. will obtain 2/7.

The 3/7 of dd. will go to her son and 2 daughters, the son taking twice the share of the daughter, thus dds. will get 2/4 × 3/7 = 6/28, and each ddd. will get 1/4 × 3/7 = 3/28.

The final distribution is—

dss. = 8/28 }
dss. = 8/28 }
dds. = 6/28
ddd. = 3/28 }
ddd. = 3/28 }

According to the system of Abū Yūsuf, we entirely disregard the intermediate ancestors and arrive at the following simple result:

As *males* { dss. = 2/8
dss. = 2/8 }
dds. = 2/8
As *females* { ddd. = 1/8
ddd. = 1/8. }

It is unnecessary to go into further details which may be found in the authorities (*j*).

Group II, Ascendants

The second group consists of ascendants. If there be no Uterine Heirs of Group I, the heritable estate will devolve upon the mother's father, who is the nearest heir in this group.

If there be no mother's father, the heritable estate will be distributed between those 'false grandparents' in the third degree who are connected with the deceased through a

(*j*) Tyabji, loc. cit.; Wilson §§244 sqq.; Mulla §71(c), ill. (a).

Koranic Heir, namely the father of the father's mother and the father of the mother's mother. Of these two, although they are both of the same sex, the former, as belonging to the paternal side, will take two-thirds, and the latter, as belonging to the maternal side, will take one-third.

In default of the relatives last mentioned, the property will be distributed between the remaining false grandparents, in the third and higher degrees.

The rules of distribution are succinctly summarized by Mulla as follows: Allot the share to the husband or wife, if any, and—

Rule 1. The nearer in degree excludes the more remote.

Rule 2. Among claimants in the same degree, those connected with the deceased through Koranic Heirs are preferred to those connected through Uterine Heirs.

Rule 3. Where there are claimants both on the paternal and on the maternal side, 2/3 is assigned to the paternal side and 1/3 to the maternal side. The portion assigned to the paternal side is then divided among the ancestors of the father, and the portion assigned to the maternal side among the ancestors of the mother.

According to Abū Yūsuf, each male receives twice the share of a female in his own group; and according to Imām Muḥammad, the complicated system mentioned in Group I of the Uterine Heirs is to be followed (*k*).

Group III, Collaterals

The third group consists of collaterals, sub-group (A) comprising nephews and nieces, and their descendants, and sub-group (B) comprising uncles and aunts and their descendants.

According to the classification of Sir William Jones in his translation of the *Sirājiyyah*, sub-groups (A) and (B) were

(*k*) Wilson §§246-8; Tyabji §719 sqq.; Mulla §72.

called Classes III and IV of the Distant Kindred. This was adopted by Rumsey (*l*), and later by Sircar (*m*), Ameer Ali (*n*), Wilson (*o*), and Mulla (*p*). Tyabji, characterically, adopts a modern and more scientific classification (*q*).

Cases relating to Uterine Heirs of Group III arise but rarely, and no new principles of social justice are established or new canons of juristic reasoning advanced; hence, after careful consideration, it has been thought advisable not to increase the student's burden by a full treatment of the subject. The practitioner and the curious reader, intent upon delving into the mysteries of this vast and complicated class, are referred to the standard works of Wilson, Tyabji and Mulla, where the simple rules laid down in the *Sirājiyyah* have been worked out with a mathematical precision and legal acumen which would have gladdened the hearts of the ancient jurists of Baghdad and Samarkand (*r*).

§95. Miscellaneous Rules

1. *Step-parent, step-child.* A step-parent or step-child is not entitled to inherit from a step-child or step-parent, respectively (*s*).

2. *Missing person as heir.* The ancient Islamic law contains some quaint rules regarding the *mafqūd al-khabar*, a person whose whereabouts are unknown. The Hanafi authorities lay down the rule that if a person dies, and his heir is missing, his share of the inheritance may in some cases be kept aside for a period of 60, 70 or even 90 years (*t*). But modern authorities hold the view that these rules have now

(*l*) *Sirājiyyah*, 52-8.

(*m*) *Muhammadan Law* (1873), 161-73.

(*n*) ii, 57-67.

(*o*) §§239-61.

(*p*) §§67-71.

(*q*) §§717 sqq.

(*r*) Reference may also be made to M. S. U. Jung, *Muslim Law of Inheritance*, Allahabad, 1934.

(*s*) Macnaghten, 99, Cases xxi and xxii.

(*t*) Ameer Ali, II, 92, 94.

become obsolete, and the presumptions contained in the Indian Evidence Act, Secs. 107 and 108 apply (*u*).

3. *Homicide.* In Hanafi law one who has unlawfully killed the deceased, whether intentionally or unintentionally, has no right to inherit any portion of the deceased's estate, Tyabji §706 (6). For Shiite Law see §100 (8), below.

4. *Death in a common calamity.* When two or more persons perish together in a common calamity and it is impossible to ascertain which of them died first, they do not inherit one from the other. For instance, if husband and wife, or father and son are killed by a bomb or lost at sea or perish in an earthquake, *neither* inherits from the other, but the property of each is distributed amongst his or her heirs, ignoring the existence of the other. Hence the husband's relations inherit his property, and the wife's relations succeed to her property. Similarly, as between father and son; the inheritance is distributed simply as if the other did not exist (*v*).

This rule is convenient in the case of Muslims; for it has recently been held by the Privy Council that when two individuals perish in a common calamity and the question arises as to which of them died first, in the absence of evidence there is in India no presumption, as in English law by statute, that the younger survived the elder. Such a question is a pure question of fact and the onus of proof lies on the party who makes the assertion (*w*)

5. *Other schools.* The law of inheritance, as stated above, is according to the Hanafi school of Sunnite law, the main authority recognized in India being the *Sirājiyyah* of Sajāwandī, translated by Sir William Jones, and published later by A. Rumsey (2nd edition, Calcutta, 1890).

(*u*) Tyabji §§708 sq.; Wilson §269A; Mulla §86. Ameer Ali's dissent, however, is worthy of careful consideration, II, 96.

(*v*) Ameer Ali, II, 76; Fitzgerald, 157-8.

(*w*) *K. S. Agha Mir Ahmad Shah* v. *Mudassir Shah* (1944) 71 I.A. 171, (1944) 47 Bom. L.R. 591.

For the law of other schools the following may be consulted.

SHĀFI'Ī LAW: Ed. Sachau, *Muhammedanisches Recht nach schafiitischer Lehre* (Stüttgart and Berlin), 1897; Th. W. Juynboll, *Handbuch des islāmischen Gesetzes* (Leiden, Leipzig), 1910; Wilson, 6th ed., pp. 425-9.

MĀLIKĪ LAW: Rarely applicable in India, but references to both the Mālikī and Shāfi'ī law will be found in Ameer Ali, II, 96-101, and in Fitzgerald throughout his treatment of inheritance in Chapters xiv to xvi and xviii; see also appendixes I and II. F. Ruxton, *Mālikī Law* (London), 1916, and D. Santillana, *Istituzioni di Diritto Musulmano Malichita*, 2 vols., Rome, 1938, may also be consulted.

ḤANBALĪ LAW: No cases seem to have occurred in India, and apparently the subject has not been dealt with in English.

N.B. Professor N. J. Coulson's *Succession in the Muslim Family* (Cambridge University Press, 1971) came to my hands only in January 1973, and, unfortunately, I was not able to use it for revising this chapter. Where his opinions differ from the text-writers on Anglo-Muhammadan law such as Macnaghten, Rumsey, Ameer Ali, Wilson, Tyabji or Mulla, it will be for the courts to decide what the correct rule for application is. The learned professor is somewhat chary of citing the original authorities for some of his propositions, and this may lead to doubt and difficulty in dealing with actual cases.

CHAPTER XIV

THE SHIITE LAW OF INHERITANCE

§96. General Principles and Classification of Heirs
§97. Class I §98. Class II §99 Class III
§100. Anomalies, Miscellaneous Rules
§101. Sunnite and Shiite systems compared

§96. General Principles and Classification of Heirs

THE principles of the Ithnā 'Asharī Shiite law—commonly known as 'Shia law' in India—are very different from the principles of Hanafi law and require separate consideration. They are also of great practical importance because the courts are often called upon to determine cases governed by the law of this school.

According to the Ithnā 'Asharī school of jurisprudence, two causes give rise to a claim for inheritance:

A. *Nasab* (blood relationship), and
B. *Sabab* (special cause).

A. *Nasab* is subdivided into two groups:

(i) *dhū farḍ* (Koranic heir) (*a*),
(ii) *dhū qarābat* (blood relation, agnate or cognate) (*b*).

B. *Sabab* is also subdivided into two groups:

(i) *zawjiyyat* (the status of a spouse),
(ii) *walā'* (special legal relationship).

Walā' is of three kinds—

1. *walā'* of *'itq* (right of emancipation),
2. *walā'* of *ḍāmin al-jarīrah* (right of obligation for delicts committed by the deceased),
3. *walā'* of Imāmate (right by virtue of religious leadership).

(1) and (2) are obsolete in India; (3) is replaced by the law of escheat (*c*).

(*a*) Usually spelt *zu farz*; plural, *dhawū'l-furūḍ*.
(*b*) plural, *dhawū'l-qarābat*.
(*c*) Ameer Ali, II, 101-6; Students' 7th ed., §§47-54 (pp. 55-8); Baillie, II, 261-3. Ameer Ali, II, 134, has a useful table.

The Fatimid Law of inheritance, which governs the Dā'ūdī and Sulaymānī Bohoras of the Musta'lian branch of the Ismā'ilī Shī'a, is similar in nature, and its main principles will be found in the *Da'ā'im al-Islām*, Volume II (*d*).

We now proceed to a detailed examination of heirs according to the principles of *nasab* and *sabab*.

A. Nasab (*Blood Relationship*)

Heirs by consanguinity are divided into three classes and each class is divided into two groups:

Class I. Section (i)—Parents.
Section (ii)—Children and lineal descendants, h.l.s.

Class II. Section (i)—Grandparents, h.h.s.
Section (ii)—Brothers and sisters and their descendants.

Class III. Section (i)—Paternal, and
Section (ii)—Maternal uncles and aunts of the deceased, and of his parents and grandparents, h.h.s. and their descendants, h.l.s. (*e*).

These classes may be illustrated by simple diagrams (see inset facing this page).

Class I excludes Class II; likewise, Class II excludes Class III. But the heirs of the two sections in each class take together, and do *not* exclude each other.

A few simple illustrations will show the difference between the Sunnite and Shiite schools.

(*d*) Qāḍī Nu'mān, *Da'ā'im*, ed. Fyzee, II (2nd ed., Cairo, 1967), pp. 365-400, §§1329-1403. See also the writer's 'The Fatimid Law of Inheritance' in *Studia Islamica* (Paris, 1958), IX, 61-9; and *Compendium of Fatimid Law* (Simla, 1969), pp. xxxvii sq. and Ch. v, pp. 97 sqq.

(*e*) Tyabji §§730 sqq.; Wilson §§450 sqq.; Mulla §§88 sqq.

Class One

F ○ M *(Section I)*

P ⊖

S ○ D

Descendants, h.l.s.
(Section II)

Class Two

↑

Higher Ancestors (paternal and maternal) } *(Section I)*

Grandparents

F ○ M

P ⊖   B ○ S

(Section II)

Class Three

FFF ○

FF ○   Father's Uncle (or Aunt) ○

F ○   Uncle (or Aunt) ○

P ⊖

Paternal uncles and aunts and their descendants constitute Section I; and maternal uncles and aunts and their descendants constitute Section II. The same diagram may therefore stand for both the sections.

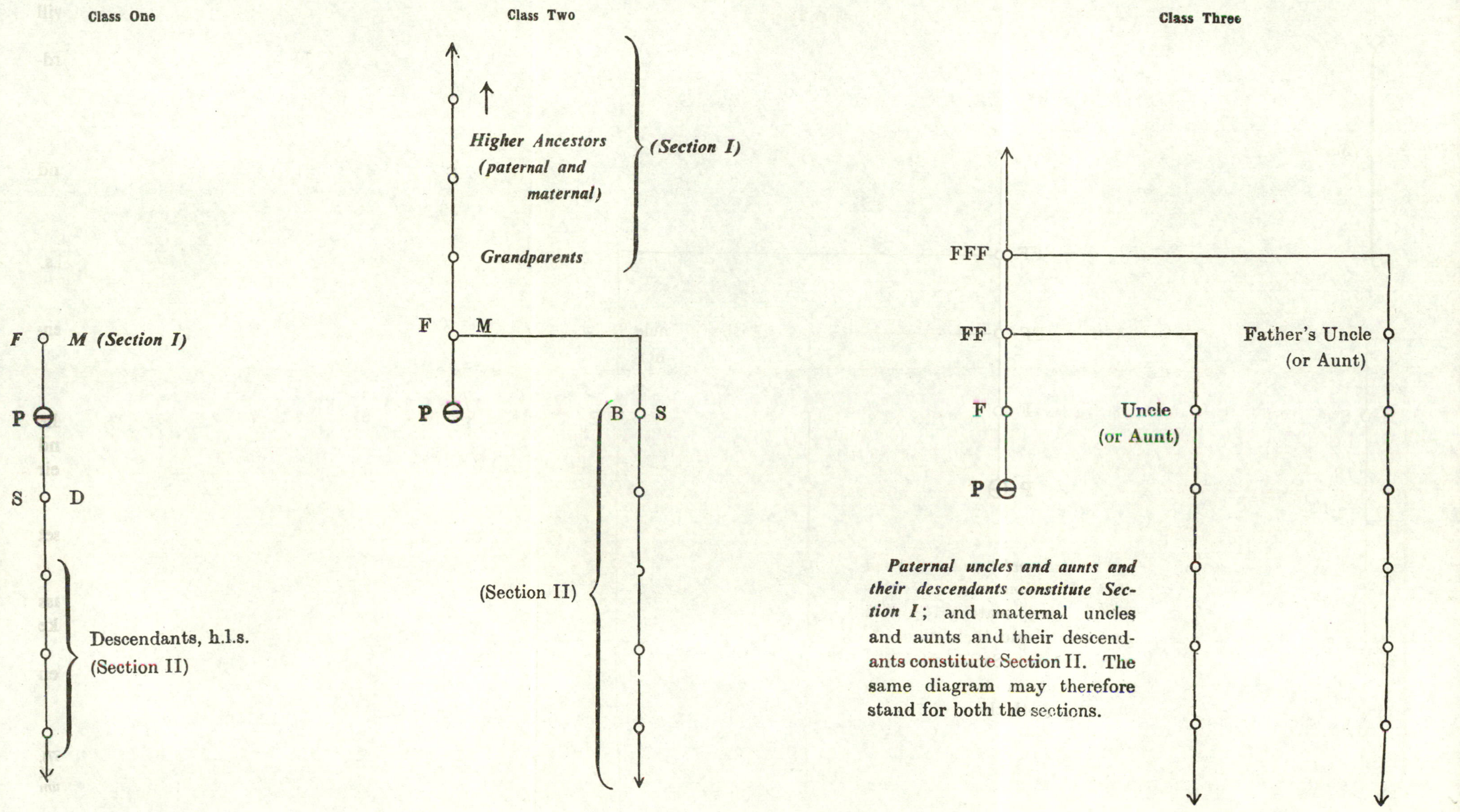

(1) Mother, daughter, brother (*f*).

By Hanafi law—m.=1/6; d.=3/6; b.=2/6.

By Ithnā ʻAsharī (Shiite) law the brother, belonging to Class II, is excluded; and the division between the mother and daughter is in proportion to their original shares. The Koranic shares would be 1/6 and 1/2 (= 3/6), respectively. Therefore, m. = 1/4; d. = 3/4 (*g*).

(2) Daughter's son, father's mother, full brother (*h*).

By Hanafi law, the daughter's son being a Uterine Heir is excluded; the father's mother, as a Koranic Heir, takes 1/6; and the full brother, as an Agnatic Heir, takes 5/6.

In Shiite law, the daughter's son, being an heir of the first class, succeeds in preference to the other two, who belong to the second class. On this point, it may be observed that in the Shiite scheme the daughter's children are in a very high category. Imām Ḥusayn was a daughter's son of the Prophet, and the Shiite law apparently pays particular attention to this relationship, and arranges the inheritance so that instead of being postponed as heirs of Class III, they come in as members of the first class (*i*).

(3) Brother's daughter, full paternal uncle.

In Hanafi law the brother's daughter is a Uterine Heir, and is postponed to the paternal uncle who is an Agnatic Heir. In Shiite law the brother's daughter belongs to Class II, and takes in preference to the uncle, who is placed in Class III (*j*).

It is unnecessary to give further illustrations, which can be

(*f*) Wilson §457.

(*g*) The illustration represents the facts in *Rajah Deedar Hossein* v. *Ranee Zuhoor-oon Nissa* (1841) 2 Moore's I.A. 441; *Cases,* 490, which is the leading case for the application of Shiite law in India.

(*h*) Mulla §88, ill. (a).

(*i*) Fitzgerald, 145; *Fat. Law* §§393-401.

(*j*) Mulla §88, ill. (b).

found in Ameer Ali (*k*), Wilson (*l*), Tyabji (*m*) and Mulla (*n*).

A modern classification of Shiite heirs is:

(I) *Koranic Heirs,* persons whose portions are fixed by the Koran, called *dhū farḍ*, for example the mother and the wife.

(II) Those who sometimes inherit as Koranic Heirs (*dhū farḍ*) and sometimes by virtue of their blood relationship (*dhū qarābat*), for instance the father, the daughter alone and the daughter with the son, the full or consanguine sister alone, and the sister with the brother.

(III) Those who take only by reason of relationship, *dhū qarābat*, for example the son, the uncle, the uncle's son, etc. (*o*).

§97. Shiite Heirs—Class I

From this general scheme, we must now proceed to enumerate the Koranic Heirs, and the following are in this category (*p*).

KORANIC HEIR—*dhū farḍ*.

By Affinity:
1. ***Husband***, always inherits, 1/2 or 1/4.
2. ***Wife***, always inherits, 1/4 or 1/8, singly or jointly.

(*k*) The illustrations given by Ameer Ali contain many cases where the distribution of the inheritance would be identical in the two systems, Ameer Ali, II, 110 sqq.

(*l*) §457.

(*m*) §§740 sqq.

(*n*) §88.

(*o*) Ameer Ali, II, 106-7; Students' 7th ed., p. 60.

(*p*) The most exhaustive and systematic treatment of Shiite inheritance is to be found in Tyabji §§740 sqq. and in Sircar, II, 165 sqq. Mulla §§88 sqq. is practical, but his use of the terms 'Sharers' and 'Residuaries' is open to question. The terms are bad enough in Hanafi law; but, to continue to use the *same* terms in Ithnā 'Asharī law, for a scheme which is totally distinct, is hardly justifiable, although he only follows in the footsteps of other eminent authors. For the student, the best summary treatment is to be found in Ameer Ali, Students' 7th ed., 55-65.

By Consanguinity:

3. *Father*, (i) when there are descendants, takes 1/6, as *dhū farḍ*;
(ii) when no descendants, takes as *dhū qarābat*.

4. *Mother*, always inherits, 1/3 or 1/6.

5. *Daughter*, always inherits, 1/2 or jointly 2/3, as *dhū farḍ*; or with son, as *dhū qarābat*.

6. *Full sister*, 1/2 or jointly 2/3; with brother inherits as *dhū qarābat*.

7. *Consanguine sister*, 1/2 or jointly 2/3 with consanguine brother, inherits as *dhū qarābat*.

8. and **9.** *Uterine brother or sister*, 1/6 or jointly and equally, 1/3.

The following heirs, classed by Hanafi jurists as Koranic Heirs, are omitted by the Shiites: (1) Son's daughter, h.l.s., (2) True grandfather, h.h.s. and (3) True grandmother, h.h.s. (*q*).

PRIORITIES (*r*). The structure of the Shiite law is much simpler than that of the Hanafi law, and it is best to begin with the husband and the wife. The practical rule is first to assign the share to the spouse, and then to proceed to examine the claims of other heirs.

1. Husband. The share is 1/2 if there are no children, and 1/4 if there are.

2. Wife. She takes 1/4 if there are no children, and 1/8 if there are.

The 1/4 or 1/8 is equally divided among the wives if there be more than one. Thus if a Shiite marries four wives, A1, A2, A3 and A4, and one of them, A4, *has children*, each of the wives will receive 1/32 of the estate (*s*). The childless widows, however, will be under certain disabilities.

(*q*) Tyabji, loc. cit. Mulla, compare tables on pp. 58A and 102.

(*r*) Tyabji §739, Principles of Priority in Shiite law.

(*s*) Sircar, II, 739.

Childless widow. A childless widow does not take her share from the immovable property of her husband; but she is entitled to her proper share in the value of the household effects, trees, buildings, and movable property, including debts due to the deceased (*t*). The exact meaning of the expression 'childless widow' is in doubt. Does it mean a woman who *has had* no children, or does it merely imply that the widow *has* no children *living* at the time of the death of her husband? This question has not yet been finally settled (*u*).

Fatimid Law. The Fatimid law does not exclude a childless widow, nor does it countenance the diminution of the widow's share, whether in movable or in immovable property, *Da'ā'im,* II §§1341-3, 1394; *Fatimid Law* §458.

The previous statement made by me in *Studia Islamica,* IX, 61, 68 was an error, which is regretted. The reasons for the error will be found in *Fatimid Law,* cited above.

Spouse as sole heir. If the widow is the sole surviving heir of the deceased, the early texts laid down that she was entitled only to her Koranic share, one-fourth (*v*) and the residue, three-fourths of the estate, went to the Imām, and by modern law would escheat to the State. But Ameer Ali says 'As there is no machinery now to take charge of the Imām's share, the ancient doctrine enunciated in the *Sharā'i' al-Islām* is completely exploded,' (w) and goes on to show that certain later jurists, in these circumstances, allowed the wife to take the residue as well. The Indian courts have adopted this humane and just course (*x*).

Thus, in the absence of all other heirs, the husband or the wife takes the whole of the property.

The Fatimid jurist Nu'mān reports two decisions from Ali who decided to give the whole of the property to the sur-

(*t*) Tyabji §740(2); Mulla §113.

(*u*) Tyabji, loc. cit., com. The author also gives some curious illustrations from ancient texts.

(*v*) The texts do not mention the husband; hence, presumably, the limitation does not apply to him.

(*w*) Ameer Ali, II, 123, footnote (3).

(*x*) ibid., II, 124; Tyabji §750; Mulla §92.

viving spouse, when no other heir existed. It is therefore clear that this rule, three centuries older than that of the *Sharā'i'*, would prevail among all branches of the Shī'a, *Da'ā'im*, II §1390, p. 393; *Fat. Law* §454.

3. Father. 4. Mother. If the deceased leaves any descendant, the father or mother or both, the parents are treated as belonging to the class *dhū farḍ*, and each of them takes 1/6.

If there are no descendants, the father is treated as belonging to the class *dhū qarābat*, and takes the residue after the allotment of the shares of the husband or wife and the mother.

The mother takes 1/3 where there are no descendants and 1/6 where (i) there are descendants, or (ii) there are the father and two or more brothers, full or consanguine, and in certain other cases (y).

For example (1) Husband, mother, father.

h. = 1/2 }
m. = 1/3 } as Koranic Heirs.
f. = 1/6 as blood relation.

(2) Wife, mother, father.

w. = 1/4 }
m. = 1/3 } as Koranic Heirs.
f. = 5/12 as blood relation.

Compare Sunnite law, Mother, Case 4, p. 407 above (z).

(3) Father, mother, son.

f. = 1/6 }
m. = 1/6 } as Koranic Heirs, Section I.
s. = 2/3 as Koranic Heir, Class I, Section II.

(4) Father, mother, 2 daughters.

f. = 1/6 as Koranic Heir, Section I, because there are daughters.
m. = 1/6 as Koranic Heir, Section I.
2d. = 2/3 as Koranic Heirs, Section II (*a*).

(y) For details, see Tyabji §741 sqq; Mulla §96.

(z) These two decisions in Sunnite law were those of the Caliph Omar, and were not accepted by the Shiites.

(*a*) Mulla §96, ills. (a) to (d); for father, see Wilson §456.

5. Eldest son. The eldest son in Shiite law enjoys certain special privileges which remind us of primogeniture and the legitimistic tendencies prevalent amongst the Shī'a as a rule. If the deceased, being a male, has left more sons than one, the eldest son is entitled to take as his special perquisite the garments of the deceased, his signet ring, sword and Koran. On the other hand, the son is solely responsible for any religious obligations, such as prayers, alms, pilgrimage, and so forth, which the deceased may have left unperformed (*b*).

The Fatimid law is identical (*c*).

6. Daughter (*d*) (i) Where there is a son, he takes the residue, after allotting portions to the Koranic Heirs.

(ii) Where the daughter survives with him, she shares the residue with him in the proportion of 1 to 2.

(iii) When the daughter survives and there is no son, she takes 1/2 alone, and 2/3 jointly with other daughters (*e*).

Daughter's share. The daughter's share, as in Sunnite law, is one half of the share of the son. This is a rule of general application to female heirs, and it is sometimes asked why there should be such a disparity between the sexes. A Shiite explanation, in the shape of a report handed down from Imām Ja'far al-Ṣādiq, is well worth repeating. It is said that some one doubted the wisdom of such a limitation, particularly as the female is the weaker vessel. The Imām replied: 'A female is excused from the performance of many duties imposed by law upon a male, such as service in the holy wars, maintenance or support of relations, and payment of expiatory fines, and for this reason her share of inheritance has been justly limited to half the portion of a male.'(*f*)

7. Grandchildren. We now come to a striking peculiarity of Ithnā 'Asharī law. In the absence of children, the

(*b*) Wilson §453; Ameer Ali, II, 111; Tyabji §742, n. 19; Mulla §112.
(*c*) *Da'ā'im*, II §1393; *Fat. Law* §457.
(*d*) It will be seen that the daughter's share is closely affected by that of the son; hence, the son has to be mentioned.
(*e*) Tyabji §742.
(*f*) Tyabji, loc. cit., citing Baillie, II, 385.

grandchildren stand in the shoes of their respective parents, and inherit in accordance with a rule of representation which requires explanation. Fitzgerald rightly observes that 'the Shia doctrine of representation is merely the *madhhab ahli tanzīl* (*g*), lifted from the position of a postscript to the centre of the scheme'.(*h*)

Principles of Distribution

'Representation' and Stirpital Succession. If the deceased leaves only one heir, the whole of the property goes to him or to her. If such heir is the wife, the older view was that she took 1/4, and the remaining 3/4 escheated to the Imām. Ameer Ali, however, took the view that the residue, in modern times, should also be inherited by the wife; and, as we have noted above, this is the accepted doctrine in the courts (*i*).

If the deceased leaves more than one heir, the *dhū farḍ* (Koranic Heir) must first be assigned his or her share; and the simplest way of beginning is to assign the share to the husband or wife.

After this has been done, we come to the second stage, and here it is necessary to determine two questions, logically distinct from each other, namely:

(i) *Who are the heirs entitled to inherit?* and

(ii) *What are their individual shares?*

Much confusion of thought can be avoided if these two questions are considered separately and understood.

The word 'representation' has several meanings in law. For instance, we may speak of representation to the estate of a man deceased, and in this context we speak of 'personal

(*g*) This is a species of representation to be found among the Shāfi'īs and briefly discussed by Fitzgerald, 145 and Appendix II, 228-9. There are very few Shāfi'īs in India, to be found mostly on the western coast, notably the Kōknīs of Bombay and the Moors of Ceylon, and the matter need not be dealt with at greater length.

(*h*) Fitzgerald, 145. For Fatimid law, see *Fat. Law* §§397, 398, 401.

(*i*) See above, pp. 417-18, and *Abdul Hamid Khan* v. *Piare Mirza* (1934) 10 Luck. 550, discussing original texts.

representatives', that is, executors and administrators. The meaning of this is made clear by a study of the Indian Succession Act, 1925, and it is unnecessary to dilate upon it.

The second meaning is the process whereby one person is said to 'represent' the share receivable by him through another person, who was himself an heir. A perfect example of this is to be found in the Hindu law of succession. For the purposes of our discussion we are concerned with the second meaning.

We may repeat that when a man dies, two questions arise: (i) which of the surviving relations are entitled to inherit, and, *after determining this question*, (ii) what are the exact shares they take?

For the purpose of determining *the right to inherit*, neither the Sunnite nor the Shiite law recognizes the right of representation. But for determining *the quantum of the share* a species of representation is employed among Uterine Heirs in Hanafi law (*j*) and in the Ithnā 'Asharī Shiite law (*k*).

We shall proceed to consider each of these *two* questions independently.

For the law in Pakistan, see Appendix E, below.

Question 1. Who is the heir?

To determine this we must apply the following rules:

Rule—The nearer excludes the more remote (*l*).

Illustration. If a person dies leaving a son Ali, and the son of a predeceased son, Bāqir, the son Ali entirely excludes the grandson Bāqir. The Sunnite and Shiite schools are unanimous on this point. This rule is entirely different from the rule of Hindu succession, and in considering 'representation' it is well to regard this as a cardinal rule (*m*).

(*j*) Called ***madhhab ahli tanzīl***, **Fitzgerald, 119, 145, Appendix II.**

(*k*) Fitzgerald, 150, shows that this is similar to Ḥanbalī, Shāfiʿī and Zaydī law. The Fatimid law is identical, *Fat. Law*, op. cit.

(*l*) Compare al-Jabarī, Rule B, p. 424, above.

(*m*) Baillie, II, 276, 280, 285; Tyabji §§730(1), 739, com. 1; Mulla §93(1).

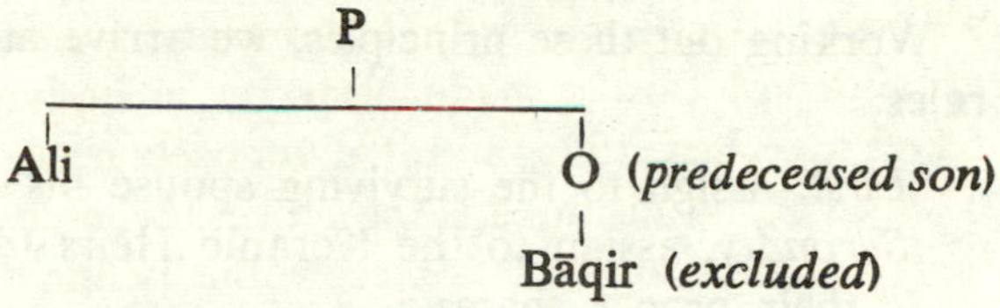

Question 2. What is his share?

Rule—Stirpital succession. When P dies leaving three grandsons, one (Ali) by a predeceased son, and two (Ḥasan and Ḥusayn) by another predeceased son; all the grandsons are heirs, and we have to proceed to distribute the estate. In such cases, to find the quanṭum of the share taken, we have to apply a rule akin to 'representation' as explained above.

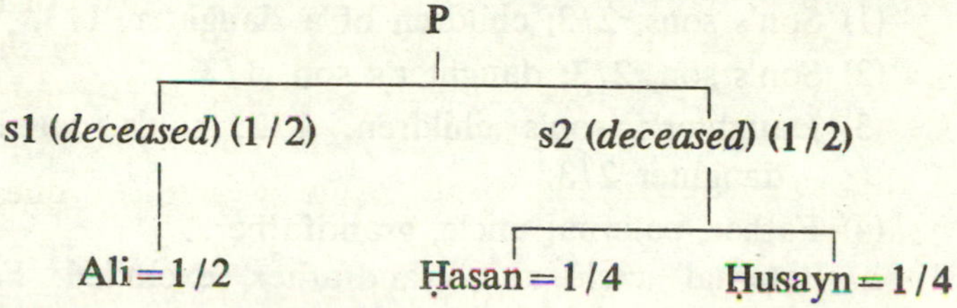

Here s1 and s2, the sons of the deceased, will be allotted a moiety each. Ali will obtain his father s1's half share; Ḥasan and Ḥusayn will receive a quarter each, dividing equally the moiety assigned to their father, s2.

This is nothing but stirpital succession (*n*); and it is therefore submitted that 'representation' as an explanatory term can and should be avoided (*o*). Thus, if there is a Koranic share fixed for some relation, then that share descends to his descendants, the residue going to the other blood relations (*dhawū'l-qarābat*). The surviving relations, let us say, are a uterine brother's son and a full brother's daughter. The uterine brother's 1/6 will go to his son, and the full brother's residuary portion, 5/6, will go to his daughter (*p*).

(*n*) Or succession by stock, or *per stirpes*.
(*o*) Ameer Ali, II, 108; Wilson §461; Tyabji §742, and esp. the rules from Sir William Jones's *Digest*, cited at p. 880. Mulla §§93-4.
(*p*) Mulla §96.

Working out these principles, we arrive at the following rules:

First, assign to the surviving spouse his or her share;
Secondly, assign to the Koranic Heirs (*dhawū'l-furūḍ*), their proper shares;
Thirdly, assign the residue among the blood relations (*dhawū'l-qarābat*), applying the Shiite rules of distribution (*q*).

The anomalous cases of 'Increase' or 'Return' will be dealt with later.

Illustrations

(1) Son's sons, 2/3; children of a daughter, 1/3.
(2) Son's son, 2/3; daughter's son, 1/3.
(3) Daughter's son's children, 1/3; son's daughter's daughter, 2/3.
(4) Father, paternal uncle, grandfather.
Paternal uncle and grandfather, excluded. Father takes the whole estate.
(5) Husband, 1/4; mother, 1/6; sons and daughters or their descendants take the residual 7/12 dividing it stirpitally, males taking twice the share of females (*r*).

§98. Shiite Heirs—Class II

The second class consists of two sections: section (i) comprises grandparents, paternal and maternal, howsoever high, and section (ii), brothers and sisters, and their descendants, howsoever low. The two sections do not exclude each other, but among the members of each section the nearest succeed. For example, the mother's mother (two degrees removed)

(*q*) Tyabji, loc. cit.; Wilson §§45 sqq.

(*r*) These and other illustrations will be found in Tyabji and Ameer Ali, II, 108 sqq.

excludes the father's father's father (three degrees removed), and the sister excludes the brother's son (*s*).

As the heirs are divided into two sections, there are three possibilities. The surviving relations may be—

(1) Ascendants, without collaterals;
(2) Collaterals, without ascendants;
(3) Both ascendants and collaterals (*t*).

1. Ascendants, without collaterals

(A) To begin with, assign the share of the husband or wife;
(B) then, *divide the residue* according to the following rules:

(i) Assign 1/3 of the ESTATE to the maternal side, and the residue to the paternal side, thus—

The surviving relations are ff., fm., mf. and mm.
Assign 1/3 to mf. and mm., and
the residue to ff. and fm.

(ii) *Maternal side*. The maternal grandparents take their portion, the one-third, and divide it between themselves, male and female sharing *equally*.
Therefore, mf.—$1/2 \times 1/3 = 1/6$;
mm.—$1/2 \times 1/3 = 1/6$.

If there is only one maternal grandparent, mf. or mm., he or she will take the entire 1/3.

(iii) *Paternal side*. Then take the *paternal side*; the residue is to be divided according to the double share to the male.
Therefore, ff. = residue × 2/3;
fm. = residue × 1/3.

If there is only one survivor on the paternal side, ff. or fm., he or she takes the entire 2/3.

(*s*) A very clear and logical discussion will be found in Tyabji §742, read with the principles at pp. 876 sqq.

(*t*) Mulla §97.

Failing immediate grandparents, the property goes to remoter ascendants on the same principles of distribution, the nearer rigorously excluding the more remote (*u*).

It should be noted that the maternal side gets its full one-third share, as the principle of *ta'ṣīb* is not recognized by the Shī'a.

2. Collaterals, without ascendants

(A) *Brothers and Sisters only*

Assign the share of the husband or wife and divide the residue in accordance with the following rules:

(i) Brothers and sisters of the full blood exclude consanguine brothers and sisters.

(ii) Uterine brothers and sisters are not excluded by full or consanguine brothers and sisters; they take 1/6 or 1/3 according to their number.

(iii) Full, and in their absence, consanguine brothers take the residue.

(iv) Full sisters (without full brothers); or, failing them, consanguine sisters (without consanguine brothers) take the Koranic share of 1/2 or 2/3 according to their number (*v*).

(v) The full or consanguine brother takes double the share of the sister; the uterine brothers and sisters take equally, brother and sister sharing *alike*.

Illustrations

(1) One full brother (or in his absence, cb.), there being no other claimant, takes the whole estate.

(2) Two such brothers divide the estate equally.

(3) Two full sisters and one full brother. Estate divided into four shares—fb. = 1/2, fss. = 1/4 each.

(4) One single sister, full or consanguine. 1/2 as Koranic Heir, 1/2 by return.

(*u*) Wilson §§462-3; Tyabji §§743-44; Mulla §98.

(*v*) Wilson §464; Tyabji §744; Mulla §99.

(5) One uterine brother (or sister); one full or consanguine sister. ub. = 1/6; s.(f. or c.) = 1/2 as Koranic share *plus* 1/3 by return = 5/6.

(6) Two uterine sisters; uterine brother; consanguine sister. Uterine brother and sisters will share their one-third equally, thus:

$$\left.\begin{array}{l}\text{ub.} = 1/9\\ \text{us.} = 1/9\\ \text{us.} = 1/9\end{array}\right\} = 1/3$$

and the consanguine sister—1/2 as her Koranic share. The remainder (that is, 1/6) will be shared proportionately by the consanguine sister, and uterine brother and sisters. See below §100, Return, Exception 3 (*w*).

(7) Husband; full brother; full sister.

$$\text{husband} = 1/2$$
$$\text{fb.—}2/3 \times 1/2 = 1/3$$
$$\text{fs.—}1/3 \times 1/2 = 1/6.$$

(8) Wife; uterine brother; consanguine brother; consanguine sister (*x*).

$$\left.\begin{array}{r}\text{w.—}1/4 = \ \ 9/36\\ \text{ub.—}1/6 = \ \ 6/36\end{array}\right\}\ \text{Koranic shares.}$$
$$\text{cb.—}2/3 \times 7/12 = 14/36$$
$$\text{cs.—}1/3 \times 7/12 = \ \ 7/36$$
$$\overline{\text{Unity}}$$

(B) *Descendants of Brothers and Sisters only*

If there are no brothers or sisters or ancestors, assign the share of h. or w. and divide the residue as follows:

(i) The principle of *stirpital succession* must be followed. The share of a full or consanguine brother is allotted to his descendants, and is divided according to the rule of double share to the male.

(*w*) Tyabji §747.
(*x*) Mulla §99.

(ii) The share of each uterine brother or sister must be allotted to his or her descendants, and is divided so that male and female share alike.

(iii) If there are no children of brothers or sisters, remote descendants take according to the above principles (*y*).

Illustrations

(1) Husband =1/2, Koranic Heir.
Uterine brother's daughter =1/6, Koranic share of her father.
Full brother's daughter =1/3, Residual portion of her father.
Consanguine brother's son—Excluded by full brother's daughter.

(2) Children of uterine brother; children of uterine sister; children of full sister; children of consanguine brother. 1/3 to uterine collaterals; 2/3 to full sister's children, who exclude consanguine brother's children (*z*).

3. Ancestors plus Collaterals

If the deceased leaves grandparents, in addition to brothers and sisters or their descendants, first, assign the share of the husband or wife, if any; and then divide the residue in the following manner:

(i) A paternal grandfather counts as a full or consanguine brother; and a paternal grandmother as a full or consanguine sister.

(ii) A maternal grandfather counts as a uterine brother; and a maternal grandmother as a uterine sister.

On failure of the grandparents, remoter ascendants inherit on the same principles; and on the failure of brothers and sisters, their descendants take *per stirpes* and inherit on similar principles (*a*).

(*y*) Tyabji, loc. cit.; Mulla §100.
(*z*) Tyabji, loc. cit., ill. (17).
(*a*) Tyabji, loc cit.; Wilson §468; Mulla §101

Illustrations

(1)	Paternal grandfather (= Full brother)	= 2/3
	Full sister	= 1/3
(2)	Paternal grandfather (= Consanguine brother)	= 2/3
	Consanguine sister	= 1/3
(3)	Uterine brother Maternal grandmother (= Uterine sister)	= 1/3 Koranic share, each takes 1/6.
	2 Full sisters	= 2/3 Koranic share.
(4)	Mother's father (= ub.) 1/6 = 3/18 Mother's mother (= us.) 1/6 = 3/18	1/3 as Koranic Heirs.
	Full brother = 4/18 Full sister = 2/18 Father's father (= fb.) = 4/18 Father's mother (= fs.) = 2/18	2/3 as blood relations.
(5)	Wife	= 1/4 Koranic share
	Uterine sister Uterine brother Maternal grandfather (= ub.)	= 1/3, each taking 1/9, Koranic share.
	Paternal grandfather	= 5/12 as blood relation.
(6)	Full brother's son	= 1/2 (being his father's share, Section II).
	Father's father	= 1/2 (Section I) (*b*).

§99. Shiite Heirs—Class III

(1) If there is not a single heir of Class I or II, the estate is inherited by heirs of Class III. The rules of distribution are as follows:

First, assign the Koranic share to the surviving spouse.

(*b*) These illustrations are from Mulla §101: others may be found in Tyabji §747, especially illustration (37), which is *Aga Sheralli* v. *Bai Kulsum* (1908) 32 Bom. 540. Texts were cited and it was held that succession in the third class, as in the first and second classes, is *per stirpes* and not *per capita*.

Next, divide the residue among the following relations in the order of priority.

Group A.—Paternal and maternal uncles and aunts of *the deceased*;

Group B.—Their *descendants*, how low soever, the nearer excluding the more remote;

Group C.—Paternal and maternal uncles and aunts of *the deceased's father and mother*;

Group D.—Their *descendants*, how low soever, the nearer excluding the more remote.

The groups are infinite in number, although the possibilities are limited by the brevity of human life. Remoter relations inherit in the like order (*c*).

(2) Each of the above groups has priority over the next; hence, no member of Group B can succeed so long as a member of Group A survives, and so on.

(3) *Historical exception.* If the only claimants are the son of a full paternal uncle and a consanguine paternal uncle, the former, although he belongs to Group B excludes the latter who is nearer and belongs to Group A.

When the Prophet died, the question arose whether Ali, the son of Abū Ṭālib, a full paternal uncle of the Prophet, had priority over 'Abbās, a consanguine paternal uncle. The Shiites, being followers of Ali, and accepting the religious headship of the Imāms descending from him, made this exception to sustain the claims of Ali and his descendants (*d*).

Principles of distribution. The most important rules are:

(i) to assign 2/3 of the estate to the paternal side and 1/3 to the maternal side;

(ii) to divide the paternal 2/3 among paternal uncles and aunts, as if they were brothers and sisters, that is,

(a) to assign 1/3 or 1/6 among the uterine uncles and aunts, male and female taking in equal proportions;

(*c*) Tyabji, loc. cit., ill. (32) sqq.; Wilson §§469-72; Mulla §102.
(*d*) Wilson §469; Tyabji §739 deals with this exception exhaustively.

(b) to assign the remainder (2/3 or 5/6) among the full paternal uncles and aunts; or failing them to the consanguine paternal uncles and aunts. In both these cases, the distribution is according to the double share to the male;

(iii) to divide the maternal 1/3 among the maternal uncles and aunts in the following manner:

(a) assign to the uterine uncles and aunts 1/3 of the maternal portion, if there be more than two, or 1/6 if there be only one; and

(b) divide the remainder (2/3 of the maternal portion) among full maternal uncles and aunts, and failing them, among the consanguine maternal uncles and aunts.

In cases (iii) (a) and (b), males and females take *equally*.

(iv) If there be no uncle or aunt on the maternal side, the paternal side takes the whole of the estate; and similarly, where there are no claimants of the paternal side, the maternal side takes the inheritance exclusively.

Illustration

2/3	Full paternal uncle—$5/6 \times 2/3 = 5/9$.
	Consanguine paternal uncle—excluded by full paternal uncle.
	Uterine paternal uncle—$1/6 \times 2/3 = 1/9$.
1/3	Full maternal uncle—$5/6 \times 1/3 = 5/18$.
	Consanguine maternal uncle—excluded by full maternal uncle.
	Uterine maternal uncle—$1/6 \times 1/3 = 1/18$.

Further illustrations and details will be found in Tyabji (*e*), Ameer Ali (*f*), Wilson (*g*), and Mulla (*h*).

(*e*) §747; in §748 he deals with the case where an heir is related to the deceased in two different ways; see also Ameer Ali, II, 120.

(*f*) II, 118-20.

(*g*) §§469-72.

(*h*) §§103-5.

§100. Anomalies, Miscellaneous Rules

Anomalies. Upon distribution the shares may (A) amount to *unity*; or (B) be *less* than unity; or (C) be *more* than unity. The second case represents *radd* (Return) in Sunnite law; the third, *'awl* (Increase). In Shiite law the problems are dealt with differently.

(A) Where the shares amount to unity, no difficulty arises and it is unnecessary to consider any illustrations.

(B) RETURN—LESS THAN UNITY

If there is a residue left after satisfying the claims of the heirs named in the Koran, and there are no blood relations in the class to which the Koranic Heirs belong, the residue reverts to the Koranic Heirs proportionately.

Illustrations

(1) Mother = 1/6 increased to 1/4;
Daughter = 1/2 increased to 3/4;
Brother—excluded. Belongs to Class II.

By Hanafi law the brother would have taken the residue as one of the *'aṣabāt*.

(2) Mother = 1/6 increased to 1/5;
Father = 1/6 increased to 1/5;
Daughter = 3/6 increased to 3/5.

By Hanafi law the residual 1/6 would have been taken by the father.

(3) Uterine sister = 1/6 increased to 1/4;
Consanguine sister = 3/6 increased to 3/4 (*i*).

There are three exceptions to Return in Shiite law: the spouse, mother, and uterine brother and sister.

Exception (1).—Spouse. Neither the husband nor the wife is entitled to a share in the Return, if there exists any other heir.

(*i*) Wilson §457; Mulla §106.

If the sole surviving heir is the husband, he inherits the whole of the property; in the case of the widow, although the texts did not permit the wife to take more than her one-quarter share, it has now been held in *Abdul Hamid Khan* v. *Peare Mirza* (*j*), that the widow is in the same position as the husband. Ali, it is said in the *Da'ā'im*, gave the whole of the property of the husband to the widow, where she was the sole surviving heir (*k*).

Exception (2).—*Mother*. If the deceased leaves his mother, father and one daughter, and also

(i) two or more full or consanguine brothers, *or*
(ii) one such brother *and* two such sisters, *or*
(iii) four such sisters,

the brothers and sisters, though themselves excluded from inheritance as being heirs of Class II, prevent the mother from participating in the return, and the surplus reverts to the father and the daughter proportionately to their respective shares.

This is the only case in which the mother is excluded from the Return.

Illustration

Mother	—1/6	= 4/24
Father	—1/6 increased to 1/4 × 5/6	= 5/24
Daughter	—1/2 = 3/6 increased to 3/4 × 5/6	= 15/24

2 full brothers—excluded (*l*).

Exception (3).—*Uterine brother and sister*. Where uterine brothers and sisters survive with full sisters, the uterine brothers and sisters do not participate in the Return. The residue is taken entirely by the full sisters. This rule does not apply to consanguine sisters. Consanguine sisters, and uterine

(*j*) (1934) 10 Luck. 550. Mulla §107.

(*k*) *Da'ā'im*, II §1390; *Fat. Law* §454; Tyabji §750.

(*l*) Wilson §458; Mulla §108.

brothers and sisters divide the Return in proportion to their shares.

Illustrations

(1) Uterine brother = 1/6 (excluded from Return)
Full sister —1/2 as Koranic Heir + 1/3 by Return = 5/6.

(2) Uterine brother, Uterine sister } = 1/3, that is, *each* 1/6
Full sister —1/2 as Koranic Heir + 1/6 by Return = 2/3.

(3) Widow —1/4 = 3/12
Uterine sister —1/6 = 2/12
Full sister —1/2 as Koranic Heir + 1/12 by Return = 7/12 (*m*).

(C) Increase—more than unity

The Sunnite (Hanafi) doctrine of Increase (*'awl*) is not recognized in the Shiite (Ithnā 'Asharī) school of law. If the sum of the Koranic shares exceeds unity, the fraction in excess is invariably deducted from the share of—

(i) the daughter or daughters;
(ii) the full or consanguine sister or sisters (but *not the uterine sister*).

Illustrations

(1) Father, mother, husband and one daughter.

f.—1/6 = 2/12
m.—1/6 = 2/12
h.—1/4 = 3/12
d.—1/2 = 6/12 - *1/12* = 5/12

13/12

(*m*) Wilson §465; Tyabji, 3rd ed., 913-15; Mulla §109.

(2) Husband, 2 full sisters.

h.—1/2 = 3/6
2 fs.—2/3 = 4/6
———
7/6

The excess of 1/6 will be deducted from the sisters' share. Hence the 4/6 of the sisters' share will be reduced to 3/6. Therefore, each sister = 1/4 (*n*).

Fatimid Law, see *Fat. Law* §§459-63.

Miscellaneous Points

1. *Subsidiary heirs.* Apart from the return to the husband or the wife, Shiite law recognizes the right of a successor by contract, and finally, escheat. Tyabji §§726-29.
2. *Eldest son,* see above, §97, 5, p. 448.
3. *Childless widow,* see above, §97, 2, p. 446.
4. *Illegitimate child,* Wilson §474 and Ameer Ali, II, 128, show the distinction between the *walad al-zinā,* the child of fornication and *walad al-malā'ina,* the child of imprecation or a child disowned. The former is a *nullus filius* and inherits neither from the father nor from the mother, but the latter inherits from the mother, Tyabji §732(3); Mulla §114.

   The Fatimid jurist Nu'mān lays down that the mother of an illegitimate child inherits from him, *Da'ā'im,* II §1364; *Fat. Law* §§238, 437. But there is no mention of the bastard's rights.
5. *Principles of exclusion* are given by Ameer Ali, II, 125-32.
6. *Double relationship.* Where a person is doubly related to the deceased, *he inherits in both capacities.* If a woman dies leaving a husband, who is also her cousin (paternal uncle's son), he will receive his share as a husband, *plus* his share as a blood relation. Ameer Ali, II, 120; Tyabji §748.

(*n*) Wilson §459; Tyabji §742, pp. 881 sq.; Mulla §110.

7. *Difference of Religion*. Nu'mān, the Fatimid jurist, lays down that a Muslim can inherit from a *kāfir*, but not *vice versa*. And the property of an apostate (*murtadd*) is distributed according to the Muhammadan law; *Fat. Law* §§442-4.

8. *Homicide*. The homicide in Ithnā 'Asharī law is excluded from inheritance only if he has *intentionally* killed a person, Tyabji §732 (1); but *aliter* among the Fatimids, where the killer is excluded whether the manslaughter was intentional or not, thus agreeing with the Hanafi jurists, *Fat. Law* §446.

§101. Sunnite and Shiite Systems Compared

After having studied the two systems (*o*), it becomes abundantly clear that the Sunnite and Shiite laws of inheritance differ widely. This seems surprising as we know that the starting-point of both is the fixed and immutable text of the Koran—for the devout Muslim, the word and the voice of God Himself. How and why have these differences arisen? What are the causes—historical, political, economic and social—which have led to this puzzling result? The answer to these questions has not yet been given in a definitive fashion by any scholar. The welter of cause and effect is undoubtedly confusing; but, for the student at any rate, a modern author, Tyabji, has made some fruitful observations, and we shall content ourselves by following mainly in his footsteps (*p*).

1. *Principle of Agnacy* (ta'ṣīb) *Destroyed*

An examination of Sunnite inheritance reveals that the Hanafi interpretation kept intact the ancient tribal structure of society. The '*aṣabāt* (Agnatic Heirs) remained in the Hanafi scheme the most important heirs. The substratum of pre-Islamic custom was not demolished.

(*o*) The Fatimid jurist Nu'mān follows, as we have seen, mostly the Ithnā 'Asharī school, but there are notable variations, *Fat. Law*, Intr. xxxv sqq.

(*p*) Tyabji, pp. 897-8 (end).

The Shiites, however, destroyed this principle completely. 'As for the *'aṣabāt*, dust in their jaws'—thus is reported from an Imām of the House of the Prophet, Imām Ja'far al-Ṣādiq (*q*). They interpret the Holy Writ as placing those who are related through women on a footing of equality with those related through men. Cognates and agnates are placed on a footing of equality. The classification of Heirs was *not* I. Koranic Heirs, II. Tribal Heirs, and III. Uterine Heirs, but with due consideration given to the provisions of the Koran, we have two main classes:

(A) Koranic Heirs (*dhū farḍ*), and
(B) all other blood relations (*dhū qarābat*).

The Fatimid law is identical and does not recognize *ta'ṣīb* (agnacy) (*qq*).

2. *Classification of Heirs*

It follows therefore that the classification of heirs is simple: Class I, Class II, Class III; and not Koranic Heirs, Tribal Heirs, Uterine Heirs.

One further word of caution: the terms 'sharer', 'residuary' and 'distant kindred' have been in use for a century and a half. But they are misleading even in respect of Hanafi heirs; much less should they be used for their Shiite counterparts. The *principles* of classification being different, the use of the same names merely confuses the issues. The Koranic Heirs remain; but the *'aṣabāt* and *dhawū'l-arḥām* are combined to form a new class, *dhawū'l-qarābat*, based on blood relationship in the widest sense. Tyabji says:

> The Shiites do not leave the old rules of law as they were, but replace them by a set of rules consisting of a fusion of the customary law and the Islamic reforms, and thus, amongst Shiites, the classification of heirs becomes important only when we have to deal with the question of the quantum of shares they take, and not for the purpose of considering which persons are entitled to

(*q*) Tyabji §730, n. 3, citing Baillie, II, 400; Fitzgerald, 147; Wilson §450, notes.
(*qq*) *Fat. Law* §§432-4.

succeed. The clue seems to be that *the Hanafis take the Koranic alterations of the pre-Islamic customs literally,* and *the Shiites take them as illustrations of underlying principles.* The former let the substratum of the customary law stand unaltered except to the extent to which it is definitely altered by express provisions of the Koran. The Shiites take each instance mentioned in the Koran as speaking not only for itself but as indicating the widest possible principles (*r*).

3. *Stirpital Succession*

The verse that a male shall have twice as much as a female is interpreted by the Shiites as changing the entire scheme of distribution. The Shiite theory of Imāmate is based upon the principle that excellence is due to heredity and a noble pedigree. Circumstances like the tragedy of Kerbela tended to deepen the feeling, and thus we see the theory of law that the *daughter's children stand in the shoes of the daughter*, and the sister's children inherit in the right of the sister; and this principle was systematically applied in every case.

4. *Females However Remote Inherit on the Analogy of the Daughter or Sister*

The Koranic provision that the daughter is entitled to succeed with the son, is interpreted by the Shiites as applicable to all heirs female. The Shiite jurists take the provisions of the Koran not as restricted to individual instances of the daughter or the sister, but as establishing a new principle for the benefit of females. As Tyabji rightly points out, probably the *most important legal reform* introduced by Islam refers to the *rights of women* (*s*).

The same author shows that the Koranic verse about the relative proximity of parents and children has received different interpretations, but the results have been far-reaching. A text of the Koran is taken, not as a particular dictate, but as a principle, capable of almost limitless expansion.

(*r*) Tyabji, 4th ed., 897. The italics are mine.

(*s*) Tyabji, ibid., 894.

An illustration is the succession of uncles and aunts, and collaterals in general.

And Tyabji finally concludes his acute analysis by discussing the principles relating to Return and the rights of the mother—questions of relatively lesser importance than those more fully discussed above.

The real cause of the difference between the principles of the Sunnite law of inheritance and its Shiite counterpart is one of the most important problems remaining unexplored by modern research; and it is the hope of the author that someone with ability and experience will take an early opportunity to proceed on a voyage of discovery.

APPENDIX A

THE MUSLIM PERSONAL LAW (*SHARIAT*) APPLICATION ACT, 1937

(ACT XXVI OF 1937)

(7th October, 1937)

An Act to make provision for the application of the Muslim Personal Law (Shariat) to Muslims[1]

WHEREAS it is expedient to make provision for the application of the Muslim Personal Law (*Shariat*) to Muslims: [1] it is hereby enacted as follows:

1. Short title and extent.

(1) This Act may be called THE MUSLIM PERSONAL LAW (*SHARIAT*) APPLICATION ACT, 1937.

(2) It extends to the whole of India (except the State of Jammu and Kashmir).[2]

2. Application of Personal Law to Muslims.

Nothwithstanding any customs or usage to the contrary, in all questions (save questions relating to agricultural land) regarding intestate succession, special property of females, including personal property inherited or obtained under contract or gift or any other provision of Personal Law, marriage, dissolution of marriage, including *talaq, ila, zihar, lian, khula* and *mubaraat*, maintenance, dower, guardianship, gifts, trusts and trust properties, and *wakfs* (other than charities and charitable institutions and charitable and religious endowments) the rule of decision in cases where the parties are Muslims shall be the Muslim Personal Law (*Shariat*).

STATE AMENDMENTS

MADRAS

For section 2 *substitute* the following section, namely:

"2. *Application of Personal Law to Muslims.* Notwithstanding any custom or usage to the contrary, in all questions regarding intestate succession, special property of females,

[1] Words 'in the Provinces of India' omitted by A.L.O. 1950.

[2] Substituted by the Miscellaneous Personal Laws (Extension) Act (XLVIII of 1959) with effect from 1st February, 1960.

including personal property inherited or obtained under contract or gift or any other provision of personal law, marriage, dissolution of marriage, including Talaq, Ila, Zihar, Lian, Khula and Mubaraat, maintenance, dower, guardianship, gifts, trusts and trust properties and wakfs the rule of decision in cases where the parties are Muslims shall be the Muslim Personal Law (Shariat)." Mad. Act. XVIII of 1949, S.2 [12.7.1949].

ANDHRA PRADESH

Same as that of Madras.

3. Power to make a declaration.

(1) Any person who satisfies the prescribed authority—

(a) that he is a Muslim, and

(b) that he is competent to contract within the meaning of section 11 of the Indian Contract Act, 1872, and

(c) that he is a resident of (the territories to which this Act extends)[3] may by declaration in the prescribed form and filed before the prescribed authority declare that he desires to obtain the benefit of (the provisions of this section), and thereafter the provisions of section 2 shall apply to the declarant and all his minor children and their descendants as if in addition to the matters enumerated therein adoption, wills and legacies were also specified.

(2) Where the prescribed authority refuses to accept a declaration under sub-section (1), the person desiring to make the same may appeal to such officer as the State Government may, by general or special order, appoint in this behalf, and such officer may, if he is satisfied that the appellant is entitled to make the declaration, order the prescribed authority to accept the same.

4. Rule-making power.

(1) The (State Government) may make rules to carry into effect the purposes of this Act.

(2) In particular and without prejudice to the generality of the foregoing powers, such rules may provide for all or any of the following matters, namely:

[3] Substituted by the Adaptation of Laws (No. 3) Order 1956.

(a) for prescribing the authority before whom and the form in which declarations under this Act shall be made;

(b) for prescribing the fees to be paid for the filing of declarations and for the attendance at private residences of any person in the discharge of his duties under this Act; and for prescribing the times at which such fees shall be payable and the manner in which they shall be levied.

(3) Rules made under the provisions of this section shall be published in the (Official Gazette) and shall thereupon have effect as if enacted in this Act.

5. Dissolution of marriage by Court in certain circumstances.

(*Repealed by the Dissolution of Muslim Marriages Act, 1939* (*VIII of 1939*), *S. 6.* (*17.3.1939*))

6. Repeals.

(The undermentioned provisions) of the Acts and Regulations mentioned below shall be repealed in so far as they are inconsistent with the provisions of this Act, namely:

(1) Section 26 of the Bombay Regulation IV of 1827;

(2) Section 16 of the Madras Civil Courts Act, 1873;

(x x x x)[4]

(4) Section 3 of the Oudh Laws Act, 1876;

(5) Section 5 of the Punjab Laws Act, 1872;

(6) Section 5 of the Central Provinces Laws Act, 1875; and

(7) Section 4 of the Ajmere Laws Regulation, 1877. ([5])

[4] Omitted as per amendment in Act XVI of 1943, Section 3(b).

[5] This Act has been brought up to date with reference to the text of the Act in A.I.R. Manual, Vol. X, 2nd Edition (1961).

APPENDIX B

(THE) DISSOLUTION OF MUSLIM MARRIAGES ACT, 1939

(ACT VIII OF 1939)

(17th March 1939)

An Act to consolidate and clarify the provisions of Muslim law relating to suits for dissolution of marriage by women married under Muslim law and to remove doubts as to the effect of the renunciation of Islam by a married Muslim woman on her marriage tie.

WHEREAS it is expedient to consolidate and clarify the provisions of Muslim law relating to suits for dissolution of marriage by women married under Muslim law and to remove doubts as to the effect of the renunciation of Islam by a married Muslim woman on her marriage tie;

It is hereby enacted as follows:

1. Short title and extent.—(1) This Act may be called THE DISSOLUTION OF MUSLIM MARRIAGES ACT, 1939.

(2) It extends to the whole of India (except the State of Jammu and Kashmir).[1]

2. Grounds for decree for dissolution of marriage.—A woman married under Muslim law shall be entitled to obtain a decree for the dissolution of her marriage on any one or more of the following grounds, namely:

(*i*) that the whereabouts of the husband have not been known for a period of four years;

(*ii*) that the husband has neglected or has failed to provide for her maintenance for a period of two years;

[1] Substituted by the Miscellaneous Personal Laws (Extension) Act (XLVIII of 1959) with effect from February, 1960.

The old sub-section (2) was as follows: "(2) It extends to the whole of India except the territories which immediately before the 1st November, 1956, were comprised in Part B States."

(*iii*) that the husband has been sentenced to imprisonment for a period of seven years or upwards;

(*iv*) that the husband has failed to perform, wihout reasonable cause, his marital obligations for a period of three years;

(*v*) that the husband was impotent at the time of the marriage and continues to be so;

(*vi*) that the husband has been insane for a period of two years or is suffering from leprosy or a virulent venereal disease;

(*vii*) that she having been given in marriage by her father or other guardian before she attained the age of fifteen years, repudiated the marriage before attaining the age of eighteen years;

Provided that the marriage has not been consummated;

(*viii*) that the husband treats her with cruelty, that is to say:

(*a*) habitually assaults her or makes her life miserable by cruelty of conduct even if such conduct does not amount to physical ill-treatment, or

(*b*) associates with women of evil repute or leads an infamous life, or

(*c*) attempts to force her to lead an immoral life, or

(*d*) disposes of her property or prevents her exercising her legal rights over it, or

(*e*) obstructs her in the observance of her religious profession or practice, or

(*f*) if he has more wives than one, does not treat her equitably in accordance with the injunctions of the Qoran;

(*ix*) on any other ground which is recognised as valid for the dissolution of marriages under Muslim law;

Provided that—

(*a*) no decree shall be passed on ground (iii) until the sentence become final;

(b) a decree passed on ground (*i*) shall not take effect for a period of six months from the date of such decree, and if the husband appears either in person or through an authorised agent within that period and satisfies the Court that he is prepared to perform his conjugal duties, the Court shall set aside the said decree; and

(c) before passing a decree on ground (*v*) the Court shall on application by the husband, make an order requiring the husband to satisfy the Court within a period of one year the date of such order that he has ceased to be impotent, and if the husband so satisfies the Court within such period, no decree shall be passed on the said ground.

3. Notice to be served on heirs of the husband when the husband's whereabouts are not known.—In a suit to which clause (*i*) of section 2 applies—

(a) the names and addresses of the persons who would have been the heirs of the husband under Muslim law if he had died on the date of the filing of the plaint shall be stated in the plaint,

(b) notice of the suit shall be served on such persons, and

(c) such persons shall have the right to be heard in the suit:

Provided that the paternal uncle and brother of the husband, if any, shall be cited as party even if he or they are not heirs.

4. Effect of conversion to another faith.—The renunciation of Islam by a married Muslim woman or her conversion to a faith other than Islam shall not by itself operate to dissolve her marriage:

Provided that after such renunciation, or conversion the woman shall be entitled to obtain a decree for the dissolution of her marriage on any of the grounds mentioned in section 2:

Provided further that the provisions of this section shall not apply to a woman converted to Islam from some other faith who re-embraces her former faith.

5. Rights to dower not to be affected.—Nothing contained in this Act shall affect any right which a married woman may have under Muslim law to her dower or any part thereof on the dissolution of her marriage.

6. Repeal of section 5 of Act 26 of 1937.—(Repealed by the Repealing and Amending Act, 1942 (25 of 1942), S. 2 and Sch. I).[2]

[2] This Act has been reproduced from the Text of the Act found in A.I.R. Manual, Vol. IX, 3rd Edition (1970).

APPENDIX C

AGREEMENT FOR DISSOLUTION OF MARRIAGE

Some years ago, at the instance of Begum Sharīfa Ḥāmid 'Alī, a prominent worker in the cause of women's rights, a leading firm of solicitors in Bombay drafted an agreement, in consultation with me, to ensure to a Muslim wife in India the fullest possible rights of obtaining her freedom by the rules of law as applied to *ṭalāq-e tafwīḍ*. This agreement, to be signed BEFORE the *nikāḥ* ceremony, is in fairly wide use among certain of the educated families in Bombay; and, as it is not well known outside, it is printed here in order to facilitate its more general use.

IN THE NAME OF ALLAH, THE ÇOMPASSIONATE, THE MERCIFUL

This agreement is made at Bombay this ...... day of .... Between 'Alī the son of Muḥammad (Hereinafter called 'the Husband') of the one part and Fāṭima the daughter of Ḥasan (hereinafter called 'the Wife') of the other part

WHEREAS the Husband and Wife both profess the— (*a*) Muslim faith and declare that they are governed by the— (*a*) Muslim Personal Law

AND WHEREAS a marriage is to be contracted (*b*) and solemnized between the Husband and Wife on .... the .... day of Hijri .... i.e. the .... day of .... A.D.

AND WHEREAS it is mutually agreed and it is of the essence of the said contract of marriage between the Husband and the Wife that the Wife should have the power of divorce as hereinafter mentioned NOW IT IS HEREBY AGREED AND DECLARED as follows

1. The Husband shall pay to the Wife by way of *mahr* a sum of Rs 11,000 such *mahr* being payable by the Husband to the Wife as to the sum of Rs 5,500 at the time of the said marriage

(*a*) Mention the school of the parties, i.e. Hanafi, Shāfi'ī, Ithnā 'Asharī, etc. If the parties differ in their schools, it is all the more necessary to say so in India and Pakistan.

(*b*) It is necessary to emphasize that the agreement should be entered into *before* the marriage takes place.

and as to the remaining sum of Rs 5,500 only in the event of his death or divorce taking place between him and the Wife.

2. Subject to the provisoes hereinafter mentioned the Wife shall have the power to divorce in manner mentioned in clause 3 below for dissolving the said marriage on any one or more of the following grounds namely

(a) That the Husband failed to observe and perform the duties imposed upon a husband by Muslim Personal Law namely

(i) kindness in general behaviour and treatment

(ii) the fulfilment of conjugal rights and

(iii) the maintenance and support of the Wife

(b) That the Husband has married or gone through the form of marriage with another woman after the date hereof

(c) That the temperaments of the Husband and the Wife are incompatible or otherwise the Husband is unable to keep the Wife happy or

(d) The grounds mentioned in Section 2 of the Dissolution of Muslim Marriages Act 1939 or any of them.

PROVIDED that the Wife shall not have the said power to divorce unless and until

(i) It has been admitted by the Husband in writing that the said grounds or ground exist or existed or

(ii) It has been certified in writing by the said Ḥasan the father of the Wife so long as he shall be alive and after his death by any two respectable persons after giving the Husband a reasonable opportunity to make such representations in the matter as he may desire that such grounds or ground exist or existed.

3. The said power to divorce shall be exercised by the Wife declaring before any two witnesses that in accordance with the power derived by her from this agreement she divorces the Husband and the said marriage shall stand dissolved as from the date of the declaration.

4. The said power to divorce shall not be revocable by the Husband and shall not be affected by the Wife having failed on one or more occasions to exercise the same.

IN WITNESS WHEREOF the parties to these presents have hereunto set their respective hands the day and year first hereinabove written.

SIGNED by the abovenamed }
in the presence of

SIGNED by the abovenamed }
in the presence of

APPENDIX D

SPECIAL MARRIAGE ACT, 1954

CHAPTER III

Registration of Marriages Celebrated in other Forms

Registration of marriages celebrated in 3 of 1872.

15. Any marriage celebrated, whether before or after the commencement of this Act, other than a marriage solemnized under the Special Marriage Act, 1872, or under this Act, may be registered under this Chapter by a Marriage Officer in the territories to which this Act extends if the following conditions are fulfilled, namely:—

(a) a ceremony of marriage has been performed between the parties and they have been living together as husband and wife ever since;

(b) neither party has at the time of registration more than one spouse living;

(c) neither party is an idiot or a lunatic at the time of registration;

(d) the parties have completed the age of twenty-one years at the time of registration;

(e) the parties are not within the degrees of prohibited relationship:

Provided that in the case of a marriage celebrated before the commencement of this Act, this condition shall be subject to any law, custom or usage having the force of law governing each of them which permits of a marriage between the two; and

(*f*) the parties have been residing within the district of the Marriage Officer for a period of not less than thirty days immediately preceding the date on which the application is made to him for registration of the marriage.

Procedure for registration.

16. Upon receipt of an application signed by both the parties to the marriage for the registration of their marriage under this Chapter, the Marriage Officer shall give public notice thereof in such manner as may be prescribed and after allowing a period of thirty

days for objections and after hearing any objection received within that period, shall, if satisfied that all the conditions mentioned in section 15 are fulfilled, enter a certificate of the marriage in the Marriage Certificate Book in the form specified in the Fifth Schedule, and such certificate shall be signed by the parties to the marriage and by three witnesses.

Appeals from orders under section 16.

17. Any person aggrieved by any order of a Marriage Officer refusing to register a marriage under this Chapter may, within thirty days from the date of the order, appeal against that order to the district court within the local limits of whose jurisdiction the Marriage Officer has his office, and the decision of the district court on such appeal shall be final, and the Marriage Officer to whom the application was made shall act in conformity with such decision.

Effect of registration or marriage under this Chapter.

18. Subject to the provisions contained in sub-section (2) of section 24, where a certificate of marriage has been finally entered in the Marriage Certificate Book under this Chapter, the marriage shall, as from the date of such entry, be deemed to be a marriage solemnized under this Act, and all children born after the date of the ceremony of marriage (whose names shall also be entered in the Marriage Certificate Book) shall in all respects be deemed to be and always to have been the legitimate children of their parents:

Provided that nothing contained in this section shall be construed as conferring upon any such children any rights in or to the property of any person other than their parents in any case where, but for the passing of this Act, such children would have been incapable of possessing or acquiring any such rights by reason of their not being the legitimate children of their parents (*a*).

(*a*) The text of the sections will be found in *India Code*, 1958, Vol. VI, Part ix, p.11.

APPENDIX E

GOVERNMENT OF PAKISTAN

MINISTRY OF LAW

Ordinance No. VIII of 1961*

Rawalpindi, the 2nd March, 1961

AN

ORDINANCE

to give effect to certain recommendations of the Commission on Marriage and Family Laws (*a*)

Whereas it is expedient to give effect to certain recommendations of the Commission on Marriage and Family Laws;

Now THEREFORE, in pursuance of the Proclamation of the seventh day of October, 1958, and in exercise of all powers enabling him in that behalf, the President is pleased to make and promulgate the following Ordinance:—

1. **Short title, extent, application and commencement.**—(1) This Ordinance may be called the Muslim Family Laws Ordinance, 1961.

(2) It extends to the whole of Pakistan, and applies to all Muslim citizens of Pakistan, wherever they may be.

(3) It shall come into force on such date as the Central Government may, by notification in the official Gazette, appoint in this behalf.

2. **Definitions.**—In this Ordinance, unless there is anything repugnant in the subject or context,—

(a) "Arbitration Council" means a body consisting of the Chairman and a representative of each of the parties to a matter dealt with in this Ordinance:

Provided that where any party fails to nominate a representative within the prescribed time, the body formed without such representative shall be the Arbitration Council;

* David S. Pearl, 'Family Law in Pakistan', *Journal of Family Law*, Vol. 9, 1969, pp. 165-89 (University of Louisevilie) contains an excellent account of how the Ordinance has been implemented.

(*a*) Came into force on 15 July 1961, by notification dated 12 July 1961.

(b) "Chairman" means the Chairman of the Union Council or a person appointed by the Central or a Provincial Government, or by an officer authorized in that behalf by any such Government, to discharge the functions of Chairman under this Ordinance:

Provided that where the Chairman of the Union Council is a non-Muslim, or he himself wishes to make an application to the Arbitration Council, or is, owing to illness or any other reason, unable to discharge the functions of Chairman, the Council shall elect one of its Muslim members as Chairman for the purposes of this Ordinance;

(c) "prescribed" means prescribed by rules made under section 11;

(d) "Union Council" means the Union Council or the Town or Union Committee constituted under the Basic Democracies Order, 1959 (P.O. No. 18 of 1959), having in the matter jurisdiction as prescribed;

(e) "Ward" means a ward within a Union or Town as defined in the aforesaid Order.

3. **Ordinance to override other laws, etc.**—(1) The provisions of this Ordinance shall have effect notwithstanding any law, custom or usage, and the registration of Muslim marriages shall take place only in accordance with those provisions.

(2) For the removal of doubt, it is hereby declared that the provisions of the Arbitration Act, 1940 (X of 1940), the Code of Civil Procedure, 1908 (Act V of 1908), and any other law regulating the procedure of courts, shall not apply to any Arbitration Council.

4. **Succession.**—In the event of the death of any son or daughter of the *propositus* before the opening of succession, the children of such son or daughter, if any, living at the time the succession opens, shall *per stirpes* receive a share equivalent to the share which such son or daughter, as the case may be, would have received if alive.

5. **Registration of marriages.**—(1) Every marriage solemnized under Muslim law shall be registered in accordance with the provisions of this Ordinance.

(2) For the purpose of registration of marriages under this Ordinance, the Union Council shall grant licences to one or more persons, to be called Nikah Registrars, but in no case shall more than one Nikah Registrar be licensed for any one Ward.

(3) Every marriage not solemnized by the Nikah Registrar shall, for the purpose of registration under this Ordinance, be reported to him by the person who has solemnized such marriage.

(4) Whoever contravenes the provisions of sub-section (3) shall be punishable with simple imprisonment for a term which may extend to three months, or with fine which may extend to one thousand rupees, or with both.

(5) The form of *nikah nama*, the registers to be maintained by Nikah Registrars, the records to be preserved by Union Councils, the manner in which marriages shall be registered and copies of *nikah nama* shall be supplied to the parties, and the fees to be charged therefor, shall be such as may be prescribed.

(6) Any person may, on payment of the prescribed fee, if any, inspect at the office of the Union Council the record preserved under sub-section (5), or obtain a copy of any entry therein.

6. **Polygamy.**—(1) No man, during the subsistence of an existing marriage, shall, except with the previous permission in writing of the Arbitration Council, contract another marriage, nor shall any such marriage contracted without such permission be registered under this Ordinance.

(2) An application for permission under sub-section (1) shall be submited to the Chairman in the prescribed manner, together with the prescribed fee, and shall state the reasons for the proposed marriage, and whether the consent of the existing wife or wives has been obtained thereto.

(3) On receipt of the application under sub-section (2), the Chairman shall ask the applicant and his existing wife or wives each to nominate a representative, and the Arbitration Council so constituted may, if satisfied that the proposed marriage is necessary and just, grant, subject to such conditions, if any, as may be deemed fit, the permission applied for.

(4) In deciding the application the Arbitration Council shall record its reasons for the decision, and any party may, in the prescribed manner, within the prescribed period, and on payment of the prescribed fee, prefer an application for revision, in the case

of West Pakistan, to the Collector and, in the case of East Pakistan, to the Sub-Divisional Officer concerned and his decision shall be final and shall not be called in question in any court.

(5) Any man who contracts another marriage without the permission of the Arbitration Council shall—

(a) pay immediately the entire amount of the dower, whether prompt or deferred, due to the existing wife or wives, which amount, if not so paid, shall be recoverable as arrears of land revenue; and

(b) on conviction upon complaint be punishable with simple imprisonment which may extend to one year, or with fine which may extend to five thousand rupees, or with both.

7. **Talaq.**—(1) Any man who wishes to divorce his wife shall, as soon as may be after the pronouncement of *talaq* in any form whatsoever, give the Chairman notice in writing of his having done so, and shall supply a copy thereof to the wife.

(2) Whoever contravenes the provisions of sub-section (1) shall be punishable with simple imprisonment for a term which may extend to one year or with fine which may extend to five thousand rupees or with both.

(3) Save as provided in sub-section (5), a *talaq* unless revoked earlier, expressly or otherwise, shall not be effective until the expiration of ninety days from the day on which notice under sub-section (1) is delivered to the Chairman.

(4) Within thirty days of the receipt of notice under sub-section (1), the Chairman shall constitute an Arbitration Council for the purpose of bringing about a reconciliation between the parties, and the Arbitration Council shall take all steps necessary to bring about such reconciliation.

(5) If the wife be pregnant at the time *talaq* is pronounced, *talaq* shall not be effective until the period mentioned in sub-section (3) or the pregnancy, whichever be later, ends.

(6) Nothing shall debar a wife whose marriage has been terminated by *talaq* effective under this section from re-marrying the same husband, without an intervening marriage with a third person, unless such termination is for the third time so effective.

8. **Dissolution of marriage otherwise than by talaq.**—Where the right to divorce has been duly delegated to the wife and she wishes to exercise that right, or where any of the parties to a

marriage wishes to dissolve the marriage otherwise than by *talaq*, the provisions of section 7 shall, *mutatis mutandis* and so far as applicable, apply.

9. **Maintenance.**—(1) If any husband fails to maintain his wife adequately, or where there are more wives than one, fails to maintain them equitably, the wife, or all or any of the wives, may in addition to seeking any other legal remedy available apply to the Chairman who shall constitute an Arbitration Council to determine the matter, and the Arbitration Council may issue a cerificate specifying the amount which shall be paid as maintenance by the husband.

(2) A husband or wife may, in the prescribed manner, within the prescribed period, and on payment of the prescribed fee, prefer an application for revision of the certificate, in the case of West Pakistan, to the Collector and, in the case of East Pakistan, to the Sub-Divisional Officer concerned and his decision shall be final and shall not be called in question in any Court.

(3) Any amount payable under sub-section (1) or (2), if not paid in due time, shall be recoverable as arrears of land revenue.

10. **Dower.**—Where no details about the mode of payment of dower are specified in the *nikah nama*, or the marriage contract, the entire amount of the dower shall be presumed to be payable on demand.

11. **Power to make rules.**—(1) The Provincial Government may make rules to carry into effect the purposes of this Ordinance.

(2) In making rules under this section, the Provincial Government may provide that a breach of any of the rules shall be punishable with simple imprisonment which may extend to one month, or with fine which may extend to two hundred rupees, or with both.

(3) Rules made under this section shall be published in the official Gazette, and shall thereupon have effect as if enacted in this Ordinance.

12. **Amendment of Child Marriage Restraint Act, 1929 (XIX of 1929).**—In the Child Marriage Restraint Act, 1929 (XIX of 1929),—

(1) in section 2,—

(a) in clause (a), for the word "fourteen" the word "sixteen" shall be substituted;

(b) in clause (c), the word "and" shall be omitted; and

(c) in clause (d), for the full stop at the end a comma shall be substituted, and thereafter the following new clause (e) shall be added, namely:—

"(e) 'Union Council' means the Union Council or the Town or Union Committee constituted under the Basic Democracies Order, 1959 (P.O. No. 18 of 1959), within whose jurisdiction a child marriage is or is about to be solemnized";

(2) section 3 shall be omitted;

(3) in section 4, for the words "twenty-one" the word "eighteen" shall be substituted;

(4) in section 9, after the words "under this Act", the words "except on a complaint made by the Union Council, or if there is no Union Council in the area, by such authority as the Provincial Government may in this behalf prescribe, and such cognizance shall in no case be taken" shall be inserted; and

(5) section 11 shall be omitted.

13. **Amendment of the Dissolution of Muslim Marriages Act 1939 (VIII of 1939).**—In the Dissolution of Muslim Marriages Act, 1939 (VIII of 1939), in section 2:

(a) after clause (ii), the following new clause (iia) shall be inserted, namely:—

"(iia) that the husband has taken an additional wife in contravention of the provisions of the Muslim Family Laws Ordinance, 1961"; and

(b) in clause (vii), for the word "fifteen" the word "sixteen" shall be substituted.

MOHAMMAD AYUB KHAN, H. Pk., H. J.,
FIELD MARSHAL,
President.

Rawalpindi, the 2nd March, 1961.

N. A. FARUQUI,
Cabinet Secretary (*a*).

(*a*) *Gazette of Pakistan, Extraordinary*. Published by authority. Karachi, Thursday, 2 March 1961, amended by Ordinance XXI of 1961, dated 19 June 1961.

APPENDIX F

PROCESSIONS AND OTHER MISCELLANEOUS MATTERS

The law of processions is not a part of the Muhammadan law, but rather of the 'common' law of India, applicable to all parties irrespective of caste and creed (*a*).

No sect has an exclusive use of the highway for its worship (*b*), and no sect is entitled to deprive others for ever of the right to use public streets for processions on the plea of sanctity of their place of worship, or on the plea that worship is carried on therein day and night; for, in affording special protection to persons assembled for religious worship or ceremonial, the law points to congregational rather than private worship (*c*).

In India there is a right to conduct a religious procession with its appropriate observances through a public street so that it does not interfere with the ordinary use of the street by the public, and subject to lawful directions by the magistrates (*d*). The right is inherent and does not depend upon custom; but it does not extend to the committing of a nuisance on the highway (*e*).

'Worshippers in a mosque or temple which abuts on a highway have no right to compel the processionists to stop their music completely while passing a mosque or temple on the ground that there was continuous worship inside it. Even if music, whether religious or not, offends against the religious sentiments of another community, it cannot be objected to on that ground. The stopping of the music would offend the religious sentiments of the processionists just as much as its continuance may offend the religious sentiments of the other. There can therefore be no right to insist on its complete stoppage.'(*f*)

An electricity supply company, having been duly authorized under the Indian Electricity Act, 1910, to place their wires across the streets of a town at a height of not less than 20 feet, the Shiite

(*a*) Constitution of India, Arts. 19 and 25-8.

(*b*) Tyabji §563.

(*c*) *Sundram* v. *The Queen* (1882) 6 Mad. 203 (F.B.).

(*d*) *Manzur Hasan* v. *Muhammad Zaman* (1924) 52 I.A. 61.

(*e*) *Muhammad Jalil* v. *Ram Nath* (1930) 53 All. 484, 491.

(*f*) ibid., at p. 490, per Sulaiman C.J. and Young J.

Muslims had no right to ask for an injunction ordering the company to raise the electric wires to such a height as not to obstruct the passage of the *ta'ziyas* in the Muḥarram procession (*g*).

A civil suit lies against those who would prevent a procession with its proper observances (*h*). 'It is a matter entirely for the District authorities to consider whether in the particular circumstances if a procession was taken out it would lead to public disturbance'; ordinarily, the High Court will not interfere with the District Magistrate's discretion (*i*).

Ramaḍān Fasting: Persons who go into hotels, after forming unlawful assemblies, to beat up others who do not fast can be prosecuted (*j*).

Pīrs, Shiite Law: The institution of Pīrs is not known among the Ithnā 'Asharī Shiites (*k*).

(*g*) *Martin & Co.* v. *Syed Faiyaz Husain* (1943) 71 I.A. 25.

(*h*) *Manzur Hasan* v. *Muhammad Zaman* (1924) 52 I.A. 61. See Tyabji §521A(3), where full citation of the Indian case law on the subject will be found.

(*i*) *Mohammad Siddiq* v. *State of Uttar Pradesh* [1955] 1 All. 121.

(*j*) *Fateh Khan* v. *Pakistan Government* PLD 1950 Peshawar 39.

(*k*) *Sardar Bibi* v. *Muhammad Bakhsh* PLD 1954 Lahore 480.

APPENDIX G

SELECT BIBLIOGRAPHY

The fullest bibliography will be found in J. Schacht, *An Introduction to Islamic Law,* Oxford, 1964.

For Indian law, see the works of Aghnides, Morley, Sircar, Ameer Ali and Wilson.

The elementary student can usefully begin with the bibliography in Anderson and Coulson, No. 15, in Sec. (a), below.

The list of books is arranged in two groups; the first deals with more general concepts and is of importance to the student of Islam no less than to the mere law student; the second restricts itself to the principal current textbooks on Indian law.

SYSTEMIC STUDY OF ISLAMIC LAW

(a) Introductory

1. HURGRONJE, C. SNOUCK, *Selected Works of,* edited (in English and French) by G.-H. Bousquet and J. Schacht. Brill, 1957. ('. . . Snouck and Goldziher laid the foundations of our science, and hence these pages are of enduring interest.'—Joseph Schacht, Foreword.)
2. GOLDZIHER, Ign., 'The Principles of Law and Islam' in the *Historian's History of the World,* VIII (1904), 294-304.
3. JUYNBOLL, Th. W., on 'Law' (Muhammadan) in Hastings' *Encyclopædia of Religion and Ethics,* VII, 858-83.
4. LAMMENS, H., *L'Islam: Croyances et Institutions.* Beyrouth, 1926. Translated into English by E. Denison Ross, London, 1929. Chapter v, on Jurisprudence.
5. MILLIOT, Louis, *Introduction à l'étude du Droit Musulman,* 1953, Paris. (For a critical review of this book, see J. Schacht, in the *American Jour. of Comparative Law* for 1956, 133-41.)
6. OSTROROG, Count Léon, *The Angora Reform.* London, 1927. Lecture I, 'The Roots of the Law'.
7. MORLEY, W. H., *Administration of Justice in British India.* London, 1858. 'The Mahomedan Law', pp. 241-323.

8. LEVY, R., *Social Structure of Islam*. Cambridge, 1957. Chapters iv and vi.

9. SANTILLANA, D., on 'Law and Society', in *The Legacy of Islam*. Oxford, 1931, p. 284.

10. SCHACHT, Joseph, 'Islamic Law' in *Encyclopædia of Social Sciences* (1932-7), VIII, 344-9.

11. ———,'Esquisse d'une Histoire du Droit Musulman', *Notes et Documents,* XI, Institut des Hautes-Études Marocaines, 1953, pp. 1-89.

12. VON GRUNEBAUM, G. E., *Medieval Islam*. Chicago, 1947. Especially, Chapters v and vi.

13. GIBB, H. A. R., *Modern Trends in Islam* (Haskell Lectures in Comparative Religion, University of Chicago, 1945). Chicago (U.S.A.), Cambridge (England), 1947. Chapter v, 'Law and Society'.

14. FYZEE, Asaf A. A., *A Modern Approach to Islam*. Bombay, 1963. (Chapters ii and iii.)

15. ANDERSON, J. N. D. and COULSON, N. J., 'Islamic Law in Contemporary Cultural Change', *Saeculum* (Munich), XVIII, 1967, 13-92. (One of the best introductions to the subject.)

16. BOUSQUET, G. H., *Le Droit Musulman,* Paris, 1963.

17. SCHACHT, J., 'Islamic Law in Contemporary States', *American Journal for Comparative Law,* 1959, Vol. 8, 133.

18. ANDERSON, J. N. D., 'The Significance of Islamic Law in the World Today', ibid., 1960, Vol. 9, 187.

19. FYZEE, A. A. A., 'The Relevance of Muhammadan Law in the Twentieth Century,' *Cambridge Law Journal*, 1963, 261.

20. DERRETT, J. D. M., *Religion and Law in the State in India*. New York, 1968. (Especially Chapters 2, 13 and 15; and Bibliographical Note.)

(b) General Discussion

1. GOLDZIHER, Ignaz, *Muhammedanische Studien,* Vol. I, 1889; Vol. II, 1890. Halle. (A truly epoch-making work. Tr. C. R. Barber and S. M. Stern, *Muslim Studies*. 2 vols. London, 1967, 1971.)

2. GOLDZIHER, Ignaz, *Vorlesungen über den Islam*. Heidelberg, 1910; 2nd edition, 1925. Trans. into French by F. Arin under the title of *Le Dogme et la Loi de l'islam*. Paris, 1920. (Recently translated into Arabic in Egypt.)

3. MACDONALD, D. B., *Development of Muslim Theology, Jurisprudence and Constitutional Theory*. London, 1903.

4. SCHACHT, Joseph, *Origins of Muhammadan Jurisprudence*. Oxford, 1950. Reprinted. (A classic. Referred to as 'Schacht'.)

5. ———, *An Introduction to Islamic Law*. Oxford, 1964. (Brief, but authoritative. Contains the most exhaustive bibliography of modern books and articles.)

6. TYAN, Émile, *Histoire de l'Organisation Judiciaire en Pays d'Islam*. Paris, Vol. I, 1938; Vol. II, 1943.

7. ———, *Institutions du Droit Public Musulman*, Tome I, Le Califat, Paris, 1954. Tome II, Sultanat et Califat, Paris, 1956.

8. JUYNBOLL, Th. W., *Handbuch des islāmischen Gesetzes*, Leiden-Leipzig, 1910.

9. ANDERSON, J. N. D., *Islamic Law in the Modern World*. London, 1959.

10. DE BELLEFONDS, Y. Linant, *Traité de Droit Musulman*. Vols. I and II. Paris/The Hague, 1965. (Vol. I—General Notions; Vol. II—Marriage. Other volumes to follow. Sunnite Law.)

11. *Encyclopædia of Islām*, by M. Th. HOUTSMA and others, Leiden-London, 1913-37, 4 volumes and *Supplement*, 1938. Articles on *Sharī'a, Fiqh, Shī'a*, etc. The *Supplement* contains a number of valuable articles, chief among which are *Adat Law*, *Ismā'īlīya* (W. IVANOW), *Istiḥsān* and *Istiṣlāḥ* (R. PARET) and *Ḳiyās* (T. J. BOER). This work was issued in English, French and German simultaneously; I have referred to the English edition. It has also been translated into Arabic, Urdu, and Turkish. A revised edition is being published.

The student is advised to refer continuously to this valuable work of reference, which is indispensable.

12. *Shorter Encyclopædia of Islām* by H. A. R. Gibb and J. H. Kramers. Leiden, 1953. Contains articles on religion and law from the parent work. Convenient and economical.

On **'uṣūl,** see especially:

13. ABDUR RAHIM, *Muhammadan Jurisprudence*. Tagore Law Lectures for 1907. Madras, 1911.

14. AGHNIDES, N. P., *Mohammedan Theories of Finance with an Introduction to Mohammedan Law and a Bibliography*. New York, 1916.

15. MAHMASSANI, S. (*Falsafat al-tashrī' fi'l-Islām*) *Philosophy of Jurisprudence in Islam*. Beirut, 1946; 2nd edition, 1952. Eng. trans. by F. J. Ziadeh (Beirut), Leiden, 1961.

(c) History of Fiqh

There is no exhaustive treatment of the history of *fiqh*. In addition to the various in the *Ency. of Islām*, the following works may be referred to:

1. SCHACHT, J., *Esquisse d'une Histoire du Droit Musulman*, Paris, 1953.

2. *Law in the Middle East*: Vol. I, *Origin and Development of Islamic Law*. Edited by M. Khadduri and H. J. Liebesny. Washington (D.C.), 1955. (Cited throughout as *LME*.)

3. MUḤAMMAD AL-KHUḌARĪ, *Ta'rīkh al-tashrī'i'l-Islāmī*, 3rd edition, Cairo, 1930/1348. (An abridged Urdu translation under the title of *Tārīkh-e fiqh-e islāmī* was published by Mawlānā 'Abd al-Salām Nadwī in Azamgadh, U.P., A.H. 1346.)

4. COULSON, N. J., *A History of Islamic Law*. Edinburgh, 1964.

5. MUḤAMMAD B. ḤASAN AL-HAJAWĪ AL-THA'ĀLIBĪ, *al-Fikr al-sāmī fi ta'rīkh al-fiqh al-islāmī*. Fās (Fez, Morocco), A.H. 1345.

(d) Bibliography

For European works:

1. PFANNMÜLLER, D. G., *Handbuch des Islām-Literatur*. Berlin-Leipzig, 1923, pp. 235-55.

2. JUYNBOLL, Th. W., *Handbuch des islāmischen Gesetzes*. Leiden-Leipzig, 1910.

3. PEARSON, J. D., *Index Islamicus,* 1906-55. London, 1958. Especially, 101 sqq., and *Supplements.* (Especially valuable for periodical literature.)

On particular topics:

4. SCHACHT, *Introduction,* see No. 5, in list (b), above.
5. *The Encyclopaedia of Islām,* and *Supplement.*
6. *Der Islam,* 1923, XIII, 349-55.

For original texts, mainly Sunnite:

(i) **Ḥanafī Law**

7. AGHNIDES, N. P., 'Introduction to Mohammedan Law' (in *Mohammedan Theories of Finance*). New York, 1916, and SCHACHT, J., *Introduction to Islamic Law.* Oxford, 1964. Pages 113, onwards.

(ii) **Mālikī Law,** see Santillana, David, *Istituzioni di Diritto Musulmano Malichita.* Two volumes. Rome, 1938; and Ruxton, F., *Maliki Law* (being a summary of the French translation of Sīdī Khalīl's *Mukhtaṣar.* London, 1916.

(iii) **Shāfi'ī Law,** see Ed. Sachau, *Muhammedanisches Recht nach schafiitischer Lehre,* Stuttgart/Berlin, 1897; Juynboll, Th. W., Number 2, sec. (d), above; Nawawī, *Minhaj Et Talibin.* Translated into English by E. C. Howard, from the French of L. W. C. Van den Berg. London, 1914; and Ahmad C. Mohd. Ibrahim (Singapore), 'Shāfi'ī Law in Indian Courts', *Islamic Culture,* XXXIX, 1965, pp. 251-69.

(iv) **Ḥanbalī Law,** in Tyabji, 3rd ed., 92; and *Ency. of Islām,* s.v: Ḥanābila.

For Ithnā 'Asharī Shiite Law:

8. *Tusy's List of Shy'ah Books,* edd. A. Sprenger, 'Abd al-Ḥaqq and Gholam Qadir. Bibliotheca Indica, Calcutta, 1853-5.
9. AL-KANTŪRĪ, I'jāz Ḥusain, *Kashf al-Ḥujub wa'l-Astār 'an asmā' al-Kutub wa'l-Asfār,* ed., M. Hidāyat Ḥusain. Bibliotheca Indica, Calcutta, 1912. Indexes, 1935.

For Fatimid Law:

10. FYZEE, Asaf A. A., *Compendium of Fatimid Law.* Simla (India), 1969.

MUHAMMADAN LAW

The following are the chief modern textbooks on Indian law in English:

1. MACNAGHTEN, William H., *Principles and Precedents of Moohummudan Law*. Calcutta, 1825 (a work of great authority).

2. AL-MARGHĪNĀNI, Burhān al-dīn, *The Hedaya* or *Guide* (a commentary on Musulman Laws). Trans. Ch. Hamilton. Second Edition by S. G. Grady. London, 1870.

3. BAILLIE, Neil B. E., *Digest of Moohummudan Law*. Part First (Hanafi law), second revised edition, London, 1875. Part Second (Ithnā 'Asharī Shiite law or Imameea Code), first edition, London, 1869.

4. SIRCAR, Shama Churn, *Muhammadan Law*, Tagore Law Lectures, 1873. Vol. I (Hanafi law), Calcutta, 1873. Vol. II, partly Hanafi and partly Imamiyah Code (Ithnā 'Asharī Shiite law), Calcutta, 1875. (Instructive and valuable.)

5. WILSON, Ronald K., *Anglo-Muhammadan Law*. Sixth edition, London, 1930. (Contains a valuable historical introduction for students.)

6. AMEER ALI, Syed, *Mahommedan Law*, Tagore Law Lectures, 1884. Vol. I, fourth edition, Calcutta, 1912. Vol. II, fifth edition, Calcutta, 1929.

7. MAHOMED YUSOOF, *Mahomedan Law Relating to Marriage, Dower, Divorce, Legitimacy and Guardianship of Minors according to the Soonnees*, Tagore Law Lectures, 1891-2. Calcutta, Vol. I, 1895; Vol. II, 1895; Vol. III, 1898.

8. ABDUR RAHMAN, A. F. M. *Institutes of Musulman Law*. Calcutta, 1907.

9. ABDUR RAHIM, *Principles of Muhammadan Jurisprudence*, Tagore Law Lectures, 1907. London-Madras, 1911.

10. MULLA, Dinshah Fardunji, *Principles of Mahomedan Law*. Sixteenth edition, Bombay, 1968.

11. TYABJI, Faiz Badruddin, *Muslim Law*. Fourth edition, Bombay, 1969.

12. VESEY-FITZGERALD, Seymour, *Muhammadan Law, An Abridgement*. Oxford University Press, London, 1931.

13. SAKSENA, K. P., *Muslim Law*. Fourth edition, Lucknow/Delhi, 1963.

14. FYZEE, Asaf A. A., *Cases in the Muhammadan Law of India and Pakistan*. Oxford, 1965. (Abbreviated *Cases*.)

INDEX OF CASES

INDEX OF NAMES AND TERMS

INDEX OF SUBJECTS